Communicational Criticism

Studies in literature as dialogue

Roger D. Sell
Åbo Akademi University

John Benjamins Publishing Company
Amsterdam / Philadelphia

^{TM} The paper used in this publication meets the minimum requirements of American National Standard for Information Sciences – Permanence of Paper for Printed Library Materials, ANSI z39.48-1984.

Library of Congress Cataloging-in-Publication Data

Sell, Roger D.
    Communicational criticism : studies in literature as dialogue / Roger D. Sell.
        p. cm. (Dialogue Studies, ISSN 1875-1792 ; v. 11)
    Includes bibliographical references and index.
    1. Criticism. 2. Literature--History and criticism. 3. Pragmatics. I. Title.
    PN81.S364   2011
    809--dc23   2011022402
    ISBN 978 90 272 1028 9   (Hb ; alk. paper)
    ISBN 978 90 272 8486 0   (Eb)

John Benjamins Publishing Co. · P.O. Box 36224 · 1020 ME Amsterdam · The Netherlands
John Benjamins North America · P.O. Box 27519 · Philadelphia PA 19118-0519 · USA

To
Alan and Karen
with love

Acknowledgements

Reworked versions of passages from my own earlier writings are incorporated by kind permission of the original publishers. Specifically from: "Two Types of Style Contrast in *King Lear*: A Literary-Critical Appraisal", in Håkan Ringbom (ed.), *Style and Text: Studies Presented to Nils Erik Enkvist*, Stockholm: Skriptor, 1975, pp. 158–171; "*Henry V* and the Strength and Weakness of Words: Shakespearean Philology, Historicist Criticism, Communicative Pragmatics", in Gunnar Sorelius (ed.), *Shakespeare in Scandinavia: A Collection of Nordic Studies*, Newark: Delaware University Press, 2002, pp. 108–141; "Blessings, Benefactions, Bear's Services: *Great Expectations* and Communicational Narratology", *European Journal of English Studies* 8 (2004) 49–80; "Wordsworthian Communication", *Nordic Journal of English Studies* 6 (2007) 17–45; "Wordsworth and the Spread of Genuine Communication", in Sibylle Baumbach, Herbert Grabes and Ansgar Nünning (eds), *Literature and Values: Literature as a Medium for Representing, Disseminating and Constructing Norms and Values*, Trier: Wissenschaftlicher Verlag, 2009, pp. 125–143; "Mediational Ethics in Churchill's *My Early Life*", in Alfred Hornung (ed.), *Auto/Biography and Mediation*, Heidelberg: Universitätsverlag Winter, 2010, pp. 207–225; and "Dialogicality and Ethics: Four Cases of Literary Address", *Language and Dialogue* 1 (2011) 79–104.

I owe an immense debt of gratitude to the Åbo Akademi Foundation for financial support from the H. W. Donner Fund. This was a major source of funding for both the ChiLPA Project ("Children's Literature, Pure and Applied") and the LitCom Project ("Literary Communication"), and it also enabled me to move to a Research Professorship while leading both projects. In addition, the Foundation has awarded me many generous travel and research grants. Without this backing, the present book would never have come into being.

For responses to earlier drafts of the work presented here I am grateful to John Creaser, Martin Gill, Jason Harding, Seamus Perry, and †Stephen Wall. I have also specially benefited from the astute but friendly comments of colleagues associated with the ChiLPA Project and the LitCom Project: Gunilla Bexar, Adam Borch, Katja Brandt, Jason Finch, Charlotta Häggblom, Anthony W. Johnson, Lydia Kokkola, Maria Lassén-Seger, Inna Lindgrén, and Helen Wilcox. The remaining shortcomings are all my own.

As on earlier occasions, I should like to thank my entire family for their patience and encouragement. This time, I address myself especially to my brother Alan and his wife Karen, who have always inspired me by their example of creative diligence.

Table of contents

CHAPTER 1

Introduction

Communicational criticism

1.1 Literary appreciation in post-postmodern times

The studies brought together here are of varying length, and deal with several different writers from several different periods of English literature, beginning with Shakespeare and ending with Pinter. In addition to a fair amount of cross-reference from one study to another, what links them together is two common denominators: they all develop a type of literary criticism which can be called communicational criticism; and they all do this as a response to the situation which, for want of a more elegant term, I call the post-postmodern condition.

"The *modern* era" is the widely accepted label for that phase of western history which included the decline of feudalism, the beginnings of parliamentarianism, the rise of the bourgeoisie, the invention of the printing press, the Reformation, Renaissance Humanism, and the birth of empirical science. Some historians would say that modernity culminated in the Enlightenment ideals of rational knowledge and control over nature, and of universal brotherhood and freedom. Others would claim that it was still at its height in the mighty engineering achievements and imperial power-games of the nineteenth and early-twentieth centuries.

By then, however, there were already clear symptoms of "*postmodernity*", a condition helpfully defined by Jean-François Lyotard (1984 [1979]) as a far-reaching crisis of knowledge, politics and culture. One main ingredient was a scepticism as to modernity's grand narratives of scientific explanation. But no less fundamental were issues of political teleology and associated problems of identity and legitimation. By the last three or four decades of the twentieth century these were becoming especially acute in multicultural urban societies, where communities and interest groupings which had hitherto been marginalized were at last finding their voice.

Seen from this point of view, the postmodern climax can be located in the so-called culture wars of the mid-1990s, during which all forms of cultural production, including literature and literary criticism, became a site for the contestation of communal differences. Literary critics of several descriptions – Marxist, post-Marxist, new historical, cultural materialist, feminist, gay or queer, ethnic, religious, postcolonial – were now tending to champion particular groupings and to speak, not of a single, universal literary canon, but of many different canons for many different readerships. In bookshops, books were actually marketed this way (with shelves for Jewish books, for black women's books, for gay men's books and so on), and in 1995 J. Hillis Miller described what he called the University of Dissensus. For Miller, a postmodern university was not a place where people from many different backgrounds came together in order to negotiate a body of knowledge and wisdom which could be generally accepted. To his mind, the difference between a person from one background and a person from another background was absolute. Difference was, as he put it, all the way down, and the function of the postmodern university was, he said, to make visible and preserve that state of affairs. This it would attempt to do by questioning common realistic representations, and by subjecting common sense and ordinary uses of language to violent interrogation. In this way he thought the postmodern university might manage to combat what he saw as a sinister commodifying hegemony.

In the new millennium, there has been a swing towards what I am calling the condition of *post-postmodernity*. This is more difficult to document than modernity or postmodernity, since it is the condition in which we are still living. Our impressions of it come from countless different sources, many of them in oral form or merely ephemerally in print. We do not yet have the distance to be able to pinpoint its most significant manifestations, and one aspect of our bias is that we ourselves are not only responding to its prevailing moods and ideas but may actually be contributing to them.

But for what it is worth, something on which I would expect many contemporaries to agree is that postmodernity was indeed a condition to which we now look *back*. The changes thrown up by the postmodern maelstrom were so radical as to propel us into a new era. It really did empower previously underprivileged groupings, so making many large societies a lot more democratic. This brought important long term benefits to the lives of many individuals, and some very exciting developments in the field of cultural production as well.

On the other hand, from what I read in newspapers, see on the television, discuss with colleagues and others, I know I am not alone in seeing the world as still riven by systematic violence and injustice on a truly shameful scale, even though political, economic, environmental, and communication-technological developments now constantly remind us that we are all denizens of just a single planet. Nor, as far as I can see, do many people think that violence and injustice on this present scale are inevitable. Though not utopian, the new mood seems to include a sense that living side by side with human othernesses not only calls for responsible and decent kinds of behaviour, but should, and could, be rewarding and enjoyable. Although we still need to be wary lest globalization promote the kind of hegemony which Miller feared in 1995, there is, I think, a growing perception that the postmodern politics of recognition, despite its emancipatory goals and achievements, was itself somewhat repressive of human ways of being and interacting. Even at the height of the culture wars, commentators such as K. Anthony Appiah (1994) were already complaining that members of a particular community could be urged to conform with a group identity script which was seriously limiting, and that an individual belonging to one grouping was all too often being discouraged from communicating with individuals belonging to another. At the same time, there was also a sense that these drawbacks could be counteracted, if only the scope for hybrid identities and rainbow coalitions could be steadily widened (Pieterse 1995). In post-postmodern times, that is sometimes what seems to be happening.

It would be naive to think that progress will be rapid. The remaining injustices are indeed widespread, and of several different kinds, operating both *between* different cultures, parts of the world and countries, and also *within* individual countries. As I write these words in February 2011, dictators in Tunisia and Egypt have just been toppled in a wave of protest that has been essentially peaceful. But elsewhere, the situation is still exacerbated by terrorist movements, perceived by their adherents as the natural response to serious grievances, and partly international in their reach. There have been appalling terrorist attacks against societies trying to make a go of multiculturalism, and in some quarters these onslaughts have been met by an upsurge of reactionary nationalism which, if it continues to make political headway, could merely lead to new inequalities, new grievances, and more terrorism.

Such worrying developments can only be reversed by measures which any well-intentioned commentator would want to see in any case: by still more resolute attempts to bring justice to every corner of the earth, and by an intensified intellectual and educational engagement with relevant ideological issues. Here the writing, reading and discussion of literary texts can make their own kinds of contribution. Students of Comparative Literature have already pointed out that in the postcolonial age "literature is becoming *immanently* global … . [I]ndividual works are increasingly informed and constituted by social, political, and even linguistic trends that are not limited to a single state or region" (Pizer 2000: 213, his italics). Some scholars have asked whether this new situation can be helpfully discussed in terms of Goethe's concept of *Weltliteratur*, which has always been so central to Comparative Literature's disciplinary identity. Certainly Goethe was thinking of literature less in the sense of "Great Books" than of a more general written production, so that he would not have encouraged antagonisms between different cultures as to their relative prestige. Not least, he believed that a significant contribution to *Weltliteratur* from his own time's German-speaking world was quite ruled out by the lack of strong political cohesion. In fact his main motivation for thinking, during the 1820s, in terms of world literature was precisely his desire for a lasting peace after all the chaos of the Napoleonic wars. Bearing in mind this eirenic origin, we could well expect his idea to become freshly seminal for post-postmodern times. The only problems are that it was unmistakably Eurocentric, and that with the later rise of nationalism its further development did come to be coloured by an element of competition. National canons of literature began to establish themselves, and only a nation's very greatest authors now had a chance of graduating to the status of world literature, a situation illustrated in North America, for example, by the "Great Books" programme pioneered by New Critics. By the 1940s literary nationalism was very widespread, and by the 1950s scholars such as

Auerbach were warning that "*Weltliteratur*" could all too easily become a euphemism for a ubiquitous standardization. "All human activity is being concentrated either into European-American or into Russian-Bolshevist patterns; no matter how great they seem to us, the differences between the two patterns are comparatively minimal when they are contrasted with the basic patterns underlying the Islamic, Indian or Chinese traditions" (Auerbach 1969 [1952]:2–3). As it happens, however, during the last decades of the twentieth century the usefulness of so-called world literature for the purposes of culturally imperialistic standardization was greatly reduced. Now there were studies of the actual facts of international literary relations – of the roles played by streams of literary influence, for instance, by literary translation, and by multilingual communities – and this kind of work was also carefully theorized, as in Dionýz Ďurišin's account of interliterary process (1989). Even more to the point, this was also the moment when postmodern critics like Homi Bhabha began to think of world literature as "an emergent, prefigurative category that is concerned with a form of cultural dissensus and alterity, where non-consensual terms of affiliation may be established on the grounds of historical trauma" (Bhabha 1994:12). In post-post-modern times, this vision of world literature as an affiliation of the different is being borne out not only in the way books are actually being circulated but also in academic discussion of the phenomenon.

Typical of the current mood within the scholarly community is a certain optimism, tempered by a sharp awareness of possible dangers. David Damrosch (2004) has pointed out that the old canonical classics may continue to attract a disproportionate amount of attention, becoming a kind of "hypercanon" against which the new authors belonging to previously "small" literatures are mustered into a "countercanon" that is merely the hypercanon's shadow. In order to remain factually accurate and politically just, literary scholarship does need to retain, as Sarika Chandra (2008) and Silvia Lopéz (2004) both argue, some insistence on national and regional distinctions. And as J. Hillis Miller (2007) and Ernst Grabovsky (2004) both emphasize, distinctivenesses also need to be maintained in the face of present-day communications technology. As channels for literary texts world-wide, the new digital media clearly have a huge potential. But their formats, and the culture of reading they encourage, could perhaps be too homogenizing.

Another topic calling for the attention of post-postmodern scholars is communicational ethics, both in the world at large and within literary writing and literary discussion in particular. Mediating criticism and communicational criticism, two types of literary discussion which were well represented (though not under these labels) among the great critics of the past, can now seek to improve the chances of fruitful relationships between both individuals and groupings by focusing, respectively, on the ethics of response and the ethics of address. This is where I myself have become caught up in post-postmodern developments, in collaboration with many other scholars world-wide, for instance under the auspices of UNESCO's *Fédération*

Internationale des Langues et Littératures Modernes (the FILLM). One typically post-postmodern happening was the FILLM's 2002 Congress in Bangkok, where my own paper was on mediating criticism and social justice (Sell 2005). Another was the same organization's symposium on emergent literatures and globalization, held in 2003 in New Caledonia. There, my contribution dealt with emergent literatures' communication-ethical development – with the fact that they first achieve recognition through a powerful assertion of group distinctiveness, but then, as they gradually enter into parity with more established literatures, become less urgently coercive (Sell 2004b).

A post-postmodern mediating critic, refusing to accept that difference is all the way down, will mediate between writers and readers of different formations, taking as a main concern the conditions for empathetic understanding and fair-mindedness. On the one hand, a reader responding to a literary text is humanly obliged to give its writer a fair hearing. If there are wide gaps between the writer's and readers' positions which make this difficult, or which tempt readers to misinterpret the writer by imposing their own world-view as the only relevant context, then the mediating critic may be able to illuminate differences of society, culture and ideology, and in this way encourage a sense of human otherness as a stimulus to self-examination, and to self-renewing mergings of horizon along the lines suggested in Gadamerian hermeneutics: "To recognize one's own in the alien, to become at home in it, is the basic movement of spirit, whose being consists only in returning to itself from the other" (Gadamer 1989 [1960]: 14). On the other hand, readers inevitably have their own historical identities, and are humanly entitled to thoughts, emotions and values of their own. If their attitude towards the writer is too servile, then the mediating critic can perhaps encourage them to an alerter independence. None of which means that the critic operates from some Archimedean point outside of history. As in any other attempt to mediate between two parties, no lasting progress will be made unless the mediator's own cards are laid frankly on the table from the start. And at best, mediating criticism will not only improve readers' relationship with particular writers taken up for discussion, but will serve as a catalyst to better communication on a larger scale. This, in a world where communicational breakdowns are extremely frequent at every level from the domestic or very local right up to that of international power politics, and where, as I say, conflict, violence, and injustice are still all too prevalent.

As for post-postmodern communicational criticism, this will draw particular attention to literary modes of address which acknowledge the human autonomy of each and every reader. For critics and teachers drawn to this task, the goal will partly recall an assumption already at work in the rhetorical treatises of the ancient world: the idea that some texts are more suitable than others as models to be emulated in language use more widely. But whereas the rhetoricians of earlier ages were often mainly looking for models of style and persuasiveness, post-postmodern communicational critics will focus on communicational ethics: on a writer's way of entering into human relationships, both with individual readers and with readers in larger groupings. By fostering a new self-consciousness about the connections between language use and human relationships, communicational criticism, no less than mediating criticism, will aim to improve the chances for peaceful coexistence and fruitful cooperation in the world at large.

I have already discussed and exemplified mediating criticism in two earlier books: *Literature as Communication: The Foundations of Mediating Criticism* (2000) and *Mediating Criticism: Literary Education Humanized* (2001). In the present book, it is the turn of communicational criticism. Yet especially when channelling a post-postmodern temperament, these two types of criticism are difficult to keep apart. Both of them represent a kind of ethical criticism which sees literature as one among other forms of real communication; in fact they can both be applied to non-literary types of communication as well (Sell 2011); and even when applied only to literary activity, they both aim to improve the conditions for human communication in general.

This makes for a tone of critical voice which, while not in the least precluding judgements that are duly frank and forthright, is on the whole more courteous and sanguine than that of some previous critical commentary. In post-postmodern times, the "rhetoric of blame and defensiveness" which Edward Said (1994 [1993]: 96) was saddened to note in so much postmodern criticism, and which Harold Bloom (1995: 31) saw as contributing to a veritable "School of Resentment", is becoming a thing of the past, and when reviewers of my own work have found it good-tempered and reasonable, they have had no quarrel with this. Rather than accusing me of soft-headed syncretism, starry-eyed day-dreams or sanctimonious smugness, they have welcomed my ameliorative aims as a potentially valuable response to current circumstances.

What they do cast doubt on is the receptivity of my likely readers. Here, from *Essays in Criticism*, is part of the lead-in to an appraisal of *Literature as Communication*:

> [I]magine a work of critical theory which is not fuelled by a will to identify opponents in order to deprecate or dismiss them; a work which states its goals and methods as clearly as does the analytic philosopher or the linguist (a device refreshingly straightforward and oddly underused); a work written in a tone suitable to academic discussion, without the vitriol of the insecure and petty – revealing a view of the academy as an intellectual community wherein ideas can be discussed reasonably in order that they may receive the benefit of even-handed criticism. Such a voice would probably be drowned in the cacophony of professorial positioning, yet Roger D. Sell's work should, for this and other important reasons, be attended to.   (Willner 2002: 155)

And here, from *English Studies*, is the last sentence of a notice of *Mediating Criticism*:

> In the end the book's value lies more in … [Sell's] analyses [of particular literary texts] than in its larger pedagogical aim, which is sadly unlikely to be met in an academic world where decency is at a discount.   (Dean 2003: 558)

That some reviewers have felt unable to be generous towards my own work without lambasting other literary scholars *en masse* may seem to suggest that the transition from a postmodern to a post-postmodern mood is not going smoothly. But such, I believe, is not the case (Sell 2004a). In *Mediating Criticism* I, too, expressed concern about the academic culture of literary studies, noting elements of over-institutionalization, dehumanizing professionalism, and elitist scholasticism, all of which could go hand in hand with an aggressively agonistic style of argument, sometimes underwritten by a general world view which I found too predominantly cynical and pessimistic. In this last connection I spoke of a widespread but rather lop-sided response to the legacy of Modernism. The sheer energy and creativity of the great Modernist writers had somewhat disappeared from view because, as I put it, so many commentators had valorized Thanatos at the expense of Eros. This prioritization, I argued, had become so routinely automated that it could operate as a kind of unquestioned prejudice, and one which, by refusing to embrace the hopefulness which may be psychologically necessary for human survival in the longer term, could make a writer such as Wordsworth seem almost unintelligible. On the other hand, each of the deleterious tendencies I diagnosed can also be seen as the mere excess of an important scholarly virtue. Any lasting consolidation of scholarly wisdom and practice is bound to entail a certain amount of institutionalization; scholarly professionialism has resulted in ground-breaking exchanges of highly specialized insights, the most significant of which have not proved untranslatable into more ordinary language; sharp argument, perhaps the quickest way to test a new idea or claim, does not preclude a switch to less coercive modes of discussion; and the valorization of Thanatos has often been, not a masochistic stock-response, but a sober recognition of grim realities which mediating and communicational critics, too, must squarely face. We inhabit, I would say, an academic culture which, though in constant need of alert self-monitoring, is still conducive to new ideas and perceptions, and is well able to promote a friendly response to a friendly initiative. Decency is not much at a discount in the two reviewers just quoted, after all, even though they themselves are working within the very culture they deplore. Why should not their colleagues have the independence of mind to be just as decent as they, and to work, if necessary, for cultural renewal?

Academic culture changes anyway. Many critics who during the late postmodern era expressed a strongly political concern on behalf of just some single identity formation are in post-postmodern times more likely to be taken up with issues – ecological, economic, cultural, geopolitical – whose implications are so global that the entire human race can figure as either plaintiff or defendant. Under these conditions, proposals for a new self-consciousness in mediating and communicational criticism can fall in fertile soil.

It so happens that the promotion of self-consciousness is already the main goal in a branch of rhetorical studies which goes under the name of communication (*sic!*) criticism. In rhetorical studies generally, there has been a very marked development beyond the traditional focus on the argumentation and style of public speaking. All types of language use can now come under investigation, plus a very wide range of phenomena which, in Kenneth Burke's sense of the term, are more broadly symbolic (Foss 2009; Hart and Daughton 2005). Many different types of message and media are viewed as thoroughly permeated with social, cultural and ideological symbolism, and rhetoric is seen as comprising, in the words of Karyn Charles Rybacki and Donald J. Rybacki (2002: 2–3), "all the ways in which human symbol can exert influence over humanity". Present-day rhetorical scholarship explores such omnipresent influence by commandeering the analytical arsenals of many different kinds of literary, cultural, social and ideological critique, and when describing itself as communication (*sic*) criticism is more than likely to be published in journals such as *Social Semiotics*, and to lay special emphasis on both the variety of phenomena examined and its own credentials as an awareness-raiser (e.g. Combs 2002). Rybacki and Rybacki (2002: 180, 225) explain that, by drawing on feminist and other postmodern frameworks of thought, communication critics seek to "uncover how the powerful elite use rhetorical activity to maintain their hegemonic power" – not least, the power of the "Euro-white-male-heterosexual hegemony". Malcolm O. Sillars and Bruce E. Gronbeck (2001: 4–5), similarly, say that a communication critic "makes an argument that describes, interprets, or evaluates the messages to which people are exposed in public or collective ways", an argument which can help them to guard against "being victimized". Or as Judi R. Cohen (1998: 204) puts it, "The communication critic evaluates how terministic screens might influence, express, represent, and/or constitute human identities, ideas, and actions". And by "terministic screen" she means: "A filter that directs and deflects our perceptions and conceptions. All language is a terministic screen" (Cohen 1998: 213). So although she does not say so, she seems to be operating on the basis of the Whorfian hypothesis in a strong form. For her, the language we speak, and more generally our society's entire symbolic structure, restrict as much as they enable, and the job of the communication critic is to open our eyes and help us build up necessary defences and counterstrategies.

Communication (*sic*) critics like Cohen, Sillars and Gronbeck, and Rybacki and Rybacki pay relatively little attention to literature, and this is probably just as well. Their shift away from rhetoricians' traditional interest in language and style is reflected in their own prose. Even some of their most central statements (such as those quoted in the previous paragraph) are poor examples of academic writing, and their manner of expression would instantly delegitimize them in the eyes of regular readers of literature. Not that such readers are innately more intelligent than communication critics, or innately more sensitive to stylistic and other literary niceties. Nor are they nowadays likely to be literary snobs. In the etymological sense of the term, the point here is itself communicational, in that it has to do with the making and consolidation of different communities. Regular readers of literature, by virtue of their reading habits, have become members of a community within which certain linguistic and stylistic norms are simply more customary than others. These, in turn, are the norms they are most likely to endorse in their own writing practice, and in their judgement of other writers. To them, scholars whose writing does not endorse those norms will seem to be on an alien wavelength.

Even so, rhetorical studies as nowadays pursued in American universities, and communication (*sic*) criticism in particular, could clearly encourage young people to be on their guard against attempts to impose upon them. Some of my own readers may see a foretaste of such efforts in Leavis and Thompson's discussion of advertising and standardization in *Culture and Environment: The Training of Critical Awareness*, first published in 1933. Since then, the hegemonic forces to which we are exposed have only increased – the fears of Miller in his postmodern phase were not without ground. So as an attempt to prevent citizens from turning into easily manipulable zombies, communication (*sic*) criticism is obviously welcome. The only risk is that it could lay itself open, as on occasion did both Leavisian and postmodern criticism, to accusations of paranoiac suspiciousness and far-fetched conspiracy theory. Its general tone is certainly rather censorious.

Granting, as we surely must, that Aristotle was right to claim that human beings learn to do things by imitating examples, critics and teachers need, not only to issue warnings, but to highlight cases of communicational good practice. Communicational good practice – as many examples of it as the available page-space or teaching hours will permit – needs to be identified, discussed, and held up for emulation. In communicational (*sic*) criticism as developed in the studies here, this upbeat task is central. And as will soon become obvious, the very theory on which I am grounding the approach is less intrinsically dystopian than the one underlying the communication criticism of Rybacki and Rybacki and their colleagues. Drawing strength from that foundation, what communicational critics will be seeking to develop is a new form of that pleasurable kind of assessment that used to be called literary appreciation. The newness lies partly in the post-postmodern ideological goal, partly in the heightened sensitivity to communicational ethics, but above all in a pleasurability now consciously stemming from a communication between writers and readers that is fundamentally dialogical.

1.2   Literature as dialogue

Anyone wishing for a full account of the theory on which I ground a post-postmodern communicational criticism will find it in *Literature as Communication*. In what follows here, I shall merely summarize some of the main points, though giving special emphasis to literary communication's dialogicality. By way of illustration, I shall often refer to Shakespeare, not only because his works have usually been the first testing-ground for literary-theoretical insights in general, but also because most of them are in the form of drama, thereby presenting a challenge to communicational accounts of literature that is usefully direct.

From antiquity onwards, many plays have communicated in what is a widely understood sense of that term: they have communicated *something*. Mystery or miracle plays, moralities, masques or masque-like plays, and pageant plays have all conveyed some sort of didactic or political message, often in allegorical form. Such plays have not begun to exploit the fuller potentialities of drama unless they have also somehow complicated their message, as did, for instance, the Second Shepherds' Play in the Wakefield Mystery Cycle. There, the play's own representation of the Virgin Mary watching over the baby Jesus in the manger was parodied by a sub-plot in which the wife of a sheep-thief disguised a stolen lamb as a baby in her cradle. In a case like this, a didactic play's message becomes more difficult to state. The odd conjunctions or disjunctions of stage image, meaning and tone leave the overall intentions of the playwright or playwrights less clear-cut.

In fact the more dramatic a play becomes, the more its writer or writers disappear from view. The writer of even a closet drama can actually seem to withdraw behind its *dramatis personae*, and in the case of a fully-fledged play that is staged in a theatre there can seem to be many additional, real-life intermediaries between playwright and audience: the actors, director and stage designer for a start. A writer who figures as the "I" of a lyric poem may possibly communicate, one might think, and so may an intrusively omniscient novelist. But even these kinds of case have been hotly disputed by some critics and theoreticians in the past, and a dramatist can often appear to have neither the desire nor the opportunity to communicate at all.

Everything depends on what we mean by "communicate". My suggestion is that the idea of communication as a matter of communicating *something* needs to be qualified. In a nutshell, communication, and literary communication especially, is often more in the nature of a dialogue. Literature can be thought of as a dialogue between writers and their public: a kind of give-and-take which has both ethical entailments and communal consequences. It is through exploring this element of dialogicality that a communicational critic seeks to evaluate writers' way of treating their addressees as human beings, and to trace the results of that interchange within society and culture as a whole.

In the case of Shakespeare, the social and cultural results have been remarkably various and far-reaching. But a possible entry into Shakespearian dialogicality is to be found in *The Siege of Krishnapur*, a novel by J.G Farrell first published in 1973 and purporting to describe one of the side-shows of the Indian Mutiny of 1857. As the sepoys' attack on the East India Company's Krishnapur station reaches its climax, the Collector is hard put to it to find adequate ammunition with which to load his cannon in reply. In the end he is reduced to using stones, but not until the supply of metal objects has been exhausted: first round objects, then less round ones, including some of his most cherished personal possessions. He is especially proud of some ornaments he acquired at the Great Exhibition in Crystal Palace six years earlier: a set of electrometallic busts of English authors, objects which reconciled within themselves, as he would have said, the wonders of Victorian technological achievement with a reverence for great literature – or, as he would probably have written it, Literature. "Without a doubt," Farrell writes,

> the most effective missiles in this matter of improvised ammunition had been the heads of his electrometal figures, removed from the bodies with the help of … [a] file. And of the heads, perhaps not surprisingly, the most effective of all had been Shakespeare's; it had scythed its way through a whole astonished platoon of sepoys advancing in single file through the jungle. The Collector suspected that the Bard's success in this respect might have a great deal to do with the ballistic advantages stemming from his baldness. The head of Keats, for example, wildly festooned with metal locks which it had proved impossible to file smooth, had flown very erratically indeed, killing only a fat money-lender and a camel stand-ing at some distance from the field of action.   (Farrell 1975 [1973]: 335)

That this passage could be interpreted as an allegory of British cultural imperial-ism would not have been lost on the postcolonial critics who were active ten to thirty years after Farrell wrote it, some of whom claimed that *The Tempest* was actually a colo-nialist text (Lindley 2002: 38–45). Whether Farrell himself (*fl.* 1935–1979) would have gone that far is open to discussion. He would perhaps have said that the reason why Shakespeare, though projected by the same imperial education system as Keats, proved to be far more overwhelming lay not in his political profile but at least to some extent in his superiority as a poet. But he would also clearly have understood Auerbach's reserva-tions about the standardizing spread of occidental cultural patterns. That Shakespeare was indeed an ideological weapon, used by the Victorians in the hope of achieving a desired effect, is certainly one of the novel's overtones here, together with a perception that the desired effect, and in no small part the effect achieved, were not entirely a matter of Shakespeare's own intentions, characteristics and efforts, but really did have much to do with the way in which he was, as it were, implemented by the institutions and personnel upholding the imperial framework.

Not that imperialists were uncomplicatedly power-hungry. As individuals their motives could be strongly altruistic – Farrell's Collector is a case in point – and the benevolent and high-minded sides of Victorian ideology were no less real than the political structures it could underpin. For one thing, Victorians saw themselves as con-veying to less enlightened peoples a sense of the universality of human nature and of its scope for noble refinement. For another, they saw the writings of great authors through the prism of post-Kantian aesthetics. Art (with a capital "A"), though alongside true religion one of the main contributors to human nobility and civilization, offered an aesthetic heterocosm that in and of itself had nothing directly to do with the world of nature as studied by science, or with the world of human interaction as explored by philosophical ethics or history-writing. Rather, Art was a pleasurable wellspring of lofty Beauty (*sic*) and ideal perfection, and *literary* Art, or Literature (*sic*), though drawing on the referential medium of language, did not straightforwardly mirror reality or state an author's own raw feelings and opinions, but was essentially imaginative and fictional. As Arnold put it, "for poetry the idea is everything; the rest is a world of illusion, of divine illusion. Poetry attaches its emotion to the idea; the idea *is* the fact" (Arnold 1888 [1880]: 1–2, his italics). Granted, Arnold also said that the reason why literature's "[c]urrency and supremacy are insured" had to do with nothing less than "the instinct of self-preservation in humanity" (Arnold 1888 [1880]: 55). He was by no means alone in believing that great authors could take over a vital spiritual role which official religion had long mismanaged. In effect, though, such respect for authors' spiritual importance could merely increase their distance from more ordinary mortals, for whom there was of course no obvious feedback channel. Then as now, an author was usually somebody quite outside a reader's own sphere of acquaintance, and in Shakespeare's and many other cases was already dead and buried. For the Victorians, this circumstance merely confirmed that Literature did not in the first instance involve interpersonal agency, whether the author's own or anybody else's. In its special timeless realm, it simply *was*.

This idea lasted well into the twentieth century, doing much to underwrite American New Criticism. But during that century's final decades, postcolonial, new historicist and several other postmodern types of criticism were vigorously re-situating literary activity within the real world of history. As a result, we are now fairly likely to view Shakespeare as the single most striking example of how literature and life in society at large can actually intertwine. Seen in a postmodern perspective, Shakespeare's texts not only conveyed the socio-ideological assumptions he held in common with his own contemporaries, but became a site for the ideological contests of later times, and not only the one between Victorian empire and its subject peoples.

Such is the background against which a literary-communicational theoretician now re-examines those discoursal features which, for nineteenth- and early-twentieth-century commentators, seemed to give literature a special aesthetic status. Pleasure and beauty, if that still seems the right word, can themselves be seen as communicational phenomena, and can arise from non-literary uses of language as well – conversation analysts have long been studying the "poetics of talk" (Tannen 1987, 1990). And although a work of art can have an attraction that is psychologically very real for us, so real that we experience it as something positively "there" in the work, and although this impression will certainly not occur unless there are features in the work which give rise to it, a great deal also depends on our own prior conditioning – on what we ourselves *bring* to our appreciation. In ways that Richard Shusterman (1992) and other pragmatist aestheticians have now explained, there are actually social contracts as to what shall count as agreeable, and as John Creaser (2001, 2002) illustrates from the interplay between prosodic discipline and rhythmic verve in the verse of Milton, much of a reader's enjoyment is the result of prior expectations being met, exceeded, or modified, a point anticipated, however surprisingly, by Coleridge. Even though Coleridge's post-Kantian account of creative imagination was seminal for the Victorians' notion of Literature as a special aesthetic heterocosm, he was himself a master of versification, and strongly sensed its contribution to an interchange between real writers and real readers that was both salubrious and decidedly conversation-like:

> As far as metre acts in and for itself, it tends to increase the vivacity and susceptibility both of the general feelings and of the attention. This effect it produces by the continued excitement of surprize, and by the quick reciprocations of curiosity still gratified and still re-excited, which are too slight indeed to be at any one moment objects of distinct consciousness, yet become considerable in their aggregate influence. As a medicated atmosphere, or as wine during animated conversation, they act powerfully, though themselves unnoticed.
>
> (Coleridge 1956 [1817]: 207)

Coleridge knew that, in a skilful piece of writing, the reassuringly old and the surprisingly new can be adapted to each other. Such co-adaptationality is a communicational principle of very wide reach, helping to explain the pleasure we take, not only in versification, but in stylistic, formal, narratological, thematic, and genre patterning of any kind at all (Sell 2000: 145–158, 178–193). Nor would this pleasure arise unless we were communicating members of an audience within which matters of taste and value are under constant, albeit often tacit negotiation. At any given time, the difference between the communally well established and the communally unexpected is something we are accustomed to recognize at first sight. When the one enters into fruitful co-adaptation with the other, our delight is itself something which can be communally shared.

Fictionality, similarly, is an element in many everyday uses of language whose communicational function nobody would question. And as I have already suggested, communication is not always transitive. It does not always communicate *something*, and is not confined to the statement of hard-and-fast facts, opinions and feelings. As I shall try to illustrate in my studies of *Great Expectations* and *Coming up for Air*, fiction is a means by which a communicator can explore general or moral truths which go beyond the detail of particular empirical cases, or can probe feelings and opinions which have yet to be stabilized into constant attitudes. In most literature which readers have felt worthy of the name, the invitation extended by any fictional elements to a truly dialogical comparing of notes is very powerful. Conversely, high literary status is not usually accorded to fictional works that are allegorical and didactic unless they expose their dogma to challenge from its own inversion, so becoming dramatic in the same sense as that Wakefield nativity play. Although Sir Guyon, the champion of Temperance in Book II of *The Fairie Queene*, resists the temptations of the Bower of Bliss according to plan, Spenser has made them so voluptuous that few readers would have been surprised if he had failed, and some may even have used them to fuel salacious fantasies of their own. Nor have Blake and Shelley been the only readers of *Paradise Lost* to feel that Milton was on the Devil's side without knowing it.

As for writing's lack of a feedback channel, this, too, does nothing to reduce literature's dialogicality. Linguists such as Edda Weigand (2009) have shown that a dialogical element is central to language activity of any kind at all, and in *Literature as Communication* I drew on text- and discourse-linguistic accounts of writing in particular as a clue to literature's inevitable element of addressivity. The facts are that all writing, like all speech, does have addressivity, and that the addressivity chosen by literary authors is not solipsistic (Sell 2000: 83–88, 158–175). Even when they have written under the auspices of a formalist aestheticism, even when they have written drama, a mode in which all the communication may seem to be happening less between the dramatist and the audience than between the characters on stage, they have written with other people in mind, their texts presenting or implying addressee personae which the real readers of a novel or a poem, the real readers or spectators of a play, can try on for size, as it were, and perhaps increasingly accept or reject as their response develops, just as with the addressee personae we all automatically negotiate in everyday conversation. By the same token, writers, including even a writer such as Shakespeare, to whom it is sometimes difficult to ascribe a definite intention, always create or imply at least a persona for themselves: an addresser persona, whose function, no less unexceptional than that of the addressee persona, is to create an impression of their own knowledge, assumptions, attitudes and values, an impression which is neither truer nor more false than any of the other self-images which they, like the rest of us, employ in life at every single moment. Writing, through its use of these and other basic communicational devices, not only connects people who are otherwise separated by space, but extends a dialogicality across time as well. Just as the stipulations of a last will and testament, whose words so obviously prompt survivors to a conscientious reading, may need to be interpreted by expert lawyers, so the readers of a literary text may sometimes hone their responses to it with the help of, say, a literary historian, who thereby takes on the role of mediating critic. Readers' sense of their human obligation towards a text's writer will at best be very pressing.

In demythologizing "Literature" into just "literature", literary-communicational theory is in harmony with an already powerful trend in the marketing and reception of published writing. Over recent decades there has been a major shift in taste and cultural perceptions. While most readers would probably still not object to the writings they admire being labelled as "literature", the term may no longer be regarded as particularly necessary, except, perhaps, by those defending a cherished institutional boundary within universities trying to rid themselves of academic archaism. In the late 1980s Bernard Bergonzi was already resigning himself to a future in which the discipline of English Studies would "explode" into many different enquiries – "cultural studies" and "communications", for instance – which would have nothing fundamentally to do with what he himself had been brought up to think of as literature. Yet he still hoped that universities would afford space to one very small and specialized rump which would devote itself to poetry (Bergonzi 1990). Where such territorial anxieties have never arisen or are a thing of the past, the word "literature" has a more neutral loading, which may even be winning back something of the concept's eighteenth century breadth. We can speculate that, before long, it may come to cover, not only popular science, philosophy and religious studies, for instance, but history, biography, autobiography, travelogue, children's books, and much else as well. With the full onset of postmodernity, the nineteenth century's aestheticist limitation of Literature to mainly poems, plays and novels was certainly much more difficult to sustain (Williams 1988: 183–188). From that point onwards, distinctions between high-, middle- and low-brow have been so steadily eroded that their decline may prove to be terminal. Although a writer such as Pinter is still perceived, especially in Britain, as "a representative of a high, bourgeois and, sometimes, avant-guarde culture" that is simply inaccessible "to those who are excluded from it by class, education and intermediaries such as the *Sun*" (Derbyshire 2009: 277), some of the other finest writers in our own time, like Shakespeare in his, have creatively hybridized genres that were basically popular, in this way greatly extending the sheer variety of texts which readers of all backgrounds like to read (Sell 2000: 271–277).

I personally still find much to discuss in poems, plays and novels. This is one of the things which most clearly distinguishes me as a communicational critic from communication (*sic*) critics like Rybacki and Rybacki. The Rybackis do cover film, television, song, public speaking, and humour. But when they speak of "large texts", they are moving in the direction of socioanthropology and urban ethnology, since their term here does not refer to novels, epics and plays, for example, but to museums, public history displays, monuments, spontaneous shrines, streets, neighbourhoods, sections of city, theme parks, and holidays. Despite their claim to an eclectic focus, they say that literature has "aesthetic properties" and therefore lock it up in a separate box of its own, which they never really re-open (Rybacki and Rybacki 2002: 141). The communicational critiques in the studies to follow here, by contrast, not only reject any view of literature so strongly marked by old-fashioned essentialism, but value the best poems, plays and novels for a quality that is also to be found in countless instances of language-in-use which no-one would ever dream of calling literature: a quality which I shall be describing as one of communicational genuineness.

These studies, then, start from a nominalistic premise. They still refer to poems, novels and plays as "literature" (albeit with a small "l"), but with only few exceptions use the term "literature" as a way of grouping together *all* the texts which many readers have *de facto* found, from whatever causes, most interesting, enjoyable and lastingly valuable. The range of media discussed is far narrower than that in the communication (*sic*) criticism of Rybacki and Rybacki. But alongside canonical literary classics, I do deal with a soldier-politician's autobiography, a popular war-time anthology of prose and verse, a teenage novel, and even one of my own attempts at mediating criticism. Each and every text taken up for discussion is evaluated within one and the same communication-ethical framework.

Although my choice of texts is more eclectic than that of many traditional literary critics, it would not have surprised Raymond Williams (1988: 183–188). But where I part company with Williams, and with other postmodern literary scholars and linguists as well, is in arguing for a communicational pragmatics that is historical without being deterministic. In trying to account for the way in which human beings actually use, interpret and act upon language in the real world, I see them as to some extent ethically autonomous. I repeat: *to some extent.* There can be no question here of a wholesale rehabilitation of the liberal humanism with which notions of Literature and its universal canon were once so tightly linked. The point is not that there is a human spirit which is independent of history but that, while we all certainly act out the consequences of our own sociocultural formation, attention must also be paid to those constant co-adaptations between the older and the newer, between the communally predictable and the communally unexpected.

Without putting writers back on Arnoldian pedestals, it can be claimed that Shakespeare's impact has indeed been partly due to his own personal qualities, though the non-Arnoldian reservation here – the "partly" – must carry due weight. People in general, and not just literary authors, can be seen as both individuals and social beings: as *social individuals* (Sell 2000: 145–158). Thoughts and behaviours which are really fairly personal can go hand in hand with traits that are far more historically representative. This was perfectly obvious to Dryden, for instance, whose literary criticism moved between the "Individual" and the "Type" with no difficulty at all. Now a similar view of human nature is emerging once again, in branches of knowledge including not only linguistic and literary scholarship, but psychology, sociology, and cultural studies. Scholarly paradigms involving extreme versions of structuralist socio-determinism and poststructuralist de-centring have come in for searching critique.

Many scholars have in fact returned to theoretical basics, pointing out that Ferdinand de Saussure, so often claimed as structuralism and poststructuralism's founding father, though he did not see *langue* as a function of the individual speaker but as a product that is assimilated by individuals within society, nevertheless regarded *parole* as a personal act that is willed and intellectual, a view which was in perfect accordance with his own training as a comparative philologist: he was an expert on how *langue*, in co-adaptation with actual *parole*, has changed over time (de Saussure 1978 [1916]: 14). So there is now an increasingly widespread sense that, no matter whether a structured system be that of language, society or culture, human beings can to some extent operate it, and are certainly not to be wholly conflated with it. Film critics, for instance, in forming an impression of some particular film-maker's complete *oeuvre*, on the one hand see many features as generic – as part of the general production culture of the film industry – but on the other hand insist on their own ability instantly to distinguish it from the *oeuvre* of anybody else. Their sense of both the generic and the distinctively personal is captured in the way they refer to a film-maker as an *auteur*, a term now sometimes borrowed into English literary criticism, precisely as a compromise between the liberal humanist "author" and Barthesian talk of "the death of the author" (Bell 1994: 35–44). Cheryl Walker (1991), similarly, has argued that even though authorship can involve formations that are typical of the culture as a whole, it can also carry the patterns of ideation, voice and sensibility of a particular individual. This duality she examines by means of "persona criticism", a persona being at once *more* personal than the endless intertextuality examined by poststructuralists and *less* personal than an original author as once seen by liberal humanists. Derek Attridge actually speaks of "idioculture": that is, of widespread cultural norms and modes of behaviour *as embodied in* a single individual. As he explains,

> [a]lthough a large part of an individual's idioculture may remain stable for some length of time, the complex as a whole is necessarily unstable and subject to constant change; and although one is likely to share much of one's idioculture with other groups (one's neighbours, one's family, one's age peers, those of the same gender, race, class, and so on), it is always a unique configuration.
>
> (Attridge 2004: 21)

In late-twentieth-century critical discourse analysis as typified by Norman Fairclough (1988), for instance, there was an emphasis on social contexts which could come a good deal closer to determinism (Sell 1991), and a similar tendency was to be seen in some of that period's most influential literary theory and criticism. While nothing could have been more thought-provoking than Bakhtin's commentaries on Rabelais and Dostoevsky, his account of such writers' dialogic imagination involved a sense of dialogicality that was counter-intuitively specialized and narrow. For Bakhtin (1981), dialogicality involved an encounter that was always less likely to be a friendly conversation than an aggressive confrontation. What it tended to promote was a communicational process whereby some word or discourse or language or culture was "relativized" or "de-privileged" by being placed in sociopolitical tension with some alternative. This varied-tonguedness or heteroglossia was said to undermine a monologism typical of more authoritarian and absolutist modes of discourse, and thereby to engage in power struggles that were latent or already active within society as a whole. Yet at the same time, the dialogicality described by Bakhtin relied on the continuing contours of those struggles for its very significance. In his kind of analysis, literary texts which hybridized or ironized by playing off one social voice against another could never reduce, but only further sharpen, the perceived differences between them. Or to put this in other, closely parallel Bakhtinian terms, dialogicality was akin to the topsy-turvydom of carnival: it was a merely temporary letting-off of steam, after which the return to status quo was all the more emphatic. What this overlooked was that literature's dialogicality, though certainly not excluding sociopolitical antipathies, does not include them necessarily, and is potentially far more dynamic. The differences it brings into play can very well originate from within one and the same sociocultural position, and the relationships it sets in motion between representatives or voicings of different positions are not pre-ordinately problematic. Sometimes the process can result in the kind of hermeneutic mergings of horizon which were theorized by Gadamer (Sell 2000: 137–149; Sell 2007), even if Gadamer himself did not see literature as communicational in any such real sense, being still tied to a nineteenth century classification of Literature under the Beautiful (Gadamer 1986: 33).

As with Bakhtin (and Bakhtinians), so with critics writing under the aegis of Foucault: post-Marxists, new historicists, cultural materialists, and postcolonial, feminist, queer and ethnic critics. In my study of Shakespeare's *Henry V* I shall be noting that, when representatives of these postmodern schools spoke of an endless ideological battle between a dominant order and potentially subversive threats to it, they, too, could minimize the scope for responsibility and for empathy with otherness. Their approaches tended to transfer agency quite away from human beings themselves to a kind of timelessly universal mechanism. This they often referred to, in Marxist fashion, as History, but it was not necessarily very historical at all. More traditional scholars complained that such reductions of history to a single ideological agonism could be historically inaccurate, a charge which sometimes prompted the poststructuralist counter-claim that historical accuracy in, say, the interpretation of a writer's words was both impossible and undesirable. According to such a view, the interest and significance of a literary text was merely something imposed upon it by particular readers or groupings of readers who were using it for their own ideological ends in their own here and now. Any sense of the text as an invitation to a dialogical comparing of notes between a writer and readers of varying positionality was conspicuously absent.

A communicational pragmatics which recognizes the moral dimension of what I am describing as our relative independence will reactivate the Greek root *pragma* (= "deed"). *Logos* is *pragma*, as we might put it, and the philological scholarship of the future would, I think, do well to include an ethical pragmatics of a kind already developed, within a sociological frame of reference, in Habermas's account of communicative action. What Habermas (1984 & 1987) specially emphasizes is that, if communication is to be genuine and effective, then there have to be certain widely accepted protocols over and above the Aristotelian logic which Nietzsche and Derrida took to be the cornerstone of western civilization. What must also come into play are ethical considerations of human equality, of truthfulness, of trust, of fairness, of cooperativeness, and of situational appropriateness.

As for literary activity, Habermas himself does not see it as one among other forms of communication, because like Gadamer he still belongs to the tradition running from nineteenth century aesthetics to twentieth century literary formalism. In his most detailed remarks on the subject, he seeks to combat what he sees in Derrida as a levelling of the distinction between communicative action and literature, a levelling which in its turn assimilates philosophy to literary criticism. To his own way of thinking, a literary work still belongs to a separate realm of purely self-referential art, and the task of literary critics is to assess it as a matter of taste, by drawing attention to features such as "artistic truth", "aesthetic harmony", and "rhetoric" in its *"pure form"* (Habermas 1998 [1985]: 396–397, his italics). On this last point he is presumably endorsing the vulgar opposition between rhetoric and truth. He seems to be thinking of truth as the prerogative of non-literary language use, and to see rhetoric in literature, not as a communicational resource, but as mere decorative embellishment. A literary author's intentions and relationship with readers are of no more concern to him than they were to American New Critics.

Even so, his profound insights into communicational ethics in general can be related to literature along lines he has not envisaged (Sell 2007). The point here is not that communicative action is to be re-conceptualized – as Habermas sees Derrida re-conceptualizing it – as literature, but that literary-communicational theory conceptualizes literature as communicative action. The single strongest support for such a view comes from readers' own gut reaction to the way a writer treats them as human beings. They do not always put this into words, but in one of his letters Keats was very explicit about it. What we really hate, he said, is "poetry that has a palpable design upon us" (Keats 1954 [1818]: 72). Like other nineteenth-century commentators, Keats actually thought that a true poet would not only abstain from such coercive intentions, but would not even have a sense of personal identity at all, an idea which had an afterlife in the Modernist valorization of impersonality, as in T. S. Eliot's essay "Tradition and the Individual Talent" (1951 [1919]). This line of thinking has always been problematic for readers who enjoy, say, Byron and Dickens for their inimitable personalities, and the truth is that all writers, Keats and Eliot included, are more personal than the two of them seem to have supposed. Yet for all that, Keats's remark on palpable design did clearly identify the ethical front on which no writer can afford to fail. Readers are understandably concerned for their own spiritual freedom.

As a result of writers' initiatives, the world is sometimes actually changed, not totally and instantaneously, but certainly in gradual stages. Readers have sufficient powers of intelligence, imagination and moral discrimination to stand back from their own situation and view it from a new angle, so that fresh insights arising from a literary text can always take their place alongside older ones. This can amount to a kind of compromise which again illustrates the principle of communicational co-adaptation. As already explained by the rhetoricians of classical antiquity, influential communicators adapt to society in order to be listened to and understood, but also with the goal of adapting society to their own project. So yes, Dickens's *Dombey and Son* really did kowtow to Mrs. Grundy's notions of decorum. To the cheek of the Victorian Young Person this novel can have brought not the slightest blush. But in those same pages Dickens also managed to deal with poverty, prostitution, adultery and marital rape, in the long run quite cutting the ground from under Mrs. Grundy's feet

(Sell 2001: 165–193). In a case like this, a literary writer's words turn out to have been a socially co-adaptational deed.

Within a culture, a writer's intentions do get interwoven with those of countless other agents. As underlined in Farrell's blackly comic parable, writers get *used* by other people. In the case of a dramatist, this process begins well before a play is seen by an audience, as actors, directors, producers, stage- and costume designers all plan, coordinate and rehearse their various contributions. As time goes by, there may be new productions, plus critical or scholarly commentaries which also affect the interpretative tradition, and a major literary work will always be cited and discussed in many other kinds of discourse as well. All of which will reflect the workings of a fundamental communicational paradox: that the more powerful individuals are as users of language, the less power they really have over their own words. The words of a major writer, though very strong in being so memorable and attracting so much notice and discussion, are also very weak, in that the more they are discussed, the more they are used by other people. They are filtered through the minds of huge numbers of individuals, who find themselves in many different kinds of situation, and who inevitably bring new emphases to bear, new understandings. Such differences of interpretation are not necessarily the result of careless or unfaithful readings, but can actually result from uncertainties, complexities, ambiguities or potentialities which were already present the mind of the writer, the kind of thing which, especially if the writer's own attitude towards it was unrepressive from the start, becomes even more noticeable as a text is read under changing historical conditions. Such interpretative developments would not deserve a writer's angry disapproval, since although the general public ought to acknowledge authors' right to their own ideas and values, and to their own understanding of what they are writing, authors are humanly bound to return the courtesy. A legitimation by which one human individual could *a priori* claim to be more worthy of respect than another is simply unavailable. Although few people nowadays would unreservedly endorse Kant's aesthetic theory, his central idea in ethics, of the universal human right to respect and fair treatment, remains foundational for our conception of justice (Kant 1998 [1785]). Agreement about which communicant's intentions, which communicant's interpretations, are the best ones cannot even be reached by discussion after the event, since the event we are talking about here will never come to an end except through the total extinction of the human species. As I shall try to show in my study of *Henry V*, this point was well understood by Shakespeare, who often disagreed with, and altered, the stories he found in his sources. In re-plotting them, he always made the strength and weakness of people's words a main focus of attention, and metatheatrically encouraged his audiences to speculate on the future of his own plays.

But a literary writer's own input remains important even so. There is a real ethical difference between literary texts which come down to us through the technologies of literacy as the works of identified writers and, say, anonymously produced ballads transmitted by oral tradition. The obligation to try to understand the human other is much more direct when the other is an individual who is specifically personalized in this way, and by using our powers of intellect and empathetic imagination, perhaps assisted by scholarly commentaries, we can at least approximate a writer's drift as best we can, complemented as it well may be by the riches of a subsequent tradition of interpretation, and inviting as it inevitably will our own assessment. In practice we do not assume, as readers, that writers are interpretable only according to their own lights, and the lights of their sociocultural fellows and contemporaries. Whether we can ever have reliable access to "the author's" or "the original audience's" interpretation is an epistemological moot point. But our minds are in any case capable of far subtler kinds of parallel processing than professionalist literary scholarship has sometimes allowed. Even when our desire to understand an author is at its most intense, our mental activity is as different as could possibly be from the monoideism which hammers out a "definitive interpretation". We cannot but react as human beings living in our own here and now, in our own time and place. And we shall probably know about some of the most significant earlier reactions as well, and understand their appropriateness to those different times and places. But none of this need for a moment distract us from an ethically motivated concern to give the writer as fair a hearing as we should like to be accorded ourselves.

On the contrary, if there is no such active juxtaposition of different points of view, literary communication is no longer taking place. When a text ceases to stimulate real discussion, it no longer inhabits the social category of literature. Conversely, our comments on a text from the past which does maintain, or which for the first time now acquires, a literary cachet will beneficially alternate between an empathy that always risks becoming historically puristic and a self-expressiveness that always risks becoming anachronistic. The very dialogicality of literature ensures that our minds do respond in both ways at once, as we live out the even-handed interchange between the writer there and then and ourselves here and now.

This is not to quibble with Farrell's perception that communication can be unidirectional. As enlisted in the consolidation or defence of empire, Shakespeare was deprived of dialogicality. It was not the Collector's intention that the sepoys should respond to the projectile, and the electrometallic head of Shakespeare obliged by simply knocking many of them flat. Or to translate the parable: those responsible for teaching Shakespeare in India did not pose questions, did not invite their pupils to a comparing of notes, but simply blasted forth a like-it-or-lump-it message of imperial determination. Whether or not this is fair comment on education under the British Raj, communication that is coercively monologic in spirit is certainly always wide-spread. So wide-spread, in fact, that it came to suggest the dominant model of communication, not only for twentieth century semioticians and linguists, but for many scholars with literary and more broadly cultural interests as well, including communication (*sic*) critics like Rybacki and Rybacki: the model, that is to say, of communication as a strongly transitive and persuasive event; as the transmission of a message from a sender to a receiver, from a speaker to a listener, from a writer to a reader, from a narrator to a narratee; as a uni-directional process, in other words, in which one party is more active, and would perhaps lay claim to a higher ideological status, while the other is more passive, perhaps more ideologically marginalized, and unable to grasp the more active party's meaning, message, or intention except by pragmatically decoding the text in relation to just a single context, a context also imposed, in effect, by the more active party. In Rybacki and Rybacki's introduction to communication (*sic*) criticism, this model is stated as follows:

> All rhetorical acts have three common elements: rhetor, rhetorical text, and receiver. The *rhetor* is the person or persons who created the message – the symbols that make up the *rhetorical text*. This rhetorical text is the collection of symbols used in a given act of communication. The *receiver*, commonly called "audience", is the person or persons influenced by the rhetorical text.
>
> (Rybacki and Rybacki 2002: 4)

In line with this, Rybacki and Rybacki also say that, when communication critics focus on narrative, they will examine the given story's ability "to serve as a reliable and desirable guide for belief and behaviour", as if narrative at best were always an allegorical dress for philosophical, religious and ethical instruction. That narratives in texts such as the Wakefield nativity play, Book II of the *Faerie Queene* and *Paradise Lost* draw communicational power from partly subverting their own didacticism is completely lost on communication (*sic*) critics, for whom literature's "aesthetic properties" simply work hand in hand with "persuasive powers of argumentation" (Rybacki and Rybacki 2002: 141–142) – like the sugar coating on a pill.

In many of the countless cases when communication does fit this kind of model, some of them helpfully analysed by communication (*sic*) critics, we can speak, with Habermas (1970), of distorted communication: of communication which is not genuine, in the sense that it does not involve an fair-minded mutual respect, but is skewed by some assumed disparity between the participants. Even though Edda Weigand's studies of dialogicality include a paper on "The Argumentative Power of Words: Or How to Move other People's Minds With Words", which brilliantly demonstrates that various techniques for exercising influence depend upon a "process of adaptation and negotiation" between one person's mind and another's (Weigand 2009: 373), such interaction is not dialogical in an ethically high sense, since it can obviously spring from selfish ends which bear no relation to its empathetic means. It can all too easily become, as one might say, an abuse of human understanding. This is not to deny that, especially when we find ourselves in positions of responsibility, some such reduced dialogicality may be almost unavoidable. Nor, in practice, need it be at all sinister. A tourist bombarded with directions to local beauty spots, or a child firmly ordered to stay on the pavement in a street of fast-moving traffic, can have reasons for gratitude. But uni-directional communication, no matter how well-intentioned at best, always tends to undermine the principle of human equality, and is often adopted for that very reason.

Now when postcolonial and other postmodern theoreticians and critics reacted against the repressive hegemony which could be buttressed by the older accounts of Literature's universality and special aesthetic status, their re-historicizing poetics sometimes assumed, in effect, that literary communication could only be communication of a strongly distorted kind. This is how, having emphasized the difference between one sociohistorical formation and another, such commentators then went on to say that literature could no longer be thought of as a single canon of great masterpieces for the entire human race, but should rather be seen as many separate canons for many differently positioned communal groupings, most of which were now to be taken as "writing back" against the older order (Ashcroft, Griffiths and Tiffin 2002). This argument fed in to the immense process of postmodern democratization and cultural empowerment within society at large. As we have seen, it has also been co-opted into communication (*sic*) criticism. Yet precisely from the point of view of communication, both as a phenomenon actually taking place between real human beings, and as a theoretical concept within scholarship, the valorization of positional difference was not exclusively beneficial (Sell 2000: 88–106). It not only insisted on distinctions between one human grouping and another, but could even suggest that different groupings had so little in common that they were incapable of mutual understanding, as if difference really did go all the way down, as Miller put it. This meant that a positional identity could in practice become a kind of prisonhouse, confining its occupants to just a limited range of taste, behaviour, and social exchange. In fact the entire human world could seem to consist of different factions ranged in unassuageable conflict – the very scenario depicted for the "culture wars". This was a climate of ideas in which truly worthwhile communication could seem to be taking place only between the like-minded, as if, in communication *between* one grouping and another, each grouping would inevitably try to assert itself and eliminate opposition. The feature most highly prized in literary texts, similarly, was a certain tendentiousness on behalf of some particular identity formation – the social script taken to be politically correct within a specific community or sub-community. Conversely, texts were excluded from the communal canon when deemed tendentious in an *un*acceptable way.

But although some of the writings that have aspired to high communal status certainly are communicationally distorted, they are unlikely to retain readers' admiration in the long term, unless, perhaps, they achieve a purely historical significance as the pioneer texts of an emergent literature. Nor were all the texts which postmodern commentators praised as, in effect, tendentious really were so, or were so to the extent alleged. To think of Salman Rushdie, Toni Morrison or Caryl Phillips along such lines, for instance, would be patently absurd.

Distorted communication will always be with us. But what many branches of late-twentieth-century scholarship failed to recognize was the availability of that more profitable kind of communication which I am describing as genuine: communication in which different parties respect each other's human autonomy. It is by emphasizing the potentiality for such genuineness that communicational (*sic*) criticism will most sharply differ from Rybacki and Rybacki's communication (*sic*) criticism. One of its main propositions is that communicational genuineness actually helps to explain why some texts attract very large audiences over very long periods of time while others do not. This claim is not a new kind of essentialism. Genuineness can never be a *sufficient* precondition for high literary status, and it frequently occurs in many other kinds of communication as well, the vast majority of it quite unrecorded. Also, readers have always applied additional, more exclusively "literary" criteria which have been specific to their own particular phase of culture. Rather, genuineness is a *necessary* precondition – a *sine qua non* – for widespread admiration, even in cases where it is not a feature explicitly praised by reviewers or literary critics. Studies published here will suggest that Wordsworth, though so often decried as egotistical, and Dickens, though so often blamed for being intrusively manipulative, both became canonical thanks to a communicational genuineness that ran far deeper than any such appearances to the contrary.

Genuine communication is not some ivory-tower fantasy. Human history is often said to have been an endless tale of violence, injustice, oppression and war, and there is more than enough truth in this to account for the frequency, and indeed the widespread institutionalization, of distorted communication in symbiosis with many different forms of coercion, divisiveness and conflict. Yet a very substantial record could also be compiled of peaceful coexistence: of human tolerance and cooperation in countless different kinds of context, within all of which the communicational situation has been, not so much a binarism of sender-receiver within a unitary context imposed by a domineering sender, as a triangular relationship between two human equals and someone or something else (though it can also be "me", "you" or "us") about whom or which they are comparing notes, both of them freely approaching this process from within their own different lifeworlds.

Not that they initially had nothing in common at all. In order to communicate, they have had to share, not only some competence in the actual means of communication, but experience of the existential basics of human life in general: the facts of birth and death, of human needs, both primary and secondary, of social allegiance and social tension, of personal relationships. These commonalities, though so variously realized in the successive phases of history's manifold cultural traditions, have always been a launching-pad for flights of imaginative empathy with otherness, and human beings have sufficient moral and intellectual self-control to step outside their own sociohistorical position and understand some other point of view, even in the innumerable cases where the final result does not turn out to be a consensus. Very often people agree to disagree. But in terms of knowledge and understanding, their genuine communication extends the overlap of their two lifeworlds all the same.

This is how communication becomes communication in the etymological sense – a "community-making": not because it forces everybody into line, but because it promotes a widening circle of discussion from many different points of view. The community resulting from undistorted communication is in principle indefinitely large and indefinitely heterogeneous.

The writing and reading of texts which become widely admired over long periods of time form one process of non-elitist, genuine communication among others, and although Damrosch (2004) is right to point out that at present world literature is still tending to fall into a primary hypercanon and a secondary countercanon, there could in fact be a canon of texts which was truly universal, not for the reasons Harold Bloom (1995, 1998) tried to resurrect from the Victorian aesthetics of Literature, not because it straitjacketed all writers and all readers into a single identity formation which it then labelled as the truly Human, not because it had been legislated into existence as a fast-fossilizing reading list authorized by self-legitimating judges, but because it showed itself able to support a dynamic catholicity, becoming a focus of dialogue within a community that was both indefinitely large and indefinitely heterogeneous.

World literature in this post-postmodern sense is what the ethical input of both mediating and communicational criticism tends to promote, even when, as in the present studies, such approaches limit their focus to works from a single cultural tradition. Even within what is perceived as one and the same culture, there will always be many positional differences that need to be brought into relationship. And habits of communicational good practice which have been thoughtfully developed within one cultural tradition can then be extended to others, and to relationships between one tradition and another.

Seen in this perspective, both Victorian and postmodern critics were partly mistaken, but also partly right. By studying the communicational dimension of texts which have already attracted, or which we think seem likely to attract, wide and lasting admiration, we can recover a sense of literature's universality without sacrificing an awareness of every writer's and every reader's historical positionality. Major writing, by communicating genuinely, is not polemically "of" a particular sociohistorical position, but neither is it in polemical denial of one. Like all genuine communication, it is at once positioned, and sensitive to the possibility of other positionings, and it can even acknowledge that its own position may involve inner uncertainties and divisions. Although it will sometimes excite even warmer admiration if the writer seems to have a strong personality, its gesture is not distortingly to convey a single, unidirectional message, but to invite readers to a comparing of notes which is dialogical in the broadest and most dynamic sense.

1.3   Literary community-making

Literary texts draw around themselves communities of addressees who do not experience themselves as receivers of a message, but who respond to what is basically an invitation to compare notes about something. The topics on which this dialogicality between writers and addressees can focus are inexhaustibly various. But as a clue to how the process of literary community-making actually gets under way, we can note that, even if the communicational self-consciousness to which I am pointing in Shakespeare was of an exceptional quality, it was of a common enough kind. In many poems, plays and novels, in many biographical and autobiographical works, and in many other kinds of writing as well, the thing about which the writer and the text's addressees compare notes is in the first instance human communication itself. Even in texts which do not tell a story or dramatize characters in action, an author's words addressed to a public can reflexively draw attention to their own style or shifting styles of communication.

This means that, as a regular course of events, communities grow up around writers' representations of, or personal attempts at, community-making. Directly or indirectly, literature's addressees compare notes, both with writers and with other addressees, about the ways in which characters "in the story", or writers themselves, are successful or unsuccessful in comparing notes and creating human relationships. Granted, when those who have engaged with a literary text give their considered opinion of it, they will often concentrate on features of some quite different nature. As I say, communication is only one of innumerable potential topics, and it often passes unnoticed. Unnoticed only in addressees' conscious mind, however. A writer's fundamental perceptions about the workings of human communication exert an immediate and crucial attraction, and the literary community becomes larger and more heterogeneous as those perceptions are experienced, subliminally or otherwise, as interesting from more and more different points of view.

So in practice, many writers are strongly concerned with human individuals as members or potential members of groupings, both smaller groupings and larger. When they portray characters in action, they are offering examples of people who somehow or other manage to make community, or who, for whatever reason, do not make community – people just like the rest of us. Romeo and Juliet are two individuals who fall in love, and we see, we hear, we understand how this feels to each of them personally. But their love's sharpness, exquisiteness, danger, comes from their membership of the two opposed families, and the play hovers between comedy and tragedy as we wait to see whether or not love will become the rule of the still larger grouping that is the entire city. Between the warring families, will distorted communication at last give way to genuine? It is this, I am suggesting, which first gets us interested, even if it is not what we explicitly discuss with other people, and even if an author's interest in community-making is not always as schematically clear-cut as in the plotting of this particular play.

Romeo and Juliet ends up as a tragedy, but from the point of view of community-making Shakespeare's tragedies and comedies work in similar ways. In *Twelfth Night*, the communal status quo is turned topsy-turvy by love, with people becoming uncontrollably, hopelessly, confusingly enamoured across class and gender boundaries. In *Macbeth*, the disruption is caused by the Macbeths' extreme ambition. In *Twelfth Night*, the disorder leads to individuals experiencing either themselves or other people as mad; Sebastian's dazed astonishment on his reception by Olivia catches the note of the entire play; and Malvolio, though he has reasons for his smiling and for his cross-gartered yellow stockings, has become sufficiently unlike himself, and sufficiently unlike a normal steward, for his incarceration in a darkroom – a standard treatment for madness – to seem reasonable enough to those who are not in on the conspiracy against him. In *Macbeth*, psychological abnormalities are no less central: the hallucinated dagger; the ghost of Banquo disrupting, in the central scene, the ceremonious banquet which Macbeth had wanted to symbolize a country united under his rule, and which for the audience can from that point onwards only mean the opposite; Lady Macbeth's compulsive hand-washing. And comedy and tragedy both lead up to a single type of ending: an emphatically reinstated sanity and communality, in comedy by way of orderly dance and marital unions, in tragedy often thanks to the prospect of new and less dangerous leaders.

What distinguishes comedy and tragedy is not so much their beginnings and endings as the precise gravity of the communal disorder which has to be lived through in the middle. Nor are the endings, though in both genres they bring some comfort, really so complete after all. The restored community does not include Malvolio, who walks off in a rage for revenge, or the Macbeths and their victims, who are all dead. The whole emphasis of both comedy and tragedy is decidedly on the middle, and on just how powerful disruption can be. The endings are "only" endings, and can even seem rather anticlimactic and unconvincing. One can come away from the theatre feeling that it is precisely communal stability that is abnormal, and that if were otherwise, then that would be the end of all good stories. Nothing of much interest is likely to happen in paradise on earth, one might well conclude. There is certainly little to suggest that Shakespeare found genuine communication more wide-spread than distorted.

His communicational realism is particularly clear his history plays. Here some of the central individuals are kings and other political figures, and the question of their relationship to groupings is a matter of whether they are going to be able to lead and dominate, which is where we get some of Shakespeare's acutest insights into the strength and weakness of words. One of his main perceptions is that words are more powerful than swords, and are at their least effective when most sword-like, as when Henry V warns the defenders of Harfleur that

> ...the fleshed soldier, rough and hard of heart,
> In liberty of bloody hand shall range
> With conscience wide as hell, mowing like grass
> Your fair virgins,   (III iii, ll. 11–14)[1]

– which is one of a whole long sequence ineffectual threats, beginning in the play's opening scene with a response to the Dauphin's present of tennis balls that might have interested Farrell's Collector: Henry instructs the French ambassadors to "tell the pleasant prince this mock of his / Hath turned his balls to gun-stones" (I ii, ll. 281–2). Harfleur falls, not because its citizens are awed at Henry's words, but because the Dauphin fails to turn up with support. Henry's threats, his most communicationally distorted utterances, are powerless because their addressees take them in their own way by totally disregarding them. Altogether more effective, at least for a time, are Henry's efforts of genuine communication, when he illustrates what Aristotle meant by a great orator's diminishing his distance from his hearers. His exhortation to his own soldiers at Harfleur is typical:

> Once more unto the breach, dear friends, once more,
> ... [T]here is none of you so mean and base
> That hath not noble lustre in your eyes.   (III i 1, ll. 29–30)

– which is doubtless the kind of thing which makes Bates say "I think the king is but a man as I am" (IV i 97), and even feel sorry for him. By acknowledging his soldiers' fellow humanity, by implicitly encouraging a dialogue, in which they respond to his thoughts about their position by starting to think about his, Henry invites all his best men into a military community, in which the hierarchy of command of course still operates, and which in this sense is still socially heterogeneous.

A polarity between distorted and genuine communication can help to shape a literary work's entire structure. In *King Lear*, for instance, there are fluctuations between, on the one hand, a manner of speech whose syntactical and rhetorical structures are balanced and cumulative and, on the other hand, utterances strongly coloured by the use of imperatives and exclamations. The balanced, cumulative style tends to be communicationally genuine, in that it correlates with characters being reasonable, calm, alive to the realities of past and present, un-self-centred, and prepared to weigh up different points of view. The imperative-exclamatory style is more likely to be communicationally distorted. It is often used by characters when, ignoring or spurning the present, they hope to stamp own will upon the future.

At the beginning of the play Lear wants to shed the cares of office by dividing his kingdom between his three daughters. He requires that they compete with each other in telling him how much they love him, and his idea is that Cordelia's love will thereby

---

1.   Quotations of *Henry V* taken from Gurr 1992.

emerge as clearly the greatest. By way of reward, he will assign to her, or to the consort
he now expects her to choose, the best share of the kingdom, plus a coronet to symbolize this. When the scheme misfires, he immediately recoups, improvising an alternative future and dictating accordingly. Throughout this entire episode, in everything
he says the peppering of imperatives and expletives is very liberal indeed: "Attend the
Lords of France and Burgundy, Gloucester"; "Give me the map there. Know that…";
"How now, Cordelia!" "Peace, Kent!"; "Hence, and avoid my sight!" (I i, ll. 34, 37, 93,
121, 124).[2] And so on, and so on. Confirming his merely twofold division of the kingdom between Goneril and Regan, his command to their husbands is: "This coronet
part between you" (I ii, l. 139). At which point the coronet becomes a stage symbol
of even greater suggestiveness than the use he had originally intended – the Fool will
later have some tart things to say about what happens if you try to split a crown down
the middle. At this point, then, Lear's communicational style is combining with stage
image to suggest that his ego-trip into the future is unadvisedly headstrong.

Cordelia, Kent and France all try to slow him down:-

> *Lear:* … Mend your speech a little,
> Lest you may mar your fortunes.
> *Cordelia:*   Good my Lord,
> You have begot me, bred me, lov'd me: I
> Return those duties back as are right fit,
> Obey you, love you, and most honor you.   (I i , ll. 93–98)

> *Lear:* This coronet part between you.
> *Kent:*   Royal Lear,
> Whom I have ever honor'd as my King,
> Lov'd as my father, as my master follow'd,
> As my great patron thought on in my prayers –   (I i, ll. 139–142)

> *Lear [to Burgundy]:* Then leave her, sir …
> … *[to France]* beseech you
> T'avert your liking a more worthier way
> Than on a wretch whom Nature is asham'd
> Almost t'acknowledge hers.
> *France:*   This is most strange,
> That she, whom even but now was your best object,
> The argument of your praise, balm of your age,
> The best, the dearest, should in this trice of time
> Commit a thing so monstrous, to dismantle
> So many folds of favor.   (I i, ll. 207–218)

---

2. Quotations of *King Lear* taken from Kermode 1997.

Each time, the resistance to Lear's will begins with a character's wresting the last one-and-a-half or two feet of a line from him, and using it for some expression which can be followed by a strong terminal pause, so allowing the actor to bring in body language suggesting a perplexed attempt to get things straight, or to appeal for understanding in others. Then follows the deliberate rehearsal of fact upon fact, to be carefully weighed together. In Cordelia's opening thrust for sanity, the stylistic bias towards accumulation with balance is especially clear: the "I" is posed antithetically at the end of the line against the line-initial "You"; the three perfect-tense verbs plus "me" syntactically mirror and semantically add to each other; and they are weighed against the three present-tense verbs plus "you" in the line following the one in which the reciprocity is explicitly stated. Yet in Kent's and France's speeches, too, a parallelism, an iconic linking of points equally worthy of consideration, is very noticeable: there is Kent's "*perfect-tense verb* as my *noun*, *perfect-tense verb* as my *noun*", and so on; and there is France's "The *noun* of your *noun*, *noun* of your *noun*", and so on. The communicational similarities between the three speakers intimate that they are all "on the same side", so strengthening the triadic narrative pattern of their unsuccessful attempts to make reasonableness prevail.

Later in the play, Lear learns some hard lessons about present reality. He begins to understand the error of his ways, the true nature of each daughter, and just how powerless he has made himself. He tries to accept all this with patience, yet can still be convulsed with fantasies of revenge. Under these circumstances, the difference between the two communicational styles becomes even more dramatic. When told that Cornwall cannot see him because of illness, and that he should bear in mind Cornwall's fiery temper, he responds:

> Fiery? the fiery Duke? Tell the hot Duke that –
> No, but not yet; may be he is not well:
> Infirmity doth still neglect all office
> Whereto our health is bound; we are not ourselves
> When nature, being oppress'd, commands the mind
> To suffer with the body. I'll forbear,
> And am fallen out with my more headier will,
> To take the indispos'd and sickly fit
> For the sound man. *[Looking on Kent* [in the stocks]*]* Death on my state!
> wherefore
> Should he sit here? This act persuades me
> That this remotion of the Duke and her [i.e. Regan]
> Is practice only. Give me my servant forth.
> Go tell the Duke, and's wife, I'ld speak with them –
> Now, presently. Bid them come forth and hear me,
> Or at their chamber-door I'll beat the drum
> Till it cry sleep to death.   (II iv, ll. 104–119)

The alternation between anger, an attempt at patience, and back again to anger could not be more marked. As always, the rhythmic changes are crucial. But also, fluent exclamations and imperatives are now in extremely sharp contrast with the three anti-thetical structures. Lear's failure to push the antitheses towards a still fuller syntactical and rhetorical isomorphism can itself suggest his difficulty in achieving anything like complete mental calm even for a moment.

Shortly afterwards, the same stylistic dichotomy helps to make our two glimpses of Lear in the storm, in scenes III ii and III iv, fascinatingly complementary. In III ii, he wants to bring about the apocalyptic end of the world; there shall be a universal judgement, which will of course take care of his daughters. As he encourages the roaring elements to this end, the exclamations and imperatives reach a kind of peak, both by their density of occurrence and by their sheer semantic strength: "Blow, winds, and crack your cheeks! rage, blow! / You cataracts and hurricanoes, spout"; "You sul'phrous and thought-executing fires / ... / Singe my white head! And thou, all-shaking thunder, / Strike flat the thick rotundity o' th'world! / Crack nature's moulds, all germains spill at once / That makes ingrateful man!"(III ii, ll. 1–2, 4–9). And so on, and so on. Yet even in this scene, it is clearly hinted that Lear's mood can swing, and that he might even achieve moments of acceptance and pity for others: "No, I will be the pattern of all patience"; "My wits begin to turn."; "Poor Fool and knave, I have one part in my heart / That's sorry yet for thee" (III ii, ll. 37, 67, 72–73). These suggestions provide a kind of bridge across to III iv, where they are realized. In this second scene he tries to control his mental anguish and desire for revenge by concentrating more on the physical sufferings inflicted by the storm, and his continued meditation on the plight of the Fool becomes the catalyst to a pity that is hardly less comprehensive than was his earlier call for doomsday. This is a context in which the cumulative-balanced style reaches, in its turn, something of a climax:

> Thou think'st 'tis much that this contentious storm
> Invades us to the skin; so 'tis to thee;
> But where the greater malady is fix'd,
> The lesser is scarce felt. Thou'dst shun a bear;
> But if thy flight lay toward the roaring sea,
> Thou'dst meet the bear i' th' mouth. When the mind's free
> The body's delicate.   (III iv, ll. 4–12)

There is a pregnant contrast between the poise of these lines and the continuing fury of the storm, a reminder of Lear's mood in the earlier scene. The dualism of mental and bodily suffering, which was only half-articulated in his attempted patience on the news of Cornwall's alleged indisposition, is now given even more marked stylistic expression by means of extended iconic interplay: between "greater" and "lesser", semantically opposite but morphologically equivalent; between "is fix'd" and "is felt", parallel morphologically, but not quite phonetically; between "Thou'ldst shun a bear"

and "Thou'ldst meet the bear"; locally, between the isomorphic yet semantically contrasting "the mind's free" and "The body's delicate"; and on a larger scale, between the
clausally isomorphic "where the greater malady is fix'd / The lesser is scarce felt" and
"When the mind's free / The body's delicate", an isomorphism pointed metrically by
the repeated use of the line-end to separate the one clause from the other. And then,
as Lear's mind reaches out into the present which surrounds him –

> Poor naked wretches, wheresoe'er you are,
> That bide the pelting of this pitiless storm,
> How shall your houseless heads and unfed sides,
> Your loop'd and window'd raggedness, defend you
> From seasons such as these?   (III iv, ll. 28–32)

– the basic facts represented by the nouns are dwelt on and explored in the accumulat-
ing adjectives; fact is weighed together with fact in a movement of mind that is lin-
guistically and rhetorically conveyed by pairings: the wretches' poverty or piteousness
is added to their nakedness by simple juxtaposition of adjectives; the storm's pelting to
its pitilessness partly by alliteration; the houseless heads to the unfed sides by parison;
and the clothes' visual appearance to their lack of weather-proofing by the two stages
of a sylleptic semantic progression. As with the first storm scene, this scene would be
less than Shakespearian if Lear's mood and style were rigidly unfluctuating. He still
shows traces of anger and of the exclamatory-imperative style – "filial ingratitude!";
"O Regan, Goneril!". But in

> ... Take physic, pomp;
> Expose thyself to feel what wretches feel...   (III iv, ll. 33–34)

he is at last commanding, albeit indirectly, himself, and the command is the more
temperate for a hint of balance in the polyptoton ("feel ... feel").

I hope this is enough to suggest that communicational contrasts are integral to
this play's entire manner of self-unfolding. My own commentary, in responding to
the varieties of communicational mode adopted by Lear and other characters, has
constantly moved outwards to character portrayal, narratological structures, and thematic significances within the play as a whole. In this respect it has mirrored the
mental processes of any spectator or reader who comes to *King Lear* with an open
mind. Consciously or not, what we first latch on to in a literary work is the words and
the way they are communicating, whether as between different characters, as a single
character's self-communion, or as the writer's own address to readers. From this we
very soon begin to draw conclusions and build larger structures of comprehension, so
that when we come to discuss the work with somebody else its actual words and their
modes of communication may no longer be the main focus of our interest. Yet there is
always a sense in which writers' preoccupation with communication and community-
making is primary.

There are actually devices which writers can use to give their public's communicational assessments a kick-start. In the case of Shakespeare's plays, there are three in particular on which he relies fairly heavily. All of them have received much scholarly and critical attention in the past. But from our present point of view, the thing to notice is how they all three work together to prompt audiences to engage in genuine communication about the genuine communication, or more often about the lack of it, on stage.

For one thing, Shakespeare uses chorus characters, the most explicit example being Chorus in *Henry V*. What Chorus does is to speak of the play's story as something that is already available as a published text, which the author of the play is now retelling. He deliberately mentions it as already part of the stuff of national legend, and clearly expects interest in it to continue. Spectators themselves, he constantly emphasizes, will have to use their own imagination and get involved in what is going on before their eyes. In other plays, in both *King Lear* and *Twelfth Night*, there are professional Fools, who comment on the insanities of the communal disturbance on stage, and who, if they are not always willingly listened to by the mad characters caught up in that, nevertheless provide the audience with suggestive benchmarks. The Old Man in *Macbeth*, similarly, comments on the unnatural happenings in the world of weather and animals, unprecedented in his long memory, and clearly emblematic of grave abnormalities in the human kingdom. His words may well prompt an audience to search their own memories, and perhaps even to test comparisons with the human kingdom of their own present time. In the ideological foreground of this particular play is of course the proposition that James VI & I has united Scotland with another country into a much larger and happier community.

A second communicationally proactive device is dramatic irony. The witches show Macbeth the vision of Banquo's heirs leading down to the monarch with twin orbs, but Macbeth interprets some of their other prophecies as cancelling this one out. Members of Shakespeare's audience have always already known, thanks to their own position in history, that the vision speaks true and cannot be so cancelled, and, well ahead of Macbeth himself, have also known that the other prophecies, about Macbeth never being killed by a man born of woman or until Birnam Wood moves, though also strictly true, are equivocal, blurring the distinction between eventualities which are absolutely impossible and eventualities which would normally have been no more than very unlikely. In *Twelfth Night*, again, the audience knows that the truth about the letter found by Malvolio is not as he assumes. Both Malvolio and Macbeth are interpreting communications according to the bias of their own community-disrupting excess, so that the audience is drawn into a kind of running disagreement with them, not only about the actual facts of the case, but about the moral lessons to be drawn from it. By corollary, every member of the audience begins to bond with every other member, for instance in assessing what the character on stage really deserves. At such points Shakespeare is uniting his audience as a community *in opposition* to the character on stage, replicating the character's isolation from normality (such as it is) on stage as well.

Thirdly, as an even stronger goad to audience involvement dramatic irony is often made more complex by Shakespeare's use of asides, soliloquies and comments by one character on another. When Macbeth and Banquo first meet the Witches and hear their greetings, Macbeth is immediately consumed by ambitious fantasies, whereas Banquo remains more sober and sceptical. In asides and soliloquies Macbeth gives the audience some idea of what he is thinking, while in another part of the stage Banquo is already conversing with other comrades in arms, to whom, glancing across at Macbeth, he says "Look how our partner's rapt" (I iii, l. 142).[3] This is how Shakespeare introduces the audience to the two completely different realities that will run along-side each other throughout the play: the public world of court and army life, the of-ficial version of events, if you will; and the private world of Macbeth, who sees public individuals and events through his own perspective, and who at first admits Lady Macbeth to his private view of things but later excludes even her. By using the device at the outset like this, Shakespeare puts theatre-goers in direct touch with both world-views, and they subsequently move backwards and forward between them. Here the dramatic irony is at the expense, not of Macbeth, but of Duncan and Macbeth's other potential victims. Nor, as the device continues to be used, is the audience's response likely to be one of straightforward condemnation of Macbeth. Their inwardness to his acute understanding of his own spiritual death may well move them to pity. In *Twelfth Night*, too, this same device can only complicate the audience's internal debate and the ensuing tradition of communal commentary. Malvolio believes that he is solilo-quizing about greatness thrust upon one (and so on) only to himself. But the theatre audience sees that he is in fact overheard by the conspirators as well, whose plans the audience have already followed in every detail. Again, then, the audience is in direct touch with the two different worlds, though this time the mitigation of their adverse judgement of the agent of disruption may come sooner – the scene can perhaps be played in such a way as to urge some sympathy for the gulled Malvolio.

At interpretative cruces like this, the whole communal process gets under way. If one production or commentator or spectator or reader or group of readers or specta-tors supports the idea that Malvolio deserves some pity, another will see him as figure of pure farce, while yet another will accommodate something of both readings. With the lapse of years, such discussion continues, and not just about the appropriate ratio of pity to condemnation for Macbeth or Malvolio. Very many other types of question are discussed as well, with some of them becoming typical for particular historical phases of the Shakespearian community's development, others recurring with dif-ferent twists in different periods. As illustrated by David Fishelov (2010), another scholar now interested in literature's dialogicality, the magnitude and variety of such interpretative interactions between a text's writer and its public are a major factor if it is to achieve canonical status.

---

3. Quotations of *Macbeth* taken from Evans *et al.* 1997.

Even in one and the same period there can be many different ways of reading just a single play. The postcolonial view of *The Tempest* as a colonialist text now seems to have modulated into a sense that, although colonization and colonialist attitudes were very much in the air, and were clearly alluded to on stage, other frames of reference were also making their presence felt; that Caliban does to some extent suggest the colonized subaltern, but can also be related to the period's fascination with prodigies and monstrous births; and that Prospero, who after all, as David Lindley puts it, "did not choose to voyage to his island, has no interest in founding an outpost of Milan, and does not desire to turn the riches of the island … into tradeable commodities", can seem "closer to Duke Senior, reluctant inhabitant of the Forest of Arden in *As You Like It*, than to Sir Thomas Gates [one of the early Governors of the English colony in Virginia]" (Lindley 2002: 43, 39). Both the postcolonialist and other recent readings of the same play have been noted by Stephen Orgel:

> [*The Tempest*] looks different in different contexts, and it has been used to sup-
> port radically differing claims about Shakespeare's allegiances. In recent years we
> have seen Prospero as a noble ruler and mage, a tyrant and megalomaniac, a
> necromancer, a Neoplatonic scientist, a colonial imperialist, a civilizer. Similarly,
> Caliban has been an ineducable brute, a sensitive savage, a European wild man, a
> New-World native, ugly, attractive, tragic, pathetic, comic, frightening, the right-
> ful owner of the island, a natural slave. The … play will provide at least some
> evidence for all … [these readings], and its critical history is a good index to the
> ambivalences and ambiguities.   (Orgel 1994: 11)

Orgel would be going too far if his notion of *The Tempest*'s openness claimed that the play's meaning is *totally* open and, as I say, Keats certainly exaggerates when he claims that a poet "has no Identity" (Keats 1954 [1818]: 172). The notion of Shakespeare's inscrutability is closely related to nineteenth century ideas of Art's unageing specialness, which could leave writers sounding oddly de-socialized. About a great many things Shakespeare had very firm opinions indeed, even if they were not of central interest to his plays but were, precisely, what the plays took for granted: commonplaces of his own time's political ideology, for instance, such as, in *Macbeth*, the benefits flowing from James's unification of the two kingdoms. All such widespread, firm assumptions contributed to his writing's addresser- and addressee personae. They are part of the communicational starting-point, the familiar given which serves as a coadaptational foil to a play's deviant new. Postmodern new historicist critics did a lot to bring this historical Shakespeare under closer scrutiny, often by showing how his plays entailed the same assumptions as all manner of other texts contemporary with them.

But postmodern notions of sociohistorical positionality were sometimes too essentialist and simplistic, seeing a particular position as, in the first place, fixed, unchanging, and completely walled off from every other position, and, in the second place, as definable in terms of features which are mutually compatible in a very strong sense. An account of genuine communication, by contrast, sees different positions as always already overlapping in terms of the existential basics of human life, and as capable of extending the area of overlap in terms of mutual understanding, sometimes giving rise to processes of transcultural change and hybridization. It also acknowledges that a position can always already involve incoherences and internal division. To repeat, a community is not at all the same thing as a consensus. And as recent work in sociology has been making clear, a culture or a subculture really is, as I was hinting, heterogeneous (Dirlik 2007). Even if we used to believe that we were dividing the human world and its history up into cultural or subcultural groupings and epochs that clearly corresponded to something in the real world, we now increasingly admit that we were merely trying to make sense of chaos. A culture or subculture is simply not real in the same sense that Mount Everest is real, but is an intellectual category imposed on a very wide range of human phenomena. The only way a culture or subculture can be seen as a homogeneous consensus is by being observed from a very high level of descriptive abstraction. The lower our level of abstraction, the greater the amount of diversity and even contradiction we shall notice.

For a glimpse of the widespread relevance of this point, think only of the place held within British culture by *Tom Jones* (Sell 2001: 309–315). From its first publication onwards, this novel was on the one hand fiercely blamed for irresponsible superficiality, and on the other hand warmly praised for humanity, realism and humour. Lady Mary Wortley Montagu said that Fielding's happy endings "encourage young people to hope for impossible events to draw them out of the misery they chuse to plunge themselves into" (Montagu 1967 [1754]: 65), and Johnson agreed with Richardson that "the virtues of Fielding's heroes were the vices of a truly good man" (Boswell 1906 [1791]: 343–344). Boswell, on the other hand, said that Fielding did not encourage a "strained and rarely possible virtue", but did favour honour, honesty, benevolence and generosity. "He who is as good as Fielding will make him, is an amiable member of society" (Boswell 1906 [1791]: 344). For Coleridge, too, Fielding was charming. "To take him after Richardson is like emerging from a sick room heated by stoves into an open lawn on a breezy day in May" (Coleridge 1960 [1834]: 496). Up until fairly recently, if we had asked Fielding's British readers for a written statement of their views, most of them would probably have opted fairly coherently for either the one account or the other. But in more genuine communication, such distorting coherence always tends to break down, as it did in the honest remarks of Thackeray. Fielding's Tom, said Thackeray, is "an ordinary young fellow, ruddy-cheeked, broad-shouldered, and fond of wine and pleasure. He would not rob a church, but that is all" (Thackeray n.d.: 60). In which, he continued, there is nothing surprising, and nothing that might not be dealt with in a novel. But how could Fielding *admire* such a fellow so blatantly? There was the rub! Fielding's novel obviously left Thackeray unable to make up his mind, a predicament with which we are all perfectly familiar.

Human beings can be very sure about a very great number of things. But within any culture or subculture there will also be questions which seem much more problematic, and the conversations that go on within literary communities inevitably reflect this. Indeed, the uncertainties and disagreements are in no small part what *constitutes* a literary community.

1.4   Negative capability and critical discussion

Postmodern historicizations of literature and literary discussion need to be complemented, then, with insights that are less stereotyping and deterministic. If Keats really believed that either Shakespeare or he himself had no substantial historical identity, he was already under the sway of post-Kantian aesthetics. But *à propos* Shakespeare's negative capability, the capability to be "in uncertainties, Mysteries, doubts, without any irritable reaching after fact and reason", he was surely right (Keats 1954 [1817]: 53). About some things Shakespeare was curious, troubled, hesitant, non-committal, and these were the issues about which he and his audiences compared, and still compare notes. They were what shaped his plays, and he was more than willing to leave scope for disagreement about them, since the disagreement was already internal to his own mind. To repeat my earlier phrasing, he was unrepressive of his own complexities. Despite the claims which used to be made by New Critics, he did not force his ambivalences and ambiguities, as Orgel calls them, into omni-synthesizing ironies or paradoxes. The plays, far from existing in contradistinction from the fissilities of ordinary discourse, reflected tensions which were typical of the early-modern lifeworld as a whole, and which are often irresolvable even now. The apparent contradictions, which became such a powerful challenge to interpreters in other times and places, emerged from the very start, through Shakespeare's own genuinely dialogical use of language. This is what Empson (1961 [1930]) so clearly grasped: that ambiguity in literature can be wholly constructive, as a lasting stimulus to discussion. The only caveat needed here is that so-called literary texts are not more hospitable to inner contradiction than communication of other kinds. Negative capability is the main psychological and ethical precondition for any genuine communication – for any uncoercive community-making – at all.

Great writers' negative capability makes critical discussion of their "meaning" problematic. After all, a "meaning" is thought of as a *something* that is communicated. The term belongs to the semiotic and linguistic model of communication as a basically transitive and persuasive process, whereby a message is unidirectionally sent from a more active party to a more passive. The message is itself the "meaning", and is taken to be interpretable by reference to a singular context, in effect also set by the sender.

The literary hermeneutician E. D. Hirsch was thinking along these lines when he made his well-known distinction between "meaning" and "significance".

> *Meaning* is that which is represented by a text; it is what the author meant by his use of a particular sign sequence; it is what the signs represent. *Significance*, on the other hand, names a relationship between that meaning and a person, or a conception, or a situation, or indeed anything imaginable.
>
> (Hirsch 1967: 8, his italics)

"Significance" here can clearly involve more than just one context. The text can of course have a significance to the author who wrote in the original context. But it can also have a different significance to somebody differently placed, whereas meaning is being thought of as authorial, and as always hard and fast. What this kind of account overlooks is the possibility that some such single authorial meaning, and an accompanying authorial significance, might not readily emerge from a literary text's complexities; that authors themselves may not be fully sure about what they mean, or about the significance of whatever they might mean; and that they may in fact be turning to readers in the very spirit of such uncertainty, in the hope of bringing the complexities they perceive into wider discussion within the community as a whole. Any unequivocal meanings and significances a work seems to convey may well belong with those contemporary opinions, attitudes and prejudices on which it draws as ingredients to the addresser and addressee personae, which are genuine communication's mere starting point.

It is perfectly true that the term "meaning", as actually used within the communal discussion of literature, becomes something more of a hold-all, involving not only Hirsch's "meaning", and not only cognitive content, but emotional and evaluative implications, and also what Hirsch calls "significance" as well. Meaning in all these senses is thought of as entering the discussion from three main sources. There can be meanings inherent to the mind, speech or deeds of divine, human or animal characters represented "in the story". There can be authorial meanings. And there can be meanings as derived from the text by any number of different, and differently positioned readers.

The meanings of characters in, say, a novel or a play will be a central focus of attention for both its author and any reader. That is why old-fashioned character criticism was so profoundly natural, and why, after so many twentieth century approaches tended to undervalue it, there is now an urgent need for its refurbishment. Some of the most important lessons to be drawn from the twentieth century objections are that characters in literature, even when they seem larger than life, are not actually real people but fabrications; that they may be strongly coloured by their creator's own intentions or ideology; but that writers may also depict human beings as very complex and difficult to pin down. Attempts to pin down a character's "essence" could today be seen as decidedly inappropriate, since human identity itself has been much problematized over the past hundred years or so, with characters in literature now often being viewed as so many cases in point. Indeed, postcolonial writers examining the condition of cultural hybridity are now beginning to seem less the exception than the norm. As post-postmodernity gathers pace, all of us are hybrid now, as one might put it. Yet the fact remains: a literary work can very much revolve around *dramatis personae*, so that to try and understand them and their meanings is a crucial part of reading it. In *Paradise Lost*, what, at any given point, does God mean? What does Satan mean? What does Adam mean? What does Eve mean? A reader is bound to try and penetrate the different characters' various kinds of meaning all the time, and no theory of literature can brush this aside. Throughout a reader's processing of the text, all the different character meanings will be essential input, and can make for many complications or even plain confusion.

Then again, good readers try to understand the cognitive, emotional and evaluative thrust of meanings thought of as authorial. They do so both for the altruistic reasons still derivable from Kantian ethics (Kant 1998 [1785]), as a kindness they owe to the writer as a fellow-human, and for more selfish reasons as well, since the writer may be able to give them pleasure and even do them some good – the writer's very otherness may be a *significant* otherness for them. One of the imperatives they observe is: "Try to read and contextualize the writer's words in a way as faithful as possible to the writer's likely intention; try to comprehend the language as used within the writer's context of writing, and within the contexts 'in the story' as the writer represents them." A readerly here-and-now-ism which has no genuine interest in authorial meanings emanating from some other constellation of time, place and culture can only short-circuit literary dialogicality, replacing interpretation with arrogant solipsism. An account of *Paradise Lost* which does not centrally recognize that Milton was aiming to justify the ways of God to men, and that he was doing so in mid-seventeenth-century England, does not deserve serious consideration, even if Milton's own conscious aim has been perceived by intelligent readers like Blake and Shelley, Waldock (1947) and Empson (1961), as out of sync with the poem's felt life.

As this example also makes clear, authorial meanings can often be thought of as the author's assessment of character meanings. Above all, Milton is weighing up his God against his Satan. And readers, too, assess character meanings, and they assess authorial meanings as well. To repeat, readers do inevitably read texts in their own way. They have their own personal and historical positions, involving their own ranges of knowledge, emotion, and value, and they have no less right than the author to influence the final result of the communicational event as they see fit. As I was hinting earlier, scholars hoping to rein literature in by means of historical or cultural purism, so restricting the significance of an author's words to their original context, would seriously underestimate a reader's ability to think, feel and evaluate in more than one way at a time, and could only detract from the human dignity of readers here and now. Mediating and communicational critics will do everything they can to ensure that literary activity involves interactive processes in which the parties on either side of the exchange enjoy a sacrosanct human equality. The imperative relating to a work's language as originally used by the author therefore has to be complemented by another imperative no less firm: "Feel free to respond to what you honestly take to be the writer's intention in whatever way is appropriate to your own world-view and preserves your own integrity." When Blake said that as far as he was concerned Milton was of the Devil's party without knowing it, this was appropriate to what, from his own point of view, and in his own time and place, he perceived as the poem's felt life, and he was perfectly within his rights. A text which did not continually come in for re-appraisal would be a work no longer really read. For us today, Blake's view of Satan gives just as much food for thought as Milton's own. As the poem actually operates within the culture, we cannot think about the one without the other.

Literature certainly does involve meanings, then, of all the different kinds and sources. Yet the more negatively capable a writer, the more the various meanings are likely to increase in sheer number, or to be in conflict with each other. In a typical process of reading, a reader may well be far less interested in regimenting them into some kind of order than in trying to feel them all upon the pulses. Indeed, the freedom to give them all a fair hearing without jumping to hasty conclusions is what a genuinely communicational writer very much endorses. Negatively capable writing makes for negatively capable reading. Conversely, academic readings aspiring to definitiveness can be counterproductive. Scholars and critics are no less entitled than Blake to state their own opinion, and are actually obliged to do so – any claim to objectivity would be instantly disqualifying. But in literary discussion, no single meaning or opinion is ever final, and claims and counter-claims are all the better for a self-conscious awareness of this.

When we think of literature as communication in the etymological sense of that term, meanings are less important in and of themselves. An exchange of words can be a making common, a making of community, even when the community gets no further than a riot of meanings allowing no agreement but an agreement to disagree. The paradox is that genuine communication, including literary communication, while involving plural meanings, results in a single circle of communicants. What can ultimately draw readers together around a writer is not so much meanings, as something for which I have already used the Leavisian term "felt life", a sense of which can be communally shared because it is recognized in the same way that Johnson said we recognize true wit: as something "which, though not obvious, is, upon its first production, acknowledged to be just; ... that which he that never found it wonders how he missed" (Johnson 1925 [1779–1781]: I, 11).

The felt life discovered in a text correlates with negative capability in both the person who wrote it and in the reader who is now sensitively reading it. It is a question of moral openness and powers of critical observation whose insights are irreducible to a single propositional meaning. This is something Keats may instinctively have grasped in coining the phrase "negative capability", as Empson certainly did in speaking of great literature's beauty in terms of its very ambiguities of thought, emotion and value (Empson 1961 [1930]: x). Also on this wavelength was the one major twentieth century critic who understood our permanent need of character criticism, John Bayley, as when he said of *David Copperfield* that Dickens, in sending off Daniel Peggoty on his tireless search for his sinful niece, was at one and the same time giving vent to fashionable sentimentality and being ruthlessly honest about that sentimentality's sometimes maudlin possessiveness (Bayley 1976:94). In more recent criticism, such keen-eyed lack of bias still appears in Jonathan Bate's *The Genius of Shakespeare* (1997), where negative capability is no less central a concept than in Bayley's *The Characters of Love* (1960). Bate's honest introspection into the way his own mind ponders over the identities and meanings of the main figures in the narrative apparently told by the Sonnets, or is teased out of thought by the balance of right and wrong, of appropriate justice and ungenerous callousness, in Hal's rejection of Falstaff, can remind us that literary experience, like human intercourse in general, resists hard-and-fast meanings and easy answers, and never more so than when readers do their utmost to be faithful to an author's language as originally used (Bate 1997:34–64, 204–209). Bate's criticism could not be more solidly grounded on historical and philological expertise, yet breathes a negative capability which responds to Shakespeare's own. A nervous reaching after definitive single meanings is not his style.

Coleridge, in seeing creative imagination as reconciling "opposite and discordant qualities" (Coleridge 1956 [1817]:174), and T. S. Eliot, in saying that the mind of the poet can bring together the noise of the typewriter, the smell of cooking, and the experiences of reading Spinoza and falling in love (Eliot 1951 [1921]:287), were no less aware than Keats, Empson, Bayley and Bate of literature's polysemous complexities, yet wanted to think of these as synthesized into new artistic wholes, basically of the heterocosmic kind envisaged in nineteenth century aesthetics. Interpreters following in their footsteps, and American New Critical interpreters especially, though admirably constating many of a text's heterogeneities, often tended towards a mechanical reductiveness, against which Susan Sontag (1966) and Jonathan Culler (1975) finally protested, and which actually ran counter to one of New Criticism's foundational texts, "The Heresy of Paraphrase" (Brooks 1968 [1947]:157–175). But Cleanth Brooks, its author, had still cherished the dream of finding in literature new aesthetic wholes which his own commentary would articulate. Hence, as he wryly confessed,

> the frequent occurrence … [in his *The Well Wrought Urn*] of such terms as "ambiguity", "paradox", "complex of attitudes", and – most frequent of all, and perhaps most annoying to the reader – "irony". I hasten to add that I hold no brief for these terms as such. Perhaps they are inadequate. Perhaps they are misleading. It is to be hoped in that case that we can eventually improve on them.
>
> (Brooks 1968 [1947]:159–160)

Uncertainties, mysteries and doubts are what literature, like genuine communication in general, for ever floods us with. Coleridge is inferior to Shakespeare because, as Keats remarked, he would "let go by a fine isolated verisimilitude caught from the Penetralium of mystery, from being incapable of remaining Content with half Knowledge" (Keats 1954 [1817]:52). The permanent interest of a major literary work will lie in its very enigmas, so that critics daring to explicate its themes or ideas cannot afford to be reductive or emphatic. In the classic debate between Wellek and Leavis, whereas Wellek wanted "to show that the romantic view of the world … underlies and pervades the poetry of Blake, Wordsworth and Shelley … [and] elucidates many difficulties", Leavis replied,

> "The romantic view of the world", a view common to Blake, Wordsworth, Shelley and others – yes, I have heard of it; but what interest can it have for the literary critic? For the critic, for the reader whose primary interest is in poetry, those three poets are so radically different, immediately and finally, from one another that the offer to assimilate them in a common philosophy can only suggest the irrelevance of the philosophic approach.   (Leavis 1962 [1952]b: 216)

Leavis, in turning to writers for their quality of felt life, was behaving like any good reader, refusing to see them as merely social beings conditioned by a current *Weltanschauung*, but insisting that they were also individuals. So as Henry James had already made clear, the felt life in their writing was a quality whose exact form could never be predicted in advance:

> Experience is never limited, and it is never complete; it is an immense sensibility, a kind of huge spider-web of consciousness, and catching every air-borne particle in its tissue. It is the very atmosphere of the mind; and when the mind is imaginative – much more when it happens to be that of a man of genius – it takes to itself the faintest hints of life, it converts the very pulses of the air into revelations. The young lady living in a village has only to be a damsel upon whom nothing is lost to make it quite unfair (as it seems to me) to declare to her that she shall have nothing to say about the military. … [She may well be] blessed with the faculty which when you give it an inch takes an ell, and which for the artist is a much greater source of strength than any accident of residence or of place in the social scale. The power to guess the unseen from the seen, to trace the implication of things, to judge the whole piece by the pattern, the condition of feeling life in general so completely that you are well on your way to knowing any particular corner of it – this cluster of gifts may almost be said to constitute experience, and they occur in country and in town and in the most differing stages of education.
> (James 1963 [1884]: 85–86)

Equally, felt life resists neat summaries in retrospect. Leavis recognizes, no less than Cleanth Brooks, the difficulties facing a commentator who tries to capture literature's heterogeneities. But unlike Brooks, he does not make matters worse by talking about artistic form and, unlike Wellek, does not go in for philosophical paraphrases. The Jamesian appeal to experience, and ultimately to life itself, has to suffice. Though a strategy entailing its own, very considerable difficulties, for a critic wishing to avoid oversimplification it is the only viable course. As Leavis himself puts it,

"life" is a large word and doesn't admit of definition. But some of the most important words we have to use don't admit of definition. And this truth holds of
literary criticism. Not only can we not, for instance, do without the word "life"; any
attempt to think out a major critical issue entails using positively the shifts in force
the word is bound to be incurring as it feels its way on and out and in towards its
fulfilment. And it would hardly be questioned that there is point in saying that a
critic who would be intelligent about the novel must be intelligent about life: no
discussion of the novel by any other kind of critic is worth attention.

(Leavis 1963: 17)

As critics, James and Leavis meet the challenge of felt life by continuing the communal
discussion, by keeping literary dialogicality going, by resisting fossilizing formulae. In
this kind of criticism, an author's every thought and perception are constantly experienced afresh, and Eliot, whose own criticism was sometimes more polemical, generously acknowledged James's openness. "James's critical genius", he wrote, "comes out
most tellingly in his mastery over, his baffling escape from, Ideas; a mastery and an
escape which are perhaps the last test of a superior intelligence. He had a mind so fine
that no idea could violate it" (Eliot 1975 [1918]: 151).

1.5   Climates of opinion and literary-critical ethics

Literary critics' responses to the negative capability of great writing can be seen in relation to another discourse, within which, from the dawn of the modern era onwards,
literature figured not for its own sake, as it were, but as a stick with which to beat
contemporary religion. In reaction against the arid theology of the late scholastics,
humanists such as Lorenzo Valla (*fl.* 1405–57) argued that sacred truth would never
mix with "tricks of dialectics" and "metaphysical quibbles" (Tracy 1987: 244). Like
Petrarch (*fl.*1307–74), what they wanted was a religion that would actually be "poetry,
poetry concerning God", and effective not by proving anything, but by touching the
human heart (Petrarch 1971 [1384]: 90).

Their wishes were not met. On the contrary, whereas "belief" in God had once
been a relationship of loving trust in the Ineffable, whereas "*credo*" had originally
meant "I give my heart", these two terms increasingly came to signify a cerebral assent
to a list of precisely articulated doctrinal propositions. After the invention of the
printing-press, and perhaps especially in Protestant countries, such take-it-or-leave-it
propositions increasingly forced themselves on the human consciousness in the form
of articles of faith in prayerbooks, for instance, and in the catechisms used by the
clergy as a way of getting people to toe an official line. With the age of Reason and the
triumph of Newtonian science, establishment religion in Britain moved even further
from belief in the older sense, towards a cut and dried Deism.

So for many Victorians the problem was: What was to become of a scientistic religion when science itself advanced still further? The German Higher Criticism and *The Origin of Species* seemed to be meeting Broad Church theology on its own rationalist ground, and to be getting the upper hand. True, back in the 1630s there had been the Laudians, with their strong attachment to sacraments, symbols and a gesticulating ceremonialism. True, too, ever since the Catholic emancipation of 1829 many of the Laudians' descendants in the Anglican High Church had been crossing over to the more numinous version of Christianity, a development with major cultural repercussions in the spiritualized Neo-Gothic of Pugin (himself a Catholic convert). But theological appeals to scientific proofs and empirically demonstrable facts were still so widespread that, when the Connecticut Congregationalist Horace Bushnell (*fl.* 1802–76) suggested that theology should have less in common with science than with poetry, he was denounced as a heretic (Edwards 1992). After four centuries of hard and fast dogmas, many nineteenth-century Christians would have found a more poetic theology simply too vague. Especially Protestants wanted to be able to refute the ever-mounting challenge from the scientific camp with clear arguments and strong certainties. Hence, in 1870, Charles Hodge and Benjamin B. Warfield pronounced a new doctrine which asserted the literal infallibility of scripture. Nor were Catholics, though generally less reliant on words, completely immune to doubt. In the same year, a new Catholic doctrine was propounded as well: the doctrine of papal infallibility.

Doctrines of infallibility, however, endorsing as they did a communicational mode that was maximally unidirectional, were not ultimately very inviting or satisfying, which brings us full circle to Arnold, who made his most famous pronouncement on the high role of literature only ten years later:

> More and more mankind will discover that we have to turn to poetry to interpret life for us, to console us, to sustain us. Without poetry, our science will appear incomplete; and most of what now passes with us for religion and philosophy will be replaced by poetry.   (Arnold 1888 [1880]:2–3)

When Keats meditated on Shakespeare's negative capability, when Leavis responded to felt life and a reverential openness in Lawrence, and when Eliot praised James for an intelligence unviolated by ideas, they were all pinpointing, in great literature and in the finest literary discussion, a quality of mind which was often missing from the modern world's officially legitimated religious practice. Pre-modern religion, however, had been different. Both the Jerusalem Talmud and the Bavli Talmud were commentaries on the Mishnah, which in turn was an addition to the older Torah, and the other two Religions of the Book nourished cultures of devotion within which God, and the relationship between God and man, were debated just as eagerly. These were discussions on which new influences were for ever being brought to bear, in a dialogicality of spirit to which no end was envisaged, least of all in the form of tidy certainties. Unlike Coleridge as seen by Keats, God's worshipers were still capable of remaining satisfied with half-knowledge. Or to be more accurate, with no knowledge at all. Across a wide range of commentary, though perhaps most markedly in the apophatic spiritualism of Denys the Areopagite and Maimonides, the notion that God's existence or God's nature could be asserted was strongly rejected, and so, too, was the notion that God's existence or nature could be denied. The religious life was not one of confident dogmas easily put into words, but of ceaselessly renewed negotiations within the community of fellow-religionists, and of humbly expectant awe in face of God's sheer ineffability. Religion's defining process was kenosis: a complete emptying of the self with all its narrowness, and a corresponding love for the utterly non-self.

With the formulation of Einstein's relativity theory and Heisenberg's principle of indeterminacy, scientists began to sound like the apophatic theologians of the premodern epoch. The physicist Percy Bridgman (*fl.* 1882–1961) wrote that "[t]he world fades out and eludes us.... We are confronted with something truly ineffable" (Smith 1989: 8), and Popper, Kuhn and Polyani all argued that science has no choice but to rely on an act of faith. Postmodern theology, too, especially as represented by Bultmann and Tillich, rediscovered uncertainties, mysteries, doubts, a development which also had parallels in postmodern philosophy. Derrida (2002) wrote of "undeconstructibles" that are never fully realized, so echoing the Kabbalah of Jewish forbears such as Isaac Luria (*fl.* 1534–72), with his sense of the unknowable Godhead's withdrawal into itself. All of which has prompted Karen Armstrong to look back on the modern lust for certainty – that "distinctively modern yearning for purely notional, absolute truth" – as a merely temporary aberration (Armstrong 2009: 302). For Armstrong, the way forward is suggested by Gianni Vattimo's advocacy of "weak thought", stemming from his dream of a society based less on truth than charity. "When somebody wants to tell me the absolute truth," Vattimo has written, "it is because he wants to put me under his control" (Vattimo 2007: 43). For Vattimo, "[f]reedom no longer lies in the perfect knowledge of and conformity to the necessary structure of reality, but in an appreciation of multiple discourse and the historicity, contingency and finitude of all religious, ethical and political values – including our own" (Armstrong 2009: 300).

It would seem, then, that some of the most typical instantiations, not only of premodern religion, but also of science, religion and philosophy in postmodern times in principle tended to make for communities in which egotism and dogmatic assertiveness enjoyed limited scope. Instead, a far higher value was placed on the same kind of even-handed comparing of notes, the same kind of negatively capable openness before life, which characterize genuine communication of any kind at all, and which literary activity in particular was experienced as preserving even during the era of modernity.

It could be that Armstrong underestimates the extent of dogmatic assertiveness in pre-modern times, and correspondingly overestimates both the spread, and the deficiencies of modern reason. Her work is clearly driven by a noble concern to combat repressive fundamentalism, and not only religious fundamentalism but the fundamentalism of atheists such as Richard Dawkins as well, which means that she is bound to warn, like Vattimo, against reason as co-opted in the service of coercive argumentation. But one of her own most helpful comments on *religious* fundamentalism may indirectly suggest a risk to be faced by anyone combating fundamentalism *of any form at all*. "Every single fundamentalist movement that I have studied in Judaism, Christianity and Islam," she remarks, "is rooted in profound fear" (Armstrong 2009: 260). What we need to guard against, it seems to me, is our own fear of the fundamentalists' fear. On the one hand, I think we can warmly welcome Armstrong's description of postmodern theology and philosophy as rediscovering apophatic kenosis, not only because it seems accurate, but because it so firmly underlines that any widespread climate of opinion will have its own distinctive communicational dimension. On the other hand, we can ask whether her religio-historiographical drift is not a little too *déjà vu*. Through her own writings she apparently hopes to achieve, in the intellectual sphere, what the nostalgically escapist Gothic Revivalists were hoping for in the architectural. To say that she wishes modernity had simply never happened, or that she disparages, lock, stock and barrel, modernity's great triumphs of human intellect, would be unfair. But in what she writes that temptation may be only just round the corner, and to yield to it would be hugely unappreciative of an entire side of human nature as it has now become. A community's only health must surely lie in its openness to every valuable human possibility as evidenced or recoverable within its own here and now. Rigid exclusions can only worsen the chances of genuine communication in the future.

At any rate for post-postmodern communicational critics of literature, this must be the key consideration. By studying communicational genuineness in so-called literary texts, where it has always prospered, they will be working to promote the same quality in other forms of communication as well.

Most immediately, their work will have implications for the discourse of literary criticism itself, which needs to be communicationally self-conscious. And although they will be most suggestive here if their own writings set a good communicational example, they will sometimes need to draw explicit contrasts with the procedures of other critics. My own earlier remarks on postmodern schools of literary criticism – post-Marxist, postcolonialist, new historical, cultural materialist, feminist, queer, ethnic – will already have hinted that their exponents were less negatively capable than postmodern theologians and philosophers such as Tillich, Bultmann, Derrida, and Vattimo, and that they expected the literary authors assigned to the various canons they advocated to be forcefully assertive. Leavis, too, despite his sensitivity to the felt life of major writings, despite his resistance to fixed meanings in a narrow sense, was not always on an ethical par with the writers he admired (Sell 2000: 233–238). Not only did he tend to arrogate to himself a superior intelligence and sensitivity. In doing so he was also guilty of the fallacy so frequent in evaluative criticism generally, the one great fallacy which Modernist critics like Leavis had in common with Neo-Classical forbears: the unitary context assumption. Leavis writing on Fielding, no less than Pope writing in what I shall be calling his Humanist mode on Shakespeare, never doubted for a moment that his own access to life and experience, his own response to the felt life in literary texts, was representative of the entire human race at its very finest, an order of pretension whose absurdity was already somewhat glossed over, as it happened, in James's appeal to the omnipercipient damsel of the village. To "a mind ... demanding more than external action", Leavis thundered, Fielding is superficial, i.e. is totally deficient in "marked moral intensity" (Leavis 1962 [1948]: 11–12). The Montagu-Richardson-Johnson line on Fielding was not more firmly stated by Johnson himself. Leavis evidently believed that mature readers of any time and place ought to agree with him, and that Fielding himself should have known better than to write as he did.

In the mid-eighteenth century Thomas Warton's *Observations on the Fairy Queen of Spenser,* and in our own time Bate's book on Shakespeare, have supplied what Pope-the-Humanist and Leavis could lack: an intuition that the sensibility of their own position could blind them to something valuable. Bate is able to help present-day English monolinguals read Shakespeare through the eyes of his admirers in nineteenth century Germany and France, while Warton could see that a taste drawing its legitimation from Homer and Aristotle – from the "example and precept of antiquity" – represented only one set of possible criteria, and that the "romantic manner of poetical composition introduced and established by the Provencial bards" was not mere "Gothic ignorance and barbarity", but had charms and excitements of its own (Warton 1762: II 11–12).

Warton was perhaps the first self-consciously mediating critic. His explicit strategy was to "search" writers contemporary with Spenser himself: to examine "the books on which the peculiarities of his style, taste, and composition, are confessedly founded". In elucidating Spenser's historical horizon of expectations, he hoped to make his own contemporaries more aware of their prejudice, so as to counteract its inhibiting effect on literary appreciation. Gently chiding Pope for reading Shakespeare too much through Augustan spectacles, he commented, "If Shakespeare is worth reading, he is worth explaining", and his entire treatise on Spenser was an exercise in the kind of positive mediation which is self-critical, deliberately fair-minded, and purposefully oriented towards a future in which people will better understand people unlike themselves. It was all very well to say that William Caxton and the mediaeval texts he printed were "rude and uncouth". But in "an illiterate and unpolished age he [Caxton] multiplied books, and consequently readers", an observation whose continuing clear fondness for Augustan polish does not, in its full context, patronize Caxton, because Warton has so unashamedly opened himself to the imaginative power of that earlier age's literature as well. (Warton 1762: II 263–264, 265, 266). Some such humble readiness to mediate will always be welcome in commentaries on literature, I have argued, quite regardless of whether the mediation operates between two different historical epochs, between two or more cultures or subcultures simultaneously embroiled in culture wars, or simply within the here and now of just some single culture – to the extent that such enclosures still exist (Sell 2000: 125–138).

Warton also clearly shows the communicational critic's concern with the *quality* of communication – Shakespeare's, Spenser's, Pope's, his own. What he strongly resists is his contemporaries' tendency to close discussion down though a distorting passivization of the human other, whether by positioning Caxton and Spenser as uncouthly mediaeval, or by praising Shakespeare in terms irresponsive to his historical and individual identity. I hinted earlier that the role of literary historians can be like that of lawyers who help to interpret a last will and testament. But there is, of course, a difference. Even Jarndyce *versus* Jarndyce was entirely verisimilar in eventually coming to an end, whereas any purported finality in literary assessments will undermine the very community of discussion. Like mediating critics, communicational critics cannot station themselves at an Archimedean point outside of history. Any pretence of doing so would make them too Leavisian, too like Pope in his Humanist mode, too little Wartonian. Rather, by examining writers' success or otherwise in establishing relationships with readers – contemporary, later, alien – they will hope to promote a literary community which is self-consciously heterogeneous, and in which the balance of genuine to distorted communication is always shifting, however slowly, in favour of the genuine, to the ultimate benefit of human intercourse at large.

Their chances of success here can seem pitifully small. In all areas of human life, distorted communication apparently triumphs time after time. Edward Said's attempts to mediate – his own word for it (Said 1994 [1993]: xxvi, xxxi) – between differently positioned readerships were accused of being partisan, by belligerents on both sides of a fence he was not so much sitting on as trying to remove. And this sad episode in the history of literary criticism has ample parallel in the sphere of international politics. When President George W. Bush began the most recent war in Iraq, he said that Iraq belonged to an axis of evil nations, and that other countries would now have to choose whether they wanted to be on the side of good or on the side of evil. Here the most powerful man in the world was using the same coercively black-and-white rhetoric as the terrorists he was professedly targeting as his enemy. Oversimplifying and diabolizing the human other, he was cutting himself off from genuine communication with it, refusing to respect its distinctive cultural memory while remaining all too rigidly imprisoned in that of his own community – or in one version of it. On top of which, he was even discouraging neutral parties from mediating in the dispute.

Literary critics can dream of a world in which political leaders would never behave in the Bush manner or, if they did, would immediately fall from power. Such a world would also be one in which Shakespeare would never be used to back up communicational distortion and ideological hegemony, but would always be the focus for agreements to disagree, as his negative capability drew communicants, with all their differences unreduced, into a shared appreciation of his texts' felt life. What Habermas foresees in his essay "Struggles for Recognition in the Democratic Constitutional State"

(1994) is a shared political culture, within which cultural differences at other levels can be readily accommodated. Inspired by this vision, and applying it, as Habermas himself does not, to literary activity, critics can hope that the level of mutual understanding and respect will always be open to improvement, and can themselves endorse an ethical politics of communication in their own sphere. In situations of misunderstanding and even conflict, whether within the present or between the present and the past, they can try to mediate. And by carefully scrutinizing the address of literary authors, they may be able to identify valuable models of communicational good practice. They will not expect to bring about general interpretative agreements, except in the form of an agreement to disagree, for then they themselves would be communicating, not genuinely but coercively, thereby depriving literature of necessary air. A literary text's mode of existence is not as a book on a shelf but as activated in the minds of readers, while they go on pondering meanings, significances, values, for ever bringing interpretations of many different origins into thoughtful comparison. What critics certainly can try to promote is a sense of literary communication as at once profoundly universal and profoundly historical – the paradox which, in their diametrically opposite ways, both Victorian liberal humanists and late-twentieth-century postmodern commentators only partly grasped and only partly failed to grasp.

Such lofty dreams will never come completely true, and lofty dreams can in any case be extremely dangerous, at least if they lose touch with reality – the reality of difference between one person or another, for instance, or the reality of human imperfectability. The history of the concept of *Weltliteratur* provides clear illustrations of such risks. Yet despite the continuing problems of under-representation and over-standardization highlighted by Damrosch, Chandra, López, Miller and Grabovsky, Goethe's idea embodies a goal which, translated from its original context of Eurocentric modernity to one of globalized post-postmodernity, is well worth the best efforts of mediating and communicational critics. Unless people of good will set their sights on a better world, the emancipatory achievements of postmodernity will not be consolidated by the post-postmodern follow-through. Instead, our societies will be trapped in a vicious circle of injustice, violence and reactionism. In contexts where justice would now be practicable, it will not prevail. And where it does prevail, it will often do so without the emotional assent of all concerned. To work through the medium of literary criticism for improved communicational practices which could result in a thawing-out of rigid attitudes, and in a more widespread solicitude for the rights and sensitivities of every individual and grouping, is not unrealistic here. Such an undertaking represents a kind of idealistic pragmatism that has helped to put an end to conflicts in the past. Writings, and the discussion which grows up around them, have often nourished a real desire for change, sometimes helping to soften even the most cynical view of human possibilities. Undermined by Addison and Steele's *Spectator*, the ethos of Hobbes and the Restoration rake eventually gave way to that of Shaftesbury and Sir Roger de Coverley.

More recently, the twentieth century's long run of cultural pessimism, fully understandable in the light of twentieth century history, but in the end too close to becoming a stock response, was finally challenged by writers such as the polymath Raymond Tallis (1997), professor of geriatric medicine, poet, theoretician, critic, and the zoologist Matt Ridley (1997), the latter arguing that virtuous behaviour may actually be natural – that virtue comes far more readily to the human being's genetic programming than Freudians and Marxists, Modernist critics and postmodern determinists, once believed. More recently still, much significance has been read into the passing of the presidential mantel from George W. Bush to Barack Obama, himself a post-postmodern writer who has championed hope (Obama 2008 [2006]). As I send this text to press in February 2011, Obama's idealism is being severely tested by social, political and economic reality. But his hope, and some of the hope it has inspired in others, is still alive.

CHAPTER 2

Henry V and the strength and weakness of words

2.1 Literary dialogicality over time

In branches of linguistics such as Relevance Theory, and in linguistic philosophy in descent from Wittgenstein, there has been much discussion as to whether or not we can ever really know what is going on in another person's mind. In Relevance Theory, for instance, the assumption that we *can* know is referred to as the mutual knowledge hypothesis (Sperber and Wilson 1986: 15–21). Relevance theoreticians and others reject this hypothesis in its most comprehensive form, but argue that through careful observation of what other people do and say, and through relating this to everything else we have experienced and know about already, we arrive at some sort of idea as to what they currently think, mean, or want. We then rely on this, the argument continues, as a kind of working assumption by which to regulate our own interaction with them, until such time as they surprise us by doing or saying something which seems to contradict it, in which case we revise it.

This line of thought is reasonable as far as it goes, but ties up with that model of communication to which these studies are recommending a complement. It tends to assume, that is to say, that a person's thought, meaning or will is a specifiable *something* which can be unidirectionally transferred to another person's mind, partly through an appeal to a unitary context within which it is interpretable.

Obviously, there are going to be countless cases in which this will apply, and in which communicants will therefore have relatively few hermeneutic difficulties. Not least in a work of literature, readers will find much that is totally unproblematic. In particular there will be all those features of the writer's identity, world-knowledge and ideological orientation which mark the writing as the product of a particular time and place, and which can therefore work as a kind of understandable social given with which the individually new and strange can enter into communicational co-adaptation.

But of what does the newness and strangeness consist? Well, in all kinds of interchange, literary and otherwise, there will also be many cases of negative capability, to use Keats's term (1956 [1817]: 52): cases, that is, where individuals themselves may not really know what they think, mean or want, and where their communicational intention is not to transmit any such hard and fast personal statement to other people, but rather to compare notes about whatever they happen to have in mind, as a way of exploring, from within more than just a single individual's lifeworld, what *might* be thinkable, *might* be meanable, *might* be wantable. This results in a dialogicality that is totally different from the type within which people think of themselves as exchanging mental, intentional and volitional certainties. At issue here is rather the kind of dialogicality which my Introduction was describing as genuinely communicational, and of which some of the most exemplary instances have resulted from the writing and reception of texts regarded as literary. In fact one way to think of a literary work's newness and strangeness is as stemming from its negatively capable problematization of received certainties.

This means that the dialogicality of a literary work over time is not straightforward. If one assumes, as very many literary scholars have assumed, that all communication, including literary communication, is nothing more than a unidirectional transfer of *something*, one will tend to think that, while the responses of readerships and audiences may possibly change with changing generations, the input of the author is a constant. There is a sense in which this is almost true. Certainly a response which does not grow out of an attempt to discern, understand and assess what the author actually wrote is not really a response at all but an instance of parthenogenesis, and one which, as long as it presents itself as a responsive reading and not as an actual re-writing (which can be very valuable kind of undertaking), is ethically unacceptable – is a candidate, in fact, for mediating criticism's most careful scrutiny. Yet even so, historical purists who claim to offer definitive re-statements of authorial intention underestimate literary communication's genuineness. By concentrating mainly on what is historically given in an author's profile, they fail to appreciate how this enters into those processes of negatively capable co-adaption. A writer's negative capability is perhaps most immediately highlighted by an Empsonian analysis of ambiguity, or by deconstructionist exercises, both of them critical methods which invite readers away from a hunt for certainties towards an engagement with a writer's full intelligence and sensitivity as reflected in a text's felt life. What historical purists overlook is that, as even Habermas (despite his literary formalism) can see, "it is the text itself that makes possible its uncontrollable effective history (*Wirkungsgeschichte*)" (Habermas 1998 [1985]: 387). The different ways in which a major literary work comes to be perceived can be partly explained by its author's own ability to be in uncertainties, mysteries, doubts, without any irritable reaching after fact and reason. The sincere attempts of successive generations to discern, understand and assess what that author actually wrote will arrive at a fair amount of agreement as to what it was, but will always result in those differences of perception as well, which are the inevitable and legitimate product of the interplay between authorial genuineness of address and respondents' own situated wisdom of hindsight.

A particularly clear example is the reception history of Shakespeare's *Henry V*. To describe the communal function of this play as that of a beautiful work of art with no possible bearing on real-world events would be not be easy. Some of Shakespeare's other plays have been more widely staged and admired. But what no reading or performance of *Henry V* can fail to acknowledge is Shakespeare's intense concern with politics and military conquest, which has stimulated every new generation to think about their own current phase of history, and indeed to perceive the play and their own life-world in each other's light. The significances felt to emerge have varied, depending on the precise historical circumstances of interpretation, and on interpreters' own way of viewing them.

As regards the very earliest performances, those between 1599 and the death of Elizabeth I in 1603, hermeneutic variation is not demonstrable from surviving comments by spectators. But by putting together the play's own textual history with what is known of the period's political history we can easily see that, within a very short space of time, one significant line of interpretation was, not so much changed as completely eliminated. Assuming that the First Folio's version of 1623 is derived from Shakespeare's foul papers and reflects the play as originally performed, in that first staging the Chorus drew a comparison between Henry's triumphant home-coming from France and a possible future return of the Earl of Essex from Ireland, "Bringing rebellion broachèd on his sword" (V 0, l. 32).[1] As James Shapiro comments, this is "an extraordinary moment and the only time in his plays that Shakespeare ... directs playgoers' attention away from the make-believe world of his play to the real world outside the theatre" (Shapiro 2005: 101). The political relevance to the present time was far more explicit than even for *Richard II*'s deposition scene, through a staging of which on February 7th, 1601 some supporters of Essex may have tried to serve his cause against the Queen. So exactly topical was the Chorus's semi-prophecy that performances closer to February 25th, 1601, the day on which Essex was executed, or performances given soon after that date, would have been likely to leave it out for fear of official reprisals. And sure enough, it was omitted from the First Quarto of 1600.

To turn to interpretative fluctuations at more recent junctures, in 1940, the second year of the Second World War, Derek Traversi argued in *Scrutiny* that *Henry V* had been

> most generally popular when least understood. Its concessions to human feeling are too few, its presiding spirit too discouraging to compel enthusiasm.... It may have satisfied the demands of patriotic orthodoxy at Elizabeth's court; but Shakespeare had the gift of fulfilling obligations of this kind without being deterred from his deeper purposes.... The inspiration of *Henry V* is, if anything, critical, analytic, exploratory. As we read it, a certain coldness takes possession of us....
> (Traversi 1940: 373–374)

War, Traversi underlined, is a very unpleasant business, requiring in political leaders no small degree of inhumanity, and this, he said, is exactly what Shakespeare makes

---

1. Quotations of *Henry V* taken from Gurr 1992.

clear. Just a few years later, by contrast, when the Second World War had still not drawn to a close, Laurence Olivier was working on his famous film version of the play, a venture much closer to war propaganda, and actually dedicated to the commandos and airborne troops of Great Britain, "the spirit of whose ancestors it has been humbly attempted to recapture" (Geduld 1973: 48). Then again, a generation or two later, in Kenneth Branagh's film version of 1989 "the predominant hues" were, in the words of John Sutherland and Cedric Watts, "grey and dirty-brown".

> [Branagh's] vision was discoloured by Vietnam, residues of the "politicized" 1970s infatuation with Brecht, and Orson Welles's epically muddy battle scenes in *Chimes at Midnight*, with its "war is hell" message. My Lai, not El Alamein, was what came to mind watching the 1989 film.   (Sutherland and Watts 2000: 108–109)

More recently still, Ewan Fernie has noted that both President Bush's speech after 9/11 and Lieutenant Colonel Tim Collins's address to his British troops on the Kuwait-Iraqi border in March 2003 have been compared to Henry's rallying-cry before Agincourt. But Fernie also suggested that under these latter-day circumstances the possible spuriousness of Henry's justification for invading France has been conveniently forgotten. For Fernie, the play is uncomfortably direct in its attention to Henry's sheer willpower – not a twentieth-century kind of topic, as he remarks – and to the rash and ruthless energy that goes with it: a violence which, he says, "is perhaps inalienable from human life" (Fernie 2007: 119). To admirers of Bush and Collins the play has meant one thing, then, while to Fernie it means something very different.

The paradox is that Shakespeare, by being negatively capable, has both gained and lost influence. He has gained influence, by allowing theatre personnel, audiences and readerships to make up their own minds. They have continued to be attracted into the worlds of his plays because they have not had the impression that he is trying to force his own certainties down their throats. He has lost influence, because they have taken his generosity at its word. Feeling free to come to their own conclusions, that is exactly what they have done, and with total legitimacy, as long as their response has genuinely been a response to aspects of his own uncertainties, mysteries, doubts.

This paradox can arise with any genuinely communicational dialogicality at all, and not just between literary writers and their audiences. But a no less widespread kind of paradox is the one whereby a communicant loses control by trying to keep it. A communicant who is not prepared to be in uncertainties, mysteries, doubts, without any irritable reaching after fact and reason, but who, as Keats said of Coleridge, lets pass "a fine isolated verisimilitude caught from the Penetralium of mystery, from being incapable of remaining Content with half Knowledge" (Keats 1954 [1817]: 52), may well say or write things which other people find too brittle, too narrow, too dogmatic, too refutable, too distant from an apophatic openness to life's complexities, and sometimes, as well, too willing to exert control over other communicants, too coercive. As Keats also said, we do hate poetry that has a palpable design upon us. And palpable designs upon us are just as unwelcome under non-literary circumstances. Whereas our likely response to negative capability is to be drawn in and think very carefully before either agreeing or disagreeing with anything, our response to more masterful modes of address is likely to be immediate rejection, unless, of course, they are backed up with other, even more unattractive kinds of pressure.

The paradoxical consequences of both negative capability and masterfulness are of central interest to literary writers, not only when they are thinking about their own behaviour towards their addressees and their own future fame and fortune, but also as they body forth the communication about which they are comparing notes with their audience: the communication of the characters "inside the story". Shakespeare's alertness to these paradoxes was exceptionally keen and sophisticated. Not accidentally, but inseparably from the main sweep of dramatic action, his plays reveal exactly the kind of communicational awareness necessary to account for their own strong but manifold influence.

That *Henry V* is no exception begins to seem likely from an observation by Andrew Gurr:

> No play of Shakespeare's makes so much use of differences in language and has more language barriers. With one entire scene in French, another half in French, and the French nobles regularly starting their scenes by making use of French phrases, plus Llewellyn's, Macmorris's and Jamy's non-standard English, Pistol's theatrical and old-fashioned quasi-verse, together with Mrs. Quickly's malapropisms, the play puts up a considerable show of non-communication.
>
> (Gurr 1992: 36)

Such features are not merely on the surface, and Gurr's list could be longer. Still more to the point, Shakespeare's communicational insight is reflexive here, prompting questions about his own choices and strategies as a dramatist, and in this way greatly raising the communicational quality of the play itself.

2.2   Listening for Shakespeare

An early pioneer in the study of Shakespeare's communicational self-consciousness was Gladys D. Willcock (1934, 1943, 1954a, 1954b). In her book *Shakespeare as Critic of Language* (1934), she carefully demonstrated that he was very sensitive to language and language use; that he made it the theme of a sustained sociocritical commentary in *Love's Labours Lost*; and that in other plays he foregrounded matters of pragmatics and style at precisely the dramatic highpoints – at just those moments when we might have expected that both he and his characters would be mainly interested in *what* was being said – in the thoughts and emotions – rather than in the *how* of it. Examples of this tendency include: Richard II's comment on the dying words of John of Gaunt, "Can sick men play so nicely with their names?"; Hamlet's reply to the outraged Laertes, "I'll rant as well as thou"; and Dolabella's interruptions of Cleopatra's poetical climaxes.

As an enthusiastic and intelligent reader, Willcock clearly grasped that the linguistic interests in Shakespeare's earlier plays are more superficial, whereas in the later ones they are integrated with a fuller study of human character and behaviour in general. Yet it was the earlier plays that she herself mainly discussed, her gift for descriptive linguistics, sociolinguistics, rhetorical studies and stylistics ensuring ample pay-offs. When Shakespeare's communicational interests offered a more complex literary-critical challenge, she seems to have pulled up short. Even today, there is ample scope for further study here.

As to Willcock's theoretical foundations, in common with most of her contemporaries she was not very explicit. But as a linguist, her focus was on interaction within social contexts, whereas, to the extent that she was a literary critic, she might have agreed with Coleridge or Bradley, not only about the individualities of Shakespeare's created characters, but about his own authorial independence. The net result can perhaps be taken as a kind of rough and ready synthesis, which in a way anticipates my own view of the human being as a social individual. Willcock's contextualizing linguistic analyses, though not based on a rigid social determinism, did somewhat qualify the assumptions of Victorian liberal humanism. She would probably have said that Shakespeare himself was not an entirely free agent, and also that this did not stop him from making a very considerable personal impact.

Certainly the contrast with a professedly postmodern critic such as Terence Hawkes (1986, 1992) is very striking. Hawkes is a wonderfully suggestive and amusing critic, with an extremely unusual gift for bringing Shakespeare to life. But in his work of the late 1980s and early 1990s, his stated aim had far less to do with bringing authors to life than with confirming the author's – any author's – death. For those of his readers wishing to avoid anachronisms, many of his theoretical and methodological pronouncements will have been hard to swallow, since exclusively presentist readings were exactly what he claimed to be offering. Invoking an extreme poststructuralist de-centring of the human subject, he denied Shakespeare's texts any authority or authenticity as the words of somebody called Shakespeare, and instead viewed them almost as a kind of anonymous ballad which, by way of a virtually oral tradition, had welled up through a collaboration within the "folk". Seen this way, Shakespeare never had any control over his own words at all, nor any right to such control, and everybody was at perfect liberty to use them as they pleased. What Hawkes was offering, in other words, was a defence of parthenogenetic misreadings.

A communicational critic can readily acknowledge that our present position in time and culture is so different from Shakespeare's that to grant him the understanding to which he is humanly entitled is sometimes difficult. Also, we ourselves enjoy human entitlements, including the right to say when our heuristic empathy with

Shakespeare is not developing into a longer-term sympathy. Both logically, psycho-logically and ethically, it is impossible to disagree with another communicant's idea or state of mind without first having tried to agree with it, to the extent that it lends itself to such experiment. But very often, despite a genuine effort of empathy, a more long-term agreement does prove to be impossible, in which case, to use terms drawn from speech-act theory, the illocutionary intent of the other communicant's words will be out of step with their current perlocutionary effect (Austin 1962; Searle 1969). Shakespeare's illocutionary intent was in any case, I am suggesting, negatively capable. He was so unrepressive of his own uncertainties, mysteries and doubts that his texts can often be seen as ambiguous or self-deconstructing. As a result, interpretations certainly can vary, especially as the plays come to be perceived from within a variety of sociohistorical positions.

Clearly, too, over the centuries since Shakespeare's lifetime such hermeneutic vari-ation has proliferated exponentially. When we go to watch one of his plays today, the chain of intermediaries includes the present production's actors, scene- and costume designers and director, plus those of earlier productions, plus critical discussions, plus editions both scholarly and less scholarly, and plus those earliest editions of all, which offer variant readings and are of varying degrees of closeness to anything Shakespeare himself may have put on paper. As time has moved on, Shakespeare's control over the impact of his own words, which was not something he strove to hold on to in the first place, could only further diminish. Nor can he himself, as an author long since dead in the most literal sense, re-assert it. On the contrary, the number of other agents with whose intentions his own become entangled gets steadily greater, sometimes with major ideological repercussions, as the historical contexts within which his words are received change as well.

All this, however, is not the same kind of cultural phenomenon as an oral tradi-tion. Because Shakespeare was already working within a literate culture which has only spread more widely since his death, and because one of the great benefits of literacy has been the growth of reasonably reliable historical, biographical and philological scholarship, his words still come down to us as his, and our empathetic interpretation of them can proceed with some confidence that both our agreements and disagree-ments with them will be responses to something reasonably close to what he actually wrote, and in something reasonably close to the way he actually understood it himself. Especially Shakespeare scholars, but also other theatre-goers or cinema-goers as well, take a decided interest in the way a current interpretation of a play seems to be in dialogue with Shakespeare, or with previous understandings of him. Interpretations do agree and disagree, both with Shakespeare and each other, in ways that are typical of the interpreters themselves and their own sociocultural formations. But within a literate culture there will always remain a sense that what is at issue here really is the handing on of *Shakespeare*, and that Shakespeare's written words can at least to some extent still act upon, and sometimes even change us here today. Our empathetic effort is something we owe not only to Shakespeare as our human fellow, but to ourselves, since empathy, in all genuine communication, is the way by which to enrich our own lives through a dialogue with otherness.

This is what, in his poststructuralist phase, Hawkes roundly denied. From his de-authorizing of Shakespeare's texts he drew the conclusion that their meaning has always been a total free-for-all. Mainly appealing to the American philosophical pragmatists William James, John Dewey, and Richard Rorty, he said that readers, directors, actors, spectators and critics are themselves pragmatists, who construct from a Shakespeare play the meaning which works best for them personally. "By" (i.e. by using) the Shakespeare play, they in fact make meanings of their own. Put another way, the play's meaning is "by" them (i.e. provided by them), in the same sense that a theatre programme might list "Cigarettes by Abdullah, Costumes by Motley, Music by Mendelssohn" (Hawkes 1992: 3). The final step in Hawkes's poststructuralist argument was to say that this meaning which readers construct is determined by their own ideological position within "the large-scale and continuing cultural dialogue or 'conversation' which constituted the very precondition of democracy" (Hawkes 1992: 7). Hence his programmatic summary:

> What passes amongst some literary critics for a text's "real" meaning can only be a temporary pause in this otherwise healthy process [of cultural dialogue or "conversation"]. And ... [a] text is surely better served if it is perceived not as the embodiment of some frozen, definitive significance, but as a kind of intersection or confluence which is continually traversed, a no-man's land, an arena, in which different and opposed meanings, urged from different and opposed political positions, compete in history for ideological power: the power, that is, to determine cultural meaning – to say what the world is and should be like. We try to make *Hamlet* mean for our purposes now: others will try to make it mean differently for their purposes then (or now). ... [T]here is no final, essential or "real" meaning at the end of it. There is no end. There is only and always the business of "meaning by".   (Hawkes 1992: 7–8)

At this point in his intellectual development Hawkes was compounding his extremist poststructuralism with a theory of literary communication which was *not* actually a theory of communication at all. He may well have been aware of this, since he calls it, not literary pragmatics but "literary pragmat*ism*" (Hawkes 1992: 6, my italics). The philosophical pragmatism he invoked was an epistemological theory, having to do with the truth or otherwise of our ideas about the world. And admittedly, the business of constructing what we hope will be true ideas about the world does involve processes of inferencing which resemble the ones we use in trying to work out what is in somebody else's mind from the words they speak. The cardinal difference, however, is that in truth-making only a single subjectivity is involved, that of the truth-maker, whereas in meaning-making at least two subjectivities are in relationship, those of the addresser and the addressee/s. Even though the significance and value an addressee places on an utterance may never be exactly the same as that placed on it by the addresser, even though the addresser's mental state may have been one of negatively capable uncertainty, mystery and doubt, the addressee is still humanly obliged to consider what the addresser could have meant, simply in order to be able to relate to it in the first place. Hawkes's professed concern to do justice to the *text* ("[a] text is surely better served if ...") deprived *real human beings* of a basic human right: the right to a fair hearing. This right he awarded instead to the mere inanimate text, as a way of refusing the reader's duty towards the text's known human writer. So although he had a lot to say about democracy, his account of readers simply imposing their own meanings was a travesty of democratic justice, because such justice can only obtain in a world of human interpersonality.

For Hawkes-the-poststructualist-theoretician, then, reading was a totally solipsistic activity – nothing more than an occasion for ideologically self-confirming ego-trips. As described by him, a reader's response was not really a response at all, because it involved no reciprocity. And with dialogicality short-circuited in this way, interpretations could only be parthenogenetic.

The irony is that Hawkes has always had such a sharp instinctive feel for communicational realities. Few critics have written with greater insight into those textual "silences" – the loose-ended treatment of, say, Hamlet's love of Ophelia – which actually baffle a spectator's movement of empathy, though Hawkes also showed how Shakespeare, in the "O" of the dying Cleopatra's "O Antony!", arouses an empathy with the character, and with all her creator's verbal and visual meanings, that is quite momentous (Hawkes 1986: 29–50, 79–85). As his theory leads us to expect, he is particularly interested in the links between a given interpretation and the larger social and ideological ambience in which it was made. But theory was never his work's be-all and end-all, and in a pre-postmodern age of scholarship he might well have been praised for very faithful readings. Given that his postmodern theory was what it was, his philological grasp of Early Modern English was not something he flaunted. Yet it would have been very difficult to trip him up on it, and in practice he did perhaps see an interpretation of Shakespeare as potentially an agreement or disagreement with a Shakespeare who still has a relative autonomy, and whose meanings can still be at least approximated with the help of philological and other historical knowledge. Despite the long and complicated chain of intermediaries which he so tellingly analysed, he time and time again, even in his poststructuralist phase, bore witness that Shakespeare can act upon us even today. His own readings *are* readings, and very responsive ones. They are not parthenogenetic misreadings.

Hawkes himself could never have entered into a debate about this without surrendering his theory's first premise. If he had said that my argument here is wrong, he would have been authorizing my text as that of a subject whose meanings can be both empathetically known and critically disagreed with. If he had said that I have misread him, he would have been doing the same thing for his own text. And from this point of view, the only difference between Shakespeare's texts and texts such as Hawkes's or mine is that Shakespeare's now come to their recipients through a longer and more complicated chain of intermediaries.

In the theorizing of less extremist postmodern critics, the communicational facts which Hawkes knew in his bones but did not always acknowledge were sometimes squarely stated. John Turner wrote:

> Two things ... happen together in the course of reading or watching a play – two different things, which it is important to try to keep separate, even though the boundary-line is always lost between them: we re-create the work in our own language in order to claim acquaintance with it, to give it symbolic meaning in our own world, while at the same time we grapple with the language in which it was originally written in order to know it in its history. These two activities have tended in their extremes to produce what Brecht called empathic [sic] and critical approaches to literature, traditional criticism tending towards the former and post-structuralism towards the latter. But, as Brecht saw, both are necessary, each complementing the other: and indeed both activities are perhaps necessarily and ordinarily involved in the complex shuttling back and forth between self and other which constitutes the apparently simple act of understanding.   (Turner 1988: 5–6)

But even in the communicative pragmatics of Turner, the sense of *logos* as *pragma* was rather weak. He did not share Habermas's sense of language-use in general as communicative action, let alone my own sense (not shared by Habermas) of literature as one type of communicative action among others. Part of the explanation may be that he was too taken up with Barthesian ideas about writing's playfulness, ideas which, given that he was studying Shakespeare's history plays, were hardly *à propos*. A corpus of dramatic texts making a more formidable intervention in the communal negotiation of power would be hard to find. Its perspective is one within which language reveals a far from ludic aspect.

As Willcock would perhaps have said, the history plays' intervention was distinctively Shakespeare's own, even though he was working within inherited ideological, historiographical and genre frameworks. And the chance that other people would be able to respond to the felt life of his communicational insights here has always been reasonably good, even though they have been bound to see him in their own distinctive and historical situated ways as well. To repeat, his negatively capable words have always had both strength and weakness.

Hawkes, in his more recent work, seems to have a clearer sense of this. Familiar as I was with his earlier poststructuralist claims, I approached his *Shakespeare in the Present* (2002) and a volume which Hugh Grady and he have edited together, *Presentist Shakespeares* (2007), with some trepidation. Their titles seemed to promise an even more blatant disregard for anything an individual called Shakespeare might have intended and attempted to do by means of his writings. In fact, though, Hawkes has mellowed. Even though he still claims to believe that we cannot really understand the past, and still refers to Shakespeare as if he were an entirely oral phenomenon (an argument he now links to a rather sentimental view of the improvisations of black American jazz players), his sharp historical sense is at last beginning to come through into his more theoretical and methodological pronouncements. The following passages could well be quotations from this present book:

> It is certainly the case that too much teaching of Shakespeare is devoted nowadays to the kind of simple-minded "sameness" (how like us the Elizabethans were), [sic] that ignores history. Too little concerns itself with the analysis of "difference" (how unlike us the Elizabethans were), which requires some serious grappling with it. (Hawkes 2002:117)

> Of course we should read Shakespeare historically. But given that history results from a never-ending dialogue between past and present ...

Thus far here, Hawkes's current approach to Shakespeare could not be in closer harmony with my own account of literature as dialogue. But then his sentence continues:

> ... given that history results from a never-ending dialogue between past and present, how can we decide whose historical circumstances will have priority in that process, Shakespeare's or our own? (Hawkes 2002:3)

And over a hundred pages later he answers this question as follows:

> On balance, it seems better to face up to the fact – recognised as a first principle by any self-respecting presentism – that the questions we ask of a literary text will always be shaped by our own concerns. To embrace that is not to abandon the past. (Hawkes 2002:117)

This statement of principle, by giving "priority" to our own agenda, involves a concept of communication as unidirectional. Instead of maintaining an openness before the mystery of the past and waiting to see what, by its very difference, it may suggest about ourselves, here we are simply supposed to adapt it to our own uses. Yet Hawkes, if we overlook some quirky distortions arising from his by now rather nostalgic resentment of the English class system and British jingoism, is such a faithful reader, and his historical sense so unusually alert, that much of what he writes could well be labelled as mediating criticism in the sense explained in my Introduction. In practice, his presentist fanfare is less a manifesto for anachronism than a self-distancing from shortcomings in current criticism of a historicist orientation – of which, more below.

In Hawkes's own best criticism, the dialogicality between the past and the present, between Shakespeare's words at their strongest and at their weakest, is exciting and important. What it tells us does not have more to do with Terence Hawkes in his own present than with Shakespeare in his, and much of it is actually devoted to identifying the blind-spots arising from what Hawkes explicitly refers to as other interpreters' presentisms. The use made by G. Wilson Knight of John of Gaunt's "scepter'd isle" speech in *Richard II* for the purposes of wartime propaganda was insensitive to Shakespeare's own nagging unease, for instance in *Cymbeline*, at the political and cultural subordination of Wales to England. Or to take another example, in 1945 the Office of Military Government in the American sector of Berlin included *Hamlet* on its "white list" of plays which might benefit a populace in need of political re-education, apparently without realizing that this play suggests, not only that crimes will be punished, but also that there may be something dangerously attractive about Claudius, the greatest criminal. With his characteristic mastery of historical semantics, Hawkes argues that Claudius, and all of Shakespeare's potentially most powerful effects, can no longer come into their own unless *we rid ourselves* of our own presentist preconceptions. Above all, we need to understand that, for Shakespeare and his contemporaries, play-acting and bear-baiting did not yet belong to two completely separate spheres. This, Hawkes warns, is where presentism can only decontextualize "the savage heart of Shakespeare's work" (Hawkes 2002: 88). For Shakespeare, playing on a stage and baiting a bear were not each other's antitheses, but would have both sorted under some such term as "wildness", whose opposite would have been something like "law" or "learning".

When Hawkes gets down to this kind of nitty-gritty, his procedures are spontaneously ethical, which is why he can be so suggestive about Shakespeare. Despite the remaining traces of wayward theorization, his chief critical instinct is to prick up his ears. This makes for an encounter in which the only "priority" is temporal, and accorded to Shakespeare. First in time came Shakespeare's words. Second in time comes Hawkes, who tries to read them as a way of listening for Shakespeare. During that process, in utter controversion of the poststructuralist slogans of twenty years ago, Shakespeare becomes actually present to him. For as Hawkes's admirer, Ewan Fernie, puts it, "any really responsive engagement with Shakespeare's inimitably and even alien presence in the present will in fact creatively confront, unsettle and transcend routine modes of thinking" (Fernie 2007: 97). In terms of human rights and autonomy, Hawkes and Shakespeare are each other's equals, which means that the dialogue between them is maximally alive.

Now to use his own phrasing, Hawkes is most suggestive about historical "'difference' (how unlike us the Elizabethans were)". But what his admirer Ewan Fernie found in *Henry V* was, as I say, a violence which "is perhaps inalienable from human life", a conclusion which to Hawkes's way of thinking might come very close to "the kind of simple-minded 'sameness' (how like us the Elizabethans were), [*sic*] that ignores history". On the other hand, both Fernie's perception of violence and Hawkes's own perception of savagely wild play relate to that area of existential overlap between one human lifeworld and another which provides the springboard for flights of empathy with sociocultural otherness.

That the violence and the savagely wild play have this important communicational function in no way contradicts the insights of the so-called evolutionary criticism recently developed by Joseph Carroll (2004) and Thomas Karshan (2009). Karshan is understandably impatient with twentieth-century criticism that invoked "a language-based model of art". Such criticism, "by treating art merely as a pointlessly obscure vehicle for meaning, unduly limited our sense of the variety of things individual poems or novels are doing". It saw them "as merely a message sent from A to B" (Karshan 2009: 300). Criticism based on a literary-communicational theory which, by contrast, makes an ethically loaded distinction between a unidirectional transmission of a message from A to B and a bi-directionally dialogical and uncoercive comparing of notes views literature as very much a field of interaction, which can involve the full range of interpersonal functions dwelt on in evolutionary criticism, plus all their attendant emotional, psychological and social dimensions as well. Seen in the communicational perspective, any such evolutionarily significant feature contributes to what, in my study of *Great Expectations*, I shall be describing as a story's primary tellability. It prompts in readers, listeners or theatre-goers a kind of gut-recognition which draws them further on into a writer's work, where they may then begin to negotiate other features which, though far more civilized, may be far less deeply familiar. The evolutionarily primitive is a bond of communicational attraction. It is one of the things that we listen for first and, in acknowledging it, we open our minds to the othernesses made accessible by its sameness.

In listening for Shakespeare, in trying to assess Shakespeare's own communicational behaviour and identify Shakespeare's own communicational insights, communicational critics, unlike mediating critics, are bound to spend more time on these atavistic matters than on those of microhistorical detail, quite simply because the difference between egotism and negative capability, between coercive communication and genuine communication, itself has roots that are far more primitive than those now traceable back to Kantian ethics, for instance. So Fernie is right, I think, to speak of a perhaps inalienably human violence in *Henry V*. His only shortcoming, I would say, is two-fold: he underestimates the *communicational* scope for violence, which leaves him rather surprised at the *coram populo* dearth of *physical* violence; and he overlooks the communicational *opposite* of violence, which occurs in movements of self-abnegation whose virtuousness, according to zoologists such as Matt Ridley (1997), is no less anciently wired.

2.3   Temporarily strong words

As Willcock hinted, by the midpoint of his career Shakespeare's linguistic preoccupations were already moving wide and deep. In *Henry V* especially, there is also a very marked interest in how people actually get things done. Dowden was neither the first nor last commentator to find it "clear and unquestionable that King Henry V. [*sic*] is Shakspere's [*sic*] ideal of the *practical* heroic character. He is the king who will not fail" (Dowden 1906 [1875]: 74, his italics). The point is, though, that high dramatic salience is given to those of Henry's actions which take the form of words. He may tell Katherine that he is a rough soldier, ungifted in eloquence. But this speech itself is very long, and achieves precisely the required effect on her.

If we look for signs of the practical hero's more hands-on practicality, we shall draw a blank. Where is his genius as an inventor of military stratagem? What about his brilliant deployment of archers, and his revolutionary use of the hedge of stakes to protect them against French cavalry? – both of these details were mentioned *twice* in the anonymous *Famous Victories of Henry the Fift* of the previous year. Or to repeat Fernie's kind of question, when, *coram populo*, does the rough soldier hero actually get round to using a sword? The only time he even comes close to it is in connection with the dual he promises Williams, who is not even a Frenchman. In the event, he passes on the gage to the bellicose Llewellyn, who in his physical assaults on both Williams and Pistol is the only character really seen to do violence on stage, and who is in any case mainly comic, just as are Pistol and Nym or Pistol and Le Fer in the only other scenes where violence is even a remote possibility (II i, IV iv).

The Chorus warns all along that the theatrical representation will give a very poor idea of the story's mighty events. But the spectacle is even more scanty than this leads an audience to expect. The only truly heroic deaths in battle are those of Suffolk and York, but these happen off-stage and are merely narrated by Exeter, as if by a messenger in Greek tragedy. The kind of thing Shakespeare does show us is: Henry giving the papers to Cambridge, Gray, and Scroop in which they read words tantamount to a death sentence; Henry inciting his men once more unto the breach at Harfleur; Henry raising Westmorland's spirits with the Saint Crispian speech; and Henry reacting to a change in the state of battle with a lightning-swift imperiousness of speech:

> But hark, what new alarm is this same?
> The French have reinforced their scattered men.
> Then every soldier kill his prisoners.
> Give the word through.   (IV vi, ll. 35–8)

According to most editors except Taylor (1982: 65), not even this command is obeyed on stage (Gurr 1992: 177), and there is a pervasive sense that words are decidedly more important than actions, almost as if they have a power of their own. This is not just because of the paucity of visible violence. Time and time again the play's own wording draws attention to it, and from the very beginning, as when the Archbishop of Canterbury remarks that if Henry speaks,

The air, a chartered libertine, is still,
And the mute wonder lurketh in men's ears
To steal his sweet and honeyed sentences,
So that the art and practic part of life
Must be the mistress to this theoric.   (I ii, ll. 48–52)

Shakespeare makes his Grace an observant communicative pragmaticist, who appreciates that Henry is a great rhetorician, and that such a person's words can truly affect the world of human reality. Henry's words have strength.

Here there are already considerations which were somewhat overlooked in postmodern historicist criticism, a kind of criticism which Hawkes, though ostensibly accusing it of puristic reductionism, in practice shows up as *insufficiently* historicist. Not that self-proclaimingly historicist critics ignored relationships between communication, context, and power. On the contrary, Stephen Greenblatt's account of *Henry IV i & ii* and *Henry V* drew parallels between literary and non-literary texts precisely as a way of suggesting literature's implication in ongoing ideological battles. No less than Thomas Harriot's *A Briefe and True Report of the New Found Land of Virginia* (1588), Shakespeare's plays were seen by Greenblatt as testing the limits of political power, as recording the way in which challenges to it can be negotiated or assimilated, and as offering convenient interpretations of events or phenomena which do not quite tally with official dogma. This led him to speak of a poetics of Elizabethan power, which was in turn bound up with a poetics of the theatre.

> Testing, recording, and explaining are elements in this poetics that is inseparably bound up with the figure of Queen Elizabeth, a ruler without a standing army, without a highly developed bureaucracy, without an extensive police force, a ruler whose power is constituted in theatrical celebrations of royal glory and theatrical violence visited upon the enemies of that glory. … Elizabethan power … depends upon its privileged visibility. As in a theatre, the audience must be powerfully engaged by this visible present while at the same time held at a certain respectful distance from it. "We princes", Elizabeth told a deputation of Lords and Common [*sic*] in 1586, "are set on stages in the sight and view of all the world."
>
> (Greenblatt 1985: 44)[2]

Yet as a gloss on *Henry V* this was not quite right. "Theatrical violence visited upon the enemies of … [royal] glory"? It is not *violence* that is staged, and many critics, taking their cue from the Chorus, have argued that no merely theatrical representation could ever have bodied forth the English victories in any case. According to J. H. Walter, Shakespeare's task was "to extract material for a play from an epic story" and to give "within the physical limits of the stage and within the admittedly inadequate dramatic

---

2. Greenblatt annotates the last sentence of this quotation with a reference to Neale 1965: II 119.

convention … the illusion of an epic whole" (Walter 1954:xv). If spectators do carry away an impression of a "brave fleet / With silken streamers the young Phoebus feigning", or of "ordnance on their carriages / With fatal mouths gaping on girded Harfleur" (III 0, ll. 5–6, 26–27), it is because they themselves have imagined this in response to the play's own words, as the Chorus continuously and very precisely urges. "Think when we talk of horses that you see them / Printing their proud hooves i' th' receiving earth" (I 0 26–7). "Work, work your thoughts, and therein see a seige" (III 0, ll. 25). Right from the play's opening lines, themselves so memorable, Shakespeare is meta-theatrically foregrounding his own word-power over his audience, and Henry is a hero who – far more than Richard II, a poet-king whose solipsistic poetry only causes his own downfall – resembles Shakespeare. Physical violence is merely secondary and almost incidental here, mere noises off. What really counts is words.

Then again, if violence wrought on the monarch's enemies is not actually shown, how much regal awesomeness is left? Henry may sometimes be a supreme lord of language, and very good at cheering people up. But what about Greenblatt's phrase, "theatrical celebrations of royal glory"? Does even this apply? How much, for instance, does the play resemble a coronation, a royal pageant or progress, or a formal court occasion? Most of all, perhaps, in I ii, where Henry, often positioned centre-stage upon his throne, confers with his advisers and receives the French ambassadors. But what happens next? The ambassadors perpetrate a carnivalistic hoax. Their diplomatic tribute turns out to be an egregious insult: the gift of the tennis balls. In the long term, the incident may redound to Henry's favour. In France he will be able to show how mistaken the Dauphin was to see him as a frivolous ne'er-do-well. More immediately, though, the impact is, first, to remind everyone on stage and in the audience of his misspent youth, already discussed in the previous scene by Canterbury and Ely, and secondly, to send Henry himself huffing and puffing into the first of the play's long series of imprecations – "tell the pleasant prince this mock of his / Hath turned his balls to gun-stones" and so on (I ii, ll. 281–2). That this brings even Henry's eloquence to the verge of the ridiculous is hinted by what is hardly a very gross parody of it in II i, in which Pistol lets fly his preposterous verbal batteries at Nym, a scene which Pope very sensibly placed *immediately after* the court scene, and *before* the Chorus's second speech. The main advantage of Pope's arrangement is usually said to be that it allows the Chorus's announcement of Henry's arrival in Southampton to run straight into II ii, which is actually set there, whereas II i is still set in London (Gurr 1992:90). But the closer juxtaposition of Henry's and Pistol's energetic threats is undoubtedly a further benefit, and helps to pinpoint what, as we shall see, is a central motif in the plotting.

Even when Henry is on the war-path, just how awesome is he? To use Greenblatt's phrases, how likely is his "visible presence" to cow beholders to "a certain respectful distance"? The rhetoric of the "Once more unto the breach" speech and the St Crispin's Day speech is wonderful beyond praise. But Henry knows exactly what Aristotle meant: great orators co-adaptationally *diminish* their distance from their hearers. At Harfleur:

> Once more unto the breach, *dear friends*, once more,
> . . . . [T]here is none of you so mean and base
> That hath not noble lustre in your eyes.   (III i, ll. 1, 29–30, my italics)

At Agincourt:

> We few, we happy few, we band of brothers –
> For he today that sheds his blood with me
> Shall be my brother; be he ne'er so vile
> This day shall gentle his condition…   (IV iii, ll. 60–3)

In the Harfleur speech, Henry positively de-mythologizes the fearsome wrath with which great warriors scare their enemies. He tells his common soldiers how to do it!

> Then *imitate* the action of the tiger:
> … *Disguise* fair nature with hard-favoured rage.
> Then *lend* the eye a terrible aspect.   (III i, ll. 6, 8–10, my italics)

To describe these speeches as instances of negative capability on Henry's part may at first seem far-fetched. It is not as if, in the heat of the campaign, he really has much time to be in uncertainties, mysteries, doubts. The life he is leading at present is that of action, not of contemplation. Yet notice the extent to which the speeches nevertheless dismantle received certainties, both about society in general and about himself and his own role in particular. His words make customary social distinctions melt away in a warmth of common humanity, surrendering his own primacy, and offering the intimate image of a fearful bluffer behind his hard-favoured public image. At such moments Henry's persuasiveness does indeed result from a negatively capable intelligence, which is acting quite spontaneously. On the spur of the moment, he is able to conjure up a thought-provoking alternative to the usual way of conceptualizing relations between king and subject, commander and soldier, and one which stirs his hearers' own imagination. There is still no guarantee that they will do what he wants. But they are a thousand times more likely to listen and truly consider what he says than if he had merely issued a straight command. By abnegating his own social authority and personal superiority, by inviting them, as fellow human beings, to see things in this new light, he does, as it turns out, win their assent, at least for the time being, even if at some later juncture his revolutionary incitements could return to plague him in the form of a popular uprising. Negatively capable wording can have enormous influence, but guarantees no permanent control.

What Shakespeare also suggests is that Henry's negatively capable re-invention of reality, insofar as it highlights the possibility of a warrior king's own inner insecurities, is close to the mark. Although, before Agincourt, the Chorus urges the audience to imagine the king "[w]alking from watch to watch, from tent to tent" in order to show a "royal face" without "a note / How dread an army hath enrounded him", this does involve a bluff, which even the enthusiastic Chorus frankly mentions: Henry "overbears attaint / With cheerful semblance" (IV 0, ll. 30, 35–6, 39–40). In his inner man, Henry is still closer to his "brothers, friends and countrymen" (IV 0, l. 34) than he encourages them to believe, and this is something the audience will again realize when, having cast aside all visible marks of kinghood, he says to Bates, "I think the king is but a man as I am" (IV i, l. 97), words whose force as dramatic irony is curiously twofold: Bates does not know that the person before him *is* the king; yet perhaps Bates is *right* to think him just a man. Henry even says that

> no man should possess him [the king] with any appearance of fear, lest he [the king] by showing it should dishearten his army,

by which time Bates is on just the same wavelength: the king

> may show what outward courage he will, but I believe, as cold a night as 'tis, he could wish himself in Thames up to the neck.   (IV i, ll. 104–6, 107–9)

So during this highly charged lull before the storm, the king is somebody whom Bates cannot find it in his heart to envy or even much respect. If anything, he feels sorry for him; if the king's cause is unjust, the blood of many men will be upon his conscience. Henry may testily counter that every man dying in battle will still have to pay for his own sins. But Bates has only repeated what Henry himself said to Canterbury at the beginning – "May I with right and conscience make this claim?" (I ii, l. 96) – and when Bates and Williams have moved away, Henry's soliloquy on ceremony is ruthlessly honest, not only with himself but, of course, towards the audience. The kingly role is hugely oppressive. The responsibility and the scope for failure hardly bear thinking of. Far from being a "theatrical celebration of royal glory", the play is a step-by-step demonstration that royal glory is *nothing but* theatricality, and very burdensome at that.

The value of late-twentieth-century historicist criticism is not in question. In exploring power in Shakespeare's England and Shakespeare's plays, Greenblatt and others showed power and its attendant ideology, discourse, roles and ceremonies to be of pressing relevance. In any society, they never simply go away. Henry may tell the Dauphin's messengers that up until now "I have laid by my majesty / And plodded like a man for working days" (I ii, ll. 276–7). He may tell Bates that when "[the king's] ceremonies [are] laid by, in his nakedness he appears but as a man" (IV i, ll. 99–100). But not even Lear's madness or Richard II's deposition is a complete laying-by. The royal function is still ideologically in place, and includes a sense of "once a king, always a king". Lear is still restorable to the throne, and Bolingbroke can never shake off his usurper's guilt. Even his victorious son still does expensive penance, and still hopes for a son of his own to beard the Turk and generally patch things up. His main point to the Dauphin's messengers is about the great expectations that in any case surround his position, and his determination to live up to them. When he speaks the words to Bates, similarly, he is not actually naked, either literally or metaphorically, but disguised. The prescribed kingly role still persists for himself and for the audience, and throughout the play is absolutely central to his own and their perceptions of everything he says and does.

Nor can he be immune to the human pain of yielding to such a mould. Given the play's explicit de-mythologization of royalty, certain configurations of events carry a poignant sub-text. Closest to deciphering this is Llewellyn:

> As Alexander killed his friend Cleitus, being in his ales and his cups, so also Harry Monmouth, being in his right wits and his good judgements, turned away the fat knight with the great belly doublet. ... I'll tell you, there is good men porn at Monmouth. (IV vii, ll. 36–43)

Nowhere in either *Henry IV ii* and *Henry V* themselves or any of the subsequent critical commentary is the rejection of Falstaff mentioned with warmer approbation. Not even Canterbury and Ely are more impressed. Yet even Llewellyn underlines Henry's appearance of coolness, and the question is: What if it really is just an appearance? What if the coolness is no less a part of the royal theatricals than we know the courage to be? Graver still, Llewellyn's words come very shortly after Henry's brusque order that the prisoners be killed, thus half-recalling Nym and Pistol's diagnosis of Falstaff's mortal ailment: "The king hath run bad humours on the knight ... . [H]is heart is fracted" (II i, ll. 97–100). Nor is this the only hint that Henry's own subjection to the kingly role turns him into his friends' virtual murderer. Scroop, one of the traitors he impassively delivers to the laws of the land, was, as Exeter remarks, his bedfellow. Scroop knew, Henry himself says, "the very bottom of my soul" (II ii, l. 94). But Scroop could never have betrayed anyone but a king so very completely. And who but a king could lead his loving York and Suffolk to their end? After Exeter's beautiful narration has squeezed every last drop of pathos and moral significance from their deaths, is there any reason for *not* believing Henry's awkward remark that he "must perforce compound" with his eyes to prevent them from weeping (IV vi, l. 33)? Could it be that the immediately subsequent order to kill the prisoners is part of the same occupational reflex? Does he have to keep on steeling himself? Or if he really is hard-hearted now, how much pleasure can he be getting from his progressive isolation? Once again there is the parodic parallel with vainglorious Pistol, who also loses Falstaff, plus Bardolf, Nym, the Boy and Nell. Nor is it very likely that the conqueror of France will make a new soul-mate out of a French princess.

Yet the fact remains: the social and the individual can enter into co-adaptation. Although the kingly function is deeply entrenched, although Henry pays an enormous human price in adapting to it, he still has the option of somewhat adapting it to himself, and he knows it. When it suits him, he even appeals to his powerful social role in the course of bringing about social change. Hearing from Katherine that "[i]t is not a fashion for maids in France to kiss before they are married", he counters: "O Kate, nice customs curtsy to great kings. ... We are the makers of manners ..." (V ii, ll. 240–45). He clearly experiences himself as reasonably autonomous, and the political machinery does not entirely sweep him along with its physical and ideological force. The violence or the celebration normally prescribed to bolster royalty does not entirely determine the course of events. His great achievements spring from the extraordinary force of his own speech, which is itself negatively capable and involves that co-adaptational shortening of the distance between his kinghood and humanity in general. As for the pomp and circumstance, it is a facade behind which we see him trembling, a facade that he himself has to struggle to keep in place. As Alexander Leggatt remarks, what Shakespeare's history plays really show is the social symbolism of kinghood becoming less effective.

> What matters now is the individuality of the man who wears the crown: the neurotic self-destructiveness of Richard II, the practical competence and panache of Henry V. The latter can rescue kingship for a while, but only by turning it into leadership; and that means that kingship is a diminished thing.
>
> (Leggatt 1988:44)

It means, in short, that the king will have to be a communicator, and Shakespeare has a very clear view of how the relationship between *logos* and *pragma* actually works.

2.4   Immediately weak words

When the communicative king is persuading other people to do things, his most successful strategy is the one already noted: a negatively capable co-adaptation between received certainties and a totally different mental universe, which enables a royal to meet non-royals half-way, and by which the sense of community is enlarged. While in no way detracting from his persuasive intent, his concessions to other people, his assertions that the humanity they share with him overrides the social distinctions, involve a genuineness of communication which would in principle leave them free to reject his promptings. Fortunately for him, they are drawn into his own thought-world, at least for the time being, and respond positively to his appeal.

Altogether more problematic are Henry's attempts to influence people by undertaking to do something unpleasant, especially when those he is threatening belong to the grouping he continues to classify as enemy and alien. Shakespeare clearly sees the paradox of communicational masterfulness: that a direct attempt to gain or keep control over a situation can be self-defeating.

As a threatener, Henry will never be the slightest bit effective unless his hearers get the feeling that his words will be backed up with deeds – that the king will be "as good as" his word. He is obviously at a huge disadvantage here. Far from having a splendid track-record to point to, he knows perfectly well that everyone, both at home and abroad, is still gossiping about his misspent youth. On top of which, the French are increasingly unimpressed by the size, equipment and medical condition of his army.

Even so, he may still manage to be convincing by the sheer intensity of his words, and by the kind of theatrical bluff he is so good at. For a warrior king, it is vital that both his own men and the enemy should feel him capable of great bravery and blood-shed. Here, then, is yet another paradox. On the one hand, Shakespeare suggests the strength of Henry's words by never staging him in the act of slaughter. On the other hand, Henry's words themselves often promise slaughter, and he is obliged to support them with a matching impression of physical prowess. In his own body, he has to sug-gest a capability to "imitate the action of the tiger". So if I may add to the terminology of the speech act theoreticians (Austin 1962; Searle 1969), what Shakespeare sees is that certain speech acts cannot be successfully carried out unless a kind of corporal felicity condition is fulfilled. Conversely, if this condition is patently not fulfilled, the speaker's words will have even less chance of winning real control – of winning hearts and minds – than masterful words usually have.

Unless I am mistaken, Theobald, in that most celebrated of all emendations, was sensitive to Shakespeare's communicational insight here. To spell out the familiar de-tails, when the Hostess describes the death of Falstaff, the Folio has her saying:

> …I knew there was but one way. For his nose was as sharp as a pen, and a Table of greene fields.

Instead of this last phrase, the Quarto has "…and talk of floures". Something to do with talking would certainly help to make sense, and "talkd" was itself suggested to Theobald by an anonymous "gentleman sometime deceased". But the Quarto's "floures" could merely be a mistaken recapitulation of the Hostess's slightly earlier mention of Falstaff playing with flowers, and "talk" seems rather un-Shakespearian in its connotational poverty. Theobald's own suggestion was of course

> … his nose was as sharp as a pen, and a babbled of green fields
>
> (II iii, l. 14, Gurr's text of 1992)

and according to palaeographers and bibliographers, the choice between "babbled" and "talked" can only be decided on aesthetic grounds (Taylor 1982:295). Well, one aesthetic detail worth pointing out is surely that "babbled" anticipates Llewellyn's description of words without substance:

> If you would take the pains but to examine the wars of Pompey the Great you shall find, I warrant you, that there is no tiddle taddle nor pibble pabble in Pompey's camp.   (IV i, ll. 66–69)

Throughout the play a simple chiasmus operates: a person without physical thrust is likely to be or to seem a babbler, and a babbler is unlikely to have much physical thrust. The Hostess goes on to report Falstaff's last effective words as a request that she lay more clothes upon his feet. Then:

> I put my hand into the bed, and felt them, and they were as cold as any stone.
> Then I felt to his knees, and so up-peered and upward, and all was cold as stone.
>   (II iii, ll. 19–22)

After which, even the babbling had to stop.

Llewellyn thinks of the French enemy as "an ass and a fool and a prating cox-comb" – quite weightless as a word-user (IV i, ll. 74–75). This is a bit unfair on the French king, but Bourbon's sonnet to his horse ("Wonder of nature!"(III viii, l. 37)) certainly points in the same direction as Constable's remark behind his back:

> ORLÉANS: I know him to be valiant.
> CONSTABLE: I was told that, by one that knows him better than you.
> ORLÉANS: What's he?
> CONSTABLE: Marry, he told me so himself, and said he cared not who knew it.
>   (III viii, ll. 92–97)

Not that Constable himself is a weighty speaker. Urging his companions into battle, he exclaims:

> …Let us blow on them [the English],
> The vapour of our valour will o'erturn them.

That a vaporous valour would be effective seems unlikely and, given the audience's prior knowledge of the impending *débâcle*, his words can only boomerang anyway. He may boast

> … What's to say?
> A very little little let us do
> And all is done.   (IV ii, ll. 23–4, 32–34)

But the dramatic irony coolly underlines that there is much more saying than doing here.

Pistol, too, has "a killing tongue but a quiet sword", as the Boy says (III ii, l. 29). Even Llewellyn is impressed at first:

> There is an anchient lieutenant there at the pridge. I think in my very conscience
> he is as valiant a man as Mark Antony, and he is man of no estimation in the
> world, but I did see him do as gallant service.   (III vii, ll. 10–13)

See him do? Llewellyn has for the moment allowed Pistol's words to have the same kind of imaginative effect on him as the Chorus hopes to have on the audience. By the time he has been exposed to a bit more of Pistol's language – "I do partly understand your meaning", he says – and has realized that Pistol wants him to help Bardolf escape being hung for having pilfered a church, what he saw is no longer quite so clear:

> I'll assure you, a uttered as brave words at the pridge as you shall see in a sum-
> mer's day.   (III vii, ll. 41–2, 53–54)

Seeing words sums it up! In the case of Pistol, physical bravery is conspicuous by its absence. This makes it only the more amusing that even he himself imagines that a person with no verbal dash at all, a Welshman who laboriously tries to interpret Pistol's own Marlovianisms like a grammar-school pedagogue on an off-day –

> By your patience, Anchient Pistol, Fortune is painted plind, with a muffler afore her eyes to signify to you that Fortune is plind,   (III vii, ll. 25–27)

– will simply have no clout. Gower's comment on Pistol's rude disillusionment is very much part of Shakespeare's study of communication:

> You thought because he [Llewellyn] could not speak English in the native garb he could not therefore handle an English cudgel.   (V i, ll. 66–68)

Llewellyn is unusual in the play for packing *more* of a punch than his words suggest. Pistol's own last words are much more typical. Solitary and deflated, back in England he will still go on boasting, swearing that he got his "cudgelled scars" in the "Gallia wars" (V i, l. 78).

One of the play's key moments is when Pistol and Henry's paths finally cross. Henry is disguised still, and they exchange names:

> PISTOL: What is they name?
> KING: Harry *le roi*.
> PISTOL: Leroy? A Cornish name. …
>
> PISTOL: My name is Pistol called.
> KING: It sorts well with your fierceness.   (IV i, ll. 46–49, 61–62)

Pistol's mastery of Romance philology is not what it might be, and he has no idea that the man in front of him may be more than he appears, not only by title but as a person who gets things done. Henry's etymological gloss is marginally better scholarship. But does he really think Pistol's name fits? Or would he already be unconvinced by Pistol's earlier threat against Nym – "Pistol's cock is up, and flashing fire will follow!" (II i, l. 43)?

Either way, the doggedness with which the parodic Pistol shadows the royal footsteps (a plot device which clearly taught Dickens something of his trade (Sell 2001: 281–286)) draws particular attention to Henry's own pledges of future action. At one point the Boy describes Pistol as no more valorous than a roaring devil in an old play (IV i, l. 56). The question is: Does Henry sometimes not come close to being just a roaring stage king?

After his victory at Agincourt, admittedly, he is hyperbolically modest: "be it death proclaimèd through our host / To boast of this" (IV viii, ll. 106–107). Whereas at the outset of the play no less a person than the Archbishop of Canterbury had said that "miracles are ceased" (I i, l. 67), Henry will now accept no other explanation for his success than divine intervention. Llewellyn, who has obviously done a lion's share of the real fighting, slightly dents the royal sanctimoniousness, ruefully asking: "Is it not lawful, an't please your majesty, to tell how many is killed?" But Henry hardly budges – "Yes captain, but with this acknowledgement / That God fought for us" – and the Chorus later drums this in still harder: Henry, "free from vainness and self-glorious pride", as little like Pistol as possible, in other words, gives "full trophy, signal and ostent / Quite from himself to God" (IV viii, ll. 109–110, 111–112; V 0, ll. 20–22).

This saintliness has not been his usual tune, though, and could be just another example of his adopting a pose for the occasion. Before Agincourt, he actually asks God's forgiveness for bragging to the French envoy (III vii, 131–132), a repetition of the minatory self-assertiveness first seen in his reaction to the tennis balls. The Chorus's opening speech encourages the audience to imagine

> ...the warlike Harry, like himself,
> Assume the port of Mars, and at his heels
> (Leashed in, like hounds) ... famine, sword and fire
> ...[crouching] for employment.   (Prologue, ll. 6–9)

What Henry usually threatens is to let the hounds off the leash, and with dreadful consequences which he is far from euphemizing away as collateral damage. Shakespeare traces the repetition and escalation of invective very closely. The Dauphin's practical joke, Henry tells the ambassadors, will mock

> ...many a thousand widows
> ...out of their dear husbands,
> Mock mothers from their sons, mock castles down,
> And some are yet ungotten and unborn
> That shall have cause to curse the Dauphin's scorn.   (I ii, ll. 285–288)

Exeter's embassy to the French king resumes the theme:

> ...take mercy
> On the poor souls for whom this hungry war
> Opens his vasty jaws ...
> [Think of] ...the widow's tears, the orphan's cries
> The dead men's blood, the privèd maiden's groans.   (II iv, ll. 104–108)

And in urging the defenders of Harfleur to yield up their city, Henry's promises of impending horrors are even more intense. The reasons maidens might have for groaning become more explicit, and are mentioned no fewer than three times:

...the fleshed soldier, rough and hard of heart,
In liberty of bloody hand shall range
With conscience wide as hell, mowing like grass
Your fair virgins ...;

What is't to me...
If your pure maidens fall into the hand
Of hot and forcing violation?

...look to see
The blind and bloody soldier with foul hand
Defile the locks of your shrill-shrieking daughters.

(III iii, ll. 11–14, 20–21, 34–35)

There is one scene in which Henry's threats are apparently successful. This, though, is when he is already the military victor and is, in effect, simply spelling out what now will happen anyway. Here his violence is wrapped up in his special brand of humour, and ostensibly transferred from war-making to love-making, except that the interview with Katherine is not really courtship but precisely the playing-out of his military conquest. He is preparing Katherine for her transfer from the rule of a father to the rule of a husband, who is going to take over her father's kingdom, and requires of her a son who will lead a new crusade. Very intelligently, Katherine asks whether it is possible that she should love the enemy of France. In reply, Henry mixes pleasantry and malice *à la* Uriah Heep: "I love France so well that I will not part with a village of it" (V ii, l. 161). Similarly, when she finally says that she will have him if it pleases her father, he gives her a crash-course in political necessity: "Nay, it will please him well, Kate; it shall please him, Kate" (V ii, l. 225). In view of the deal Henry's diplomats are at this very moment forcing on Katherine's father, the semantic progression from "will" to "shall" carries a sinister echo of the old sense of "shall" as entailing obligation (Blake 1989:93–94). In Henry's subsequent bawdy conversation with her father and Burgandy, similarly, the memories of the siege of Harfleur are sufficiently strong – both the threats to penetrable virgins and the spectacle of the English army finally penetrating the central door or discovery-space in the tiring-house.

KING: ... And you may, some of you, thank love for my blindness, who cannot see many a fair French city for the one fair French maid that stands in my way.

FRENCH KING: Yes, my lord, you see them perspectively, the cities turned into a maid, for they are all girdled with maiden walls that war hath never entered.

(V ii, ll. 283–288)

Obviously, the threats Henry directed at Harfleur were quite enough to send a shiver down a father's spine. Not even the hippophil Bourbon wants to be a base pander, cap in hand, holding

> the chamber door
> Whilst by a slave, no gentler than my dog,
> His fairest daughter is contaminate.   (V v, ll. 15–17)

But when, exactly, does this self-knowledge dawn on him? Not until he and his fellow-countrymen are already well on their way to losing the final battle. Up until the siege of Harfleur, Henry's threats have not made the slightest impression on the French, and perhaps not even then. The Governor gives a perfectly plausible reason for his surrender: the Dauphin has let him down. Oddly enough, Pistol will be far more visibly successful in scaring Le Fer, and Henry's very repetitiousness here may suggest an underlying desperation on his part, as if he simply cannot think of anything else to say or do. Certainly Shakespeare shows that the relationship between saying and doing has become very precarious, for one of the things Henry does say is:

> …Therefore, you men of Harfleur,
> Take pity of your town and of your people
> Whiles yet my soldiers are in my command,
> Whiles yet the cool and temperate wind of grace
> O'erblows the filthy and contagious clouds
> Of heady murder, spoil and villainy.   (III iv, ll. 27–32)

At one and the same time he uses images of future violence as a threat to his enemy, and confesses that his verbal hold on his men, his true forté, could come to an end. This in itself is perhaps the most terrifying of all his threats. Yet how can he contemplate such an access of verbal weakness without being terrified himself?

2.5   Communication in the longer term

So how communicative a king is Henry overall? How much did his words change the world? And how, in consequence, will words be used *about* him afterwards? Not least, what about Shakespeare's own words, and the way they have been taken?

Is Henry a better communicator than a woman would have been, for instance? Well, with men so boastful and power-hungry and women so much their pawns and targets of battery, the only thing women can do is to try to calm things down and work for peace. At the beginning of the play, the Hostess, herself newly wrested from Nym by Pistol, pleads for what the audience may recognize as the Falstaffian variant of valour: "Good Corporal Nym, show thy valour, and put up thy sword" (II i, ll. 36–7). In the last scene, the Queen, too, knows her role. Going off with the diplomats who are to settle the final terms of the deal, she says

> Happily a woman's voice may do some good
> When articles too nicely urged be stood on.   (V ii, ll. 93–4)

She also makes the scene's penultimate speech, in which she warns against any "divorce of ...[the] incorporate league" between the two kingdoms (V ii, l. 329). But how much power does her language harness? The Chorus's final speech follows closely on her words, and is terse and very grim. Henry, "[t]his star of England", ruled "[s]mall time", and left a son, Henry VI, "Whose state so many had the managing / That they lost France and made his England bleed" (V iii, ll. 5–6, 11–12). The divorce came soon enough, and in the worst possible way.

But then again, is a woman's voice any more powerless than a man's? As a man, Henry can be a major player in his time's power politics, and may also better fulfil the corporal felicity condition which applies to threats. Yet apart from in his militarily supported sexual conquest, his threats are not demonstrably productive. And although his more co-adaptive rhetoric of encouragement gets his men, for the time being, to win his battles for him, that, it would seem, is that. The Chorus does not let the audience leave the theatre thinking that the whole future course of history was changed.

So if Henry is remembered, one might almost ask why. Some of Shakespeare's most fascinating insights into the relation between *logos* and *pragma* are tied up with Henry's own thoughts on just this matter. In his threats, we have seen, he uses the prospect of future action as a way of trying to influence the present. But sometimes, his incitements go one step further still into the future, to a point from which later generations are *looking back* on deeds which at the time of his speaking have still not been performed.

At the beginning of the play, for instance, he characteristically boasts that he will "bend ...[France] to our awe / Or break it all to pieces" so as to achieve a "large and ample empery". Then, however, he suddenly conjures up the possibility of failure, and in very specific terms: he would be tombless; so there would be no remembrance over his bones; history would not "with full mouth / Speak freely of" his acts; his "grave / Like a Turkish mute shall have a tongueless mouth" (I ii, ll. 224–232). His verbalized prospect of such verbal desolation is what gives him a final adrenalin kick before receiving the French ambassadors.

Another example works rather differently. Just before Agincourt, when the chance of failure seems very real, Henry again verbalizes it in order to inspire forthcoming action, and again by taking that extra imaginative step into the future. This time, though, he can conceive of posterity as glorifying failure itself:

> This story shall the good man teach his son ...
>
> Dying like men, though buried in ... [French] dunghills,
> They shall be famed, for there the sun shall greet them
> And draw their honours up to heaven.   (IV iii, ll. 56, 88–101)

Now if their dream of being remembered either for breaking France to pieces or for dying bravely inspires Henry and his fellow-soldiers in their efforts now, then future generations, if such memories really do come about, will themselves be inspired by them. Such ancestral memories figured in the powerful words of persuasion used by Canterbury and Ely in the play's beginning:

> Awake remembrance of these valiant dead,
> And with your puissant arm renew their feats.   (I ii, ll. 115–116)

And this, we saw, is how Henry himself is remembered in the Olivier film.

Shakespeare's meta-theatricality extends to actually foregrounding the audience's own reception of the national legend of Henry. The Chorus conveys a clear sense of the story as a narrative tradition already existing in written form ("Vouchsafe to those that have not read the story / That I may prompt them" (V 0, l. 1–2)), which the author of the present play has adapted ("with rough and all unable pen / Our bending author hath pursued the story"(V iii, ll. 1–2)). At the end of his first speech he entreats the audience:

> Admit me Chorus to this history,
> Who, Prologue-like, your humble patience pray,
> Gently to hear, kindly to judge our play.   (Prologue, ll. 32–4)

Notice that the Chorus does *not* say "Who, Prologue-like, your patience humbly pray", but "Who, Prologue-like, your humble patience pray". With the very best of manners, he is asking the audience to make a truly humble effort of empathy: not to exalt themselves over the story – not to engage in the solipsistic type of reading championed by Terence Hawkes in his poststructuralist claims. Yet at the same time, he so constantly harps on the need for the spectators' own generous imagination, on the sheer despicableness of the things actually shown *coram populo* ("four or five most vile and ragged foils / Right ill disposed in brawl ridiculous"(IV 0, ll. 50–1)), that the audience's disbelief, if it is not completely disarmed, may take a rather disrespectful tack. What if the "true things" of Agincourt were not really much better than the theatrical "mockeries" of them (IV 0, l. 54)? For the time being, the audience hears of Henry and his men's valour only from the Chorus himself, who so pointedly draws attention to his own powers of verbal deception. Spectators in the theatre, like Llewellyn as he comes to know Pistol better, will perhaps get tired of having to "see" nothing but words all the time. Resisting the Chorus's appeal for empathy, they may even begin to suspect that Granpré – no less a part of Shakespeare's play than the Chorus, after all – comes closer to the truth:

> Description cannot suit itself in words
> To demonstrate the life of such a battle,
> In life so lifeless as it shows itself.   (IV ii, ll. 52–4)

Granpré is saying that no words are powerful enough to describe the utter powerlessness of the English army. Even the Chorus's own final speech not only contains all his usual apologies for "confining mighty men" in "little room", but brings about that crushing anti-climax after the Queen's final words (V iii 3). There is no covering up the short time-span of Henry's empire. His end sounds almost as ignominious as the sight of Pistol slinking back to London with his "cudgelled scars". And the play's very last lines do not even make sense: "so many had the managing" of Henry VI's state

> That they lost France and made his England bleed,
> Which oft our stage hath shown – and for their sake,
> In your fair minds let this acceptance take.   (V iii, ll. 12–14)

For *whose* sake? For the sake of the bunglers who lost France and made England bleed? For the sake of productions of earlier plays? Well, perhaps. But in that case, this is the Chorus's way of confessing that the "Muse of fire" he summoned at the beginning of the play (Prologue 1) has finally been extinguished. For a disaffected spectator, there may be more than a hint that the theatrical mockery of true things was not such a mockery after all. It may even have been a mite too flattering. On Shakespeare's showing, Henry was not a great practical handyman; his army was pathetic; and his *non nobis* humility is perhaps ingenuous after all. That the Dauphin did not relieve Harfleur, that the French made such a cock-up of Agincourt, was hardly Henry's doing.

   Shakespeare knows that communication is always touch and go. Either his audience will empathize as he humanly deserves or they will not. But even if they do empathize, John Turner is right: their response will be mixed with criticism as well. In this play so centrally *about* communication, Shakespeare often shows characters going through the motions of what amounts to a kind of philological interpretation – Henry and Pistol's onomastic speculations are part of this large pattern. Canterbury gets things off to a good start with his speech on Salic Law, which reads rather like a learned article on, say, the identity of the Eotenas in *Beowulf*. Other instances include Katherine's English lesson, and the Boy's translations of Le Fer for the benefit of Pistol. And in every case, Shakespeare draws the audience into the characters' philological efforts, highlighting, above all, the scope for both error and disagreement. We are alerted to the fact that Canterbury's philology is itself a power of words, strongly underwritten by the church's temporal interests, and directed towards getting Henry off to battle. As a result, we cannot help wondering whether the scholarship is as unimpeachable as Henry says it has got to be. If we try to unravel it, we are probably nonplussed. During Katherine's French lesson, again, spectators ignorant of French may find themselves starting to learn the French words for finger, hand and so on, while Alice's pronunciation of English may make some members of the audience feel amusedly superior – and Katherine's imitation even more so. As for the Boy's glossings of Le Fer, one extraordinarily insightful passage pinpoints the sheer one-sidedness of Hawkes's poststructuralist notion of "meaning by":

> [LE FER] ...*je m'estime heureux que je suis tombé entre les mains d'un chevalier –*
> *je pense le plus brave, vaillant, et très distingué seigneur d'Angleterre.* ...
> PISTOL: Expound unto me, boy.
> BOY: ... he esteems himself happy that he hath fallen into the hands of one (as he
> thinks) the most brave, valorous and thrice-worthy seigneur of England.
>
> (IV iv, ll. 43–50)

In "(as he thinks)", the genuine interpretation's inevitable interplay of empathy and criticism is definitively registered.

Shakespeare, we can therefore assume, knew the exact limits of his own words' power. He could do nothing to stop his acting company from omitting the allusion to Essex, and he would not have expected his powerlessness to diminish over time, as indeed it did not – nothing could prevent Laurence Olivier from leaving out almost 1700 lines, including, of course, the hint that Canterbury has cooked the philology, Henry's appalling threats to Harfleur, and the concluding mention of his disastrous successor. Shakespeare may even have calculated that, if some of the very first spectators would admire Henry immensely, and admire Essex by association, others might be less than thoroughly convinced by the Chorus's panegyrics. He would certainly have realized that the Chorus's own meta-theatrical apologies were a bold artistic gamble. Either they would boost the power of poetry – his own power. Or they would backfire, in which case neither Henry nor Essex would seem quite so wonderful after all.

True, the Chorus does say that Henry's achievements gave "much more, and much more cause" to Londoners to turn out for him than could Essex's possible subjugation of Ireland. But perhaps Shakespeare hedged his bets. Perhaps he was not even sure what he thought himself. If Essex succeeds, all well and good, and *Henry V* gives ample pretext for patriotism. If Essex fails, look again, and you may find that *Henry V* is saying, "I told you so!" This would certainly help to account for the later swing from, say, Dowden's idealization of Henry the practical hero to Gerald Gould's indictment of Henry the cold-blooded, lying cynic (Gould 1969 [1919]). The text as a whole, I am arguing, is fundamentally ambivalent. Just because it is authored by a relatively autonomous and identifiable human being, it will not necessarily be completely intelligible and coherent – not more coherent than is humanly possible, anyway. In Keats's view, as I noted, the intellectual coherence of a Coleridge could overlook important complexities, and as both Jonathan Bate and, at his best, Hawkes have shown, there are things in Shakespeare's plays which resist empathy and baffle explanation (e.g. Bate 1997: 34–64, 204–209; Hawkes 1986: 27–50). Here was a writer with more than enough negative capability to let the "the art and practic part of life" be the mistress of the "theoric" in a far less submissive sense than that intended by Canterbury. Words, Shakespeare knew, cannot net everything in. If they could, communication would have come to an end long ago.

But even if his words give warrant for both Dowden and Gould's readings, Shakespeare, no less than Hawkes, would have recognized that readings are linked to their particular context and to interpreters' own intentions, just like Canterbury's possibly tendentious interpretation of Salic Law. Dowden was writing in the age of empire-building. Gould was evidently traumatized by the war that brought it to an end. In the 1940s, Olivier's film was patriotic propaganda for a mass audience, whereas Traversi was writing for *Scrutiny*. A few decades later still, Kenneth Branagh was recalling the war in Vietnam, while in 2007 Ewan Fernie was reading the same play as an indirect critique of the Anglo-American War on Terror.

What, then, if Shakespeare could have seen all this? Or what if he had seen Phelps's or Macready's or Kean's lavishly spectacular stagings, with their vast hordes of actors, their pageantry, their realistic mediaevalism – their attempt, in short, to make the Chorus's descriptions redundant? On the one hand, the nineteenth-century emphasis on action and ceremony *coram populo* would certainly have registered with him. Oddly enough, this made the Victorian theatre a bit like the Elizabethan theatre as seen by Greenblatt. Shakespeare's own focus, I have suggested, was much more on the king's use of language. On the other hand, there was probably enough of the Chorus in him to have enjoyed his continuing appeal to the public imagination, and he would certainly have recognized later generations' right to respond to his works in their own ways, just as he himself regularly differed from his sources, as when he left out the archers and the hedge of stakes. To the communicational intelligence that produced the Boy's "(as he thinks)", the Victorians' combination of empathy and disagreement with his texts would have seemed quite inevitable. And if Henry is least effective when most verbally forceful; if his entire invasion of France is motivated by mere ideological dogma, and in the longer term quite futile; and if his moments of more successful community-making are when he softens his own selfhood and imaginatively undermines received certainties: then Shakespeare really did understand, and himself exercised, negative capability, even though he knew that it, too, guaranteed no final control. That he would have expected of posterity a one-hundred-percent conformity to some single meaning or interpretation located in his own mind is utterly inconceivable. Despite all his certainties as a historical individual, his mental life was not finally amenable to simplistic reduction, and he would have regarded the interpretative variations of the entire tradition of reception as just one more illustration of the communal strength and weakness of any individual's words. That, he knew, was how genuine dialogicality works.

CHAPTER 3

Pope's three modes of address

3.1 A complex profile

Pope can be seen as England's last great Humanist poet, on a line descending from Spenser through Milton and Dryden. This view of him was supported by the tradition of literary-historical and biographical scholarship which culminated in Maynard Mack's *Alexander Pope: A Life*, published in1985. By that time, post-modern commentators such as Laura Brown (1985) had begun to challenge the Humanist label as taking Pope's own ideological constructions too much at face value, and as exaggerating his social centrality, complaints in a way corroborated by Roger Lonsdale's two anthologies, *The New Oxford Book of Eighteenth-Century Verse* (1984) and *Eighteenth-Century Women Poets: An Oxford Anthology* (1989), both of which made it quite obvious that Pope was not the only early eighteenth century poet of interest and merit. As a mediating critic would point out, however, Pope, like any other writer, does deserve to be understood in his own terms and in the light of his own contemporaries' impressions of his role, even if we ourselves are equally entitled to our own opinions and values, and even if we were finally not so much to agree with him and his first admirers as agree to disagree. Nor does a due recognition of the achievements of other eighteenth century poets have to be at Pope's expense. As a matter of fact, the real drawback to calling him a Humanist is that it vastly *underestimates* his breadth and impact.

My reason for insisting on the Humanist label all the same is that, as well as being at least partly accurate, it also has important communicational corollaries. It can help us tackle the question: What exactly, *vis à vis* both contemporary and later communities of readers, has been Pope's appeal? That his writing did, and does tend to create communities around itself, and that the communities have been, despite the post-modern qualifications and a more long-standing grouse about his alleged prosaicness, appreciative is not in question. But what I shall try to assess are his ways of bringing the communities into being. More precisely, how does the dialogicality he initiates between himself and readers play out in ethical terms?

His complex communicational profile was indeed bound up with his being, not only one of the great Humanist poets, but also England's last. Yet we completely miss his true scope, it seems to me, unless we acknowledge that, in addition, he was the first of England's great Romantics. Thomas Woodman remarks that "[i]f we knew Pope only by 'Eloisa to Abelard' (1717) we would think of him as an extraordinarily anticipatory poet, since the poem is 'romantic' in scenery, in gothic and medieval elements, and in the popular sense of being a passionate poem about romantic love" (Woodman 2006: 478). My own suggestion is that Pope, here and elsewhere, was *already* Romantic, mainly because of everything he was doing to bring about that age of sensibility described by Northrop Frye (1956). Perhaps partly because his Humanism and his Romanticism are each other's foil, in places I actually find his Humanist emphasis far sharper than that of any English predecessor, and his Romantic emphasis far sharper than that of any English successor.

I shall not be exploring the literary-historiographical consequences of my take on him, even though, if fully fledged Romanticism could appear by the eighteenth century's second decade, then the controversy about how to label literature written in the four decades running up to *Lyrical Ballads* and *Songs of Innocence and of Experience* – "Pre-Romantic" (Griffin 1995)? "Preromantic" (Brown 1991)? "Early Romantic" (Woodman 1998)? "Post-Augustan" (Sitter 1982)? – could perhaps be defused. Instead, I am interested in the Humanist-Romantic dualism only for its communicational consequences in Pope's own work, a topic which I hope to concretize by describing him as, in two different senses, a decidedly *nervous* writer. As a Humanist, he was nervous in a sense of the word which is now largely archaic, traceable mainly in expressions such as "to have the nerve to do something" or "What a nerve!" His Humanist writing, that is to say, was strong and forceful. As a Romantic, he was nervous in something closer to the present-day sense of the word, which is more or less the opposite of the older meaning. His Romantic writing, in short, was the product of delicate sensitivity and feeling. What I shall try to demonstrate is that these two types of nervousness resulted in two very different modes of address, inviting two correspondingly different modes of response. The dialogicality arising from his writing was never going to be all of a single kind.

It would be misleading to say that either the Humanist or the Romantic nervousness finally triumphed. Their two communicational modes are in evidence across the entire span of his writing career, often within one and the same poem. And another of my main suggestions is that some of his greatest writing was in any case in a third, sublime mode, which in some ways actually combined these other two, and which engaged with readers in distinctive ways of its own.

His three modes of address are, we might be tempted to say, interesting enough in themselves. Yet nothing is ever interesting except to human beings, who always occupy some particular sociohistorical position. Ultimately the question raised by the following pages is: What is the bearing of Pope's three kinds of addressivity on community-making in the phase of post-Humanist culture to which we ourselves belong?

3.2   Humanist nervousness

In post-Humanist times, the most serious legitimations offered for the writing of new literature, and also for the institutionalized study of literature, have been difficult to reconcile with dominant socioeconomic forces. Many good authors have seen themselves, and have been seen by readers, as writing very much from within society and, to the extent that their activities have called for justification, as performing the role of either entertainer or informative realist. On the whole, these two explanations have cut little ice with post-Humanist intelligentsias, who have tended to view significant writers in a very different light: as exceptional or even prophetic individuals standing outside of society and its philistinism; as artists creating an aesthetic world completely separate from the real one; or as spokespersons for groupings which have been under-privileged within society as a whole.

So although Tennyson, the enormously popular Poet Laureate of Victorian England, was condemned by elitist Modernist critics as, in T. S. Eliot's phrase, "the surface flatter of his own time" (Eliot 1951 [1936]: 338), Eliot also hinted a line of argument by which his work could gradually be rehabilitated in literary-academic circles. *In Memoriam* was remarkable, he said, as a religious poem of a very particular kind: "It is not religious because of the quality of its faith, but because of the quality of its doubt. Its faith is a poor thing, but its doubt is a very intense experience" (Eliot 1951 [1936]: 336). The consolations of Victorian Christianity; the Victorian ideal of marriage; the Victorian work ethic: from Eliot's remarks onwards, twentieth-century intellectuals began to praise Tennyson as having undermined such publicly endorsed certainties. W. W. Robson, for instance, found that in "Ulysses" Tennyson "the responsible social being, the admirably serious and 'committed' individual" was up against Tennyson "the most un-strenuous, lonely and poignant of poets" (Robson 1960: 159).

By the 1940s, a similar mantle of alienation was being draped around the shoulders of Dickens, who in his own time had been, as it were, the favourite uncle at every family hearth, but whom Edmund Wilson was now describing as a veritable Jekyll-and-Hyde (Wilson 1941; Sell 1994: 3–11). Such unsettling lines of interpretation became increasingly routine as the discussion of modern European literatures established itself ever more firmly within twentieth century universities. Many academic critics, and some postmodern critics in particular, themselves adopted an outsider stance, sometimes deliberately biting the hand which fed them. This was one form of a larger postmodern paradox: that institutions enjoying strong social endorsement, and often public funding as well, became the fora for social subversiveness. In Britain during the Thatcher years, this phenomenon may have helped to compensate for the perceived inadequacy of the parliamentary opposition. Within the English departments of British universities – the workplace of scholars such as Terence Hawkes, who as we have seen can still give vent to that period's anti-establishment animus even today – literary texts were often seen as a site for ideological critique.

During the period 1450–1750, attitudes had been different. Throughout Europe Humanist educationalists were praising the literature of ancient Greece and Rome for what they chose to see as ethical insights that were in total harmony with their own societies' most central ideals. Here, the argument went, was an enduring supply of ennobling wisdom on how to live, how to treat other people, and how to endure life's hardships, wisdom which, if duly embraced, was said to maximize the chances for individual contentment without upsetting the body politic. New poetry in the European vernaculars was deemed capable of the same beneficial consequences, and this was a rationale which Renaissance patrons of the arts were willing to understand, even if, or partly because, their generosity to poets could also be self-aggrandizing.

Echoing claims already lodged in classical times, Humanist poets figured their own writings as the trump of Fame, responsible for broadcasting the reputations of those whose merits they celebrated. When the individual so honoured happened to be the poet's own Maecenas, patronage could lead, as Shakespeare may have hinted in Sonnet 18, to a kind of tit for tat, by funding the composition of lines which would immortalize patron and poet simultaneously:

> So long as men can breathe or eyes can see,
> So long lives this, and this gives life to thee.   (Sonnet 18, ll. 13–14)[1]

Granted, Shakespeare may have written this at a time when the theatres were closed and he was dependent on other sources of income, for basically he was a "new" man in both economic status and ideology – a writer who, as Pope saw him,

> For gain, not glory, wing'd his roving flight,
> And grew Immortal in his own despight.
> > (*Imitations of Horace*: Ep. II i, ll. 71–72)[2]

Certainly Pope himself wanted to be seen as proudly independent of patrons, and in effect did mainly earn his living as the publisher of his own books (McLaverty 2007). Yet one of the curiosities of his pivotal position in English literary history was that this loyalty to the bourgeois ethos of his father, who despite Pope's regular description of him as a gentleman had traded as a linen-merchant, could be fully counterbalanced by a commitment to the other, non-economical and ethical side of the Humanists' cultural dispensation. His haunting imitation of part of Horace's Ode IV ix, for instance, was in one sense a far more ringingly Humanist text than a close translation would have been:

---

1.   Quoted from Duncan-Jones 1997.

2.   All quotations of Pope's poems from Butt 1963.

Lest you should think that Verse shall die,
Which sounds the Silver Thames along,
Taught on the Wings of Truth, to fly
Above the reach of Vulgar Song;

Tho' daring Milton sits Sublime,
In Spencer native Muses play;
Nor yet shall Waller yield to time,
Nor pensive Cowley's moral Lay.

Sages and Chiefs long since had birth
E're Caesar was, or Newton nam'd,
These rais'd new Empires o'er the Earth,
And Those new Heav'ns and Systems fram'd;

Vain was the chief's and sage's pride [*sic*]
They had no Poet and they dyd!
In vain they schem'd, in vain they bled
They had no Poet and are dead!   (*Imitations of Horace*: Od. IV ix, ll. 1–16)

One thing this left out was Horace's mention of sung or unsung lovers, whom Pope replaced with the sung or unsung scientists, so that connotations of erotomania gave way to those of reason, towering intellect, and the world of learning. And at least by ironic implication, a similarly Humanist linkage between worthy achievements, poetry and fame underlay his imitation of Horace's epistle to Augustus (Ep. II i). Here Pope, who as I say spurned patronage, pretended to go through the motions of homage to George II, a dedicatee whose understanding of the arts, and whose general suitability as a theme for Fame's trump, were in fact both zero.

Pope's determination to be a self-made man meant that, to a far higher degree, I think, than any earlier poet, classical or Humanist, he brought his own integrity as a blower of that trump right into the foreground, where it sometimes jostled for place with the ways and days of the individuals who were ostensibly his topic. As early as 1711 he not only imitated and completed the unfinished third book of Chaucer's *House of Fame*, but in his conclusion to it firmly rejected the prospect of literary fame for himself unless his life turned out to be duly unimpeachable:

Unblemish'd let me live, or die unknown,
Oh grant an honest Fame, or grant me none!   (*The Temple of Fame*, ll. 523–524)

In many later poems he would again devote climactic final lines to a demonstrative scrutiny of his own role and credentials.

For Humanists, then, and for Pope especially, poetry was a lofty and very public calling. The classics of Greek and Roman literature were a source of consensually acceptable wisdom. Humanist poets were expected to emulate them in vernacular languages by producing more wisdom of the same kind. In turn, their achievements were to be recognized by Humanist critics, who would praise them for the honesty of their own praise of great ones, and for having consolidated the inherited understanding of how to live a human life. Literature, and the community which grew up around it, were taken to be ideologically consubstantial with society's community at large, which in its turn was assumed to be educationally and experientially uniform. As Mack put it,

> [p]oetry for ... [Pope], as for his great predecessors, is emphatically more a social than a personal institution; its proper audience a cross section of educated readers; its proper subject the shared common life. To write in a public idiom, and always within a program of reference calculated to draw poet and reader into a community of experience, first with each other and then with other poets and readers of a valued past (or, as it was put the other day in a dialogue between two American poets, to "carry the culture with you"): this was the poet's task, as Pope understood it.   (Mack 1985:87)[3]

True, poetry was also felt to be delightful, and in many different ways. Sometimes its delights were almost overwhelming. Johnson, the last and greatest of the English Humanist critics, freely acknowledged that the argument set forth in Pope's *Essay on Man*

> was never till now recommended by such a blaze of embellishments, or such sweetness of melody. The vigorous contraction of some thoughts, the luxuriant amplification of others, the incidental illustrations, and sometimes the dignity, sometimes the softness of the verses, enchain philosophy, suspend criticism, and oppress judgment by overpowering pleasure.   (Johnson 1925 [1779–1781]: II 227)

But even this poem did have an argument, after all, and poetic pleasure in general was seen less as a distraction than as a sweetener to culturally sanctioned edification. Horace's dictum in his *Ars Poetica* was widely invoked:

> *omne tulit punctum qui miscuit utile dulci,*
> *lectorem delectando pariterque monendo.*   (*Ars Poetica*, ll. 343–4)[4]

By way of locating his efforts within what Mack called the publicly recognized programme of reference, Pope regularly introduced his longer poems with prefatory materials in which their instructional aims came in for special attention. Often this took the form of a prose summary of the poem's argument, and sometimes there were comments on the pedagogical value of the chosen genre or style. A preliminary note

---

3.   Mack does not identify the two, apparently neo-Humanist American poets.

4.   "He has won every vote who has blended profit with pleasure, at once delighting and instructing the reader." Quotations and translations of Horace's satires, epistles and *Ars Poetica* taken from Fairclough 1966.

to *The Temple of Fame* justified the use of allegory against a *"pretended Refinement of Taste"* in *"[s]ome modern Criticks"*:

> [I]f Fable *be allow'd one of the chief Beauties, or as* Aristotle *calls it, the very* Soul *of Poetry, 'tis hard to comprehend how that Fable should be the less valuable for having a Moral.*   (*Temple of Fame*, Note)

An introductory note on "The Design" of *An Essay on Man* tacitly rebutted the note on "The Verse" with which Milton had introduced the second edition of *Paradise Lost* in 1674. The measure of his poem, Milton had explained, was

> English heroic verse without rhyme, as that of Homer in Greek, and of Virgil in Latin; rhyme being ... the invention of a barbarous age, to set off wretched matter and lame metre; graced indeed since by the use of some famous modern poets, carried away by custom, but much to their own vexation, hindrance, and constraint to express many things otherwise, and for the most part worse than else they would have expressed them. ... [Rhyme is,] as a thing of it self, to all judicious ears, trivial and of no true musical delight; which consists only in apt numbers, fit quantity of syllables, and the sense variously drawn out from one verse into another, not in the jingling sound of like endings, a fault avoided by the learned ancients both in poetry and all good oratory.[5]

Pope's own note, also echoing another piece of Horatian advice,

> *quidquid praecipies, esto brevis, ut cito dicta*
> *percipient animi dociles teneantque fideles,*   (*Ars Poetica*, ll. 335–336)[6]

explained that

> [t]his I might have done in prose; but I chose verse, and even rhyme, for two reasons. The one will appear obvious; that principles, maxims, or precepts so written, both strike the reader more strongly at first, and are more easily retained by him afterwards: The other may seem odd, but is true, I found I could express them more *shortly* this way than in prose itself; and nothing is more certain, than that much of the *force* as well as *grace* of arguments or instructions, depends on their *conciseness*. I was unable to treat this part of my subject more in detail, without becoming tedious; or more *poetically*, without sacrificing perspicuity to ornament, without wandring from the precision, or breaking the chain of reasoning.
>   (*Essay on Man*, "The Design")

---

5. Quotations from Milton's poems taken from Carey and Fowler 1968.

6. "Wherever you instruct, be brief, so that what is quickly said the mind may readily grasp and faithfully retain."

In the poems themselves, the values endorsed were as clearly apparent as such preliminaries would have led a reader to expect, and their social acceptability was equally unmistakable. Although he strongly disapproved of many of the people he mentioned, and although some of them held positions of enormous power and influence within the cultural or political establishment, he did not adopt the stance of an outsider, but presented such individuals as themselves monstrous aberrations from an otherwise universally embraced ideal of the *vir bonus*, and as far more damaging to the common weal than his own merely physical abnormality.

Important in his personal background here, as very much a Tory sympathizer during the long Whig ascendency under Walpole, were some of his closest associations (Rogers 2010): with Henry St. John, Lord Bolingbroke, who, though a major Tory figure, and for a time thought of as a Jacobite, wrote a treatise arguing that political parties were actually outdated; with several large-minded Whigs, some of whom, such as Richard Temple, Viscount Cobham, came to oppose Walpole; with the Patriots, an organized political grouping of Walpole's opponents from both the Tory and Whig parties; and with the Freemasons, who fostered a form of spirituality and fellowship which political differences were not allowed to disrupt.

The Freemasons also ruled out religious differences. Pope's Catholicism entailed real limitations to his rights as a citizen and, as with his Toryism and his bodily afflictions, he openly mentioned possible sources of grievance in his poetry. The London Monument, with its inscription to the effect that the Great Fire of 1666 had been started "by the Treachery and Malice of the Popish Faction", was like "a tall bully" who "lifts the head, and lyes" (Mack 1985: 41; *Epistle to Bathurst*, l. 340). But no less characteristically, he did not allow such frankness to mark his position as adversarial. God he described as a divine, benevolent, but otherwise mysterious Creator – an entity in some respects akin to the God of Christianity, but certainly not to the God of either Catholicism or Protestantism specifically. When *An Essay on Man* was accused of impugning traditional doctrines about the free will of both man and God, he gratefully permitted William Warburton, another Whig friend, and later Bishop of Gloucester, to explicate the orthodoxy of what the prefatory note had called its chain of reasoning. But although as a teenager he had spent long hours poring over the tomes of theological controversy in his father's library, an engagement in apologetics would not have suited his own chosen public image, and by allowing God to be more or less the supreme being of Deism, the religion of gentlemen, as it has been called, and of admirers of the polite philosophy of Shaftesbury, some of whom were strongly critical of Catholicism (Young 2003: 125), he had in practice used the *Essay* to bolster his own social centrality. "The Universal Prayer", similarly, written in 1715 and subsequently used as a pendant to the *Essay*, resembled that fine hymn by his Dissenter contemporary Isaac Watts, "From all that dwell below the skies / Let the Creator's praise arise" (Watts 1808 [1719]: 238), in offering a dignified public channel for a personal faith that was far from narrowly denominational. Apostrophizing the "Great First Cause" which is "in every

Age, / In every Clime ador'd, / By Saint, by Savage, and by Sage" (ll. 5, 1–3), Pope's text was actually rather undemonstrative in its Christian gestures. It did speak of Grace and damnation, and did allude to the language and ideas of the Lord's Prayer. But there was no direct equivalent of Watts's "Let the *Redeemer's* Name be sung" (my italics). Instead, trust was placed in the activated moral fibre of human beings themselves. To find the "better Way" and bow to the divine will was merely to know the difference between "Good and Ill", to avoid "foolish Pride / Or impious discontent" (ll. 32, 10, 33–34), and to pursue an unjudgemental solidarity with society as a whole:

> Let not this weak, unknowing hand
> Presume Thy Bolts to throw,
> And deal Damnation round the land,
> On each I judge thy Foe.   ("The Universal Prayer", ll. 25–28)

So instead of condoning a use of religious categories as an excuse for sorting fellow-citizens into sheep and goats, the poem set great store by empathy:

> Teach me to feel another's Woe;
> To hide the Fault I see;
> That Mercy I to others show,
> That Mercy show to me.   (ll. 37–40)

In publicly favouring, despite his own openly acknowledged Tory and Catholic allegiances, a humane reasonableness that was cross-party and ecumenical, Pope was leaving room for an ultimate grounding of his writerly persona on values immediately recognizable, to anyone in the know, as Humanist. More conspicuously and systematically than any English predecessor, he confirmed that spiritual fulfilment and true virtue were for ever retraceable to the pristine wisdom of the ancient world, above all as formulated by Horace on the Sabine farm, the antetype of that villa in still rural Twickenham which he so painstakingly converted into a personal statement (Mack 1969), its facade Palladian but on a modest scale, its grotto conceived as a Golden Age setting (albeit enhanced by mirrors) in which

> Unpolish'ed Gemms no Ray on Pride bestow,
> And latent Metals innocently glow,
>   ("Verse on a Grotto by the River Thames at Twickenham", ll. 5–6)

a place where his trusted friends could enjoy the kind of hospitality described in his imitation of Horace's Satire II ii, "[p]lain, but not sordid, tho' not splendid, clean" (l. 48). Pope's was the Horace who had similarly distanced himself and his boon companions from the imperial city with all its vice and show, yet who had also been smiled upon by Augustus, just as Pope himself hung in at the very centre of English life and would doubtless have welcomed the smiles of George II, had they been forthcoming and worth the having. Such a Horace, the Horace of

> *insani sapiens nomen ferat, aequus iniqui,*
> *ultra quam satis est Virtutem si petat ipsam,*   (Ep. I vi, ll. 15–16)[7]

would have been readily understood by educated readers as a model of sociable probity and *media via* prudence. Nor would they have thought any the less highly of a contemporary writer whose Horatian pedigree was so meticulously displayed. After all, what could be more convincing than Pope's adaptation of Horace to their own unfanatically Christian age? –

> For Vertue's self may too much Zeal be had;
> The worst of Madmen is a Saint run mad.
>   (*Imitations of Horace*: Ep. I vi, ll. 26–27)

True, in many places his own preaching of virtue was not exactly lukewarm. But how could genteel readers possibly object to moral teachings with which, despite the adaptation to eighteenth century England, they could think themselves already familiar, or at least vaguely familiar, from their own classical education? In adapting Horace, and in writing his own new poems in Horatian modes, Pope scored some sharp hits on many of his contemporaries, yet under the appearance of saying almost nothing which Horace had not said already. This involved a rhetorical stratagem which, though he spelt it out for the benefit of would-be literary critics, was of wider application:

> Men must be *taught* as if you taught them *not*;
> And Things *unknown* proposed as Things *forgot*.
>   (*Essay on Criticism*, ll. 574–575)

His frequent appeal to a shared grounding in the classics was the main ingredient in a charmingly coercive social cement, which tended to bind him and his readers together into what he was proposing as the moral consensus. Readers whose educational background was up to scratch would take pleasure in spotting the learned allusions (when these were not, as in the footnotes to *Pastorals* and *The Dunciad*, spelt out), and in generally identifying with the Humanist thought-world. Other readers might be cowed into to trying or pretending to do so, too ashamed to confess their cultural gaps. Basically, such writing's gesture was: "We all know our Horace, don't we? We're all temperate and civilized human beings, aren't we?"

I say "charmingly coercive social cement". It *was* coercive, and Pope was too communicationally intelligent not to know this. But he obviously thought that he was doing the right thing and that England would be the better for it. Had we been his contemporaries, the chances are that we would have agreed with him, even if it would be very pleasant to assume that the ideology of our own society today is ethically superior. Then again, in toning down his own Tory and Catholic sympathies, in not

---

7.   "Let the wise man bear the name of madman, the just of unjust, should he pursue Virtue herself beyond due bounds."

expecting his illness and deformity to be accorded special treatment or a release from normal responsibilities, Pope was subjecting himself to the same communal discipline as he envisaged for his readers. This partly explains why the coercion could indeed be truly charming. Not to have encouraged his readers to set their sights on the same ideal of human life and civilization as he himself adopted would have implied that they were his inferiors in character and refinement. His witty deference of address is the proof that in laying claim to the ethical and cultural high ground he did not view it as necessarily too steep a climb for other people.

"Other people" was not just men. Although the Humanist ideal could seem masculine in tone, and sometimes represented women as less rational and civically responsible than their brothers, husbands or sons (Rumbold 1989), Pope recommended Horatian prudence and common sense in several poems dedicated to female readers, plus a feminized version of Horatian companionability. As for charming coerciveness here, when the woman addressed was already said to display the qualities valorized, the poem might seem to apply no pressure at all, so that charm would not really have been needed. But any such impression would have missed Humanist poetry's fundamentally public mode of operation. *Epistle II: To a Lady*, for instance, characteristically ended with a sudden zooming-in on the poet who had written it. Having praised Martha Blount, its dedicatee, for embodying a golden mean between several pairs of opposed character traits, Pope concluded:

> The gen'rous God [i.e. Phoebus], who Wit and Gold refines,
> And ripens Spirits as he ripens Mines,
> Kept Dross for Duchesses, the world shall know it,
> To you gave Sense, Good-humour, and a Poet.   (*Epistle to a Lady*, ll. 289–292)

Martha's good sense and good humour were to be the foundation of her Fame, trumpeted abroad as a model for others by Pope himself. As didacticism these lines were not particularly heavy-handed, and the path hither had in any case been smoothened by the poem's earlier gallantry about Martha's age, which was forty-four at the time of its publication in 1735. After some harsh enough detail about the faded charms of other women, it had claimed that the excellent qualities brought together in Martha were something which

> ... Phoebus promis'd (I forget the year)
> When those blue eyes first open'd on the sphere.
> (*Epistle to a Lady*, ll. 283–284)

In the "Epistle to Miss Blount, With the Works of Voiture", written for Martha's elder sister Teresa in 1710, when she was twenty-two, the same qualities of character were urged more directly on the addressee herself (presumably because Pope thought she had not yet permanently achieved them), and the poem's charm was at first less ingratiating. The lines

> Trust not too much your now resistless Charms,
> Those, Age or Sickness, soon or late, disarms;
> *Good Humour* only teaches Charms to last,
> Still makes new Conquests, and maintains the past.
>
> ("Epistle to Miss Blount", ll. 57–62)

did acknowledge Teresa's beauty, but with a reference to her passing years that was not chivalrous but sermonizing. Having thus candidly lodged his ethical argument, however, and not only for Teresa's benefit, of course, Pope rounded things off with a delightful fantasy of Voiture contemplating his latest new reader from beyond the grave:

> Now crown'd with Myrtle, on th'*Elysian* Coast,
> Amid those Lovers [his female correspondents], joys his gentle Ghost.
> Pleas'd while with Smiles his happy Lines you view,
> And finds a fairer *Ramboüillet* in you.
> The brightest Eyes of *France* inspir'd his Muse,
> The brightest Eyes of *Britain* now peruse,
> And dead as living, 'tis our Author's Pride,
> Still to charm those who charm the World beside.
>
> ("Epistle to Miss Blount", ll. 73–80)

Here the hints of bodily decay no longer applied to Teresa but to Voiture, who was positively dead, and in re-affirming Teresa's irresistible beauty Pope now explicitly acknowledged the beauty of other women as well, and without the slightest trace of the earlier reservations. With unabashed gracefulness, he was seeking to charm his women readers by professing himself charmed by their charms.

He employed the same very ancient ruse in *The Rape of the Lock*, but even more gracefully and on a far greater scale. In dedicating the poem to Arabella Fermor, he claimed to have written it "only to divert a few young Ladies, who have good Sense and good Humour enough, to laugh not only at their Sex's little unguarded Follies, but at their own". Even in the first version (1712), the little unguarded follies did not escape notice, and when he later (in 1714) added Clarissa's speech his own ideal of womanhood became as explicit as in the poems to the Blount sisters:

> Why round our Coaches crowd the white-glov'd Beaus,
> Why bows the Side-box from its inmost Rows?
> How vain are all these Glories, all our Pains,
> Unless good Sense preserve what Beauty gains:
> …
> What then remains, but well our Pow'r to use,
> And keep good Humour still whate'er we lose?
> And trust me, Dear! good Humour can prevail,
> When Airs, and Flights, and Screams, and Scolding fail.

Beauties in vain the pretty Eyes may roll;
Charms strike the Sight, but Merit wins the Soul.

(*Rape of the Lock*, V, ll. 13–16, 29–34)

As with Pope's other long poems, Warburton was not slow to point up the instructional argument. In his footnote of 1751 he explained that Clarissa was introduced "*to open up more clearly the* MORAL *of the Poem*" (Tillotson 1962: 195). But Pope's own footnote of 1736 merely noted that Clarissa's lines were "*in a parody of the speech of Sarpedon to Glaucus in Homer*". They were of course part of a larger mock-heroic design which was at once dazzlingly imaginative and disarmingly light-hearted. Pope really was seeking to move his readers to a happy laughter, and the hints of own male susceptibility to Belinda's charms could not have been more charmingly adroit. For all his alertness to little unguarded follies, he cheerfully aligns himself with the crowd of white-gloved beaus:

… graceful Ease, and Sweetness void of Pride,
Might hide her faults, if *Belles* had faults to hide:
If to her share some Female Errors fall,
Look on her Face, and you'll forget 'em all.   (*Rape of the Lock*, II, ll. 15–18)

The genesis of *The Rape of the Lock* is well known. Pope responded to John Caryll's request that he write something to heal the breach between the Fermor family – Arabella Fermor having a pretty head of hair – and the Petre family – Robert Lord Petre having helped himself to a love-lock from it. Pope was hoping that the laughter generated by his poem would "laugh them together" (Mack 1985: 248). Both the Fermors and the Petres, however, were Catholic families, and elsewhere Pope wrote with a view to reconciling Catholics with Protestants or, what sometimes amounted to the same thing, Tories with Whigs. *Windsor-Forest*, the earliest major example, was more or less silent about the Tudor monarchs responsible for introducing Protestantism, but did perhaps see the depredations of William I as a type of Henry VIII's dissolution of the monasteries, certainly referred to the execution of Charles I as a fatal crime, and clearly implied that Anne, as a Stuart, was the first legitimate monarch since the expulsion of James II. As always, then, Pope did not hide his religiopolitical affinities. But here, too, he was not prepared to let them be a deal-breaker. The poem's lovingly detailed rural setting was strongly opposed to the city, and thereby strongly Tory in implication. Yet Pope's affinity with his merchant father was again reflected, perhaps, in the poetical vision of London as a free port, the very hub of world trade:

The Time shall come, when free as Seas or Wind
Unbounded *Thames* shall flow for all Mankind,
Whole Nations enter with each swelling Tyde,
And Seas but join the Regions they divide.   (*Windsor-Forest*, ll. 397–400)

Walpole and his Whigs would have drunk to that! And with a touch of the fancifulness which was writ large in *The Rape of the Lock*, Pope even proposed a witty compromise between the Whigs who opposed the peace of Utrecht and Anne's Tory government which had brought it about. Old Father Thames remarks:

> No more my Sons shall dye with *British* Blood
> Red *Iber*'s Sands, or *Ister*'s foaming Flood;
> Safe on my Shore each unmolested Swain
> Shall tend the Flocks, or reap the bearded Grain;
> The shady Empire shall retain no Trace
> Of War or Blood, but in the Sylvan Chace,
> The Trumpets sleep, while chearful Horns are blown,
> And Arms employ'd on Birds and Beasts alone.   (*Windsor-Forest*, ll. 367–374)

That the sheer delightfulness of such visions mercantile and mock-heroic really would bring the Whigs on side was hardly likely. But Pope's desire for harmony was unmistakable, even if his most convincing example owed everything to a leveller far grimmer than either trade or huntsmanship: in the Chapel of St. George at Windsor Castle, both Henry VI and Edward IV lay buried –

> The Grave unites; where ev'n the Great find Rest,
> And blended lie th' Oppressor and th' Opprest!   (*Windsor-Forest*, ll. 317–318)

Such binary oppositions were everywhere apparent in Pope's writing, which often did seem to establish a kind of coming together, or golden mean, between the two terms opposed. In addition to all the other charms, and especially in the moralizing poems, a crucial element in the persuasion here was the versification. To all intents and purposes, there could seem to be a total symbiosis between the spirituality and ethics of the classical *media via* and his own verse couplet, whose rhetoric, syntax and rhythm sustained a refinement unprecedented in Sir John Beaumont, Waller, Denham or even Dryden and later neither equalled nor, except by Johnson, attempted. Through its structures of line against line and half-line against half-line, Pope's couplet enhanced figures such as antithesis, parison, chiasmus and zeugma which sharply highlighted the polar extremes between which the rational compromises were to be attempted, or which could reinforce their prudence once proposed. So insistently did the carefully sculpted verse and the balanced ethical stance seem to require each other that it would have been impossible to say whether, in Pope's view, a controlled artistic perfection imitated a temperate perfection of life, or *vice versa*.

Some forceful examples involved what readers would immediately acknowledge was a whole spectrum of possibilities between two extremes on either side of a clear mid-point. In *Epistle III: To Allen Lord Bathurst*, the range was from parsimony to extravagance.

> The Sense to value Riches, with the Art
> T'enjoy them, and the Virtue to impart,
> Not meanly, nor ambitiously persu'd,
> Not sunk by sloth, nor rais'd by servitude;
> To balance Fortune by a just expence,
> Join with Oeconomy, Magnificence;
> With Splendour, Charity; with Plenty, Health;
> Oh teach us, BATHURST! yet unspoil'd by wealth!
> That secret rare, between th' extremes to move
> Of mad Good-nature, and of mean Self-love.   (*Epistle to Bathurst*, ll. 219–228)

And the criterion of prudent balance enforced by a poem's couplets could be further buttressed in its entire structure, through a series of character sketches contrastively ranged along the same ethical spectrum. The golden mean embodied in Bathurst himself was mirrored, on a lower rung of the social hierarchy, in the Man of Ross, who is a veritable mainstay of the community in his part of the country, engaging in major afforestation and civil engineering projects, providing for the old and the sick, putting quacks and "vile Attornies" out of business (l. 274), generously dispensing hospitality and well-being, and all this on an income of a mere £500 a year. In this portrayal of the Man of Ross, the linen merchant's son was transmogrifying the Humanist country house poem as represented by Jonson's "Penhurst Place" into an idyll rather less aristocratic (which is not to deny that Jonson and his stepfather had both worked as bricklayers). An altogether more dystopian transmogrification of that same genre occurred in the lines on Cotta, whose stinginess "sham'd his fortune and his birth" (l. 179):

> Like some lone Chartreux stands the good old Hall,
> Silence without, and Fasts within the wall;
> No rafter'd roofs with dance and tabor sound,
> No noontide-bell invites the country round;
> Tenants with sighs the smoakless tow'rs survey,
> And turn th' unwilling steeds another way:
> Benighted wanderers, the forest o'er,
> Curse the sav'd candle, and unop'ning door;
> While the gaunt mastiff growling at the gate,
> Affrights the beggar whom he longs to eat.   (*Epistle to Bathurst*, ll. 189–198)

Then in contrast to both the balance of Bathurst and the Man of Ross and the tight-fistedness of Cotta, there was the profligacy of the Duke of Buckingham, who (at least according to contemporary gossip and Pope's poem here) died in the most sordid of Yorkshire inns:

> There, Victor of his health, of fortune, friends,
> And fame; this lord of useless thousands ends.   (*Epistle to Bathurst*, ll. 313–314)

As for the end of the poem, the merchant's son offered the fiercely realistic parable of Balaam, whose career traverses the entire spectrum from one end to the other, at first a good citizen, "Religious, punctual, frugal, and so forth", constant both "at Church, and Change [the Stock Exchange]", a man whose "gains were sure, / His givings rare, save farthings to the poor" (ll. 343, 347–348), but later in life a man of enormous influence, a knight and MP, his son commissioned as an officer at his expense yet whoring, drinking and duelling himself to death, his daughter be-poxed through her marriage to a Viscount, his wife addicted to gambling away vast sums of money, and he himself thereby driven to accept a bribe from France, for which he was impeached and hung, his remaining wealth all forfeit to the Crown.

Elsewhere, though, Pope seemed to be assuming similar scope for movement along what, on reflection, may have struck some readers as an unlikely spectrum from chalk to cheese. To return to his public endorsements of dialogue between Whigs and Tories, of the Deists' syncretic higher being, and of a kind versification that would be neither exactly prose nor exactly poetry, in each and every case his preference would have recommended itself for its amenable politeness, but at the risk of displeasing those for whom the relationship between the opposed terms was not scalar but disjunctive. To adamant Tories or Whigs, to died-in-the-wool Protestants or Catholics, or to the many readers, both then and later, for whom writing was *either* prose *or* poetry, amenable politeness was not necessarily the highest good, and the differences on which they insisted could feel as absolute as that between life and death. Invested with all the force of Pope's couplet, however, these potentially awkward compromises could come across as the most natural thing in the world, even when, in amused embroidery upon Horace's already laconic description of himself in Satire II i as not exactly a Lucanian and not exactly an Apulian,[8] all three of them were rattled off in quick succession, a paradox per couplet:

> My Head and Heart thus flowing thro' my Quill,
> Verse-man or Prose-man, term me which you will,
> Papist of Protestant, or both between,
> Like good *Erasmus* in an honest Mean,
> In Moderation placing all my Glory,
> While Tories call me Whig, and Whigs a Tory.
>
> (*Imitations of Horace*: Sat. II i, ll. 63–68)

---

8. "*Sequor hunc, Lucanus an Apulus, anceps*" (l. 34). "He [i.e. the poet Lucilius] it is I follow – I, a Lucanian or Apulian, I know not which".

In cases like this, Pope's couplet and the associated ethical mean were clearly in the nature of a pre-prepared mould, designed to regulate every imaginable kind of recalcitrance in the interests of harmonious decorum. To resist the sheer power of such writing, even readers who were usually sticklers for the distinctions in question would have had to be on their toes.

Nor was versification the only factor. Diction, too, had a key communicational role, but a less conspicuous one, which actually had two, complementary aspects. For one thing, there were the proportional relationships between the different parts of speech (adjectives, nouns, verbs and so on), together with the matter of word positioning. The finest insight into this came from the commentator whose understanding of the word "nervousness" I am hoping to rehabilitate, Joseph Warton, in the second volume of his *Essay on the Genius and Writings of Pope*, published in 1782. Discussing a particular sequence of lines from one of Pope's poems, Warton commented:

> There is not a useless word in this passage: there are but three epithets [i.e. adjectives] … ; and they are placed precisely with the very substantive [i.e. noun] that is of most consequence; if there had been epithets joined with the other substantives, it would have weakened the nervousness of the sentence. This was a secret of versification POPE well understood, and hath often practised with peculiar success.   (Warton 1806 [1782] 102–103)

By "nervousness", Warton meant something like "strength, vigour, force" (*OED*, sense 1), a meaning of which the *OED* gives no example later than 1895, but which I should like to extend to the entire arsenal of rhetorical and stylistic devices through which Pope so formidably sought to enforce the Humanist mind-set, and also to the sheer strength of character valorized by that mind-set. To adapt Warton's more limitedly stylistic observation to the six-line passage just quoted, ("My Head and Heart thus flowing …"), the only nouns to be allocated an adjective were "*Erasmus*" and "Mean", which really were the substantives of most consequence here. Then there is the other side of diction's communicational strength, which involved an application to the writing process of the *media via* so typical of Horace's entire mode of being:

> viribus, ingenio, specie, virtute, loco, re
> extremi primorum, extremis usque priores.

Pope, whose imitation of Epistle II ii was at this point as close as he ever came to actual translation –

> In Pow'r, Wit, Figure, Vitrue, Fortune, plac'd
> Behind the foremost, and before the last.
> (*Imitations of Horace*: Ep. II ii, ll. 302–303)

–, made the link to diction in *An Essay on Criticism*, recommending that in the choice of words one

> Be not the *first* by whom the *New* are try'd,
> Nor yet the *last* to lay the *Old* aside.   (*Essay on Criticism*, ll. 334–335)

And Johnson, describing a stylistic principle which actually went well beyond diction, was very shrewd about Pope's own style: Pope "excelled every other writer in poetical prudence; he wrote in such a manner as might expose him to few hazards" (Johnson 1925 [1779–1781]:212). The diction of the "My Head and Heart" passage was poetical prudence in a nutshell. The adjectives linked to "*Erasmus*" and "Mean" were "good" and "honest", two words which, despite a powerful ethical loading, were neither archaic nor new-fangled, and drew absolutely no attention to themselves as words in any other way either. There was consequently a fair chance that readers would take on board the ethical loading almost without thinking, a chance further improved by Pope's characteristic yoking together of diction and versification. The two halves of the single line –

> Like good *Erasmus* in an honest Mean

– matched the two unostentatious nominal expressions in a parison ("Like *adjective* + *noun* in an *adjective* + *noun*"). By somewhat slowing down the verse's onward movement, this ensured that ethical points nevertheless would register, almost calling attention to themselves, but not quite. Such was the intricate power with which Pope strained every nerve – every last ounce of communicational strength – to urge his readers into the grouping of those for whom the three awkward compromises he was proposing were totally unproblematic instances of the Humanist *media via* as pursued by any decent member of society.

In Pope this Humanist nervousness was uniquely forceful, its seems to me, but also uniquely charming, and thereby – a most signal case of sweet pleasure and useful instruction mixed – only the more forceful. Casting his friend William Fortescue in the role of Trebatius, Horace's conversation partner in Satire II i, his imitation had all the warmth and casualness of convivial talk. Yet to suggest, as he so engagingly suggested in this "My Head and Heart" passage, that the differences between Tories and Whigs, Protestants and Catholics, prose and verse were more or less immaterial was to perform, with the lightness of a butterfly indiscriminately flitting from clover to cornflower, the function of a steamroller. Although the tone seemed relaxed and pleasingly deferential, this was ultimately *not* an instance of negative capability – the capability of being "in uncertainties, Mysteries, doubts, without any irritable reaching after fact and reason" (Keats 1954 [1817]:53). Pope's aim was rather to bring about that civilized consensus within which other people's hesitations or reservations would be given as little room as he allowed to his own natural grievances as a Tory, a Catholic, and an invalid. Superficially, his coupleteering could perhaps seem to resemble the balanced, cumulative style in which Cordelia, Kent, France and, at some points, even Lear himself reasonably dissociated themselves from a blind stampede into the future (see Section 1.3 above). But if so, that was precisely the trick of it. Even though a stylistic feature can often be associated with just one particular semantic or interactional implication, such conventional expectations are sometimes triggered only to be thwarted, most noticeably in mock-heroic writing, perhaps, but potentially in any kind of communication at all. Everything depends on the context and overall drift, and Pope's well-weighed reasonableness, his concessions to different points of view, could sometimes be less real than apparent. Differences existed to be smoothed away.

He was not, in fact, as totally bland as some of his own literary-critical pronouncements can lead us to expect. Even at his blandest, even at his most decorously tempered, he could be breaking new ground. Yes, he did recommend that writers be neither the first nor the last to use a word, and we have seen that he practised what he preached here, and that this was merely one aspect of his Horatian *via media* through life in general. But how boring a writer would be whose language, to echo Johnson, never exposed him to more hazards! The truth is that, even if Pope's individual words were never very old or very new, in terms of whole phrases and aphorisms no other writer apart from Shakespeare has so deeply enriched the English language. His didacticism, similarly, was certainly not always very blatant. And yes, this was partly because the ethical values he endorsed were so often the ones his readers remembered, or had only half-forgotten, from the classical authors they had studied when young. But again, how boring a writer would be who came across as merely reminding! Pope did not merely remind. In making himself the Horatian poet of his own time's England, he was constantly opening his readers' eyes and stirring their grey matter. In his accounts of the Man of Ross and Sir Balaam, for instance, the merchant's son was pioneering a social realism to which the nearest comparisons are in the novels of Defoe and Smollett, or in the etchings, engravings and paintings of Hogarth. As already partly noted, elsewhere he could significantly *change* a Horatian original.

One such change itself reveals his own firm understanding of the co-adaptational principle involved here. He clearly saw that *media via* prudence, whether poetical prudence or prudence in other spheres of life, was not necessarily just a matter of satisfying the tastes and expectations of a polite *beau monde*. It could also involve concessions offered in the hope of counter-concessions. Horace, in addressing Maecenas in Epistle I i, had said that he was going to give up writing, because it was time to cure his sickness of soul with the spells and charms of philosophy. He would not rely on just a single guru, however, but would turn for comfort wherever the storm happened to drive him. At one moment he would be a fierce champion of virtue. Next moment, he would slip back into the rules of Aristippus (the Cyrenaic philosopher who held that pleasure was the chief good), and in this Cyrenaic phase would "*mihi res, non me rebus, subiungere*" (l. 19).[9] Pope, just as he elsewhere said he could be both Whig and Tory, Catholic and Protestant, so here, in casting himself in the role of Horace, and St. John in the role of Maecenas, did nothing to weaken the stress on the temperate man's readiness to draw wisdom from several different quarters:

---

9. "bend the world to myself, not myself to the world".

> As drives the storm, at any door I knock,
> And house with Montagne now, or now with Lock.
> Sometimes …
> Still true to Virtue, and as warm as true:
> Sometimes with Aristippus…
> Indulge my Candor. …

In fact by adding allusions to I Corinthians X 22 ("I am made all things to all men") and Philippians IV 5 ("Let your moderation be known unto all men") he positively underlined his own amenable eclecticism:

> Sometimes with Aristippus, or St. Paul,
> Indulge my Candor, and grow all to all;
> Back to my native Moderation slide, …

But then suddenly, quite unlike Horace, whose relapse into Cyrenaic philosophy would make him want to bend the world to himself, not himself to the world, Pope clearly stated that his own moderate stance would be both a winning and a yielding. Yes, like Horace in his Cyrenaic mood he would get his own way with the world. But he would get it precisely because he was letting other people get their way as well:

> Back to my native Moderation slide,
> And win my way by yielding to the tyde.   (*Imitations of Horace*: Ep. I i, ll. 25.34)

Most obviously through his gallant yielding (as in the poems to the Blount sisters and *The Rape of the Lock*) to the tide of feminine vanity, but equally through all his many other ways, argumentational, rhetorical, stylistic, of not upsetting readers, Pope was all the time trying to win ground for what the Humanists chose to see as the socially acceptable ethical insights of the ancient Greeks and Romans, even though some readers, both then and later, refused to be swayed.

Coleridge, himself a domineering conversationalist, could not but resist the element of congenial coerciveness in another writer, and in doing so foreshadowed my comments here. On the one hand, he mentioned a particular form and ideal of society. On the other, he noted a didactic manner of coupleteering sophistry, his exact terms suggesting that he was indeed reacting against the kind of potentially problematic compromises I have specially highlighted. Describing in *Biographia Literaria* his earliest encounter with Popeian textualities, he wrote:

> I saw that the excellence of this kind consisted in just and acute observations on men and manners in an artificial state of society as its matter and substance – and in the logic of wit, conveyed in smooth and strong epigrammatic couplets as its form. Even when the subject was addressed to the fancy or the intellect …; nay, when it was a consecutive narration …; still a *point* was looked for at the end of

each second line, and the whole was as it were a sorites or, if I may exchange a logical for a grammatical metaphor, a *conjunction disjunctive*, of epigrams.

(Coleridge 1956 [1817]:9)

In recalling this assessment in 1817, he half-suggested that it should be written off as youthful lack of experience. But in one of his lectures on Shakespeare in 1818, he was still not sure that Pope deserved the name of poet:

> This I must say, that poetry, as distinguished from other modes of composition, does not rest in metre, and that it is not poetry, if it makes no appeal to our passions or our imagination. One characteristic belongs to all true poets, that they write from a principle within, not originating in anything without; and that the true poet's work in its form, its shapings, and its modifications, is distinguished from all other works that assume to belong to the class of poetry, as a natural from an artificial flower, or as the mimic garden of a child from an enamelled meadow.

(Coleridge 1885 [1818]:232)

Coleridge summed up the feeling of many critics, from Joseph Warton to Arnold and beyond, that Pope's reasoning restraint and paradoxical combination of artificiality with matter-of-factness cramped their own autonomy as readers. Confronting his texts, they did not feel sufficiently encouraged to have feelings and to use their imagination. Their main variation of emphasis was merely in how they lodged the charge of unnaturalness. Whereas Coleridge disliked writing that did not well up from inner sources, others, though seeing human nature – Pope's professed forté ("The proper study of Mankind is Man" (*Essay on Man* II, l. 2)) – as an important dimension of nature in general, trumped his wisdom here with that of Shakespeare. Not gifted, according to Hazlitt, with "the capacious soul" of a Shakespeare, he allegedly lacked "an intuitive and mighty sympathy with whatever could enter into the heart of man in any circumstances" (Hazlitt 1818:139). In the eyes of such critics, the main tendency of his work was in effect to endorse just one, uncomprehensive view of human life in society.

But the protest against Pope's control was by no means wholesale. Even for Coleridge the translation of the *Iliad* was an "astonishing product of matchless talent and ingenuity" (Coleridge 1956 [1817]:9); even Hazlitt was deeply moved by *Eloisa to Abelard* (Hazlitt 1818:149–150); and for some of their contemporaries Pope's entire socio-artistic ethos was unobjectionable. Accordingly to Hazlitt's essay "Of Persons one would wish to have seen", Charles Lamb (referred to as "B___") particularly admired Pope's "friendly Epistles and his compliments", seeing the latter as "[t]he finest … that were ever paid by the wit of man. Each of them is worth an estate for life – nay, is an immortality" (Hazlitt 1826:36). Byron, too, was an vigorous apologist for Pope at his most eighteenth-century, roundly denouncing what he saw as "the vulgar and atrocious cant against him".

> [B]ecause his versification is perfect, it is assumed that it is his only perfection; because his truths are so clear, it is asserted that he has no invention; and because he is always intelligible, it is taken for granted that he has no genius. We are sneeringly told that he is the 'Poet of Reason', as if this was a reason for his being not poet.   (Byron 1933 [1820]: 26–27)

Above all, said Byron, grasping the Humanist nettle, Pope is "an *ethical* poet": the highest kind of poet, that is, who

> does that in *verse*, which the greatest of men have wished to accomplish in prose.... He who can reconcile poetry with truth and wisdom, is the only true '*poet*' in its real sense, 'the *maker*', 'the *creator*'.   (Byron 1933 [1821]: 27)

3.3   Romantic nervousness

Now Byron's comments were published in 1820 and 1821, by which time Byron himself was living in expedient exile, his own private life having long been an object of public outrage in England. The year 1821 also saw the publication of *Cain*, his poem about the guilt-ridden outcast, which along with *Childe Harold's Pilgrimage* did so much to encourage perceptions of Romantic poetry as a channel for emotionally sensitive protest against society. That a post-Humanist poet so much the archetype of the rebellious outsider should champion, and champion on ethical grounds, a Humanist poet so deeply self-rooted at the very centre of English society may at first seem curious. One possible explanation would be that Pope and Byron were not actually contemporaries – that the society which Byron criticized was no longer the one with which Pope had identified. Perhaps Byron even allowed himself a fantasy of having been born, not in 1788 but 1688, the same year as Pope. But a more likely explanation, it seems to me, is that Byron was not nearly so enamoured of Walpole's England, and saw in it anticipations of the social phenomena with which he was battling in his own time. Pope, he could have felt, had already submitted them to an appropriate ethical critique, which he himself still needed to continue.

Pope the Humanist insider and Byron the Romantic outsider did have a lot in common, and it went deeper than the often noted similarities of tone and phrasing. As Thomas Woodman (2005) has begun to suggest, there could even come a point by which Pope the insider was virtually also an outsider. Although he did not allow himself to be more than necessarily marginalized by his own religio-political background and invalidism, in satirizing powerful men as monstrous by the standards of all *viri boni* he was appealing to a criterion whose practical endorsement by the establishment of the day was patently far from total and whole-hearted. This, in such cases, was precisely his point, and was doubtless why in several passages he continued a line of questioning started in some of the poems he imitated from Horace: Was it better for a satirist to attack identifiable individuals or generalized types? – types such as the immensely wealthy but utterly tasteless Timon in the *Epistle to Burlington*, for instance. One of the disadvantages of general satire was said to be that it made too many enemies – "A Hundred smart in *Timon*", as Pope himself put it in his imitation of Horace's Satire II i (l. 42) – though he also said, in a letter to Arbuthnot of 1734, that "General Satire in Times of General Vice has no force" (Sherburn 1956: III 423). Whether vice ever seemed so general as to make him feel, in spite his public displays of solidarity, actually alienated from his own society we cannot know. But he did say that its sheer awesomeness outstripped his own poetical creativity –

> Vice with such Giant-strides comes on amain,
> Invention strives to be before in vain.   (*Epilogue to the Satires: Dia. II*, ll. 5–6)

– and during the worst periods of anti-Catholic hostility he probably did think about following friends such as St. John and Francis Atterbury into religiopolitical refuge in France. The only thing holding him back from foreign travel would have been, not so much his physical handicaps, as that canny instinct, so clearly traced throughout Mack's biography, for remaining at least as close as possible to the movers and shakers in English affairs. The distance he wished to have between himself and the society for and about which he wrote was no greater than the few miles from parliament and court to Twickenham, easily negotiable both on land and by river. But even though some of the rich and the powerful themselves came out to Twickenham, there could well have been times when that distance seemed a good bit longer, times when he felt himself an exile in all but fact.

All writers of real communicational power are both insiders and outsiders. A writer who was too exclusively an insider would merely endorse the status quo. To this extent, the prejudice of post-Humanist intelligentsias against literary entertainers and realists has not been entirely groundless. But a writer who was too exclusively an outsider would also make no difference, through being so alien. To this extent, post-Humanist intelligentsias have sometimes tended to promote a literature for the relatively few. At issue here is once again the principle of communicational co-adaptation, which made it possible for Pope to win his way by yielding to the tide. A communicant, by meeting other communicants half-way, by being, or by becoming for the purposes and duration of communication, so like them as to win their trust, stands a better chance of introducing them to something new, or to a new way of thinking or feeling. Schematically: A adapts to B in the hope that B will adapt to A. Result? With a bit of luck, a process of communication that is co-adaptational. Clearly, some major writers concede rather more to their prospective readers' expectations, and others rather less. Writers come across as either more easy-going or more challenging, more of an insider or more of an outsider. But what is so striking about Pope's pivotal role in English literary history is that he ended up, not only as both insider and outsider, but as both insider and outsider to a quite exceptional degree.

As an extreme insider, his emphasis was above all on those socially acceptable ethical values which the Humanists chose to derive from the classics. But as throughout this study, I do insist that they *chose to* derive them. There was no reason why Horace should not have been embraced as a model for sociable probity and *media via* prudence, as I have put it. But to have that kind of take on classical authors was certainly to filter them. The Humanist ideal was a sociocultural construct rooted in the Humanists' own, still basically Christian epoch, and when Humanist scholars invoked the life and civilization of that earlier age they were consciously selective, since they were by no means as ignorant of its conditions and mores as their own time's idealizations of it could suggest. Humanist artists, too, were well aware of an interplay that could arise between the cultures of different times and places, and consequently had a sense of their own creativity as, in the words of T. M. Greene (1976), a kind of "double groping": they were groping *back* towards those ancient remains, and groping *forwards* to "a modern sensibility" which would be able to mediate that otherness. But in mediating for their own time the gods and goddesses, the heroes and heroines, of classical literature and myth they certainly chose to emphasise some moral and emotional qualities at the expense of others. A wide range of ancient virtues was perfectly acceptable. But anger (unless righteous) and (as I hinted earlier) erotomania were problematic for a start. This was why Ovid, no less than in mediaeval times, had to be moralized, so helping to create a climate of ideas in which the Elizabethans' own salaciously Ovidian narrative poems had the appeal of forbidden fruits. Love could never be ruled out altogether, but always tended to figure not only as the unpredictable bliss and agony it had already been in Ovid, but as very much a threat to the temperate individual's peace of mind – a passion to be channelled as decorously as possible in accordance with prevailing taboo. In Pope's own exquisite imitation of Horace's Ode IV i, sexual fantasy was a deranging, painful magic even for a fifty-year-old.

> But why? ah tell me, ah too dear!
> Steals down my cheek th' involuntary Tear?
> Why words so flowing, thoughts so free,
> Stop, or turn nonsense at one glance of Thee?
> Thee, drest in fancy's airy beam,
> Absent I follow thro' th' extended Dream,
> Now, now I seize, I clasp thy charms,
> And now you burst, (ah cruel!) from my arms,
> And swiftly shoot along the Mall,
> Or softly glide by the Canal,
> Now shown by Cynthias's silver ray,
> And now, on rolling Waters snatch'd away.
>
> (*Imitations of Horace*: Od. IV i, ll. 37–48)

Astonishingly, poignantly, and quite without precedent in Horace's Latin, in the single word "burst" the anticlimactic shattering of the dream usurped an orgasmic climax. But this was as far as Humanist frankness went, for what Pope's lines did not divulge (to readers not familiar with the original) was that the object of Horace's desire was the boy Ligurinus. In translating the *Iliad* and the *Odyssey*, similarly, whatever else he was doing (which was of course a very great deal) Pope took care to air-brush not only the characters' sentiments and morals but Homer's language. "What was barbarous, he softened," as Mack wrote, "and what was gross or vulgar he mitigated" (Mack 1985: 352). So much so, that Coleridge, despite that praise for Pope's "matchless talent and ingenuity" here, clearly saw the Homer as a major contribution to the early eighteenth century's "artificial state of society".

> I do not stand alone in regarding [his translation of Homer] as the main source of our pseudo-poetic diction. And this, by the bye [*sic*], is an additional confirmation of a remark made, I believe, by Sir Joshua Reynolds, that next to the man who formed and elevated the taste of the public, he that corrupts it is commonly the greatest genius.   (Coleridge 1956 [1817]: 22n.)

In the end the Humanist idealization of both ancient and modern life could no longer hold. Not only was the Battle of the Books beginning to raise the question of whether contemporary writers might have qualities actually superior to those of the ancients. Not only were scholars such as Richard Bentley penetrating the ancient world ever more deeply, including its less salubrious aspects. In a Europe, in a Britain so torn apart by the violence of both international and civil wars, so sullied by all forms of vice and lust for power, the most accurate comparisons with classical literature would have been with everything the Humanists toned down. That their central exhibit was a sanguinary epic was deeply troubling, for, as Claude Rawson has shown, Dryden's claim that "[a] heroic poem, truly such, is undoubtedly the greatest work which the soul of man is capable to perform" was becoming increasingly difficult to square with anxieties about the morality of wars, which "hitherto", as Milton put it, had been "the onely Argument / Heroic deemd" (Rawson 2000: 45–47). Pope tried to make his English version of *The Iliad* somewhat more agreeable than a direct translation would have been, and as editor of Shakespeare he was also hoping to whitewash the greatest poet of modern England, whose work had suffered, he claimed, from "his endeavours solely to hit the taste and humour that then prevailed. The Audience was generally composed of the meaner sort of people" (Pope 1933 [1725]: 152). But the truth about both the ancient world and modern Britain could no longer be suppressed. To Pope's chagrin, Theobald quickly supplied a less interventional edition of Shakespeare, and Pope himself, despite the almost perverse magnificence of his Homer, and despite his desire to write a great new Humanist epic in English, the ambition which had already proved too much for Dryden, never completed his projected

Brutus. Even if his politely prudent manner was actually a way of winning as well as yielding, in other words, by the early eighteenth century the ethical programme to which it spoke was seriously under question. Pope was the last major English writer who even tried to keep it alive, an impossible task which helped to win him that post-humous reputation for unnaturalness.

This was one main part of the larger culture-historical background to the Popeian psychomachia – to the extreme tension in his work between a Humanist and a Romantic nervousness. Despite his most charming and most powerful efforts, the Humanist nervousness was increasingly less viable. The other crucial background factor was that Romantic nervousness was a phenomenon for which there was already beginning to be a language. Thanks to pioneers such as Thomas Willis and George Cheyne, the study of neurology and psychology was well under way in Pope's England, so that the sense of the word "nerve" as "sinew" or "tendon", and with it Joseph Warton's sense of "nervousness" as "strength, vigour, force", though still widely evidenced, were starting to become obsolete, making way for the new kind of nervousness which, by the time of what Woodman (1998) calls the early Romantic period, was already a recognized phenomenon: nervousness as "Mental agitation; apprehension, anxiety; heightened or excessive sensitivity", for which the *OED*'s first entry is from 1798, even though in 1744 Mark Akenside's poem *The Pleasures of Imagination* had already dwelt on the role of the nervous system within the creative process. George Rousseau has shown that Pope, too, who was himself treated by Cheyne and had a life-long invalid's familiarity with medical thinking and gossip, felt the importance of nervous input to his own writing. He could have been forgiven, Rousseau thinks, for seeing his supernormal propensity for "high imaginative states" (Cheyne's term) as compensating for his physical subnormalities. Rousseau actually suggests that, with nerves so "taut and tonic" (Cheyne's terminology again), Pope could well have imagined that "there was nothing flaccid or effeminate, soft or weak, in his body, let alone lacking the masculinity he sought" (Rousseau 2007:218). Rousseau is mainly concerned with psychobiography, and by drawing on his knowledge of Pope's medical case history suggests a personal vibration behind some of the poetry, whereas my own approach is to read the poetry first and give it a chance to work in the ways Pope was entitled to expect. Read thus, it is a nobler achievement, in a few places openly presenting itself as the work of an invalid, but of an invalid who in his address to the public is not a hypochondriac, and whose fiercely satirical pen is not a compensation for a possibly dysfunctional penis but the means to raise ethical questions of sometimes national importance. Rousseau does valuably confirm, however, just how typically, in the poetry itself, what Pope supplies is additional, or even contradictory to the cut-and-dried order of an ostensible chain of reasoning. And no less valuable is his stress on Pope's own sense of this.

The new nervousness involved the liberation and positive cultivation of sensitive perceptions, fine feelings, powerful emotions. Its long-term human and social consequences could hardly be entirely beneficial. But Pope seems to have assumed that it was note of the future and, in everything he did to foster its development within the culture as a whole, did not think of it as just a superficial fashion. If widely perceived as merely a social expectation, it would have been unlikely to arise in the first place. When it did arise, it would have to do so from deep within each individual.

So whereas the thrust of his satires and verse essays was on the whole deontic or persuasive, in the writing where the new sensibility came into play his relationship with his readers was very different. They were not being urged to be polite good citizens, to join the ranks of the right-minded, to tread the ethical *media via*. Here he was altogether less coercive than in his Humanist mode, and also much less of a showman or master of ceremonies than in what I call his sublime writing. Instead, his method was to describe human fates, experiences and concerns very feelingly, but also gently. His offering was submitted to readers in the hope of a sympathetic response, which would be of no value unless it were voluntary. To the extent that he did seek to shape a community here, it was one of delicate and spontaneous sensitivity to the plight and perceptions of others. Like the speaker in "Elegy to the Memory of an Unfortunate Lady", he valued those whose breast had "learn'd to glow / For others' good, or melt at others' woe" (ll. 45–46).

Partly thanks to the heroines of Rowe's tragedies and Richardson's novels, and to the many fictional representations of benevolent men and men of feeling, notions of sensibility and sentiment did become fashionable, of course, and Pope's own *Eloisa to Abelard* was itself influential, for instance on many of the many women novelists who portrayed their heroines' lovers as generously wise and sympathetic figures, well able to recognize female personhood and depth of emotion (Wikborg 2002) – Eloisa apostrophizes Abelard as "my father, brother, husband, friend!" (l. 153). Pope sensed, however, that the new nervousness, in direct opposition to the older, ethical nervousness of the politely Humanist citizen, was fundamentally unsuited for display. In cases where its cultivation did have beneficial consequences for the public sphere, this would be by supplying individuals with a new, but semi-secret source of energy to carry them through a life of responsibilities and socializing. To attempt to cultivate it *in* public would be to risk inauthenticity. Ostentation could all too easily take off the edge of genuinely personal feelings, and if the public-private distinction were not most carefully preserved the new kinds of intuition would simply not occur.

On the other hand, those developing the new nervousness, or recognizing its presence and validity in the lives of others, could themselves take part in a public life within whose discourse the phenomenon was in some way bound to be noted. In his own social role as a man of letters, the thing Pope himself mentioned was a matter of tone, and precisely a hint of the *non*-public.

What he approved of in a literary critic, for instance, was a truthfulness and a candor such

> That not alone what to your *Sense* is due
> All may allow; but seek your *Friendship* too.   (*Essay on Criticism*, ll. 564–565)

The sheer impossibility of every reader of a literary critic, or even of every author criticized, literally establishing contact and becoming friends with that critic was obvious enough. Even in the eighteenth century, the overlap between the community of all those who read and wrote books and the private circle of any individual critic would be very small. Truthfulness and candor in a critic certainly are attractive. They do inspire readers to value not only the common sense of the judgements offered but, exactly as Pope implied, underlying qualities of human warmth and genuineness to which a friendship would allow fuller access. This was how Pope himself was drawn into friendship with Joseph Spence, whom he esteemed as a most honest critic of his own poetry. But a critic who was friend to all the world would run the risk of being, not only a rather anæmic critic, but actually nobody's friend at all – or at least no better a friend than Belinda:

> Bright as the Sun, her Eyes the Gazers strike,
> And, like the Sun, they shine on all alike.   (*Rape of the Lock*, II, ll. 13–14)

The good critic should by all means have an intimate privacy of tone, but one to which access was normally possible only though the critic's publications.

In a poet, similarly, Pope could discern features appealing to the new sensibility which arose *in spite* of conventional public norms, so that to this extent Romantic nervousness was in parallel with the Sublime. But whereas the Sublime in, say, an epic or a Pindaric ode could be a very demonstrative break from the accepted rules of writing, the private was altogether less conspicuous and more endearing. Of Cowley Pope wrote,

> Forget his Epic, nay Pindaric Art,
> But still I love the language of his Heart. (*Imitations of Horace*: Ep. II i, ll. 77–78)

Here too, then, Pope's sense was that public, literary activity could sometimes allow a glimpse into an almost sacrosanct domain, where writing individuals had their most essential life, and into which they once again entirely withdrew every time a reader finished reading them. To use phrasing from one of his letters, the private was the domain of "one's self, one's time, one's quiet, (the very Life of Life itself)" (Sherburn 1956: II 194).

In his own poetry, the private was sometimes aligned with the rural in the countryside-city dichotomy and said to be altogether preferable to the urban. But this was never going to be a convincing gesture unless the Humanist aura of loudly trumpeted achievement completely gave way to the new, domestic intimacy. Such was not the case when he characteristically ended *Windsor-Forest* by discussing his own writing:

Here cease thy Flight, nor with unhallow'd Lays
Touch the fair Fame of *Albion*'s Golden Days.
The Thoughts of Gods let *Granville*'s Verse recite,
And bring the Scenes of opening fate to Light.
My humble Muse, in unambitious Strains,
Paints the green Forests and the flow'ry Plains,
Where Peace descending bids her Olives spring,
And scatters Blessings from her Dove-like Wing.
Ev'n I more sweetly pass my careless days,
Pleas'd in the silent Shade with empty Praise;
Enough for me, that to the listning Swains
First in these Fields I sung the Sylvan Strains.   (*Windsor-Forest*, ll. 423–434)

Granville was George Granville, Lord Lansdowne, who, like Sir William Trumbull, belonged to the circle of older men who encouraged Pope as a young writer. Especially with the benefit of hindsight, we may find Pope's deference to Granville's own poetry somewhat disingenuous. Although he himself was young, and although this present poem and the *Pastorals* certainly *were* pastoral, there was nothing to prevent a young poet from emulating Virgil in the usual Humanist manner by later moving on to the grander kinds of poetic task here ceded to Granville. Even for some of the poem's first readers, the escapist quietism of the ending could have been difficult to reconcile with its earlier surveys of national history, its vision of a British empire of trade, its attempts to mediate between the country's two great parties. Pope did like to put a distance between himself and the centre of power, but I have noted that it was a very short one. Although his poetry of feelings was nothing if not a poetry of privacy, this passage unintentionally reminds us that he was also England's last great Humanist poet, a breed which, as blowers of Fame's trump, could simply not thrive in obscurity. Within a few years, if not immediately, Granville must surely have blushed at the young tiger's fawning.

In the *Pastorals*, by contrast, Pope's poetry of the private was neither self-referential nor idealized. Far more than often acknowledged, not least by Wordsworth (Griffin 1995), these poems anticipated *Lyrical Ballads* in making the countryside a setting for some of the most basic human emotions. But neither living close to nature nor giving vent to strong feelings was a panacea for all of life's ills. Even if many readers have seen this writing as Pope's most artificial, there was a verisimilitude of not only joy but sorrow here, and considerable intensity as well.

In practice the artificiality functioned, not as a distancing of the poetry's subject-matter, but as a pleasant inducement to the reader. In his introductory "Discourse on Pastoral Poetry" Pope had engaged to write something which "consists in simplicity, brevity, and delicacy; the two first of which render an eclogue natural, the last delightful", and the delightful delicacy was intricately interwoven with the artificiality, which was also quite compatible with simplicity and brevity. As the poems unfolded, he kept his promise by means of exquisite descriptions of natural scenery and weather, and with a lyricism that was utterly ravishing even before Handel set "Where'er you walk" to music. Thanks to his characteristic paratextual commentaries, we can sometimes even see where a small revision has made all the difference. "While silent birds neglect their tuneful lays" became "While silent Birds forget their tuneful Lays" ("Winter", l. 7). And the fact that the voice was lyric rather than narrative or discursive gave a maximum immediacy, not at odds with the delicacy, to the most private kind of feelings about some of the most life-defining experiences any individual can face: love, unrequited love, the death of a loved one. In this way, rather than using the genre as, say, a vehicle for religious or political allegory, a ploy which the "Discourse" denounced in the pastorals of both Mantuan and Spenser, and rather than letting the artificiality be a self-sufficient and delusive prettification, Pope was able to develop a head-on emotional realism of the highest human relevance. So much so, that, whereas Mack (1985:133–134) described the *Pastorals* as the last effete gasp of what had once been a major Humanist convention, they can equally well be seen as the first truly Romantic poetry in English, and very powerful at that, the relevance being precisely to individuals in their most intimate lives, quite beyond the reach of social help or interference.

In "Spring", Strephon and Daphnis alternate their quatrains in joyful praise of, respectively, Delia and Sylvia, and their experiences of love, and their claims for their sweethearts, are similar. But not even their participation in the singing contest really puts them in touch with each other, or with Damon, who awards the prizes, since love, though a great leveller and no respecter of persons, is a dimension of their life in which they stand alone. Basically they are soliloquizing side by side. In "Summer", the stress on the individual is even stronger, since Alexis, after Pope's introductory referral of his sad case to his friend Dr. Samuel Garth (himself a literary man and this poem's dedicatee), is the sole speaker, and neither Garth with all his medicines nor anyone else can help him:

> On me Love's fiercer Flames for ever prey,
> By Night he scorches, as he burns by Day.   ("Summer", ll. 91–92)

In "Autumn", the pattern is attractively varied, with Hylas and Ægon each singing a song of unbearable desire, Hylas for Delia, Ægon for Doris, Hylas at first wondering "Do lovers dream, or is my *Delia* kind?" and in the end ecstatically exclaiming "She comes, my *Delia* comes", Ægon desperately deciding that "One leap from yonder Cliff shall end my Pains" (ll. 52, 53, 95). Yet this contrast between them merely strengthens the sense that Fate deals every human being their own particular hand. In "Winter", Thyrsis, at the request of Lycidas, sings "of *Daphne*'s Fate, and *Daphne*'s Praise" (l. 8), and is clearly doing so partly on behalf of many others who also mourn her passing. By a beautiful pathetic fallacy he even intensifies the communal grief by figuring birds and breezes, trees and rivers as joining in. He also offers some consolation, in a vision of Daphne now resting in "*Amaranthine* Bow'rs", "Above the Clouds, above the Starry

Sky" (ll. 73, 70). But then, in the earliest of Pope's long series of shocking conclusions which was to end with Universal Darkness burying all at the end of *The Dunciad*, the poem closes with a wintry prospect to which we must all accustom ourselves in isolation, each alone:

> But see, *Orion* sheds unwholsome Dews,
> Arise, the Pines a noxious Shade diffuse;
> Sharp *Boreas* blows, and Nature feels Decay,
> Time conquers All, and We must Time obey.
> Adieu ye *Vales*, ye *Mountains, Streams* and *Groves*,
> Adieu ye Shepherd's rural *Lays* and *Loves*,
> Adieu my Flocks, farewell ye *Sylvan* Crew,
> *Daphne* farewell, and all the World adieu!   ("Winter", ll. 85–92)

In one sense, the grave does unite Henry VI and Edward IV in St. George's Chapel, Windsor. Yet we shall not actually share our own death with anybody else. It is Thyrsis' own sheep, his own loved-ones, his own world of which he is taking leave, and Pope was inviting a Romantically nervous response as part of which readers would consider corresponding points of reference in their own most personal lives. In a life of feeling, the thoughts and emotions of others always stir a sympathetic vibration, an unselfish self-reference. In communal terms, poetry of this kind would tend to strengthen what *An Essay on Man* describes as a chain of Love running through the entire universe.

Death's absoluteness was what the Humanist poet's trump of Fame was supposed to counteract, and I have already pointed out that Pope's imitation of Horace's Ode IV ix was more Humanist in character than a strict translation would have been, at least in so far as it replaced sung or unsung lovers with sung or unsung scientists. In another respect, however, the imitation did not exploit this Ode's own Humanist potential. Horace was addressing himself to Marcus Lollius, a wealthy supporter of Augustus who was consul in 21 BC, and the Ode's last four Alcaic stanzas were all devoted to Lollius' praise. It so happens that Lollius had something of a reputation for corruption, so that Horace was perhaps tongue-in-cheek here. But even so, it is very striking that Pope, in a text where he was making the Humanist claim about the immortal reputations of those praised in poetry, did not imitate these last stanzas as well, replacing Lollius with a suitable contemporary, and capitalizing on opportunities suggested by the Latin phrasing ("… *est animus tibi / rerumque prudens et secundis / temporibus dubiisque rectus*")[10] for nicely weighted antitheses and parisons on the theme of an ethical *media via*. Because he did not, his imitation is not only that much less Humanistic, but that much closer to the post-Humanist nervousness of the pastorals. Death seems rather more difficult to come to terms with, and more intimately intrusive.

---

10. "A mind thou hast, experienced in affairs, well-poised in weal or woe." All quotations and translations of Horace's Odes and Epodes taken from Bennett 1964.

In other poems, death's insidiousness becomes explicit. In the "Epistle to Mr. Jervas: with Dryden's Translation of Fresnoy's Art of Painting", a characteristically jarring conclusion directly undermines Humanist hopes for the trump of Fame. Having first dwelt on the skill in painting demonstrated by both Jervas and Dufresnoy, and on the writing abilities of both Dryden and – this with due modesty – himself, and having claimed that such artistry certainly can perpetuate the memory of people painted and praised, Pope suddenly seems to lose faith:

> Alas! how little from the grave we claim ? [= !]
> Thou [i.e. Jervas] but preserv'st a Face and I a Name.
>
> ("Epistle to Mr. Jervas", ll. 77–78)

And a similar concern is especially disturbing in "Elegy to the Memory of an Unfortunate Lady", a poem likely to arouse in Romantically nervous readers the most acute embarrassment on behalf of the sufferer remembered, whose very namelessness is one key to her misfortune. As for the male speaker who laments her fate in the poem, some of the emotions it stirs in him are so alarmingly anti-social that readers may find themselves assuming that he cannot be Pope himself. Given the new nervousness, however, this is open to question, since the valorization of the intimately personal clearly could have disconcerting consequences, no less in Pope than in any other normally law-abiding citizen. At all events the speaker, identifying the lady only as a victim of love, and as a suicide whose restless ghost still haunts the glade in which she is buried, champions her cause in no uncertain terms, and with a bitterness against other mortals, high and low, which soon becomes very apparent. It was not her fault, he says, that her soul aspired "[a]bove the vulgar flight of low desire" (l. 12). Ambition can even be a good thing, he argues, at least if you happen to be a king or a hero. And is it really so surprising that she chose not to resemble the vast majority of other people? – whose souls

> … peep out but once an age,
> Dull sullen pris'ners in the body's cage:
> Dim lights of life that burn a length of years,
> Useless, unseen, as lamps in sepulchres ?
>
> ("Elegy to the Memory of an Unfortunate Lady", ll. 17–20)

What chance did she have, after all, when her guardian failed to support her? – a man whose entire family in the speaker's view deserves to die, because their "breast ne'er learn'd to glow / For others' good, or melt at others' woe" (ll. 45–46). With no friends or relations present at her funeral, the unfortunate lady was "by strangers honour'd, and by strangers mourn'd", an exile, now lying in unhallowed ground, "without a stone, a name", who "once had beauty, titles, wealth, and fame" (ll. 54, 69, 70).

> A heap of dust alone remains of thee;
> 'Tis all thou art, and all the proud shall be!   (ll. 73–74)

At which point, in perhaps the most astonishing of all Pope's remarkable conclusions, the fact of death characteristically comes together with the question of the power or weakness of poetry itself:

> Poets themselves must fall, like those they sung;
> Deaf the prais'd ear, and mute the tuneful tongue.
> Ev'n he, whose soul now melts in mournful lays,
> Shall shortly want the gen'rous tear he pays;
> Then from his closing eyes thy form shall part,
> And the last pang shall tear thee from his heart,
> Life's idle business at one gasp be o'er,
> The Muse forgot, and thou belov'd no more!   (ll. 75–82)

Both the unfortunate lady herself and her lover-poet are completely helpless in face of their intimately personal agonies, completely anonymous and, like countless other souls in pain, completely alone – there is no mention of her even knowing of his love for her, let alone of her reciprocating it. Here all talk of reasoning, or of choosing carefully, or of a *media via* endorsed by a polite society, would be totally beside the point. Polite society is a parallel, but separate universe. The lady's ambition was absolute. Her victimization was absolute. Her suicide was absolute. The speaker's fantasy of revenge is absolute. His continuing love is absolute, until his last breath, when his own death, too, will be absolute, and both of them be absolutely forgotten. The only life that was real for them was one of extreme anguish, experienced in utter alienation from society. And that predicament, so closely akin with the one depicted in *Childe Harold* or – perhaps an even closer parallel – in Tennyson's *Maud*, has in Pope the shocking, concentrated clarity of a hyper-Romantic nervousness, marking the sharpest possible contrast with nervousness of the older Humanist kind.

Because the unfortunate lady's guardian has shown that he is not man of feeling, the speaker, who is perhaps Pope, and who is certainly in his own view himself a man of feeling, feels passionately that the guardian and all his family should die. In his mind's eye he actually sees their "long fun'rals blacken all the way" (l. 40). That really is how un-socialized feelings can sometimes work. The lady herself, driven by high desires, came to grief. That, too, really can happen when social norms are side-stepped. The new nervousness was clearly extremely dangerous from the start. The sympathies to which it gave rise could be very selective, the emotions destructive. It dissolved the older social cement without offering the slightest guarantee that under its own sway human beings would in practice be able to live side by side in happiness.

This is a problem which in the late-twentieth-century phase of the post-Humanist era became even more acute, to the extent that the postmodern politics of recognition compartmentalized society itself into many different groupings. This was an emancipatory strategy designed to promote the rights of individuals belonging to communities hitherto underprivileged. As such, it was not only commendable but highly successful. But in terms of overall social cohesion, and of communications between one grouping and another, democratization came at a price here. As post-postmoderns, we may find ourselves wishing that Pope, who bore so much responsibility for the birth of the new era, had thought about such risks and built in some sort of safeguards from the start. This, though, would be doubly unfair. First, it would overlook the possibility that some of today's remaining areas of social friction could result from remaining injustices. Terrorist suicide bombers, whose sense of exclusion and desire for retribution were so strikingly anticipated by the speaker in "Elegy to the Memory of an Unfortunate Lady", make claim to grievances which, though never legitimating acts of violence, must at least be seriously investigated. Secondly, the fundamental dilemma was something that Pope certainly did think about. All those features in the satires and the verse essays which I have described as hyper-Humanist can be seen as his own personal qualification to this potentially dangerous new trend he was opening up elsewhere. His difficulty was that even if one did embrace received ethical codes, even if one did value common-sense prudence and polite behaviour, and even if, for good measure, one did go in for religion as well, one would still have feelings in any case, sometimes feelings so powerful that they would vent themselves with no cultural encouragement at all. Nor was it as if one could actually choose *which* feelings one had. Perhaps, then, a self-culture which acknowledged the facts of emotional life was, however threatening to society, at least preferable to a regimen which acceded to social order by denying them. Or perhaps not. The dilemma was very real, and we are still wrestling with it today.

More particularly, Pope was thinking about it when he wrote *Eloisa and Abelard*. Here he was working in a genre which, both in its classical form in Ovid's *Heroides* and in the Renaissance form of Drayton and Daniel's heroic epistles, had already challenged the Humanist cautiousness about erotic feeling, and had in this sense offered precedents for the literature of sensibility which developed with the rise of the eighteenth century's new kind of nervousness. Not that Pope's Eloise is the least bit undignified or irrational. On the contrary, she represents the highest Humanist ideal of womanhood as expressed in the poems to the Blount sisters or in Clarissa's speech in *The Rape of the Lock*, and she is also truly religious. Because of her religious feelings, and also because of her strong ethical principles, she has decided to give up her love relationship with Abelard and become a nun. And with both her religion and her morality pointing her in the same direction, she could have been forgiven for hoping she would find peace and happiness. The only problem is that her love, her passionate desire for Abelard, lives on, so that, no matter how she may seem to the other nuns, her inner life is a most terrible torment. In one sense her ostensible life as a nun is a kind of lie. Yet it is not an out-and-out lie, since if she had been re-united with Abelard she would probably have found herself pining back to the state of God's votaress, so genuine is also her religious motivation. As Pope represents her case, in the historical period during which she lived there was no way for her to be both wholly in love with God and wholly in love with a man. That is what she would have preferred emotionally, and her emotions were simply not of her own choosing. By taking the course dictated by religion and duty she could never be totally happy, but no other historically available option would have made her totally happy either. As for Horatian talk of prudent moderation, any such notion would have been absurdly out of place. A spectrum of possibilities running from nun to wife, and with a mid-way point of convenient compromise, did not exist. As with the unfortunate lady in that other poem, in Eloisa's world there are only incompatible absolutes, from which her only release will be through the absoluteness of death.

Mack (1985: 324) pointed out the similarity with French neo-classical tragedy. "[T]he poem means us to pity a protagonist trapped like a Racinian Bérenice or Phèdre in a world where nothing desirable is possible and nothing possible desirable". But for Eloisa, even the imaginary voice prompting her towards what seems the path of duty is gentle and kind. She does love God, and she does love her life as a nun. Nor, despite her low self-esteem, does Pope encourage us to think of her as a sinner, or as having failed in the way that Sir Guyon so nearly failed in the Bower of Bliss, or that Adam and Eve did fail in Milton's Eden. True, several of the women authors who wrote poems in response to *Eloisa and Abelard* did so in order to reassert the virtue of chastity which they themselves had been brought up to follow, and in which they felt Eloisa was deficient (Thomas 1994: 190–193). Pope, by implication, they were seeing as a libertine. But he himself would perhaps have described his spiritual temper here as closer to that of *An Essay on Man*, with its benevolent universe held together by that chain of Love. Even if the life-choice between wife and nun was absolute and in that sense black and white, for a wife to dream of nunhood, or for a nun to dream of wifehood, was not, the poem seemed to be suggesting, reprehensible. With the noblest will in the world, one simply cannot deny that such hopeless fantasies are the emotional life's reality. And both love of God and love for a man are, to Pope's perception, ennobling emotions in and of themselves, even within a culture which made them contradictory. In a different historical period they might have been not only psychologically compatible, as they already clearly were for Eloisa, but compatible within society as well.

As we have now learnt almost to expect, in the poem's very last lines Pope raised the question of his own role as poet. Eloisa looks forward into the time after her own death:

> And sure if fate some future Bard shall join
> In sad similitude of griefs to mine,
> Condemn'd whole years in absence to deplore,
> And image charms he must behold no more,
> Such if there be, who loves so long, so well;
> Let him our sad, our tender story tell;
> The well-sung woes will sooth my pensive ghost;
> He best can paint 'em, who shall feel 'em most.   (*Eloisa to Abelard*, ll. 359–366)

That Pope, who produced that miraculous improvement on Horace's Ode IV i ("And now you burst, (ah cruel!) from my arms"), who put words into the mouths of Alexis, Hylas and Ægon in the Pastorals, and who created, or may even be, the speaker in "Elegy to the Memory of an Unfortunate Lady", had indeed spent many years in a private agony of frustrated love seems entirely possible. Biographical corroboration is hard to come by, but commentators such as Patrick Cruttwell (1966: 32–35) have assumed that a sensitivity about his own physical handicaps would have put the damper on any amatory overtures he might otherwise have made, the main candidates for his interest perhaps including Lady Mary Wortley Montagu and both of the Blount sisters. The point here, though, is not biographical, but has to do with his self-presentation within the poem. By implication, he, who has already shown his mettle in the 350 previous lines, is indeed the kind of poet Eloisa is foreseeing. He will understand the sadness of her story, and the tenderness of it. He will feel her woes. As for his soothing her pensive ghost, Eloisa's wish here reflects her own belief that she will be excluded from heaven, a fate which Pope may not have thought she deserved, even if, as a Catholic in private life, he may have thought it perfectly possible, and even if he spoke of the ghost of the unfortunate lady in the other poem as entirely real, or at least as entirely real to the excitable sensibility of the poem's speaker. If his poetry of feelings begins to hint that his religious beliefs were not fully represented by "The Universal Prayer" and An Essay on Man, this is no accident. But the hint is no more than a hint. If he really did believe in heaven, and if he really believed that after death these two women would be excluded from it and haunt the earth as ghosts, that fate can only have seemed infinitely more sad to him than the already very sad stories of their lives-before-death. But his distinction between a poet's public and private life, the distinction on which the cultivation of Romantic nervousness entirely depended, remained in place here, and the writing did not divulge exactly where he stood. Some readers might have thought less highly of him if he had seemed to require a response assuming the literal reality of ghosts, while others might have been in two minds about where they stood themselves. Many Catholic readers would have been likely to take the infinitely sadder view. Others may have concluded that the two poems' talk of ghosts involved a merely literary belief, drawing its most obvious cultural sustenance from the ghost of Hamlet's father. Communicationally, the point to notice is that the poem's last couplet could spur absolutely any kind of reader to review their own most intimate graveside hopes and fears in any case, and that Eloisa's imagined instructions to her painterly poet also suggested the general spirit in which the poem's own lines should be taken, a reading style well represented by De Quincey, for example: "The self-conflict – the flux and reflux of the poor agitated heart" places the reader "in tumultuous sympathy with the poor distracted nun" (De Quincey 1933 [1848]: 29).

As I say, Hazlitt was also very struck by Eloisa and Abelard. But both he, Coleridge and Arnold did not fully respond to Pope's invitation to the sensitively minded. None of them really appreciated the freedom which much of his best writing allows to a reader's own imagination, feelings, and sympathies, and none of them picked up the clue he issued through Eloisa's lips to one of his most distinctive qualities: to the tenderness with which he wrote about tenderness, or about its absence. Eloisa had known tenderness in her relation with Abelard, and the tenderness continued for her, both as a memory and an attitude. As a result, even if her historical circumstances prevented an optimal fulfilment, she was a great deal happier than the society of Pope's own time allowed many people to be, to whom tenderness was quite unknown. In the early eighteenth century, just as Eloisa had appealed to a tenderness in her imagined poet, so a tender poet could try to stir a tenderness in his imagined reader.

Some of Pope's very greatest writing is about the lack of tenderness in the life-experience of contemporary women. Society ensured that women were above all denizens of the non-public world – "A Woman's seen in Private life alone" (*Epistle to a Lady*, l. 200) – and private life could be pure hell for them. With an ur-feminist forthrightness that would not have surprised us in Blake or Shelley, Pope analysed the sociopolitical background to their psychological formation:

> In Men, we various Ruling Passions find,
> In Women, two almost divide the kind;
> Those, only fix'd, they first or last obey,
> The Love of Pleasure, and the Love of Sway.
>   That, Nature gives; and where the lesson taught
> Is but to please, can Pleasure seem a fault?
> Experience, this; by Man's oppression curst,
> They seek the second not to lose the first.   (*Epistle to a Lady*, ll. 207–214)

To the extent that they are in the public eye, the main social imperative is that they appear chaste when young and promiscuous when old. And Eloisa would have counted herself richly blessed if she could have foreseen the sheer misery of their domestic life:

> See how the World its Veterans rewards!
> A Youth of frolicks, an old Age of Cards,
> Fair to no purpose, artful to no end,
> Young without Lovers, old without a Friend,
> A Fop their Passion, but their Prize a Sot,
> Alive, ridiculous, and dead, forgot!   (*Epistle to a Lady*, ll. 243–248)

Except, of course, that they were not, and are still not forgotten, at least as a grouping. Just as *Eloisa and Abelard* countered Humanist poetry's trump of Fame by preserving a sad and tender story of socially embarrassing unhappiness, so here Pope's writing was bringing the tragedy of women's lot into unforgettably sharp focus, and with unrelenting publicity. Because he intuited the structural reason for their plight, in this form the poetry of Romantic nervousness could have nothing but positive consequences, by offering his insights for reciprocally frank and private consideration by every other claimant to sensibility. At first these magisterial couplets may sound like a sequence of general truths. But because the injustice they identify was in principle eradicable through discussion and politics, they were general truths for only a certain phase of history (which in all too many contexts has still not come to an end). Not that he was preaching a message of reform. He was rather tending to assume that true change would come when enough sensitive minds were ready for it. His lines were merely showing, merely revealing, and his nervousness was not Humanist here, but Romantic. Nowhere in his writing was he more profoundly concerned, but the writing is also ethically consistent. In pinpointing oppression, the poet of feeling did not seek to oppress his own readers with explicit didacticism. They were free to draw their own conclusions.

In a poem such as the "Epistle to Miss Blount, on her leaving the Town, after the Coronation", the tone was lighter, even though life's vexations were here seen as afflicting both men and women, and irrespective of whether they found themselves in town or in the country. With glowing memories of the excitements of London during the coronation festivities, Zaphanalinda (Teresa) now went

> ... to plain-work, and to purling brooks,
> Old-fashion'd halls, dull aunts, and croaking rooks,
> She went from Op'ra, park, assembly, play,
> To morning walks, and pray'rs three hours a day;
> To pass her time 'twixt reading and Bohea,
> To muse, and spill her solitary Tea,
> Or o'er cold coffee trifle with the spoon,
> Count the slow clock, and dine exact at noon;
> Divert her eyes with pictures in the fire,
> Hum half a tune, tell stories to the squire;
> Up to her godly garret after sev'n,
> There starve and pray, for that's the way to heav'n.
>
> ("Epistle to Miss Blount, on her leaving the Town", ll. 11–22)

Such lines themselves were tenderly affectionate, of course. But what they, too, captured was a lack of meaningful tenderness in the world they describe, this time the correlative, not so much of social injustice, as of a gruelling, minute-by-minute, day-by-day boredom, here documented with a realistic precision we nowadays expect in novels, films and television. As was also very typical of Pope's poetry of feelings, differences were not scalar here, as in much of his Humanist poetry, but absolute. You were either in the town or in the country, and there was no half-way house. Ending, no less characteristically, with himself, Pope wrote that he was still in town; that he fantasized about being in the country with Zaphanalinda and Parthenia (Martha), just as Zaphanalinda still dreamed of being back in town; but that then

Gay pats my shoulder, and you vanish quite;
Streets, chairs, and coxcombs rush upon my sight;
Vext to be still in town, I knit my brow,
Look sow'r, and hum a tune – as you may now.   (ll. 47–50)

Like *Eloisa to Abelard*, the poem was about two different ways of being, which could not both be chosen at one and the same time. However playfully, the question Pope was raising again had to do with the quality of life as frankly experienced in the heart, and the jocular references to praying and fasting again encouraged readers to make whatever they would of the religious dimension. The poem was very unlikely to change anything, except by offering readers who had endured similar vexations an amusing form of self-recognition and community. That, though, was no mean gift.

Pope's best gift was of himself, when he opened his heart to his readers far more intimately than any of the poets usually thought of as Romantics, because more quietly, less fussily, more prosaically, more novelistically. To begin with some of the things which troubled him personally, he never so totally rejected Humanist stoicism as to feel sorry for himself in public. But he was no stranger to suffering, and had certainly been denied some tendernesses, sometimes, he could well have felt, at the hands of society as a whole. Although he did not complain, for a Catholic child to have deciphered that inscription on the Monument must have been an unnerving experience, and the deprivations he and his parents suffered for the sake of religion were also hurtful. One thing he did complain about, presumably because he had to bear it in common with members of any church or party, was the impositions of costly vanity. Compared with his own modest but genuine comforts in Twickenham, the style of living to be found in more stately residences could rub him up the wrong way. In *Epistle IV: To Richard Boyle, Earl of Burlington*, he has nothing against wealth *per se*, as long as it is wisely used. In the poem's magnificent climax he approvingly notes that vast sums of money have been spent on containing dangerous waters – as with his portrait of the Man of Ross in the *Epistle to Bathurst*, one imagines he would have admired the great civil engineering projects of the Victorians. What he does criticize is status symbols, and especially those which cause positive discomfort and unease. As he pinpoints the yawning gap between the ostentatious finery of Timon and the private irritations of Timon's guests, the poetry combines a journalistic sharpness with the intimacy of an encoded diary:

The rich Buffet well-colour'd Serpents grace,
And gaping Tritons spew to wash your face.
Is this a dinner? this a Genial room?
No, 'tis a Temple, and a Hecatomb.
A solemn Sacrifice, perform'd in state,
You drink by measure, and to minutes eat.

> So quick retires each flying course, you'd swear
> Sancho's dread Doctor and his Wand were there.
> Between each Act the trembling salvers ring,
> From soup to sweet-wine, and God bless the King.
> In plenty starving, tantaliz'd in state,
> And complaisantly help'd to all I hate,
> Treated, caress'd, and tir'd, I take my leave,
> Sick of his civil Pride from Morn to Eve;
> I curse such lavish cost, and little skill,
> And swear no Day was ever past so ill.   (*Epistle to Burlington*, ll. 153–168)

Writing like this would have prompted readers to generalize from his experience, inviting them to look into their own hearts, and to ask themselves just how much true satisfaction they were receiving from their current manner of living, whether consciously chosen or simply culturally determined. It could well seem that a social life totally lacking in sensitive tenderness between one human being and another was not really worth the living. But it is precisely at points like this that, in Pope's view, true tenderness of feeling was too much to hope for in the public sphere. To quote that letter again, there were simply too many "Forms, Complaisances, and amusements, which do not inwardly please me", too many affronts to "one's quiet, (the very Life of Life itself)" (Sherburn 1956: II 194). If and when tenderness did arise, it was simply more sequestered. Of course the *Epistle to Burlington is* satirical, and several powerful men did think they saw themselves in Timon. But above all, Pope was here offering an extraordinarily honest and personal response to what he had experienced, with which readers could compare notes. Once again, he was treating them as men and women of sensibility, or at least as credible aspirants to sensibility, and as people whose minds were open for discussion.

Even more generous with his own most private feelings were some of the imitations of Horace in which, while preserving Horace's low-keyed wryness of tone, and while anglicizing features of Horace's life-style on the Sabine farm, he also found striking parallels with his own family and domestic situation. This permitted him to adopt a confessional mode, albeit still under the dignified guise of imitation. Horace's neighbour Ofellus, whose words Pope adopts for his own voice, has been forced from his own lands and now rents from a landlord, just like Pope, who has lost his right to family property because of religion, and both Ofellus and Pope cheerfully accept their fate, Pope himself being also calmly resigned to bachelorhood and childlessness, finding so much to enjoy in a round of simple pleasures among his friends. The difference between Timon's dinner which is not a dinner and the fare on the Sabine farm as imitated in Twickenham could not be greater:

'Tis true, no Turbots dignify my boards,
But gudgeons, flounders, what my Thames affords.
To Hounslow-heath I point, and Bansted-down,
Thence comes your mutton, and these chicks my own:
From yon old wallnut-tree a show'r shall fall;
And grapes, long-lingring on my only wall,
And figs, from standard and espalier join:
The dev'l is in you if you cannot dine.

(*Imitations of Horace*: Sat. II ii, ll. 141–148)

The "Epistle to Dr. Arbuthnot" was still more revealing and, in the respect and tenderness with which it speaks of Pope's dead father, and in divulging Pope's experience of nursing his aged mother, anticipated the poetry of primary emotions in *Lyrical Ballads* even more directly than did the *Pastorals*. I not suggesting, as did the Preface to *Lyrical Ballads* and other exercises in Romantic historiography (Griffin 1995), that Wordsworth and Pope are in competition. But the fact is that Wordsworth, for whom the bonds between parents an children were such a major poetic theme, wrote hardly anything about it in the first-person singular. His mother died when he was seven, his father when he was thirteen, and they may never have been particularly close to him. If they had been, his feelings for Ann Tyson, his landlady and substitute mother when he attended school in Hawkshead, might have been weaker, and so, too, might have been his later need to conceptualize himself as a child brought up by Nature. Pope's approach to the theme, by contrast, was quietly direct and intimate. To the extent that the label retains any meaning at all, it is Wordsworth who was "eighteenth century" on this front, whereas Pope's filial tribute ends as follows:

Me, let the tender Office long engage
To rock the Cradle of reposing Age,
With lenient Arts extend a Mother's breath,
Make Languor smile, and smooth the Bed of Death,
Explore the Thought, explain the asking Eye,
And keep a while one Parent from the Sky!

(*Epistle to Dr. Arbuthnot*, ll. 408–413)

A poet of feelings indeed! The gentle, painstaking affection speaks for itself, and without the slightest gush. Even though he was himself such a major public figure, here he was offering a quiet glimpse of himself as finding meaning, happiness and inspiration in the most private of spheres. By writing with such intimacy of friends, family, the things of the heart, he was doing a very great deal to valorize the personal in the public mind, so bringing into being among his readers a whole community of sensitive individuals.

3.4   Sublimity

At the end of my Introduction I emphasized the inspirational value of ideals. Ideals which lose touch with reality can be very dangerous. Yet if we had no dream of a better world, and if we did not struggle to bring that better world into being, then the real world would get even worse.

Some ideals, however, are less likely than others to make lasting headway, and the Humanist ideal, though by no means short-lived, and though seminal to some of the world's greatest writing, painting, sculpture, architecture, and music so far, was in the long run trebly doomed. In the first place, there was the eighteenth century's steady valorization of feelings: the gradual accommodation with enthusiasm; the rise of a Methodism discontented with the rationalistic aridities of the Anglican Broad Church; and, more generally, the steady move towards Romanticism, with its associated kind of nervousness. Secondly, and quite regardless of whether we believe in the availability of redemption as promised within Christianity, Watts's "From all that dwell below the skies" was more realistic than Pope's "The Everlasting Prayer" in recognizing the limits of human self-improvement. Human beings, though sometimes independently a good deal nobler, it seems to me, than acknowledged in the dourer versions of Christianity, are simply not as perfectible as the Humanist ideal tended to propose. Thirdly, this was something which the Greek and Roman literature invoked by the Humanists as their very foundation itself made blatantly obvious. Try how they would, in Homer's Achilles, for example, there were traits on which Humanists simply could not build. As Steven Shankman has observed,

> George Chapman – Pope's daunting Renaissance predecessor in the field of Homeric translation – tried consistently to rationalize Achilles' wrath and to turn Achilles into an ideal Renaissance hero who, from the opening moment of the poem, is largely in control of his emotions. Achilles is no ideal hero in Book IX, however, when he commits a fatal mistake by not re-entering the battle at once in order to save his fellow Greeks from destruction. Odysseus, Phoenix, and Ajax arrive as an embassy to Achilles's tent and try to reason, but to no avail. Achilles is coming slowly around to reason, but he is not yet there. He is still obsessed with his passionate hatred of Agamemnon, even after Odysseus, on Agamemnon's behalf, makes a more than generous offer to compensate Achilles for the loss of his prize. In Chapman's version, Achilles explains to Ajax at length that, in order to teach Agamemnon a lesson about the art of kingship, he has consciously chosen to "loose the reines" of his anger.   (Shankman 2007:65)

Pope, though he tried to make Homer polite, in other ways clearly rejected the option of Humanist idealization. As Shankman continues, in Book IX of Pope's translation Achilles was far less restrained than in Chapman's. Pope's own comment on the passage was that Achilles owns that reason would induce him to a reconciliation, but his anger is too great to listen to reason. … Anger is nothing more like madness, than that madmen will talk sensibly enough upon any indifferent matter; but upon the mention of the subject that caused their disorder, they fly out into their usual extravagance.

And of an earlier description of Achilles' anger at Agamemnon Pope remarked:

His rage … is like a fire blown by a wind that sinks and rises by fits, but keeps continually burning, and blazes but the more for those intermissions.

(In Shankman 2007:66)

When Sir William Trumbull first mooted the idea of a translation of Homer, he had wanted Pope to render the ancient classic as "useful and instructive" to readers in their own time's England as it had once been to Horace (Mack 1985:350). But although Pope's Preface to his *Iliad* dutifully trotted out the Horatianism of "Pleasure and Profit join'd to make it valuable", that was that, and no more was said on the matter. Instead, the Preface can best be read as confirming that Homer positively undermined the Humanist ideal, and not only through the unreasonable behaviour of some of the characters in his story. Pope, like Longinus, of whose treatise *On the Sublime* Europe had become aware through Boileau's French translation of 1674, and on whom he himself had drawn in his *Essay on Criticism*, strongly felt that the greatest writing was itself irrational – ultimately inexplicable in terms of rules or qualities of judgement. In which connection, his Preface to the *Iliad* resorted to the very same metaphor as he used to suggest Achilles' anger, so establishing a literary hierarchy within which Virgil, for all his greatness, was less great than Homer by being cooler, more judicious, more controlled:

The Course of … [Homer's] verses resembles that of the Army he describes, … *They pour along like a Fire that sweeps the whole Earth before it.* … [T]his can over-power Criticism, and make us admire even while we dis-approve. Nay, where this appears, tho' attended with Absurdities, it brightens all the Rubbish about it, 'till we see nothing but its own Splendor. This *Fire* is discern'd in *Virgil*, but discern'd as through a Glass, reflected, and more shining than warm, but every where equal and constant … ; But in *Homer*, and in him only, it burns every where clearly, and every where irresistibly.   (Pope 1933 [1715]:146–147)

Towards the end of Pope's lengthy development of this contrast, the similarity between Homer and Achilles is actually made explicit:

When we behold their Battels, methinks the two Poets resemble the Heroes they celebrate: *Homer*, boundless and irresistible as *Achilles*, bears all before him, and shines more and more as the Tumult increases; *Virgil*, calmly daring like *Æneas*, appears undisturb'd in the midst of Action, disposes all about him, and conquers with Tranquillity.   (Pope 1933 [1715]:148)

Memories of these passages may have prompted Johnson, both in his claim that *An Essay on Man* suspended criticism and oppressed judgment through the overpowering pleasure it afforded, and in his extended description of Pope as, in effect, the Virgil to Dryden's Homer, a critical *tour de force* which culminated in Pope's own metaphor:

> If of Dryden's fire the blaze is brighter, of Pope's the heat is more regular and constant. Dryden often surpasses expectation, and Pope never falls below it. Dryden is read with frequent astonishment, and Pope with perpetual delight.
>
> (Johnson 1925 [1779–1781]: 215)

For what it is worth, my personal impression is that Johnson got this wrong, and not only because, as a patriotic Humanist, he wanted to portray his own England as a new Greece and Rome rolled into one. There was also what Hazlitt called the "periodical revolution of his [Johnson's] style" (Howe 1930–1934: IV, 177), or what W. K. Wimsatt described as his antithetical "habit of meaning", his cultivation of antithesis as an expressive form for its own sake (Wimsatt 1941: 44, 49), a mannerism which, ironically enough, doubtless reflected his profound admiration for Pope's balanced couplets. This, too, could have made him over-keen to re-apply the structure of assessment in Pope's Preface to *The Iliad* to Pope himself and Dryden, which in turn would have meant that the one great poet would have to be contrasted against the other, even in the face of substantially equal merits. Pope's poetry, it seems to me, does perpetually delight, but I think it sometimes blazes and astonishes as well. Estimates of sublime genius, however, of which the Preface's rankings of Lucan, Statius, Shakespeare and Milton provided further examples, are of their nature subjective, and my main concern is not to engage in delusive calibration, but to enlist Johnson as a contemporary witness to, at the very least, a heat and attractiveness in Pope which defied rationality.

In part, it was presumably Pope's sense of his own irrational potential which led him to gird up his Humanist nervousness: for instance, through those prose paraphrases of his longer poems; through that claim for the didactic power of *The Temple of Fame*'s fantastic allegory; and through publicly pledging that the verse-form of *An Essay on Man* could not lure him into a poeticality which would "sacrifice perspicuity to ornament" or "wander from the precision, or break the chain of reasoning". So keen was he for that poem's reasoning to be seen as firmly logical and orthodox that he even risked the consequences bound to flow from a public defence of it by Warburton. In Mack's unforgettable words, "[t]o be defended by Warburton was rather like being defended by a giant saurian, whose thrashing tail could inflict as much damage on the object defended as its savage muzzle on the assailants" (Mack 1985: 745). Interestingly enough, in beginning his "Epilogue to the Satires: Dialogue I" in partial imitation of Horace's Satire II iii, Pope put into the mouth of his imagined critic a complaint against his own writing that had no precedent in Damasippus's challenge to Horace: "You grow *correct* that once with Rapture writ" (l. 3). But to Humanist nervousness, rapture could only be a threat, because it was so contrary to the *media via* selected for admiration in Horace. If a volume of poetic raptures was smashed to shreds by the tail of a giant saurian, so much the better!

The chain of reasoning in *An Essay on Man* not only argued for the traditional idea of a chain of Being, but in one of its main climaxes conceived of this as the previously mentioned chain of Love in the universe as a whole. Perhaps this is not the first claim one would expect from a work with this particular poem's title, and the opening apostrophe to St. John, its dedicatee, had certainly promised to "[e]xpatiate free o'er all this scene of *Man*" (I, l. 5, my italics). But Pope clearly felt a need to explain man's place in the larger context, and just as his preliminary note had a relationship with Milton's note on "The Verse", so in the poem's sixteenth line he aspires to "vindicate the ways of God to Man", an unmistakable echo of Milton's aim as stated in the twenty-fifth line of *Paradise Lost*: to "justify the ways of God to men". Nor was he unimpressed by Milton's sublime fire. According to his Preface to the *Iliad*, "it glows like a Furnace kept up to an uncommon Fierceness by the Force of Art" (Pope 1933 [1715]: 147). Yet I have already noted the difference between the higher being of his own public statements and the God of Christianity, and he could also make delightful fun of Milton for his literalness in matters metaphysical. When the Peer attacks Belinda's lock of hair with the scissors, one detail parodies the heavenly battle of Milton's good and bad angels, in which Satan's "ethereal substance", having been pierced by Michael's "griding sword", "closed / Not long divisible" (*Paradise Lost*, VI, ll. 329–220):

> A wretched *Sylph* too fondly interpos'd;
> Fate urg'd the Sheers, and cut the *Sylph* in twain,
> (But Airy Substance soon unites again).   (*Rape of the Lock*, III, ll. 150–150)

In *An Essay on Man* there is accordingly no narrative of fall and redemption, and no peeping into whatever may lie beyond human ken. Instead, the mode is one of philosophical argumentation, adducing only attestable points of reference, including some of the physical phenomena dealt with in modern science, such as the force of gravity in Newton:

> Look round our World; behold the chain of Love
> Combining all below and all above.
> See plastic Nature working to this end,
> The single atoms each to other tend,
> Attract, attracted to, the next in place
> Forc'd and impell'd its neighbour to embrace.
> See Matter next, with various life endu'd,
> Press to one centre still, the gen'ral Good.
> See dying Vegetables life sustain,
> See life dissolving vegetate again:
> All forms that perish other forms supply,

(By turns we catch the vital breath, and die)
Like bubbles on the sea of Matter born,
They rise, they break, and to that sea return.
Nothing is foreign: Parts relate to whole;
One all-extending all-preserving Soul
Connects each being, greatest with the least;
Made Beast in aid of Man, and Man of beast;
All serv'd, all serving! nothing stands alone;
The chain holds on, and where it ends, unknown.   (*Essay on Man*, III, ll. 7–26)

At first glance this could never be mistaken for "Tintern Abbey", a poem which my next study here will praise for its communicational genuineness. Pope's imperatives seem to boss us around. His writing apparently tells us what to think and what to think about, and instead of merely presenting descriptions of the world or religio-philosophical ideas as arising from the personal experience of the poet, it seems to be asserting them as indisputable facts and general truths. Nor is that all. As Pope foretold in the preliminary note, the work's principles, maxims and precepts become even more forceful and memorable because of the couplet form. When he uses his characteristic weighting of line against line or half-line against half-line as a way of emphasizing figures of chiasmus or antithesis, the appearance of didacticism can feel rather overbearing:

Made Beast in aid of Man, and Man of beast.

On the other hand, Wordsworth, too, though in his best poetry not wishing to *preach* his philosophy, would have been pleased enough to meet with agreement, and there is actually a strong similarity between his and Coleridge's sense of "one life in all" and Pope's main idea in the lines just quoted. In addition, there is a fairly obvious continuity from Wordsworth's plan for *The Recluse* to explore "the creation (by no lower name / Can it be called)" which arises from the "blended might" of the "external World" and "Mind" (*Prospectus to* The Recluse, ll. 63–71),[11] back through this passage in *An Essay on Man* to the creation narrative in Book VII of *Paradise Lost*.

Nor, despite appearances, are Pope's couplets necessarily "too self-contained to invite dialogue or argument", as John Sitter puts it. Impressions of their tight closure can actually be somewhat qualified as we become aware of the larger structures – verse paragraphs and entire poems – within which they work, structures which, as Sitter continues, "do invite active engagement and response" (Sitter 2007: 45). In point of fact, this particular passage has a lower proportion of typically "Popeian" couplets than the satires, and its verse, rather than constantly pausing to underline judiciously weighed assessments, does flow, and does fall easily into three verse paragraphs (beginning "Look", "See Matter next", and "Nothing is foreign").

---

11. Quotations of Wordsworth taken from de Selincourt and Darbishire 1952–1959.

Even more to the point, over and above the aphoristic vigour promised by Pope's introductory note, a verse norm involving end-stopped lines and rhymed couplets offered opportunities which in both Miltonic and Wordsworthian blank verse were quite unavailable. Once again, I am not suggesting there is any competition. Wordsworth's lines seem likely to win praise for a very long time to come:

> And I have felt
> A presence that disturbs me with the joy
> Of elevated thoughts: a sense sublime
> Of something far more deeply interfused,
> Whose dwelling is the light of setting suns,
> And the round ocean and the living air,
> And the blue sky, and in the mind of man:
> A motion and a spirit that impels
> All thinking things, all objects of all thought,
> And rolls through all things.   ("Tintern Abbey", ll. 93–104)

The power of this stems partly from the way in which the enjambements, registering as such because many lines are still end-stopped, enact the impelling motion of the interfused "something" as it overcomes all barriers. In Pope, however, precisely because enjambements are so much *more* rare, and because they are quite *exceptionally* rare between the second line of one couplet and the first line of the next, the similar philosophical idea, when processed by a reader within the norm-setting passage as a whole, acquires a quite extraordinary force. The universal soul even connects one couplet with another!

> One all-extending all-preserving Soul
> Connects each being, greatest with the least.

Wordsworth's emotional sign-posting – "disturbs", "joy", "elevated", and (just in case we had still not registered the elevation, or he himself were in danger of sinking) "sublime" – can seem almost crude by comparison, and there is surely a sense in which Pope was right after all:

> My Head and Heart thus flowing thro' my Quill,
> Verse-man or Prose-man, term me which you will.
> (*Imitations of Horace*: Sat. II i, ll. 63–64)

His apparently prosaic, apparently rationalistic, apparently didactic manner admits an un-self-advertising sublimity for which the only precondition is the reader's own cooperatively sensitive attention to the verse.

At the end of the passage this takes a further, paradoxical turn, when the form of the self-contained and aphoristically assertive couplet is used, after eighteen lines of ostensible didacticism, to confess to an area of complete ignorance:

> All serv'd, all serving! nothing stands alone;
> The chain holds on, and where it ends, unknown.

In the larger context of the passage as a whole, that last word, underlined by the rhyme, is quietly but totally strange, and John Sitter, though adducing other, complementary features, arrives at what is surely the only possible assessment here: that the chain of reasoning which culminates with the chain of Love being beyond human imagination "rests less on sight than on something approaching mystical vision" (Sitter 2007: 48). In the terms I was proposing in my Introduction, what we have here is a coercive impulse in synergy with an apophatic. Or in the parallel terms of this present study, the Humanist nervousness of reasoning is in synergy with the post-Humanist nervousness of heightened sensitivity. The higher being's ultimate unknowability comes with the stealthy force of what we now call nervous shock, the effect again depending on a collaborative nervousness in the reader currently processing the words and versification. At points like this, the poetry is not simply telling readers what to think, but is inviting them into a community of the sensitive, who might well have independent intuitions of their own.

The chain of Love, though so carefully reasoned for in this passage, *is* a chain of Love, and not merely of Being, so encouraging sentiments towards it which are that much warmer. At its higher end it is totally incomprehensible but, in view of hopeful signs at the lower end, without being frightening. As an ambience within which human beings are to live their lives, this was already less stark, more conducive to pleasure, than the one presupposed by Pope's Humanist predecessors. It was almost as if Adam and Eve and their descendants had been allowed to stay on in the Garden of Eden after the Fall, and had continued to enjoy the delights so wonderfully described by Milton. For Milton, the reality of postlapsarian life was one of constant confrontations between willpower and temptation, and the temptations to which Adam and Eve succumbed while still in Eden were a foretaste, in that the only means of resistance was through the exercise of rational virtue. In Book II of *The Faerie Queene*, where Sir Guyon championed Aristotelian temperance, the outlook had already been basically similar, and Dryden was still appealing to the same ethical framework when he embodied the excesses of the first Earl of Shaftesbury in Achitophel:

> A daring pilot in extremity;
> Pleased with the danger, when the waves went high
> He sought the storms; but for a calm unfit,
> Would steer too nigh the sands, to boast his wit.
>
> (*Absolom and Achitophel*, ll. 159–162)[12]

---

12. Quotations of Dryden taken from Conaghan 1978.

Very pointedly – one sees where Pope learned the effect of running on couplet to couplet – Achitophel did not represent the Humanists' moral self-discipline and prudent
media via. Yet Dryden was himself so fascinated that the same character sketch also
anticipated Pope's sublime fire metaphor, in lines which explode even more gloriously
out of the couplet's confinement, into an iconic triplet:

> A fiery soul, which, working out its way,
> Fretted the pigmy body to decay,
> And o'erinformed the tenement of clay.   (ll. 156–158)

Many readers, quite against the grain of Milton's effort to justify the ways of God
to men, have felt that his Adam and Eve would have been mad not to yield to their
temptations, and have said, like Blake and Shelley, Waldock (1947) and Empson
(1961) in the era of Romantic nervousness, that his Satan is sublimely magnificent,
or that the Bower of Bliss into which Acrasia invites Spenser's Sir Guyon is genuinely delightful. For the Humanist argument to work, the temptations did have to feel
real: real for the characters in the story, real for the readers, real for the author – the
reason why Milton did not believe in censorship was that he could not praise "a fu-
gitive and cloister'd virtue, unexercis'd and unbreath'd, that never sallies out and sees
her adversary" (Milton 1644:12). But truly tempting temptations were not without
risk to the Humanist project, and efforts such as those of that gloomy old superego
the Palmer, Guyon's tutor, to keep him and the poem's readers on the straight and
narrow could hardly solve the problem. The plain fact was that Horace's prudent
advice in Epistle I vi, "*Nil admirari prope est una ... / solaque quae possit facere et
servere beatum*", imitated by Pope as

> "Not to Admire, is all the Art I know,
> To make men happy, and to keep them so",
>
> (*Imitations of Horace*: Ep. I vi, ll. 1–2)

was very contemptuous of riches, gluttony, and so forth, but without offering an alternative motivation that was really inspiring. Human beings do like to have feelings
of wonder and enjoyment, and more generally do appreciate a freedom to have feelings in the first place, and to act upon them. In his Horatian poems, I have argued,
Pope insisted on the virtue of self-control even more emphatically than did his great
predecessors. But even better than they, he also knew how basically unattractive, how
crampingly unsublime, such a regime could feel. This, after all, was the great drawback of a Humanist education as satirized in *The Dunciad*, where Bentley boasted that
he and his fellow-dons could "petrify a Genius to a Dunce":

> With the same Cement, ever sure to bind,
> We bring to one dead level ev'ry mind.
>
> (*The Dunciad in Four Books*, IV, ll. 267–268)

In some parts of *An Essay on Man*, as also in "The Universal Prayer" associated with it, Pope seemed to believe in a benevolent creator of a benevolent universe and, while not forgetting that a chain is of course a chain, to think that man, as a link in a chain of *Love*, could perhaps hope for lenience, and even afford to be lenient towards himself. In contradiction to "Elegy to the Memory of an Unfortunate Lady", the implication was apparently that man, too, could be relied on to be naturally benevolent, and that a freedom from external restraint would entail no risks for either individuals or society as a whole.

In the early eighteenth century this un-Wattsian, un-Christian assumption was defended by two main arguments. One was the die-hard Humanist claim, so central for Pope, that man is naturally capable of virtuous conduct thanks to his powers of reasoning. The other was the claim that we have an innate moral sense which makes us naturally love virtue and hate vice, an argument eloquently expounded in *An Inquiry Concerning Virtue, Or Merit*, published the third Earl of Shaftesbury (grandson of the Shaftesbury satirized by Dryden) in 1699, an important contribution to post-Humanist nervousness – to the culture of sentiment as opposed to reason – and clearly invoked in *An Essay on Man*:

> Vice is a monster of so frightful mien,
> As, to be hated, needs but to be seen.   (*An Essay on Man*, II, ll. 217–218)

Both arguments also had a larger dimension, in that they not only suggested grounds for human conduct, but represented different attitudes to joy and sorrow. For the Humanists, joy tended to be the reward of self-discipline, sorrow the result of weak character. With the aid of reason, life's natural griefs could be stoically endured. For a Shafestesburian, decorous politeness could still be very important, but all kinds of emotions were on a freer rein. Happiness and sadness were both to be expressed and shared, a sharing which could heighten joy and perhaps alleviate sorrow. To the extent that Pope's poetry was appealing to the Humanist mindset, he was inviting readers to take their place in the ranks of the rationally virtuous, with their nervousness, in the older sense of nervousness, duly braced. To the extent that it appealed to Shaftesburian assumptions, he was inviting them to join a circle of the emotionally cultivated and tender-hearted, who would draw on the new, sensitive kind of nervousness.

In fact, however, and despite the at times optimistic note of *An Essay on Man*, he often wrote about the inadequacy of both the Humanist and Shaftesburian philosophies, neither of which really accounted for what actually happened in life. People did not seem to be able to control themselves. Nor was there much evidence that they could be virtuous spontaneously. For all we know, in his private devotions as a Catholic he may have accepted sin as an undeniable fact and, like Watts after all, pinned his hope on Christ's redemption. Even in his publications, he clearly showed the influence of Pascal. But Pascal's method of shooting off both Sceptical and Stoical arguments as a way of confusing himself or his readers into faith has left many readers at the stage of mere confusion, and the optimistic Deism of Pope's public statements is often outbalanced by a sense of disappointment and surprise. Ian Jack caught this, when he said that Pope's greatest poetry "is as sombre as that of Dante ... . Sainte-Beuve said of Molière, 'il a au cœur la tristessse' : the same words might form the epitaph of Pope" (Jack 1954: 27). Communicationally speaking, the net result might seem to be utterly disorienting. Or rather, the effect might apparently be to invite readers into a *community* of the utterly disoriented, for whom certainties have fallen away and nothing taken their place, and who simply try to muddle along as best they can, trusting and distrusting both head and heart.

But muddling along as best one can does not feel true to the spirit of what Pope offers, just as the sadness of Molière cannot eclipse his sheer *brio*. Jack was suggestive again, I think, when he commented:

> Hazlitt was right when on reading *The Rape of the Lock* he did not know whether to laugh or cry. Pope often reminds one of Mozart: there is in his work the same depth of emotion, perfectly restrained by the strict patterning of art:
>
> > ...since Life can little more supply
> > Than just to look about us and to die.   (Jack 1954: 27)

More exactly, this was suggestive as long as one remembers not only the Symphony no. 40 in G-minor but also *The Magic Flute*.

Here, in fact, is where Pope was closest in spirit to Dryden, who was at once so appalled and so dazzled by the first Earl of Shaftesbury's foolhardiness that in Achitophel he rendered it sublime. The collapse of reason was profoundly disturbing, but was also a heady stimulus to the imagination. Through sheer hyperbole, through a reduction of irrationalities to an awe-inspiring ludicrousness, Pope offered wonderful entertainment to readers comfortably astride an ethical high horse and, to readers who felt themselves hit, a playful challenge they were far more likely to remember than a mere plodding reprimand.

It was all very well for *An Essay on Man* to advise

> Know then thyself, presume not God to scan;
> The proper study of Mankind is Man.   (*Essay on Man* II, l. 1–2)

But in the continuation of this same passage, it emerged that the human end of the chain of Love was not really all that much more knowable than the divine end. Man was

> Plac'd on this isthmus of a middle state,
> A being darkly wise, and rudely great:
> With too much knowledge for the Sceptic side,
> With too much weakness for the Stoic's pride,
> He hangs between; in doubt to act, or rest,
> In doubt to deem himself a God, or Beast;

> In doubt his Mind or Body to prefer,
> Born but to die, and reas'ning but to err;
> Alike in ignorance, his reason such,
> Whether he thinks too little, or too much:
> Chaos of Thought and Passion, all confus'd;
> Still by himself abus'd, or disabus'd;
> Created half to rise, and half to fall;
> Great lord of all things, yet a prey to all;
> Sole judge of Truth, in endless Error hurl'd:
> The glory, jest, and riddle of the world!   (*Essay on Man* II, 3–18)

At first the epigrammatical zest of these well-known couplets may deafen us to Pope's negatively capable willingness to live in uncertainties, mysteries, doubts, without any irritable reaching after fact and reason. The couplets sound so certain: so undoubting, reasonable, knowing. Yet if we ask what they are so certain *about*, it is man's doubts, man's irrationality, man's ignorance. Man's sheer erroneousness is highlighted by the epigrams as something utterly wonderful and astonishing. Man, by being no less unreasonable than the higher being is *beyond* reason, has become equally sublime.

Here and in many other places, Pope was inviting any member of the human race who happened to be reading him to a veritable carnival of non-reason, which from now on, however, could no longer be expected to come to an end through reason's re-instatement, because of the particular historical watershed at which he was writing. Looking back, this passage was not without all precedent. The allusion to Pascal's method of playing off Stoic against Sceptic will be clear enough, and many of Pope's first readers would have remembered similar lines of thought in Erasmus, Montaigne, *Hamlet*, and Fulke Greville, whose couplets of 1609 can at first seem a truly remarkable anticipation:

> Vainly begot and yet forbidden vanity;
> Created sick, commanded to be sound.
> What meaneth nature by these divers laws?
> Passion and reason, self-division cause.
> ("Chorus Sacerdotum" from *Mustapha*, ll. 3–6)[13]

On the other hand, while Pope noted such predecessors for their clear-headed reasonableness about man's unreasonableness, and for the qualification they thereby offered to the Humanist ideal they otherwise so warmly embraced, by his own time English culture and society had lived with man's self-contradictoriness for over a century longer, and the rational side of human nature, though ostensibly taken to an extreme form

---

13. Quotation of Greville taken from Bullough 1939.

in the Augustans' own self-image, no longer seemed so resilient. Greville's note had been one of puzzlement and trouble – "O wearisome condition of Humanity!" (l. 1). It was as if, to him, the struggle between passion and reason seemed likely to drag on indefinitely. Pope, in this famous passage, and in much of his other most memorable writing, was overcoming his terror at passion's now indisputable triumph. He was presenting – celebrating, almost – irrationality as the major fact of life, and welcoming readers into a grouping which would react to this as buoyantly as possible.

Sometimes his psychologizing here was indeed less than negatively capable. In places he certainly did reach after fact and reason, and a more forceful attempt to impose order than his notion of the ruling passion, propounded in both *An Essay on Man* and several other places as well, would be difficult to imagine. One statement of it is in *Epistle I: To Richard Temple, Viscount Cobham*:

> Search then the Ruling Passion: There alone,
> The Wild are constant, and the Cunning known;
> The Fool consistent, and the False sincere;
> Priests, Princes, Women, no dissemblers here.
> This clue, once found, unravels all the rest. (*Epistle to Cobham*, ll. 174–178)

And a main difference between this and a Jonsonian humour or a Shandean hobby-horse is that, although Jonson and Sterne wisely grounded their characters in contemporary medical and psychological theory, their basic aim was to produce comedy, whereas Pope was not in the first place looking for comic effect but trying to recommend a framework for understanding. The closeness to comedy very much threatened the didactic goal, however, predisposing readers to expect, and Pope himself to come up with, oversimplifications.

On the whole, though, his suggestion was not only that human beings are so irrational as to be guided by a ruling passion, but that even the guidance of a ruling passion can be hard to see. Quite simply, man is radically inconsistent, so that self-knowledge, let alone knowledge of others, is a lost cause. Again in the *Epistle to Cobham*, he wrote:

> Oft in the Passions' wild rotation tost,
> Our spring of action to ourselves is lost:
> Tir'd, not determin'd, to the last we yield,
> And what comes then is master of the field.
> As the last image of that trouble heap,
> When Sense subsides, and Fancy sports in sleep,
> (Tho' past the recollection of the thought)
> Becomes the stuff of which our dream is wrought:
> Something as dim to our internal view,
> Is thus, perhaps, the cause of most we do. (*Epistle to Cobham*, ll. 41–50)

As we have seen, a further complication was that, even at their most intelligible, half the human race in any case had not just one ruling passion but two. And human nature, whether by being completely chaotic or by being completely channelled in a ruling passion (or two), was always quite irrational enough to make for sublimity. Although the Humanistic ideal was on the point of total collapse, the cultural memory of it still provided a criterion by which to suggest the awesome and entertaining strangeness to which readers now needed to adapt themselves in society as a whole. The greatest portraits – Wharton (*Epistle to Cobham*, ll. 180–207), Attossa and Chloe (*Epistle to a Lady*, ll. 115–150, 157–180), Atticus and Sporus (*Epistle to Dr. Arbuthnot*, ll. 193–214, 305–333) – are all instances of a satirical sublime which, far from attempting to whip readers and the satire's butts into to the paths of reason and virtue, encourages, in readers of any colour, a rumbustious acclimatization to the way of the world in all its scary, entertaining oddity. This, as the most practical first step, for the individual reader and society as a whole, towards survival.

Nor would this work nearly so well without an element of self-projection in the writing. Pope is at least as irrational as anybody else, and knows it. He constantly confesses to this in his more serious poems, where it can partly be seen as a rhetorical ploy to forestall satire of the satirist. But something akin to the irrational sublime of the great portraits is also to be felt in the delightful self-description in "A Farewell to London: In the Year 1715" (not published until 1775), a little piece which Mack (1985:286) aptly described as a "rollicking tavern poem":

> Why make I Friendships with the Great,
> When I no favour seek?
> Or follow Girls Seven Hours in Eight? –
> I need but once a Week.
>
> Still idle, with a busy Air,
> Deep Whimsies to contrive;
> The gayest Valetudinaire,
> Most thinking Rake alive.
>
> Solicitous for others Ends,
> Tho' fond of dear Repose;
> Careless or drowsy with my Friends,
> And frolick with my Foes.　　　　　　　　　("A Farewell to London", ll. 29–44)

Sometimes he mentions the possibility that his satire may be an attempt to wreak vengeance on his enemies. In places he admits the scope for George Rousseau's kind of readings, which see the animus in the writing as stemming from a bitterness at his own handicaps. But as I say, he is on the whole far nobler than that, and he is also more honest. In describing the self-destructive chaos of Attossa's life and psyche he does not distance himself from her, but readily empathizes with the inner feel of it, seeing her life not only as it seems to others but also as, in moments of truth, it must seem to Attossa herself –

> Strange! by the Means defeated of the Ends,
> By Spirit robb'd of Pow'r, by Warmth of Friends,
> By Wealth of Follow'rs! without one distress
> Sick of herself thro' very selfishness!   (*Epistle to a Lady*, ll. 143–146)

Wharton's fatal love of excessive praise, similarly, could not fail to strike a chord with a poet so concerned for his own fame, a biographical detail which is supererogatory here, however, since the writing again itself conveys an inwardness of knowledge. Chloe's burning resentment, and the jealousy of Sporus, physically an object of contempt, socially both an insider and an outsider, were if anything still nearer the bone for Pope, and if he vehemently wanted to avoid becoming even more like them, this can only have intensified the writing's venom. As for Atticus, by general consent the most magnificent portrait of all, Mack (1985:280) notes that it not only describes Addison but imitates him. The entire passage, in accusing Addison, who is apparently so true to a judicious *media via*, of damning with faint praise, damns Addison himself by that very method, and for motives no less opaque to the eye of reason than Addison's own.

In satire of this order Pope's own irrationality itself became sublime, most conspicuously when he wrote more as an outsider to the vice, corruption and greed of those at the centre of power. Here he sounded correspondingly less Horatian, coming closer to the *saeva indignatio* of Juvenal or Persius. The awe-inspiring animosity of the writing drew no less attention to itself than to the degeneracy it lambasted, and Pope himself parodied what was likely to be the most common complaint against it:

> But *Horace*, Sir, was delicate, was nice;
> *Bubo* observes, he lash'd no sort of *Vice*.
>   (*Epilogue to the Satires: Dialogue I*, ll. 11–12)

His self-righteousness could be truly extraordinary:

> Yes, I am proud; I must be proud to see
> Men not afraid of God, afraid of me:
> Safe from the Bar, the Pulpit, and the Throne,
> Yet touch'd and sham'd by *Ridicule* alone.
>   (*Epilogue to the Satires: Dialogue II*, ll. 208–211)

A passage like this shows just how willing he sometimes was to throw the Almighty's bolts and deal damnation round the land, just how reluctant to hide the fault he saw and show some mercy. Here the good citizen of "The Universal Prayer" was achieving sublimity by mutating into a forerunner of the highly strung Childe Harold. The prudent Horatian who advised against too great a zeal for virtue, was now a saint run

gloriously mad, blasphemously proud of being more feared than God. This had little
to do with an invalid's attempt to get his own back on the healthy. Above all it really
was human pride, such as we all can muster, and his diatribes were the more sublime
for the clear hints that they could at any moment descend to the ridiculous, though in
a way they were ridiculous already. Pride of this order can only herald a shocking fall,
as Pope well knew. At the close of this same poem, his friend was allowed to recommend that he calm himself. Why not "write next winter more *Essays on Man*"?

So much for portraits and self-portraits. In narrative verse, irrationalities found
additional paths to sublimity. In *The Rape of the Lock*, there was the response of the
other characters to Clarissa's warmly sensible advice:

> Beauties in vain their pretty Eyes may roll;
> Charms strike the Sight, but Merit wins the Soul.
>   So spoke the Dame, but no Applause ensu'd;
> *Belinda* frown'd, *Thalestris* call'd her Prude.
> To Arms, to Arms! the fierce Virago cries,
> And swift as Lightning to the Combate flies.
> All side in Parties, and begin th'Attack;
> Fans clap, Silks russle, and tough Whalebones crack;
> Heroes' and Heroins' Shouts confus'dly rise,
> And base, and treble Voices strike the Skies,
> No common Weapons in their Hands are found,
> Like Gods they fight, nor dread a mortal Wound.
>
> (*Rape of the Lock*, V ll. 33–44)

The human defiance of reason could not be more sharply dramatized or, as the mock-
heroic scrum continues for several pages, with more playful sublimity, until in the
poem's final lines – that position in a poem which he so habitually used for maximum
impact – the spectacular overthrow of Humanist dignity and sense is marked in a very
particular way. With Belinda's missing lock now a new constellation in the night sky,
Pope addresses her directly:

> Then cease, bright Nymph! to mourn thy ravish'd Hair
> Which adds new Glory to the shining Sphere!
> Not all the Tresses that fair head can boast
> Shall draw such Envy as the Lock you lost.
> For, after all the Murders of your Eye,
> When, after Millions slain, your self shall die;
> When those fair Suns shall sett, and sett they must,
> And all those Tresses shall be laid in Dust;
> *This Lock*, the Muse shall consecrate to Fame,
> And mid'st the Stars inscribe *Belinda*'s name.
>
> (V, ll. 141–150)

Despite all the mock-heroic claims for Belinda's fatal charms, the grave, which Pope's charmed gallantry so often, but not always, failed to mention, will be her own ultimate resting place. And what then? As we have seen, a Humanist poet's answer was often self-referential here. "My lines, in trumpeting your fame, will be co-eternal with it." But as Arabella Fermor and any other reader would be well aware, Belinda could only be remembered, if at all, for her "little unguarded Follies", for rejecting sensible self-control. Yes, the poem had made this the cue to a dazzling feat of artistic imagination, which posterity would be insane not to love and admire. But was it not the poetry itself that they would take to their hearts here, rather than the poetry's historical only begetter? Whether the reference in the penultimate line was to Belinda's lock or Pope's own *Rape of the Lock* he was perhaps still too gallant to clarify. But by making her irrationality sublime, the poem itself did certainly become a more sublime ado about nothing than could ever have been expected.

Pope had a sense of proportion. The *little* in "little unguarded Follies" was gallant, but without, he might have said, being inaccurate, and in *The Rape of the Lock* reason's conquerors were accordingly sublime, not by terrifying, but in the quite staggering inventiveness of their petty priorities. *The Dunciad* also rendered irrationality sublime, and thereby also became sublime itself. But here the irrationality was on a stupendous scale and, more in accordance with the observations of Longinus, the poem's dazzling sublimity connoted genuine fear, plus not a little of Pope's deepest sadness. As the "secret might" of Dulness steadily spreads,

> *Art* after *Art* goes out, and all is Night.
> See skulking *Truth* to her old Cavern fled,
> Mountains of Casuistry heap'd o'er her head!
> *Philosophy*, that lean'd on Heav'n before,
> Shrinks to her second cause and is no more.
> *Physic* of *Metaphysic* begs defence,
> And *Metaphysic* calls for aid on *Sense!*
> See *Mystery* to *Mathematics* fly!
> In vain! they gaze, turn giddy, rave, and die.
> *Religion* blushing veils her sacred fires,
> And unawares *Morality* expires.
> Nor *public* Fame, nor *private*, dares to shine;
> No *human* Spark is left, nor Glimpse *divine*.
>
> (*The Dunciad in Four Books*, IV, ll. 640–652)

This, from the poem's climactic vision of the final return of universal Darkness and primaeval Chaos, is comparable to some of the finest cartoons of Gerald Scarfe: at once hugely enjoyable as an imaginative invention, and terrifyingly portentous as an intelligent mind's assessment of the world's current direction. With the Humanist valorization of reason breaking down; with the older, civilizing nervousness giving way to the newer nervousness of free-for-all spontaneities, whose consequences for social cohesion could be negative; with the upper classes and the country's entire world of letters succumbing to shallow vulgarity, mindless vanity and greed: under such circumstances, all fully present in the poem's concretizations, Pope's mock-heroic *sprezzatura* was paradoxically channelling a genuine horror at Humanism's final demise.

F. R. Leavis's account of Pope *lacked* proportion, it seems to me, but was not completely misguided. In *The Dunciad* he found "Augustan sublimities", by which I think he meant sublimities arising from threats to Augustanism, rather as I am speaking of sublimities arising from a defiance of reason. He also made a further, crucial observation:

> [W]e don't, for the most part feel the total effect [of *The Dunciad*] to be negative, expressing a hostile and destructive will. The force of this judgment comes out when we look by way of comparison at Swift. The final impression that Swift, in any representative place, leaves us with is one of having been exposed to an intense, unremitting and endlessly resourceful play of contempt, disgust, hatred and the will to spoil and destroy. The contrast brings home to us the sense in which Pope, in practising his art of verse, in engaged, whatever his materials, in positive creation.   (Leavis 1962 [1952]a: 89)

Pope would have felt this was unfair to his friend. Here, though, I commend it for what it says about Pope himself. Leavis's intuition seems to be similar to my own sense of the sublimity's entertainment value and relative gentleness as a reprimand. What Leavis completely failed to recognize, however, was that the phenomenon immortal-ized by this poem's sublimity was of such a different order from that which promoted sublimity in *The Rape of the Lock*, and that Pope, while treating it in a positive and entertaining manner, was also shocked and terrified. Leavis spoke of the poem's pre-dominant feeling as genial, which in a way it is, and of a predominance of creativeness which delights "in the rich strangeness of what it contemplates", which is also true as far as it goes. But by the time he remarked that

> there is nothing repressive about the Order that commands his [Pope's] imagina-tion. His sense of wonder has been richly and happily nourished, and can invest what offers itself as satiric fantasy with the enchantment of fairy-tale.
> (Leavis 1962 [1952]a: 96)

his unqualified beatification was seriously misleading. Agreed, in *The Dunciad* there was nothing repressive about Augustan Order. But that was because Augustan Order was completely breaking down, both in society as a whole and in the mind of Pope himself, its sometimes reluctant champion, who knew he could never reconstruct it. Within the establishment sphere of high culture, its place was now being usurped by all the extraordinary irrationalities which he was making so amusingly, but also so awesomely sublime. Leavis's terminology – "fantasy", "enchantment of fairy-tale" – was far too anodyne, and surprisingly close to that Bloomsburian "cult of the *dix-huitème*" which he so despised (Leavis 1964 [1936]b: 62). He simply did not catch the frisson, the excitement, the very grave danger.

Why, then, my concern with Leavis's comments of sixty years ago, especially if they have this blind spot? My hunch is that to ponder Leavis's blind spot can help us clinch the significance of Pope's two-fold nervousness for us today. Here, though, Leavis himself must be placed in his context.

His commentaries on Pope were of a piece with his pamphlet *Mass Civilization and Minority Culture* of 1930 and his book *Education and the University: A Sketch for an "English School"*, first published in 1943. Here he linked the plight of minority culture within mass civilization to "the decay of the Common Reader [*sic*]". This Common Reader he described as a reader on whom Johnson had been able to rely: a competent, cultivated reader, whose good taste involved the "more-than-individual judgement" of "a homogeneous culture" (Leavis 1948 [1943]: 106–107). In *Revaluation's* chapter on Pope, he further specified that the homogeneous culture was based on

> the ideal (generally shared and not hopelessly removed from the actual) of a civilization in which Art and Nature, Beauty and Use, Industry and Decorum, should be reconciled, and human culture, even in its most refined forms, be kept appropriately aware of its derivation from and dependence on the culture of the soil.

Quoting from the *Epistle to Burlington* (ll. 170–180),

> 'Tis Use alone that sanctifies Expence,
> And Splendor borrows all her rays from Sense,

Leavis continued:

> Pope was at one with a society to which these were obvious but important truths. So supported, he could sustain a formal dignity such as, pretended to, would make a modern ridiculous. "Use" represents robust moral certitudes sufficiently endorsed by the way of the world, and "Sense" was a light clear and unquestionable as the sun.   (Leavis 1964 [1936]b: 71–72)

Not to mince words, this was myth-making. Leavis was very sensitive to some of the dimensions of Pope I have covered in describing him as a Humanist, and as a self-rooting insider to the polite *beau-monde*. But he apparently did not see, or did not want to see, just how small that subsection of eighteenth century English society really was, or just how uncommon the so-called Common Reader was in a country where most people could still not read. Given which, his failure to sense the precariousness of what he calls Augustan Order, or to see Pope's personal sense of this in face of his own outsider-like doubts and the surrounding deluge of mindless, rapacious vulgarity, is perhaps less surprising.

As for the need which generated Leavis's myth, it was, I believe, a mixture of nostalgia and idealism at a particular moment of English history. By the early twentieth century it was gradually becoming possible to speak of universal literacy. Modernist writers and Modernist literary critics responded by closing ranks and becoming more elitist or, to speak more generously, by encouraging first- and second-generation readers to aim very high (Sell 2001: 1–13). Leavis, certainly concerned with standards, found it inspiring to look back to what he liked to see as a golden age in which society was united in shared tastes and values, a community which he could then try to re-invent through his own crusade as a critic and educator. Here again, then, we are speaking of an idealistic dream, and in fact of an oddly belated continuation of the Humanist dream itself. Leavis saw Pope as a critical intelligence enjoying a centrality within a homogeneous community, the kind of position to which he himself aspired, for instance when proposing English studies, his own field, as the queen of university disciplines (Leavis 1948 [1943]). This prevented him from seeing, not only that the problem of minority culture within mass civilization was one with which Pope was already wrestling in *The Dunciad*, but that, as the twentieth century rolled on, the civic virtues of Humanist nervousness could only be relegated every more firmly to the past.

By the time of Leavis's death, the postmodern politics of recognition was, as I say, carrying the destabilizing centrifugality of Romantic nervousness to new extremes, invaluably identifying the rights and identities of countless individuals, but at the heavy social price of strict boundary-lines between one community or subcommunity and another. In post-postmodern times, centripetal compensations are coming into play, often grouped under the heading of "globalization". Yet in some respects globalization may even increase the risk of Romantic solipsism. In particular, there is the question of digitally globalized communication. Cyberspace is of course open to everybody who can use the necessary equipment, and its social media offer forms of association and interaction which many users have welcomed as sovereign remedies for loneliness. Yet cyberspace itself can be a lonely habitat. Some of the virtual realities it makes possible are desperately sad, and no two individuals follow the same cyberpath for very long in any case. In a way which Leavis's idealizations quite ignored, *The Dunciad*, through confronting head-on the results of two centuries of exponential development within print culture, was one of the first English texts to face up to the root political problem always raised by major advances in communicational technology: the problem of personal liberty *versus* social cohesion.

Pope's own strategy for dealing with this is still suggestive. His first step was to face up to the facts by making them unforgettably sublime: the facts, above all, of social and cultural meltdown viewed from the standpoint of Humanist reason. Nothing could take away the sadness and horror of this. But Pope, through bold ridicule, was tending to acclimatize his readers to it. By which I do not mean that he was making them uncritically resigned to what was going on, but that he was brazening them into getting through a good day's work in spite of it, just as, today, a devastating Scarfe cartoon may cheer us up at breakfast.

The poem was also sublimely cacophonic. This was Pope's way of giving community a chance to re-invent itself, not by force, not by reason, not by religion, but through sheer talk. Especially in the final version of 1743, it was as if he had decided, "Let people say whatever they want to say! Then let's see what happens!" It opened:

> The Mighty Mother, and her Son who brings
> The Smithfield Muses to the ear of Kings,
> I sing. Say you, her instruments the Great!
> Call'd to this work by Dulness, Jove, and Fate;
> You by whose care, in vain decry'd and curst,
> Still Dunce the second reigns like Dunce the first;
> Say how the Goddess bade Britannia sleep,
> And pour'd her Spirit o'er the land and deep.
>
> (*The Dunciad in Four Books*, I, ll. 1–8)

These lines referred to forms of popular entertainment which, with the approval of the Goddess of Dulness, were threatening to take over the polite theatres as the entertainment of royalty and aristocracy, and also to those responsible for this lamentable development, including some great Whigs who had bolstered the witless regimes of George I and George II ("Dunce the first" and "Dunce the second"). Also mentioned was some criticism and cursing that had been heaped upon such potentates, and it would have been immediately obvious to any reader of the poem that Pope himself was the kind of person who could have made such complaints. Here, though, he purports to believe that such bickering is absolutely pointless, and invites – with emphasis ("Say you", "Say") – the powerful Whigs to tell the story from their own point of view, a pro-Dunce account which through the course of the poem will be expressed by both a wide array of individual dunces themselves and the presiding voice of Dulness. Then, only a few lines after this passage, the poem apostrophizes Swift, now living in Ireland, and invites him to think about what is happening in England, which he is bound to do along much the same lines as his friend Pope. In addition, there is all the paratext, which takes up many pages before the first and after the last pages of the poem proper, and whose learned or mock-learned commentaries occupy a very large amount of space underneath the running verse, all of this purportedly authored by several different people, real or imaginary: in particular, by Pope himself and some others who might agree with him, such as "Scriblerus" and Warburton, plus commentators more hostile, such as Bentley and Theobald.

Throughout the poem, then, many different people are set in motion, some of them rational, most of them not, all of them doing absolutely their own thing, and therefore often talking past each other, as characters are sometimes said to do in the plays of Pinter. As an exercise in cultural reconstruction this might seem doomed to failure. But Pope has not lost control, even though his control is extremely gener-ous and un-self-assertive. His main concern is to have the story and its characters refracted through so many different lenses, as it were, that what takes place in the mind of readers will be an exercise of personal judgement. It is impossible to read the poem without in a sense trying on all the different points of view for size, and without sometimes reacting in more than one way at once.

What then actually emerges from the free-for-all is the possibility of some rather unexpected alliances. Think, for instance, of all the scatological humour. Or even bet-ter, perhaps, think of the pissing competition between Osborne and Curll. Osborne and Curll are not exactly being extolled for their contribution to British culture here, and Swift and other Scriblerians would have shared Pope's disapproval. On the other hand, Osborne and Curll have sufficient reality in the poem to establish that their own opinion of themselves is far higher than Pope's, and if Pope's reduction of them to the level of rivals in urination at first seems wounding, it also redounds to Pope's own disadvantage, as he must have known it would, because it makes him, too, seem puerile. Then again, Osborne and Curll, and all their supporters, might actually enjoy a bit of puerility, and a reader such as Swift (whose Gulliver extinguished the fire in the apartment of the Empress of Lilliput with a deluge which even Curll might have envied) would have nothing against it either. Shit-and-piss jokes at the furthest pos-sible remove from any ideal of high civilization can actually, when civilization is felt to be under threat, unite both satirist, butt and wider audience as well, just as is still the case with Gerald Scarfe and *Private Eye*. At the same time, *The Dunciad* also draws on another, very different common denominator, in the heroic language by which the pissers and their pissing are mock-heroically described – "One on his manly con-fidence relies, / One on his vigour and superior size" (II, ll. 169–170), and so on. Communicationally, this style would have worked as a shared cultural memory, a left-over from the age of Humanism which binds together Pope and Swift with Theobald, Bentley and most of the other the Dunces as well.

In short, from whatever position readers came to the poem, their processing of it necessarily involved them in a dialogicality, and to some extent a uniting dialogical-ity, with others unlike themselves. New relationships could arise, in ways perhaps still promotable through the content- and value-neutral media of the latest communica-tional technology today. *The Dunciad*'s many-voicedness, which was such a formid-able challenge to the compositors who had to set its pages (McLaverty 2001: 82–106), gave a foretaste of the hermeneutic and interactional opportunities nowadays avail-able to users of digital hypertexts and social media (Snead 2010). In his own publish-ing activities Pope had already made himself, in economic terms, a master of the new bourgeois culture of print. But in writing and seeing *this* poem through the press, he was boldly asking whether that culture's soul was to be nothing more than cash, and whether its main ideological hallmark would be merely an opposition to the old patri-cian Humanism, or whether it could result in some totally uncharted kind of deeper communality. This means that, seeing, as we now do, the implications of our own cyberspatial culture for, say, the workings of local, national and international politics, we can go back to *The Dunciad* as a way of sharpening our wits for speculation on the human future.

3.5   Pope today

Pope wrote a large body of poetry in pentameter couplets, but much work in other verse forms as well, and he also contributed to a wide range of genres. But even in his most disturbing poems, the single most obvious common denominator was the sheer pleasure he offered. To some extent I have dwelt on this, quoting the delighted appreciation of earlier critics, mentioning the centrality of pleasing to a Horatian poetics, and here and there drawing attention to various kinds of charm, to delicacy of sentiment, to ravishing lyricism, to unobtrusive language skills, to subtle versification, to congenial humour, and to sublimely satirical comedy. I hope this has at least been enough to suggest my own endless enjoyment of his writing, and by implication its potential appeal to my contemporaries.

Perhaps I should have said more. After all, communicationally speaking Pope's willingness to please was the first clause in his unwritten contract with readers, and a precondition for everything else. The pleasure was what attracted them, and they came to rely on him for it. Admittedly, Patrick Cruttwell (1966: 13) was exaggerating when he claimed that in Pope's work "the object of it all, the purpose of 'each talent and each art,' is simply to 'please.'" In listing poetic roles which Pope did *not* undertake – "to express oneself, or to reform the world, or to be an unacknowledged legislator of mankind, or a trumpet to sing to battle" – Cruttwell failed to recognize some functions which he certainly did fulfil: not least the three main types of community-making I have been trying to highlight here. But in all Pope's modes of address, pleasingness is so much the *sine qua non* that Cruttwell's overemphasis is understandable.

Granted, in both earlier and later times countless other writers have, as it were, signed up to the same hedonistic contract, and have been thanked and admired for holding to it. So in Pope or any other writer, pleasingness *per se* is not a distinctive feature, even though the ways in which authors please in practice are widely various. But at our own post-postmodern moment of time, pleasingness in writers is noteworthy, in that so many postmodern literary commentators wrote as if it had passed them by. If that impression is correct, if they really did find literary texts unenjoyable, then their sheer perseverance, both as commentators and above all as readers, was bizarrely heroic. If the impression is incorrect, we can suspect that their exclusion of pleasure as a topic of discussion was simply the current way for a post-Humanist elite to portray literary writers as self-distanced from society's small-mindedness.

For all its charm, Pope's own work can itself be seen as hastening the advent of such post-Humanist accounts, since he was, if I am right, the first great English Romantic, and an extremist Romantic at that, sometimes virtually, though not literally, occupying a position of ur-Byronic exile. At the same time, he was also the last great English Humanist, and an extremist one, especially in tending to root himself at the very heart of English society. Throughout a career which was pivotal for the entire course of English literary history, his Romantic and his Humanist tendencies were constantly in evidence. Some poems were more predominantly Humanist, others more predominantly Romantic, while the poetry I have described as sublime was somewhere in between. There were even cases where all three modes alternated with each other, so leading to the rich tonal variety of a poem such as the *Epistle to Dr. Arbuthnot*, which began with Horatian common sense on the deluded ambitions of amateur writers, which then rose to the satirical sublime of the portraits of Atticus and Sporus, and which rounded everything off with the gentle privacies of the tributes to Pope's father and mother.

Whether considered in a single poem or throughout his entire oeuvre, all such tonal variation was *ipso facto* a variation in his relationship with readers. This is the aspect of his writing to which I have been drawing special attention, with the communicational dimension of his Humanist tendencies as my starting-point. Here I have spoken of a Humanist nervousness, deliberately drawing on the older sense of "nerve" and "nervousness", which involved ideas of strength, vigour, force. As a cultural formation, Humanist nervousness cherished a cross-party, ecumenical ideal of ethical strength. This was taken to serve as a kind of spiritual cement which would hold society together and maintain order, when necessary by smoothing out abnormalities. It took the form of a civilized politeness, a rational probity, and a *media via* prudence, for all of which classical authors were taken to supply models. For Pope as a writer, Humanist nervousness also involved a corresponding strength of rhetoric, diction and versification in speaking to the ideal. In complete accordance with the Horatian tag, his stance *vis à vis* his readers here was at once coercively instructional and very charming. Coleridge and Hazlitt both resisted this sweet force, claiming that the society reflected in his work was narrow or artificial, whereas Byron admired him as an ethical poet of permanent relevance.

Such disagreement among readers during the early nineteenth century was the continuation of the major cultural shift that was already under way in Pope's own time. The Humanist ethos was beginning to lose credibility, its scholarly foundations re-examined, its idealizations questioned, and its standards challenged by what its own adherents saw as a rising tide of irrationality, bad taste, immorality and ignorance. In many of his satires, epistles and imitations of Horace, Pope's efforts were fuelled by the hope that mankind's capacity for civilization, reason and self-control would prevail. But his optimism could also give way to fear and great sadness, which is where he could begin to come across as an outsider, sometimes an irate and proudly contemptuous outsider, even while still close to the centre of cultural and political power. At other points, and in the greatest satirical portraits in particular, his writing became sublime, and in *The Rape of the Lock* and in *The Dunciad* comically sublime, even if *The Dunciad*'s comedy was still unmistakably interlaced with fear and sadness. Rather than trying to rehabilitate reason, virtue and taste along Humanist lines, he here accepted the time's sociocultural and ethical upheaval as a fact and, by making those he saw as responsible for it much larger than life and totally ridiculous, was tending, no longer to coerce readers, but to help them be more resilient and clear-sighted, rather in the manner of a great political cartoon. By allowing the chaos of values to blare out in its many different voices, he was creating a space within which some new form of community might emerge, even if the first common denominators to be tossed into a new, post-Humanist cultural cement were nothing more than shit-and-piss humour and, ironically enough, the fading memory of classical poetic diction.

That the new, Romantic kind of nervousness – nervousness more in our own usual sense of the term – would be as socially constructive as Humanist nervousness was in principle unlikely. The phenomenon involved an empowerment of personal sensitivity, feelings, emotions, intuitions, and was thus extremely individualistic. There was no guarantee that the sentiments which came to expression would not be partisan or destructive, a risk alarmingly apparent in the speaker in "Elegy to the Memory of an Unfortunate Lady", who may be Pope himself. The main hope of a new kind of social bonding lay in Shaftesburian benevolism: in the idea that human beings have an innate moral sense which predisposes them to love virtue. So just possibly, by cultivating the new nervousness many different individuals would find themselves sharing similar sentiments, and responding in sympathetic ways to the plight of others. Pope himself wrote a fair number of lines in which, leaving aside the more public ethos of Humanist poetry, he suggested the sorrows and joys of human life – including his own life – in intimately private areas. Here the single most important factor was tenderness: its presence or absence in the life-experiences described, and the delicate tenderness of the writing itself. In work of this kind Pope was not trying to persuade his readers to virtue. Neither was he trying to brace them to weather out the tempestuous confusions in ethical and moral values. And if, as was surely the case, he was encouraging them to find new commonalities, then here this had nothing to do with puerile humour or an archaic classical tradition. Rather, he was offering his own most delicate observations, and inviting readers to a sympathetic comparing of notes. To the extent that he succeeded, he was bringing to birth a new, in principle limitless community of sensitive individuals.

Some of his most interesting writing, however, did not simply alternate between the Humanist and Romantic nervousnesses but fused them together. This is where we come back to the prose-poetry dichotomy, which he himself discussed in the preface to *An Essay on Man*. For many nineteenth-century readers, most notoriously for Arnold, his verse was so prose-like as to be nothing *but* prose. In the early and mid-twentieth century, with the admiration of Edith Sitwell (1930) and G. Wilson Knight (1954), the pendulum looked as if it might swing to the view that it was nothing but poetry. But in an exciting and socially significant way, some of his finest writing – the passage on the chain of Love, for instance – really does have the virtues both of what we see as prose and of what we see as poetry. Exciting: because it brings our responses to argumentation and persuasion into dialogical synergy with our capacity for apophatic sensitivity. Socially significant: because all societies have to strike a balance between order and freedom. Pope's way of communicating here, his taking responsibility by arguing for something he felt to be a truth of wide relevance, while at the same time behaving ethically in allowing readers considerable freedom of imagination and response, was, and remains, unusual. Public discourse would always benefit from more input of this kind.

By the time Pope was born, the printing press had already been in operation for two centuries, permitting a huge proliferation of texts, and thereby presenting a formidable challenge to individuals and institutions aspiring to regulate knowledge and taste. The press was also beginning to enable writers to earn a living independently of the patrons who earlier might have called their tune, an independence of which Pope himself was a historically important instance. This is not to say that writers could now write whatever they pleased. Their books still needed to be sellable, and customers' tastes did exercise an influence. But throughout Europe, small cultural elites were certainly losing their grip, *pari passu* with the decline of the Humanistic ideal which since the beginnings of the modern era had usually been their ideological backbone. As more and more readers from within more and more different sociocultural settings came into the market for printed materials, democratization could only accelerate. In part *The Dunciad* channels Pope's terrified dismay at what he could not help seeing as raging sea of vulgarity, but in part, too, it reveals his awareness of the inevitability of what was happening, and his hope of some sort of social continuity in spite of it. The ability of this poem's comic sublime to outface the cultural bad weather and encourage readers to do the same marked it, we might say, as the creation of a merchant's son. And in other poems, too, his emphasis on the new, Romantic nervousness of the private and individual, even at the occasional risk of social disruption and violence, was no less bourgeois. By the time Leavis was coming to prominence in the 1930s, the bourgeois sensibility had reached a literary high-point in the Victorian novel and the dramatic monologues and domestic poems of Browning and Tennyson, but also a low-point in a Victorian sentimentality against which Modernist writers and critics reacted with new forms of elitism. Leavis developed his myth of the eighteenth century as a homogeneous society, and attempted to re-shape the culture of his own time according to that pattern. But neither Leavisian criticism nor the new universities of the late twentieth century could impose a lastingly viable authority on the many kinds of life-experience still coming to expression for the first time, and the reaction of postmodern critics against potentially hegemonistic tendencies was very strong.

Paradoxically, the different sociocultural groupings they championed were not only emancipatory but repressive, enforcing a conformity within the grouping to its favoured identity script, and sometimes putting a damper on communication between one grouping and another. But in our post-postmodern new millennium, the culture wars so typical of the 1990s have abated, and there would seem to be a wide-spread sense that political, economic and environmental factors could result in just a single human world, though one where differences could still be recognized. As for the no less global phenomena of computer-mediated discourse and the Internet, these are the first major technological developments in communication, apart from the telephone, the radio and the television, since the printing press; they are value-free and content-neutral; and they have thereby vastly increased, not only the scope, but also the need, for both social coercion and liberation. The root form of this situation can be seen in the tension between Humanist and Romantic nervousness in Pope. And if *The Dunciad*, in some ways so like a digital hypertext, was the work in which he faced it most directly as a theme, then the more general synergy in his writing between the pedagogically prosaic and the liberatingly poetic is a clue to communicational strategies which, appropriate then, could still be viable today.

If we did seek to emulate Pope's communicational achievement, it would obviously be with a view to building or consolidating a community of our own. In the process, we could hardly fail to be struck by his variegated ideological colouring, which in a small way anticipated the eclectic multi-perspectivism of post-postmodern societies. There were the three main shades: religion, Humanism, and Shaftesburian benevolism. In Pope's time, benevolism was still actively innovatory within society as a whole, very much in key with the new nervousness, and strongly conducive to an emphasis on the private and domestic. In terms of literary history it coincided with the shift from the aristocratic valorization of the heroic epic poem to the more bourgeois ethos of the novel, already strongly anticipated by the tender intimacy of Pope's tribute to his dead father, the linen merchant, and his dying mother. As for religion, the process of secularization was already setting in, so that, however gradually, religious beliefs and practices were acquiring the status of cultural memory. Whatever the private truth about Pope's own beliefs and practices as a Catholic, in his public statements he went in for Deistic dilutions of the earlier dogmas. Yet as an important element in his approach to readers he still appealed to ecumenical religion, and to the ethical corollaries of religion, and had a very sharp eye for religion as merely a matter of rote, and as merely an ingredient to display or sex appeal –

> On her White breast a sparkling *Cross* she wore,
> Which *Jews* might kiss and Infidels adore.   (*The Rape of the Lock*, II, ll. 7–8)

In the same way, he was already beginning to exploit Humanism as a further source of ethical guidelines, even after its highest aspirations as an intellectual movement had come unstuck.

As so often in these studies, then, I am speaking of inspirational ideals, but this time also of ideals which survive their own cultural death. If some of my own readers have had difficulty grasping that Humanism did indeed die in Pope's lifetime, this may have been because of their awareness of, and probable participation in, Humanism's cultural afterlife. In the long run, the distinction between the life and the afterlife of an ideal may be of little practical importance, since it can sometimes be imaginatively recuperated, just as Humanism itself had sought to be an imaginative recuperation of the ancient world. In Pope's writing, the moribund ideals of religion and Humanism could still work as a valuable counterbalance to the more dangerous potential of the life of feelings, and without impeding the blossoming forth of that new ideal in its more positive forms.

In our own post-postmodern era, too, ideals of widely different character and origin could perhaps more fruitfully complement each other than in the recent past. If that is something we should like to happen, then the immensely enjoyable case of Pope can strengthen our belief in its possibility, and help us better understand the necessary pre-condition: a communicational environment within which responsible coercion and a liberal comparing of notes can credibly alternate and even interweave.

CHAPTER 4

Wordsworth's genuineness

4.1 Universal or historical?

For a post-postmodern communicational critic, Wordsworth's sustained presence within the culture is reassuring, but for reasons which earlier admirers would not have articulated. His poetry has always had a bearing on a world where dangerous divisions between different political and cultural constellations are easily exacerbated by communicational dysfunction. But although a long line of sensitive critics have offered insights and terminology which permanently affect the way we talk about him, they inevitably seized on features which seemed important to them as representatives of their own particular historical formation. For over a century and a half his idea of the poet as a man speaking to men came in for much attention, but within an ideological framework which rather toned down the difference between one grouping of human beings and another. As a result, the extent to which he tried to engage his readers in genuine communication, the dialogical kind of communication which enlarges the scope of community precisely by recognizing and embracing such differences, was underestimated, and so were his efforts to promote such communication in the world at large. True, his achievement here was far more modest than he himself would have hoped, but only because his hopes were pitched so high that their realization would have completely changed the course of history. His attempts were none the less impressive for being inspired by a dream, and were underwritten by his own generosity of spirit and sheer loving-kindness. It is these efforts and these virtues which make him a poet for our time.

His popularity was not instantaneous. Reviewers of *An Evening Walk* (1793) and *Descriptive Sketches* (1793) were unwelcoming, and to some early readers the interest displayed by *Lyrical Ballads* (1798, 1800) and its Preface (1800) in simple country-folk seemed dangerously Jacobin. But once there was a gradual upswing in his fortunes, it proved to be irreversible. Despite fluctuations caused by the widening fame of Scott, Byron and Tennyson, before his death his audience was already large and variegated: of both sexes and of every reading age; not only both country- and city-dwellers, but also upper-class, middle-class and lower-class readers; both readers with a long family tradition of reading behind them and readers whose forbears were illiterate; both more secular and more religious-minded readers – Catholic, high-church, middle-church, low-church, nonconformist; readers of differing political persuasions; and, even if he never challenged Byron's popularity in continental Europe, readers not only in Britain but North America. Forty years after his death, partly in step with the further spread of literacy, partly thanks to Arnold's insistence that he was the third greatest English poet after Shakespeare and Milton (Arnold 1888:132), his reputation was still growing. Nor was there any parallel to the Modernist "dislodgement" of Milton, to use Leavis's word (Leavis 1964 [1936]a:42). Leavis himself, far from challenging Arnold's ranking, complained that his more detailed comments had paved the way for a Georgian trivialization of Wordsworth (Leavis 1964 [1936]c:154–159). More recently Christopher Ricks, who also admires both Tennyson and T. S. Eliot, has said "[t]here has been no greater poet [than Wordsworth] in the two centuries since he was born" (Ricks 1987b:134). And such consistently favourable verdicts have been well matched by the level of attention he receives more generally. Wordsworth experts have done a very great deal to illuminate his life, his thought, and the many different versions of his texts, and there is a steady stream of interpretations of particular poems and of his opus as a whole. He is often taken up in schools and universities, and in any anthology of English poetry is guaranteed a central place. Some of his poems are common points of reference, and widely known by heart. Some lines and phrases have entered into the English language as regularly used.

Many admirers have attributed his unusual breadth and longevity of appeal to universal qualities of the kind he himself described in the Preface to *Lyrical Ballads*:

> In spite of difference of soil and climate, of language and manners, of laws and customs: in spite of things silently gone out of mind, and things violently destroyed, the Poet binds together by passion and knowledge the vast empire of human society, as it is spread over the whole earth, and over all time. … Poetry is the first and last of all knowledge – it is as immortal as the heart of man.
>
> (1850 text, Owen and Smyser 1974:I, 141)

That they were responding to something "as immortal as the heart of man" has been the unquestioning belief not only of countless ordinary readers but of commentators in the central liberal humanist tradition of Wordsworth criticism. Empson (1952), Donald Davie (1955), Christopher Ricks (1987a, 1987b), and Susan J. Wolfson (1997) have all detected a timeless subtlety and force, a timeless pleasurability and beauty, in his use of language and versification. Leslie Stephen (1876), Arnold (1888), A. C. Bradley (1909), Helen Darbishire (1972 [1926]), Leavis (1964 [1936]), and Geoffrey Hartman (1971 [1964]) have all found permanent and far-reaching insights in his particular kinds of story, his perceptions, his introspection, his emotionality; in his portrayal of the beauty and sublimity of nature; in his idea of a human life in harmony with nature; and in his other philosophical interests, shading sometimes into religious intuitions, and sometimes into ethics, as his writing comes to be a criticism of life in a more general sense.

On this traditional view, his only real blemish was his egotism. His poetry's beauty and universality was said to be flawed by the impurities of an authorial selfhood that was too intrusive. That his writing expressed his own feelings and was extensively autobiographical was acceptable only as long as it maintained an exalted degree of human representativeness. As early as 1805 Wordsworth himself could see that *The Prelude* in particular might be accused of "self-conceit" (Wordsworth 1805). For Keats, his sublimity was so badly tainted by egotism that, in marked contrast with Shakespeare's negative capability, it was nothing short of unethical. His readers were "bullied into a certain Philosophy engendered in the whims of an Egotist". Much too ready to "brood and peacock" over his own speculations, he failed to realize how much "[w]e hate poetry that has a palpable design upon us" (Keats 1954 [1817, 1818]: 51–54, 71–72).

With what they regarded as his greatest poetry, Wordsworth's nineteenth century admirers did not experience this problem, and in the twentieth century he was sometimes commended as impersonal even by stringently Modernist standards. For critics whose buzzwords included "symbol", "image", "epiphany" and "haiku", his best verse was so unspoilt by authorial intrusion that it resembled, as we might put it, the prose of Henry James as described by T. S. Eliot: "a baffling escape from … Ideas", and the work of mind "so fine that no idea could violate it" (Eliot 1975 [1918]: 151). Eliot himself, it has to be said, was unenthusiastic. Judging from his essay "Tradition and the Individual Talent" (1951 [1919]), he thought that Wordsworth's talk of the overflow of powerful feelings recollected in tranquillity came too close to seeing poetry as personal self-expression, and he perhaps felt that Wordsworth's own verse illustrated the shortcomings of poetry so conceived. But to the extant that any such view was based on *The Prelude,* he would have relied on the version of 1850, since the 1805 version was unavailable in print until Ernest de Selincourt's parallel-text edition of 1926, and he clearly found Wordsworth a force to be reckoned with even so. He did not actively seek to "dislodge" him, and neither, as I say, did his contemporaries. On the contrary, when Helen Darbishire reviewed de Selincourt's edition, she immediately found in the 1805 *Prelude* a

> poetry of spiritual experience so intense, so pure, and so profound that it holds the essence of all religion. … [It] gives us … elemental experience freed from the gloss of later interpretation … . And it shows us, further, how its roots lay … in the sensuous life which is our common heritage.
>
> (Darbishire 1972 [1926]: 98)

By 1970 Jonathan Wordsworth was going back a few years further still, drawing attention to the Two-Part *Prelude* of 1799, "a poem of much smaller scope but also much more concentrated power than the thirteen-Book version of 1805" (Wordsworth 1979 [1970]: 568). The mid-twentieth century's progressive discovery, in ever earlier drafts of *The Prelude*, of the pure, the intense, the elemental, and of all this "freed from the gloss of later interpretation", gives a good idea of what readers of that time were looking for, and finding, in Wordsworth's poetry.

Even so, received wisdom about his best writing was always qualified by a sense that much of his production falls to a far lower level. Especially in the wake of Arnold's essay of 1888, readers tended to feel that there was an early, greater Wordsworth and a later, lesser Wordsworth, and that the lesser Wordsworth certainly can be egotistical and, to boot, intrusive, fussily preachy, and banal. Sometimes such faults were found even in early poems, the most notorious example being "The Thorn", in the first printed versions of which Wordsworth wrote of the muddy little pond beneath the tree that "I've measured it from side to side; / 'Tis three feet long, and two feet wide" (de Selincourt and Darbishire 1952–1959: II, 239n), a couplet which Coleridge had publicly numbered among the "unpleasant sinkings from the height to which the poet had previously lifted [his readers]" (Coleridge 1956 [1817]: 194–195). Confronted with authorial interventions of this calibre, readers felt that the sublime was giving way to the ridiculous, and the temple of beauteous imagination throwing wide its portals to prosaic bathos. As James Kenneth Stephen put it, the impression could arise that Wordsworth had two voices, the one which "learns the storm-cloud's thunderous melody", the other that of "an old half-witted sheep / Which bleats articulate monotony" (Stephen 1891).

As both his incessant revisions and his anxiety about self-conceit in *The Prelude* partly suggest, Wordsworth could be unsure of his own touch. In the 1798 version of "Old Man Travelling; Animal Tranquillity and Decay, A Sketch", the arresting description of the old man is followed by a passage in which the poet enters the poem in his own person in order to ask him where he is going and why. The old man tells him that he is on his way to Falmouth, where his mariner son has been hospitalized after a sea-fight. But in the 1800 *Lyrical Ballads*, Wordsworth shortened the poem's long title so as to concentrate on "Animal Tranquillity and Decay" and converted the old man's reply from direct to indirect speech. In 1815 he went much further, entirely deleting both his own intervention and the old traveller's response, so whittling the poem down to just the description of the old man walking, an uncannily suggestive epiphany, which in due time gave Modernist readers exactly what they wanted.

For a communicational critic today, the earlier commentators' strong polarization between the ideal and the real, between the universal and the personal, does not offer the most promising starting-point. On the one hand, talk of Wordsworth's poetry as representing an ideal impersonality suggested that his address was to a correspondingly ideal and universalized humanity. On the other hand, the condemnation of his egotism conveyed the quite contrary impression of a capacity for extreme solipsism on his part. There was no obvious middle ground where critics could have spoken of his writing as it actually worked and works in the real world, of its role, that is, as a form of communication between the real Wordsworth and particular real readers or groups of readers.

The consequences of this conceptual impasse were especially unfortunate for *The Excursion*, as when Hazlitt (1814) remarked that Wordsworth's "intense intellectual egotism [here] swallows everything up. … It is as if there were nothing but himself and the universe," or as when Jeffrey complained that the poet who here betook himself to "retirement" was not so much above society as out of touch with it (Baker 2001: 328). But elsewhere, too, Wordsworth's community-making was either misrepresented or quite unmentioned in earlier criticism. The assumption that there was an absolute dichotomy between selfhood and poetry, and correspondingly between Wordsworth and Shakespeare, was simply too deeply entrenched. The plain facts are that Shakespeare's capability is *not* so negative as to leave us entirely to our own devices, and that Wordsworth's sublime is *not* so egotistical as merely to force upon us his own selfhood. Although we are certainly more aware of Wordsworth's presence in, say, the sublime passage about crossing the Alps in Book VI of *The Prelude* than of Shakespeare's during the no less sublime heath scenes in *King Lear*, this is in no small part a consequence of Shakespeare's writing in a dramatic as opposed to an autobiographical mode, and does not mean that Shakespeare's sublime bears no imprint of his own sensibility, as if it were not clearly distinguishable from the sublime of other writers. Yet although nineteenth-century commentators did recognize that even Shakespeare's work might have at least some autobiographical vibrations, in Shakespeare's case, as Edward Dowden expressed the standard view, "to pass through the creation of the artist to the mind of the creator […] by no means prevents our returning to view the work of art simply as such, apart from the artist, and as such to receive delight from it." In fact there was not felt to be much of a choice, since Shakespeare, "[j]ust when we have laid hold of him, […] eludes us, and we hear only distant ironical laughter" (Dowden 1906 [1875]: 3, 6). To Shakespeare, then, Dowden more than once applied the line from *Troilus and Cressida*, "The secrets of nature have not more gift in taciturnity", whereas the same could hardly be said of Wordsworth, whose personal appearances in his own writing were quite blatant, and far more difficult to reconcile with the Victorian notion of Art.

As for a less lofty literary-critical notion which might have exculpated them, it did not help that the post-Humanist view of writers as outsiders, boosted not least by Wordsworth and Coleridge's theory of a special kind of creative imagination, gradually overshadowed the eighteenth century's sense of polite letters. This only reinforced Wordsworth's self-promotional criticism of the Popeian style as unnatural (Griffin 1995). As a result, readers' ears were closed to his own resourceful extension of eighteenth century modes of address, not only beyond Pope's appeal to readerships that were civilised or sensitive, but also beyond the more affable cosiness of Cowper in *The Task*. A writer who came before them as somebody prepared to be a good-humoured friend, frankly saying what he thought and felt as a person of his own background and temperament, but with varying degrees of emphasis and certainty, and deferentially inviting them to compare notes with him: such a writer, even when his community-making overtures won him a huge audience, could not be welcomed in language drawn from either the Preface to *Lyrical Ballads* or any of the Romantics' other literary-theoretical *tours de force*. If the triumph of Romantic historiography prevented readers from seeing that Pope was already a fully-fledged exponent of Romantic nervousness, who in his *Pastorals* and in his verse tributes to his own parents, for instance, was on the same wavelength as Wordsworth in *Lyrical Ballads*, then it also deafened them to a congeniality of address which was not only one of the main hallmarks of literary culture in Pope's day, but which was also Wordsworth's own most effective mode, his Romantic protestations notwithstanding.

The theoretical upheavals within late-twentieth-century literary scholarship improved this situation, but not straightforwardly. As with postmodern criticism in general, so in Wordsworth criticism from the late 1970s onwards there was a pervading element of historical re-contextualization, precisely as a way of bringing aestheticist and universalist accounts of authorship and readership into question. Some criticism now went to the opposite extreme, however, heavily stressing the *difference* between one sociocultural formation and another, and tending to suggest that the chances of communication between different formations were deterministically restricted. Jon Klancher argued that the traditional view of Wordsworth as a quintessential "Romantic" quite unsituated in time and social space was an ideological construction designed to conceal Wordsworth's failure to bridge "social and cultural difference in a powerful act of cultural transmission", a failure attributed by Klancher to deepening divisions within audiences themselves (Klancher 1987:150). Marilyn Butler attempted a similar demystification by adducing the context of England after the French Revolution. If the widespread fear of Jacobinism was one reason for Wordsworth's initial unpopularity, Butler saw his later work as successfully adopting "the public mantle of the poet of counter-revolution, celebrating the Burkean conservative ideology of personal humility and service, domesticity, hearth and home, the English plot of ground" (Butler 1981:65–66). John Barrell (1988) and Mary Jacobus (1994) saw specific gender limitations in Wordsworth's writing, while for Thomas McFarland his devotion in both his poetry and his daily life to his own nearest and dearest – something by now of considerable interest to biographers (Gill 1989:203) – was "in one way ... [a] deepening ... [of] human commitment, [but also] involved ... a lessening of concern with what, from our twentieth century perspectives, may be called the liberal myth of the *a priori* value of mankind in general." Under the pressure of personal sorrows and political disillusionment, Wordsworth's strong feeling for humanity came in McFarland's view to be "more and more concentrated in the idea not of people in general but in that of a *significant group* of people", significant for him personally, that is to say, and sharing his own sometimes conservative views, plus a background in firmly upper-middle-class culture (McFarland 1981:141, his italics).

The earlier commentators on Wordsworth had underestimated his communicational achievement through their liberal humanist assumption that all men, by which they meant all human beings, were basically the same. This had made communication seem rather too easy. Readers acculturated within that older paradigm simply took for granted that Wordsworth was addressing them, and while they were actually responding to his generous deference were seldom consciously struck by it, except when they condemned his friendly approaches in his own person as just another proof of egotism. Here the postmodern historicization of Wordsworth and his readers was potentially a valuable corrective, by bringing the poetry as a whole more down to earth. Yet it sometimes made poetic communication with all sorts and conditions of people sound impossibly difficult – as if the allegedly Burkean Wordsworth could not have spoken to radically minded readers, for instance, or as if women readers could not have negotiated his alleged gender handicap, or as if lower-class readers could not have embraced a writer whose ethos was allegedly so genteel. If the older, universalizing criticism could not explain why Wordsworth's poetry was so much slower to catch on in Europe than Byron's, then the postmodern historicization could not explain why it had nevertheless reached as far as it had.

4.2   Hybridity

To the extent that postmodern criticism drove wedges between Wordsworth and readers not made in his own image, it calls for qualification on two counts. First, it too readily assumed, as I say, that people who do not share the same position cannot communicate with each other. For a different view of communication, I would point to the present book's Introduction and, for a fuller exposition, to my *Literature as Communication* (Sell 2000). Secondly, the postmodern account of Wordsworth's own image as patriarchal, conservative, and genteel was too simplistic. A better way to describe his formation, it seems to me, is as significantly hybrid. Is he an educated person with civilized tastes, or a person with deep roots in folk culture? He is both. Is he urbane, or is he rustic? He is both. Is he politically reactionary, or is he progressive? Again, he is both. The truth is that his mode of being undermines all such dichotomies, and any critic who fails to recognize this will make the historical impact of his poetry that much more difficult to explain. Especially for communicational critics, his sociocultural and ideological flexibility is a matter of prime concern, as a factor predisposing him to empathize with a considerable variety of human beings, and broadening the scope of his own address.

Temperamentally and by conviction, he was generously democratic, but he did belong to a particular epoch. As a young man he looked on in confused anguish as the longed-for Revolution turned into Terror. Together with many of his contemporaries he was therefore saddled with that visceral fear of the mob which is sometimes mistakenly thought of as peculiar to thoroughgoing political conservatism. This in turn could affect the way his writing brought in the classical dichotomy between city and countryside. In view of the sheer crowdedness of cities, he sometimes saw them as extremely dangerous places, whereas the countryside could figure as the refuge of pristine simplicity and true freedom.

The countryside's appeal could be further heightened by the powers and charms of nature. So at several points in *The Prelude* Coleridge is an object of pity because he spent his formative years at Christ's Hospital School in London, far away from "rivers, fields / And groves". Taking his cue from autobiographical details in Coleridge's own poem "Frost at Midnight", Wordsworth comments that

> [thou, while] yet a liveried schoolboy, in the depths
> Of the huge city, on the leaded roof
> Of that wide edifice, thy school and home,
> Wast used to lie and gaze upon the clouds
> Moving in heaven, or haply, tired of this,
> To shut thine eyes and by internal light
> See trees, and meadows, and thy native stream,
> Far distant – thus beheld from year to year
> Of a long exile.   (*The Prelude* (1805), VI, ll. 274–284)[1]

At the very beginning of *The Prelude* he describes how he himself, having been a "discontented sojourner" in the "vast city", has now finally escaped. With a "gentle breeze" blessing his cheek, he passes through "green fields" beneath an "azure sky", "[f]ree as a bird to settle where ... [he] will" (*The Prelude* (1850), I, ll. 1–9). And as in "Frost at Midnight", where Coleridge describes himself as "reared / In the great city, pent 'mid cloisters dim" (ll. 51–52),[2] so here in *The Prelude*, the city-country contrast is sharpened by a particular Miltonic intertext. In *Paradise Lost* Book IX there is an epic simile describing somebody who, having been "long in populous city pent", finally sallies forth on a summer morning to enjoy "each rural sight, each rural sound" (ll. 445–466).[3] The simile equates this urbanite's pleasure on getting out into the countryside with Satan's overwhelming delight on arriving in Eden from Hell.

Elsewhere in *The Prelude*, however, Wordsworth is fascinated by London's sheer bustle – the dazzling variety and energy of Bartholemew Fair, for instance. Throughout his adult life, he was more than happy to give himself up to a whirl of parties, visits, and theatre-going in the nation's capital, and although he had a quick eye for instances of human tragedy on its crowded streets, urban realism of an unpleasantly

---

1.   Quotations from the 1799, 1805 and 1850 versions of *The Prelude* taken from Wordsworth, Abrams and Gill 1979. In the present study, I am not consistently discussing just one version of this poem. The version chosen for quotation at any particular point sometimes depends upon the argument in hand, and sometimes is simply the version I take to offer a poetically superior reading. In this second kind of case, I do not automatically concur with Darbishire's Modernist preference for the 1805 version over the 1850 but have assessed all versions on what seem to me to be their merits.

2.   Quotations of Coleridge's poetry taken from Keach 2004.

3.   Quotations from Milton's poetry taken from Carey and Fowler 1968.

sensuous kind is quite absent from his writing. Nowhere in his writing is there anything quite like the second line of that simile in *Paradise Lost* –

> As one who long in populous city pent,
> Where houses thick and sewers annoy the air … .   (IX, ll. 445–456)

On the contrary, London can be so far from physically distasteful as to be positively lovely. The most famous example is in the sonnet "Composed Upon Westminster Bridge, Sept. 3, 1803", where city and countryside are not so much contrasted as found to make an equally miraculous impression on both eye and soul. Captured at its most country-like, London is here quiet and virtually depopulated, with the boundaries between architecture and the natural world much softened. "Ships, towers, domes, theatres, and temples lie / Open unto the fields, and to the sky", and in the very foreground there glides a river "at his own sweet will" (ll. 5–6, 12). While as a matter of everyday fact the city air would often have been full of smoke, in the sonnet it is unpolluted, just as it seems to be when, on his escape into the countryside at the beginning of *The Prelude*, he casts a "backward glance upon the curling cloud / Of city smoke, by distance ruralised" ((1850) I, ll. 88–89). Even if the city can be ruralized only by special lighting conditions, or at a particular hour of the clock, or by a distance which turns out to be an aesthetic distance, such writing bears not the slightest trace of anti-urban bias. It speaks nothing but open-hearted wonder.

Conversely, his descriptions the countryside are often far from idealistic. In "Home at Grasmere" he writes

> I came [to Grasmere] not dreaming of unruffled life,
> Untainted manners; born among the hills,
> Bred also there, I wanted not a scale
> To regulate my hopes. Pleased with the good,
> I shrink not from the evil with disgust,
> Or with immoderate pain. I look for Man,
> The common Creature of the brotherhood,
> Differing but little from the Man elsewhere,
> For selfishness, and envy, and revenge,
> Ill neighbourhood – pity that this should be –
> Flattery and double-dealing, strife and wrong.
>   ("The Recluse. Part First. Book First. Home at Grasmere", ll. 347–357)[4]

---

4. Quotations from ll. 1–753 of this poem are taken from MS D, the final version, as edited and adopted in de Selincourt and Darbishire 1952–1959: V, 313–338. MS D does not contain the conclusion of the poem but indicates that it is to be found in the form of the Prospectus to *The Recluse* as a whole which was published in 1814. For quotations from the poem's conclusion, that 1814 text is the one used here, as given by de Selincourt and Darbishire 1952–1959: V, 3–6.

Himself originally a denizen of the countryside, he expects to find countryside people no worse or better than anyone else. They may even engage in kinds of behaviour – flattery and double-dealing – which the Preface to the *Lyrical Ballads* might suggest is the monopoly of urbanite "social vanity" (1800 text, Owen and Smyser 1974: I, 234).

And if city smoke can be ruralized to a curling cloud, the countryside can be urbanized. Not its physical appearance, however. Its people, rather. And not its people in every respect. But above all the language of its people. When in the Preface to the *Lyrical Ballads* he explains his interest in "[h]umble and rustic" characters, he is at pains to mention that "[t]he language, too, of these men has been adopted", and to give reasons for this policy:

> [S]uch men hourly communicate with the best objects from which the best part of language is originally derived; and because, from their rank in society and the sameness and narrow circle of their intercourse, being less under the influence of social vanity, they convey their feelings and notions in simple and unelaborated expressions. Accordingly, such a language, arising out of repeated experience and regular feelings, is a more permanent, and a far more philosophical language than that which is frequently substituted for it by Poets, who think that they are conferring honour upon themselves and their art in proportion as they separate themselves from the sympathies of men, and indulge in arbitrary and capricious habits of expression, in order to furnish food for fickle tastes and fickle appetites of their own creation.   (1800 text, Owen and Smyser 1974: I, 234)

Coleridge's discussion of these claims in Chapter XVII of *Biographia Literaria* listed some forceful counterarguments:

> Rustic life (above all, low and rustic life) especially unfavourable to the formation of a human diction – The best parts of language the products of philosophers, not of clowns or shepherds – Poetry essentially ideal and generic – The language of Milton as much the language of real life, yea, incomparably more so than that of the cottager.   (Coleridge 1956 [1817]: 188)

Wordsworth thinks of the most important aspects of language as beginning with hourly communication with the best objects, and with simple expressions which can subsequently become more sophisticated. Coleridge thinks of the most important aspects of language as beginning with the discourse of philosophers and great poets, and then gradually percolating downwards to the rest of the human race. Both of them have clearly grasped something vital. But a text produced in accordance with Coleridge's ideal will always have to guard against obfuscation and elitism, while a Wordsworthian text will need to avoid bathos and coarseness. Even in the Preface itself, Wordsworth anticipates the Coleridgean point of view with a parenthetical concession:

> The language, too, of these men has been adopted (purified indeed from what appear to be its real defects, from all lasting and rational causes of dislike or disgust) …   (1800 text, Owen and Smyser 1974: I, 124)

And as Coleridge was the first to recognize, the entire controversy about language was really a red herring. After all, the *Lyrical Ballads* were not Robert Anderson's *Cumbrian Ballads* of 1805, which so strongly foregrounded dialect features (Baron 1995: 16–20). In Wordsworth's major poetry, the speech of rustic characters is not really very prominent at all, and to the extent that it does come in, both as direct speech within inverted commas, and even more obviously when in the form of indirect or free indirect speech, it is mediated through his own educated sensibility, in a style which also absorbs philosophical terminology from Hartley and Burke, and poetic diction from Cowper, Thompson, Akenside, and Milton. Country-folk are observed through the same imaginatively refining perspective as that by which a view of London can be synthesized to natural landscape.

Regardless of what the Preface may in places seem to suggest, Wordsworth did not turn to countryside people either for their language or for what he and Coleridge called their manners. In both language and manners, countryside people were impolite in ways which he knew might cause offence. The other side of the coin was that they also lacked that "social vanity" by which, in cultivated people, genuinely human thoughts and feelings can be masked. At first our own sophistication as present-day students of literature, many of us with memories of deconstructionist literary theory, for instance, may tempt us to accuse Wordsworth of naive essentialism here. But if so, we need to expose ourselves more frankly to his challenge, for he, if anybody, knew about the close interrelationship between environment and human individuation. If, in the culture-versus-nature controversy, he had been an absolute naturalist, the choice between rustic and urbane characters would have been a matter of pure indifference to him. As it was, he always remained at least enough of a Godwinian to believe that upbringing did count. Yet on the other hand, he would also have understood what Lord Chesterfield, that paragon of politeness, had in mind when he remarked that, at court, "if enemies did not embrace, they would stab. … The guile of the serpent simulates the gentleness of the dove" (Stanhope 1755). What Wordsworth wanted to lay before his readers was instances of love and hate, joy and despair, guilt and forgiveness, and of moral qualities such as strength or weakness, unselfishness or selfishness, kindness or unkindness, all of this captured in nakedly spontaneous modes of action, even though recollected within a process of poetic creation that was tranquilly meditative and civilizing. His underlying assumption does not rule out culturalist recognitions that the human being is always already socially formed, and that the objects of thought and feeling, and the contexts within which moral qualities come into play, inevitably vary from one social milieu to another. But he is always sufficiently naturalist to insist, as in "The Old Cumberland Beggar", that "we have all of us one human heart" (l. 153), a claim which in existential terms is still defensible. Primary needs and secondary needs; social bonds and social conflicts; birth and, above all, death: these human basics, though open to infinitely varied cultural realizations, are common to us all, and provide an experiential springboard from which to launch ourselves on flights of imaginative empathy with people whose very otherness may be significant for us. So in seeing the genre of the epitaph as, in effect, the archetype of all poetry, Wordsworth's instinct was sound. A good epitaph, he said in the first of his three essays on the topic, is not a case of "proud writing". It is not "shut up for the studious: it is exposed to all – to the wise and the most ignorant; … the stooping old man cons the engraven record like a second horn-book; – the child is proud that he can read it; and the stranger is introduced through its mediation to the company of a friend: it is concerning all, and for all" (Wordsworth 1814:453–454). Its very occasion is of course the ultimate levelling.

A good epitaph, he argued, is not circumstantially particular, but will have a certain human generality, and all his own best poetry is similarly "ideal and generic", to use Coleridge's terms. If his cityscapes leave out the sewers which annoy the air, realistic detail from the countryside never comes with the raw brutality of Crabbe, but is observed by a sensibility that is delicate and kindly. Sometimes, rural sordidness is seen with the eye of sorrow, as when the Pedlar in Book I of *The Excursion* notices that Margaret, in her grief for the husband who has taken the King's shilling never to return, no longer bothers to keep her cottage and garden tidy –

> … looking round me, now I first observed
> The corner stones, on either side the porch,
> With dull red stains discoloured, and stuck o'er
> With tufts and hairs of wool, as if the sheep,
> That fed upon the Common, thither came
> Familiarly, and found a couching-place
> Even at her threshold.   (*The Excursion*, I, ll. 742–748)

At other times, there is a note of transforming consolation, as when the Pedlar, now thinking of Margaret at rest in her quiet grave, again contemplates the sordid disarray of her garden –

> Those weeds, and the high spear-grass on that wall,
> By mist and silent rain-drops silvered o'er,
> As once I passed, into my heart conveyed
> So still an image of tranquillity,
> So calm and still, and looked so beautiful
> Amid the uneasy thoughts which filled my mind,
> That what we feel of sorrow and despair
> From ruin and from change, and all the grief
> That passing shows of Being leave behind,
> Appeared an idle dream…   (*The Excursion*, I, ll. 943–952)

Yet Wordsworth's treatment of the rural had none of the pretty emptiness and artificiality of pastoral motifs in so much of the verse, painting and china of the eighteenth century, for which Wordsworth and other Romantics in part blamed Pope (Griffin 1995). As I argued in the previous study, Pope's *Pastorals*, though exquisitely charming and fanciful, were in fact deeply moving in their treatment of some basic human feelings and concerns. But although this made Pope, despite his more open engagement with erotic love, the most recent significant predecessor here, Wordsworth's failure to acknowledge a debt was perhaps understandable, in that his temperamental affinity with Spenser and Milton was certainly much closer. *The Shepheardes Calender* and "Lycidas" belonged to the European line in descent from the New Testament's allegory of shepherds as the pastors of human souls. In this kind of poetry, a shepherd was a significant moral agent, and a good or a bad shepherd was to be emulated or shunned accordingly. What was striking in Wordsworth own contribution, moreover, was his literalness. When he presented a clergyman, he presented, not a clergyman disguised as a shepherd, but a country clergyman. His rural characters, submitted to close ethical and spiritual scrutiny, were country people who in real life would have been, as he claimed, exactly as he described them. Pope's Strephon and Daphnis, Hylas and Delia, Ægon and Doris, by contrast, carry with them an obviously literary colouring from the pages of Theocritus and Virgil, even though they are fully charged with Romantic nervousness, and even though Pope, too, avoided pastoral allegory.

Another way to say this is that, as an observer of country people, Wordsworth was very different from Lockwood in *Wuthering Heights* (1847). Disappointed in love, Lockwood travels northwards in order to get away from the falseness and artificiality of the *beau monde* down in the south. In his melancholy, he believes that he is a true man of feeling, and he now wishes either to isolate himself from the human race altogether, or at least to have dealings only with people who are as genuine as he believes himself to be. He might almost have got his ideas about life in the rural north from the Preface to the *Lyrical Ballads*. Yet the human drama which confronts him in Yorkshire shows him up as the shallow literary sentimentalist he has always been. Wordsworth, on the other hand, was perfectly accurate in claiming to have had a rural upbringing himself. Despite being the son of a gentleman, despite his grammar-school- and Cambridge education, and despite his strong affinities with many earlier poets, travel writers, and philosophers, he had grown up, not only surrounded by impressive natural scenery, but in the very heart of a rural community. During his years at Hawkshead Grammar School, he had been a lodger in the tiny cottage of Hugh and Ann Tyson, Hugh a master joiner, Ann formerly a draper. Here was the woman – "my old dame, so motherly and good", so full of her "parent's pride" in him (*The Prelude* (1805), IV, ll. 17–18) – who took the place of his own dead mother. At her fireside, he drank in true stories such as the one mentioned in Book VIII (ll. 223–311) of the 1805 *Prelude*, the story of a Lakeland shepherd and his son looking for a lost sheep, of the son's remembering that sheep often return to the place where they have grazed as lambs, of the son's actually finding the sheep but then being stranded on a rock in the middle of a stream, and of the father's final coming to the rescue.

The Pedlar in *The Excursion* has something of the same hybridity as Wordsworth himself. When, by 1798, Wordsworth had completed one version of the story of Margaret and her ruined cottage, the Pedlar who narrated it was little more than a narrative convenience – the poet's ostensible source of information, and an entirely secondary character. But Wordsworth become dissatisfied with this and more than doubled the poem's length, in order to explain how the Pedlar, a man of simple countryside origins, could have come to acquire the insight required in order to give Margaret's story its full due. Wordsworth's description of the Pedlar's childhood and youth amid the sights and sounds of the natural world, and of his response to a "sentiment of being, spread / O'er all that moves, and all that seemeth still" ("The Ruined Cottage", MS B, ll. 243–244), were the first steps towards writing his own spiritual autobiography in the shape of the Two Parts version of *The Prelude*, completed in 1799, which co-opted hundreds of lines originally applied to the Pedlar, including the phrase just quoted. The other main aspect of his increased interest in the pedlar figure had to do with more formal education: with the Pedlar's early upbringing in the Scottish kirk; with the centrality of the Bible for him; with the books he borrowed from the Schoolmaster; and with his fascination with arithmetic and geometry, for which he found examples in natural phenomena – "His triangles, they were the stars of heaven, / The *silent* stars; his altitudes the crag / Which is the eagle's birthplace" ("The Ruined Cottage", MS B, ll. 210–213). By the same token, between 1801 and 1804 Wordsworth gave more and more thought to his own immersion in literate culture, now becoming dissatisfied with the Two Parts *Prelude*, which brought his own life-story only as far as the end of his Hawkshead schooldays, and writing a new, five-book *Prelude* so as to cover his studies in Cambridge. In other words, for nearly twenty years before the Pedlar's narration of Margaret's story finally appeared in 1814 in Book I of *The Excursion*, Wordsworth personally had had not the slightest doubt that a man of humble countryside origins could be deeply in tune with the world of nature, could have a finely empathetic understanding of human beings, and could even be intellectually sharp and ethically sound in apprehending fundamental questions of science and philosophy.

Well aware that such a take on the Pedlar would shock "the prejudices of artificial society", he added a footnote to ll. 340–341 of *The Excursion* Book I ("From his native hills / He [the Pedlar] wandered far; much did he see of men"), in order to bring in a long passage from Robert Heron's *Observations made in a journey through the Western Counties of Scotland in the autumn of 1792*. This he offered as collateral evidence of the "class of men, from whom my own personal knowledge emboldened me to draw this portrait [of the Pedlar]" (de Selincourt and Darbishire 1952–1959: V, 411). What Heron reported was that, both within the Roman Empire and in colonized North America, travelling merchants had done much to bring civilization to indigenous savage peoples; that they had become "eminently skilled in the knowledge of the world";

that their lonely wanderings in thinly-inhabited districts had given them "habits of reflection and of sublime contemplation"; and, to crown it all, that it

> is not more than twenty or thirty years since a young man going from any part of Scotland to England, of purpose *to carry the pack*, was considered as going to lead the life and acquire the fortune of a gentleman. When, after twenty years' absence, in that honourable line of employment, he returned with his acquisitions to his native country, he was regarded as a gentleman to all intents and purposes.
>
> (de Selincourt and Darbishire 1952–1959: V, 412)

As figured in *The Excursion*, Wordsworth the educated poet experiences himself as actually the Pedlar's inferior in intellect and spiritual wisdom, and when the two of them come across the Solitary's copy of *Candide*, a work soon to enter into a fascinating intertextual relationship with the Solitary's own life-story, the Pedlar's verdict has a ring of Johnsonian authority. *Candide*, he says, is the "dull product of a scoffer's pen, / Impure conceits discharging from a heart / Hardened by impious pride!" (*The Excursion*, II, ll. 485–486).

Coleridge shared "the prejudices of artificial society". He could never grasp the sheer sociocultural range of either Wordsworth himself or the Pedlar in *The Excursion*.

> Is there one word … attributed to the pedlar in the *Excursion* characteristic of a pedlar? One sentiment that might not more plausibly, even without the aid of any previous explanation, have proceeded from any wise and beneficent old man of a rank or profession in which the language of learning and refinement are natural and to be expected? Need the rank have been at all particularized, where nothing follows which the knowledge of that rank is to explain or illustrate? When on the contrary this information renders the man's language, feelings, sentiments and information a riddle …?
>
> (Coleridge 1956 [1817]: 257)

He could quite see that Wordsworth was interested in rustic life,

> not *as* low and rustic, or in order to repeat that pleasure of doubtful moral effect which persons of elevated rank and of superior refinement oftentimes derive from a happy imitation of the rude unpolished manners and discourse of their inferiors.
>
> (Coleridge 1956 [1817]: 189)

But he incurably believed that gentlemen closely identified with urban civilization were the people most in touch with the great questions of life, and most capable of shouldering responsibility for the general human weal. True, his own poem "Reflections on Having Left a Place of Retirement", written in 1796, the year before the beginning of his close intimacy with Wordsworth, does not underestimate rural delights. Its description of the Clevedon cottage and garden in their "Valley of Seclusion" is lovingly detailed (l. 9), and his rambles along the hills and cliff-tops of the southwest coast have prompted intuitions which may soon have helped Wordsworth to articulate, in "Tintern Abbey", his own sense of the One Life in all things. Yet for Coleridge, rural pleasures, even at their most uplifting, were marred by his truant's sense of guilt. The poem figures him as now leaving Clevedon in a rush to get back to the city, and to political activity on behalf of "unnumber'd brethren" who have "toiled and bled". No longer willing to

> ... dream away the entrusted hours
> On rose-leaf beds, pampering the coward heart
> With feelings all too delicate for use,

from now on he will "revisit thee, dear Cot" only in the spirit, "when after honourable toil / Rests the tired mind" (ll. 45–48, 63–65).

At first sight Wordsworth's "Home at Grasmere" might just as easily have been entitled "Reflections on *Reaching* a Place of Retirement". It opens with a statement of his powerful childhood memories of Grasmere and of his profound longing for a home in such a place. Some passages involve the same polarization of city and country, and the same straightforward preference for the countryside, as in the *Prelude*'s Miltonically reinforced description of the pent-up urbanite's escape. Another parallel is with the passage in "Tintern Abbey" which tells how memories of the rural scene have persisted as a source of spiritual strength "in lonely rooms, and 'mid the din / Of towns and cities" (ll. 25–26). And as in that poem, so here, he describes himself as accompanied by his sister Dorothy. Their "beautiful and quiet home" in Grasmere will also be enriched by the occasional sojourns of their brother John, the Hutchinson sisters, and Coleridge himself,

> ...a Brother of our hearts,
> Philosopher and Poet, in whose sight
> These Mountains will rejoice with open joy.   ("Home at Grasmere", ll. 659–661)

Grasmere, then, will draw to itself Wordsworth's significant group, to borrow Thomas McFarland's phrase. According to Kenneth J. Johnston, the poem's ethos is actually becoming too cosy, which would explain, if Johnston were right, why most of it was not published during Wordsworth's own lifetime. Wordsworth, says Johnston, reluctantly came to acknowledge "the social responsibility he was shirking"; his thoughts of poverty, death and evil punctured the idyll and disrupted his bonding with nature; the poem as a whole shows his "clear awareness that his greatness as a poet could never be built on Grasmere, the Lake District, or even all of Nature"; the only spiritual community he could vouch for was the extended family; and Grasmere was simply not the right place from which to save the human race (Johnston 2003: 79–83). Johnston, then, has unquestioningly adopted the mind-set of Coleridge's "Reflections on Having Left a Place of Retirement". In fact, however, the expression "place of retirement" would have been totally inappropriate in the title of Wordsworth's poem, since it might have suggested that the central focus of life, both of human life in general and of Wordsworth's own life in particular, was really in some place *other* than Grasmere. For Wordsworth, Grasmere really is both home and workplace, in a way that, for Coleridge, Clevedon or any other village could never have been. At the same time, and by extension, Wordsworth really is writing for readers situated anywhere at all. For him, life and literature can be geographically polyfocal in a way which, to a generation conversant with the World Wide Web, is likely to seem much less dated than Coleridge's metropolitanism.

Taken as a whole, "Home at Grasmere" suggests that William and Dorothy's hopes of Grasmere will not have been misplaced. Already, Wordsworth has his familiars: the breezes that "[p]ursue each other through the yielding plain / Of grass or corn, over and through and through, / In billow after billow, evermore / Disporting"; the "small grey horse that bears / The paralytic Man"; the whooping "Owl that gives the name to Owlet-Crag" (ll. 28–31, 505–506, 521). And stating in the sharpest possible terms the contrast with

> ... the vast Metropolis ...
> Where pity shrinks from unremitting calls,
> Where numbers overwhelm humanity,
> And neighbourhood serves rather to divide
> Than to unite [,]

he can affirm that

> ... Society is here
> A true Community, a genuine frame
> Of many into one incorporate.   (ll. 597–601, 614–616)

Above all, Grasmere is the place where he knows he will be able to do his distinctive work. Johnston's aggressively Coleridgean verdict is that "Home at Grasmere" makes claims for the place that are completely unrealistic – that Wordsworth "ultimately backs himself into a corner, out of the poem, and breaks off" (Johnston 2003: 81). Yet the poem's final section begins,

> Yet 'tis not to enjoy that we exist,
> For that end only; something must be done.
> I must not walk in unreproved delight
> These narrow bounds, and think of nothing more,
> No duty that looks further, and no care.   (ll. 664–668)

Coleridge would agree, of course, which is why he himself left Clevedon for Bristol or London. But for Wordsworth, the great thing to be done can only be done here in Grasmere, by writing, as his life-long participation in the world of polite letters had equipped him to write, for the readers of literature everywhere, but also by writing in intimate harmony with the precise natural and social world from which he personally drew most strength. With the modest frankness so characteristic of the entire poem, he wants to avoid "ill-advised Ambition and … Pride", yet also confesses his belief that "an internal brightness is vouchsafed [to him] / That must not die" (ll. 673–676). Gaining self-confidence as he goes along, he continues,

> Possessions have I that are solely mine,
> Something within which yet is shared by none,
> Not even the nearest to me and most dear,
> Something which power and effort may impart,
> I would impart it, I would spread it wide,
> Immortal in the world which is to come.   (ll. 686–691)

He immediately apologizes for so bold a claim but, now quite unstoppably, goes on to tell of his thirst for conflict, struggle, and ultimate victory in life. The poem ends, not with the embarrassing whimper reported by Johnston, but with the prodigious thunderclap of the final 107 lines, a passage much better known than the rest of "Home at Grasmere", because he actually published it, in the 1814 Preface to *The Excursion*, as the Prospectus to the now publicly promised *Recluse*. *The Recluse*, his poetic and philosophical *magnum opus* on "Man, Nature, and Society", was to consist of a preparatory autobiographical part (posthumously published as *The Prelude*), a Part I (including "Home at Grasmere" itself), a Part II consisting of *The Excursion*, and a concluding Part III. All in all, *The Recluse* would proclaim

> How exquisitely the individual Mind
> (And the progressive powers perhaps no less
> Of the whole species) to the external World
> Is fitted: – and how exquisitely, too –
> Theme this but little heard of among men –
> The external World is fitted to the Mind;
> And the creation (by no lower name
> Can it be called) which they with blended might
> Accomplish.
> (*Prospectus to* The Recluse (= conclusion to "Home at Grasmere"), ll. 63–71)

Especially when read with these and the rest of the final 107 lines in place, "Home at Grasmere" expresses little doubt that he will be able to complete this work of awe-inspiring and universal significance, and to complete it at home in Grasmere. As I shall later illustrate, the rhetoric of this poem itself is a most remarkable specimen of his literary-communicational power.

Coleridge's commentary on Wordsworth's poetry in *Biographia Literaria* is generous and helpful. Twenty years previously, through his conversation and writing he had crucially helped Wordsworth to formulate some of his most fruitful ideas. They had often lived in close proximity, and for well over a year under one and the same roof, at Allan Bank, Grasmere. Coleridge himself remains a significant poet, and in his prose writings shows himself an exceptionally gifted polymath, and a most energetic champion of social justice. Yet despite all this, Coleridge's own social formation was much more monomorphic than Wordsworth's – the analysis of his formative London years in both "Frost at Midnight" and *The Prelude* is psychologically accurate –, and he was socially unimaginative. For people whose formation was different from his own, his empathy was not immediately forthcoming. As a result he never really grasped Wordsworth's way of being in the world, and was ultimately deaf to Wordsworth's most distinctive mode of address.

The irony is double: that Wordsworth could never have written a single word of his greatest poetry if Coleridge had not been his early sparring partner; and that he had no real opportunity to perceive Coleridge's ultimate deafness to his most distinctive writing until 1815. When he wrote the 1814 Preface to *The Excursion*, he still thought that to finish *The Recluse* would be, quite literally, to write and publish a complete and self-contained work of that title. Coleridge, who thought the same, had been expecting him to produce "the *first* and *only* true Phil[osophical] Poem in existence" (Coleridge 1815:329). Wordsworth had constantly looked to him for advice on how to write it in practice, albeit largely in vain. Especially in 1804, when Coleridge had set off on his long Mediterranean trip still without leaving clear guidelines, Wordsworth had been much discomforted. Finally, eight months after publication of *The Excursion* Coleridge broke this 18 years' silence, in a letter to which students of both Wordsworth and Coleridge have devoted much attention. The key passage opens as follows:

> [In *The Recluse*] I supposed you first to have meditated the faculties of Man in the abstract, in their correspondence with his Sphere of action, and first, in the Feeling, Touch, and Taste, then in the Eye, & last in the Ear, to have laid a solid and immoveable foundation for the Edifice by removing the sandy Sophisms of Locke, and the Mechanic Dogmatists, and demonstrating that the Senses were living growths and developements [*sic*] of the Mind & Spirit in a much juster as well as higher sense, than the mind can be said to be formed by the Senses.

As for the conclusion:

> In short, Facts elevated into Theory – Theory into Laws – & Laws into living & intelligent Powers – true Idealism necessarily perfecting itself in Realism, Realism refining itself into Idealism. – Such or something like this was the Plan, I had supposed that you were engaged on.   (Coleridge 1815:330)

According to Juliet Barker, this was

absolutely devastating. It cut the ground from under William's feet as a man, as a philosopher and as a poet. Quite simply, it told him that he had failed in the most important work of his life. And reading this critique, this prospectus for a poem of which a third was already written, William must have been forced to accept his failure. ... [I]t was the end of the dream which had motivated almost the whole of his literary life.   (Baker 2001: 330–331)

But Barker's "William must have been forced" is unconvincing, not only because it is unsupported by any detailed references to Wordsworth's spoken or written reactions (Barker herself (2001: 331) conscientiously notes that "[i]f he responded, or made any sort of protest, the letter has been lost"), but also because here for Wordsworth was the clearest possible demonstration of what his own genius did *not* entail. Judging by the 1805 *Prelude*, "Home at Grasmere", *The Excursion* and all his other great work hitherto, he now had more than enough self-knowledge and self-confidence to recognize this without regret. Even though, for the rest of his life, he was certainly unhappy at Coleridge's disappointment in him, and actually caught something of Coleridge's own penchant for self-accusation, a work with the addressivity and content expected by Coleridge's letter would have been totally unWordsworthian, and incomparably less valuable than the greatest work that Wordsworth did produce. He could simply have no wish to address himself so exclusively to readers of philosophy, or to seem to write so narrowly from the life-experience of a typical philosopher, and his types of illustration and argument were not so purely philosophical either. In particular, he did not share philosophers' monological preoccupation with truth. In his own thoughts about his great project, he frankly saw himself as offering "the sensations and opinions of a poet living in retirement" (Preface to *The Excursion*), and throughout his entire career as a writer he was perfectly aware that his sensations and opinions were very much subject to variation, not only as his personal feelings alternated between joy and despondency, but as he drew on kinds of experience, thought, and feeling which, however much synthesized by style and imagination, could either be more rural or more urban in their affinities. The uncanny inwardness with which a poem such as "The Old Cumberland Beggar" successively penetrates the mind-sets of the most abject of countryside figures and of the nation's great and good in Westminster is profoundly characteristic, and totally un-Coleridgean.

In every sense except the literal, he did complete *The Recluse*. "Home at Grasmere" is already a deeply felt reverie on the mutual compatibility of mind and nature, and on their blending in rural communities. The same applies still more obviously to *The Prelude* and *The Excursion*. And even before he read Coleridge's allegedly devastating letter, in the Preface to *The Excursion* he had clearly stated his sense that his more "minor Pieces", poems such as "The Old Cumberland Beggar", for instance, "which have long been before the Public, when they shall be properly arranged, will be found by the attentive Reader to have such connection with the main Work [*The Recluse*] as may give them claim to be likened to the little cells, oratories, and sepulchral recesses, ordinarily included in [the larger body of a gothic church]". His own arrangement of collected editions of his poems, not by chronology, but according to affective, psychological, and thematic categories, is an important clue to the coherence of his opus overall, even if it has annoyed readers by making the poems of what Arnold described as the golden decade more difficult to find amid the bulk of the later ones. Every word of his poetry really is the sensations and opinions of a profoundly thoughtful and sensitive poet, living in a state which, even when he does describe it as one of rural retirement, is not an abnegation of social responsibility but nourishes his most distinctively manifold qualities, thereby greatly extending his outreach.

4.3   Community spirit

In moving beyond postmodern stereotypes of Wordsworth's formation as restrictively monocultural I am not alone. Frances Ferguson, too, has picked up on his view of epitaphs, for instance, commenting that, for him, "the epitaph registers an insistence that human attachment … continues in the absence of agreement" (Ferguson 2003: 106), an observation in close harmony with my view of community as a grouping within which sub-groupings and individuals can agree to disagree. Michael Baron goes one stage further, pointing out that Wordsworth's eclectic sense of community did not limit itself to the here and now but also had a diachronic dimension. *The Prelude*'s dream of the Arab horseman (in Book V) asks to be read as a lament for the fragility of poetry, not only as an inscription on perishably physical paper, but as an aesthetic creation which may not withstand the vicissitudes of taste (Baron 1995: 134–135). Lucy Newlyn, in similar vein, traces the same poem's own attempt to guard against this danger through self-confessed affinities with Shakespeare, Milton, Fox, Bunyan, Wesley, Paine, Priestley, Hartley, Cowper, Rousseau and Coleridge. Here Newlyn finds evidence of "the collaborative nature of Wordsworth's interaction with the audiences – past, present, and future – which he imagines and addresses. It makes of the poem a vast web of literary connections, expanding from the individual imagination towards an 'outermost and all-embracing circle' of precursors and readers" (Newlyn 2003: 61) – the "one great society alone on earth: / The noble living and the noble dead" (*Prelude* (1805) X 968–9). Taking all his predecessors for what they were, when and where they were, and not envisaging just one particular type of reader either now or in the future, he hopes to bring about a literary community that will be large but heterogeneous.

Wordsworth's historically differentiating community spirit, as we can perhaps call it, was so strong that it inevitably came across in his writing, even though for well over a century his admirers interpreted him in terms of lofty-minded aestheticism and de-historicized universality. The main point missed by that tradition of commentary was that the hybrid complexity of his attitudes feeds in to an ethically principled rhetoric, warmly inviting readers into fellowship while still allowing them to retain all their difference from himself. The nineteenth century ideal of poetry did not valorize such generous friendliness and tended to assimilate some of its manifestations to the egotism as a cause for regret. Postmodern critics, again, while valuably puncturing the traditional notion of poetry's universality, could not grasp that just a single reading community could be both historical and very large without being hegemonic, or that just a single writer could address it. And whereas traditional critics had complained that Wordsworth could be too wilfully present in his own writing, some postmodern critics tended towards the opposite extreme, almost seeing him as the mere auto-mated mouthpiece of one fairly narrow segment of society.

The theoretical spadework for a more adequate view of Wordsworthian com-munication has been commenced by Baron. Particularly relevant is the contrast he draws between Wordsworth's own view of communication and Herder's notion of the *Volk*. Although both these writers saw language as a power which could bring people together, Wordsworth was less mystical and more pragmatic, very much anticipating Habermas's concept of communication as social action. As noted in my Introduction, Habermas stresses that, for communication to be genuine and effective, there have to be certain social protocols over and above the Aristotelian logic which Nietzsche and Derrida took to be the cornerstone of Western civilization. What is also called for is a common willingness to speak or write in ways that are comprehensible, true, truth-ful, sincere, and socially appropriate. And despite Bakhtin's claim that Romanticism is essentially monologic, a charge which certainly applies to the Romantic theoriza-tion – including Wordsworth's own – by which the eighteenth century culture of polite letters was so firmly demoted, Baron detects in Wordsworth's actual poetry a strong wish to reach out across sociocultural divides, plus a gut feeling that the ordinary everyday virtues of good will, honesty and tact will be communicationally decisive (Baron 1995: 133–134). True, Baron also says that "[i]t is difficult to see what force could *produce* such a [communicational good] will on a wider basis except an appeal to political identity" (Baron 1995: 133, his italics). But here, I think, he is relapsing into the determinist historicism of some of his postmodern predecessors, thereby contradicting the force of his own main argument. The will to communicate does not confine itself within some pre-existent grouping of political look-alikes. As Baron's own analysis skilfully shows, Wordsworth himself saw communication as making a community beyond the grouping as presently defined. Even when in the first instance addressing what McFarlane described as the significant but socially narrow group of his own nearest and dearest, he hoped for a wide audience. In fact the "Poems on the Naming of Places" were experiments deliberately designed to test whether the place-names invented and cherished by his own loved-ones and himself could also have a resonance for other people as well (Baron 1995: 59–69). His fervent desire was that his own thought- and life-world would indeed become public, the initial privacies notwithstanding. For his own part, the communicational good will could not have been stronger, and like Habermas he sensed that this in itself was more than half the battle.

Often the eager good will translated into an importunate urge to bring his un-customary perceptions within the scope of customary language. Hence, to use Helen Darbishire's phrase, his glosses of later interpretation, which readers have in many cases found so anticlimactic, over-intrusive and self-centred. But to repeat, there is no absolute distinction between poetry and self-centredness. There is rather a sliding scale, which means that verdicts on any particular instance will be a matter of taste. And since taste, in turn, is a matter of what preconceptions and expectations readers bring to their reading, their verdicts will vary, depending on how much they are pre-pared to enjoy the sense of Wordsworth addressing them as person to person. Even the readers most willing to welcome him in this role – even I myself – will always feel that many of his interventions go too far. By any standard, bathos is fairly frequent. But if we squarely admit this, it should be that much easier to see that many passages which were bathos on a strictly idealist criterion, on a communicational criterion are not bathos after all.

If we take the full measure of Wordsworth's desire, not to create ideal poetry, not to bully or talk down to his readers, but to offer friendly communion, then the first and longest version of the poem about the old man travelling is of considerable inter-est. Here, without detracting from the old man's fascinating initial appearance, Words-worth also seeks to explore his personal background, to find out what makes him tick, and to see if there are similarities with other, less unusual-seeming human beings. What he discovers is that the reason for the old man's tranquillity of settled purpose, and for his apparent immunity to discomfort, is his longing to see his wounded son. There have probably always been some readers who, as Wordsworth anticipated in his stout defence of the "elementary feelings" observable in "[l]ow and rustic life" (Preface to *Lyrical Ballads* (1800), Owen and Smyser 1974:I, 124), will have found such straightforward paternal love a little naive or even incredible. But to Wordsworth when he first wrote the poem, it was very real, and perhaps the most important thing of all. It was this that he wanted to share with his readers, and if they were prepared to listen to him, if they took his reported investigation as perfectly natural, if they did not want to think of the old man as just an exotic curiosity, if they wanted, with Wordsworth himself, to deepen their understanding of him, by *recognising* his human sameness and otherness in the sense recently explained by A. C. Goodson (2009) in terms of the ethical theory of Levinas, then in practice the circle of community was already expanding. What was going was a process of bonding, between Wordsworth and his readers and the old man himself, as it were, or people like him.

Wordsworth's own ideas about such processes can be deduced from the portrait of Michel Beaupuy in *The Prelude* Book IX. While living in Blois in 1792, it was from Beaupuy that he received his most important political education. But he was not more taken by the man's ideas than by his way of treating other people.

> Man he loved
> As man; and, to the mean and the obscure,
> And all the homely in their homely works,
> Transferred a courtesy which had no air
> Of condescension; but did rather seem
> A passion and a gallantry, like that
> Which he, a soldier, in his idler day
> Had paid to woman: somewhat vain he was,
> Or seemed so, yet it was not vanity,
> But fondness, and a kind of radiant joy
> Diffused around him, while he was intent
> On works of love or freedom ...   (*Prelude* (1850) IX 306–17)[5]

These democratic kinds of courteous warm-heartedness are brought into play in Wordsworth's own communication. Not only did his hybridity of personal formation allow him, in everyday life, to be at ease with people from a far wider social range than Coleridge was, for instance. In much of his writing his joyfulness and sensitive openness come across as also a matter of temperament, springing from an irrepressible delight in human pursuits of almost any description. In fact the poetry draws on something which to Modernist readers under the sway of Thanatos and anomie could seem, as Lionel Trilling put it, too unabrasive to be real (Trilling 1967; cf. Sell 2001: 217–222). It brings into play what the Preface to *Literary Ballads* described as "the grand and elementary principle of pleasure, by which ... [man] knows, and feels, and lives, and moves" (1850 text, Owen and Snyser 1974: I 140).

He certainly can cast himself as a solitary, and the Preface to *The Excursion* was fair game for Bagehot's delicious parody: "Now it came to pass in those days that William Wordsworth went up into the hills" (Bagehot 1972 [1852]: 55). Yet what Hazlitt (a better portrait-painter than critic of Wordsworth's poetry) found in his physiognomy was a striking juxtaposition of introvert high seriousness and mirth:

> There was a severe, worn pressure of thought about his temples, a fire in his eye (as if he saw something in objects more than the outward appearance), an intense high narrow forehead, a Roman nose, cheeks furrowed by strong purpose and feeling, and a convulsive inclination to laughter about the mouth, a good deal at variance with the solemn, stately expression of the rest of his face.
>
> (Hazlitt 2000 [1823]: 523)

---

5.   The wording of the penultimate line here in the 1805 version is less suggestive of the communicational force of Beaupuy's attitude: "a kind of radiant joy / That covered him about when he was bent / On works of love or freedom."

Wordsworth, who so delighted in the London round of social calls, parties and theatre-going, instinctively perceives solitude as a negativity that is poignantly exceptional, a state whose inner eye may well bring exquisite pleasures, but which is almost inhuman in being cut off from the responses of others. This is part of the aura of "Old Man Travelling", as also of "She dwelt among th' untrodden ways", and although it is the Solitary Reaper's very solitariness that makes her song so audible, and perhaps even gives rise to it, her music, though doubtless satisfying some private need of her own, becomes a sound which Wordsworth bears in his own heart, and a memory which his poem of course shares with an ever widening circle of readers. When he, too, wanders "lonely as a cloud", he is similarly drawn into a "laughing company", albeit of daffodils, with whom, even in his imagination's most exquisite "bliss of solitude", he will still – of all things! – dance ("I wandered lonely as a cloud", ll. 1, 10, 16). Solitude is necessary to the tranquil recollection from which his poetry flows, but does not correlate with standoffishness or selfish irresponsibility. Recent complaints that he failed to acknowledge the voice of Dorothy in his writing – for instance, her journal's wonderful description of laughing daffodils (Butler 2003:42, 51) – overlook some of the general laws of communication and human creativity, and fail to grasp Wordsworth's own deepest feelings. One of the ways in which communities grow is precisely through our borrowing other people's perceptions, often quite unconsciously. And to appreciate Wordsworth's loving respect for Dorothy one need only compare, as I shall below, his way of treating her in "Tintern Abbey" with Coleridge's way of treating Sara in "The Eolian Harp". At its most distinctive, Wordsworth's poetry empathizes with, and itself expresses, different modes of being, flowing naturally between pleasurable self-withdrawal and warmly welcomed social bonds, of whose pleasures music and dancing are the archetypes. Typically enough, *The Prelude*'s great moment of solitary self-dedication to the lofty calling of poetry immediately follows upon a jolly evening whose survival in the memory is just as vibrant:

> ... dancing, gaiety and mirth–
> With din of instruments, and shuffling feet,
> And glancing forms, and tapers flittering,
> And unaimed prattle flying up and down,
> Spirits upon the stretch, and here and there
> Slight shocks of young love-liking interspersed
> That mounted up like joy into the head,
> And tingled through the veins.   (*Prelude* (1805) IV 316–27)

4.4   Ambition and humility

The austerity deduced by Hazlitt from the upper regions of Wordsworth's face is at its most awesome in those closing lines from "Home at Grasmere" which were published in 1814 as the Prospectus to *The Recluse*. Clearly apparent here is Wordsworth's Miltonic level of ambition, as he adopts Milton's stance of addressing the entire informed world of his time. Alluding to Milton's invocation of Urania, he even seems prepared to go one better:

> Urania, I shall need
> Thy guidance, or a greater Muse, if such
> Descend to earth or dwell in highest heaven!
> For I must tread on shadowy ground, must sink
> Deep – and, aloft ascending, breathe in worlds
> To which the heaven of heavens is but a veil.
> All strength – all terror, single or in bands,
> That ever was put forth in personal form –
> Jehovah – with his thunder, and the choir
> Of shouting Angels, and the empyreal thrones –
> I pass them unalarmed. Not Chaos, not
> The darkest pit of lowest Erebus,
> Nor aught of blinder vacancy, scooped out
> By help of dreams – can breed such fear and awe
> As fall upon us often when we look
> Into our Minds, into the Mind of Man –
> My haunt and the main region of my song.   (ll. 25–41)

Seen one way, the risk he runs here is of coming across as a literary braggart. The personnel and vistas of the hitherto greatest epic in the language leave him evidently unintimidated, an apparent hubris which readers may well find difficult to swallow. Seen in another light, the entire Prospectus is truly sublime, with Wordsworth setting himself up as the greatest of all prophets, and seeming to pull it off. Yet readers who do admire him here will not necessarily have been bowled over by a sheer effrontery. His open reliance on Milton's language and style of versification, his confessed eagerness to copy Milton in appealing to the most powerful muse available, can hint at an altogether more sober self-evaluation, for as in Milton, so too in Wordsworth, invocation itself contains an element of modesty, very like that of an apology. Neither Milton nor Wordsworth believed in the existence of muses in any literal sense. Yet both of them, in purporting to think that their own mighty themes could emerge under the inspiration of a supernatural being, were indicating a willingness not to take personal credit. They were not putting themselves forward in order to win praise for their own achievement, but in the hope of conveying insights which they honestly

hoped would benefit the entire human race. Despite their afflatus, they were humble
of spirit, acutely concerned lest their vision become dim, or their modes of expression
prove inadequate, as in Wordsworth's case becomes even clearer in the final lines of
the Prospectus. Here he entreats help, no longer from a mere creature of the literary
imagination, but from the "dread Power ... / Whose gracious favour is the primal
source / Of all illumination" (ll. 101–102), or in another version: from "great God / ...
who art breath and being, way and guide, /And power and understanding". At which
point some readers may even be inclined to forgive the appearances of boasting altogether, because of the plain prose sense of what he is actually saying. Given the mighty
task he proposes, he really does feel that he needs the strongest kind of support. After
all, if he finds the subject-matter of *Paradise Lost* no longer quite so stupendous, that
is perhaps because Milton has already mastered it. The mind of man, by contrast, has
yet to be grappled with.

The knife-edge this passage treads between self-importance and humility is very
Wordsworthian. But it seems to me that the only way to find fault with the writing
here is through an exclusive adherence to the older mode of Wordsworth criticism: by
requiring that it be a perfect instantiation of the Beautiful, the Sublime, the Imagination, that it be Poetry, that it be Art; and by simply not expecting or wanting it to be
frank about his own ambitions and self-doubt. If we, by contrast, take the lines as a
frank statement of his own hopes and fears as a writer, as a huge promise to us, his
readers, which he has not always thought he will be able to fulfil, then we will surely
feel their power to engage our thoughts and sympathies for him as one who, despite
an understandable solemnity, invites us to be his fellows in conversation.

4.5   "Home at Grasmere"

To repeat the point yet again, the published Prospectus to *The Recluse* had actually
been written as the last section of "Home at Grasmere", the first 958 lines of which,
unpublished during Wordsworth's lifetime, bear such striking witness to his sociocultural hybridity. I have already rejected Kenneth J. Johnston's suggestion that he refrained from publishing them because he came to see them as escapist. At first a better
explanation might seem to be that he planned them as an integral part of *The Recluse*
itself, which he never completed. Yet *The Excursion*, too, was to be part of the *magnum
opus*, and was published together with the Prospectus in 1814. So perhaps the real
reason for self-censorship here was the same hesitation about lengthy autobiography
to which he confessed *à propos The Prelude* ("a thing unprecedented in Literary history that a man should talk so much about himself" (Wordsworth 1805)), and which
may have led him to hold that poem back as well. To *keep himself out of* the public eye
would have been a natural enough response to the accusations of egocentric intrusiveness and bathos, and in point of fact an analogous self-withholding was effected

through his cuts to "Old Man Travelling". "Home at Grasmere" would obviously not have qualified as pure Poetry uncontaminated by selfhood, and his assessment was perhaps that, to a taste now increasingly nurtured by his own Preface to *Lyrical Ballads*, continuities with the personalizing congenialities of eighteenth century loco-descriptive poetry, for instance, or of Cowper on domesticity, would not appeal.

Given the passion and philosophical depth of the poem's grasp of natural beauty, and given its moments of tense soul-searching, those continuities were not of a predictable kind. But in its warm confidentiality of address there certainly was an eighteenth-century flavour, and one which called for readers who were less the devotees of consummate art than friendly, sympathetic fellow-beings. Such are the readers implied by the writing itself, and in addressing them Wordsworth's ethical sensitivity is very alert. His less articulable insights, his colossal spiritual project, and his downright honesty are all quite undiminished, for the main theme is indeed his own desire to find a *modus vivendi* which will reconcile the world of letters with a rural life lived close to nature. For him personally, nothing was at the time more crucial, since his entire future as a writer, and above all his chances of ever completing *The Recluse*, seemed to hang upon it. Yet these considerations, and all the attendant hopes and fears, are voiced with an extraordinary delicacy which, though inviting the warm approval of communicational critics today, during Wordsworth's own lifetime might have fallen, as he possibly expected, on deaf ears – on ears as deaf as those of Coleridge to what in post-postmodern times must seem his true distinction.

Although the poem describes him and Dorothy as finally returning to settle in the region where he spent his childhood, he cannot think of himself as *merely* returning. The experiences he has had elsewhere, and in other social circles, make him also a "Newcomer" to Grasmere. Their journey hither through the Yorkshire dales was a blustery one, and for two whole months the weather of Grasmere itself continues to test their resolve. During that period they are particularly fascinated by the birdlife of the place, and above all by two white swans who, like themselves, seem rather isolated from the rest of their kind, in a "small open space / Of blue unfrozen water, where they lodged, /And lived so long in quiet, side by side" (ll. 258–260). When one day the two swans are suddenly no longer to be seen, the human newcomer resorts to a euphemistic periphrasis which, especially to present-day readers, may seem precious and even ludicrous, but which nevertheless recalls Augustan modes of congenial discursiveness, its rather strained attempt at fanciful urbanity perhaps also marking the awkwardness of his still incomplete re-assimilation with the countryside: what he and sister now fear is that

> The Dalesmen may have aimed the deadly tube,
> And parted them [the two swans]; or haply both are gone
> One death, and that were mercy given to both.   (ll. 266–268)

According to Johnston (2003: 81), "William and Dorothy had drastically over-invested themselves in their symbolic identification with the swans" and the poem's "extreme symbolism" here descends to "ridiculous literalism". But such a reading, so exclusively the product of the older, idealist tradition of Wordsworth criticism, and so strongly biased in favour of Coleridgean metropolitanism, is irresponsive to the care with which the poem is following the newcomers' tense weeks of trial, as they seek to build up relationships with both the natural and human worlds of Grasmere, passionately hoping for a welcoming embrace, yet always secretly fearing rejection as outsiders. The fantasy of one or – was it? – both of the swans being killed by the dalesmen even begins to grapple with the possibility that one of them – would it be William? would it be Dorothy? – would survive the ordeal of re-acclimatization better than the other, and that they might actually be separated, a thought so unsettling, and so out of key with his high hopes of Grasmere, that Wordsworth immediately tries to disown it:

> Recal [*sic*] my song the ungenerous thought [of the dalesmen killing the swans];
>
> > forgive,
>
> Thrice favoured Region, the conjecture harsh
> Of such inhospitable penalty,
> Inflicted upon confidence so pure.   (ll. 269–272)

In the full context, these lines attribute the same complete purity and innocence of intention as seen in the swans, the same need of protection, to Wordsworth and his sister themselves, yet without risking the gauche simple-mindedness or arrogance that might vitiate a more direct moral self-appraisal. Nor is the indirectness a form of dishonesty. For thoughtfully sympathetic readers it will not hide, but positively reveal exactly what Wordsworth and Dorothy have been feeling. It is a fine truthfulness which is also finely modest: a frankness that is prepared to intimate their sense of vulnerability, but tempered with a decent unwillingness to overstress it, or to indulge in priggish self-pity.

4.6   *The Excursion*

A certain modesty must also underlie many of the poems which, like the first version of "Old Man Travelling", dramatize conversations between Wordsworth himself and other people. I say this because in the cases I have in mind the conversation comes across as real and untendentious, the longest and most impressive example being *The Excursion*, where we have Wordsworth, the Pedlar, the Solitary, and the Pastor spending a lot of time walking and eating and conversing together against a Lakeland backdrop.

Coleridge was unhappy with this set-up, complaining that Wordsworth had an undue predilection for the dramatic form in certain poems, from which one or other of two evils must result. Either the thoughts and diction are different from the poet, and then there arises an incongruity of style; or they are the same and indistinguishable, and then it presents a species of ventriloquism, where two are represented as talking while in truth one man only speaks.

(Coleridge 1956 [1817]: 258)

But, at the risk of stating the obvious, people do have different cultural backgrounds; even people whose cultural backgrounds are similar can have different opinions; and even one and the same person can be in two or more minds at once. This last is the disposition which Keats praised in Shakespeare as negative capability – the capability of "being in uncertainties, Mysteries, doubts, without any irritable reaching after fact and reason" (Keats 1954 [1817]: 53) – and although Keats was the first to pit Shakespeare's negative capability against Wordsworth's egotistical sublime, he may also have sensed the limitations of too absolute a distinction. Certainly he found *The Excursion* to be one of the "three things to rejoice at in this Age" (Keats 1954 [1818]: 58), and here could well have been responding to what is at times a most thought-provoking philosophical dialogue. Whereas its four speakers each give vent to some very strong certainties, the poem as a whole does not. Seamus Perry's description of Book I would in fact apply throughout: it is certainly "a curiously double-minded poem" (Perry 2003: 165) – and "double" may be an understatement.

Granted, the Pedlar would like to cheer the Solitary up; absolutely sure that the Solitary's attitude is mistaken, he goes to great lengths to explain why; and Wordsworth-the-poet, too, rather like Milton in his report of Satan's conversation with Eve, is judgemental, for instance in describing the Solitary's smile as unpleasantly sarcastic. Yet the Solitary's depression is not without cause, as the Pedlar himself recognizes in preparing Wordsworth-the-poet to meet him, and as the Solitary himself explains much more extensively. The Solitary's voice here is not authorially silenced, and in fact speaks of sorrows which Wordsworth could all too easily understand: not only the loss of close family members, but also a bitter, life-changing disappointment with the outcome of the Revolution. Then again, the Solitary is also allowed moments when he still responds to beauty in the world of nature, and when his smiles become more amicable, as his frozen heart gradually thaws to his companions. And when the Pedlar, in exasperation at his own failure to convert the Solitary to a more lasting joy, requests that the Pastor back him up, the Pastor is given some lines whose wisdom is of a very different order from that which Coleridge hoped for from *The Recluse*, because it intimates that different individuals' apprehension of the world can differ, and can even vary from one situation to another. Our personal sense of truth and rightness can be complicated even at best, and is relative to the particular point in life's journey at which we find ourselves:

… when in changeful April fields are white
With new-fallen snow, if from the sullen north
Your walk conduct you hither, ere the sun
Hath gained his noontide height, this churchyard, filled
With mounds transversely lying side by side
From east to west, before you will appear
An unillumined, blank, and dreary, plain,
With more than wintry cheerlessness and gloom
Saddening the heart. Go forward, and look back;
Look, from the quarter whence the lord of light,
Of life, of love, and gladness doth dispense
His beams; which, unexcluded in their fall,
Upon the southern side of every grave
Have gently exercised a melting power;
Then will a vernal prospect greet your eye,
All fresh and beautiful, and green and bright,
Hopeful and cheerful:- vanished is the pall
That overspread and chilled the sacred turf,
Vanished or hidden; and the whole domain,
To some too lightly minded, might appear
A meadow carpet for the dancing hours.   (*The Excursion*, V, ll. 531–551.)

This is not the type of passage which attracted much praise or blame in traditional Wordsworth criticism. It is not what came to be thought of Literature at its highest – not the Beautiful, not the Sublime, not Imagination-Poetry-Art. But neither is it exactly egotistical bullying or bathos. Moving in an area where any sharp disjunction between the ideal and the ego is quite without relevance, the writing does offer, to use the Modernist term, an epiphany of the world of nature – of the snow and the sunshine – in everyday but poignant interplay with the world of human settlement – with the rows of burial mounds. But this is interwoven with a discursiveness whose rational argument is surely interesting, and frank without being coercive. Companionably low-key, the Pastor's acknowledgement of a mind-set with which he strongly disagrees, his willingness to concede that the gloomy view from the north is just as real as the vernal revelation from the south, encapsulates the communicational ethos of the entire poem.

From the very outset, Wordsworth's own reluctance to force wisdom down his readers' throats has been unmistakably channelled in the dramatization of different voices. And here the Pedlar's voice, too, has been one of warm-hearted understanding. In Book I, he tells his tragic tale of Margaret and her ruined cottage to Wordsworth-the-poet in the here and now, much of what he says being a matter of his own earlier anguish in following the events as they unfolded in real time. Wordsworth-the-poet, as he now listens to this story, is so overwhelmed by grief that he walks away to wrestle with his feelings alone. Then he comes back to hear the story's no less disturbing climax. Yet the Pedlar also mentions how, already some time ago, he himself has come to embrace those more comforting thoughts, of Margaret now resting in the grave's peace, and of the beauty of her neglected garden's weeds, "[b]y mist and silent rain-drops silvered o'er" (I, l. 944) – another lovely instance, this, of quiet epiphany working hand in hand with an ongoing rational argument. In the end, the Pedlar's own bitter grief for Margaret's sake simply ran its course, so that he is now that much further along in life's journey than Wordsworth-the-poet, who, though still protesting out of intense fellow-feeling for Margaret and her family, can perhaps draw strength from the older man. The younger man is helped, but not pushed. The Pedlar is just "there" for him, less of a preacher, perhaps, than in and of himself something of an epiphany, like the Old Man Travelling.

4.7   "Tintern Abbey"

There is a close ethical kinship between *The Excursion* at its finest and other poems in which, rather than dramatizing the conversation of friends, Wordsworth directly addresses his own intimate circle – his significant group, as McFarland called it – or some particular member or members of it. It is here that his genuine communication can most readily be experienced as a kind of politeness. Not politeness in the sense of an elegant and perhaps elitist refinement, however, not politeness as Chesterfield understood it, the serpent simulating the dove, and certainly not politeness as discussed by our own time's anthropological linguists either (Brown and Levinson 1987) – genuine communication is *not* a strategy for exercising power while allowing some other, perhaps disempowered person merely to save face (Sell 2000: 107–138; 2001: 107–138). A much closer affinity is with politeness as described by Fielding in his "Essay on Conversation":

> Good-breeding …, or the Art of pleasing in Conversation, … may be reduced to that concise, comprehensive rule in Scripture: Do unto all men as you would they should do unto you.   (Fielding 1903 [1743]: 249–250)

Wordsworth's address in these poems, then, is both intimate and strongly benevolent. Yet if it were only that, the poetry would be too saccharine, insufficiently co-adaptational between a social given and a more individual new. What is so extraordinary about the writing here is its combination of the very strong friendliness with quietly steady originality. Wordsworth's pre-eminence of address lies in the way he warmly appeals to common ground while making not the slightest pretence of being ordinary. In relating to his readers he strikes an uncanny balance between closeness and distance, between human equality and unasserted mental superiority. In the last analysis, his New Testament loving-kindness, his ethical politeness, is a matter of his neither under- nor over-estimating his readers' capacities.

All major literary texts have something of this same co-adaptational duality (Sell 2000: 207–230). For one thing, at whatever point of sociocultural history a writer happens to be writing, there will be available a certain range of stylistic and formal options. A writer cannot ignore these and is bound to use them as a resource. Otherwise, the text will completely confound readers' expectations, and defeat their attempts to assimilate and categorize it. At the same time, no major writer leaves the repertoire of pre-existing styles and forms unchanged, but makes a personal imprint which experienced readers can come to recognize by its interesting and often pleasurable distinctiveness from everything which has gone before.

One of the most admired of all the poems addressed by Wordsworth to his loved-ones is "Tintern Abbey" (1798), which in stylistic and formal terms is similar to Coleridge's "The Eolian Harp" (1796), even if the latter is a good bit shorter. Both poems are addressed to a beloved woman and fall into five verse paragraphs of blank verse – of unrhymed iambic pentameter. Yet there are differences, too, a study of which can greatly sharpen our sense of Wordsworth's communicational distinctiveness.

Although the dominant verse form in Pope and other poets of the earlier eighteenth century had been the iambic pentameter couplet, pentameter blank verse had already been reintroduced by admirers of Milton, and in a poem such as Cowper's *The Task* (1785), much loved by both Wordsworth and Coleridge, had already been associated with quotidian and domestic matters at a very far remove from Milton's high epic. Milton is likely to be remembered for something such as the fall of Lucifer:-

> Him the almighty power
> Hurled headlong flaming from the etherial sky
> With hideous ruin and combustion down
> To bottomless perdition, there to dwell
> In adamantine chains and penal fire,
> Who durst defy the omnipotent to arms.   (*Paradise Lost*, I, 44–49)

Rather than moving back to such bold enjambements and rhythmic fluidity, Cowper's *The Task* still had clear traces of Pope's end-stopping and medial caesura. But through relinquishing rhyme, Cowper did draw less attention than Pope to his verse *as* verse, so that its effect was somewhat like that of his period's colloquial yet well-turned conversation. It allowed a familiarity of tone which went hand in hand with some markedly un-sublime diction, of a kind already present in Pope's mock-heroic *The Rape of the Lock* (1712, rev. 1714). Take, for instance, the passage which for many readers has become Cowper's signature tune:

> Now stir the fire, and close the shutters fast,
> Let fall the curtains, wheel the sofa round,
> And, while the bubbling and loud-hissing urn
> Throws up a steamy column, and the cups,
> That cheer but not inebriate, wait on each,
> So let us welcome peaceful ev'ning in.   (*The Task*, IV, 36–41)[6]

Given such stylistic and formal precedents, then, how did Coleridge and Wordsworth each bring them into a dynamic co-adaptation with the unexpected?

In clear anticipation of Keats, Coleridge's main deviance from the recent example of Cowper was to make the note of friendly familiarity more sensuous, more emotionally appealing, more "romantic", more erotic, even, and as one aspect of this development to return to a more Miltonic irregularity of rhythm, the wind of the spirit playing over his poetic lyre in complete sympathy with the subject-matter of this particular poem:

> And that simplest lute,
> Placed length-ways in the clasping casement, hark!
> How by the desultory breeze caressed,
> Like some coy maid, half yielding to her lover,
> It pours such sweet upbraiding, as must needs
> Tempt to repeat the wrong! And now, its strings
> Boldlier swept, the long sequacious notes
> Over delicious surges sink and rise,
> Such a soft floating witchery of sound
> As twilight Elfins make, when they at eve
> Voyage on gentle gates from Fairy-Land,
> Where Melodies round honey-dropping flowers,
> Footless and wild, like birds of Paradise,
> Nor pause, nor perch, hovering on untamed wing!
> O the one life within us and abroad,
> Which meets all motion and becomes its soul,
> A light in sound, a sound-like-power in light [*sic*]
> Rhythm in all thought, and joyance every where [*sic*] –
> Methinks, it should have been impossible
> Not to love all things in a world so filled;
> Where the breeze warbles, and the mute still air
> Is Music slumbering on her instrument.   ("The Eolian Harp", ll. 12–33)

But Wordsworth's verse in "Tintern Abbey", though on first hearing apparently more chaste and cool in diction and imagery, and in this sense closer to Cowper, is nevertheless as sensuous as it is possible to be without being sensual, and thereby ultimately

---

6.   Quotation of Cowper taken from Milford 1906.

more complex. It embodies an emotional and moral decorum that is very bracing, because at once so finely controlled and so responsive to beauty and pleasure, so thoroughly a blend of unpompous dignity and utter joy. As for sound and rhythm, the excitement is more immediate, as the verse moves even further away than Coleridge's from Popeian regularities, sometimes to swell with quite torrential force. Astonishingly, then, while some lines have the Cowper-like lowness of key –

> The day is come when I again repose
> Here, under this dark sycamore, and view
> These plots of cottage-ground, these orchard-tufts,
> Which, at this season, with their unripe fruits,
> Are clad in one green hue and lose themselves
> 'Mid groves and copses.   ("Tintern Abbey", ll. 9–14)

– other passages completely re-invent the Miltonic grand style:

> And I have felt
> A presence that disturbs me with the joy
> Of elevated thoughts: a sense sublime
> Of something far more deeply interfused,
> Whose dwelling is the light of setting suns,
> And the round ocean and the living air,
> And the blue sky, and in the mind of man:
> A motion and a spirit that impels
> All thinking things, all objects of all thought,
> And rolls through all things.   ("Tintern Abbey", ll. 93–102)

And in the closing address to Dorothy, everything comes together into a beautifully sensuous and affectionate sublime which was totally unpredictable but, once ventured upon, inimitably appropriate:

> let the moon
> Shine on thee in thy solitary walk,
> And let the misty mountain-winds be free
> To blow against thee; and, in after years,
> When these wild ecstasies shall be matured
> Into a sober pleasure; when thy mind
> Shall be a mansion for all lovely forms,
> Thy memory be as a dwelling-place
> For all sweet sounds and harmonies; oh! then,
> If solitude, or fear, or pain, or grief,
> Should be thy portion, with what healing thoughts
> Of tender joy wilt thou remember me,
> And these my exhortations!   ("Tintern Abbey", ll. 134–146)

On the one hand, then, "The Eolian Harp" was an exceptionally interesting poem, offering readers a stylistic and formal challenge that was quite complex enough to merit the literary cachet, and in all likelihood providing Wordsworth with a crucial stimulus to his poem of two years later. On the other hand, when "Tintern Abbey" did come before the public, it was even more daringly well-judged.

Nor was its co-adaptational tact confined to matters of style and form. Wordsworth's poem is no less finely judged in matters of thought and feeling. Here, too, a comparison with "The Eolian Harp", while revealing some striking similarities, is to Coleridge's disadvantage.

Both poems are usually thought of as belonging to a particular genre, for which in 1928 George McLean Harper mentioned two possible labels, each suggesting a rather particular range of associations. One label, now the more widely established, was "the conversation poem", which may lead readers to expect that such a poem will directly report a two-way dialogue between the poet and a friend or loved-one. Approached with this expectation in mind, both "Tintern Abbey" and "The Eolian Harp" are somewhat surprising, since the words they present are those of the poet only, with no explicit feedback from the immediate addressee. If readers making this observation also happened to know that Coleridge himself believed that "The Eolian Harp" was the first historical instance of the genre, and that it was from the title of another poem by Coleridge that Harper took the term "conversation poem", then they might well conclude that such a poem is always going to be a basically Coleridgean mode, perhaps even to the extent of exhibiting a conversational style like that of Coleridge himself, of whom Madame de Staël remarked that "[h]e is very great in monologue, but he has no idea of dialogue" (Perry 2000: 148) and De Quincey (1893: 18) that his talk "defeats the very end of social gatherings". The other possible label mentioned by Harper was "the poem of friendship". This will not raise the expectation of an actual dialogue, but could rather hint at parallels with the undomineering affection of a friendly letter. Nor will readers approaching a poem with this kind of expectation be surprised if a monologic surface leaves scope for a deeper dialogicality of spirit. In such a case they may even find themselves wondering whether the poet's loving kindness towards the immediate addressee does not somehow carry over to themselves as well. The implied reader persona of the poet's loved-one may channel a considerate addressivity of wider scope.

But before considering how the two available genre labels suit or fail to suit these particular poems, it will be as well to recall their basic chains of argument:-

> In paragraph 1 of "The Eolian Harp" Coleridge welcomes the peacefulness of evening in the garden of his country cottage, which he is enjoying in the company of his beloved Sara. Paragraph 2, which I earlier quoted in its entirety, draws Sara's attention to the ecstatic sound of the wind playing over the Eolian harp in the window, and sees this as an instance and symbol of a single life which permeates the whole of creation, including humankind, so drawing us into universal love.

Paragraph 3 mentions the reveries he has about such matters when he is alone on the hillside during the daytime. Paragraph 4 again suggests that the whole of animate nature is swept by an intellectual breeze. But in paragraph 5, Sara's sober eye is said to reprove "Philosophy's aye-babbling stream", and to make him feel that his pantheistic free-thinking has been heretical and sinful; from now on he will be more grateful for his peaceful home, and for Sara herself.

In paragraph 1 of "Tintern Abbey", Wordsworth comments on his return to the beautiful scene near Tintern after an interval of five years. Paragraph 2 says that during that interval he has greatly benefited from his memories of the scene. Paragraph 3 says that these memories have in fact provided him with an imaginative retreat from the burdensome world of everyday life. In paragraph 4 he hopes for similarly sustaining memories of the scene during the years to come; his passion for nature is not now as strongly physical as it was at the time of his first visit here, but is calmer, and gives him that sense of a spirit informing the whole world of nature and the mind of man. In paragraph 5 he adds that the scene is also valuable to him because, from now on, it will be associated with his sister Dorothy, his present companion here; he tells her that she reminds him of his younger, more passionate self, and that she, too, will perhaps remember the beautiful scene in the future, and be sustained by it through times of difficulty; after his own death, perhaps she will also remember this return visit of his to Tintern, and his love of the scene both for its own sake and for hers.

In addition to the similarities of style and form, then, the two poems have three central similarities of thought and feeling: in both, the climax has to do with the poet's relationship with the beloved woman to whom the writing is in the first instance directed; in both, the poet has a profound interest in the pantheistic philosophy of the "one life in all"; but in both, the beloved woman and the poet are not really on the same philosophical wavelength.

In these respects, both Coleridge and Wordsworth were again making an interpersonal impact that was at once sufficiently reassuring and sufficiently challenging to warrant the literary cachet. To take only two of the more obvious precedents, in *Epistle to a Lady* (1735) Pope, too, had addressed some serious subject-matter to a close female companion, and in *An Essay on Man* (1733–34) he had propounded a rationalist providentialism or chain of Love that was not totally unlike the mutuality of love between humankind and nature now envisaged by the two Romantics. At the same time, the kinds of sentiment and emotion welling up in conjunction with the philosophizing of both Coleridge and Wordsworth were clearly of a new and very different order.

Once again, however, the originality of Wordsworth, though sacrificing no necessary deference, was far more boldly radical than that of Coleridge, and in a way which makes "Tintern Abbey" a poem of generous Wordsworthian friendship, whereas "The Eolian Harp" is a poem of characteristically Coleridgean conversation. The contrast is apparent at the very heart of the poems, in the writers' reactions to the beloved woman's mental distance from their own philosophical interests.

As it happened, when writing in his Humanist mode Pope's attitude to women had always been somewhat double-edged. The *Epistle to a Lady* had sought to engage the intellect of Martha Blount not only very affectionately, but as that of an equal. But we can perhaps ask whether the equality here had not been exceptional, the result of this particular woman's having been perceived as thinking like a man. Certainly the other women about whom Pope shares his perceptions with her are mainly the objects of his pity or scorn. This less egalitarian, more conventional orientation, which Pope himself overturned in his Romantic mode, still underlies the assignation of gender roles in Coleridge, who in the passage quoted earlier compares the sound produced by the Eolian harp under the caresses of the desultory breeze to the sweet upbraiding of a coy maid half-yielding to her lover. This analogy aligns the man with the all-infusing spirit of nature, the woman with the inanimate and purely responsive instrument. Perhaps unsurprisingly, then, the unmalleability of Sara's different mind-set is a problem for Coleridge, which he tries to solve by ostensibly surrendering to the woman's view of things, and by apparently demonizing his own habitual philosophizing as sinful, wilful, heretical, foolish, and much in need of forgiveness. The poem envisages no possibility that both parties might actually be right in their own different ways, no possibility that Sara might not really mind him philosophizing as long as he found a way to combine this with family responsibilities, and no possibility that either of them might ever really change. The qualification of his own bias is not so much willing and frank here, as too conspicuous and even downright disingenuous, foreclosing on any possibility of a friendly comparing of notes by assuming a far more agonistic model of communication, and by seeming, within that framework, to cede victory to Sara while in fact hoping that she and/or other readers will feel as sorry for him as he feels himself. In publishing the poem, in tacitly inviting an extended circle of readers to sympathize with him as a brilliantly gifted philosopher-poet enchained to a stubbornly sensible and God-fearing woman, his behaviour was, and remains embarrassing. Publication of this particular text was already a betrayal of lovers' trust – a nasty foretaste of the later long separation and ultimate divorce.

So if James A. Butler had placed the Wordsworthian addressivity alongside the Coleridgean, he would perhaps have been less inclined to complain that in "Tintern Abbey" Dorothy "is not given her own voice" (Butler 2003:42). In strictly formal terms, "Tintern Abbey" is no more a dialogue than "The Eolian Harp". But at a less superficial level, the dialogicality is at least as warm, generous and unconventional as Pope's in addressing Martha Blount. Although, as is clear from lines quoted earlier, Wordsworth likes to imagine Dorothy as for ever surrounded by the mountain winds, his implication is not that the winds will caress and make her in any sense – literally or metaphorically – compliant, but that she herself will be just a free as the winds' own blowing: "let the misty mountain-winds be free / To blow against thee". Wordsworth's prepositions can be quietly surprising and semantically crucial (Ricks, 1987b), and "against" here, by insisting on the woman's autonomy at all, is totally un-Coleridgean, and by insisting on it in such a slightly marked, matter-of-fact way, which takes it so very much for granted, is the spontaneously democratic Wordsworth at his most characteristic. Correspondingly, he neither professes disingenuous guilt about his own pantheism, nor tries to bring Dorothy round to that way of thinking. Instead, he positively rejoices in her mental difference from himself, which – even if "outside the poem" he protected her as an unmarried sister – he sees as quite unconnected with gender, and as quite possibly a mere difference of age. His only assumption is that human beings really can change over time, as the poem reports that he himself has changed. In places the phrasing is negatively capable even to the extent of acknowledging that his own present beliefs, firmly held though they certainly are, may turn out to be mistaken – "If this / Be but a vain belief", "I would believe", "If I were not thus taught" (ll. 49–50, 87, 112).

At his greatest, Coleridge, too, was genuinely dialogical. The Ancient Mariner's guilt-ridden coerciveness, though unmistakably a Coleridgean disposition, is dramatized as that of a character in a narrative poem. His spell-binding defiance of the wedding guest's natural predilection for genuine communication within joyous social gatherings is something about which Coleridge actively compares notes, leaving readers equal scope for sympathy and horror.

But as author of "The Eolian Harp", he allows less hermeneutic freedom, as the contrast with the in many ways so similar "Tintern Abbey" makes especially clear. To the Wordsworth of that poem, neither the world of nature nor his own philosophical belief is ultimately more important than is his first addressee herself. His loving concern for her future is very evident, and on the poem's publication for a wider audience Dorothy could have had not the slightest cause for resentment, or other readers for embarrassment – unlike readers of "The Eolian Harp", they were not being cajoled into an adjudication. *Vis à vis* both Dorothy and all subsequent readers, Wordsworth's writing is communicationally genuine in the highest degree, whereas "The Eolian Harp", for all its virtuosity and sheer loveliness, is a ploy in a power struggle, with Sara herself and with other readers, too.

4.8   *The Prelude*

In 1986 *The Prelude*, as the most extensive example of Wordsworth's poems of friendship, the poem for Coleridge as Wordsworth habitually called it, came under the scrutiny of Lucy Newlyn, who at that time saw its long series of addresses to Coleridge as reflecting an antagonism that had run through the whole history of the two authors' relationship (Newlyn 2004: 165–194). Coleridge, she said, had helped Wordsworth find his voice, and Wordsworth, still feeling a debt of gratitude, tried to preserve a myth of their continuing close collaboration and equality, as if the Alfoxden days of 1797 had never ended. In fact, though, Wordsworth was now in complete command of his art, needing no support in his solitary quest, and also very aware of Coleridge's human shortcomings. Coleridge in *The Prelude*, Newlyn said, is sometimes idealized beyond all recognition in order to preserve the fantasy of the past living on into the present, while at other times he is portrayed as altogether more flawed, and very much second fiddle to Wordsworth himself.

Newlyn's close readings did much to support this analysis, but in a preface to the second edition of her book (Newlyn 2004) she considerably qualified the picture. Her new perception was that Wordsworth's treatment of the friendship is related to Romantic ideas about personal chemistry as illustrated in Goethe's novel *Elective Affinities* of 1809. Seen this way, temperamental opposition and intellectual disagreement might actually result in strong attractions and amalgamations. And although Newlyn's talk of amalgamations perhaps risked making the communicational ethics of *The Prelude* sound coercively Coleridgean, the poem certainly does describe the friendship *as* a friendship, a communion within which, as always in Wordsworth, difference is an integral part of the human other who is loved.

In directing his words to his nearest and dearest he was endowing his poems of friendship with an implied reader towards whom his own feelings were strongly affectionate. This reader persona was an element no less crucial to these poems' construction than whatever story, ideas, perceptions, or feelings they might be dealing with, or whatever verse-form they might be written in. It was also a crucial rhetorical property, determining a poem's entire tone from start to finish, and offering any readers at all, and not just readers who belonged to the poet's own intimate circle, a generous image of themselves with which to identify for the purpose and duration of reading it. Not that members of the general public have ever mistaken themselves for Coleridge when reading *The Prelude*, or for Dorothy when reading "Tintern Abbey". The point is rather that the mode of address is such that, in order to read the poetry at all, you cannot help becoming a vicarious beneficiary of Wordsworth's kindness, even if, in another part of your mind, you make a firm distinction between his reader persona and the person you think you really are yourself. Especially for a writer so often moved by a sense of mission, and thereby so likely to launch into a dictatorial monologue, this text-internal dramatization of deeply friendly relations between himself and his readers was a most promising starting-point.

The poems of friendship contain some his loftiest and most powerful passages, the lines of a visionary intensity which most closely answered to the nineteenth century sense of Poetry in its ideal purity, and for which some of the older critical vocabulary still seems unlikely to be bettered. Many of them originate from what Arnold described as the "golden prime" of the years 1798–1808; they most certainly did not belong with the "mass of inferior work", the "great deal ... of poetical baggage" of which Wordsworth needed to be editorially "relieved" (Arnold 1888: 136). Yet here, too, Wordsworth himself often figures within the writing in very much the same way as was so often blamed for intrusiveness and bathos. Even the short, Two Parts *Prelude* of 1799, in which Jonathan Wordsworth found such concentrated power, can shift from the almost inarticulable to the far more obvious, from the virtually un-authored suggestiveness of epiphany-symbol-image-haiku to the prosy terminologies of, say, psychology, aesthetics, and rhetoric.

At their best, such shifts into the mundane are deeply companionable and interesting, channelling a discussion which is neither trite nor pompous in the least, and which even takes its bearings on the more impersonal kind of observation at its most powerful. An example from *The Prelude* of 1799 is the following:

> ... I saw
> A naked pool that lay beneath the hills,
> The beacon on the summit, and more near
> A girl who bore a pitcher on her head
> And seemed with difficult steps to force her way
> Against the blowing wind. It was in truth
> An ordinary sight, but I should need
> Colours and words that are unknown to man
> To paint the visionary dreariness
> Which, while I looked all round for my lost guide,
> Did at that time invest the naked pool,
> The beacon on the lonely eminence,
> The woman and her garments vexed and tossed
> By the strong wind.   (First Part, ll. 314–347)

Wordsworth's rather cerebral little disquisition, in the middle of this passage, on his rhetorical and linguistic difficulty, with its slightly assertive claim for the visionary dreariness of what he saw, is surrounded on either side by the imagistic impersonality of the lines in which the problem is actually solved, as his eye takes in the ordinary scene twice over, but without imposing ordinary preconceptions or conclusions. This interplay amounts to an engaging dialogue in which both the impersonal and the personal voices retain their distinctive qualities. The primitive power of the nearly inarticulate has not been prosified away, yet has nevertheless become a topic of discussion between the intelligent and cultivated writer and readers who are also credited with some sophistication. The net result is a poetry which at once pierces to the marrow and takes us into the poet's friendly confidence, almost as if in mitigation of the starkness of the incident described: the total separateness of the two human existences, Wordsworth's and the girl's, each enclosed within their own desolate universe, Wordsworth having lost his guide, the girl's defining relationship being merely with the wind – rather as "Tintern Abbey" imagines Dorothy after Wordsworth's death. As so often in Wordsworth, solitary individuality and social bonding are actually brought very close together. Within the poem's mimetic world, Wordsworth is isolated and the girl is isolated, and in its discoursal world, too, readers who register the visionary dreariness of this, who fully absorb this double dose of loneliness, do so in their most private being. Yet at the same time, the poet's more self-conscious and prosaic intervention can, as it were, draw readers into discussion, even about the very difficulties which beset attempts to turn personal perceptions into common property.

The Prelude draws its readers in throughout. As readers, we are free to relate in our own personal way to both the author persona and the persona of Coleridge, the immediate addressee and loved-one. But there is also that real possibility that, in one part of our mind, we will allow the loved-one's persona to serve as our temporary surrogate. Obviously, the poem's Coleridge, so strongly called to the religion of nature, yet so inveterately drawn back into the great city, so powerfully health-giving and inspiring in his own life-work for liberty and justice, yet so often a cause of friendly anxiety in his sufferings and illness, is uniquely the historical Wordsworth's portrait of the historical Coleridge. Yet it has real potential as an implied reader of wider scope, precisely because Wordsworth's feelings for Coleridge are just as warm as for any other reader of his close acquaintance. In his urge to share with him something of vital interest to himself, his sheer affection for Coleridge – for all that individual's most wonderful and problematic difference from himself – is so impulsive that the question of whether or not to tolerate such a difficult friend simply never arises. Even readers other than Coleridge himself, and not even belonging to the poet's own immediate circle or period of history, can feel implicitly welcomed by a generosity so capacious.

So when a version of *The Prelude* was eventually published in 1850, it could first of all have positioned readers as, in one part of their minds, its Coleridge, and could then have tended to invite that Coleridge, as it were, to join in spirit with its Wordsworth. Its concluding vision of Wordsworth and Coleridge as joint labourers in the heroic work of humankind's salvation was not a nostalgic throwback to 1797, but really could be read as a hope for the future, treading that typically Wordsworthian knife-edge between self-aggrandizement and genuine humility. Readers struck by a tendency to self-aggrandizement could have been noting that by 1850 Coleridge was long since dead, that Wordsworth was now dead as well, and that this was presumably the situation which he had predicted and planned for. After his own death, nothing was left of himself and Coleridge but the texts they had written, and although the poem apparently asked to be back-dated as addressed to Coleridge some time before his death in 1834, a more natural reading was arguably that those remaining texts continued to fuel discussion, so that both writers could still indeed be thought of as the momentous project's powerful leaders, albeit in a rather metaphorical sense. Readers more inclined to acknowledge a tendency to humility might have been responding to the fact that, in Wordsworth, the metaphorical is often less true and less surprising than the literal. More literally, and less arrogantly, after the year 1850 the poem's concluding hope could apply to no one but human beings still alive or still unborn. Viewed in this way, Wordsworth's stance was a good deal less embattled. Rather than seeing his mission as unrelentingly uphill work, he had simply been hoping that future readers, having enjoyed the poem and having empathized with Coleridge and himself, would henceforth fill the gap created by the deaths of the two prime movers, and fully devote themselves to their own spiritual well-being, all readers their own prophets, all joint labourers in a shared salvation. Democratically, salvation would start to spread among the poem's own readers by a kind of happy literary infection – a kind of radiant joy diffused.

4.9   Puzzlement and doubts, sorrows and fears

Perhaps Wordsworth's egalitarian dream is sometimes too heady, veering towards euphoric bombast. Yet on the whole his hopes for a spread of joy by infectious diffusion went together with an awareness that, as *The Excursion*'s Pedlar came to remember in his conversation with the Solitary, and as the Pastor had never forgotten, the grand and elementary principle of pleasure is not something you can just drum into people. The uplift of *The Prelude*'s conclusion can be approached only by way of the immediately previous lines, which confess to "[t]imes of much sorrow, of a private grief / Keen and enduring", and which contemplate the possibility that, "too weak to tread the ways of truth, / This age [will] fall back to old idolatry", that "men [will] return to servitude as fast / As the tide ebbs", that they will "to ignominy and shame / By nations sink together" ((1805) XIV, ll. 416–417, 431–435). One of the most distinctive hallmarks of Wordsworth's best writing is not only that it is inalienably personal, but that, even at its most joyful, the personal voice so honestly allows concessions and counterarguments.

   A clear example is "My heart leaps up / When I behold / A rainbow in the sky". This poem begins with a simple enough pleasure, but is not one-track-minded, since its ostensible argument that the child is father of the man is radically and permanently problematic. By proposing it so forcefully Wordsworth is inviting dialogue with very different kinds of view. In his own day, the poem apparently agreed with Rousseau, but only by challenging long centuries of Western thought, including the church's doctrine of original sin. In our own time, the Rousseauistic view of childhood as a quite separate spiritual and moral preserve, an idea so convincing, or at least so attractive, to Victorians, has itself come under question, not only from the Freudian hypothesis of infantile sexuality, but because of growing concerns about child criminals, alterations in children's habits of play, and the accelerating onset of puberty. As for the poem's hope of a pure and happy adult life, from the moment of publication onwards this was, if anything, an even greater affront to many readers' sense of real-life possibilities. But if Wordsworth himself had not been deeply aware of such difficulties, difficulties expressed in grimly pessimistic lines allotted to *The Excursion*'s Solitary,

"My heart leaps up" would never have been written in the first place, because it would simply have had no point for him. As things are, the poem's optative modality ("So be it", "I could wish" (ll. 5, 8)) is clear enough, and is an explicit resistance to what can only be the all too powerful thought of an adulthood worse than death. As he clings to his hope, such acknowledgements of the alternative, gloomier view defuse any hint of banality by gently prompting us to introspection. Despite the up-beat affirmations of a very audible lyric selfhood, a fair degree of negative capability is also at work.

With such a short lyric, this observation, once made, may seem particularly obvious. But in the longest poems, too, Wordsworth's own perceptions, feelings and thoughts are not a uniform totality that is counterposed to a greater variety of readerly views. The four speakers in *The Excursion* are so many Wordsworthian alter egos, with a wide variety of his own moods and intuitions distributed between them, an arrangement which countenances heterogeneity on the part of readers only the more gladly. As for *The Prelude*, recent analysis has often been in the spirit of Kenneth R. Johnston's remark on a feature I have already glanced at in "Tintern Abbey". After the famous lines about seeing into the life of things, Wordsworth suddenly breaks off: "If this / Be but a vain belief, yet, oh! how oft / [have I returned to the River Wye in my thoughts]" (ll. 49.59). Registering this and the other similar details, Johnston says that "Tintern Abbey", though "usually read as a deeply affirmative statement of secular or existential faith, ... achieves its affirmation in ways that are shot through with signs of their own deconstruction" (Johnston 1998: 595). In *The Prelude*, similarly, critics have found: a belief that paradise is the produce of the common day, but also the belief that our true home is with infinitude; a belief that as human beings we act in interchange with nature, but also the belief that what we find in nature comes from our own minds; Wordsworth's sense of his own calling as a prophet of mighty nature, but also his strong belief that the mind of man is far more beautiful than nature; and so on (Gill 2003: 150–151). One certainly can find such major alternations of opinion in Wordsworth's personal interventions. But what is happening here is not self-deconstruction. Nor is Wordsworth simply contradicting himself. First and last, he is community-making, which is seldom an entirely easy and painless process. When we are genuinely community-making, we cannot pretend that we have sorted out all of life's great questions and made ourselves intellectually ship-shape. Our willingness to offer words that are comprehensible, true, truthful, sincere, and socially appropriate can extend even as far as admitting what we cannot after all deny: our puzzlement and doubts, our sorrows and fears. We freely confess that many of the disagreements we find within the community at large are also internal to our own mind, and we fully accept that any extension of the community we ourselves may bring about is likely to involve still further heterogeneity. What holds a community together is nothing more, but also nothing less, than a generous agreement to disagree when unavoidable, plus a common determination not to insist on impossible certainties. Of community in this sense, potentially so significant for our post-postmodern times, Wordsworth is surely the supreme poet.

CHAPTER 5

Great Expectations
and the Dickens community

5.1   Blessings, will-power and pleasure, or their absence

How is it that Dickens's writings have brought about such a large and enduring community of readers? Despite all the critical and scholarly attention devoted to him, this phenomenon has not, I think, been fully explained. My suggestion is that it has something to do with a genuine dialogicality which his texts can foster between himself and his readers, and that this in turn is bound up with the way he tells a story. What I shall try to bring into focus is his story-telling in its communication-ethical dimension.

Among earlier commentators likely to offer clues here are those with interests in narratology, a well developed branch of scholarship which has greatly improved the exactness with which many aspects of story-telling can be described. It can sometimes seem a dehumanizingly scientistic discipline, however, and has given few clues as to how the forms and structures it so accurately describes can be ethically evaluated as deployed in any particular story. A more deliberately communicational narratology can, I believe, remedy this deficiency and lead to a fuller appreciation of a wide range of story-tellers, including Dickens. More specifically, such an approach can draw attention to aspects of Dickensian dialogicality which have not come within the purview of other kinds of commentary, but to which our culture in its post-postmodern phase could be very hospitable.

Great Expectations is especially instructive here, because its plot so directly foregrounds *blessings*, which in a humanizingly communicational narratology must be a central factor. By blessings, I simply mean circumstances or events which bring happiness. In real life, people have usually thought of blessings as coming about either through blind chance, or through the workings of some supernatural power, or through the deliberate deed of a human being, in which case the deed can be called a "benefaction", and the person who performs it a "benefactor" – as the etymology suggests, benefactors are people who deliberately try to do good to somebody else. Sometimes we also speak of "blessings in disguise", which arise when what at first seemed an unfortunate turn of events in the long run proves to have brought some unexpected benefit, or when somebody's attempt to do harm to somebody else – the "malefaction" of a "malefactor" – somehow or other backfires and accrues to that other person's good. Equally important can be the bane in disguise, as we might call it, of a benefaction which in practice is a malefaction. In some Germanic languages, though not in English, there is an expression which ironically describes this as the kind of help or kindness you might expect from a bear: a *Bärendienst* (German), a *björntjänst* (Swedish) – or bear's service, as I shall be calling it. Ostensibly a bear's service *is* a service. But intentionally or otherwise, it is really a disservice.

Even in the early days of narratology, blessings, benefactions and bear's services did not pass entirely unnoticed. Vladimir Propp (1968 [1928]) mentioned characters who could have the roles of "donor" and "helper", and later scholars suggested that the helper-characters in a story could be in tension with "opponent"-characters (Greimas 1977). But *who* helped or opposed *whom* here? Answer: Ancillary characters helped or opposed the hero. There was typically only one hero, and narratological accounts of his task or quest or adventure did not present it as first and foremost a matter of his own helping or opposing somebody else, even when it certainly could have been seen in that light as well. Instead, the main narrative focus was said to be on the challenge to the hero's courage or ingenuity, and on whether or not events, supernatural powers or other people helped *him*.

That the pioneering narratologies took this form was partly, I shall argue, the result of their overall methodology and underlying ideology. But there was also a much more obvious explanation. The narratives which Propp examined were folk tales, and the pattern he discovered was really there.

And just as, in the history of western linguistics, the analytical framework forced upon all languages was for many centuries the one originally developed for the grammar of Latin, so, in narratology, many major literary narratives would simply not fit into the available scholarly scheme. Right up until *Great Expectations*, and for a few decades longer as well, literary plots often basically centred on the exchange of benefactions and malefactions between *several* main characters at once. Such stories could not be described in terms of the earliest narratological models without distortion. As compared with such a story itself, the narratological analysis of it always tended to make one of the characters emerge with undue prominence, yet also with a diminished degree of moral responsibility.

The fact is that, in *Portrait of a Lady* (1881), Isabel Archer's inherited money is not something received from a minor character in a donor- or helper role in order to assist her in some pre-given heroic purpose. The legacy's implications for Isabel personally do seem crucially important, since as readers we seriously wonder whether it will turn out to have been a blessing or a bear's service for her. But more to the point, the money itself gives rise to a sense of purpose in Isabel, and also implicates other main characters as well. She can now bestow riches on somebody else, who may then repay her, so to speak, in whatever sort of coin. True, the novel is focalized through Isabel's own point of view, and even its title may seem to make her the most important character of all. But read another way, the title suggests that we should not only look through Isabel's eyes, but should also look *at* her, just as she might be seen by the other characters in the novel, for instance, whose goals and interests are in fact the main object of our curiosity all along. Madame Merle's deliberately intended bear's services towards Isabel are part of what both we as readers and Isabel herself simply have to find out about. And as for the novel's awe-inspiring climax in the scene where she and Caspar Goodwood finally kiss, this culminates with Isabel's drawing back, out of principled self-subjection to the terrible will of Osmond, the man she has married in the mistaken belief that he would be a worthy recipient of her financial backing. In now rejecting Goodwood after the kiss, she is rejecting the offered blessing of a new and truly valuable life with him, even though Goodwood's very name underscores this point with an obviousness still carrying over from Dickens. As far as Isabel is concerned, Goodwood's desire for her is now another blessing that is *not* a blessing. Whatever readers may feel about it, Isabel feels that it is very much a bear's service. "'Do me the greatest kindness of all,' she panted. 'I beseech you to go away!'" (James 1968 [1881]:644).

By the time of high Modernism, novel-writing was changing in ways which can still excite astonished admiration. But this went together with a certain loss of interest in blessings, benefactions and bear's services. Goodwood's kiss had been

> like white lightning, a flash that spread, and spread again, and stayed; and it was extraordinarily as if, while she took it, she felt each thing in his hard manhood that had least pleased her, each aggressive fact of his face, his figure, his presence, justified of its intense identity and made one with this act of possession.
>
> (James 1968 [1881]:644)

Both in subject-matter and figurative language here, James was anticipating the Lawrence of *Women in Love*, who spurned "the old stable *ego* of the character" (Lawrence 1967 [1914]:18) and created fictional people who were often less marked by some personal continuity than by an unpredictable changeability, for which a major means of representation was thought-provoking similes and metaphors. A character's identity was constant, Lawrence explained, only in the sense that coal and diamond are both forms of carbon (*ibid.*). Yet James's continuation of the kiss episode was probably not to Lawrence's taste. Before the lightning simile, another figure of speech is already in motion: in being drawn towards Goodwood's force, Isabel feels she is drowning, and that she needs to "catch herself, to feel something to rest on." This is continued immediately after the revelations of the lightning-kiss: "So had she heard of those wrecked and under water following a train of images before they sink." But then, within the next two sentences, the crisis is over: "But when darkness returned she was free. She never looked about her; she only darted from the spot" (James 1968 [1881]:644). This darkness and this freedom are not those attained by a person who drowns. The lightning-kiss has merely given way to ordinary darkness; she has escaped drowning; and it is almost as if her body itself removes her from the place. Her moral determination to be faithful to her monstrous husband, her sheer act of will here, seems as instinctively physical as her experience of the kiss itself. In *Women in*

Love, by contrast, questions of morality and willpower are altogether more disembodied and distant, except when characters such as Mrs Crich, Gerald, or Hermione carry out some premeditated intention, so bringing down upon themselves the full weight of Lawrence's disapproval. Having spurned "[t]he certain moral scheme" which he found in Turgenev, Tolstoy and Dostoevsky (Lawrence 1967 [1914]: 17), Lawrence erected a new one of his own, whose valorizations were just as certain. As far as he was concerned, the greatest good was spontaneousness, and projects involving moral exertion, or choices involving moral principles, were all too likely to involve a conscious deliberation which made them suspect. Joyce and Woolf were less preachy here, as if they viewed spontaneousness as simply a fact of life. Yet their treatment of character was in this respect Lawrentian. In *A Portrait of the Artist as a Young Man*, Stephen may worry about filial duty. In *To the Lighthouse*, Mr Ramsay may hope to march his mind towards some tiny new advance in philosophical thought, and Mrs Ramsay to create a special aura of home and family. But in the fictional worlds to which these characters belong, human beings, certainly as compared with James's Isabel, are rather passive. Undisturbed by any shaping ethical resolve, their consciousness simply streams, and so, of course, does their unconscious.

One way to read this development is as a novelistic correlative of an ever more secularized and science-driven culture, within which, by the time of late-twentieth-century postmodern critics, any attempt to legitimate some particular scheme of values would be challenged by manifold interest groupings, and anyone suggesting that a human being might have a certain moral autonomy would be obliged to argue against biological, psychoanalytical, sociological, cultural, and linguistic forms of determinism. Lawrence's sense of the human being's widely varied "allotropic states which … are states of the same single radically unchanged element" (Lawrence 1967 [1914]: 18) sounds very conservative as compared with 1980s-style deconstructionists, who might have accused his phrasing of essentialism here, and who routinely argued that both meaning and personality are totally unstable and for ever in need of construction or reconstruction. To think in terms of human beings and their choices or actions was now said to be even more irrelevant than ever. Postmodern literary texts which could be read as avoiding such "irrelevance" were duly praised, whereas literary texts whose characterization encouraged it were said to be the artificial relics of an outdated ideology.

Nor was it as if Modernism and its continuing cultural impact were even hedonistic. In *Women in Love* Birkin was admittedly

> happy in the wet hill-side, that was overgrown and obscure with bushes and flowers…. He took of his clothes, and sat down naked among the primroses, moving his feet softly among the primroses, his legs, his knees , his arms right up the armpits, lying down and letting them touch his belly, his breasts. It was such a fine, cool, subtle touch all over him, he seemed to saturate himself with their contact.
> (Lawrence 1960 [1921]: 119)

But the more ecstatically Paterian the cult of sensuous spontaneity became, the less it really had to do with human relationships. Birkin's moment of bliss is only a brief respite from his dealings with the un-primrose-like Hermione, and in Modernist representations of human life in general, difficulty and discord were endemic. Influenced by this, Modernist readers were likely to welcome Isabel's rejection of Goodwood as an avoidance of an all too obvious happy ending. On this view, the forbidden fruit of adultery would simply have been too tasty, not only for Goodwood and Isabel themselves, but for readers. Or as Lionel Trilling was to put it, the truest representative of twentieth century culture was Dostoevski's Underground Man. Why? Because the principle of pleasure had no weight for him. In previous ages, said Trilling, people who cultivated painful and "unnatural" emotions or ways of life, people who attempted to know those "psychic energies which are not to be summoned up in felicity", were exceptional. In the twentieth century, "unpleasure" was itself the norm. Modern literature and the "extruded 'high' element" in the general culture had subversively undermined all ideas of peace and bliss, which now seemed utterly lifeless. According to Trilling, the only Christian concept he and his contemporaries really understood was that of the *felix culpa*, and even this they interpreted in their own way: through sin and death, the seductions of peace and bliss could be avoided. Eden was to be dreaded. Or as Trilling also put it, nothing was now more incomprehensible in Wordsworth than his talk of a "grand and elementary principle of pleasure" which constitutes "the naked and native dignity of man", by which man "knows, and feels, and lives, and moves" (1850 text, Owen and Snyser 1974: I 140). Pleasure nowadays, said Trilling, made people feel *un*real. As a confirmation that they actually existed, they needed the abrasions of pain (Trilling 1967 [1963]: 84, 80). The very idea of blessings was, to say the least, unfashionable.

5.2   Narratology hitherto

The de-ethicizing masochism of much twentieth century culture left its mark, not only on some strands of deconstructionist criticism, but on other scholarship in the humanities (still so called), including narratology. But to say this is not to claim that narratology was worthless. Scholars charting its history now distinguish two main phases (Nünning 2000): the phase of "classical" or structuralist narratology in descent from Propp's morphology of the folk tale; and a "postclassical" phase of sociocultural and various other "new" narratologies, as seen for instance in Fredric Jameson's account of narrative as socially symbolic act (Jameson 1981). The issues dealt with in both phases were very real, and the progress made is something which can still be built on.

Classical narratology concentrated on narrative texts, without doing much in the way of contextualizing them. Its achievement was vastly to expand the range of narrative patterns and devices to which we can give a name. Granted, it is possible to feel that once a feature has been detected and described, the next question is: "So what?" I once had a very diligent student, who wrote a very accurate analysis of point-of-view and the time dimension in certain novels by a certain novelist. But then he ground to a halt, because he could find no way of saying – as he felt he needed to say – whether a very elaborate narrative design was good for its own sake, or whether it was good in terms of some more all-embracing rationale, or whether on some such larger view it might even have had some drawbacks. Here was a question of judgement, calling for modes of enquiry over and above his energetic positivism. But obviously, an elaborate narrative design is not at all the same thing as a simple narrative design; it is important to be able to pin such differences down; and if there is then a challenge to criticism, so much the better!

The challenge is one to which the finest classical narratologists in any case began to rise. In making visible the narrative sophistication of *À la recherche du temps perdu*, Genette (1980) was constantly asking or implying the question: "How, if the arrangement had been different here, would the net result have been different as well?" In the same spirit, twentieth century accounts of *Great Expectations* sometimes dwelt on various consequences of Dickens's use of a first-person homodiegetic narrator. Anny Sadrin even hinted how, if the focalization had instead been entirely from the point of view of Magwitch, the same story would have resulted in a totally different reading experience (Sadrin 1988: 59–63).

In Chicagoan narratology, the question of affect was foregrounded even more directly, precisely in terms of the reader's likely judgements of characters' actions, and with an explicit interest in the reader's pleasure or pain. Perhaps there was a tinge of Chicagoan behaviourism here, as if a literary work were a mechanical device, and its reader a rather judgemental, manic-depressive robot. Whether a narrative could also be something more than just an invitation to "goody-or-baddy?" verdicts, and a stimulus to pleasure or pain, was not exactly clear. On the other hand, a satisfactory answer to the big "So what?" will always have to include affect as at least one dimension, and R. S. Crane's suggestive essay on *Tom Jones* (Crane 1952) was doubtless seminal for James Phelan's no less suggestive account of *Great Expectations* (Phelan 1994 [1989]). Phelan discussed both plot and characterization, carefully tracing how readers will probably come to like or dislike certain characters, and showing that Wemmick, in particular, not only has a role in forwarding events, but acts as a focus for feelings and attitudes, both Pip's and readers' own. By responding to the case of Wemmick, readers actually become clearer and firmer in their verdict on Pip, not least on Pip's behaviour towards Joe – on Pip's malefaction, as we could also phrase it, towards the man whose generosity had confirmed him in his own practice of benefaction, the man who had told the re-captured convict that "[w]e don't know what you have done, but we wouldn't have you starved to death for it, poor miserable fellow-creatur [*sic*]. – Would us, Pip?" (p. 36).[1] In the hands of Chicagoans like Phelan, then, narratology was certainly becoming sensitive to Dickens's own moral universe.

---

1. All quotations of *Great Expectations* taken from Rosenberg 1999.

As for postclassical narratology, it not only focussed on texts, but also related texts to something else. More specifically, it tried to answer the "So what?" arising from classical narratology by presenting narrative form as semantically loaded *per se*. Such and such a story type or device was said to reflect such and such a psychological dynamism, or sociopolitical constellation, or ideological structure, or cultural epoch. This, too, could be very illuminating. Granted, it is possible to feel that once such a relationship has been pointed out, the "So what?" merely regresses one stage further. Such approaches may even tend to *assimilate* a narrative to the relationship's other term, so that, especially if the other term is easily observable in quite different connections, there will be no particular reason for studying the narrative at all, since its semantic loading will merely be something we knew already, so to speak. Or worse, the thing we knew already – the Oedipus complex, the patriarchy, Victorianism, or whatever – will have been a Procrustean bed onto which the narratologist has tried to force the narrative. Clearly, though, something as fundamental in human life and society as narrative is very likely to have wide-reaching ramifications, and the contribution of postclassical narratology's contextualizations to our larger understanding of narratives, literary and non-literary alike, was potentially considerable. How could I say less? – when in the opening pages of this study I myself have linked the twentieth century's narrative marginalization of blessings, willpower and pleasure to certain broader trends in the culture.

In Peter Brooks's analysis of *Great Expectations* (Brooks 1994 [1980]), postclassical narratology's potentiality began to be realized. Brooks's starting point was his quarrel with some classical narratologists' premise that plotting is mainly a matter of drawing on received story paradigms, or of re-shaping a *fabula* into a *sjuzet*. In Brooks's view, this obscured a vitally dynamic psychological dimension, which he illustrated by using Freud's *Beyond the Pleasure Principle* as a kind of master narrative. Seen this way, all plots begin with the pleasure principle or Eros, which entails a desire for activity and movement, which can in turn set up tensions and be narrated. No less universally, plots end with the death wish or Thanatos, which connotes quiescence, non-happening, non-narratability. Yet a plot has to keep Eros and Thanatos in some sort of balance, and this means that the plot's middle, as well as being a stage on the path towards its end, will also be a kind of detour, delay or arabesque, which doubles back upon its beginning. So Pip struggles to create a version of his own life-story and identity, and in doing so has to grapple with the fact that two different versions of his origins are for ever competition, the one seeing him as naturally vicious, the other seeing him as a fairy-tale hero. But at the same time he also keeps returning from London to his native village and the marshes, and finally the suppressed Magwitch himself returns. At which point the perplexities of the story's middle become less distressing, as any attempt to plot his life into some sort of coherence and significance begins to seem pointless. Eros is giving way to Thanatos, and Pip is finally "cured" of plotting altogether. Here again, then, narratology was centrally concerned with pleasure and pain, this time the main character's pleasure and pain rather than readers', and was describing that character as himself partly instrumental in his own destiny.

But even if narratology, in both its classical and postclassical phases, could be helpfully descriptive, and had not lost all sense of the human dimension of narratives, it always involved at least a certain de-humanization, for reasons no less ideological than methodological. In a nutshell, its analyses of both the story-teller and the story-internal characters tended to underestimate the scope for human decision-making. Classical narratology emphasized that a teller used forms and devices which were hereditary. Or when a teller's particular intervention in tradition did attract notice, the logic of the resulting constructs was often thought of in formalistic terms as auto-telic. Story-internal characters, similarly, were represented as going through motions which were impersonally self-sufficient, even when they were apparently motions of choice, a style of explanation which became even clearer when carried over into cultural anthropology. "We are not ... claiming," said Claude Lévi-Strauss, "to show how men think the myths, but rather how the myths think themselves out in the men and without men's knowledge" (Lévi-Strauss 1970 [1964]: 46). And with Lévi-Strauss, we have already arrived at the deterministic ethos of some postclassical narratology, which attributed the form of both a narrative itself and of its characters' narrative-internal days and ways to that other term – to the psyche, the state, the ideology, the culture, or whatever – with which the narrative form was said to be related.

Eiichi Hara (1994 [1981]), for instance, felt that Brooks had made Pip's destiny too much a matter of Pip's own choosing. By drawing on Bakhtin, Hara was able to speak about Pip as caught up in a number of different story-lines, none of which is peculiar to him since they all pre-existed within Victorian culture, reflecting different zones of the socio-ideological spectrum. One such story, instantiated by certain remarks of Pumblechook and Wopsle, casts Pip in the role of a criminal who will come to a sticky end. And Wopsle also starts another familiar story-line, by representing Pip as a bad apprentice, like George Barnwell in George Lillo's popular play, *The London Merchant* (1731). Since, on Hara's view, Pip does not actually find or make such plots for himself, he cannot – *pace* Brooks – be "cured" of plotting either. Rather, what happens at the end is that the various stories simply collapse, leaving a vacuum which could only be filled by the sheer irrationality of Pip's desperate passion for Estella. The dialogism between the competing story-lines could only climax as a carnival of misrule, after which, as with both dialogism and carnival as conceptualized by Bakhtin, the status quo will presumably be restored with fresh emphasis. In short, what happens is an entirely social and circular process, on which the novel's main character has no willed influence.

When viewed by either classical or postclassical narratology, an individual's own intentions and feelings could actually be dissociated from his or her actions – to the minimal extent that those actions could even be regarded as actions in the first place. Not only that, but the intentions and feelings of all other individuals could be correspondingly omitted from any discussion of what the first individual's actions might have by way of consequences. Narratives were represented as revealing so little control on the part of either tellers or their characters, and so little felt impact of one human being on another, that even stories stopping very far short of tragedy were likely to come out sounding a bit dispiriting. Everything was apparently so random and amoral.

Indeed, the concepts of both tragedy and comedy, so centrally concerned with the absence or presence of blessings, could actually be drained of meaning. Happy endings were duly noted when unavoidable. But in narratological analysis happiness could come across as either rather abstract, or downright delusory. That narratology's somewhat depersonalized human beings would fully relish even a chance blessing was unlikely from the start, and that they themselves would actually confer a blessing by beneficent design was even less likely still. Especially in the thought-world of postclassical narratology, blessings were much more likely to be written off as bear's services straight away. The tendency was to ascribe them to the workings of psychological, ideological or sociocultural forces which were sinister and impersonal, much as Marx portrayed the comforts of religion as the opiate of the masses. So although Brooks's analysis does see Pip as plotting his own pleasure and his own identity, it also describes him as in both respects being swept along by the Eros-Thanatos dynamism, a psychological mechanism which is really just as impersonal as the culturally pre-existent story-lines detected by Hara. That pleasure might result from another human being's act of kindness; that Pip, at least as a young boy and a grown man, if not as an Estella-struck teenager, is himself capable of such kindnesses; that his generosity is finally established as a permanent trait in his mental make-up, and is its own rich reward; but that the difference between genuine benefaction and intentional bear's services can often be hair-fine: these are some of the things which make this novel so intensely interesting to readers, but which narratology has so far hardly discussed.

If narratology is to consolidate its twentieth century achievements, then that same century's de-humanization and anti-hedonism must once and for all be rejected. Otherwise, narratological accounts of pre-Modernist literary texts, in which blessings, benefactions, and individuals' willed bear's services have such a central position, will continue to risk anachronistic misrepresentations. Accounts of numerous twentieth century narratives, in which blessings, benefactions and willed bear's services have lived on against the grain of Modernist fashion, will also be distorting. And the entire narratological project will come to seem more and more passé, in its insensitivity to the many ways in which pre-Modernist attitudes, perceptions and values are already being re-cycled as the post-postmodern condition becomes ever more prevalent.

Trilling's essay on Modernism's devalorization of pleasure was first published in 1965. But by then, literary and artistic norms in general were already changing again. By 2005, with the postmodern challenge to established legitimations having now undermined the very distinction between the Arts (*sic*) and popular culture, the elitist austerities of Modernism could seem even more dated, and there had been a rising tide of scholarly books and articles on the aesthetics of enjoyment (e.g. Shusterman 1992). In addition, the human subject whose pleasure could now once again be legitimately cultivated was increasingly seen as exercising at least a certain relative autonomy. Although there could be no going back to a pre-twentieth-century sense of reason's or the will's absolute sovereignty, there was certainly much discussion of structuralist and poststructuralist theoreticians' frequent neglect of the following words of de Saussure: "Language [*langue*] is not a function of the speaker; it is a product that is passively assimilated by the individual ... . Speech [*parole*], on the contrary, is an individual act. It is wilful and intellectual" (de Saussure 1974 [1916]:14). Especially articulate was Raymond Tallis, who aimed to assert

> the centrality of individual consciousness, of undeceived deliberateness, in the daily life of human beings. We are not absolutely transparent to ourselves but we are not utterly opaque either; we are not totally self-present in all our actions but nor are we absent from them; we are not complete masters of our fates, shaping our lives according to our utterly unique and original wishes, but neither are we the empty playthings of historical, political, social, semiological or instinctual forces.   (Tallis 1997:228)

Simultaneously with such carefully qualified re-assertions of human agency, there was also a widespread rehabilitation of ethical consciousness in general, and of virtue in particular – that notion so closely associated with the "certain moral scheme" which Lawrence had wanted to overthrow. In Matt Ridley's best-selling popularization of zoology, the dichotomy between virtue and spontaneity, which had been presupposed, though to such different effect, by both Lawrence himself and the predecessors against whom he was rebelling, finally broke down. Benefaction, it now appeared, may come much easier to our actual genetic programming than either scientists or Modernists once believed. Virtue itself may be natural (Ridley 1997). So we can, I think, be fairly sure that new readers will soon be finding their way to Anthony Ashley Cooper (1671–1713), third Earl of Shaftesbury, the Platonist who spoke so eloquently of the human being's innate moral sense, the benevolist doctrine so attractive, though by no means unproblematic, to Pope in what I have called his Romantic mode, as also to the Fielding of *Amelia* (Sell 2001:291–352).

5.3   Positionality and ethics

Narratology can become more humanized, hedonistic, and generally up-to-date through a cross-fertilization with a historical but non-deterministic theory of communicative pragmatics. As explained in the Introduction, and at greater length in my *Literature as Communication* (2000), the very keystone to such a theory is a view of the human being as a *social individual*: a social animal, yes, and very much subject to cultural and ideological formation; but still in a real sense an individual as well, with sufficient powers of intellect and imagination to empathize with somebody whose formation is different, and with sufficient willpower to form judgements and take decisions not necessarily in harmony with the surrounding society, especially when the "other" encountered through communication turns out to be a significant other. As human beings, we are at once positioned, and capable of ethical engagement.

On such a view, people do strongly reflect their own culture and society, but also have a certain relative autonomy. And people do change from moment to moment, but do not change entirely. They bear a continuing responsibility for the things they do and say, and they also instantiate a certain continuity of memory, thought, and evaluation. In consequence, not only a story's teller, but also its represented characters, and particular people who hear or read it, will usually be found to have perfectly discussable identities, in which more representative and more personal traits can be thought of as combined.

Dickens, then, was very much a man of his time, with more than enough inner knowledge of bourgeois aspirations to gentility to render Pip's hopes and dreams believable, yet could also distance himself, so as to show gentility's darker side. Pip himself, so carried away by the culturally available fantasies of place as to desert Joe for Estella or, more comically, to inform Trabb the tailor that "Mr Pip must decline to deal further with one who could so far forget what he owed to the best interests of society, as to employ a boy who excited Loathing in every respectable mind" (p. 189), also despises others for toadying to displays of gentility and, by the time he comes to write his story down, sees it as having so constantly presented him with real moral choices that he now habitually reprimands himself for cowardly wavering between right and wrong, and for weaknesses and meannesses of which he has made himself guilty in order to curry favour with people he despises. Very similar tensions between social pressures and a certain personal autonomy would also be experienced by readers, both Victorian and later readers, in their own lives. Even if readers today are less likely to feel the attraction exercised on many of Dickens's first readers by gentility, they will inevitably find that their spiritual integrity is threatened by the fashions of our own time. In the fairly recent past, there was something of a fashion for renouncing moral responsibility altogether, in the name of the various dehumanizing determinisms.

The difference between readers then and readers now is just one example of a much wider communicational phenomenon. The different participants in a process of communication do not share one and the same context, and the contextual dissimilarities fundamentally affect the interaction taking place between them, including any story-telling. This may be obvious enough when the communicants belong to quite separate cultures or to different periods of time, in which second case one of them will be already dead and buried. But with the proviso that communicants' different contexts must overlap at least to the extent of their sharing at least a linguistic medium (if necessary through translation) and experience of the human condition, communication *always* takes place between different positions. Even two people apparently representing one and the same cultural formation will always do so with somewhat different inflections, since when they enter into communication with each other, the knowledge, memories, experiences, attitudes, values, and prejudices which they bring to the process will not be identical. No matter how much they already have in common, their contexts of operation will not be completely coterminous.

Dickens, for his part, was a Victorian writer who was writing for Victorian readers, yet he was a writer whose own thoughts, experience, and imagination were leading him to create the story of Pip, a conception previously non-existent, and his adopted narrative set-up made no detectable distinction between Dickens and Pip himself, so that the ironies at Pip's expense are the middle-aged Pip's own ironies. Pip's own positional difference from many of the first readers of 1860–1861 lay not only in the sheer range of his social experience – from the blacksmith's forge to polite receptions in Richmond – but also in the relative shortness of his time in London. Until his teens he lived in the marshland village, and his London period came to an end when, in his early twenties, he went to live for eleven years in Cairo. London did not have time to become softened by a veil of familiarity for him, which helps to explain the intensity with which he observes Little Britain, Newgate and the more suburban Walworth, and also the disillusioned sharpness of his critique of fashionable gentility, though actually, of course, Pip is also the cover for Dickens, the inveterate novelist of London, whose perceptions of it were so much livelier than those of an ordinary denizen. Pip's and Dickens's positional distinctiveness was likely to make them something of a challenge. Its slight unfamiliarity was something which readers had to get used to, and which gave the story part of what it had to say for them.

That positional differences can be negotiated is entirely thanks to the human being's relative freedom of mind. Communicants habitually, and often very successfully, try to empathize their way into each other's worldview for the sake of mutual understanding. Yet as all the present book's studies are arguing, sometimes the best way to think of a communicative situation is not just in terms of its two differently sited participants, but as a triangle. To say that a speaker or writer or narrator sends a message to be received by a listener or reader or narratee can be somewhat misleading, since any account involving this kind of uni-directionality and cut-and-dried binarism risks prioritizing the binarism's first term, so making the sender a more active party, while the receiver figures as much more passive. Very often indeed, communication in the real word certainly does take this form, sometimes for reasons explored by Habermas in terms of distorting social relations (Habermas 1970, 1972, 1984 & 1987, 1998a, 1998b). But the triangular reality of what I am calling genuine communication is that the two communicants are always in consultation, and that what helps to keep them in consultation is some third entity, which they are in consultation *about*. Granted, the third entity can actually be one or both of the consulting parties themselves, since they themselves are part of what they can talk about. It can also be something quite fictional, as in the case with much communication through narrative, since as Aristotle's and Sir Philip Sidney's different arguments both showed, to make up a story can be an excellent way to deal with some very real issue (Sell 2000: 33–38). But whatever the third entity is, the two communicants can be thought of as comparing notes about it, which means that they are both contemplating the third entity itself and allowing for each other's view of it. So the net result of any particular process of communication between a given initiator and a given respondent may represent a victory, as it were, for either view, or for neither. What, if anything, prevails may even be some quite new view, arrived at through the very interaction.

Like all too much twentieth century linguistic and literary scholarship, classical and postclassical narratology was often guilty of the unitary context fallacy: the usually quite unconscious assumption that a context, even at the outset of communication, can be identical for the two or more people involved (Sell 2000 65–71, 119–145). In the case of narratology, it was the assumption that those hearing or reading a story share exactly the same context of operation as its teller. In point of fact, communication is a historically linear process, between participants operating in contexts which are to a greater or lesser extent non-coterminous, even though there must always be at least that minimal contextual overlap of shared language proficiency and experience of the human condition, and even though, as a net outcome, the area of overlap can be permanently expanded, in the form of an increase in mutual understanding, if not agreement.

One possible expression of the unitary context assumption is a presentism which can come dangerously close to arrogance. Brooks and Hara interpret *Great Expectations* so entirely in terms of the Freudian master script and the Bakhtinian social calculus that they tend to ignore Dickens's own interest in Pip's degree of moral autonomy. They risk forcing their own context of reading onto Dickens's context of writing. The other main expression of the unitary context assumption is an unrealistic historical or cultural purism. I should now be guilty of this myself, if I were to say that the only way to read Dickens is in his own terms, and that Brooks and Hara have no right to think about him in Freudian and Bakhtinian terms, and should therefore hold their peace. This I emphatically do not say, because if I did, I should be trying to silence Brooks and Hara's difference as responding parties, so that my historical purism would simply be the mirror image of their own presentism, which tends to silence the difference of Dickens as the initiating party. In both its forms, the unitary context assumption fundamentally distorts communication, even though the role of linguists, literary scholars and narratologists should arguably be to promote it, by offering any necessary mediation between the different positionalities involved. So when Brooks and Hara choose to read Dickens through the eyes of Freud and Bakhtin, our reaction needs to be both affirmative and questioning – something along the lines of: "Yes, truly interesting! And what would Brooks, Hara, Freud and Bakhtin all look like when seen through the eyes of Dickens?" Genuine communication involves seeing the other in the light of the self, and the self in the light of the other. When we read Dickens, we owe it to ourselves to let him read us as well, so to speak. It is up to us to ensure that the dialogicality remains genuine. Otherwise, we may be missing out on something from which we could greatly profit.

5.4   Primary tellability

Given that genuine communication is so fundamentally reciprocal, a communicant will not normally launch into a story unless the other communicant, no matter how differently situated, is likely to find it worth the telling (Pratt 1977). And one way to discuss a story's tellability is in terms of a kind of ritual equilibrium that gets disrupted (Sell 1985). Discourse analysts have long been able to show how in normal social intercourse people often contribute apparently empty remarks simply in order to preserve group solidarity, to establish alignments of opinion, or to mitigate disagreements (Stubbs 1983: 188). More generally, human beings seem to have some instinct for peaceful relations, and for things being done in a regular, usual manner. We do have a considerable interest in ritualizing a secure status quo. On the other hand, human beings sometimes seem to have another instinct, perhaps equally strong, for quarrels or adventures, and sometimes their lives are unsettled by circumstances quite beyond their own control. Human behaviour and experience become worth putting into a story when these two different tendencies are seen in opposition, so that the ritual equilibrium of daily life is threatened. A stable situation does not in itself constitute matter for narrative, unless as a starting-point for, or background against which to assess, those departures from normality which make for story proper.

This kind of primary tellability, as we can call it, often involves close personal relationships, and in one sense *Great Expectations* thrusts its readers *in medias res*, since the opening pages clearly tell us that the ritual equilibrium of any life Pip might have had together with his biological parents and siblings has already been rudely interrupted by the deaths of all of them except his sister, Mrs Joe. Mrs Joe's bringing up of him "by hand" is itself marked as a tellable abnormality, and a distressing one at that. But after she has been pacified by Orlick's brutal attack, things stabilize a good deal. With Biddy now living in the forge and filling it with so much sweetness and calm, the possibilities for story would actually be coming to an end, were it not for the further disruptions already building up as a result of Pip's increasing obsession with gentility and Estella, and through the opening moves in Magwitch's benefaction. The "second stage of Pip's expectations", the novel's twenty middle chapters, is dominated by Pip's hope that all his uncertainties will eventually be resolved in a genteel marriage with Estella. The "third stage", having detailed the further disequilibriums following upon the shattering of that dream, including his vague and unrealistic alternative vision of marriage with Biddy, leaves him in the subdued equilibrium of two *ménages à trois*, one of them with Herbert and Clara in Cairo, and the other back in England with Joe and Biddy, whose little Pip he borrows almost as if he were his own son. Both the published and unpublished versions of the novel's final pages then raise the question of whether Estella will once again unsettle a status quo. In the unpublished version, she does not, whereas in the revised, published version an opening is hinted towards a new and altogether more blessed equilibrium, which would reward both parties for all their earlier sufferings.

Primary tellability of this kind means that personal relationships are very highly valorized. Throughout *Great Expectations*, disturbing relationships such as those of Joe's parents, of Joe himself and Mrs Joe, of Mr and Mrs Pocket, of Magwitch and Molly, of Estella and Drummle, of Miss Havisham and Compeyson, and of Jaggers and Molly are very sharply contrasted with the happy hearths of Herbert and Clara, of Joe and Biddy, and of Wemmick, the Aged Parent and Miss Skiffins. It is no accident that, just when Pip is beginning to resign himself to Estella's union with Drummle, the "vague something lingering in my thoughts" (p. 335) should define itself as his hope of marrying Biddy precisely thanks to Wemmick's having roped him in to be his best man. His joy at Wemmick's marital bliss only makes Biddy's disinclination and unavailability more of a disappointment. No less poignant is his immediate and unselfish recognition that Biddy and Joe are a perfect match. The blessings seem to be falling to everyone but himself.

In Dickens, the ritual equilibrium whose disruption and restoration begins and ends a story does often takes the form of marriage. But the same is true of many later novelists as well. Will Isabel leave Osmond, or will she not? Could Birkin's marriage with Ursula have been complemented, as he had so intensely hoped, by a close tie with Gerald, or not? And even in Dickens, other types of relationship can also serve the same role. In fact his novels include such a huge variety of stable domestic arrangements that Lawrence seems, by comparison, narrow-minded. If it were not for the risk of falling into classical narratology's schematic disregard of humanizing particulars, I might even have suggested that the creator of the Herbert-Clara-Pip threesome would have wondered what all Birkin's fuss was about.

5.5   Secondary tellability

So to claim that Dickens's primary tellability was too bound by the ideology of the Victorian bourgeoisie for the subsequent, less hedonistic century to become interested would be wide of the mark. But it was certainly tellability of a very obvious kind. Other novelists have been less obvious, or have apparently set altogether less weight on sheer story. Sometimes tellability and literary realism can even seem strange bedfellows.

Here, though, it is important to recognize two different kinds of readerly satisfaction, which in the case of Dickens are not mutually exclusive. According to Aristotle, stories are satisfying to the extent that they are probable, an observation which may at first suggest that they involve nothing but the equilibrium of life as usual. But what is actually involved is rather a kind of secondary tellability: tellability as the ultimate "point" or "moral" of a story, something which is much more open to interpretation. Primary tellability, to the extent that a teller does develop it, seeks to get listeners or readers hooked. It is what Chicagoan narratology was very good at pinpointing through its attention to readers' hopes and fears. Secondary tellability is what makes people think. And whereas pulp fiction may have plenty of primary tellability but not much secondary, and whereas E. M. Forster expressed a Modernist scorn at the "gaping audience of cavemen or ... [the] tyrannical sultan or ... their modern descendant the movie-public" who only ask "And then?" (Forster 1974 [1927]: 60), Dickens offers both an obviousness of primary tellability, and a secondary tellability which, though just as strong, is intelligently subtle.

Not even Chicagoan narratologists explored this to the full. Perhaps the step from the residually behaviourist ethos of Chicago to something more like Gadamerian hermeneutics was too intimidating. Even in the fine account of *Great Expectations* by James Phelan, the assessments readers were said to make of characters and their actions came across as rather black and white, and there was little sense that, as Gerald Prince (1983) was one of the first narratologists to point out, differently sited interpreters might assess a story's point in different ways.

Admittedly, many of the things which happen in *Great Expectations* are the result of coincidence, and readers' judgements of whether a coincidence is likely or not will have very little to do with their own sociocultural situationality. In the novels of Hardy, coincidence is also, and notoriously prominent. But in Hardy, the coincidences tend to happen as the story is running on under the reader's direct observation, so to speak, whereas in a late Dickens novel many coincidences have already happened in the distant past, and have had far-reaching consequences for the story's present time, in which a main character is now digging them up again as a way of explaining everything. In *Great Expectations,* the central cluster of coincidences has been that Miss Havisham, Molly, and Magwitch all had one and the same lawyer, Mr Jaggers, and that not even Jaggers knows all there is to know about his clients. He knows that Estella is Molly's daughter, and he himself arranged for her to be adopted by Miss Havisham. But he does not know that Estella's father is Magwitch, whom he defended at a different point in time, and whose benefaction towards Pip he facilitates at a still later point. Magwitch himself, similarly, thinks that his daughter is long since dead. Pip, partly helped by the quite arbitrary "link of association" through which he guesses who Estella's mother is (p. 292), works everything out for himself, and then tells it all to Jaggers, much to even Jaggers's surprise. Whether or not readers will also be surprised, and in a derogatory sense, will depend partly on their own most personal experience of life, and even on their temperament, though I should also note that, here more than in some of his other novels, it is almost as if Dickens had pondered another of Aristotle's remarks, to the effect that a fiction which might otherwise strain belief can actually work very well, as long as its potentially incredible elements are made to seem even more credible than everyday ordinariness (Potts 1968: 58). Jaggers, as Dickens shows him, is so much at the heart of the legal world that he really might have come into contact Miss Havisham, Molly, and Magwitch. And Magwitch's desire not to implicate Molly through guilt by association fully accounts for his absence at the time of her trial, which in turn perfectly explains Jaggers's ignorance of Estella's paternity.

But most of the novel's happenings result from characters' own acts of benefaction or malefaction, and benefaction has a clear tendency to be, not good works in the sense of the holy fool's impulsively natural generosity as seen in Joe, but bear's services, involving impure motives, and leading to outcomes that are deeply problematic. It is here that positional differences between different participants in the process of narrative communication certainly can go with profound differences of interpretation.

Brooks and Hara were by no means the only twentieth century commentators to read the plot's progression in terms of large, impersonal forces. Edmund Wilson (1941), George Orwell (1964 [1939]), Humphrey House (1948), Lionel Trilling (1950) and Robin Gilmour (1981) all discussed gentility as a major Victorian social phenomenon, and there was a tendency to see Magwitch's desire to avenge himself on the genteel Compeyson by making a gentleman out of Pip as serving a representative or symbolic function, almost as if Magwitch had no control over himself. Then, at least by the end of the twentieth century, there were several postmodern critics, most of them feminists, perhaps the most eloquent of whom was Linda Raphael (1994 [1989]), who saw Compeyson as setting in train another drama of symbolically representative bear's service: Miss Havisham's efforts, through nurturing Estella, to get her own back for Compeyson's sociotypically male abuse of her own sociotypically female vulnerability. In Dickens's time, a social critic such as John Stuart Mill – who actually disliked *Bleak House* for treating the rights of women with what he saw as vulgar ridicule (Mill 1970 [1854]) – might already have understood such readings, and Dickens himself, though certainly no revolutionary, was a radical in a rather deeper sense than perceived by Trollope (1970 [1870]). Trollope, as both a rival novelist and an efficient civil servant, saw Dickens as a populist, with no true understanding of society's need for coordinated government. But Dickens also had a much stronger sense than, say, his beloved Fielding that social injustice is systematically structured (Sell 2001: 347–352). Indeed, the plot's bringing together of Magwitch's and Miss Havisham's so different yet so similar responses to Compeyson can seem even less coincidental, to the extent that such broader social reverberations certainly do get clearly suggested.

On the other hand, neither Mill nor Dickens was a postmodern social determinist. They both were high Victorians, with the high Victorians' sense of the upright human being's willpower as quite strong enough to resist social pressure, and to be unselfish and principled. Even Jaggers, who is at first so contemptuous of Joe's generous affirmations, and so cynical in his own pursuit of professional power, is finally shown to have had more than merely business motives in arranging for Estella's adoption. Here had been "one pretty little child out of the heap, who could be saved" (p. 307). Other characters, too, perform what are explicitly described as either personal acts of benefaction – Wemmick's endless solicitousness of the Aged Parent's happiness and well-being, Herbert's efforts to get Pip a place in the Cairo office, and so on – or benefactions with very personal strings attached. In bringing Pip up by hand, for instance, Mrs Joe did literally save Pip's life, but at the considerable price of holding him indebted to her for ever afterwards – the kind of dependency which a self-respecting person like Matthew Pocket is, in his turn, willing and able to avoid.

Communicational narratology can here join forces with mediating criticism, helping readers of our own time to grasp that aspect of Dickens's secondary tellability to which our culture, in its post-postmodern phase, is ready to be re-sensitized. What can be usefully pinpointed is the very large extent to which the novel raises questions of personal moral choice, and the extent to which, even within the Victorians' own thoughtworld, such questions were less straightforward than Pip's regular use of the right / wrong binarism might suggest. This kind of scholarly service is not to be confused with what used to be called a thematic interpretation, since it is not really an interpretation at all, and certainly not a holistic one. Instead, its focus is still on how the story's teller tried to get an audience interested, and in particular, here, tried to start them thinking. The emphasis is on the kind of ethical questions readers were likely to ask themselves, and especially on those questions' fascination and difficulty.

To begin with Magwitch's benefaction, Pip's own response to the full revelation is itself complex. At first he is horrified at having been the protegé of somebody now his social inferior, and horrified at Magwitch's having shaped him as a mere instrument in his scheme of symbolic revenge on the gentleman-villain Compeyson. His horror, moreover, goes hand in hand with a strong physical dislike – "What I was chained to, and how heavily, became intelligible to me as I heard his hoarse voice" (p. 248). He therefore decides that he will make no further personal use of Magwitch's money. This resolve he maintains quite consistently, yet not without coming to see something altogether more noble in Magwitch's motives, and not without beginning to question his own – "I felt a kind of satisfaction – *whether it was a false kind or a true, I hardly know* – in not having profited from his *generosity* since his revelation of himself" (p. 258, my italics). The fuller context here includes his recognition of his own complicated emotions in his similarly secret patronage of Herbert. He several times describes his payment of money to get Herbert fixed up with a job as the only good act he has ever performed, and the Wemmick of Walworth also says this "is devilish good of you" (p. 224), a verdict apparently all the more trustworthy in that the Wemmick of Little Britain has previously told him that to invest in a friend like this would be tantamount to throwing the money off of any of London's six bridges. Yet as Pip also confesses to Wemmick, his desire to help Herbert partly sprang from his guilty belief that he had ousted Herbert from the favours of Miss Havisham, and when, a few pages later, he writes about his pleasure at Herbert's joy in believing that he has finally achieved something, one of the words he uses is surely rather jarring: "I had the greatest difficulty in restraining my tears of *triumph* when I saw him so happy" (p. 226, my italics). This is not just joy at his friend's joy. It is also tinged, however slightly, with self-satisfaction at having relieved his own guilt, and at having masterfully engineered a cunning scheme. Not only that, but he uses exactly the same striking word in suggesting what riles him so much in Magwitch: he speaks of Magwitch's "*triumph* in my story" (p. 225, my italics) – Magwitch's triumph in the rags-to-riches story which he (Magwitch) has engineered by means of his money. Pip's increasing recognition of the degree of "false" satisfaction mixed up with his own "true" satisfaction, and of the degree of "true" satisfaction mixed up with Magwitch's "false" satisfaction, whose falsity Magwitch himself has the honesty to condemn on several occasions as "low", eventually leads to a judgement whose animus is completely turned away from Magwitch onto himself: "in the hunted wounded shackled creature who held my hand in his, I only saw a man who had meant to be my benefactor, and who had felt affectionately, gratefully, and generously, towards me with great constancy through a series of years. I only saw in him a much better man than I had been to Joe" (p. 332). Given all of which, for a reader to arrive at anything remotely resembling an objective assessment of Magwitch will not be easy. Dickens could almost be taken as saying that objective assessment is not worthwhile or even possible: that in such cases the only judgement is the heart's judgement – the heart's judgement as it arises at some particular moment, in consequence of some particular combination of earlier and current experience. Even if readers are in places drawn into provisional verdicts, these constantly turn out to be inadequate. Such, to use Keats's phrase, is the negative capability of narrative's secondary tellability. Uncertainties, mysteries, doubts are not tidily bundled away.

In the case of Miss Havisham, her benefaction of £25 pounds on the occasion of Pip's becoming articled to Joe was obviously well meant. And when, after the final shattering of his great expectations of her, Pip tells Jaggers that she "was *good enough* to ask me" if she could nevertheless help him (p. 305, my italics), he is using what may nowadays seem an old-fashioned and politely formulaic expression in the full sense which ideas of goodness always have in this novel. "Can I only serve you, Pip, by serving your friend?" she had asked (p. 296). Her desire to serve was genuine, and her service, for Pip's sake, to Herbert was readily forthcoming. But in between these real benefactions, there has been her more problematic behaviour towards Estella and, through her, towards Pip himself. In the scene in which she finally starts to contemplate the full consequences of this, she becomes distraught by the most harrowing sense of guilt, which readers may for the moment think quite justified, if very pitiful. Yet her words repeatedly carry another meaning as well: "I did not know what I had done"; "[W]hen she first came to me, I meant to save her from misery like my own. At first I meant no more"; "I wanted a little girl to rear and love, and save from my fate" (p. 298). In which there was surely nothing more harmful than in that rough diamond in *David Copperfield*, Aunt Betsey, another abused woman, who nursed exactly the same dream. Nor was Pip's own suffering at Miss Havisham's hands by any means entirely of her making. He was predisposed to fall into her trap, both personally and socially predisposed, as Dickens clearly suggests, and assessments of her degree of responsibility and power are not consistent even from the lips of Estella. "I am what you have made me", Estella tells her coldly (p. 230). Yet when Pip accounts for Estella's behaviour in precisely the same way, she asks, "Why do you injuriously introduce the name of my mother by adoption? It is my own act" (p. 271). Or to take another contradiction, on the one hand Estella tells Pip "we are not free to follow our own devices, you and I" (p. 202), as if they were a benefactor's mere puppets, while on the other hand she can produce the anomalous semantics of a sentence such as "*You are to* take me there [to Satis House from Richmond] and bring me back, *if you will*" (p. 228, my italics). The text as Dickens has written it is constantly prompting readers to make judgements of Miss Havisham's actions. But hard and fast judgements such as those which serve within the legal system so familiar to Jaggers and Wemmick are really not easy.

As for Pip himself, the triumph he feels on having conspired to help Herbert is a characteristic emotion. The exercise of power is something he does not shrink from, and even relishes. He no sooner learns that he is coming into some money than he has a fantasy of "bestowing a dinner of roast beef and plum-pudding, a pint of ale, and a gallon of condescension, upon everybody in the village" (p. 115). Much later on, he lets slip the sentiment, "I would not have undone the engagement between her [Clara] and Herbert, for all the money in … [Magwitch's] pocket-book" (p. 281). The very idea of trying to undo it is surely rather surprising, and even shocking. Yet Pip does seek to alter other people's lives. At the ostentatious funeral which Trabb, doubtless in hope of his approval, laid on for Mrs Joe, he registers the absence of Trabb's boy, but without further comment, even though he had earlier written that letter expressing the "Loathing" excited by the boy in "every respectable mind", a comment which Trabb has presumably not forgotten. Later, Pip speculates on how Trabb's boy would have felt if he had known that his actions had saved him (Pip) from being thrown by Orlick into the lime kiln, "[n]ot that Trabb's boy was of a malignant nature, but that he had too much spare vivacity, and that it was his constitution to want variety and excitement at anybody's expense" (p. 321). This is somewhat disingenuous, because Trabb's boy would have some reason to regard him as not just "anybody", and to want to get revenge, just as Miss Havisham, Magwitch and Orlick all want to get revenge on those who have done them harm. As for Orlick's grievance, the reasons for it are made very clear. If it had not been for Mrs Joe's strange fondness towards her assailant, Pip's machinations against Orlick would have started at the forge. As things are, he has to wait until he can get Jaggers to dismiss him from Satis House, though by that time he has already, as Orlick puts it, come "betwixt me and a young woman I liked" (p. 316), just as it later becomes his ambition to come between Drummle and Estella. In both these last instances, he claims to have purely protective motives towards the young woman herself. "It makes me wretched," he tells Estella, "that you should encourage a man so generally despised as Drummle" (p. 234). But he himself is stalking her just doggedly as Drummle, and in the end, as his mind wrestles with that "vague something", his hopes of Biddy are hardly more appropriate than Orlick's. In which fuller contexts, the motives for his interventions seem even more open to discussion.

Just as in the cases of Magwitch and Miss Havisham, a blanket verdict is not possible. If his service to Herbert was not, as he sometimes suggests it was, a spontaneously good deed, neither was it, despite what he also says, his only benefaction. But either because of his characteristic guilt feelings, or out of a real sense of modesty, even his most genuinely good deeds come across as simultaneously qualified. As a young child, for instance, he felt an instinctive pity for the escaped convict he met on the marsh, and went to great trouble to help him, in the way Joe so warmly endorses, yet he was also, and very pointedly, acting out of terror at the man's threats. And on three much later occasions, his generosity, though able to bestow blessings beyond all price, is still ethically problematic.

First, when Miss Havisham fears she may have caused him as much pain as she herself has suffered, she "dropped on her knees at my feet; with her folded hands raised to me in the manner in which, when her poor heart was young and fresh and whole, they must often have been raised to Heaven from her mother's side" and implores his forgiveness (p. 297), which his mercy is godlike enough to grant. Yet there *is* a qualification. A page or so later he re-experiences his childhood hallucination of seeing her dead body hanging from the beam in the brewery, and only a page later still, he cannot perform the continuing great kindness of rescuing her from the fire except by being very cruel: "I still held her forcibly down with all my strength, like a prisoner who might escape" (p. 300), almost as if her were avenging himself on her after all.

Secondly, when he has finally pieced together the story of Estella's parentage and adoption, and knows, as neither Estella herself, Molly, nor Magwitch knows, that they are all alive, and all resident within a short distance of each other, he has the three of them in the palm of his hand. If he so chooses, he could bring about a family reunion by which the novel might seem to achieve the kind of primary tellability we expect from Smollett – another of Dickens's eighteenth century favourites. Seen this way, the huge coincidence that Miss Havisham, Molly, and Magwitch all used the same lawyer is not merely an incredible coincidence that Dickens has made more credible than everyday ordinariness. Nor is it just a symbolically sociotypical conjunction of the revenges against Compeyson as both a gentleman and an abuser of women. It also puts Pip, as very few other plots could conceivably have put him, in a position of absolute power to bestow or withhold what many readers might feel would be the most important blessing of all, perhaps the kind of blessing which only God can give. Yet Pip decides not to bestow it, because, having listened to the arguments of Jaggers's "wiser head" (p. 303), he judges that it would actually be the greatest bear's service of all. Magwitch would have no joy of Molly now. Molly herself is probably best off as she is, under Jaggers's firm protection and control. And a reunion with these two particular parents would do nothing to help Estella in her already dreadful marriage with the snobbish Drummle. The greatest benefaction he can give all three, Pip concludes, is through doing absolutely nothing. The only possible blessing arising from a family re-union, and one which Jaggers and Pip do not even discuss, is that Magwitch might be pleased to know that his daughter is still alive and has become a lady. But here, precisely, is the qualification. This possible blessing is something an alert reader may easily think about, perhaps wondering whether Pip might at least have considered it as well.

But Pip's information about Estella's life and condition is what he then uses for the third and greatest benefaction of all, when he assumes the role of *deus ex machina* in the life-story of the dying Magwitch.

> "Dear Magwitch, I must tell you, now at last. You understand what I say?"
> A gentle pressure on my hand.
> "You had a child once, whom you loved and lost."
> A stronger pressure on my hand.
> "She lived and found powerful friends. She is living now. She is a lady and very beautiful…".

And just so that the story will have all the primary tellability a dying man could wish:

> "… And I love her!"   (p. 342)

– as if she loved him and were free to love him, too, and as if the sound of wedding bells could be confidently expected. Even for less alert readers, Pip's benefaction to Magwitch here will perhaps be slightly tarnished by the element of deception, and others may even ask themselves whether his end justified his means.

5.6   Politeness

Now just like other forms of communication, narrative involves co-adaptations between the individual and society and between one individual and another (Sell 2000: 145–158, 198–193). As these studies frequently emphasize, every social individual has to adapt to the communicative resources which the particular society offers – the language, the genres, the intertextualities – but will naturally do so in the hope that the society will adapt to his or her own personal project. Similarly, communicants always tend to meet each other half way, and to give and take. This is the key to persuasive rhetoric: if you want your audience to become more like you, then you have to become more like them, but not too much like them, because in that case you would lose the difference you were hoping to contribute.

In their most visceral form these co-adaptive gambles are experienced as a matter of politeness, or more accurately, as a tension between too much politeness and too little (Sell 2000: 107–138). Politeness can be thought of as involving a communally sustained scale of evaluation, calibrated from extreme offensiveness, through a more neutral central range, to extreme obsequiousness. It is a scale which registers any kind of speech or action at all. But given that the human being is a social individual, conventional notions of politeness may not be entirely binding, and communication, including story-telling, can involve a kind of interpersonal tightrope act, discussable in terms of both selectional politeness and presentational politeness. Selectional politeness is more or less an anthropological notion, having to do with the choice of things to say, and of words to say them with, choices which relate to questions of taboo and fashion. Presentational politeness is more of a psycholinguistic notion, having to do with the manner of presenting the subject matter. Is the communicant being helpful towards fellow-communicants? Is it easy for them to see what the point is, what is happening, what the general bearings are? And in terms of both selectional and presentational politeness, a narrator can afford to concede neither too much, because that would be simply boring, nor too little, because that would be simply shocking.

Because politeness is a social phenomenon, it also has a history. What counts as polite and impolite has varied from one age to another. Here, then, is another area where the communicational narratologist can join hands with the mediating critic. The presentational politeness of *Ulysses* is so different from that of *Moll Flanders* that *Moll Flanders* may even strike present-day readers as boring, unless they are sensitized to the ways in which, within his own culture, Defoe, too, was balancing too little against too much. Presentationally, however, *Great Expectations* has never been disliked. Readers have always faced enough of a challenge in trying to work out the fore-plot before the main story time, but as Thomas Loe (1994 [1989]) suggested, the kind of task involved may well have been familiar from their prior experience of mystery and suspense novels. Also, it is the same task as Pip himself has to perform within the story, who can act as readers' representative, as it were, and help to keep them going. There are so few shifts of time perspective and voice, and they are so clearly marked, that Pip's own narration moves on steadily and perfectly intelligibly, even when he is reporting his experiences of fever and hallucination. On the other hand, it is never facile, and as Chesterton remarked, you have no sooner come to a clear understanding of what has been going on in a Dickens novel than you begin to forget it again (Chesterton 1970 [1906]). Especially a late-Dickens plot creates a teasing but pleasing difficulty in retrospect, which permanently invites re-reading. And on each re-reading, the novel's secondary tellability will come home with renewed force, because the plot so much constates it. When our memory of the actual story and pre-story of *Great Expectations* has become somewhat blurred, we have thereby inevitably forgotten some of the enormous weight and moral complexity of Pip's benefactions as well.

Really to get the novel's point, we have to be actually in the process of reading it here and now. A so-called definitive interpretation of a literary text is always out of place, because it forecloses on the communicative partnership of all readers subsequent to the reader who pronounces it. But in the case of late Dickens, a definitive interpretation would be even more insensitive than usual, because it would so totally fail to capture the way his complicated intrigues can precipitate a secondary tellability that is so ethically provocative.

So no, with Dickens the issue of politeness has never been one of presentation, but, in historically varying ways, of selection. In the case of *Great Expectations*, he himself can perhaps be said to have foreseen this. By 1860, many readers were complaining that his recent novels had become too serious and gloomy in the choice of both settings, subject-matter and story-lines. Dickens, never insensitive to feed-back, but perhaps less than frank here, told Forster that his new novel had a "grotesque tragi-comic conception" and an "exceedingly droll" opening: it "put a child and a good-natured foolish man in relations that seem to me very funny". Forster allowed himself to be convinced, later writing that "Dickens's humour, not less than his creative power, was at its best in this book" (Forster 1928 [1872–1874]: Book 9, Chapter 3). But not all the early commentators saw it as a return to vintage quality; most fellow writers were cool or simply silent; and by the time *The Portrait of a Lady* began to appear in *Macmillan's Magazine* in 1880, *Great Expectations* belonged with *A Tale of Two Cities* among Dickens's "minor" and least popular works (Morris 1882; Cook 1879: 26), and this in spite of its revised, less sober ending, supplied on the recommendation of Bulwer Lytton. Even Forster found the changed ending less "consistent with the drift, as well as natural working out, of the tale", and many readers clearly felt that the novel's "drift" really was too dismal. After all, Pip is for the most part in an agony of frustrated longing, his head hopelessly turned by both Estella and the dream of gentility, and he finally spends the eleven years of only rather circumspect happiness in the Cairo *ménage à trois*. Against this background, the revised ending could well have struck readers as no less dubious than the happy ending Pip intimates to the dying Magwitch. Indeed, that episode in the book itself could positively have alerted them to their reasons for deeming the entire work a bit off-putting. If they felt that the primary tellability should have involved some more emphatic blessings, then the bittersweet portrayal of Magwitch's deathbed delusion could well have seemed like an assault on their own fondest desires, after which the very beautiful published ending might actually have come across as all too obviously the sop that Dickens intended. James's tale of Isabel's disappointed expectations, so unthinkable without the Dickensian precedent, and at least as dour, was immediately less offensive, because *Great Expectations,* and Dickens's other later novels, had already broken the selectional norms confirmed by his earlier ones. Late Dickens himself involved a fair amount of anti-hedonism, and by 1880 such an ur-Modernist trait could be developed with much less risk and more consistency.

With the full advent of Modernism, James's reputation continued to rise, and Dickens no longer looked the same. By the middle of the twentieth century many critics were praising *Great Expectations* as his supreme creation, precisely because its selections were now seen as basically unpleasurable. By that time, readers also knew, what Forster's biography had still concealed, that Dickens had kept the actress Nelly Ternan as his mistress, and they were accordingly admiring the gloomy later novels for a disturbing innerness to Victorian duplicities, and for a healthily disillusioned view of life in general. George Bernard Shaw, in his edition of *Great Expectations*, went the whole hog, by restoring the original, less pleasant ending, and Lionel Trilling, that connoisseur of pain's abrasive reality, found plenty of "sordid, hidden reality" in this same novel. "The real thing," he explained, "is not the gentility of Pip's life but the hulks and the murder and the rats and decay in the cellarage of the novel" (Trilling 1950:211), a reading whose sense of literary decorum had clearly been nourished on the early Eliot – on the rat's feet over broken glass in the dry cellar of the Hollow Men. What critics complained of now was the goodness of Joe and Biddy and, more generally, the novel's assumption that a human being can try, by instinct or by personal resolve, to pursue a good end. Numerous commentators psychoanalysized Pip as not knowing his own deepest drives, or as the helpless victim of ideology. By seizing so enthusiastically on the gloomy and darker elements which had not pleased Victorian taste, they were downplaying the primary tellability's more cheerful aspects, and ignoring the extent to which its secondary tellability involves a moral axis.

Given the notion of selectional politeness, the tellability of *Great Expectations*, both primary and secondary, can be reformulated. Its primary tellability involved a tension between ritual equilibrium thought of as pleasantly cheerful and ritual equilibrium thought of as unpleasantly gloomy. This tension, so completely encapsulated in the equilibrium of the Cairo threesome ("I lived happily with Herbert and his wife, and lived frugally, and paid my debts" (p. 355)), was always bound to test the patience both of readers preferring pleasure and of readers preferring gloom. The novel's secondary tellability involved a tension between, on the one hand, the radical's sense of human beings as influenced by forces larger than their own individuality and, on the other hand, the upright Victorian's sense of them as exercising willpower. Again, readers preferring either view to the other were bound to feel provoked. Such were Dickens's co-adaptive gambles – his attempt to cater, somewhat but not entirely, for the predispositions and sensitivities of many possible readers.

To repeat: somewhat but not entirely. If Dickens had immediately and entirely satisfied every reader, he could never have hoped to bring about change. He would have been making so many polite concessions that his valuable distinctiveness would have been quite lost. He would have been adapting to society, but in no expectation that society would adapt to him.

5.7 Community-making

Communication, including story-telling, does change the status quo. It is a semiotic process by which people negotiate the world and each other. Especially when it is the kind of communication that Habermas would describe as undistorted by power and inequalities, part of the outcome is that the amount of overlap between the two contexts within which the communicants are operating actually gets larger. So what then takes place is communication in the etymological sense: a making common, a making of community. Even in a case of persisting and extensive disagreement, the new measure of understanding can strengthen human bonds. Without ever bringing about some glorious and universal human consensus, and even though conflicts be-tween different individuals and groupings are probably, as Heraclitus and Blake and Stuart Hampshire have all thought, a sign of life and a stimulus to creativity, commu-nication nevertheless holds out the hope of a more peaceful co-existence.

It also tends to remind human beings that, despite all the countless shades of sociocultural difference, some of their deepest feelings and experiences result from those existential common denominators. We are all born; we shall all die; we all have needs, primary and secondary; we all form relationships, with individuals and within society at large; we are all susceptible to pleasure; we all dislike pain; we are all capable of giving and receiving both pleasure and pain. Communication, and perhaps story-telling especially, tends to reinforce the sense of fellowship. Alongside acts of positive benefaction, of which it can of course be the channel, a story offers, in and of itself, a major opening for goodwill. Which is not to say that communication, and least of all story-telling, will always be ecstatically joyful. Fellowship is just as likely to take the form of sharing burdens and sorrows.

A sense of literature as communicational in this profound sense is nothing new. It was very real for the first readers of seventeenth century devotional poetry, for in-stance (Sell 2001: 139–164). It was also what prompted some admirers of Dickens to form the appropriately named Dickens Fellowship, which ever since 1905 has pub-lished *The Dickensian: A Magazine for Dickens Lovers*. By 1925, a new venture of this kind would have been impossible. It would have sounded too cosy, too much like hero-worship, too antiquarian, too out of touch with grim twentieth-century reali-ties, too hedonistic, too interested in *early* Dickens. Yet *The Dickensian* continues to be read, because there are people who still find, and want to find, Dickens enjoyable, and who want to continue comparing notes about the third entities which he brought within the communicative set-up.

On the one hand, and like any other communicants, readers of *Great Expectations* will negotiate these third entities from within their own positionality and on the basis of their own experience. This will inevitably mean that they do not all emphasize and de-emphasize precisely the same features. A reading here and now which turned out exactly the same as a reading there and then would not be the product of an intelligent and socialized mind. That Modernist readers lost track of Dickens's tellability was almost inevitable, just as for us now it has become much easier to overlook what were once the most salient features of Modernist writing.

On the other hand, readers have never had anything to gain from blinding themselves to the very large amount of existential and emotional reality they actually share with Dickens, nor from a refusal to try and empathize with his sociohistorical difference, which may well turn out to be a significant difference for them. So much so, that a commucational narratologist who alerts post-postmodern readers to the nature of Dickens's primary and secondary tellability can hope to confirm our culture in its renegotiation of the postmodern determinisms: in its ongoing rediscovery of pleasure, and of the human being's own power – for better and worse – of action.

This is a process of change in our entire orientation to life, which will in turn affect our response, not only to the novels of Dickens, but to any narrative at all. We may now have entered a period in which *Women in Love* is likely to be valued, not for itself suggesting a suitable orientation, but, among other things, for having called in question the nineteenth century's orientation in ways which can lead to its firmer recuperation, albeit with inevitable differences, in the twenty-first. Isabel Archer will probably be ever more warmly admired for her force of resolution, and ever more whole-heartedly pitied for the misery it ensured her. And always, telling and responding to stories will be more clearly perceived as a dialogical activity, taking place within a community of many differently positioned, different-minded, often wildly disagreeing human beings, whose endlessly variegated fellowship a story can itself enlarge.

CHAPTER 6

The Waste Land
and the discourse of mediation

6.1   Mediating *versus* conflictual discourse

To a critic who evaluates instances of language use as communication, the discourse of mediation presents itself as a prime object of study. To the extent that a person honestly trying to mediate between two parties in a conflict listens to what they are both saying, tries to do full justice to both sides, has no foregone conclusions as to exactly how the situation can be improved, and has no sense of being personally in a position to pronounce some absolute truth or judgement, mediation pre-eminently belongs to the kind of communication I describe as genuine. Its very aim is to promote dialogicality in a full sense.

One way to point up its fundamental features is by contrasting it with the discourse of conflict, which is no less interesting to a communicational critic, but for opposite reasons. Perhaps the most noticeable difference between them is that they each tend to imply their own attitude to history. The discourse of conflict, although it arises in, and because of particular historical circumstances, and although it can be greatly preoccupied with them, can also be very selective and unrealistic in the way it refers to them, and even downright unhistorical. As a result, conflicts only become more intense and long-drawn-out. The discourse of mediation, by contrast, requires that its practitioners have a sense of the course of history as extremely powerful, but as nevertheless partly re-directable by human volition. In fact anyone engaged in trying to mediate in a conflict could almost be forgiven for wishing that the opposed parties would simply forget their previous history. Yet mediation which totally ignored historical considerations would hardly succeed, since in that case both of the opposed parties would feel that their interests and rights were being overlooked, especially if their own sense of history were mythologically tinged by a discourse of conflict.

Conflictual discourse is by no means confined to politics, propaganda, or generals' pep talks. There can also be literary manifestations, which is why I shall begin with a discussion of Robert Bridges as a wartime anthologist of poetry and prose. Conversely, mediation can be an important task, not only for a diplomat, but for a literary critic, and especially for a literary critic faced with the condition of post-postmodernity. Hence my attempt here to move beyond some *fin de siècle* interpretations of T. S. Eliot.

6.2   Robert Bridges' *The Spirit of Man*

In both 1916 and 1940 the world was heading towards a state of maximum conflict. By 1916, the First World War was already well under way, and the Second World War was the major fact of European life by 1940, the year in which Derek Traversi published his dour interpretation of *Henry V* in *Scrutiny*. Another item published in 1940 was a reprint of a little book which had first appeared in 1916, and which now carried the title: *The Spirit of Man: An Anthology in English & French From the Philosophers & Poets made in 1915* [sic] *by Robert Bridges, O. M. Poet Laureate & dedicated by gracious permission to His Majesty King George V.*

The title-page also boasted a 3 cm. × 2 cm. drawing based on Michaelangelo's image of the creation of Adam in the ceiling of the Sistine Chapel. The naked Adam, reclining on the earth, receives the touch of life from the hand of God, which points downwards from the sky. The reason for printing this here is hinted by Bridges's Preface:

> To put it briefly, man is a spiritual being, and the proper work of his mind is to interpret the world according to his higher nature, and to conquer the material aspects of the world so as to bring them into subjection to the spirit.
>
> (Preface (unpaginated))

Bridges was engaged in the same kind of ideological exercise as Olivier in his film of *Henry V*, and the antithesis between the spiritual and the material was his propaganda's very keystone. To put it crudely, the reclining Adam, like any imperialist male worth his salt, has the world squarely under his backside. But if, in the second decade of the twenty-first century, readers were now to wonder about the title's promise of texts in only English and French, perhaps thinking that something humanly valuable may have been lost by the exclusion of, say, Immanuel Kant and Goethe, the point was not just that, in both 1916 and 1940, Germany was the enemy. Becoming the enemy was a matter of forgetting God's touch of life, of making oneself insensible to the breath of the spirit, and of being too involved in matter. To quote the Preface again, "The progress of mankind on the path of liberty and humanity has been suddenly arrested and its promise discredited by the apostasy of a great people, who, casting off as a disguise their professions of Honour, now openly avow that the ultimate faith of their hearts is in material force." Up until now, "[w]e had accounted our [German-speaking] cousins as honest and virtuous folk; some of us have well-loved friends among them whom we have heard earnestly and bitterly deplore the evil spirit that was dominating their country." But now it is impossible not to suspect that Prussia has not only subjugated, but infected and morally enslaved the various Teutonic states, and that "a vision of world-empire" is deluding or tempting them. We, meanwhile, "turn to seek comfort only in the quiet confidence of our souls; and we look instinctively to the seers and poets of mankind, whose sayings are the oracles and prophecies of loveliness and lovingkindness." We are not as perfect as we might be, perhaps. "Our national follies and sins have deserved punishment." But we are still free and true at heart, and can "take hope in contrition, and in the brave endurance of sufferings that should chasten our intention and conduct." We soundly desire "brotherhood and universal peace to men of good-will", and in fighting for our country are fighting for freedom and honour. "That fairest earthly fame, the fame of Freedom, is inseparable from the names of Albion, Britain, England: it has gone out to America and the Antipodes, hallowing the names of Canada, Australia, and New Zealand; it has found a new home in Africa: and this heritage is our glory and happiness" (Preface (unpaginated)).

The *British* imperialists, in other words, have a very great chunk of the earth under their collective backside, but have not forgotten the higher things of the spirit. There is more than a suggestion that their solid terrestrial seat is their reward for being at least a bit purer in spirit than the Germans.

Bridges' Whiggish talk of progress and his Enlightenment ideal of universal brotherhood give his text a particular period flavour. But this blends in very smoothly with the far more ancient rhetoric of conflictual disjunction. On the one hand there is spirit, eternity, humanity, universal brotherhood, friends, relatives, loved-ones. On the other hand there is matter, history, bondage, inhumanity, diabolic monstrosity, enemies – enemies who insert wedges of greedily nationalistic difference between themselves and a universal humanity. Here is a discourse which envisages no *media via*. Whereas, to look at the positioning of Adam in Michaelangelo's image, you might equally well have thought that he was striking some kind of compromise between God and Mammon, any such idea is firmly ruled out by Bridges's rhetoric.

Fully in keeping with this, his selections of uplifting verse and philosophy are themselves presented as a-historically disembodied. As the book's Table of Contents makes clear, they are arranged, not chronologically but according to theme. In Book I: Dissatisfaction, Retirement, Spiritual Desire, Idea of God, Spiritual Love and Praise. In Book II: The Muses, Beauty is Truth, Fairyland, Romance, Childhood, Ideal Love, Nature, Spring and Lovers, Youth and Age. In Book III: Mortality, Melancholy, Sorrow, Sin, Ethics and Conduct, Philosophies and Humanities. And in Book IV: Lovingkindness, Sympathies, Christian Charity, Myths, Christian Virtue, Vocation and Active Virtue, Social Virtue and Freedom, Heroism, The Happy Warrior, Life in Death, The Heavenly Kingdom. For purposes of identification, each extract of prose or verse is merely headed with a number. The authors' names, and the titles of the texts from which the extracts are taken, are listed only at the back of the book. And the rationale for such arrangements can be derived from No. 83, a passage from the Preface to *Lyrical Ballads* which, as pointed out in my study of Wordsworth, was seminal for nineteenth century ideas about Poetry (*sic*) in general:

In spite of difference of soil and climate, of language and manners, of laws and customs, – in spite of things silently gone out of mind, and things violently destroyed, the Poet binds together by passion and knowledge the vast empire of human society, as it is spread over the whole earth, and over all time … . Poetry is the first and last of all knowledge – it is as immortal as the heart of man.

(No. 83)

Still buying into this in 1940, the publishers Longman Green and Co. Ltd. and the Readers' Union Ltd. saw no reason why the same spiritual treasures should not remain just as valuable as they had been in 1916. Historical differences were neither here nor there.

This idea of the essential oneness of all humanity was not peculiar to the British and their allies. The German soldiers with whom Henry Williamson chatted during the 1915 Christmas truce believed that "they were fighting for the same causes and ideals as we were" (Glover and Silkin 1990: 151). Despite the idea's usefulness to imperial propaganda, it could still summon up the thought-world of Enlightenment egalitarianism, and for any free-spirited European living between 1789 and 1945 was likely to be a cardinal belief.

The British poets who reacted most strongly against the First World War were no exception. For them, the notion of a universal humanity was a key stimulus. They figured the war as providing absolutely no benefits, except in finally intensifying the sense of common humanity which it had begun by disrupting. Addressing first British, and then German womanhood, Siegfried Sassoon wrote,

You [the British women] can't believe that British troops "retire"
When hell's last horror breaks them, and they run,
Trampling the terrible corpses – blind with blood.
O German mother dreaming by the fire,
While you are knitting socks to send your son
His face is trodden deeper in the mud.

("Glory of Women", in Parsons 1965: 97)

What both the British and the German wives, mothers and daughters experience and feel is fundamentally the same. Difference of soil and climate, of language and manners, of laws and customs might just as well not exist. Or in the words of the ghost who confronts Wilfred Owen in "Strange Meeting", "I am the enemy you killed, my friend" (Lewis 1977: 35–36), almost as if real historical reasons for an armed conflict are unimaginable.

As long as everybody in a conflict – not only the people fighting on both sides, but the people actually opposed to the fighting – are locked into this mental separation between a timelessly universal spirit of humanity and something altogether more material, historical and evil, the conflict will continue, even at the cost of enormous suffering and loss of life, until both sides are exhausted or one of them is beaten.

Nor does this rhetoric suddenly come into being with a formal declaration of war. The outbreak of physical hostilities merely sets the seal on an antagonism which has already made itself felt, and which has been no less real for being verbal. The conflictual discourse will actually have been so powerful that conventional attempts to defuse the danger of armed combat have simply made no headway. As pointed out by Kalevi J. Holsti in his *Peace and War: Armed Conflicts and International Order*, "there are no cases on record where formal mediation actually prevented a war" (Holsti 1991: 112).

6.3   Conceptualizing mediation

One of the reasons for this is that the role of mediators has often been too narrowly conceived. Or more exactly, too little attempt has been made to keep the language of mediation sufficiently distinct from the language of conflict. Mediation has not been seen as an undertaking calling for empathy, creativity and foresight. Its perceived scope has rather lain in the sorting out of conflicts that have already begun to take their toll of warriors' and innocent victims' lives. Professional mediators, even when schooled on textbooks with titles such as *Positive Diplomacy* (Marshall 1997), have been encouraged to promote peace by means of threats, sops, and bribes, or through the embattled parties' own rhetorical disjunction between the purity of universal humanity and an evil historical separatism.

For mediation to be successful, that disjunction must be broken. Now that the postmodern reifications of barriers between one community and another are, in the post-postmodern era, giving way to the ideal of a globalized world that is nevertheless still sensitive to difference, it should become easier for mediators to apply insights arising from a study of genuine communication. The facts of human and social diversity have to be seen as potentially energizing, and dialogue across perceived lines of sociocultural demarcation as potentially illuminating and non-coercive. What is needed is a language in which peaceful human co-existence would *not* be in binary opposition with the historical facts of difference between one human grouping and another. Then the opposed parties might be persuaded to engage in a genuine attempt to negotiate each other's otherness.

Even during the postmodern era, a way forward was suggested by research carried out into water disputes. These clearly showed that cultural differences, instead of assuming their more traditional role as obstacles to agreement, can actually provide clues to conflict resolution (Faure and Rubin 1993). It is all a matter of improving mutual understanding, which as long as the discourse remains full of unbridgeable dichotomies of spirit / matter, God / Devil, friend / enemy, eternity / history, universal / local can never happen.

Then again, mutual understanding and non-disjunctive discourse are most likely to thrive within political frameworks of a particular kind. By the end of the twentieth century, Western liberal philosophers were responding to the centrifugal fragmentation of postmodern society, not only with Blakean notions of the positive energies flowing from powerful oppositions, but with calls for a rational justice which would check and de-fuse potential hostilities (Hampshire 1992 [1989]: 189). In this they were already sounding a post-postmodern note, since their aim was to steer the postmodern politics of recognition in the direction of a society that would be egalitarian, and in that sense blind to difference, yet with no hegemonic encroachment on the rights and human dignity of the very many kinds of people who nevertheless do differ from each other. When Stuart Hampshire pinned his hopes on "a recognisable basic level of common decency" which would feed into "a minimum procedural justice", he was seeing "evil, in the form of the drive to domination, ... [as] the uncompensated violation of this basic justice" (Hampshire 1992 [1989]: 186).

Both within individual states and internationally, there are already many bodies of arbitration whose procedural justice seeks to prevent such violations through processes of negotiation. As for mediation within the literary sphere, readers who venture on texts from alien milieus may well need help, and a sociocultural difference is *always* a difference, regardless of whether its main axis is diachronic or synchronic. Whether we realize it not, we can all have problems with texts from some earlier historical period of what we may think of as our own tradition, and we can be just as strongly challenged by texts emanating from what we may perceive as some other communal grouping within contemporary multicultural society. As noted in my Introduction, one critic who clearly recognized this was Edward Said, who described his mediating aims quite explicitly (Said 1994 [1993]: xxvi, xxxi).

Critics like Said, however, have been unable to draw support from the main traditions in twentieth century literary theory (Sell 2000: 29–118). Especially in the earlier part of that century, a great deal of literary theorization and criticism was carried out within the de-historicizing paradigms of Freudian or Jungian criticism, New Critical formalism, Leavisian moral criticism, and so-called practical criticism in general. I. A. Richards' influential *Practical Criticism* (1929) de-contextualized and de-authored poems in exactly the same manner as Bridges' *The Spirit of Man*. The student guinea-pigs whose wayward interpretations prompted Richards to recommend the discipline of careful close reading had been told nothing about the provenance of the poems they were asked to discuss, and many teachers drew the conclusion that the literature classroom was supposed to be a kind of laboratory, hermetically sealed off from society and social change (Sell 2000: 127–129). Then in the later twentieth century, Marxist, post-Marxist, new historicist, cultural materialist, feminist, ethnic, queer-theoretical, and ecocritical approaches to literature brought history back into the picture, but rather too forcefully. Within, say, Barthesian or Foucauldian structuralism, there was sometimes an element of social determinism, to the effect that human individuals are completely circumscribed by their milieus or language. So whereas the earlier approaches had seen literature as so universal and unworldly that mediation could never even be *necessary*, there were now approaches which, by throwing doubt on our intellectual, imaginative and moral ability to get beyond our own social formation, suggested that mediation between different situationalities was not *possible*. This contrast between early and late twentieth century paradigms was in its own way just one more example of the counterproductive dichotomy between eternal spirit and historical materiality.

In order to mediate, whether in a pub brawl, between warring nations, between different historical phases of the same tradition, or between different types of reader within post-postmodern society, the counterproductive dichotomy must be replaced by a particular kind of view of human nature: an account such as that advanced in my *Literature as Communication* (2000: 145–158) and, more briefly, in my Introduction here. Such a view frankly takes a middle path between historicist determinism and liberal humanist universalism, on the one hand firmly stressing sociocultural differences, on the other hand insisting on existential common denominators, and on the human capacity for empathy with otherness, for imaginative agency, and for moral integrity. Seen in this light, human beings, even while they are adjusting themselves to society's expectations, can co-adaptationally bring about changes in society itself, which thereby adjusts to *them*. In a nutshell, such an account recognizes not only the historical likelihood of conflicts, but the human potentiality for negotiating them. It sees mediation as both necessary and possible.

Mediators, including mediating literary critics, also need a clear sense of communicative pragmatics, another area in which earlier scholarship was sometimes unhelpful. The assumption of much twentieth-century work in linguistics, semiotics, narratology and literary theory was that two people engaged in communication can actually share a single context. And granted, communication between two individuals will never take place unless their contexts of operation overlap to at least some extent. Most importantly, they will share an experience of those existential fundamentals of the human condition, which are their springboard to empathetic understanding of people they perceive as unlike themselves. But even those existential common denominators will be realized in widely different ways in different times and places, and even two people ostensibly representing one and the same sociocultural formation will come to the communicative interchange with different constellations of knowledge, perceptions, attitudes and interests, so that their ways of interpreting and evaluating the words used will be different as well.

The present studies are describing genuine communication as a historical process by which we explore the human other in its own position, and allow the human other to explore us in ours. As a result, perceptions can change, since we shall have seen ourselves through the eyes of the other, and the other will have seen itself through our eyes. We and the other may even become more alike, so that communication will have been a process of self-discovery by self-alienation. When we are communicating genuinely, otherness can always be charged with such suggestions for our own future lives, whereas our more coercive and conflictual moves take no interest in the other's point of view at all. At worst, we see the other as merely diabolic, materialistic, inhuman, something to be destroyed, while we ourselves hold on to our positions, remaining always the same, and perhaps believing that God is on our side. Our follies and sins may have deserved punishment, as Bridges puts it. But our own thought-world, our own community's empire, if it has one, is closer to purity and truth than anybody else's. It is only when communication is genuine, when it is *not* locked into this dysfunctional and rhetorically buttressed disjunction between us and them, that it can change the world. And *how* does it change the world? By allowing people to try on each other's difference for size, a process which can be undertaken in literary communication as much as in any other. To use terms suggested by T.S. Eliot, a reader's act of provisional poetic *assent* can sometimes become an element of the reader's more permanently embraced philosophical *belief* (Eliot 1951 [1929]: 257–258).

The task of mediation is to enhance the dialogicality of communication by improving the conditions for such heuristic self-projection into otherness. A mediating critic's view of *The Spirit of Man* will be that it fuelled the fires of war precisely by reducing the level of dialogicality between self and otherness. This was not just a matter of excluding German writers. There was the still more fundamental disjunction introduced between the English and French texts actually quoted and those same texts' own historicity. Not that their significance should have been seen as wholly confined to their original context of composition. The point is rather that, in a genuine interchange between writer and reader, neither the context of composition nor the context of current reading will dominate the outcome. Thanks to the way Bridges presented his extracts, they conveyed the impression of a "vast empire of human society, as it is spread over the whole earth, and over all time". Wordsworthian phrasing, when used within a venture such as *The Spirit of Man*, though far less often when used by Wordsworth himself, reflects an inclination to overlook the historical facts of difference altogether. The necessary corrective is to be found in one of the more sharply realistic pronouncements of Shelley, which actually turned up in Bridges' extract No. 86: "A man, to be greatly good, must imagine intensely and comprehensively; he must put himself in the place of another and of many others" (Shelley 1954 [1840]: 283). An imaginative going-out from the self in its own position is what Bridges' own unchronological and depersonalizing arrangement of his extracts did not encourage. If anything, he was inviting readers to an exercise in solipsism. The various poets and philosophers' co-adaptations with the world of their own particular time were obscured, so that their words could indeed become infused with a pathos and significance deriving entirely from the distressful context of reading in 1916, a presentist take-over of the past on which the publishers again relied in 1940.

To wish that Bridges' anthology had been otherwise than it was would risk the same error of which he can be accused himself. It would be to read his book as if it had not belonged to a particular phase of history, during which people's mind-set simply was what it was. Similarly, to suggest that *The Spirit of Man* was *not* inspiring to his contemporaries, or that that they *ought not* to have been inspired by it, or that it would have been *far more* inspiring if it had been put together in some other way – any such claims would be absurdly arrogant.

All we can say is that, if Bridges had indeed allowed his selected writers to retain more of their historical distinctiveness, both from each other and from his own time's readers, then the net result would have been different. The inspiration would not have been to keep up the war effort. The book would have offered readers a dialogue with a fundamental human "sameness" which nevertheless took different forms in different times and places, rather like the experience enjoyed by Henry Williamson when he chatted with the German soldiers, who did not thereby suddenly lose their German identity. That experience became available to Williamson only under the conditions of the Christmas truce. The human relationships it involved were not of enemies at war.

6.4   Enhancing dialogue with Eliot

A dialogical type of reading experience is what mediating criticism tries to encourage and reinforce. Such a criticism's hallmark is a solicitude for the human parity of the writer under discussion with every new reader of that writer. It is a criticism which, moving sharply away from conflictual dichotomies, will seek to help readers relate both to the multicultural present and to the many different phases of cultural history.

How, then, will it approach T. S. Eliot, arguably the most important English poet to emerge between 1916 and 1940, yet not, of course, included in the second edition of *The Spirit of Man*? I have already discussed Eliot in *Mediating Criticism* (Sell 2001: 107–138), and anyone interested in my more detailed thoughts about his strategies, his textures, and his reception history can find them there. These present reflections, because less directly concerned with Eliot *per se*, will merely summarize a few of his characteristics. The main focus will be on questions of critical approach. How, in principle, do mediating critics go about their task?

First and foremost, perhaps, the reading glasses available in the here and now must not be allowed to blind readers to the there and then. Time and time again, the so-called culture wars of postmodernity were fuelled by a literary criticism that was fundamentally uncircumstantial or anachronistic, with critics of opposed parties aggravating their quarrels by a solipsistic disregard of considerations of context (Sell 2000: 88–106).

Given the postmodern politics of recognition, one of the discourses within which Eliot came to figure was that connected with anti-Semitism. And that Eliot used anti-Semitic topoi and clichés, did not apologize for doing so, and never campaigned against anti-Semitism is all true enough. From our own position in time we can readily grant that the example he set was unenlightened here. If a figure of his stature had taken a stand against anti-Semitic attitudes, the world would have been a somewhat better place, in which those nurturing and acting upon such sentiments would have had even less excuse. Perhaps unsurprisingly, then, Anthony Julius spoke in 1995 of passages in Eliot which "make a Jewish reader's face flush", and which "insult Jews: to ignore these insults is to misread the poems" (Julius 1995: 1–2).

Yet in this kind of response the pragmatics of reception is actually distorted. In this particular example, the distortion is very clear from Julius's use of the present tense: Eliot's writings "*make* a Jewish reader's face flush" and "*insult* Jews". In 1995, when Julius published his remarks, Eliot had already been dead for thirty years; the passages and poems in question had been written even longer ago; and times and attitudes had changed. Without question, the expressions to which Julius objected, written or spoken in 1995, would not only have insulted Jews, but would have attracted widespread condemnation for doing so. But Eliot did not write or speak them in 1995. When he wrote them, they may well have been insulting to Jews but, however regrettably from Jews' own point of view, and from the point of view of any responsible person in 1995 (or later), they would not have been generally regarded as reprehensible, and even many Jews might have taken them in their stride. From a moral point of view, the case of Ezra Pound needs to be distinguished as different, not just as a matter of degree, not just, that is, because his anti-Semitic statements were more blatant, comprehensive and vituperative than Eliot's, but because he was still making them in what could already be called our own epoch, at a time when the naivety or ignorance or hate or self-confidence which knew no better was even more obviously misplaced, as he himself may eventually have recognized – "Too late came the understanding" (Pound 1963).

At the most general level, the point is that our notions about prejudice, and about the "common sense" which is sometimes used to justify prejudice, need to be sufficiently historical. We all exhibit the prejudices and common sense of our own particular time and place and formation – of our particular "thrown-ness", to use Heidegger's language. Some of our most routinely automated assumptions will make future generations shudder, but we cannot be straightforwardly blamed, since, as Gadamer (1989: 265–307) pointed out, we have nothing else to go on. Without our prejudices and common sense, in situations demanding a swift response we should be quite incapacitated. And even when we do have more time to think, common sense and prejudice are still our only starting point. This line of thought is not as reactionary as it may at first sound, and my aim is certainly not to condone the politics of Heidegger. What Gadamer also stressed is that, when we do think, and when we are confronted by new kinds of situation, our common sense and prejudices are open to revision. Although they may still offer us a certain support, Gadamer's point was not that our critical faculty should be allowed to go into abeyance. On the contrary, he saw today's common sense and prejudices as having resulted from a criticism of yesterday's.

Now as a young man, Eliot was evidently a dreadful snob – or rather, a dreadful snob as seen by somebody now reading him with my own, different set of prejudices. One of the student essays he wrote at Harvard was about Kipling, and it blamed Kipling, an older member of something rather like his own mandarin class, but also an immediately popular writer, for being immature (Ricks 2001). Here the foretaste of I. A. Richards and F. R. Leavis's Modernistic chastisement of stock responses was very strong, and in the critical essays through which Eliot later prepared the ground for his own literary breakthrough one of the key arguments was that "it appears likely that poets in our civilization, as it exists at present, must be *difficult*" (Eliot 1951 [1921]: 289, his italics), a sentence which rapidly became a *locus classicus* of Modernist elitism. Yet the connotations evoked by the Jewish characters in his own early poems can seem at least as facile and unquestioning as Kipling's alleged jingoism, and were also, of course, just as acceptable to contemporaries of varied class backgrounds. But then again, given the subsequent course of twentieth century history, and given Eliot's indisputable intelligence, and his later, entirely credible Christian humility, did he remain unswervingly anti-Semitic for the rest of his life? Or did he begin to scrutinize and readjust his own prejudices in the way that Gadamer suggested is natural? According to Christopher Ricks's *T. S. Eliot and Prejudice* (1994), Eliot really did subject his own views to criticism, and from fairly early on. Ricks's handicap, however, was his own apparent unawareness of Gadamer, which meant that his revisionist account of prejudice, courageous and profoundly thoughtful in itself, was more uphill work than it need have been, and correspondingly more open to attack. According to Julius, Ricks actually trivialized the issues. For Julius, it would seem, a prejudice was always evil in and of itself, and extremely unlikely to be changed.

Elsewhere I have already recommended that mediating critics should be conversant with Gadamer (Sell 2000: 137–145; 2007). If they are, it will be that much easier for them to re-assess such controversies. When a prejudice that is nowadays unacceptable colours the author-reader relationship proposed by a literary work from the past, this is part of what has dated in it. Even if there had been no evidence for a mid-life change of views on Eliot's part, to assume that, if he were still alive today, he would have had a continuing intellectual and emotional investment in a now outdated prejudice would not credit him with much sense. Similarly, when Julius implied that we are as shocked by Eliot's anti-Semitic sentiments as if his texts had been written today, and that we would also have been shocked by them if we had been alive to read them when first published, he was committing the unitary-context fallacy in a very gross, albeit common form. To repeat, Eliot was not writing today, and did not address himself to readers of today. If we ourselves had been among his first readers, the chances are that we should have reacted as other people did.

The point is not *tout comprendre c'est tout pardonner*. It rather has to do with hermeneutic and communicational realism. We have to try to empathize with a writer, including a writer's prejudices. Otherwise we shall not understand, and communication will not be taking place. But communicational empathy with a historical formation will very seldom develop into total sympathy on a long term basis. On the contrary, communication will also fail to take place unless we register some response of our own. In any major writer there will be qualities which we can only admire, and may even try to imitate. An outdated prejudice we shall simply reject, even if, logically, psychologically and ethically, we cannot disagree with it without first having tried to penetrate the mind-set from which it sprang. In some cases the qualities we admire may only stand out only the clearer for the presence of the prejudice, almost suggesting that, in contrast to the work's newness, its prejudice was passé from the start.

There are actually cases, including, I shall suggest, Eliot's anti-Semitism, in which prejudices have functioned as a kind of rhetorical concession: a co-adaptational *quid pro quo*, as it were, such that by indulging the current prejudice authors have met the general public half-way, so increasing the likelihood that something of their more original creative initiatives, or of their less old-fashioned perceptions, will be more widely accepted. This is an uncomfortable truth, but needs to be faced. Such beneficial outcomes cannot relieve an author of responsibility for the prejudice concerned, even if that responsibility would have been assessed more lightly when the prejudice was still widespread. My point is only that the sheer *communicational* workings of prejudice are what present-day critics of, say, Harriett Beecher Stowe would be overlooking, if they blamed her for not sharing our own time's attitudes on colour and ethnicity, so turning a blind eye to her diplomatically radical impact on her own contemporaries. Similarly unhistorical were a number of postmodern feminist critics who in effect condemned Dickens for not being a postmodern feminist. A graver injustice is hard to imagine. Dickens, by both representing and challenging his own time's prejudices, by saying both Yes and No to Mrs Grundy, arguably did more than any other Victorian public figure to improve the lot of women (Sell 2001:286–290). Stowe and Dickens were no less influenced by nineteenth century prejudices than we ourselves by the prejudices of our own time. But they also had it in them to be fundamentally more progressive than most of their contemporaries and, even more remarkably, to bring the two kinds of mind-set into dialogue.

As this may already suggest, a post-postmodern mediating critic's most typical line of argument is that in debates about Eliot, Dickens, Stowe or any other writer, a readership can come into communication not only with the writer, but in effect with other readerships (cf. Sell 1999). As within society at large, so within the sphere of literary activity, newer communicants and their situationalities are for ever commenting on older ones, and receiving in return, as it were, queries or confirmation. A community is not a static consensus, but can be dynamically heterogeneous through space and time. In a disagreement such as that between Julius and Ricks, the depth and sincerity of feeling on both sides is perfectly apparent. Yet literature was nevertheless bringing them into communication, and a mediating critic inspired by Habermas will hope that levels of mutual understanding and respect can always be raised.

In dealing with Eliot's prejudices, the post-postmodern mediating critic will describe them as, in and of themselves, having slowed down the pace of necessary historical change, but also as an aspect of the co-adaption which was needed in order to harness Eliot's powerful creativity. Part of the critic's difficulty here is in helping present-day readers conceptualize twentieth century culture before Eliot had made his astonishing and lasting mark upon it. One way to begin would be by asking why, if Longman Green and the Readers' Union had tried to bring the 1940 edition of *The Spirit of Man* up to date by including *The Waste Land*, that poem would have looked so odd there. Of its first 41 lines no fewer than six were in German, and this was only the beginning. *The Waste Land*'s many different languages and many different voices can have left readers with no choice but to "try out" difference, for it allowed no stable subject position for either an I-persona or an implied you-persona. The fragmentation, the decay of imperial hegemonies, was even explicitly thematized. Fragments were here being shorn against the ruins, and new juxtapositions, new potentialities for human sensibility and identity, were explored through a whole long sequence of remarkable co-adaptations between cultural tradition and the poem's present moment.

In particular, the vision of a golden world of Poetry that is universal and eternal, the nineteenth-century vision still upheld by *The Spirit of Man*, was at once recreated and destroyed. On the one hand, there was the Spenserian loveliness of "Sweet Thames run softly till I end my song": on the other hand, "A rat crept softly through the vegetation" (ll. 176, 187).[1] Or the echoes of eloquent Shakespearian pentameter collapsed into a ragtime parody of bardolatry (l. 128). And while some passages could easily have been included in *The Spirit of Man* under "Idea of God", "Ideal Love" or "Spring and Lovers" –

> … when we came back, late, from the hyacinth garden,
> Your arms full, and your hair wet, I could not
> Speak, and my eyes failed, I was neither
> Living nor dead, and I knew nothing,
> Looking into the heart of light, the silence.   (ll. 37–41)

–, all such poignancy and visionary wonder was rudely challenged by the flushed assault of the young man carbuncular on the bored typist. In places, the poet seemed to withdraw, un-self-importantly, into the poem and its many voices. In other places, readers could not but sense him as a formidable agent, who was radically disregarding polite preconceptions as to what poetry ought to be about, what language it ought to use, and by what narrative or discursive structures it ought to be organized.

---

1. Quotations of Eliot from Eliot 1969.

To crown it all, these mind-stretching co-adaptations between old and new, between correctness and offensiveness, extended from the writing itself to Eliot's public image, so creating a decisive new context within which the poetry came to be read and understood. In the London of 1922, nothing could have been more outrageous than a brash young American, and the author of *The Waste Land* was certainly that. Yet he was rapidly becoming even more of an establishment figure than Bridges himself: founder-editor of *The Criterion* in that same year and, thanks also to his job with Fabers from 1925 onwards, the single most important arbiter and patron of contemporary poetry; not slow to associate himself with conservative and even reactionary sentiments, including anti-Semitism; deliberately old-fogy in manner; and consequently the butt of countless jokes – as when Virginia Woolf wrote to her brother-in-law, "Come to dinner. Eliot will be there in a four-piece suit" (Gordon 1977: 83–84). In both his writing and his role as a celebrity, the latter reinforcing the former, Eliot was making the old-buffer thought-world of *The Spirit of Man* less viable, while still co-adaptationally deferring to its powerful sway.

A mediating critic can help today's readers empathize with Eliot's first audience as regards his conventionality and shockingness alike, which may be the only way to enable younger generations to grasp the extraordinary historical achievement of his rhetorical co-adaptations between the two. Then another main task is to sensitize today's readers to a dead writer's continuing interpersonal charge within their own here and now; in the case of Eliot, to highlight the continuing exemplariness of his style as a style which, to echo Empson's "This Last Pain" (Empson 1962: 32–33), he had learned from despair, yet which was also bursting with ebullient energy. As a response to chaos, to a world in which values had been fundamentally challenged and old identities, social scripts and legitimacies were falling away, *The Waste Land*'s stylistic coadaptations between old and new can still hint, especially to emergent or threatened groupings, that disparate world-views can actually co-exist. For more firmly established groupings, they can still suggest that changes to a status quo may also bring about a self-enlargement. Whereas the notion of communal identity conveyed by Eliot's own explicitly cultural and ideological criticism could be coercive and authoritarian, *The Waste Land* enthusiastically accords a large amount of space to difference. Traditional order is fragmented here, and the fragmentation is ultimately not more worrying than stimulating. It is the spur to Eliot's dazzling creativity.

Lastly, there is an even more fundamental feature, which is not peculiar to Eliot's poem, but typical of any genuine communication at all, a feature in which the communicational genuineness of mediating criticism finds, as it were, a mirror image of itself. The characteristic at issue here is at least as uplifting as anything in Bridges's anthology, but the mode of appreciation it calls for is totally different. The point is not that literature embodies gems of spiritual purity which will help us to maintain a battle against the materialistic otherness of an enemy, but rather that literature, like all other genuine communication, not only calls upon a willingness to negotiate otherness, but implies a hope that everybody, no matter how various their positions, would wish to enter into the spirit of this, and to live side by side in reasonable happiness, even when the chances for such an outcome seem very slim. Mediating criticism, which is itself hopeful, will encourage readers to be responsive to the basic hopefulness of literary authors. This quality underlies even their grimmest texts, in that to publish any text at all is to invite readers into dialogue, and sometimes into a fellowship in suffering, whereas a true pessimist might choose the ultimate self-silencing of suicide (Sell 2001:213–352). Eliot, despite the terrible times through which he had lived, despite the anguish of his own private life – historical and personal circumstances whose mention by mediating critics may help new readers to appreciate his sheer ethical strength – , had a writer's faith in the power of words to communicate, and to communicate in the fullest sense by bringing people within a community.

In so strongly exhibiting communicational hope Eliot was further undermining his own conservative political views, since this kind of hope does not involve a prospect of hegemony. On the contrary, in any genuine community there will still be disagreements, often serious and extensive. More particularly, the old and the new will always be in co-adaptational tension. So like the discourse of mediation itself, other types of genuine communication, including the texts which come to be accorded the status of major works of literature, place neither too great, nor too little a stress on history. Bridges' discourse of conflict in *The Spirit of Man*, though strongly tied to a particular historical juncture, in another sense allowed history no weight. It separated the communicating word's timelessly universal hopefulness from the real contingencies within which it plays its part. In Eliot's *The Waste Land*, and in a mediating criticism which offers it for the appreciation of readers today, the relationship between the old and the new is more fully dialogical.

CHAPTER 7

Churchill's *My Early Life* and communicational ethics

7.1 A Nobel laureate

When Churchill was awarded the 1953 Nobel Prize for Literature, it was not in recognition of *Savrola* (1900), his one and only novel. Rather, the committee commended him for "his mastery of historical and biographical description as well as for brilliant oratory in defending exalted human values" (Nobelprize.org. 25 Aug 2010).

In one sense this accolade is unsurprising. Churchill's historical and biographical works – his record of the Nile campaign, for instance, his histories of the two World Wars, his biographies of his ancestor, the Duke of Marlborough, and of his own father, Randolph Churchill – sold remarkably well during his own lifetime and are still admired today, even if not so often read. As for the speeches to which the citation refers, some of them – the wartime radio broadcasts especially – not only helped to change to course of world history but hold a central place within anglophone cultural memory, contributing a wealth of phrasing to English idiom.

Yet seen within the framework of Anglo-American literary thought, the Nobel judges either still had their heads in the eighteenth century, or were well ahead of their own time. In 1953, most literary scholars and general readers in the English-speaking world accepted the distinction drawn in Victorian and Modernist theory between the realm of "Literature" (capital "L") and the "real" world of history. They also tended to accept the Victorian and Modernist limitation of Literature mainly to the genres of poetry, drama, and the novel. While Clarendon's *True Historical Narrative of the Rebellion and Civil Wars in England* (1702–1704), Gibbon's *Decline and Fall of the Roman Empire* (1776–1788), Boswell's *Life of Johnson* (1791), and the speeches of Edmund Burke (*fl.* 1729–1797) were all recognized as most remarkable works of their own kind, they were not perceived as literary texts with anything like the centrality of, say, *The Waste Land*, *King Lear* and *Middlemarch*. As noted in my Introduction, however, by the end of the twentieth century the notion of literature (now lower-case "l") was regaining something of its pre-nineteenth-century breadth. So much so, that the term may soon have outlived its usefulness.

Under these new circumstances, the 1953 verdict of the Nobel Committee is likely to be more widely and enthusiastically endorsed. Earlier on, there was not only the question, at least for anglophone readers, as to whether the genres in which Churchill usually wrote were really literary. Even though his worst enemies could see that he was a polymathic genius, there was also a feeling that his accounts of his illustrious forbears and of the two World Wars (in both of which he had played such a central part) were actually apologias for past and present Churchills. This complaint, though easy enough to substantiate, was rather disingenuous. Of this particular writer, on these particular topics, what do readers really expect? – and perhaps really want? Over the next few decades, it could well be that such objections will pale into ever greater insignificance, and his works come to be viewed as supreme glories of a broad-based canon of "English literature" or, more simply, as some of the most admirable and wonderfully enjoyable texts ever written in English. If so, this will happen, I suggest, not only because of his golden language, and his sheer command of facts, narrative and argument, but also, and crucially, because of his instinctive feel for communicational ethics, even if, taking him as a whole, and bearing in mind his keenness for apologetics, this claim at first seems rather preposterous.

I shall not deal with his major works in the genres mentioned by the Nobel citation. His distinctive communicational traits are all to be seen in *My Early Life* (1930), his most explicit venture into autobiography, a genre in which apologetics could even more easily get the upper hand. As a way of highlighting the book's ethics of address, and its consequent value as a model for post-postmodern times, I shall argue that he here displays the qualities we expect in a trustworthy mediator. Mediation is not merely one of the modes of diplomacy, or of linguistic or literary criticism, but can also occur within many other kinds of interchange as well, both spoken and written. In his autobiography, Churchill's turn of mind is mediational in a strong sense: energetically flexible and judicious; constantly negotiating different sociohistorical positions and different ways of looking at the world; and congenially prompting readers to follow suit in thoughtful dialogue with him.

7.2   Simply an egotist?

As pointed out in my Introduction and the foregoing study of *The Waste Land*, mediators provide information and commentary in an effort to extend the area of overlap between different life-worlds. Their task involves being maximally unbiased towards the various positions involved, yet without laying claim to an impossible objectivity. No matter how skilled they may become at empathizing with many different types and conditions of humanity, they do not themselves occupy some Archimedean point outside of history, but will always have some entirely terrestrial position of their own, which they will do well to confess. Otherwise their enterprise will become just as dubious as any other pretence to homogeneously human universality.

Seen from this angle, the special interest of mediational tendencies arising within an autobiography stems from that genre's defining characteristic: its strong foregrounding of the viewpoint associated with the single individual who is both protagonist and narrator. *Ceteris paribus*, the genre is itself biased in favour of just a single position, and this risk can be aggravated by an autobiographer's own personality. At least in the Western tradition, outstanding autobiographies are seldom the work of very shy people, and most autobiographers assume that a reader will expect their thoughts, emotions, experiences and achievements to have some broader relevance. They feel themselves obliged to show that, in some respect or other, they are rather important or interesting, just as the genre's own narratological set-up implies. As far as I know, Keats had not seen drafts of lines which Wordsworth eventually included in *The Prelude*. But he strongly reacted to what he experienced as autobiographical undertow in some of Wordsworth's other work, and coined his own interesting label for it. Somewhat critically, yet not without admiration either, he spoke of Wordsworth's "egotistical sublime" (Keats 1954 [1818]: 170). In an earlier study here I have suggested that this was not entirely fair, or relevant, in a critique of Wordsworth. But in many autobiographers, some such quality is certainly present.

My Early Life is the work of a man whose egotism was, in the words of Geoffrey Best, of "Himalayan vastness", and whose history of the First World War, *The World in Crisis*, was described by Balfour as "an autobiography disguised as an history of the universe" (Best 2002 [2001]: 33, 83). Very conscious that his gifted and ambitious father had died at the untimely age of 46, Churchill was quick to see himself, not only as a man of destiny, but as a man of destiny with all too little time to make his mark. In the opening stages of his career, he pulled every possible string, bent every possible rule, so as to ensure that he would be in the right place at the right time. His formidable pushiness could both infuriate and amuse his contemporaries, and he himself later made rumbustious jokes about it. *My Early Life* reports that some his comrades in arms were

> actually abusive, and the expressions "Medal-hunter" and "Self-advertiser" were used from time to time in some high and some low military circles in a manner which would, I am sure, surprise and pain the reader of these notes. It is melancholy to be forced to record these less amiable aspects of human nature, which by a most curious and indeed unaccountable coincidence have always seemed to present themselves in the wake of my innocent footsteps, and even sometimes across the path on which I wished to proceed.   (p. 168)[1]

His capacity for self-irony is something to which I must return. But the first thing to note is that, as a soldier and politician, his egotistical drive could often seem to be bolstered by an extremely straightforward and pragmatic sense of ethics. As John Keegan says, Churchill's

---

1.   Quotations of *My Early Life* taken from Churchill 1959 [1930].

beliefs had simple origins, in the piety and goodness of his beloved nanny, Mrs Everest; in the code of schoolboy fair play; in the ethic of manliness learned at the Royal Military College … at Sandhurst and in his regiment; in the strictures of the Commandments, preached in the Old Testament language … in the Harrow School chapel. From all those sources Churchill derived an undoubted sense of sin; his horror of wrongdoing was to inform his political life.   (pp. 11–12)

At the same time, says Keegan, he appears "to have carried no burden of personal sinfulness, that besetting affliction of thinking Victorians". Britain, too, we might add, had little to be ashamed of in Churchill's view. It was truly *Great* Britain, and the British Empire was the single most important influence for good in the world at large, backed up by force when called for – whatever force was needed for the particular job in hand. Imperial and Churchillian self-assertiveness were apparently of a piece.

In *My Early Life* egotism and bull-at-a-gate benevolent imperialism may at first seem to be the dominant inspiration, at least if we concentrate on the actual story. The book describes his life in basically chronological order up until 1902. He was born, in 1874, into an aristocratic political elite. His father, Lord Randolph Churchill, was an especially prominent Conservative politician. Churchill himself, despite early educational setbacks, achieved some distinction during his Sandhurst training as a cavalry officer, and in 1895 was commissioned in the prestigious Fourth Hussars regiment. Thirsting to see some action, he managed to get himself to Cuba, where he was treated as a distinguished observer of the war between the Spanish and the island's indigenous rebels, but where he also for the first time came under fire – on his twenty-first birthday, as he is at pains to mention. After this blooding, life was less exciting for a while. From 1896 onwards the Fourth Hussars were stationed at Bangalore in the south of India, where Churchill, apart from doing some extensive reading, also played a lot of polo, the cavalry officer's sport par excellence, and was involved in military drills and operations of a merely routine character. Much more challenging were the postings he then wangled for himself to bloody campaigns on India's north-west frontier, and in the Sudan, where he took part in Kitchener's long march on Khartoum and in the great Battle of Omdurman. In Cuba, north-west India and the Sudan alike, he also acted as a war journalist, and he further cashed in on his north-west Indian and Sudanese experiences by publishing, very shortly afterwards, books on the entire campaigns. It was the writings which first established his name, and on the strength of this he resigned his commission and started to aim at a political career. But then in 1899 came the Boer War, and he once again got himself to the scene of action, in both journalistic and military capacities. His totally fearless courage enabled him to save an armoured train from the hands of the enemy, and he also pulled off an astonishing escape from a prisoncamp, exploits which he duly reported to his own newspapers, but which were also taken up in news media internationally. As a widely acclaimed hero, he then took part in the so-called Khaki election of 1900, entering parliament as one of the Conservative members for Oldham, the Lancashire mill town. The book's final pages describe his parliamentary debut, and his increasing reluctance to accept Conservative Party orthodoxies.

Is *My Early Life*, then, really the kind of autobiography which readers today are likely to enjoy? As I have just summarized it, probably not. The apparent intellectual and moral oversimplifications; the apparent embrace of life-goals having mainly to do with the exercise of military and political power; the primitive certainties apparently shared with imperialistic boys' adventure stories such as H. Rider Haggard's *King Solomon's Mines*, a book which the young Churchill read at least a dozen times (d'Este 2010:13): such qualities, if allowed unmitigated rule, would have been fair game for postcolonial critics in the postmodern era, and to post-postmodern critics less worried about globalization *per se* would still seem to connote a global vision that was too hegemonic. The *Pax Britannica*, after all, was supposed to be a world peace achieved by Britain's world domination. In fact, however, Churchill is not on a one-track-minded rampage here. The book does embody imperialist ideology. But just as *The Dunciad* is problematizing the demise of Humanism, so *My Early Life* is in a way re-opening questions of both the past and future. Although its author, as a nursling of the mid-Victorian period, was never going to be politically correct in the manner of, say, Barack Obama, he does give clear signs of having thought about his own world view, and about other people's as well. What he offers readers is the amusing companionship of a well read and widely experienced individual who, to use Keats's other term, is well endowed with negative capability (Keats 1954 [1818]:170). This, running alongside, and qualifying the elements of egotistically sublime jingoism, is what underwrites Churchill's gift for mediation, which can nowadays invite readers into dialogue in at least five dimensions. His value for our own time is not that his *ideas* are post-postmodern – how could they have been? – but that this dialogue which he instigates is so exemplary in its genuineness. Though in no way damping down his own indomitable personality, he is for ever encouraging readers to think in several different ways at once.

7.3   Mediation between 1930 and 1874–1902

In identifying the most obvious dimension of mediation we can take a cue from Churchill himself, whose writerly self-consciousness is very alert. In *My Early Life* he quite deliberately mediates between his readers of 1930, the "new generation" to whom the book is explicitly dedicated (p. 4), and his own now distant youth. As he explains in the Preface,

> When I survey this work as a whole I find I have drawn a picture of a vanished age. The character of society, the foundations of politics, the methods of war, the outlook of youth, the scale of values, are all changed, and changed to an extent I should not have believed possible in so short a space without any violent domestic revolution. I cannot pretend to feel that they are in all respects changed for the better.   (pp. 7–8)

"Full allowance for such changes", he adds, "should be made by friendly readers". But he does provide readers with ample assistance.

The differences between 1930 and the vanished age of 1874–1902 are brought into sharp relief by his narratological framework, which leaves the stretch of time from 1902 to 1930 fairly blank. It would have been unnatural if he had made no proleptic reference to these intervening years at all. He does frequently say that the First World War – still known in 1930 as the Great War – was to involve a totally different kind of warfare from what he experienced in Cuba, India, the Sudan and South Africa. On occasion he does mention that men he met with during his youth were to die in that war, two of them at Gallipoli, or that they played some role in his later life as well. Mentioning his difficulties with Latin at school, he does fast-forward to Asquith's pained expression whenever he ventured one of his few Latin tags during a cabinet meeting. In recounting the death of his beloved nanny Mrs Everest, who in her later years had been more or less cast off by his mother, and whose funeral arrangements he made and paid for himself, he does mention his pleasure at subsequently being able to introduce what in 1930 was still an unrivalled national pension and insurance system. He does add a footnote to the effect that in 1910 he managed to get the Albert Medal for Civilian Gallantry awarded to the driver and fireman of that armoured train in South Africa. And in writing of his anguish at being imprisoned by the Boers, he does remember the improvements he has subsequently been able to introduce into British prisons. But the only prolepsis of any considerable length has to do with his dealings with the South African leader Louis Botha, who he believes was the soldier who captured him after the armoured train episode, and who later made trips to London in order to negotiate new constitutional arrangements with him during his time at the Colonial Office. Here he pointedly apologises for the disruption of his tale's straightforward chronology, and all other major happenings between 1902 and 1930 are quite unmentioned: not only the comet-like progress of his own political career, with his switches from Conservatives to Liberals and back again, and his handling of a succession of senior ministerial portfolios, but also wider historical developments as well. There is nothing about the causes of the First World War, nothing about his own warmongering as First Lord of the Admiralty and his possible share of responsibility for those deaths in Gallipoli, nothing about his key role in the patrolling and partitioning of Ireland, nothing about the self-destruction of the Liberal Party, nothing about his restoration of the Gold Standard in his budget of 1925, nothing about the related social and industrial tensions resulting in the General Strike of 1926, nothing about the correspondingly rapid rise of the Labour Party (though he does complain about increased taxes), nothing about the Conservatives' consequent fall from power, and nothing about his own exile – from 1929 to 1939, as it was to turn out – in the political wilderness. In short, the disjunction the book makes between the then of 1874–1902 and the now of 1930 is more or less total. Certainly there is absolutely no sense that the world has moved from its state in 1902 to its state in 1930 by any normal sort of historical process. If he had not known otherwise, as he puts it in the passage just quoted from the Preface, the only credible historical explanation for the huge changes that have taken place would have involved a violent domestic revolution.

Brightly visible across the yawning chasm of the intervening years, one of the main phenomena he sees a need to mediate is the theory and culture of Victorian warfare.

> The minds of this generation [i.e. his readers of 1930], exhausted, brutalized, mutilated and bored by War, may not understand the delicious yet tremulous sensations with which a young British Officer bred in the long [European] peace approached for the first time an actual theatre of operations.   (pp. 84–85)

> [Cavalrymen,] [t]he Dragoon, the Lancer and above all, as we believed, the Hussar, still claimed their time-honoured place upon the battlefield. War, which used to be cruel and magnificent, has now become cruel and squalid. In fact it has been completely spoilt. … Instead of a small number of well-trained professionals championing their country's cause with ancient weapons and a beautiful intricacy of archaic manoeuvre, sustained at every moment by the applause of their nation, we now have entire populations, including even women and children, pitted against one another in brutish mutual extermination, and only a set of blear-eyed clerks left to add up the butcher's bill. From the moment Democracy was admitted to, or rather forced itself upon the battlefield, War ceased to be a gentleman's game.   (pp. 72–73)

In India, "the deities of a hundred creeds were placed by respectful routine in the Imperial Pantheon" (p. 120), and even the elephants had a recognised place in the great scheme of things, for at the end of a military parade there would come

> a score of elephants drawing tandem-fashion gigantic cannon. It was then the custom for the elephants to salute as they marched past by raising their trunks, and this they all did with exemplary precision. Later on the custom was abolished because vulgar people tittered and the dignity of the elephants or their mahouts was wounded. Later on still, the elephants themselves were abolished, and we now have clattering tractors drawing far larger and more destructive guns. Thus civilization advances. But I mourn the elephants and their salutations.   (p. 126)

Even during the Boer War, the dignity and gentlemanliness survived. Bitterness against the enemy was still considered unprofessional, and there was a "grace and amenity about this war singularly lacking fifteen years later on the Western Front" (p. 329). The very idea of another war occurring between civilized European nations would have been regarded as quite absurd.

Then there were the workings of Victorian society and politics. In between Sandhurst and his first posting abroad, he had half a year in which he could give himself over to

> the amusements of the London Season. In those days English Society still existed in its old form. It was a brilliant and powerful body, with standards of conduct and methods of enforcing them now altogether forgotten. In a very large degree every one knew every one else and who they were. The few hundred great families who had governed England for so many generations and had seen her rise to the pinnacle of her glory, were interrelated to an enormous extent by marriage. Everywhere one met friends and kinsfolk. The leading figures of Society were in many cases the leading statesmen in Parliament, and also the leading sportsmen on the Turf. Lord Salisbury was accustomed scrupulously to avoid calling a Cabinet when there was racing at Newmarket, and the House of Commons made a practice of adjourning for the Derby. In those days the glittering parties at Lansdowne House, Devonshire House or Stafford House comprised all the elements which made a gay and splendid social circle in close relation to the business of Parliament, the hierarchies of the Army and Navy, and the policy of the State. Now Lansdowne House and Devonshire House have been turned into hotels, flats and restaurants; and Stafford House has become the ugliest and stupidest museum in the world, in whose faded saloons Socialist Governments drearily dispense the public hospitality.
>
> ... I am glad to have seen, if only for a few months, ... [that] vanished world.
>
> (pp. 96–97)

Not that Churchill is as opposed to democracy as his sneers at the Labour Government and democratic warfare may suggest. On the contrary, thinking back to his own election campaign in Oldham in 1900 he worries about what is happening to democracy in 1930.

> I must explain that in those days we had a real political democracy led by a hierarchy of statesmen, and not a fluid mass distracted by newspapers. There was a structure in which statesmen, electors and the Press all played their part. ... [At a public electoral] meeting what pleased the audience most was that ... [Mr Chamberlain], having made a mistake in some fact or figure to the prejudice of his opponents, ... went back and corrected it, observing that he must not be unfair. All this was before the liquefaction of the British political system had set in.   (p. 365)

Churchill's mediation of his own youth for his first readers did stress certain aspects of it at the expense of certain others, as we shall soon see. Even so, it was in my view ethically unimpeachable. He did nothing to hide his strongly remaining attachment to the ideology within which he had grown up, yet clearly recognized the enormous changes which had taken place, and without expecting or even hoping to turn the clock back. On the contrary, he was well aware that the wheels of history were not going to grind to a halt in 1930 either. In fact the book also richly *invites* mediation, between his own moment of writing and later readerships which had not yet come into being.

7.4   Mediation between today and 1930

So this is a second dimension of mediation into which the book enters, and here the ethical challenge is to historians of the period and to Churchill's biographers. Such scholars can above all try to unravel for us today Churchill's own sense of the "anxious and dubious times" in which he was writing (p. 8), his possible reasons for writing, and intelligent ways for us to evaluate the book in our own here and now.

By general scholarly agreement, the main political dilemmas which concerned him at the beginning of his wilderness years had to do with: the rise of Socialism; employment and economic problems in the wake of his restoration of the Gold Standard, the General Strike, and the Wall Street crash of 1929; the conflict between Keynesian ideas about state intervention in the interests of social justice and the free trade liberalism for which, in contrast to his father, he had come to feel so passionately; the closely related question of whether social welfare ought to have a higher priority than re-armament, a question in its turn linked to the ongoing controversy about whether or not to see post-war Germany as still a threat; the further question of whether or not Ireland, as Churchill himself hoped, would be re-united and accept dominion status under London; but above all, India, the most splendid jewel in the imperial crown, and Indian aspirations to greater autonomy, the issue on which, as commentators both then and now agree, Churchill's vehemently reactionary views had by the mid-1930s almost totally destroyed his own political credibility.

A good bit more tricky to mediate is the exact connection, if any, between these concerns and *My Early Life*. Ian S. Wood is one of several biographers to point out the paradox that Churchill, "in a long life, apart from army service in India and relatively short periods in Africa, … seldom visited the empire he extolled, giving preference for travel and recreation to France and the United States" (Wood 2000: 157). His view of India in particular, Wood says, remained that of a cavalry subaltern, complete with the racial prejudice and imperialist's social Darwinism of that vanished age (Wood 2000: 157–170). If he did revisit India, it was only on the wings of memory and imagination, re-creating the saluting elephants and so on for inclusion in *My Early Life*. The book's own mediation of 1874–1902 was clearly not just helpful information for his own first readers, but was also self-expressive. Partly it was a chance to blow off nostalgic steam. Partly, perhaps, he was charging himself up for continued battle in the great cause. Partly, for all we know, it may have been an indirect channel for anxiety, and for some incipient strategic thinking, about the up-and-coming Adolf Hitler, for as Richard Holmes, another recent biographer, points out, it was thanks to its continuing links with Britain that India was in 1939–1945 to raise the largest all-volunteer army in history (Holmes 2005:15). Yet when Holmes goes on to claim that *My Early Life*, along with everything else Churchill wrote up until 1940, actually "served the purpose of making himself the man to whom the country would turn in an emergency" (Holmes 2005:296), he surely goes too far. Granted, when *My Early Life* explains to readers of 1930 that Lord Cromer had had "the phlegm and composure which used to be associated with high British administrators in the East", it does also add that "[w]e do not see his like nowadays, though our need is grave" (p. 222). But the level of Churchill's own remaining political ambition during his early wilderness years is far from clear. He was engaged in a very large number of remunerative literary projects, and spoke to L. S. Amery in terms of retiring from politics altogether in order to devote himself entirely to money-making. Amery reports:

> He had been all that he wanted to be short of the highest post, which he saw no prospect of, and anyhow politics were not what they had been. The level was lower; there no longer were great men like Gladstone or Salisbury ...
>
> (In Jenkins 2002 [2001]:424)

In *My Early Life*, not only are his references to his own political achievements during the period 1902–1930 very few and very brief. Still more to the point, he makes no attempt to defend his record's more controversial episodes. Whereas his biographies of his Marlborough and his father were indeed strongly apologetic, and whereas his history of the First World War partly defended his own strategies as First Lord of the Admiralty, *My Early Life* was, as Roy Jenkins puts it, not designed "to prove a point or to advance a theory but to entertain." Jenkins especially enjoys Churchill's "most agreeable mockery of himself" (Jenkins 2002 [2001]:420). Of which, as promised, more below.

As for intelligent ways of evaluating the book in our own here and now, all the biographers suggest hints for mediation of this kind, one of the most explicit coming from Geoffrey Best:

> "Glory" to Churchill's way of thinking was not only something within the reach of individual fighters and cohesive small groups like regiments and crews of warships, it was what entire peoples could attain through shared achievement and self-assertion in the world, which historically meant by force of arms. ... [Nowadays] [a] Briton may ... wonder how much of larger value has gone with the cult of arms. One might not lament the end of "glory", but what about "chivalry" and "honour". There must be improvement of some kind in the fact that the concept of "dying for your country" no longer provides the model of an ideal death; but

there may not be much of an improvement in not knowing whether there is any-thing in your country worth fighting for, whether you belong to this country or to that, or even whether you belong to any distinctive country at all.

In Best's final words his own aim in mediation aim is spelled out with complete frankness:

> I hope my book may help to make his values intelligible and his achievements respected. ... I am persuaded that, in this later time, we are diminished if, admit-ting Churchill's failings and failures, we can no longer appreciate his virtues and victories. (Best 2002 [2001]: 335–336)

And it is easy enough to imagine how Best's take on the entire life and works could be applied to *My Early Life* as a representative case in point.

7.5   Mediation between today and 1874–1902

But the mediation which can be offered by scholars today is not only of *My Early Life* as a Churchillian work of 1930. Scholars also discuss the book's own mediation of the years 1874–1902, a third mediational dimension into which it enters.

When it comes to Victorian war, society, and politics, Churchill's own account still broadly stands the test of time. His biographers do little more than add supple-mentary information, some of it statistical and relating to those intervening years (1902–1930) during which the momentous changes took place, as when Holmes doc-uments the passing of the old ruling class:

> Thirty-two peerages and 35 baronetcies became extinct in 1914–1920, not all as a result of the war, although some 300 peers or their eldest sons (of the 1500 who served) were killed of died as a result of war service. The 1914–1915 battlefields of Flanders have some cause to be regarded as the cemetery of the pre-war aristo-cracy. The gentry were heavily concentrated in the Territorials and, although they were specifically excluded from service abroad, in 1914 the great majority voted to go overseas and in the process suffered dreadful losses: 47 heirs to peerages were killed in action before the end of the year. Double death duties levied when a father and heir died soon after each other crippled many landed estates, and 25 percent of land in England and Wales changed hands in 1918–21. Another, prob-ably more significant, change was the decline in the participation of the gentry in public life. With so many of the sons who traditionally stood for Parliament still serving in the armed forces, the candidates for the 1918 election tended to be older men with backgrounds in business. The character of politics changed so greatly thereafter that the squirearchy never really got back into it.
> (Holmes 2005: 126)

A good bit more controversial is Churchill's mediation of his own inner life as a child and young man. Holmes, true to form, says that the autobiography tries to re-launch his political career by holding up his early life as a great triumph over personal disadvantage. Holmes claims that in point of fact Churchill was "excessively indulged" as a child, and himself displayed the lack of empathy and the sheer unmanageableness of a child suffering from Asperger syndrome, while his parents gave him "superficially fond or narcissistic rather than indifferent parenting", so that he got "more than the normal attention a boy of his age and social standing had a right to expect in those days" (Holmes 2005: 21–27). A reading of other biographies, and especially of the one by his son Randolph Churchill, which contains a wealth of revealing letters, suggests that Holmes is seriously at sea here, and that if anything *My Early Life* dutifully tones down his parents' thoughtlessness or downright harshness, even if it is entirely open about his substitute mother, his nanny Mrs Everest, the "dearest and most intimate friend" of the first twenty years of his life (p. 80).

As for his love-life, the autobiography does not even mention it until the impishly throw-away last eight words:

> Events were soon to arise in the fiscal sphere which were to plunge me into new struggles and absorb my thoughts and energies at least until September 1908, when I married and lived happily ever after.   (p. 378)

Keegan and Jenkins, however, hint that he was undersexed, and Holmes that he was abstinent because he assumed his father died of syphilis, while his son Randolph's account is again more detailed (though not salaciously so), especially about the relationship with Pamela Plowden, whose privacy, together with that of other old flames, Churchill in 1930 may still have wished to protect.

There is much to suggest, too, that in retrospect Churchill significantly minimized the breadth and sophistication of his early political interests. Indeed, his political bent was already so strongly marked by 1896 that, as is obvious from some of the letters quoted by Randolph, he was far from excited at the thought of going to India. That he was unable to get a job that would have kept him in London, at the very heart of empire, was a great disappointment.

Nor were all these details just a matter of the autobiography's handling the truth about him as a private individual. In one way or another, each and every one of them contributes to an image of Churchill himself as a central representative of that vanished age. As he writes about his own feelings, the sheer historical typicality he sees in them may have taken off their more acutely personal edge.

There is, of course, a huge body of other historical and biographical scholarship relating to the second and third mediational dimensions into which the autobiography enters. But perhaps my handful of examples has hinted at least something of the ethical range. Biographers like Best, Jenkins, Keegan and Wood come across as on the whole balanced. To recall Best's phrasing, they seem to admit Churchill's failings and failures while appreciating his virtues and victories, even though, as genuine communicators within a large and heterogeneous scholarly community, they agree to disagree with each other on particular points. Holmes, too, seems often very fair, and it is he who even offers some serious mitigation of Churchill's reluctance to lose India. On Churchill's infancy, however, and on his reasons for writing his autobiography, Holmes seems less judicious, almost as if he had an axe to grind. At the opposite extreme is Randolph Churchill, whose account, partly thanks to its quotations from the letters, has a unique inwardness to Churchill and his world, but who, both as loyal son and as official biographer, always runs the risk of favourable bias, even if his text is never seriously marred by it.

7.6   Mediation between our wisdom of hindsight and Churchill's ignorance of the future

Moving on now to a fourth dimension of mediation, this is less the prerogative of scholarly historians and biographers than a type of reaction which can come from any present-day reader at all. The point is simply that, in relation to Churchill's text of 1930, we all now have the wisdom of hindsight. As a result, a genuine dialogicality can arise between us and Churchill himself, a spiritual communion that is egalitarian and bi-directional in spirit, even though it can never be a literal dialogue.

Take, for instance, his reflections on his father's politically suicidal resignation from the Chancellorship in Salisbury's cabinet.

> I can see my father now in a somewhat different light from the days when I wrote his biography. I have long passed the age at which he died. I understand only too plainly the fatal character of his act of resignation.... Lord Salisbury represented to the nation what it needed and desired. He settled down heavily to a long steady reign. Naturally he was glad to have the whole power in his own hands, instead of dividing it with a restless rival.... It is never possible for a man to recover his lost position. He may recover another position in the fifties or sixties, but not the one he lost in the thirties or forties. (pp. 54–55)

Here we "tell" Churchill he is wrong. In 1939 he himself recovered the position he had been forced to resign at the age of 41 in 1915: he once again became First Lord of the Admiralty. Not only that, but in 1940 he achieved the supreme position, as Prime Minister, and having lost it in the general election of 1945 at the age of 71, in 1951 recovered it, too, in his late seventies. When, recapturing the spirit of his vivid youth he says to readers in 1930, "Come on now all you young men, all over the world. ... You have not an hour to lose. You must take your places in life's fighting line", or when he writes of the Boer War that "[t]he British nation was smarting under a series of military reverses such as are so often necessary to evoke the exercise of its strength" (pp. 67, 305), we "tell" him he is warming up for his great radio broadcasts of ten years later. When, in 1930, he writes that he had believed he had seen in South Africa the "last projectile I should ever see fired in anger" (p. 360), we "tell" him that his irony at his own naivety is not nearly ironic enough; the "Great War" was not to remain the greatest. And most of us, I take it, will react to his description of an injured Sikh soldier – "He shouted with pain; his turban fell off; and his long black hair streamed over his shoulders – a tragic golliwog" (p. 148). Here we may "tell" him that his racist attitudes were later to make him completely underestimate the imperial ambitions and military might of Japan, so leading, in 1942, to the loss of Singapore, the British Empire's main bastion in the Far East. We may also "tell" him that in the early 1950s, when he had already accepted Indian Independence, he was to confess to his personal physician,

> When you learn to think of a race as inferior beings it is difficult to get rid of that way of thinking... [W]hen I was a subaltern the Indian did not seem to me to equal the white man.   (Wood 2000: 170)

With mediation in this fourth dimension, it is up to each and every one of us to be as balanced as possible. In 1930 Churchill, despite his sense of destiny, could not know just how great he would later become. But in "telling" him about this we shall not lose sight of his weaknesses and prejudices. Then again, in facing up to his prejudices we shall be duly chastened by the thought that, thirty years from now, some of our own most deep-seated assumptions will no longer be *comme il faut*. By then, those of us who are still alive may well have changed our minds, as Churchill did.

7.7   Mediation between Churchill's different selves

Churchill's own response to information about the, for him in 1930, unknown future would have be one of utter non-surprise. He fully accepted that "it is not given to human beings ... to foresee or to predict to any large extent the unfolding of events" (Churchill 1942: 1–2), and the older he had become the more totally unpredictable changes he observed, both in the world and large, in military technology, in political issues, and in himself personally. *My Early Life* is completely permeated by these insights, which means that the first-dimensional mediation, by Churchill himself between readers in 1930 and the vanished epoch of 1874–1902, is constantly complemented by mediation in a fifth dimension. Fifth-dimensional mediation is instigated by Churchill himself within the writing, and mediates between one position, one kind of identity formation or attitude and another, in effect by setting them in dialogic juxtaposition with each other, as we have already partly seen in the contrast between his earlier and his later way of understanding of his father's resignation. His critical awareness of his own literary strategy is, as always, complete. Once again, the

Preface clearly alerts readers to what is going on: "I have tried, in each part of the quarter-century in which this tale lies, to show the point of view appropriate to my years, whether as a child, a schoolboy, a cadet, a subaltern, a war-correspondent, or a youthful politician" (p. 7).

In this he has evidently been influenced by another text involving strong auto-biographical elements: *David Copperfield*. I am not thinking of the obvious similarities between Peggoty and Mrs Everest or between the mystery of Lord Randolph and Churchill's adored mother and that of Murdstone and David's. More fundamentally, Churchill has learnt from Dickens how to bring two different points of view into tension with each other, often a humorous tension, especially when the contrast is between a child's-eye view and an adult's:

> … we paid a visit to Emo Park, the seat of Lord Portarlington, who was explained to me as a sort of uncle. Of this place I can give very clear descriptions. … The central point in my memory is a tall white stone tower which we reached after a considerable drive. I was told it had been blown up by Oliver Cromwell. I understood definitely that he had blown up all sorts of things and was therefore a very great man. (p. 10)

From such self-ironic beginnings Churchill's prose develops a self-mediating momentum all of its own, the most obvious symptom being its virtuoso versatility of style.

Sometimes there is a huge set-piece of unflaggingly lofty description, the magniloquence informed by Churchill's painterly love of gorgeous colour, with firm composition yet delicate line and texture. An unforgettable example is his overview of the Battle of Omdurman:

> The armies marched and manoeuvred on the crisp surface of the desert plain through which the Nile wandered in broad reaches, now steel, now brass. Cavalry charged at full gallop in close order, and infantry or spearsmen stood upright ranged in lines or masses to resist them. From the rocky hills which here and there flanked the great river the whole scene lay revealed in minute detail, curiously twisted, blurred and interspersed with phantom waters by the mirage. The finite and concrete presented itself in the most keenly-chiselled forms, and then dissolved in a shimmer of unreality and illusion. Long streaks of gleaming water, where we knew there was only desert, cut across the knees or the waist or marching troops. Batteries of artillery or long columns of cavalry emerged from a filmy world of uneven crystal on to the hard yellow-ochre sand, and took up their positions amid jagged red-black rocks with violet shadows. Over all the immense dome of the sky, dun to turquoise, turquoise to deepest blue, pierced by the flaming sun, weighed hard and heavy on marching necks and soldiers. (p. 178)

Sometimes, as if in a separate compartment, he turns war into pure farce, anticipating Evelyn Waugh or even Black Adder.

> As he rose he rose to leave us, Lord Marcus Beresford said with great earnest-
> ness, "Good-bye, old man, mind the V. C." To this our poor friend, deeply moved,
> replied, "I'll do my best to win it." "Ah!" said Lord Marcus, "you are mistaken, I
> did not mean that, I meant the Vieux Cognac!"
>
> I may here add that these cases of champagne and brandy and my share in
> them fell among the many disappointments of the war. In order to make sure that
> they reached the headquarters intact, Lord Gerard took the precaution of label-
> ling them "Castor Oil". Two months later in Natal, when they had not yet arrived,
> he dispatched an urgent telegram to the base at Durban asking for his castor oil.
> The reply came back that the packages of this drug addressed to his lordship had
> by an error already been issued to the hospitals. There were now, however, ample
> stores of castor oil available at the base and the Commandant was forwarding a
> full supply forthwith! (p. 239)

But there are also many occasions when intratextual mediation becomes supremely lively, as Churchill's self-mockery brings the two styles, the two attitudes to
war, together into a single paragraph. At one point he tells how, during his sea passage
back from the Sudan campaign, he was already turning his recent memories into the
glorious prose of the campaign history he was later to publish. On the ship he also
struck up a friendship with "the most brilliant man in journalism I have ever met",
G. W. Steevens. One day,

> I was working in the saloon of the Indiaman, and had reached an exciting point in
> my story. The Nile column had just by a forced night march reached Abu Hamed
> and was about to storm it. I was setting the scene in my most ceremonious style.
> "The dawn was breaking and the mists, rising from the river and dispersing with
> the coming of the sun, revealed the outlines of the Dervish town and the half
> circle of rocky hills behind it. Within this stern amphitheatre one of the minor
> dramas of war was now to be enacted." "Ha! Ha!" said Steevens, suddenly peering
> over my shoulder. "Finish it yourself then," I said getting up; I went up on deck.
> I was curious to see how he would do it, and indeed I hoped for a valuable con-
> tribution. But when I came down again I found that all he had written on my nice
> sheet of paper was "Pop-pop! pop-pop! Pop! Pop!" in his tiny handwriting, and
> then at the bottom of the page printed in big letters "BANG!!" I was disgusted at
> this levity. (p. 219)

Churchill was perfectly capable of trumpeting the certainties and simplistic ethics
of Empire. Yet his mind was anything but simple. In one sense the most clubbable of
men, in another sense he was as little gregarious or fixed in either his own or other
people's ways as it is humanly possible to be. *My Early Life* frankly shows his early development in exactly this direction. As a young child he had clearly felt an enormous
need to belong to the "world" of his parents and the Conservative Party, but what

filtered down to him of his father's rejection by Salisbury clearly shook his faith in this. By the time he is at prep school in Brighton, although he can still march with the rest of the class to church (with Dickensian echoes here from *Dombey and Son*), he can now decline, for his own reasons of principle, to turn to the East during the recitation of the Creed. A similar complexity of stance recurs throughout. As a young subaltern self-educating himself in Bangalore, he works out his own philosophy as a man of thought but also a man of action, "believing whatever I wanted to believe, while at the same time leaving reason to pursue unfettered whatever paths she was capable of treading", not fully believing in Christianity, but sensible enough not fully to reject it either: he would pray for special protection when about to come under enemy fire and be "sincerely grateful when I got home safe to tea". Heart and reason should "run smoothly together in double harness" (pp. 120–122). Or to take another example, during the Boer War he was absolutely passionate for an all-out pursuit of victory, but when victory was achieved he was no less passionate for magnanimity towards the defeated foe, a kind of alternation which he explains as typical of him, and as having always brought him into conflict with both the great political parties, one of which is always more pacifist and the other more Jingoistic. Why are the parties like this?

> It is all the fault of the human brain being made in two lobes, only one of which does any thinking, so that we are all right-handed or left-handed; whereas if we were properly constructed we should use our right and left hands with equal force and skill according to circumstances. As it is, those who can win a war well can rarely make a good peace, and those who could make a good peace would never have won the war. It would perhaps be pressing the argument too far to suggest that I could do both.   (p. 339)

As psychology, this may seem rather rough and ready. But we should remember the date and recognize, as always, his sharp self-understanding. His disclaimer of political ambidextrousness is of course merely good manners. As Holmes points out, his handling of Ireland in 1920–1922 had shown exactly this kind of positive bi-lobality (Holmes 2005: 135).

This power of mediating between different positionalities, ideologies, styles, phases of his own life, aspects of his own mind is what makes *My Early Life* so distinctively different from a run-of-the-mill autobiography by an imperialist soldier or politician. On both war and politics he even expresses himself in a way which would sound self-contradictory in most other writers. Explaining his thirst for action as a young officer, he speaks of "[t]he general peace in which mankind had for so many years languished", and of the vital importance of grabbing any "little titbits of fighting" there might happen to be. On the other hand, when one such titbit, in Peshawar, fails to materialize because of an unexpected and lasting peace agreement, he says that "as a budding politician I was forced to approve" the wisdom of this. But then "the South African War was to attain dimensions which fully satisfied the needs of our small army. And after that the deluge was still to come" – a passage in which "needs" is the pugnacious young soldier's word and "deluge" is the word of the responsible politican and older man, who has now lost most of his youthful comrades in the trenches of that Great War – at times Churchill's sense of the horror and pathos of that war bring Wilfred Owen to mind (pp. 83, 167). As for a political example of complex writing, he explains how in his early days in parliament

> I was so untutored as to suppose that all I had to do was to think out what was right and express it fearlessly. I thought that loyalty in this outweighed all other loyalties. I did not understand the importance of party discipline and unity, and the sacrifices of opinion which may be lawfully made in their cause.   (p. 377)

He certainly does believe in party discipline, as much in the book has shown. He does mean the words seriously. But much else in the book has impressed on us his maverick intelligence, and will have reminded us that in his subsequent political career he crossed the floor of the House not just once but twice. So there is simultaneously irony in the words as well. And in all such cases, the writing reveals his capability for being in uncertainties, mysteries, doubts, without any irritable reaching after fact and reason. It follows both head and heart, or comes from both lobes of the brain.

For us as readers now, the interaction of all this fifth-dimensional mediation with mediation of other dimensions can be especially challenging. There is, for instance, a longish section of dazzlingly light-handed farce which describes how Churchill, while still a Sandhurst cadet, makes his very first public speech, as the leader of a campaign for the abolition of a recently built wall in the promenade area of the old Empire Theatre. The campaigners' objection to the wall is that it blocks off access to the bars, thereby preventing gentlemen theatre-goers from taking a drink during the interval and associating with ladies of the town. The energy and ingenuity Churchill musters in this cause are truly formidable, and what is happening here is certainly fifth-dimensional mediation. Churchill's negatively capable self-parody pricks the bubble of his later imperialistic schemes and self-importance in advance – how delicious that the name of the theatre whose amenities he wanted to save should actually have been The Empire! But fourth-dimensional mediation also comes into play, because there are things we could "tell" him about the (for him in 1930) unknown future. He would *not* be able to save India. As early as five years later he could *not* block the Government of India Bill. But on the other hand, how straightforwardly can we today accept self-parodying mock-heroics from the man who, *ten* years later, really did, in the eyes of even the most recent commentators, both popular (Johnson 2009:109–140) and scholarly (Hastings 2009:598), save the entire world? – a man of destiny if ever there was one! Does he, in places like this, now seem – well, almost a little too modest and unassuming?

7.8   Communicational potential

Churchill's fifth-dimensional mediation between his different selves complements his first-dimensional mediation beween 1930 and the period 1874–1902. His silence on the historical processes by which 1902 became 1930 can make the vanished epoch of his youth seem very strange and distant, and the period qualities he chooses to see there – the moral and intellectual uprightness, the sheer courage, the relaxed elegance – make it a veritable golden age, to which his own continuing attachment is clear, and of which his own younger self emerges as the shining exemplar. At times his self-portrayal does indeed smack of the egotistical sublime, and it carries the strong imperialist overtones as well. Certainly as compared with his biographers, he tends to emphasize his sense of duty and his heroism at the expense of his intimate personal feelings, as both a little child and a young heterosexual male, and the intensity and sophistication of his early political thinking is similarly overshadowed. But even though the book is in many senses a simplistically imperialist adventure story, there is also that basic absence of reactionary drive. Though perfectly frank about his nostalgic preferences, and about his contempt for some aspects of the age in which he now writes, he is not trying to force his readers back into old ways. Despite the vehemence of his subsequent efforts to hang on to the imperial crown's supreme jewel, the autobiography's Indian sections are a self-indulgence which readers, too, and readers of any time, surely, can enormously enjoy, quite simply because the saluting elephants and all the rest of it are so completely void of palpable design upon us. Churchill knows that history moves on, and he positively undercuts the egotistical and imperialistic resonances through mediation in the fifth dimension. His often self-ironic juxtapositions of different viewpoints and ideologies in his own lifetime, and of different aspects of his own complex self, do make the book rather unusual. Whereas mediation corresponding to that of the first four dimensions can arise with any autobiography at all, and also, I should add, with many other forms of communication as well, the number of communicators who can sustain the high level of genuineness to be found in Churchill's playful self-dramatizations has always been small. Conversely, the community of readers from which it is likely to win recognition will always be potentially large and heterogeneous.

The uncertainty as to whether or not Churchill's crystal ball underestimated his own future career clearly underlines our obligation as present-day readers to keep our fourth-dimensional "conversations" with him as fair as humanly possible. But judging by the track-record of mediators in the second and third dimensions – of biographers and historians as they assess his aims or performance as a writer in 1930 and his own mediation of the vanished age for his first readers – the chances are that new readings of him will indeed be even-handed. There will never be a full consensus on every aspect and detail, and the risk of readerly bias will never go away. In practice, though, the most well-informed and articulate commentators do seem to be engaging in the kind of genuine dialogicality to which Churchill's own writing is itself an invitation, conscientiously comparing notes with him, and agreeing to disagree where necessary.

CHAPTER 8

Orwell's *Coming up for Air*
and the communal negotiation of feelings

8.1 Sensibility in Modernist novels

During the Modernist period, by no means all novelists were as openly experimental as Joyce, Woolf and Lawrence. The early novels of George Orwell, in particular, have often been taken as merely a continuation of nineteenth century realism. Yet in Dickens, realist traits had been closely interwoven with imaginative grotesquerie, plangent emotionality, and hints of mythical archetypes. And the early Orwell, for whom Dickens was a powerful forbear, did not purvey documentary detail for its own sake, and was actually far less interested than Dickens himself in the feel of everyday human interaction. Even in *Great Expectations*, which as a first-person narration could have allowed Pip as dominant a presence as Churchill in his own autobiography, Dickens characteristically traces a series of benefactions and malefactions exchanged between *several* main characters. In Orwell's *Coming up for Air*, George Bowling is far more central than any other character in the same book, yet has nothing even remotely resembling Churchill's decisiveness, and actually never confronts difficult moral dilemmas. He does do things, needless to say, and some of the things he does may cause pain to other people. But he does them unreflectingly. Rather than deliberately making choices and carrying out courses of premeditated action, he is above all a person to whom things happen. His only real initiative is the decision to return to Lower Binfield, his natal village, and what he finds when he gets there is a complete travesty of his desires (insofar as he has any), and quite beyond his own control. It is something to which his response can only be one of emotional and intellectual re-adjustment.

So one way to describe *Coming up for Air* would be along the lines of Propp's morphology of the folk tale, albeit as a folk tale *manqué*. Bowling is the hero of a quest narrative, whose grail, if only he could have found it, would have been the world of his own childhood in rural England before the First World War.

In effect, his story involves such a total breakdown of any grand and elementary principle of pleasure, to use Wordsworth's phrase (1850 text, Owen and Snyser 1974: I 140), that it qualifies for a place among the Modernist classics as described by Lionel Trilling (1967 [1963]: 84). Especially his relative passiveness – the fact that his energies largely remain psychic, with little translation into a world of relationships and action – seems thoroughly Modernist as well. What Orwell highlights are the man's qualities of memory and sensibility, so recalling, despite the obvious stylistic differences, Proust's more celebrated *rechercheur du temps perdu*, or Stephen Daedalus, Mrs Ramsay, and Rupert Birkin.

Especially because the writing is apparently so close to standard notions of realism, *Coming up for Air* can help us see that, in Modernist novels generally, imaginative, emotional and mythical elements could become even more central than in Dickens. The death of little Paul Dombey within earshot of the Channel's mighty rollers was already a recycling of Wordsworth's "Immortality Ode" (Sell 2001: 185). But in the early twentieth century, novels were taking over the function of nineteenth century lyric poetry still more completely. Whereas the first Modernist poets presented themselves under the banners of "difficulty", of unsentimental impersonality, of imagistic tightness; whereas the "Macspaunday" poets contemporary with the early Orwell (Louis MacNeice, Stephen Spender, W. H. Auden, C. Day Lewis) could accommodate Bowlingesque observations of a blade of grass piercing the city's pavement without relinquishing their wry intellectuality; and whereas Dylan Thomas did not cultivate the expressiveness of "Fern Hill" until the mid-1940s: throughout the first four decades of the twentieth century it was precisely the writers of novels who provided a forum for the negotiation of values, attititudes and emotions which readers could, as it were, try on for size. Orwell, in this novel of 1939, was communicating very substantially, opening up possible paths for a common sensibility at an extremely disconcerting moment in world history.

"Opening up possible paths for a common sensibility". Not: "Telling readers what to think and feel". The immediate and enduring value of Orwell's communication has above all been that it resists oversimplification. He opens up not just one main possible path, but two very different ones, and without suggesting that a straightforward choice between them is either desirable or possible. The reaction of both Bowling and his creator to sociocultural and political developments during the 1920s and 1930s seems to veer from an extrovert hard-headedness to a soulfulness that is introvertedly poetical. In allowing wide scope to both these kinds of response, in acknowledging that they both have their own kind of legitimacy, the writing has a negatively capable dialogicality which, without making the lives of readers the least bit easier, can certainly help them to articulate, and then perhaps to question, some of their own ideas and emotions. The dialogue going on within the psyche of Bowling reflects the dialogue going on within Orwell himself, which in turn opens out into what is potentially a very rewarding dialogue with his readers.

8.2 An apparently unpoetical protagonist

Part of Bowling's communal role as a character in this novel was to express, through his detailed first-person narration, how it felt when, having finally realized that you needed to come up for air, you then discovered that there was no air left to come up to, or not, at any rate, air of a kind you would have liked.

So far so good. Yet Bowling is an unlikely channel for refined sensibility, we are allowed to think, and not least because of all the attention paid to his waistline. Forty-eight inches, last time he measured it. Or was it forty-nine? Not "one of those bellies that sag half-way down to the knees", we are to understand. Merely a certain broadness in the beam, "a tendency to be barrel-shaped". Let us agree, then: he is "the active, hearty kind of fat man, the athletic bouncing type that's nicknamed Fatty or Tubby and is always the life and soul of the party". Not much over fourteen stone, if we will believe him (p. 8).[1] Or if we do some mental arithmetic, fourteen stone seven pounds even *before* his re-appearance in Lower Binfield. There, the penny-in-the-slot machine registers: "*Weight: 14 stone 11 pounds*". An increase, he reflects, of four pounds in three days, doubtless thanks to all the booze (p. 202). Which can only mean that his new suit – "blue flannel with a thin white stripe", and with something "the tailor calls a 'reducing effect'" – must be sitting all the tighter (p. 182).

Granted, some of the weighing machine's other verdicts are more ingratiating:

> "*You are the possessor of exceptional gifts, … but owing to excessive modesty you have never received your due reward. Those about you underrate your abilities. You are too fond of standing aside and allowing others to take the credit for what you have done yourself. You are sensitive, affectionate, and always loyal to your friends…*"
>
> (p. 202, Orwell's italics)

But Bowling, though he does not comment here, will hardly be impressed. Fat men who are the life and soul of the party, and who, to boot, are salesmen, with butter-coloured hair, a bright red face, and still a trace of Cockney accent, are not *supposed* to be fine, delicate souls. At one point he remembers *Wasted Passion*, a novel he borrowed from a Boots library, about "one of those chaps you read about in novels, that have pale sensitive faces and dark hair and a private income". When his girl did a bunk with some other chap, it went roughly like this:

> *David paced up and down the room, his hands pressed to his forehead. … Sheila untrue to him! It could not be! Suddenly realization rushed over him, and he saw the fact in all its stark horror. It was too much. He flung himself down in a paroxysm of weeping.*   (p. 22, Orwell's italics)

Well, what if Hilda disappeared for

> a weekend with somebody else – not that I'd care a damn, in fact it would rather please me to find that she'd still got that much kick left in her – but suppose I did care, would I fling myself down in a paroxysm of weeping? Would anyone expect me to? You couldn't, with a figure like mine. It would be downright obscene.
>
> (p. 22)

---

1. Quotations from *Coming up for Air* taken from Orwell 1962 [1939].

No, "I'm vulgar, I'm insensitive, and I fit in with my environment", most typically the bar of a public house or commercial hotel. We are dealing, he would have us know, with a thick-skinned type who will always land on his feet, and who is always sure to have his little adventure. "[F]at men have more luck with ... [women] than people seem to think". Why? Because "a woman doesn't look on *any* man as a joke if he can kid her that he's in love with her" (p. 23). So obviously Elsie, sweetheart number one, did not desert *George*. George, after two or three months away in the army, "of course" stopped writing to Elsie (p. 112). After all, a girl is not a girl for ever, particularly if she is lower class. When he finally sees Elsie again, twenty-four years later, in Lower Binfield, "the girl I'd known, with her milky-white skin and red mouth and kind of dull-gold hair, had turned into this great round-shouldered hag, shambling along on twisted heels" (p. 204). From behind the counter of her husband's ramshackle tobacconist's shop, she hands him a pipe for inspection, and their fingers just touch. But "[n]o kick, no reaction. The body doesn't remember" (p. 208). And come to think of it, even middle-class girls, even the Hildas of this world – or, no, *especially* the Hildas! – have no sooner won the frightful battle of getting their man to the altar than "the woman kind of relaxes, and all her youth, looks, energy, and joy of life just vanish overnight," leaving her "a depressed, lifeless middle-aged frump" with, to crown it all, a cunning, restless kind of jealousy, something which the poor unfaithful husband can only find rather odd, "considering how little that kind of thing means to her" (pp. 136, 138). Marriage is certainly not what it is cracked up to be, and "[w]hen a woman's bumped off, her husband is always the first suspect – which gives you a little side-glimpse of what people *really* think" about it (p. 135, my italics). Put another way, there is "nothing ahead of you this side of the grave except sweating your guts out to buy boots for the kids" – for those little bastards the very sight and sound of whom are usually quite unbearable (pp. 142, 11–12, 87).

Which raises another point. The *poetry* of childhood? Wordsworth? "There was a time when meadow, grove, and all that"? Baloney!

> The truth is that kids aren't in any way poetic, they're merely savage little animals, except that no animal is a quarter as selfish. A boy isn't interested in meadows, groves, and so forth. He never looks at a landscape, doesn't give a damn for flowers, and unless they affect him in some way, such as being good to eat, he doesn't know one plant from another. Killing things – that's about as near to poetry as a boy gets. (pp. 73–74)

All things considered, *any* poem – say, "Keats's 'Ode to a Nightingale' (or maybe it was a skylark – I forget)" – is nothing more than "a voice, a bit of an eddy in the air" (p. 158). Yes, poetry is just the sort of bunk that prevents an elegant old ghost like Porteous – Oxonian classicist and retired public-school master (no horrible kids of his own, of course) – from facing up to the facts of life in 1938. Old Hitler, for instance, and this Joe Stalin. At least a beer-swilling fatso has got more sense.

8.3   A poetical protagonist after all

But has he, though? And is the difference between fat and thin quite so absolute? George Bowling himself, at any rate, says that he is "not altogether fat." The remark is immediately followed by a jovial caveat – "No! Don't mistake me. I'm not trying to put myself over as a kind of tender flower, the aching heart behind the smiling face and so forth." But all the same, it does introduce the idea that one can be "fat, but ... thin inside". A fat man may even have some history of quite literal thinness, which may actually leave him with a kind of psychological hangover of thinness from his own past (p. 23). George was born in 1893, married Hilda in 1923, at first sometimes felt like strangling her, but later stopped caring, got fat, and settled down. "It must have been in 1930 that I got fat" (p. 143). Yet a residual, inner thinness does seem quite possible.

In one part of his mind women, for instance, have never been divided into just temptresses and gaolers. He has felt plenty of guilt about ditching Elsie, and in point of fact their relationship had been an education in quite the opposite of callousness. "I'm grateful to Elsie, because she was the first person who taught me to care about a woman. I don't mean women in general, I mean an individual woman" (p. 103). As for Hilda, the thought that "at this moment she might be lying somewhere in ghastly pain, or even dead, for all I knew[,]" sent "a most horrible pang of fright through me, a sort of dreadful cold feeling in my guts" (p. 226). Not a paroxysm of weeping, admittedly. But certainly something, something for which most novels available from a Boots library would not even try to suggest the language.

> So I'm fond of Hilda after all you say? I don't know what you mean by fond. Are you fond of your own face? Probably not, but you can't imagine yourself without it. It's part of you. Well, that's how I felt about Hilda. When things are going well I can't stick the sight of her, but the thought that she might be dead or even in pain sent the shivers through me.   (p. 226)

Despite everything, Hilda, it would seem, has become flesh of his flesh, bone of his bone, and his feelings can be just as Old Testament, just as blindly elemental and visceral, towards his often so insufferable children:

> Sometimes I've stood over their cots, on summer evenings when it's light, and watched them sleeping, with their round faces and their two-coloured hair, several shades lighter than mine, and it has given me that feeling you read about in the Bible when it says your bowels yearn. At such times I feel that I'm just a kind of dried-up seed-pod that doesn't matter twopence and that my sole importance has been to bring these creatures into the world and feed them while they're growing up.   (p. 12)

Which is very close to the uneroticized family values of *Lyrical Ballads,* and leads directly into a rather meadow-grove-and-all-that kind of account of his own childhood. The Wordsworthian perceptions and sentiments are quite clear enough, even if the fat man's recurrent "sort of" and "not giving a damn" do try to tone them down:

> It was a wonderful June morning. The buttercups were up to my knees. There was a breath of wind just stirring the tops of the elms, and the great green clouds of leaves were sort of soft and rich like silk. And it was nine in the morning and I was eight years old, and all round me it was early summer, with great tangled hedges where the wild roses were still in bloom, and bits of soft white cloud drifting overhead, and in the distance the low hills and the dim blue masses of the woods round Upper Binfield. And I didn't give a damn for any of it.
>
> (pp. 58–59)

Perhaps he did *not* give a damn at the time. But he certainly does now, as his mind's eye re-creates his former self in such surroundings. And once he is *literally* on his way back to Lower Binfield, there is a sudden compulsion to stop the car – to "get out and have a smell of the spring air, and perhaps even pick a few primroses if there ... [is] nobody coming." As it happens, he is almost caught in the act. Rather than let the occupants of a passing vehicle think that a fat middle-aged man has broken his journey just to pick some primroses, he chucks the bouquet out of sight behind the hedge and pretends to be buttoning up his flies. But he has already spent quite some time there, just leaning on the five-barred gate and taking it all in:

> The grass under the hedge was full of primroses. Just inside the gate a tramp or somebody had left the remains of a fire. A little pile of white embers and a wisp of smoke still oozing out of them. Farther along there was a little bit of a pool, covered over with duckweed. The field was winter wheat. It sloped up sharply, and then there was a fall of chalk and a little beech spinney. A kind of mist of young leaves on the trees. And utter stillness everywhere. Not even enough wind to stir the ashes of the fire. A lark singing somewhere, otherwise not a sound, not even an aeroplane. (p. 162)

As he struggles to overcome his fat man's embarrassment, the moment of epiphany is confirmed:

> What I felt was something that's so unusual nowadays that to say it sounds like foolishness. I felt *happy*. I felt that though I shan't live for ever, I'd be quite ready to. If you like you can say that that was merely because it was the first day of spring. Seasonal effect on the sex-glands or something. But there was more to it than that. Curiously enough, the thing that had suddenly convinced me that life was worth living, more than the primroses or the young buds on the hedge, was that bit of fire near the gate. You know the look of a wood fire on a still day. The

sticks that have gone all to white ash and still keep the shape of sticks, and under the ash the kind of vivid red that you can see into. It's curious that a red ember looks more alive, gives you more of a feeling of life, than any living thing. There's something about it, a kind of intensity, a vibration – I can't think of the exact words. But it lets you know that you're alive yourself.   (p. 163)

The words he does think of are pretty exact even as they stand. What helps us to approve of them, and what perhaps helped him, more than he knows, to find them, is the poem underlying *Dombey and Son*, that original poem about "meadow, grove, and all that":

> O joy! that in our embers
> Is something that doth live,
> That nature yet remembers
> What was so fugitive!

> ("Ode: Intimations of Immortality from Recollections
> of Early Childhood", ll. 131–134)[2]

And if old Porteous's mellifluous incantation had not put him off, the "Ode to a Nightingale" might also have registered with him. Even though Keats's illness did not allow him to grow either fat or middle-aged, he, too, was sometimes labelled as a Cockney, and he, too, was looking for an escape from a distressing everyday reality.

8.4   A poetical and unpoetical author

So Bowling certainly does have feelings, and his feelings, though he does not always realize it, are of unimpeachably literary pedigree. Nor is this all. No less than *À la recherche du temps perdu*, *Ulysses*, *To the Lighthouse*, and *Women in Love*, Orwell's novel comes close to lyrical *self*-expression. Despite Modernist ideas about the impersonality and objectivity of art in general, early-twentieth-century novels not only supply feelings, but sometimes give them the ring of author-autobiographical truth, even when the author might attempt to tone this down.

Keats was thin. But another thin writer was Eric Arthur Blair, a six-foot-two-and-a-half beanpole of man, whose body, by the time he created George Bowling, had already fallen victim to the same wasting disease as Keats's. By that time, too, he had also created another George: George Orwell. True, the difference between Blair and Orwell should not be overstated. In real life, Blair often seemed to use his original name and his *nomme de plume* quite interchangeably. When he was working at the BBC, he would sometimes sign the one name over the typed form of the other,

---

2.   Quotations of Wordsworth from de Selincourt and Darbishire 1952–1959.

apparently without thinking (Davison 1996: 39). Yet at the very least, the coexistence of the two names set up a constant potentiality for differences, and in both the novels and the essays "Orwell" might well connote a self-fashioning, and even a self-muting, of some particular kind.

To the extent that this hypothesis has been tried out already, critics have spoken mainly in terms of class. Raymond Williams commented on Orwell's "continual mobililty, his successive and serious assumption of roles. When he is in a situation, he is so dissolved into it that he is exceptionally convincing" (Williams 1971: 88). Basically, Williams was hinting that if Orwell was Blair in any sense at all, then he was a kind of Blair in exile, a Blair who had uprooted himself from the public-school-educated British ruling class in India, in order to go slumming in Paris or to sample the life and work of a Wigan coalminer.

Now granted, the ability to move from breeding to vulgarity, to write a "good bad poem" which is "a graceful monument to the obvious", is one of the things Orwell himself admires in Kipling, so much a man of Eric Blair's own background, even though Kipling remained ideologically loyal to it. Yet in Orwell's view, the hybridization of civilized and uncivilized would not be possible unless, between instances of humanity which are, socially speaking, so widely different, there were an underlying kinship of temperament. If anywhere, indeed, it would be in the area of temperament that real differences would have to be located, except that a temperamental difference can be at once real and rather deceptive.

> The fact that such a thing as good bad poetry can exist is a sign of the emotional overlap between the intellectual and the ordinary man. The intellectual *is* different from the ordinary man, but only in certain sections of his personality, and even then not all the time. (Orwell 1965 [1942]: 60)

This helps to explain why Orwell rubbed his fellow-intellectuals' noses in the art of the dirty postcard. What the drawings of Donald McGill illustrate is "the Sancho Panza view of life, the attitude to life that Miss Rebecca West once summed up as 'extracting as much fun as possible from smacking behinds in basement kitchens'". As Orwell saw it,

> the two principles, noble folly and base wisdom, exist side by side in nearly every human being. If you look into your own mind, which are you, Don Quixote or Sancho Panza? Almost certainly you are both. There is one part of you that wishes to be a hero or a saint, but another part of you is a little fat man who sees very clearly the advantages of staying alive with a whole skin. He is your unofficial self, the voice of the belly protesting against the soul. His tastes lie towards safety, soft beds, no work, pots of beer and women with 'voluptuous' figures. He it is who punctures your fine attitudes and urges you to look after Number One, to be unfaithful to your wife, to bilk your debts. Whether you allow yourself to be influenced by him is a different question. But it is simply a lie to say that he is

not part of you, just as it is a lie to say that Don Quixote is not part of you either, though most of what is said and written consists of one lie or the other, usually the first.   (Orwell 1964 [1941]: 151–152)

So my own suggestion is that Blair-Orwell, though one and the same individual, was endowed with a certain duality of temperament, which Orwell here urges us to see as typically human. In the Orwell persona, one striking feature is indeed the intellectual's thinness, as he himself might have put it. Yet even though the Orwell persona is given no personal pre-history of literal fatness, metaphorically speaking he has always been quite fat enough to find intellectuality somewhat suspicious. To parallel Bowling's amusing self-description, Orwell is perhaps not "altogether" thin. Total thinness may be something we can usefully think of as the consumptive Eric Arthur Blair's alone, as it were.

On the face of it, Orwell is far more gaunt than Bowling at least. Orwell, and some of Orwell's readers, will know how close *Coming up for Air* is to the "Immortality Ode" and the "Ode to a Nightingale", whereas Bowling himself does not quite know it, so that readers can only smile behind his back. Not that Bowling is an illiterate ignoramus. Until the collapse of his father's seed and corn business, he was one of the more gifted pupils of Walton Grammar School, and was expected to go on to Reading University and become a schoolteacher. Sometimes he professes uncertainty about learned words ("my pituitary deficiency, or whatever it is that makes you get fat" (p. 47)). But he always gets them right, and having avidly devoured, as a boy, the tales of Donovan the Dauntless, Nick Carter, and Sexton Blake, he later graduated to reading experiences involving a fuller intellectual engagement. In fact serious reading was his only relief from the futility of two lonely years of wartime army service devoted to the protection of eleven cans of bully beef – property of the secret or even non-existent West Coast Defence Force. Here again, though, he is very careful to play down his own soulfulness. One favourite book was Compton Mackenzie's *Sinister Street*, and what he liked most of all was Wells's *The History of Mr. Polly*. While parts of Conrad's *Victory* had also been quite readable, other parts merely bored him, and a story by D. H. Lawrence left him feeling he would like to read more of the same, but not sure why. What we really must *not* do is to "run away with the idea that I suddenly discovered Marcel Proust or Henry James or somebody" (p. 120).

This warning, though, gives pause for thought. According to one possible reading, Bowling's hungover thinness is, here more than ever, a far greater part of him than he wants to admit. For how can he say that he never discovered Proust or James, and how can he and his audience agree about what he thereby missed out on, unless, by now at least, he *has* discovered them? His meaningful production of the sentence presupposes that Proust and James are now part of his mental universe. According to a different explanation, this is still a bit unlikely, and the sentence's oddness is a momentary break-down in the dramatization of a first-person-singular Bowling. Orwell, that is to say, is dropping his guard in order to talk about his main character virtually in the third person, from the more cultivated viewpoint of a man who is a lot thinner. But either way, there is also a further difficulty, since the question often arises: Is Orwell really so very much thinner after all? At times it is almost as if he, too, simultaneously knows, and does not know, Proust and James. As in his other realistic pre-war novels, and as again in the two post-war dystopias, the shadow cast by H. G. Wells can often seem much longer.

At least to a certain extent, "George Orwell" could have been a fiction by which Eric Blair sought to deny his psychological thinness – his quixotism, his masochistic devotion to causes which were possibly lost from the start. Seen this way, Blair was no less embarrassed by his own passionate soulfulness than Bowling, and therefore sometimes saw to it that George Orwell comes across as pretty tough and wordly-wise – if not positively crass and superficial. This is the Orwell who, in the essay "Why I Write", purports to confess that one of his main driving forces is an exceptional degree of self-centred vanity and sheer egoism. Blair even made him say that "one can write nothing readable unless one constantly struggles to efface one's own personality" (Orwell 1965 [1947]: 187). This echo of Eliot's influential essay "Tradition and the Individual Talent" was presumably intended to make us think that here is a Modernist writer who struggles to overcome his own feelings. Yet the echo is sounded at precisely the point where Blair, I suggest, was most firmly using the Orwell persona in order to conceal his own self-sacrificing idealism. As another reason for writing, the Orwell persona was made to mention an enthusiasm that was essentially aesthetic. "As long as I remain alive and well" – or, we might paraphrase, as long as Blair could keep a stiff upper lip about the tuberculosis – "I shall continue to feel strongly about prose style, to love the surface of the earth, and to take pleasure in solid objects and scraps of useless information" (Orwell 1965 [1947]: 186). But this last phrase is already rather shame-faced, and on the whole the essay presents an aesthetics of writing that is not very Eliotian at all. Aesthetics, it would seem, is a form of mild self-indulgence, partly a kind of Georgian pastoral, and partly a mere elegant dress for matters of down-to-earth reportage and analysis. The writerly impulses which the Orwell persona was made to value most were the "[d]esire to see things as they are, to find out true [historical] facts and store them up for the use of posterity", plus a strong and all-embracing political purpose. More specifically:

> The Spanish war and other events in 1936–7 turned the scale and thereafter I knew where I stood. Every line of serious work that I have written since 1936 has been written, directly or indirectly, *against* totalitarianism and *for* democratic socialism, as I understand it.   (Orwell 1965 [1947]: 184–185)

8.5   Realistic observations and social engagement

In *Coming up for Air*, the passages where we pick up allusions behind Bowling's back are actually the exception rather than the rule. Sometimes, we may simply be imagining things. Bowling, for whom fishing is more pleasurable than sex, and who could literally "write a book on the technique of fishing" (p. 69), was educated at Walton Grammar School. A joke on Orwell's part? (An allusion, that is, to Isaak Walton's classic *The Complete Angler* of 1653?) Or just coincidence? For most of the time, irony is not even hinted. Even if Bowling's narratorial style is decidedly colloquial (Fowler 1995: 148–158), whereas Orwell, as a writer, would be thought of as more formal, the voices of the two Georges are basically indistinguishable, almost as if they had the same waistline – somewhere between a barrel and a beanpole.

One of the main aims is apparently nothing more, though certainly nothing less, than factual accuracy. The descriptions of the countryside in which Bowling grew up, though rich in detail of flora and fauna, and of human pursuits and occupations as well, are never lush or over-sentimental, and are always meticulously dated as reflecting precisely the early-twentieth-century phase of civilization. No less carefully observed are the cultural innovations and ecological depredations of the 1930s: the decor and gustatory offerings of a milk-bar; the spread of suburbia; the untidy explosion of a rural village into a town; the disappearance of trees for the sake of sham-Tudor; the former secret fishpool now dried-out and filled with old tin cans; the Thames contaminated. To an ear that is sociologically alert, the distinction which Bowling's mother used to make between man's work and woman's work is also just as central, and so is his father's utter incomprehension when honest dealings and sheer hard work did not protect his business from the competition of bigger players with new ideas about marketing. Nor is there any doubt about the precise bearing of the English class system on Bowling's own marriage. The £5-a-week commercial traveller, almost a gent as compared with his shopkeeper father, falls for a girl whose background he "only knew by hearsay": "the poverty-stricken officer class", a background closer to Eric Blair's, in which the evening meal is dinner.

> For generations past her family had been soldiers, sailors, clergymen, Anglo-Indian officials. They'd never had any money, but on the other hand none of them had ever done anything that I should regard as work.   (p. 133)

Also duly noted is the situation's potential for social comedy or tragedy:

> I looked on them as my social and intellectual superiors, while they on the other hand mistook me for a rising young business man who before long would be pulling down the big dough. To people of that kind, "business", whether it's marine insurance or selling peanuts, is just a dark mystery. All they know is that it's something rather vulgar out of which you can make money.   (p. 135)

And yes, sometimes the analytical gaze is certainly turned on larger-scale political issues, at which points the writing's negative capability can certainly give way to a pretty strong desire to shape public opinion. The mass hysteria which the speaker at the branch meeting of the Left Book Club tries to stir up against the Nazis is just the kind of thing which Orwell – though no lover of the Nazis! – was still warning about in his "Notes on Nationalism" in 1945.

All this is the writing of the Wellsian Orwell. Put another way, the Orwell persona here is the one who diagnosed Dickens as not a real revolutionary; as an upholder of private property; as a commentator who thought that the existing power structure would be perfectly satisfactory if only everybody were better behaved; as a writer who, mainly familiar with the south of England, and especially with the world of the Cockney and the *petit bourgeois,* was unable to empathize with either industrial workers, farm labourers, gentlemen, aristocrats, the holders of real power, or criminals; as a novelist whose soft-handed heroes gravitate towards "radiant idleness" and "feather-bed respectability", whose heroines must never marry beneath themselves, and whose servant characters are still basically feudal; as, to sum up, a man who "knows very little about the way things really happen", and who, though certainly not a highbrow, and though very sharply aware of other human beings, nevertheless sees them "as 'characters', not as functional members of society", so that "[e]xcept in a rather round about way, once cannot *learn* very much" from one of his novels (Orwell 1965 [1939]: 123, 124, 115, 135).

In turn, Orwell-the-critic-of-Dickens taught others how to pick holes in Orwell's own novels, presenting Raymond Williams, for instance, with an entire structure of argument ready-made. Orwell, said Williams, is a wonderful reporter "in terms of differences and snobberies in accent, clothes, tastes, furnishing, food." But it is all so shallow! Orwell does not understand the things he sees. He "does not develop any kind of thinking which can sustain and extend a critical analysis of structures". He imagines that there is a basic English decency which requires no fundamental change; England is merely a family in which the wrong members are in control; all that is needed is for people to become "more civilised, more humane, more generally and equitably prosperous". By defining class in terms of mere externals, says Williams, Orwell effectively masks the fact that "class is a powerful and continuing economic relationship – as between the owners of property and capital and the owners only of labour and skill", and that "money in the pocket" is not at all the same thing as "capital, which is the ownership and creation of the means of social life itself". Furthermore, complains Williams, Orwell does not really feel for people outside of Blair's own class. Blair's attempt to uproot himself merely left him as the exile who, in spite of, but also because of that "continual mobility" – that "constant and serious assumption of roles" – had no true allegiance, and no true sense of the proletariat's own potentiality for education and progress. Not least in *Animal Farm* and *Nineteen Eighty-Four*, his analysis, according to Williams, was simply wrong, and much too pessimistic. His critique of totalitarianism encouraged a kind of stock-response opposition to any kind of collective effort at all (Williams 1971: 22, 84, 24).

A socially engaged writer who is strong on reportage will always be discussed like this. Both Dickens and George Orwell were writers of that kind, and to ask whether their writing was historically accurate and analytically correct makes a great deal of sense. But to say that either of them did not understand the world in which he lived does seem a bit rich. For Williams, writing in 1971, to blame Orwell for being pessimistic during the period 1936–1949 was just as anachronistic as for Orwell to blame Dickens for, in effect, not using Marxian concepts. A much fairer course would be to ask whether Dickens's and Orwell's documentation and analysis were intelligently observant by the standards of their own day. And even this would be only one kind of question, the answer to which could never do justice to their texts as a whole.

8.6   Deeper and more particularized experience

The immediate point is that *Coming up for Air* is not only Orwell's book but Blair's, whom I am seeing as quixotically thinner and more soulful. Not only is the writing much closer to Wordsworth and Keats than George Bowling would ever want to recognize. It is also closer to Proust and James than would perhaps be admitted by even George Orwell. In "Why I Write" Orwell does say that he has tried to make political writing into an art" (Orwell 1965 [1947]: 186). But the art of *Coming up for Air* goes far beyond the matters of natural description and stylistic externals foregrounded by that essay. Above all, there is a use of fiction to explore and express profound realities of the individual psyche. Whereas, at their fattest, Orwell and Bowling are both interested in putting people into little sociological boxes – Bowling himself, for instance, as a £5-a-week commercial traveller who married into the class of poverty-stricken army officers –, and whereas Raymond Williams, having first found fault with some of these categorizations, then provides the notion of the class exile as a little box of his own in which to place Orwell – "Orwell was one of a significant number of men who …" (Williams 1961[1958]:279) –, what Blair makes Orwell make Bowling also say, as we might express it, is not just that Elsie taught him to appreciate the personal uniqueness of a lover, but that *any* human being both definitely is, and definitely is not, one of the crowd:

> The usual crowd that you can hardly fight your way through was streaming up the pavement, all of them with that insane fixed expression on their faces that people have in London streets, and there was the usual jam of traffic with the great red buses nosing their way between the cars, and the engines roaring and horns tooting. Enough noise to waken the dead, but not to waken this lot, I thought. I felt as if I was the only person awake in a city of sleep-walkers. That's an illusion, of course. When you walk through a crowd of strangers it's next door to impossible not to imagine that they're all waxworks, but probably they're thinking just the same about you.   (p. 28)

So if we think of Orwell's eye as the eye which registers the course of sociocultural change, then what Blair discerns will be a particular individual's response to it. This makes for a wonderfully slow-motion story, which has its own indelible logic: the young man's embrace of sudden and unexpected opportunities for upward social mobility; his willingness to forget his humble origins; his later disillusionment with the brave new world; the concomitant stagnation in his most intimate private life, only underlined by an ageing body's need for more capacious clothing and false teeth; the consequent re-emergence of thoughts about his childhood; his attempt, by actually taking himself to his birthplace, to return entirely to his own and the country's past; the inevitable disappointment; the final resignation to the unalluring present; and some rather anxious fears about the future. In short, the story which Blair makes Orwell make Bowling tell could be the story of almost *anyone's* life on earth, and is the same story whose archetypal power informs the two great first-person narrations of Dickens. The plots of *David Copperfield* and *Great Expectations*, so different from Orwellian plots in foregrounding interpersonal relationships and moral choice, nevertheless anticipated Orwell's kind of poetry here, and were thereby more humanly coherent than his comments on Dickens's "rotten architecture, but wonderful gargoyles" would seem to allow (Orwell 1965 [1939]: 133). In point of fact, *Coming up for Air* draws tellingly on their mythopoetic detail – from the child's experience of church-going or family gravestones, through the young snob's self-display on revisiting his former haunts, to that willed forgetfulness of his first love. What Orwell does at his most "Orwell", by contrast, is merely to make the linkage – which will always operate in any individual life – between the universal story and some particular phase of a certain culture.

In this matter of linking the historically particular with the humanly general, and especially in the matter of particular childhoods, Orwell is one of Dickens's main rivals in English, and very consciously so. In places, his critique of Dickens's social understanding was positively cranky, clearly reflecting the inverted snobbery of a left-wing intellectual's valorization of manual labour. ("It is difficult to imagine him [Dickens] digging a cabbage patch" (Orwell 1965 [1939]: 119)). Yet he was far too generous not to acknowledge Dickens's more universal dimension, and in doing so can alert us to qualities in his own novel of the same year as the Dickens essay:

> I must have been about nine years old when I first read *David Copperfield*. The mental atmosphere of the opening chapters was so immediately intelligible to me that I vaguely imagined they have been written *by a child*. And yet when one re-reads the book as an adult and sees the Murdstones, for instance, dwindle from gigantic figures of doom into semi-comic monsters, these passages lose nothing. Dickens has been able to stand both inside and outside the child's mind, in such a way that the same scene can be a wild burlesque or sinister reality, according to age at which one reads it. (Orwell 1965 [1939]: 93)

As it happens, in both Dickens and Orwell the understanding of historical particularities is far more suggestive than an anachronistic left-wing critique will ever give them credit for. But in any case, a novel's sociocultural detail and analysis, though a necessary consequence of its embodiment of the universal in historical form, is not its be-all and end-all, and will be none the worse for being controversial. A novel is not a science textbook. It claims to offer nothing more than just the single author's personal assessment, and at best to offer it for a comparing of notes.

Even in the most realist of novels, the deepest relevance will be very much a matter of mood and general attitude, on which readers' verdicts are likely to be even more erratic than on its more particular historical commentary. Raymond Williams, a Welsh railwayman's son who became a professor at Cambridge, thereby forcing himself upwards where Blair had forced himself downwards, had a rosy picture of the proletariat, which affected his overall tone, whereas Blair was increasingly saddened and disappointed. If we were to indulge in gossip and guesswork, we might suggest that Williams was prey to the meritocrat's guilt, and that this made him idealize what he had risen above, whereas Blair was simply peeved at having given up so much for so little. Needless to say, biographical speculation can also be less cynical than this. But the far more important point here is that Williams-like optimism and Blairian pessimism are both humanly possible. In at least a mild sense we are all manic-depressives, presumably, and to express pessimism can often seem a no less reasonable response to the facts of a situation than to express optimism. Not only that, but it can be just as valuable socially. Optimism runs the risk of being naively unconvincing, even if it can sometimes be a genuine inspiration to action. Pessimism, even if it, too, can become, as Williams said, a stock response, may also be a catalytic irritant. The determination to improve things is no less likely to arise from a thorough-going dissatisfaction than from a utopian vision. And anyway, pessimists who go public are actually not as pessimistic as pessimistic can be. The despairing solipsism of a wordless suicide is a very different thing from the gesture of Eric Arthur Blair, who not only laid pessimism open to inspection, qualification or even refutation, but also as an invitation to fellowship.

8.7   Communal perspectives

In accusing Blair of fostering a disbelief in communality of any kind, Williams underestimated the collectivity of successful literary communication itself. Both writers and readers share that capacity for empathy with different shades of human otherness which Blair's own life so clearly illustrated, and on which Williams himself so grudgingly remarked. As I have been suggesting in other studies here, it is precisely by bringing this imaginative power into play that literature, no less than any other form of communication, can constantly widen its own social circle. To make this claim is,

I am saying, not to return to nineteenth century notions of human nature as having just some single formation. In an age of post-postmodern polyculturality, to think of literature in a way which so nearly condones a hegemonic consensus is no longer possible. Instead, our hope is likely to be that literature will bring together different readerships while at the same time leaving some of the differences between them intact. As a result, the writing and reading of literary texts may well improve the chances for peace and understanding, yet without eliminating creative tensions between the manifold forms of human fulfilment. By the same token, the antagonistic rhetoric of an Orwell-on-Dickens or a Williams-on-Orwell has lost its bite.

The political antagonism of Orwell was in any case at odds with what we might call the deeper intuition of Blair. Orwell's claim that all his writing after the Spanish war sprang from a political desire "to push the world in a certain direction" (Orwell 1965 [1947]: 184) can hardly account for *Coming up for Air*, which has much more to do with the individual's own experience of being pushed, by the world itself, in a direction quite unchosen. What Williams saw in Blair as a dangerously influential and peculiarly mid-twentieth-century disbelief in communality could just as easily be described as a much older stance of individual protest against powerful pressures, a kind of protest just as instinctive as that "good-tempered antinomianism" which Orwell was again generous enough to recognize in Dickens (Orwell 1965 [1938]: 139). An unfailing sympathy for the underdog is a quality this novel itself explores from early on, as in Bowling's outrage at the humiliation of the chemist's-shop assistant by her supervisor. And when resistance seems of no avail, there is also the no less human resort to mythologization: to the idyll of a childhood in a golden past when time, though so historical, seemed stationary; or to those nightmare guesses at the future – "The barbed wire! The slogans! The enormous faces! The cork-lined cellars where the executioner plugs you from behind!" (p. 165), scenarios which were to be further developed in *Animal Farm* and *Nineteen Eighty-Four*.

Even if neither the myth of the past nor the myth of the future were necessarily accurate in detail or implied analysis, even if neither of them would render a present experience of change more palatable, even if, inevitably, a counter-myth comes into circulation, a myth more in tune with, for instance, Raymond Williams's way of thinking, there could still be no excuse for stopping these Blairian myths from coming to the surface, any more than Fancy's failure to cheat so well as she is famed to do could ever be a pretext for censoring the "Ode to a Nightingale". Cushioning his own vulnerability within the greater fleshiness of both his fictional Georges, Blair speaks to, and for, a vulnerability, an ultimate thinness, which could be our very own. Whoever we happen to be, no matter where and when we happen to be alive, we can read him for the paradoxical reminders that we are not alone in being lonely in the crowd, and that perhaps *nobody* is either altogether fat or altogether thin. If Bowling, without even realizing it, has learned from Wordsworth how to connect his deepest feelings with a heap of glowing embers, then our communion with Blair-Orwell can do the same kind of thing for us. His negatively capable solicitude for shared and contradictory possibilities of feeling would not normally be mentioned as an instance of social and political reform. Yet it represents a very substantial communal gain, and one that is not restricted to any particular class or nation or period, even if distinctions between one human grouping and another will never be eroded, and will remain the stuff of novelistic mimesis.

CHAPTER 9

Lynne Reid Banks's *Melusine: A Mystery* (1988)

The ethics of writing for children

9.1   The writer's dilemma

The dialogicality intrinsic to genuine communication does not require that communicants are co-present or have feedback channels to each other. In both the author and the reader of a literary work, the dialogicality is recognizable as a quality of mind: as a generous deference which, with no sacrifice of frankness or personal identity, acknowledges the rights, concerns and sensitivities of other communicants.

The rights, concerns and sensitivities of other communicants always call for due care. But to an adult hoping to communicate with children this responsibility can sometimes seem particularly heavy. Think, especially, of a children's writer who is dealing with very painful subject matter. As Lydia Kokkola (2003) stresses in her book on Holocaust literature for children, to pitch a novel containing traumatic details at child readers does call for the greatest possible tact. At best, such a book may help children start to think about some of life's most difficult questions. But if it overestimates their level of intellectual and emotional maturity, it may do more harm than good.

Not every book for children has tactfully respected child readers. Some of the earliest texts published for the young were positively sadistic in their didacticism. There was Heinrich Hoffmann's *Struwwelpeter* (1848 [1845]), for instance, in which the thumb-suckers were punished by having their thumbs cut off. Even in much more recent times, some of the most popular reading matter for children has endorsed a more or less total disempowerment of young readers, seriously undermining their autonomy as individuals, and showing little sensitivity to their fears and spiritual vulnerability. It is in these terms that Maria Lassén-Seger (2002) has analysed K. A. Applegate's Animorphs series, for instance.

That children's books have so often had a bullying streak is unsurprising. All over the world, children are exposed to cruelty, exploitation, and abuse. Although societies do not officially endorse these conditions, they have not succeeded in putting a stop to them, and even people whose behaviour towards children is not criminal can be unloving and unsupportive. In some quarters there is still a belief, which Hoffman would have applauded, that in the raising of children the only way to be kind is by being cruel. No society will survive which allows its members to do whatever they want, the argument goes, and because civil rights entail civil responsibilities, children must learn to accept a fair amount of regulation, stern regulation if necessary, as did their parents and grandparents before them. The older generation, it is claimed, does know best, and would be shirking its duty if it did not put children firmly in their place. Such disciplinarianism may sometimes be well-intentioned, but can also turn vicious. As channelled through children's literature, the worst examples would be writers who, under the pretext of bracing children for the harsh realities of life, not only availed themselves of shock tactics, but used trauma-laden subject matter as a kind of threat by which to reinforce an adult regime.

It was against this background that many postmodern commentators argued that literature for children is fundamentally and inevitably unfriendly towards them. Perry Nodelman, for instance, taking childhood as above all a social construction, analysed children's literature in Foucauldian terms as an exercise in discoursal control. Seen this way, adults "write books for children to provide them with values and with images of themselves [i.e. of children] *we* approve of or feel comfortable with" (Nodelman 1992: 30). In Nodelman's work, then, the theoretical concepts which other postmodern critics had used to set up dichotomies between the establishment and underprivileged communities defined in terms of gender, sexual orientation, class, ethnicity and religion were now brought in to represent children as an interest grouping that was systematically repressed by power-holding adults.

It so happens that a truly shocking book such as Miriam Steiner Aviezer's *The Soldier with the Golden Buttons* (1996 [1964]), in which a child character has to watch three other children being burned alive, breaches the mimetic conventions of children's literature, which have not prioritized such thorough-going realism (Kokkola 2007). Traditionally, trauma has been avoided, sometimes as a danger towards which the story might have seemed to be leading, but which peripeteically gives way to the rounded closure of a happy ending.

According to postmodern critics, however, even children's writers who did supply happy endings had not always done so out of a concern for their young readers' spiritual well-being. Jacqueline Rose (1984) argued that the tradition's hedonistic bias was at least partly driven by adult wish-fulfilment. To her mind, some of the matters at issue in children's literature had nothing to do with children at all and were actually imperceptible to them. Precisely by blocking out violence and suffering, children's books vented, she argued, a nostalgia for their authors' own childhood as an age of innocence long since passed, a sweetly melancholic notion which she saw as appealing to many adult readers as well. Above all she pointed to Edwardian children's classics such as *Peter Pan*, but then the postmodern sociologist Chris Jenks (1996) added that the Rousseauistic idyll of a golden childhood has had a special place within the social symbolic of later times as well. One of Jenks's claims was that, by the late twentieth century, acts of murder committed by children seemed exceptionally frightful, whereas in earlier periods of history the same phenomenon had occasioned no more consternation than murder by adults. His explanation was that, within a secularized *Weltanschauung*, the image of the pure and beautiful child had become the adult's last relic of spiritual wholeness.

In some respects adult disregard for real children may still be on the increase, with the Internet now offering a global scope to paedophiles, for instance. But in post-postmodern times, just as postmodernity's other power dichotomies are being reconceptualized in terms of a globalization that is more beneficial and non-hegemonic, so the postmodern assumption that adults always and necessarily maltreat or ignore the young was bound to be qualified as well. Given the new mood, commentators are increasingly ready to acknowledge that the finest writing for children does indeed involve an ethically motivated dialogicality, within which children and adults are each other's equals (Sell 2002). Such writing welcomes children into a human circle by comparing notes with them, fully recognizing that they have their own ways of seeing things, frankly offering entries into a more adult understanding for those of them who may be interested and ready for it, but also still allowing a child's-eye view to run alongside such maturer perceptions. Such communicational genuineness is even to be found in children's books that were written when the postmodern theoretical paradigms were still in their zenith.

So without underestimating the possible force of adult escapism, some critics are now stressing that juvenile literature's avoidance of unpleasantness certainly can reflect a real concern for its readers' mental health. Maria Nikolajeva (2002) robustly assumes that a happy childhood is precisely what children deserve, and describes the "prelapsarian" or "Arcadian" plots of traditional children's literature as intimating the child's still undiminished potentiality to become or to do absolutely anything. This, she says, can only boost young readers' self-confidence in a manner wholly appropriate to the early stages of their initiation into life and society at large.

By implication, Nikolajeva is appealing to attitudes already enshrined in that whole raft of legislation by which any civilized society seeks, on the best available expert advice, to shelter children from potentially harmful forms of cultural production. Probably for most of us, trauma is not something we would wish upon either ourselves or other people, and least of all upon children. One does not become a better human being as a result of it, and although the experience of it can promote a kind of knowledge and even wisdom, one can also be knowledgeable and wise without it, and a lot happier, too, without thereby becoming either unduly pampered or insensitive to the plight of those less fortunate. Presumably there would be widespread recognition that a degree of happiness does sometimes prove to be possible in life, and that although billions of human beings live in conditions of poverty and exploitation which make happiness much less likely for them, it is actually something to which everyone is entitled, and especially in life's earliest stages, since a happy childhood offers the best foundation for later years.

That said, these benevolent sentiments can exist in tension with a very different kind of assumption, both in the minds of individuals and within the culture as a whole. Especially in the field of literary criticism, one Modernist legacy which fed into the various forms of postmodern criticism, and which still exerts considerable influence even today, is a certain valorization of suffering, not as something enjoyable, needless to say, but as an incontrovertible reality. One *locus classicus* for this is still the article by Lionel Trilling to which I have referred in previous studies here: "The Fate of Pleasure" (Trilling 1967 [1963]). This argued that pleasure nowadays made people feel *un*real. As a confirmation that they actually existed, they needed the abrasions of pain.

To repeat, the two kinds of assumption co-exist. In extreme forms, the one can become a naively wish-fulfilling utopianism, the other a masochistically addictive dystopianism. But they both contain enough truth not to cancel each other out. Suffering can certainly be all too real, painful and widespread. And in point of fact, trauma has been a central focus in some of the most powerful literary works from ancient Greek tragedy onwards. But trauma is neither more humanly authentic than untraumatic experience, nor more intrinsically deserving of literary treatment. While some very great writers take us to some extremely disturbing places, others are deeply rooted in the calmer, sometimes pleasurable ordinariness of the everyday.

As for children's writers, those who recognise their responsibilities and do not try to uphold an adult tyranny will always face an ethical dilemma. On the one hand, there is the imperative of truth to their subject matter. On the other hand, there is the imperative of sensitivity towards their young readers. In the case of trauma literature for children, this two-fold duty becomes acutely problematic, since here very serious forms of suffering must somehow be recognized for what they are, but without enlisting the rawest kinds of verisimilitude. While to overprotect child readers might actually incapacitate them for life as it really is, writers hoping to engage them in genuine communication will hardly offer disclosures that are too disturbingly abrupt. The frankness and the tactfulness of a children's trauma novel are likely to be in inverse ratio to each other. At some points, the only way for a writer to remain tactful without being positively dishonest may be by going silent, in which case child readers will be left guessing. This, too, is problematic, since it may arouse fears and anxieties which some children may be unable to discuss with an adult. But for a writer to tell lies or half-truths about trauma – in any way to play down or even beautify away the likely severity and likely duration of suffering – is arguably less defensible.

9.2   Tactful but honest indirectness

During the last decades of the twentieth century, this dilemma did not deter a fair number of writers from taking up trauma as a motif in novels for teenagers and young adults. In cases such as Ruth White's *Weeping Willow* (1992), Cynthia D. Grant's *Uncle Vampire* (1994), Cynthia Voigt's *When She Hollers* (1994), Jacqueline Woodson's *I Hadn't Meant to Tell You* (1994), Francesca Lia Block's *The Hanged Man* (1994), and Lynne Reid Banks's *Melusine: A Mystery* (1990 [1988]), the challenge to the prelapsarian conventions of traditional children's literature was all the sharper in view of the precise nature of the trauma dealt with. The traumas of flood or earthquake victims result from *force majeure* – at least as long as all possible measures have been taken to reduce the consequences of such natural disasters. Equally difficult to blame on identifiable human individuals is trauma deriving from, say, the general conditions of life in the twentieth century, or from the human condition *tout court*, and the same thing partly applies even to the trauma of a Holocaust survivor: particular human beings may have been its immediate cause, but their guilt will also have been collective, involving the political power structure of an entire state. Child characters in the aforementioned novels by White, Grant, Voigt, Woodson, Block and Banks, by contrast, are the victims of incestuous paedophilia, which means that they suffer at the hands of a very specific individual, a nameable member of their own family, and an individual whose behaviour would not only fail to win official approval, but is also a serious abuse of a member of the reader's generation by a member of the writer's generation. The injury involved is a complete travesty of the adult-child relationship which genuinely communicational children's writers themselves attempt to foster.

Some of these novels were fairly well received. Michael Cart's praise of Block's *The Hanged Man* drew on some comments by Chris Crutcher, himself a writer of teenage books but also a practising family therapist who had worked with child-abuse victims. "I believe stories can help," Crutcher had written, because they can prompt teenagers to "look at their feelings, or come to emotional resolution, from a safe distance. If, as an author, I can make an emotional connection with my reader, I have already started him or her to heal... . *I am not alone* is a powerful medicine" (in Cart 1996: 211, Crutcher's italics). In short, Cart was commending Block because, to readers who were themselves victims of incestuous paedophilia, she was offering a heartening sense of solidarity with fellow-suffers, and because she was making their voice more publicly audible, their wound more readily perceptible.

From an ethical point of view, this was clearly a noble achievement. But what Cart refrained from discussing was the ethical dilemma I am raising here. He did note that other critics' responses to *The Hanged Man* had been rather cooler than his own, and he did attribute this to the book's "mature and subtle ideas and themes", and to its "powerful dark material" (Cart 1996: 210). But what he did not examine was the appropriateness of Block's addressivity to that large majority of her readers who had *not* been subjected to incestuous paedophilia in their own lives. Most strikingly of all, he did not consider the likely impact of the novel's narratological structure, which made the trauma victim herself the single main protagonist, and which told the story entirely as experienced by her, in her own unfiltered voice.

To be fair, Cart may simply have taken for granted that this structure could not possibly harm the book's most likely readers, because Block so clearly envisages them as young people already in their mid- or later teens. The teenagers addressed by Banks's *Melusine*, on the other hand, a novel which more clearly illustrates the dilemma I am raising, are a few years' younger. Here Block's kind of narratological structure would certainly have been more risky, and Banks's own solution is indeed different. Her book opens with Roger, an English teenager whose voice is just on the point of breaking, arriving with his mother, father and twin sisters, Emma and Polly, at a French chateau in which they are going spend their summer holiday as paying guests. What subsequently happens there is not narrated in the first person singular, but everything in the book is nevertheless seen through Roger's own eyes. In one very real sense, the story told is Roger's story. Yet Roger, far from emerging as the only centre of attention, focalizes the victimized Melusine, whose trauma, though obviously the book's *raison d'être*, is thereby dealt with indirectly. Readers are not taken straight into the mind of the abused girl. They can only draw inferences about her experiences from the puzzled observations of the pubertal boy.

The chateau is the isolated and decaying ancestral home of the Serpe family, two surviving members of which are normally its sole occupants: M. Serpe and Melusine, his daughter, who is perhaps slightly older, and certainly *seems* mysteriously older, than Roger. It is late at night when Roger and his family first arrive, and they are welcomed – though "welcome" is hardly the right word – by M. Serpe alone. At first, then, they know nothing of Melusine's very existence. But as they eat a snack amid the dirt and flies of M. Serpe's squalid kitchen, they ask him if he is all on his own, and he replies that, no, he has a daughter living with him. Then, in a nervous attempt at humour, Roger's mother asks him whether he has no more than just the one girl living with him. M. Serpe, when this question is translated for him into French, becomes very angry. Though receiving no explanation of his rage, his paying guests do at least gather that he also has another daughter, but that she no longer lives with him. Soon after this little incident, the English holidaymakers move through into their own rooms in the chateau, which are cleaner, much better furnished, and rather imposing. The door between their quarters and M. Serpe's kitchen and other accommodation is normally locked.

Over the days which follow the mystery thickens, as Banks draws on some of the same Gothic conventions as Poe in *The Fall of the House of Usher* and Hitchcock in some of his films. The dilapidated chateau contains a dark secret, which as it gradually reveals itself has to be mentally and emotionally processed by Roger. The crux of the matter is M. Serpe's sexual abuse of Melusine, and his earlier abuse of her older sister, who actually killed herself as a result. The older sister's mortal remains now lie in a coffin in the chateau's gloomy tower, in a room which M. Serpe has turned into a kind of shrine. At the climax of the story, Roger and his father have crept through a secret tunnel which brings them into the tower, where they duly discover the shrine and the coffin in it, though they are still unaware of the full explanation. M. Serpe surprises them there and fires a gun at them, with inaccurate aim, however, because he is thrown strangely off balance, so falling backwards through the high tower's window to his death. As he falls, he screams out something which Roger and his father later come to realize was: "*Pardonnez moi, mes filles!*" (p. 160).[1]

---

1. Quotations of *Melusine* taken from Banks 1990 [1988].

Despite the book's title, then, it is still very much about Roger, himself on the threshold between childhood and sexual maturity, and forced to come to terms with adult sexuality in a very disturbing manifestation. Having soon become friends with Melusine through helping her milk the large herd of goats, he at one point starts to wonder where she is. Peering in through a window, he finally locates her in the gloom of the Serpes' kitchen, where she is sitting in her father's lap, apparently against her will. Roger quickly draws back from the window, but what he has seen still lingers in his mind, leading the same night to a dreadful nightmare. The next day's events revolve less directly around Melusine and her father, but do nothing to calm him down. Noticing how disturbed he is, his parents suggest that he should sleep in the parental bed with his father, and his mother sleep in another room. His own awakening sexuality is now so nervously on edge that the questions of whose bed is where and of who is sleeping with whom are actually becoming curiously insistent in his story as a whole. As he is lying beside his father, a huge storm is raging outside, water starts coming in through the roof, and there is a power-cut. Roger gets up to fetch a torch from his own bedroom, a room associated, as I shall soon explain, with strange experiences which strongly reinforce his apprehension about being there. But his mother, too, is upset by all the commotion, and Roger suggests that she could sleep on the sofa in the big room, and offers to go and sleep in his own room after all. At which point his father announces that he has "moved the [double] bed to a place where the floor seemed dry and with a bit of juggling with the bedclothes at least one person could sleep in it. Maybe two 'if they were very fond of each other', which was a family joke" (p. 96).

As Roger becomes more confused and worried, on three separate occasions he manages to elicit from his parents a response to his anxieties that is both truthful and tactful, a diplomatic honesty which by extension carries over to Banks's own stance *vis à vis* her young readers. The first such conversation occurs as father and son lie listening to the storm. With much hesitation, Roger wonders whether M. Serpe is "nice to Melusine", and whether or not it is "okay for a father to – well, to kiss his daughter, and – you know, sit with her on his knee". When he explains what he saw through the kitchen window, his father does not much like the sound of it, because "[a] man who lives without a wife, like Monsieur Serpe, can get very lonely. Especially in a remote place like this, with no adult company. And if he's got a young daughter, sometimes he can get – a bit fonder of her than he ought to." Roger immediately asks whether he is talking, as people do on the television, about child abuse, and if so, how such a thing can possibly happen, not with a stranger, but with a child's own father. The paternal reply is, "Nobody likes to tell kids this, but I'm afraid it happens a lot inside families as well. Especially between fathers and daughters." Roger's father agrees with him that this would be "really wrong", although "we mustn't jump to conclusions" (pp. 89–91). During the second conversation, when Roger has now seen Melusine bitterly crying, and she has told him that she understands his desire to know what is happening between her father and herself, he asks his own father about the problem of suffering.

> "...if a person – if she were suffering, really badly so that she couldn't bear it, and
> God and – I mean, not God or anybody else did anything to stop it, even though
> she believes in Him, would that explain ... I mean, if you really can't bear some-
> thing, and it keeps on happening, you might – you might change, something
> could break out in you, you could become – something completely different.
> Could that happen, d'you think?"
>   His father looked into his eyes.
>   "What are you trying to tell me, son?"
>   Roger looked down.
>   "I don't know... I just thought...
>   "There's no doubt that suffering can change people. And nobody can tell me that
> it always makes them better."   (p. 117)

During the third conversation, which ostensibly begins as one of Roger's moves in a
parlour game he is playing with his parents and Polly, he asks, "If you suspected that
a child ... – a neighbour's child was being ill-treated by her p-parents, would you tell
the police?" His father and mother intelligently realize that his question is in earnest,
but say that a lot would depend on the meaning of "ill-treated". Supposing it meant
"abused", Roger suggests, a term which Polly then blandly glosses with the single
word "Sex", so arousing in Roger a sudden apprehension. As he dashes out of the
room, he shouts, "I'm going to look for Emma! ... She shouldn't be out in the dark
by herself" (pp. 126–127). Emma, it emerges, is in the goatshed with M. Serpe, but
has come to no harm.

But if, partly as a result of pondering these conversations with his parents, Roger
would eventually be in a position to adopt a grown-up perspective, during the story
he also has ideas which seem far less down to earth. The long and the short of it is
that he perceives Melusine herself as frequently changing shape to become a huge
snake. Although nobody else sees her this way, Emma does say "She doesn't walk. She
glides" (p. 83), and there is also a local legend about a much earlier female member of
the Serpe family, supposed to have been a witch complete with animal familiars, who
could change herself into a snake. One annotation to Banks's novel would be that the
Vendée region in which she sets it (with references to the towns of La Rochelle and
Poitiers) was actually homeland to the Melusine whose supernatural story was first
popularized by Jean d'Arras and Coudrette around the end of the fourteenth century,
subsequently to become widespread within Western culture as a whole – from Goethe
through Mendelssohn to Proust and A. S. Byatt. But be that as it may, Roger keeps the
apparent metamorphoses of the latest Melusine entirely to himself, not even reporting the strange rustling he thinks he hears in his bedroom on the very first evening.
When, on the next day, he actually meets Melusine for the first time, her skin already
looks strangely cold to him, and her eyes somehow like buttons. During a visit to
the nearby town, he sees her dancing in the street to a tune somebody is playing on
a pipe, and thinks that her undulating movements are not really human. Later on,

when he, Melusine and Polly get into difficulties in a rowing boat on the river, Polly is rescued from drowning by, as Roger cannot help believing, Melusine transformed into a mighty water serpent, and he is just as certain that the reason why M. Serpe is thrown off balance and falls out of the tower is that Melusine, in the form of the snake, comes to the aid of his father and himself. No less surprisingly, he has also perceived the huge snake as coming down through a hole in the ceiling from Melusine's room above and actually laying itself on his own bed. Then after M. Serpe's death, Melusine at first seems to have vanished into thin air. But what Roger does find is the sloughed-off skin of a large snake, which he promptly buries in a compost heap. When Melusine eventually re-appears in human form, he thinks that her skin now has a much warmer glow to it, and that her eyes are no longer button-like, her lips less straight and thin.

On the one hand, then, Roger is struggling to understand the phenomenon of sexuality and incestuous paedophilia as seen from a more adult perspective. On the other hand, he is still experiencing emotions and unusual perceptions or fantasies with a childish intensity. This epistemological disjunction is at its sharpest in the penultimate chapter, when he is back in England. His parents had offered to take the orphaned Melusine home with them prior to her going to live with an uncle in Canada, but Melusine mysteriously disappeared after a car crash on their way up through France. Roger is still so seriously disturbed by the whole business that his parents have arranged for him to see the school psychologist, who regards incestuous paedophilia as simply a matter of fact.

> [Roger] told her his suspicions about what the ogre [M. Serpe] had been doing to Melusine, and she didn't turn a hair about that. She said she thought it was entirely possible. She didn't underrate the damage that such a thing might have done to Melusine, though she didn't dwell on it. She said that in all probability, the reason why Melusine's older sister had killed herself was because her father was abusing her in the same way; and that that would explain why he was so obsessed with guilt that it drove him mad. Roger asked why he did the same thing to Melusine, if he felt so guilty about his first daughter. The psychologist told him that people didn't do these sorts of things because they decided to, rationally and logically, but because in many cases they just couldn't help it. She said probably Melusine realized this and that was why she put up with it.   (p. 179)

But the very cool-headedness of her approach here finally forces Roger into blurting out the whole secret of Melusine's apparent metamophoses. On hearing his narrative, the psychologist pricks up her ears and starts to think about referring his case to a psychiatrist, a response which may or may not help Roger to keep his secret to himself once again, or perhaps even to switch to the more adult view once and for all. This suggestive uncertainty is a fine culmination to the development of Roger's inner turmoil throughout, and here, I think, the novel could interestingly have ended, precisely *without* the rounded closure so typical of traditional children's literature.

As in one of the passages quoted above, Roger has all along been wondering why or how Melusine had seemed to be changing shape. In particular, was it her response to suffering? The fact that such a question is explicitly raised within the text means that readers, too, may ask themselves whether Roger's fantastic perceptions might actually mean something in more naturalistic terms. And indeed, to read the novel as a pure fantasy would underestimate its hermeneutic complexity. For an adult reader, Melusine's apparent metamorphoses could well be the early symptom of a psychosis on Roger's own part, as the psychologist perhaps begins to suspect. Or even more plausibly, Roger's strange impressions could be a kind of defence mechanism which, while cashing in on the imagery of the colourful local legend, basically reflects the pubertal boy's hypersensitivity to sado-sexual vibrations in the new and strange environment. Certainly in reporting Roger's perceptions, Banks is allowing considerable leeway to the book's youngest readers, who if they wish can come to terms with Melusine partly along the same lines as Roger himself, and at their own pace. By at first believing that her suffering takes the form of having to endure a switch from the human into the reptilian, not only Roger, but also any child who reads his story can imagine their way towards a kind of provisional understanding of the dehumanizing subjection into which Melusine has been forced.

Roger's mother, for her part, though never told of his extraordinary experiences, takes his evident preoccupation with Melusine in her stride. She even mentions that she herself had at the same age had an uncontrollable crush on an older man. Her instinct is pretty much on target here, since at one level Roger clearly experiences M. Serpe as a detested rival. The latency of Roger's own sexuality itself becomes a central motif, with some of the writing even veering towards a kind of soft pornography with Melusine as its object. While luxuriating in a soapy warm shower Roger "wondered suddenly if Melusine had a shower. When this thought occurred to him, a picture came into his mind of her body, straight and slim with her strange face turned upward to the shower-head, her black hair wet and loose around her shoulders. The details were blurred by the spray as if she were veiled" (pp. 38–39). Further proto-erotic hints occur in the episode where he sees her dancing in the street, "swaying her hips, … [h]er mouth … slightly open, her tongue between her lips" (p. 49). Next, when he sees her crying so bitterly, she is actually lying on her bed and he, having furtively climbed up a ladder and in through the bedroom window, is on the bed with her, trying to comfort her – in this story where beds are so curiously foregrounded. When, a bit later on, Melusine, in snake form, visits or seems to visit his own bed,

> he felt he must touch her now, let her know that he was with her, not afraid of her, that, as much as an ordinary person could, he understood, and did not shrink from her in this awful form.
>
> Besides. He wanted to touch her. Even like this. (pp. 119–120)

But clearly here, Roger's development is not being treated only in sexual terms. The physical attraction runs side by side a sense of moral responsibility, similar to the unselfish consideration he is also starting to show for his mother and sisters. Banks is at pains to emphasize that, in local legend, the Melusine figure has symbolized both evil and good, an ambiguity also apparent, we might note, in its occurrences within both folklore and high culture more generally (Krell 2000). In his dealings with the contemporary manifestation, Roger has the insight to see through the diabolically reptilian appearances to an innocent vulnerability and need of love. His feelings for the snake-girl he believes he sleeps with are strongly protective, and after Serpe's death he can even see that Melusine, though now released from the abusive relationship, may actually be mourning a loss. Not that he has always managed to understand her. On the contrary, readers whose initiation into life's darker sides is already more advanced than his will have guessed at explanations still beyond him. When, for Melusine's benefit, he tried to imitate the writhing of her hips as he had seen her dancing in the street, she became quite distraught, her own experience leaving her only too apt to pick up the sexual overtone of which he himself was not yet fully conscious. And when, during the excursion on the river, he wilfully distanced the children's boat from the parents' boat despite his father's instructions to the contrary, Melusine was overwhelmed by an extreme, and for Roger completely incomprehensible dread of what filial disobedience might lead to. Yet even so, throughout the novel his thoughtful and honest attempts to understand her will constantly stimulate readers to try to empathize with her for themselves.

9.3   The risk of dishonest overtactfulness

Banks clearly means there to be a sense in which Melusine, no less than Roger, matures towards adulthood. Her true metamorphosis is evidently supposed to be from an abused girl, not into a huge snake, but into a chatelaine. In the novel's last chapter, when Roger's parents have realized that the only way to help him is to take him back to La Vendée and let him try to find Melusine again, there, sure enough, she is in the old family home, but newly happy and triumphant. Or to put this another way, with the dramatic death of M. Serpe and the burying of the snakeskin in the compost heap, the novel's Gothic elements have come to an end. The ancient chateau does *not* finally go up in flames. Instead, Melusine has started to make herself the mistress of it, moving pieces of furniture back into their rightful places, and opening doors and windows to let in air and sunshine. It is not clear how she will be able to restore the place to its full glory. Yet by refusing to go and live with the Canadian uncle, by simply being where she feels she belongs, she has already prevented a certain rapacious lawyer from selling the estate from under her and pocketing the money. She is turning into an agent to be reckoned with.

For most adult readers this conclusion will probably seem pure fantasy. But here the fantasizing is no longer dramatized as Roger's but is unapologetically Banks's own. She is presenting the episode, not as something weird and wonderful experienced by Roger when Melusine's suffering was at its height, but as something that really could have followed when the immediate cause of the girl's suffering had been removed. Adult readers may enjoy this attractive turn of events without being the least bit convinced by it. But there is a considerable risk that in child readers it could implant too optimistic a notion of the prognosis for incest victims.

Admittedly, some of the older clinical findings suggested that sexual abuse during childhood made psychological difficulties in later life neither less nor more likely, and could even be benign (Briere and Elliott 1994:54, fn. 4). And although by the time Banks was writing *Melusine* this comfortable conclusion had already been widely rejected, clinicians were still saying that roughly a third of all survivors were reporting no long-term negative effects (Kendall-Tackett *et al.* 1993). In addition, there was an increasing awareness that nomethetic research methods could easily result in generalizations which would not apply to every particular case. "[A]lthough ... survivors tend, as groups, to have more problems than their non-abused peers, there is no single universal or uniform impact of sexual abuse, and no certainty that any given person will develop any posttraumatic responses to sexual abuse" (Briere and Elliott 1994:63). For reasons which were still not fully understood, some victims managed to cope with what had happened to them far better than most others (Spaccarelli 1994).

But although Banks's Melusine could in principle have been one of these more fortunate individuals, clinical findings still make amply clear that the dice are loaded against such happy outcomes (Kendall-Tackett *et al.* 1993; Briere and Elliott 1994; Hilton and Mezey 1996). Incestuous paedophilia leaves the large majority of victims with severe problems, ranging from low self-esteem and feelings of guilt, to a bitter sense of betrayal, painfully obsessive memories and dreams, and radically distorted attitudes and behaviour, sometimes including violently destructive tendencies which, as in the case of Melusine's sister, can also be self-destructive. In order to achieve some degree of spiritual well-being, most survivors need the proactive support of either a professional therapist, close family members, or friends, and preferably support of all three kinds, often over a long period of time.

In self-justification Banks could certainly appeal to the need to protect her young readers, and even to offer some hope to the small minority of them who are themselves the victims of incest. Yet the trade-off between such tactful benevolence and the demands of truth is very problematic here, since in a child who has recently endured a prolonged exposure to incestuous paedophilia, and who also knows that her elder sister took her own life as a release from that same fate, Melusine's degree of uncrushed self-reliance is so very far from likely. Whereas Roger's fanciful perceptions of her reptilian metamorphoses were well in accordance with the disnaturing torment of her ongoing suffering, the fanciful authorial description of the young chatelaine's abrupt and total recovery is not truthful to anything like the same extent, and this in a novel where, as I say, the fundamental truthfulness of some very strange happenings is explicitly raised as an issue. The protective pleasantness which Banks maintains by way of Roger's snake fantasies goes hand in hand with a basic honesty towards her young readers. That further kind of legitimation is something which the protective hedonism of her final chapter conspicuously lacks.

Melusine's unlikely success in fending so well for herself might have emerged as less of a fantasy if accompanied by some glimpses of her own most intimate thoughts and feelings. Although literary writers are sometimes forgiven for telling stories which are not only improbable but downright impossible, such poetic licence is conditional, as Aristotle noted, upon the writing's being powerful enough to render the impossible convincing. Indeed, said Aristotle, "[a] convincing impossibility is preferable to what is unconvincing even though it is possible" (Potts 1968: 58). Banks, by not taking readers inside Melusine's own mind here, fails to make the victim's improbable though not impossible resilience really believable for an adult reader, or really trustworthy for a much younger one.

Here I am close to echoing a complaint lodged by Maria Lassén-Seger, who finds this novel unsatisfactory because it inscribes Melusine's experiences so entirely within the discourse of other people, and of Roger in particular (Lassén-Seger 2006: 176–182). It marginalizes Melusine in her own story, at least as seen by Lassén-Seger, who would perhaps have preferred, throughout the entire novel, something more like Francesca Lia Block's narratological set-up in *The Hanged Man*. If so, on that particular point I should disagree with her for the reason already indicated: Banks's own narratological set-up is well gauged to her somewhat younger target audience. But Lassén-Seger's more general implication that Banks ultimately trivializes Melusine's sufferings must, I think, be upheld. Whereas Roger's interview with the psychologist would have been an ending that was well-judged and finely suggestive, the final chapter Banks then goes on to offer is a utopian excess which even wrenches the ancient legend of the original Melusine against the grain, completely reversing its traditional narrative logic. That first Melusine, having married Raymondin on condition that he will never try to see his wife on a Saturday, rewards his compliance by bearing him children and contributing to his more general prosperity. In particular, she uses her magical powers to create his fabled castle of Lusignan. But when Raymondin, during one of his wife's Saturday transformations into a snake-woman, finally spies on her, what ensues is a family tragedy, and very much to the accompaniment of Lusignan's collapse into ruins. Although Banks's fantasy of the ancient chateau re-awakening to the touch of the newly radiant young chatelaine is just the kind of happy ending for which Roger was so keen to return to France, Banks would arguably have done much better to leave both him and her young readers with such desires unsatisfied, since, given the nature of an incest victim's most likely prognosis, they could not be satisfied except by implying half-truths.

The most appropriate way for an early-teens novel to deal with Melusine's ultimate fate would have been, I think, through silence. If the story had ended simply
with Roger's visit to the psychologist, it would not have had the hedonistic closure
of a traditional children's novel, yet would still have been, not only undamaging, but
also completely honest as far as it went. Without confronting young readers head-on
with the most disturbing kind of subject-matter, it would nevertheless have firmly
intimated that cases of incestuous paedophilia do occur, and involve suffering about
which there would be more to be said if and when they are ready to take it in. In this
way, the facts of traumatic pain would have been treated with no less consistent a
respect than that accorded to the intellectual and emotional capacities of the book's
target audience.

9.4   Genuine communication despite age differences

Minus its last chapter, Banks's novel is, I would claim, a most notable instance of
genuine communication, and especially in its use of indirect narration through the
eyes of Roger, a narratological arrangement in which it happens to resemble another
very good children's trauma novel from the same period: Gillian Cross's *Pictures in
the Dark* (1996), which is told from the point of view of Charlie, who thinks he sees
his classmate, the paternally bullied and terrorized Peter, transforming himself into an
otter. The justification for such indirectness is partly mimetic, in that, although some
children do suffer traumatic experiences, most children do not. As Aristotle might
have put it, the non-traumatic point of view is the more probable. Yet mimetic claims
quickly merge into ethical considerations. I have already said that traumatic experience is not humanly superior. In principle, every human being's story, Roger's no less
than Melusine's, is equally deserving of attention. And I have also tried to show that
Banks's presentational indirectness suitably protects young readers from ideas and experiences with which they are not yet ready to grapple, but without preventing readers
who are already more mature from getting to grips with the realities which Roger's
lively fantasy still embroiders in its own way.

But then there is one further ethical consideration, it seems to me. Even children
who are normally friendly, even children like Banks's Roger or Cross's Charlie, are
themselves in a position to exacerbate the psychological damage suffered by trauma
victims of their own age. As clinicians have known for a long time, even a victim "who
was relatively unstigmatized by the molestation itself may undergo serious stigmati-
zation if later rejected by friends" (Finkelhor and Browne 1985: 538). Although most
children are not traumatized, when they come into contact with children who are,
they often perceive them as "strange", and may therefore make them the targets of
their own bullying or instinctive drives, as when Roger is surprised by his burgeoning
lust for Melusine. The tussle between the adolescent Roger's strengthening desire to

understand, help and protect her and his persistently superstitious, alarming and libidinous fantasies about her dramatizes issues which are bound to arise between child
victims of trauma and other children who are more fortunate. It is a dramatization
through which Banks, without resorting to outright didacticism, could well be doing
a very great deal to stimulate thought and sensitivity in her young readers, drawing
them gently into a mode of response that is genuinely dialogical.

Trauma literature for teenagers is presumably here to stay, and the balance it calls
for between frankness and tact, between ethical sensitivity in the representation of
trauma victims and ethical sensitivity to young readers, will continue to offer an awesome challenge to writers' powers of judgement. Banks's novel, I have argued, is not
immune to serious reproach, because her final chapter involves, as I see it, far too
complete a victory of tact over frankness. But her unfailing tact is itself noteworthy,
especially since all her previous chapters are unfailingly frank as well. What they give
us is a story about incestuous pedophilia which, by being seen through the eyes of an
*un*victimized child whose own initiation into sexuality is more ordinary, can make
large concessions to child readers' most primitive psychological mechanisms, while
also gently suggesting a more adult view of things. This kind of uncoercive communication is both mirrored and promoted though the conversations in which Roger, his
parents and the psychologist compare notes against the continuously running background of Roger's atavistic fantasy-life. Such plotting creates a mental space where
the different generations can enter into an undamagingly genuine dialogue about extremely difficult issues, a dialogue which, as the book's own literary community goes
on growing, may well do something to reduce the amount of the real-world suffering
caused through unempathetic ignorance. The community is in principle a large one,
after all, including as it could, not only both children and adults, but individuals whose
experiences of pain and pleasure may have been in widely varying proportions.

CHAPTER 10

Communicational ethics
and the plays of Harold Pinter

10.1 Coercive or genuine?

The previous studies here have voiced a post-postmodern interest in communicational, and especially literary-communicational ethics. This they have located in a dialogical comparing of notes which takes place between authors and their audiences, not least on the topic of communicational ethics in general as represented in their literary texts. It will therefore be fitting, I think, to devote a final study to the plays of Pinter, in which the human interaction of characters on stage is so peculiarly foregrounded *as* interaction, and which have led to such persistent comment on Pinter's own way of relating to his audiences.

A perusal of existing criticism suggests that the two key questions now calling for discussion can indeed be framed in language familiar from earlier pages here. First, to what extent are relationships between characters on the Pinter stage infused with communicational coerciveness, and to what extent with genuineness – with a negatively capable respect for the human other? Secondly, in comparing notes with his audience about his characters' communication on stage, how coercive, and how communicationally genuine, is Pinter himself?

The terms of the discussion so far can be traced back to Pinter's own comments on his work. But it would be inaccurate to say that his pronouncements actually *created* his audience. After the flop of *The Birthday Party* in 1958, many theatregoers soon found themselves entertained and engrossed by his work quite spontaneously, even when theatre critics remained somewhat nonplussed. What his self-description and -analysis did do, whether in letters to newspapers, in interviews with journalists, critics and scholars, in speeches acknowledging the receipt of literary prizes, or in the remarks he addressed as an actor or director to other actors or directors, was to put words into the mouths of puzzled reviewers and other professionals, from whom lines of explanation and interpretation could then percolate downwards to such members of the general public who wished to cultivate their enthusiasm in a more articulate form, even if articulacy brought no guarantee of overall coherence.

That the plays themselves did not make clear what to say about them was one of the most fundamental features on which he commented. Here he resorted to a claim which, even if totally honest, had deep roots in both ancient and Romantic accounts of poetic inspiration and was that much less likely to seem strange and unconvincing. The genesis of a play, he said, was something over which he had no personal control. It simply came to him, presumably from his unconscious mind, sometimes in the form of a memory. Most typically it was a phrase or an image or a constellation of initially nameless and sometimes sexless characters, which then irresistibly demanded that he meditate upon its implications and draw them out into a full-blown text. Even when a new play was completely written and ready to be staged, he would often profess great intellectual uncertainty as to what it was about. As a director of his own plays, although he sometimes gave actors a fairly detailed idea of the biographical and emotional background to the characters they were supposed to represent, he could also be cagey in the extreme. He could say, for instance, that on such and such a point "the playwright" did not seem to have been very specific. Or speaking *as* Pinter the playwright, he could protest that he knew nothing more about some particular character than what the character actually says and does after coming in on stage: "I have no fucking idea. I know everything about McCann [in *The Birthday Party*] after he walks through that door – I know nothing about him on the other side" (Billington 2007: 107).

To use the term discussed in my Introduction, his suggestion was in effect that his work included a strongly apophatic dimension, a line of argument subsequently taken up by some of his most influential admirers. Peter Hall, perhaps the greatest of all directors of the plays apart from Pinter himself, commented that "[t]he mystery to me is that there is communication in the theatre which is beyond words" (Hall 2005 [1974]: 137). Michael Billington, author of the magnificent Pinter biography, sees a telling similarity with mystical elements in T. S. Eliot's *Four Quartets*, of which Helen Gardner remarked that

> Mr Eliot has not at the back of his mind an idea or argument which could have been expressed quite simply, and which he is purposely disguising. These poems do not begin from an intellectual position or a truth. They begin with a place, a point in time, and the meaning or the truth is discovered in the process of writing and in the process of reading.   (In Billington 2007: 242)

– even if Pinter, at least in reference to some of his own work, would perhaps have added that a comprehensive meaning or truth might never be discovered at all.

When he was still no more than a little known provincial actor, and well before the staging of his first play, *The Room*, in 1957, he wrote down some private thoughts which, since coming into the public domain, can only have confirmed admirers in their sense of his writing's apophaticism. A note dating from 1950, when he was 20 years old, contained an inimitable re-wording of Keats's description of Shakespeare's negative capability. In writing of human life, Pinter commented, Shakespeare is essentially dealing with a huge wound. In the wound, "[a]ll postures are contained", and

> Shakespeare does not attempt to sew up or re-shape [the wound], whose pain he
> does not attempt to eradicate. He amputates, deadens, aggravates at will, within
> the limits of a particular piece, but he will not pronounce judgement or cure. Such
> comment as there is is so variously split up between characters and so contradic-
> tory in itself that no central point of opinion or inclining can be determined.
>
> (Pinter 2009: 14–15)

Then in 1955, having read *Murphy*, *Molloy* and *Malone Dies* for himself, but relying
for his knowledge of *Waiting for Godot* on a letter from his friend Mick Goldstein
which had described its London debut, he wrote back to Goldstein suggesting that the
central question raised by the new play was *not* one which Beckett could have been
expected to answer.

> It seems to me that as he does not answer his question, his message can only be
> that he, for one, can not see, or is not prepared to hazard, an answer. In other
> words, surely the sole and necessary answer to the question is the play itself. ... If
> the question was answered explicitly, the question would cease to exist, it would
> be consumed in the answer. There would be no impulse, no work, no play.
>
> (Pinter 2009: 17–18)

That the young Pinter greatly admired what he saw in Shakespeare and Beckett as a
fundamental abstention from definitive statement is beyond doubt. The likelihood
that he would try to emulate it in his own future work could not have been stronger.

Sure enough, in a letter to *The Times* in 1959, by which point *The Room*, *The Birthday Party*, *The Dumb Waiter*, and *A Slight Ache* had all received their first performances, he made public exactly this ambition:

> In many British plays I find myself put off by the spectre of the author looming
> above his characters, telling them [the audience] at every stage just what they are
> to think about them. I want as far as possible to leave comment to the audience;
> let them decide ...   (Billington 2007: 107)

Then, in a now published letter to his friend Guy Visayan in 1965, by which time he
had notched up further triumphs such as *The Caretaker*, *The Collection*, *The Lover*, *Tea
Party* and *The Homecoming*, he seemed to suggest that at least one important aspect of
negative capability came quite naturally to him. Speaking of his own plays, he noted:
"I don't feel myself more critical of any one character as opposed to another. I love and
detest the lot of them" (Billington 2007: 64–65).

These and other similar remarks are often quoted in the Billington biography,
where individual plays are discussed in their light. Describing Pinter's typescript
re-drafting of *The Homecoming*, for instance, Billington notes that "anything that
pre-empts the audience's judgement" was systematically altered, as when Teddy's

originally very patronizing attitude towards his wife Ruth on their arrival at his child-hood home in London's East End was much toned down (Billington 2007:167). At one point Billington somewhat loses his sense of proportion, it seems to me, writing almost as if neither Shakespeare's plays nor Keats's remarks on their negative capability had ever seen the light of day:

> The American writer Paul Auster in *The Art of Hunger* claims: "The one thing I try to do in all my books is to leave enough room in the prose for the reader to inhabit it. Because I finally believe it's the reader who writes the book and not the writer." In the same way, Pinter suggests that it's the audience that completes the play. In the light of structuralist criticism, which at its most extreme banishes the idea of the author, that may not seem especially heretical. But when you recall the extent to which drama has always traded in biographical specifics, fixed conclusions and consequential speech, you realize the revolutionary nature of Pinter's breakthrough. This does not preclude the dramatist having strong political convictions or charting his own private landscape. But in banishing the notion of the omniscient author and transferring moral responsibility to the audience, Pinter even in 1958 was starting to change the whole nature of the dramatic experience.
> (Billington 2007:95)

In the present book I have been suggesting that all great literary authors, most certainly Shakespeare, and even the omniscient and intrusive Dickens, allow audiences and readers an ample freedom. But if Billington were to say that Pinter abstained from coerciveness to a very striking degree, he could well be on safer ground, and I shall later be examining aspects of Pinterian dramaturgy which support such a view. Billington is more judicious, it seems to me, in his comments on *One for the Road*, in which Nicolas, the main character, is a sadistic interrogator employed by the powers that be. Here Billington suggests that "one of the many reasons why *One for the Road* works is that Pinter, while detesting everything Nicolas stands for, is able to enter into his consciousness and understand both his fanaticism and fear – in short, to turn what might have been a didactic tract into drama" (Billington 2007:297). In effect Billington is arguing that, in this play, Pinter's uncoercively negative capability achieves drama and avoids dogma precisely by keeping things complicated, a claim which is perfectly plausible. In my Introduction I mentioned just such a case, in the very different form of that mediaeval nativity play from Wakefield.

Accounts of Pinter's negative capability would seem to be corroborated by the variety of responses which the plays arouse in audiences. Among the actors who have commented on this, Douglas Hodge is particularly suggestive:

> You rehearse and rehearse, and you get into this bitter, sour world, and then it astonishes you the laughs you get when you get into the theatre! But there are moments on some nights where it's almost unstoppable, and you just have to go with it and ride the waves. And that's a wonderful experience.

> But there can be another night, when the play's as potent, when there's utter si-
> lence, and you come off and say, "We didn't do anything different then!" And yet
> you could hear a pin drop the whole evening.   (Hodge 2005: 203)

There is also ample evidence that even different members of one and the same audience
can react in different ways at one and the same time. In the words of Sam Mendes,
who directed the National Theatre's revival of *The Birthday Party* in 1995,

> when the work is being played properly what the audience takes is different, case
> to case, audience member to audience member. Because it has resonances in all
> directions and therefore you're seeking *not* to be reductive about simple meaning.
>   (Mendes 2005: 221)

Perhaps even more to the point, a simultaneous activation of varied responses can
go on within the mind of just a single theatregoer. Speaking as one such individual,
Alastair Macaulay has testified that "[t]o feel the elusiveness of … [Pinter's] meaning
is, in fact, to come very close to its essence". Indeed, "not understanding a Pinter play
is a very great pleasure" (Billington 2007: 384).

Macaulay and many others have come to think of that pleasurable incomprehension as stemming from what they describe as Pinter's keen sense of human beings'
inscrutability. According to Macaulay, "[t]he poetic beauty of his art" lies in his baffling characters (*ibid.*). This was another line of commentary started by Pinter himself,
and it has often culminated in the claim that his plays pioneered a new kind of realism
here, by portraying human beings who are just as confused or confusing as people in
ordinary everyday life. One of Pinter's seminal comments was:

> A character on the stage who can present no convincing argument or informa-
> tion as to his past experience, his present behaviour or his aspirations, nor give a
> comprehensive account of his motives is as legitimate and as worthy of attention
> as one who, alarmingly, can do all these things. The more acute the experience the
> less articulate the expression.   (Pinter 2009: 28)

And in any case,

> I've always been aware that my characters tend to use words, not to express what
> they think or feel but to disguise what they think or feel, to mask their actual
> intentions, so that words are acting as a masquerade, a veil, a web…
>   (Billington 2007: 371)

Conversations in his plays are effective, he suggested, "because people fall back on
anything they can lay their hands on verbally to keep away from the danger of knowing and of being known" (Pinter 2005 [1966]: 58). Taking its cue from such authorial
remarks, part of the received wisdom is now that characters in Pinter, either because
of an inner turmoil and failure of self-understanding, or because they sense that the
true lie of the land is too embarrassing, painful or dangerous to be acknowledged,

are authentically mystifying: mystifying to each other on stage, and mystifying to the audience as well.

This, though, seems to presuppose an underlying psychic reality which could in principle be *de*-mystified and made quite intelligible. Here all the talk about Pinter's negative capability is, as it were, forgotten, and when this line of discussion is further elaborated the anomaly becomes even more striking. In 1962 Pinter himself said that his characters, despite their inarticulacy or lack of frankness, can understand each other perfectly well, and are also perfectly intelligible to audiences.

> We have heard many times that tired, grimy phrase: "failure to communicate", …and this phrase has been fixed to my work quite consistently. I believe the contrary. I think that we communicate only too well, in our silence, in what is unsaid.
>
> (Pinter 2009: 34)

His suggestion was that, as human beings, we are all perfectly well aware that both we and other people constantly evade the truth, both about other people and about ourselves: "To enter into someone else's life is too frightening. To disclose to others the poverty within us is too fearsome a possibility" (*ibid.*). In part the critical consensus is now that not only such fears, but also other emotions as well are indeed conveyed by Pinter's characters, and in such a way that any human being would be able to grasp them. The gestures performed, and the words spoken, may well not carry their normal, default significances. A character who says, like Disson in *Tea Party* or Stott in *The Basement*, something such as "I am a very happy man" will almost certainly be on the verge of total breakdown and simply singing in the dark. Yet neither other characters nor the audience will have any difficulty in spotting a camouflaged emotional state, as long as their take on the actual words being used is not too literalist. As Peter Hall put it, "At first sight … [what is going on in a Pinter play] is an enigma, but the situation, if you attend to the play, is blindingly clear" (Hall 2005 [1974]: 135). Or to give that other remark of Hall's in a fuller form: "The mystery to me is that there is a communication in the theatre which is beyond words, *and which is actually concerned with direct feeling*" (Hall 2005 [1974]: 137, my italics), which is another point at which the critical orthodoxy came to praise Pinter for a new kind of realism. The penetrable mystery of emotional communication is, the argument goes, not a mystery confined to the theatre alone but one that is very common in everyday life. *À propos* the 1964 film version of *The Caretaker*, Penelope Gilliatt said that

> [t]he fact that people often talk like this, replying not to the meaning of the speech but to what they can guess about motives, is such a simple and compassionate observation that it is hard to think how so many writers of dialogue have managed without it for so long. For unless your characters are Jesuits, to follow a question by an answer that makes logical sense is actually a very stylised way to write lines. It is one of the things that gives Shaw's plays, for instance, their rather inhuman surface. But this is the way most dramatists have written, even when they intend to be realistic.
>
> (Billington 2007: 125)

That human beings easily understand words and behaviour involving non-default meanings or illogical oddities such as "the repetitions, hesitations and lacunae of everyday speech" (to borrow a phrase from Billington (2007: 391)) is certainly confirmed by linguistic research. Saussure's foundational insight was that the relationship between the two halves of the sign, the signifier and the signified, is arbitrary and conventional, and that any human being, by pragmatically processing an utterance in relation to the circumstances under which it is used, can readily see whether the significance to be attached to it is this conventional one or something different. So there is no earthly reason why a canine quadruped should be called a "dog"; in English this denomination is simply the well established norm; and when somebody calls their enemy a "dirty dog", the fact that the real reference is no longer to a canine quadruped is entirely unproblematic for anybody who happens to be listening, because the interpretation of metaphorical implications is one of the most routine aspects of all pragmatic processing. Similarly, if a teacher in a stuffy classroom were to say to one of the pupils, "Do you think you could open a window?" this utterance would not entail the same meaning as these same words would have if used by a doctor examining a patient with a hand injury. In the terminology of speech act theory, the doctor's use of these words would be a direct speech act. In conformity with its logical and syntactical form, it would be a real question, inviting the patient to answer "Yes" or "No" or "I'm not sure". The teacher's use of the words would be an indirect speech act. It would not really be a question at all, and the pupil addressed would have no difficulty in pragmatically interpreting it as a politely implicated command. Pinter's stage, linguists would say, is an arena of active pragmatic processing, of frequent speech-act indirection, and consequently of heavily loaded implications as well, and is to this extent life-like. And when Peter Hall influentially supplemented Pinter's own comments on the masquerade of words by noting that we can all make masks of our own faces, this was again in total conformity with current linguistic wisdom, which takes full account of body-language, and speaks of paralinguistic indirection no less readily than of the more purely verbal variety. Our facial expressions, said Hall, do not directly represent our thoughts and feelings, but are rather a kind of constant modification of ourselves in relation to others. "We are playing the game – that is, social intercourse. ... You have this storm of emotion inside you, and you change tack ... from second to second, behind the mask" (Hall 2005 [1974]: 143, 151). Everybody knows about this, he continued, because everybody does it, and everybody bears it in mind when confronted by other people, realising that, if they do not, they can expect some unwelcome surprises. Such observations have been amply corroborated by sociolinguistic and dialogue-analytical research in descent from Ervin Goffman's *The Presentation of the Self in Everyday Life* (1959).

In continued agreement with scholarship not only in the Goffmanian traditions of sociology and linguistics, but within branches of research as diverse as psychology and psychoanalysis, ancient and modern rhetorical studies, political science, and economics, Pinter and the critics he influenced have tended to suggest that such linguistic and paralinguistic deceptions are even easier to decipher if your view of human nature is of a particular kind. In a nutshell, their claim has been that in any process of human interaction you can be fairly sure that what is really going is some sort of power struggle. This is the assumption which was very common in postmodern criticism written under the aegis of Foucault, and which in earlier studies here I have challenged by arguing that human beings are also capable of what I call genuine communication: a manner of communication which respects the autonomy of the human other. In the present study, one of my main concerns is to inspect any signs of genuine communication between the characters on Pinter's stage, and in Pinter's own way of treating his audience. But despite all the commentary to the effect that he does write complex plays and does allow spectators to think about them for themselves, there is a wealth of other commentary suggesting that the action on stage is always a power struggle, and that once an audience takes this for granted everything else falls into place quite unambiguously. One of Pinter's own most influential remarks here was his point about verbal masquerade in its full form:

> I've always been aware that my characters tend to use words, not express what they think or feel but to disguise what they think or feel, to mask their actual intentions, so that words are acting as a masquerade, a veil, a web, *or used as weapons to undermine or terrorise.*   (Billington 2007: 371, my italics)

Sometimes he claimed he was dealing with a human lust for dominance whose forms of expression were far less extreme, albeit frequently in evidence. "[B]attling for position", he said, is "a very common, everyday thing" (Pinter 2005 [1966]: 61). Yet in the interviews and essays where he most fully commented on the nature of human interaction, the emotional colouring of his language – the recurrent image of the great wound of human life, and vocabulary such as the already quoted "danger", "frightening" and "fearsome" – was unmistakably alarmist, which doubtless gave a cue to one of Peter Hall's most striking remarks:

> [In discussing his plots] [m]y vocabulary is ... about hostility and battles and weaponry, but that is the way Pinter's characters operate, as if they were all stalking round a jungle, trying to kill each other, but trying to disguise from one another the fact that they are bent murder.   (Hall 2005 [1974]: 139)

This line of comment can almost seem to be associating Pinter's plays with the black-and-white of Victorian melodrama, or with the whodunits he knew so well from his early days in provincial rep. In fact Hall's advice to would-be directors of Pinter is that there have to be two different kinds of rehearsal: first, rehearsals which help actors to grasp a play's underlying truth, which Hall explicitly calls the play's melodrama; and then, rehearsals in which the melodrama is totally covered up again and the surface re-ambiguated.

> [H]ot passions have to be understood and then resolutely masked. … Most actors yearn to let some of this emotion out, to reassure the audience by telling them what they are feeling. It is an anxiety to communicate, but it is not only unnecessary, it is dangerous. … Excess must be avoided.   (Hall 2009: 168)

And the Hall tradition was perpetuated in Sam Mendes' handling of *The Birthday Party*. Mendes said that

> you have to discuss the secret play. Because in the end the actors must know what *they* mean. But I don't want the production to make that clear. The mystery of the play remains for the audience.   (Mendes 2005: 220)

If members of the audience do ever come to some sort of clarity about a Pinter play, Hall and Mendes would presumably say that this will be by replicating the search for the melodrama or secret play that has already been undertaken by the actors in rehearsal. Their line of thought seems to be that in real life people disguise the brutely selfish things they are up to; that Pinter and anybody else can see through such disguises; that in his plays he has a hard and fast idea of what is really going on; that he allows the characters to mask this over, perhaps even stretching the bounds of realism; that during rehearsals the director and actors both strip off this disguise, but only to put it back on again; and that the audience will at first be pleasurably mystified by it, but are in principle no less capable of eventually seeing through it than the playwright, the director and the actors before them. In other words, at least on the question of the interaction taking place between characters on stage, this approach to directing does not ultimately see a Pinter play as involving a negatively capable indeterminacy. Rather, what Pinter writes is viewed as a kind of cover-up, undertaken in order titillate the audience in somewhat the same way as a novel by Agatha Christie. The questions raised by the play are assumed to contribute to nothing more than a simple hermeneutic mystification, as we might call it. To switch metaphors slightly, the characters on stage, in collaboration, as it were, with Pinter himself, are thought of as having buried some rather unpleasant, but typically human secrets, which the theatre audience can then have the thrill of digging up again. Any dimension of, say, sociological, philosophical or ethical complexity is taken to be not very pressing at all.

In this kind of commentary, then, the criterion of negative capability seems to be very much in abeyance. Nor is this the end of it. Much Pinter criticism focuses even more exclusively on coerciveness: a coerciveness in the characters on stage, and coerciveness in Pinter himself *vis à vis* his audience.

One circumstance to register here is that over the years Pinter's own public pronouncements increasingly emphasized, in complete harmony with the findings of critical discourse analysts and communication (*sic!*) critics such as Rybacki and Rybacki (discussed in my Introduction), that disturbing and often well camouflaged conflicts take place, not only in the sphere of private life, but within relationships between the human individual and concentrations of social or political power. Pinter was never greatly concerned with the ideology of particular political parties or move-ments. He seldom went in for talk of political left and political right. But in 1988 he was at pains to argue that even his earliest plays had contained more essentially political tensions and subterfuges than had at first been noticed, in that they took "an extremely critical look at authoritarian postures" (Pinter 2005 [1988]: 85). In a letter of 1958 to the director Peter Wood, who was then about to begin rehearsals for that ill-starred first production of *The Birthday Party*, he had already explained that, in the shape of Goldberg and McCann, "the hierarchy, the Establishment, the arbiters, the socio-religious monsters arrive to effect alteration and censure upon a member of the club" – upon Stanley, that is – "who has discarded responsibility … towards himself and others" (Pinter 2009: 23–24). And not only in many of the poems and speeches written during the last twenty-five years of his life, but also in the contemporane-ous plays *Precisely* (1983), *One for the Road* (1984), *Mountain Language* (1988), *The New World Order* (1991), *Party Time* (1991) and *Ashes to Ashes* (1996), he came to focus on such broadly political coercion with even greater intensity. In several of the speeches – by no means only in his Nobel acceptance speech of 2005 – he particularly inveighed against the language of American and British foreign policy, as the velvet glove on an intransigently iron hand. "[W]ords like freedom, democracy and Chris-tian values are still used to justify barbaric and shameful policies and acts" (Pinter 2009: 219–220). And in all such contexts, whether early, middle or late, he was no longer thinking of the verbal obfuscation of ulterior motives as inevitably endemic to all language use and more or less negotiable. He was rather seeing it as a most grave aberration which needed to be robustly challenged and rectified. Though still invok-ing the image of masquerade, here he could rage against what he felt was

> a disease at the very centre of language, so that language becomes a permanent masquerade, a tapestry of lies. The ruthless and cynical mutilation and degrada-tion of human beings, both in spirit and body, the death of countless thousands – these actions are justified by rhetorical gambits, sterile terminology and concepts of power which stink. Are we ever going to look at the language we use, I wonder? Is it within our capabilities to do so? (Pinter 2009: 219)

It is in discussing the plays' representation of human interaction as falling within this broadly political perspective that both Pinter and the commentators following in his wake have been at their furthest remove from that emphasis on negative capability which is so prominent in many of their other remarks. Billington, in particular, says that it is futile to complain that the most openly political plays are lacking in "poly-phonic richness". They should rather be seen as

> public acts designed to draw attention to the bureaucratic euphemisms sur-rounding nuclear war (*Precisely*), the abuse of human rights (*One for the Road*), the oppression of minorities (*Mountain Language*), bourgeois complicity in gov-ernmental cruelty (*Party Time*). (Billington 2007: 289)

Firmly endorsing Shaw's claim that *A Doll's House*, though unlikely to outlive *A Midsummer Night's Dream*, will have "done more work in the world" (*ibid.*), Billington is representing Pinter as a writer determined to convey a reformer's message. "Pinter's point is ..." is one of his biography's most frequently recurring expressions. True, this is often hedged with concessions to a negatively capable Pinter: the plays are "not essays – they don't make statements or advance theses – but..."; "[n]o Pinter play is ever a statement, but ..."; "Pinter, consciously or not, exposes ..."; and so on and so forth (Billington 2007: 156, 175, 170) . But Billington, who so enthusiastically credits Pinter with revolutionizing "the whole nature of the dramatic experience" by "banishing the notion of the omniscient author and transferring moral responsibility to the audience", and who so interestingly argues that *One for the Road* is rescued by Pinter's complex empathy with Nicolas, the bad guy, from a tract-like dogmatism, can also lambast the idea that drama expresses multiple viewpoints as a "liberal fallacy" (Billington 2007: 289). Having warmly praised Pinter's emulation of Shakespeare and Beckett's alleged abstention from definitive statement, and having approvingly noted, too, that in mid-career Pinter came to admire Proust for his view of art itself as the only supreme truth, Billington then exculpates him for having apparently turned tail, and begins to celebrate him for having increasingly questioned Proust's detachment from a social and political purpose, and for having written plays of an altogether different tendency: a play such as *Party Time*, for instance, whose "central point" is said to relate to bourgeois privilege, to narcissistic materialism and indifference, and to the power of the state, a play which instead of offering "multivalent richness" is "a deadly assault on our own moral myopia", making the "point" that "the myopic acceptance of suffering and oppression in the name of order and stability is morally unforgivable"; or plays such as *Mountain Language* and *One for the Road*, with their allegedly "jolting effect on the lazy liberal conscience" (Billington 2007: 330, 331, 334, 229). This, despite *One for the Road*'s allegedly negative capability, which in his more Shavian moments Billington presumably sees as nothing more than the lazy liberal's escape clause.

Without Billington's work, my own would have been impossible. Apart from Pinter's second wife, Antonia Fraser, nobody writes about Pinter so humanely and readably. And as far as I can see, nobody has a more accurate and comprehensive grasp of the complex life-story, of the entire range of his writing in different genres and for different media, of the by now very substantial history of stage production, and of the tradition, already formidably voluminous, of Pinter commentary. Yet Billington is himself both a product and upholder of that tradition, and his biography is the most eloquent and extended expression of what at first seems to be a foundational contradiction within the entire critical orthodoxy. In Billington we see writ large the same apparent paradox that arises in a large number of other commentators whose authority or aims are on a smaller scale. We need only return to Alastair Macaulay, for instance, who despite claiming that to feel the elusiveness of Pinter's meaning is to come close to its essence, and that "not understanding a Pinter play is a very great pleasure," also wrote a letter to Pinter in which he offered a precise definition of a deeply political implication in *Ashes to Ashes*: that no man is an island.

One way to get a grip on this state of affairs is to place Billington on Pinter side by side with Thackeray on Fielding, even if the communicational pre-history of Thackeray's comments was not entirely similar. As noted in my Introduction, Thackeray's remarks on *Tom Jones* reflected two very different lines of commentary on that novel which had been endemic within Anglophone culture ever since its first publication: that it was superficial and immoral; and that it was realistic, warm-hearted and entertaining. Earlier commentators on Fielding, unlike Billington's predecessors within Pinter criticism, had tended to opt entirely for the one claim or for the other. Thackeray now clearly felt that there was a strong element of truth in both of them, and he had the honesty to say so in a public forum. From that point onwards, there was a likelihood that other commentators would follow suit, and an orthodoxy develop within which the two different claims, even if they continued to be perceived as contradicting each other, or as at least in tension, would both be experienced as true in their own way. Or still more likely, perhaps, the perceived truth of both claims would perhaps tend to remove any sense of contradiction or tension altogether, as has been the situation with regard to the two main claims within the Pinter orthodoxy ever since Pinter's own remarks helped it to get under way: the claim about negative capability and the claim about coerciveness.

The emphasis on negatively capable genuineness of communication and the emphasis on communicational coerciveness certainly can seem incompatible. But the fact is that Billington and other commentators within the Pinter community have clearly *not* experienced much of a contradiction here. To my knowledge, they have not gone in for a self-conscious assessment of their own arguments according to the criteria I have been applying here. But if they did, they might well end up saying that the emphasis of their commentary on genuineness and its emphasis on coerciveness are both perfectly appropriate.

This claim would be plausible. To stay with Thackeray for a moment, one of the strengths of his composite comment on Fielding was that, on mature consideration, it could not be dismissed as an impossibility in nature. From everything we know about human beings in general and authors in particular, it seems perfectly likely that some individual author could be superficial, immoral, realistic, warm-hearted and entertaining all in one go. Similarly, the present book has been taking for granted that negatively capable genuineness of communication and communicational coerciveness are both real possibilities, which can both be evidenced by one and the same human being.

On the one hand, and as those numerous scholars in the fields of linguistics, rhetoric, psychology, psychoanalysis, economics, sociology and political science have demonstrated, coerciveness is very widespread indeed. Whether in personal relationships or in relationships between the individual and larger social entities, it is deployed in the interests of controlling the human other. Often this is blatantly unethical, and there can be much sinister deviousness as well. But not necessarily so. As I was arguing in connection with Pope's Humanist nervousness, coercion can also stem from a sincere and responsible concern for a private or a public good. Certainly literary authors whose depiction of life overlooked the coerciveness of much human interaction would be unconvincing, and unable even to get a tellable story off the ground. As I suggested *à propos Great Expectations*, tellability will seldom arise from a collection of characters who simply leave each other alone. Usually a story does not start until peace and tranquillity have come to an end. And as for writers who themselves try to be completely uncoercive *vis à vis* their readers, they will come across as far too insubstantial, as would also have been the case with the negatively hyper-capable poet fantasized by Keats in his epistolary self-portrait:

> A poet is the most unpoetical of any thing in existence; because he has no Identity – he is continually … filling some other Body … . [H]e has no self … . When I am in a room with People if I ever am free from speculating on creations of my own brain, then not myself goes home to myself: but the identity of every one in the room begins to [*for* so] to press upon me that I am in a very little time an[ni]hilated – not only among men; it would be the same in a Nursery of children.
> (Keats 1954 [1818]: 172)

As shown in different ways by John Bayley (1976: 107–156) and Christopher Ricks (1974), Keats's own greatest writing was far more Keatsian than he himself seems to have realized. The negative capability of a writer who achieves the status of a major literary author does not result from some kind of self-denying ordinance, and writers aiming at a historically impossible impartiality will strike readers as either lightweight or dishonest.

On the other hand, to the extent that the aforementioned numerous scholars in many different fields claim that all human interaction is a power-play, and a power-play within which verbal expression and gesture seldom directly entails its normal, default significance, they are certainly distorting reality in the way I was trying to pinpoint in my Introduction. By the same token, a dramatist whose stage representation of human interaction was entirely along those same lines would be risking a mannerism no less extreme, albeit of a diametrically opposite kind, than that of George Bernard Shaw, whose characters can as Penelope Gilliatt noticed be so relentlessly transparent and articulate. As for dramatists whose own addressivity is predominantly coercive, they make little headway and are soon forgotten. That *The Doll's House* actually seems to be bearing up no worse than *A Midsummer Night's Dream* is because Ibsen was far more negatively capable than his social and ideological concerns had led Shaw to assume.

Bearing in mind, then, literary-communicational considerations and the complications of Pinter criticism to date, what might a communicational critic expect from a new examination of the plays? Most obviously, perhaps, there is a strong likelihood that the characters on stage will be decidedly coercive communicants. In theory, any human being is also capable of more genuine communication. But Pinter's characters have not usually been seen as examples of this and, as a motif in narrative, genuine communication in any case has low tellability. As for Pinter's own communication with his audience, the omens are ambiguous. On the one hand, it would not be at all surprising to find that, like other writers accorded high literary status, he addresses spectators in a spirit of negatively capable genuineness. There has been much comment to the effect that his writing does leave his audience free to make up their own minds. On the other hand, there has also been much discussion of the interpretative problems this raises for them, so that we can perhaps begin to wonder whether the freedom has actually been *forced upon* them as an empowerment for which they were not necessarily ready. In his public role as a celebrity and political activist, Pinter was not self-depreciating in the slightest (Derbyshire 2009). His plays, too, could well bear a clear stamp of his own identity, and his political plays in particular have already been loudly blamed in some quarters for a strong coerciveness. Under these circumstances, the main critical questions might even become: Is there a risk that his coerciveness may finally override his genuineness? Could it be that he is ultimately no more ethical a communicant than his on-stage characters are often said to be?

10.2   Different types of play, ideology, and character

Pinter's exceptionally long career as a playwright is often divided into three main phases: "menace", from 1959 to 1967; "memory", from 1968 to 1981; and "politics", from 1983 to 1996. These phases correspond with three major foci in commentary on his manner of writing: his scarily enigmatic writing, some of which is generally found to be very funny as well; his more poetical writing; and his more readily understandable and overtly committed writing (Zarhy-Levo 2009). They also parallel the three main kinds of influence he is said to have had on other dramatists: as a comic writer; as a Modernist writer; and as a political writer (Waters 2009). It is to such discussions of dramatic genres and styles that Billington is contributing, for instance, in some remarks on differences between menace and memory:

> Up to and even including *The Homecoming* [1965], his stage plays are still formally derived from his work [as an actor] in rep; the works after 1965 … are more clearly influenced by his experience of film and television. He attempts in dramatic form something very close to what James Joyce and Virginia Woolf accomplished in the novel: the theatrical equivalent of the interior monologue.
> (Billington 2007: 191)

Equally, Billington's emphasis on the "points" Pinter is trying to make in the political plays, and on their consequent lack of "multivalent richness", classifies them, too, as a clearly separable group.

This chronological tripartition of his career is useful for my purposes, and I shall often use the labels menace, memory and politics as if they were unproblematic. In fact, however, the following plays, listed here with dates of first performance as given in the Faber and Faber editions, fit the scheme a good bit more tidily than others:

Plays of Menace
A Slight Ache 1959
A Night Out 1960
Night School 1960
The Caretaker 1960
The Collection 1961
The Lover 1963
The Homecoming 1965

Plays of Memory
Landscape 1968
Silence 1969
Night 1969
Old Times 1971
Monologue 1973
No Man's Land 1975
Betrayal 1977
Family Voices 1981
A Kind of Alaska 1981

Political Plays
Precisely 1983
One for the Road 1984
Mountain Language 1988
The New World Order 1991
Party-Time 1991
Ashes to Ashes 1996

The plays which do not fit this scheme so comfortably are of several different kinds. First, there are three plays written during the years of the menace phase which strongly anticipate the political plays: *The Hothouse*, written in 1958 but not actually staged until 1980, and dealing with a state-run institution for experimental psychiatric care; *The Birthday Party*, first performed in 1958, and again dealing, as emphasized by that letter of Pinter's to Peter Wood, with an officialdom which seeks to control the individual; and *The Dumb Waiter*, first performed in 1960, where the overarching collective power belongs to some sort of mafia. Secondly, also during the years of the menace phase, Pinter wrote four plays, *The Room*, *The Dwarfs*, *Tea Party* and *The Basement*, first performed in 1960,[1] 1960, 1965 and 1967 respectively, all of which strongly anticipate the memory plays. Their menace is caught through the prism of an interior monologue or personal dream- and fantasy-life, sometimes involving strange transvaluations of blindness and sight and a vagueness about many facts and names. Thirdly, during his middle and late career there were occasional throwbacks to menace. In *Victoria Station*, a sketch first performed in 1982, a telephone controller unsuccessfully tries to elicit cooperation from a London cabby who, as it turns out, may still be on a high after apparently murdering a female passenger. In the longer and more important *Celebration*, first performed in 2000, the menace has considerably mellowed, as if in proportion to the festive gathering's resolute consumption of alcohol. And fourthly, there is *Moonlight*, first performed in 1993, but in many ways a throwback to memory.

Under these circumstances, it is important to recognize continuities between the phases of menace, memory and politics, and I shall often need to supplement the conventional tripartition of Pinter's career with an alternative grouping, into plays of the private sphere and plays with a more public dimension. These can be listed as follows:

Plays of the private sphere
A Slight Ache 1959
The Room 1960
A Night Out 1960
Night School 1960
The Caretaker 1960
The Dwarfs 1960
The Collection 1961
The Lover 1963
Tea Party 1965
The Homecoming 1965
The Basement 1967
Landscape 1968
Silence 1969
Night 1969
Old Times 1971
Monologue 1973
No Man's Land 1975

---

1. This is, as I say, the date given in the Faber and Faber edition. In fact *The Room* was first performed by the Drama Department of Bristol University in May 1957.

Betrayal 1977
Family Voices 1981
A Kind of Alaska 1981
Victoria Station 1982
Moonlight 1993
Celebration 2000

Plays of the public sphere
The Birthday Party 1958
The Dumb Waiter 1960
The Hothouse 1980
Precisely 1983
One for the Road 1984
Mountain Language 1988
The New World Order 1991
Party-Time 1991
Ashes to Ashes 1996

In the plays of the private sphere which have usually been grouped under "menace", access to a character's psyche can be rather difficult. To use the metaphor of orthodox Pinter criticism, both the audience and other characters on stage have to penetrate behind the mask. In *The Room*, *The Dwarfs*, *The Basement* and *Tea Party*, on the other hand, and in those plays of the private sphere which have usually been grouped under "memory", a character's psyche is far more readily accessible to the audience than that of other people in real life. Here spectators wrestle, not with a dearth of information, but with what can easily feel like an excess. But in plays of both these sub-varieties, the most prominent relationships dealt with are those between husbands and wives, between parents and children, between siblings, between lovers, and between male friends, and the dominant value system by which characters judge themselves and each other, and which Pinter offers as a criterion to the audience as well, is based on bourgeois ideals of family, love, and friendship.

In the plays of the public sphere, the presentation of characters is more straightforward, with neither a shortage nor a superabundance of clues to their inner life, so that a playgoer will have little difficulty in assessing what they are feeling and trying to do. Here, too, some characters are motivated by the ideals of family, love and friendship. But such characters tend to be the victims of other characters who are, or who aspire to be, members of some kind of some larger enterprise: a gang, a firm, some sort of official body or authority or institution, or a nation state. These are characters who, by appealing to the example of tradition, to the safety, prosperity or political rights of the people, to the dictates of reason, or to the will of the official religion's God, seek to legitimate an extreme coerciveness, which can take the most obscene forms of physical and psychological violence.

There can be no mistaking that Pinter's own sympathies here are with those of the private individuals under threat from the ruthless collective. Indeed, throughout his work the dictates of reason in particular are invoked only by unsympathetic characters, as when two officials discuss the acceptable level for a death toll in *Precisely*, or by characters in their more unsympathetic moments. In *Moonlight* the dying Andy tells his wife Bel to forget about rationalism altogether:

> Rationality went down the drain donkey's years ago and hasn't been seen since. All that famous rationality of yours is swimming about in waste disposal turdology. It's burping and farting away in the cesspit for ever and ever. That's destiny speaking, sweetheart! That was always the destiny of your famous rational intelligence, to choke to death in sour cream and pigswill.   (IV, 322–323)[2]

Granted, Andy's scatological savagery must be seen in relation to his own dysfunctional family. With his daughter childless and already dead, and with his two sons refusing to come to his own deathbed, his mind will have been searching around for extra-familial sources of comfort, and has presumably found a rationalistic atheism unhelpful. But many other Pinter characters would agree with him. In fact if they could have read Austin Quigley's account (2009) of their own communication with each other as negotiating, through a more or less reasonable process of trial and error, contractual arrangements for how to live side by side within a community, they would probably have said that it greatly underestimated the role of emotion in human life.

Not that many Pinter characters are driven by religious feelings. The dying Hirst in *No Man's Land* describes religion as merely a "glorious misery" which used to influence people in the old days (III, 382). For the dying Andy in *Moonlight*, religion is apparently as unsatisfactory as rationalism, and little more than window-dressing. When Bel says that, thanks to her convent school education, his expression "taking the piss" leaves her "somewhat nonplussed", Andy retorts: "Nonplussed! You've never been non-plussed in the whole of your voracious, lascivious, libidinous life" (IV, 321). And a similar attitude underlies some of Mark's comments in *The Dwarfs*. Mark's friend Len had been wondering why, although his own house is older than Mark's and has been in his family for many years, he does not feel that he has roots or a home. Then he suddenly switches to religion:

> LEN: Do you believe in God?
> MARK: What?
> LEN: Do you believe in God?
> MARK: Who?

---

2.   All quotations of Pinter's plays taken from the Faber and Faber edition: Pinter 1986 (= vol. I), Pinter 1991 (= vol. II), Pinter 1997 (= vol. III) and Pinter 1998 (= vol. IV).

LEN: God.
MARK: God?
LEN: Do you believe in God?
MARK: Do I believe in God?
LEN: Yes.
MARK: Would you say that again?   (II, 99)

Like rationality, God in Pinter is for authorized bullies such as Nicolas, that official interrogator in *One for the Road*, and for others, too, who lack a strong sense of attachment to families, lovers, friends. So the insecure Len, who may have contemplated religion as a way to boost his ego, later betrays both Mark and their mutual friend Pete. In most Pinter characters, religious identity is simply weak or nonexistent. Goldberg in *The Birthday Party* has a Jewish name, but in his treatment of Stanley behaves like the Nazi persecutors of Jews. And although many commentators have said that the family in *The Homecoming* seems as Jewish as the one Pinter himself grew up in, any Jewishness here is matter of sociocultural markers rather than of faith.

This is not to say that as private individuals Pinter's characters never have serious thoughts about ethics or a possible afterlife, for instance. But here such concerns are quite unattended with the trappings of official religion. Good behaviour is a question of being a good member of the family, or a faithful friend or lover, and eschatology, as so often in folklore, involves ghosts who revisit the earth out of an anxiety for their loved-ones. In *Moonlight* Andy and Bell actually see their daughter's ghost, who as a dramatis persona also has the last words of the play, and seems to be hoping for a full union with her parents' own ghosts in due course. In *Family Voices* a dead father is still longing to get in touch with his wayward son. In *Party Time* Dusty's brother Jimmy may already have been murdered by the authorities, so that his dazzling appearance at the end of the play would also be that of a ghost. And in *No Man's Land* Hirst, who is himself so close to death, speaks with loving reverence of friendly ghosts from way back when.

But if the domestic ideals of family, love and friendship are the supreme values for many characters, this is by no means the whole story, since in the plays of the private sphere these ideals can entail obligations no less demanding than, in the plays of the public sphere, those of the more broadly collective ideologies of an institution or business enterprise, or of politics, rationalism or religion. Unlike John Stokes (2009), I would not say that Pinter dramatizes Sartrean existentialists who refuse to believe in any right doctrine and simply feel social reality and individual experience on the pulses. Many of Pinter's characters positively believe in ideals of family, love and friendship. The only problem is that they fail to live up to them. Instead, as members of a family, as lovers, as friends, they become basically coercive on their own behalf.

10.3   Characters' coerciveness as plotted

As I say, much commentary hitherto has argued that what Pinter called the battling for position is his characters' most important driving force. This claim has been made for his plays of both the private and the public sphere, and has been well backed up with comments on the effect of particular words as used within particular dramatic microcontexts. Often the battle takes the form of a more power-hungry individual actually questioning a potential victim's use of language. As a result, the meanings of words can be twisted from their default harmlessness into implications, many of them metaphorical, which are more sinister.

One of numerous excellent comments on this kind of interchange comes from Katie Mitchell, who directed *Ashes to Ashes* at the Royal Court, London in 2001:

> Think of the pen sequence in *Ashes to Ashes*. She [Rebecca] starts off with: "Well, I put my pen on that little coffee table and it rolled off." He [Devlin] immediately plays very light, and she says, "It rolled right off, onto the carpet. In front of my eyes," and he says, "Good God!" At that point, he's just playing along; and then suddenly she comes in sideways by saying something else: "This pen, this perfectly innocent pen". And he replies, "You can't know it was innocent." He's still playing in a light word-play zone, but actually he's cutting under because he's using the pen as a vehicle to get to *her* about the lover. So the pen becomes *her*. When she says, "Why not?" she is still playing innocent. But then he says, "Because you don't know where it had been. You don't know how many other hands have written with it, what other people have been doing with it. You know nothing of its history."
>
> It's an exquisite piece of writing, but it's about a marriage breaking down. There was a tendency – because there were lots of other signs and signals in the text – to lighten it, as if the couple were playing a game as opposed to actually dealing with separating. They have the skin of the subject, the pen, to protect each other from what they're really transacting, which is: the man's really saying, "How dare you betray me?" and the woman is trying to soften and lighten the betrayal, because it's not about betrayal. It's about these other things that are starting to stir and alter.
>
> (Mitchell 2005: 192)

That there is already a wealth of sensitive analysis along these lines is fortunate. The indirectnesses, the implications, and what one might call the instant agonistics of Pinter's linguistic and paralinguistic surfaces can no longer be lost on serious students of his work. But if discussion of the key communicational issues is substantially to advance, such insights need to be complemented by a sharper focus on the place of individual sequences within the macrocontexts of a play's entire plot. In *Ashes to Ashes*, for instance, one of the things calling for examination is the relationship between the pen sequence and those "other things that are starting to stir and alter", as

Mitchell herself is the first to recognize. By developing this approach to every play, by not allowing ourselves to be permanently buoyed up by the fascinating surfaces of particular interchanges, by also diving down to the longer-term currents and countercurrents underneath, we can develop, not only a sense of the general tendency of communication in each individual play, but a differentiating overview of the communicational tendencies depicted by Pinter's dramatic writing as a whole. A number of the plays actually fall into five different groups, according to the types and outcomes of the coercion gradually unfolded by their plotlines.

One such group consists of seven of the plays of the public sphere: *The Birthday Party*, *The Dumb Waiter*, *The Hothouse*, *One for the Road*, *Mountain Language*, *The New World Order* and *Party-Time*. Here, the collective ideology, or the Machiavellian bravado of those who either serve it or, in serving it, turn it to their own personal advantage, wins hands down, or at least stands a very good chance of doing so. Collective coercion is indeed at a maximum, collective concern for the autonomy of the human individual at an absolute minimum.

True, in *The Birthday Party* the interrogators-cum-detention-officers, Goldberg and McCann, both have moments of unnerving doubt about their unpleasant tasks; Stanley, their victim, does try to fight back; the young woman Lulu and Petey, the man of the house, do lighten the atmosphere with a breath of everyday ordinariness; and Petey not only tells Stanley's tormentors to "[l]eave him alone" but encourages Stanley not to "let them tell you what to do" (I, 79–80). But there is no overcoming their sheer force, both physical and psychological. Stanley is reduced to an inarticulate animal, while Petey's wife Meg, who as a wannabe mother could perhaps have mounted a more robust private-life challenge to the public law-and-order mandate invoked by Goldberg, is totally unaware of what is going on, carried away as she is by her infantile fantasy of being belle of the ball at the nightmare birthday party she has planned for baby Stan, as she thinks of him.

In *The Dumb Waiter*, Gus's qualms about the violent missions he and Ben have to carry out for their organization are more insistent than those of McCann in the earlier play. Ben, too, though he would never admit it to Gus, has his doubts. He cannot deny, when Gus mentions it, that while driving to their present assignment at some unearthly hour of the morning he had suddenly stopped the car in the middle of the road for no real reason that he can think of. But when he does get his final orders from higher up, his job is now to kill none other than Gus, his old buddy, whose loyalty to the cause has presumably become too suspect. The closing curtain leaves the two of them staring at each other, Ben with his gun raised. Will he shoot? Or will he not? There must be at least some chance that at this point he will finally revolt against his superiors. But he is under huge collective pressure.

In *Hothouse*, the focus is on a far higher level of organizational machinery. Gibbs, the manipulative second-in-command, uses the institution's official ideology of caring for the patients and promoting civil peace as a way to usurp the place of Roote, his loquaciously canting boss. In this he is indirectly assisted by Lush, who is as gleefully cruel a cynic as he himself, and by Miss Cutts, who longs to go on enjoying the thrills of assisting him in the experimental terrorization of "volunteers", though she also grants sexual favours to Roote as the local supremo. Although they are basically on his own wavelength, Gibbs does not hesitate to bring about the deaths of both Lush and Miss Cutts, as also of Roote and all the other senior staff, by triggering a patient uprising. This he then explains to the Ministry as the result of a spectacular dereliction of duty on the part of Roote, which has culminated in one patient being killed and another made pregnant, misdemeanours perpetrated, according to Gibbs, by Roote himself. As for Lamb, the connotation "lamb to the slaughter" is fully appropriate. Lamb, completely duped by all the institutional cant, and desperate to play his part in the greater scheme of things, becomes the uncomplaining victim of Gibbs and Miss Cutts's vicious interrogations, and is also saddled with the blame for the patients' fatal release from their cells.

In *Precisely*, the prospect is again of inhumanity and lies under official auspices, as the two boffin-bureaucrats convince themselves that a predicted death toll of twenty million will be perfectly acceptable for reasons of national security, even if one of them would be prepared to admit in public that millions more may be killed in reality. In *One for the Road*, *Mountain Language* and *The New World Order* such horrors are brought even closer, as the interrogators and soldiery unhesitatingly expose harmless citizens to physical and psychological torture in the name of the greater good, even when, in *Mountain Language*, the muddles of state bureaucracy target individuals who are obviously innocent of the ethnic "impurities" from which the body politic is being cleansed. The official mind-set is that things can never be too clean. As Lionel, one of the interrogators in *The New World Order* puts it, "I love it. I love it. I love it. [...] I feel so pure", an outburst on which his colleague Des comments, "You're right to feel pure. [...] Because you're keeping the world clean for democracy" (IV, 277).[3]

In *Party Time*, the chronologically last play of this group of seven, while members of the ruling elite are knocking back drinks and priding themselves on their luxurious new health spa, civil unrest is being firmly quashed on the streets outside, and the high-flying men in the room are clearly just as prepared to exercise physical or psychological dominion over their female partners. Charlotte's husband, however, has mysteriously died, and Dusty's brother Jimmy has mysteriously disappeared. Not perceived by the other characters on stage, but dazzlingly visible to the audience, Jimmy finally appears in an utterly dehumanized state, perhaps, as I say, already another victim of authorized murder: "The dark is in my mouth and I suck it. It's the only thing I have. It's mine. It's my own. I suck it" (IV, 314).

---

3. In quotations from Pinter's plays, three dots are authorial punctuation, whereas three dots within square brackets indicate that I have made a cut.

A second group consists of two plays of the private sphere, *Night School* and *The Dwarfs*, in which individuals are in their own way just as straightforwardly coercive as collective ideology in the political plays, and very successfully so. In *Night School*, Willy returns to his old aunties' home after his latest spell in prison, only to discover that they have rented his room to Sally, a schoolteacher, whom they believe to be broadening her own education by taking courses at night school. In fact Sally's evenings are spent as a dancer and escort at a sleazy nightclub, and Willy recognises her from a photograph taken of her in that setting. When Mr Solto, his aunts' landlord, tracks Sally down to the club in question and truthfully tells her that he has done so at Willy's bidding, Sally, rather than allowing herself to be shamed by a loss of gentility in the eyes of Willy's aunts, packs her bags and leaves. Final score: The usurper is ejected and Willy gets his room back.

In *The Dwarfs*, there are the three close male friends, Len, Mark and Pete, but the stage set consists of only Len's home and, with a space in between, Mark's home, which is perhaps one home too few, as it were. Certainly all three men are at times in both homes, and the idea of usurping another man's home is never far away. In the very opening scene in Mark's home, Len and Pete seem to have taken possession during Mark's absence, even though there was no fresh milk in the fridge. And even when a home's owner *is* in residence, a visitor may suddenly offer him one of his own nibbles – a quintessentially Pinterian motif! As this kind of thing continues, and both of Len's friends suggest that he is mentally unstable, Len's insecurities only grow more pressing. In the end he gets on top of the situation by sowing seeds of suspicion between Mark and Pete, so that their bond of friendship breaks, and he himself is left feeling confidently victorious. In his lively fantasy life, he imagines that a team of dwarfs have tidied all of life's filth away for him, which suggests that the attitudes exploited by a collective ideology in plays of the public sphere can also have deep roots in a person's private life. In words with which Lionel in *The New World Order* would have sympathized, the triumphant Len exclaims at curtain, "Now all is bare. All is clean. All is scrubbed." (II, 105).

Just as Willy in *Night School* has no respect for either the public law or more domestic obligations to his aunts, so Len's egoism here is fiercely solipsistic. The mutual loyalty of closely bonded males has a strong attraction for him, but in the end he is insufficiently generous or sure of himself to do anything other than betray that ideal. At the level of plot, both these plays are like tricksters' tales in which cunning individuals force everything into alignment with their own will, for the sake of some rather mean advantage. Manipulativeness of this calibre is, *per se*, no more attractive than the bullying sanctioned by an institution or a state.

A third group consists of four other private-sphere plays, *The Caretaker*, *No Man's Land*, *A Slight Ache* and *A Night Out*, in all of which there are main characters who are energetically coercive, but whose coerciveness does not have the results they are hoping for. The clearest cases of this pattern are Davies the tramp in *The Caretaker* and Spooner the would-be literary man in *No Man's Land*, between whom there is a striking similarity. Both of them are invited home by a man they have met quite casually, Davies by Ashton, Spooner by Hirst, and then they both try to sponge on their generous new acquaintance. In both plays, there also comes a climactic moment when the tone they adopt towards their envisaged benefactor is unmistakably commanding, but to no ultimate avail.

In *A Slight Ache*, the main character is Edward, an upper middle class writer, who wants to get his wife Flora under firmer control. The immediate trigger to his outbursts of sexual insecurity and jealousy is a match-selling tramp, who every day stations himself at their garden gate. Edward invites the match seller in to his study, where he tries to pull rank and give him what Pinter would have called a good bollocking. The match seller himself remains completely silent throughout, but is by now a crucial pawn in the ongoing marital battle. Flora feels so humiliated by Edward's suspicions and misogynist language that she takes the vagrant under her wing, which includes coming on to him sexually. It is Edward who is left holding the tray of matches.

In *A Night Out*, Albert has difficulty adjusting both to the private values of life at home with his mother and to the collective ideology of the workplace and the company football team. A more meaningful bonding could perhaps occur between him and his workmate Seeley, but it would possibly have a homosexual undertone, which would leave Arthur feeling even more awkward and embarrassed than ever – the Wolfenden Report was published only three years before the play's first performance. At all events, his poor showing on the football field has turned the sadistic team-captain against him; he is teased for not flirting with girls at the staff party; he tries to kill his possessive and recriminating mother, and believes he has succeeded; and when he is propositioned by a girl on the street and they go back to her place, his murderous instincts flare up once again. His moment of fiercest joy comes when, having seen through the girl's genteel pretensions (shades of Walter and Sally in *Night School*), he compels her down on her knees to put his shoes on for him. On leaving, he tries to prolong the thrill by throwing her half a crown, as if for the sex they never had. Yet he is already blinking and uncertain, and on returning home finds his mother still very much alive, and now better equipped than ever, of course, to douse him in guilt.

Davies, Spooner, Edward and Albert are the main losers in their respective plays, but in a fourth group, consisting of two other plays of the private sphere, *The Collection* and *Old Times*, coercion's failures are more widely distributed. In *The Collection*, Stella is less than happily married to James and tells him, perhaps in the hope of arousing a bit more interest, that she has cheated on him with Bill, partner of the older Harry. Only she and Bill can know how much truth there is in this, needless to say, and much of the play's surface interaction has to do with their attempts to conceal or reveal, and with James and Harry's attempts to discover and re-position. Harry is increasingly on edge about an erotic attraction which he sees developing between his own Bill and Stella's James, and is correspondingly sympathetic towards the plight of Stella. Both he and she, though in the end ostensibly hanging on to their original part- ners, have clearly lost their affection, if they ever really had it – the well-to-do Harry is particularly conscious that he is merely buying the "slum slug" Bill's favours (II, 143). But Bill and James must be equally discontented, since both of them are chafing at a self-imposed bit, James because he is too inhibited to act out his full sexuality (as possibly with Arthur in *A Night Out*), Bill as the price for Harry's patronage. On the final balance sheet, then, there are losses all round. Unwilling to allow each other an autonomous freedom, all four characters have wilfully tried to force the run of events, but to no true personal advantage.

In *Old Times*, the final reckoning is if anything even bleaker. Here the married couple Deeley and Kate are visited in their house on the coast by Anna, who years ago was Kate's flatmate and only friend in London. In sequences which blend the here and now with each character's memories or fantasies of the past, Deeley sometimes tries to assert his hold over Kate in face of what he sees as a threat from Anna; Anna some- times pays him back in the same coin, implying that Kate is fundamentally hers; Kate sometimes responds negatively to their talk of her as if she had no will of her own; an alleged sexual bond between Deeley and Anna is sometimes flaunted by the one or the other of them, sometimes in an attempt to rile Kate; and Kate finally hits on ways to humiliate both Anna and Deeley, to alienate them from each other, and to exclude them, it would seem, from her own present and future life. Perhaps, then, she is like Len in *The Dwarfs*: too insecure or ungenerous to sustain lasting human bonds with the other two members in the triangle. In which case, her final self-isolation would bring her pleasure of the only kind she can manage. Or perhaps she will feelingly pay the price of her triumph, and be just as desolate as the other two. During the course of the play, all three of them have tried to exert extreme interpersonal force, but none of them ends up with anything worthwhile to show for it.

Kate's dubious achievement belongs to a world in which coercion's victories are sometimes Pyrrhic, and of this there are still clearer examples in the fifth group of plays, all three of them dealing with the private sphere: *The Basement*, *The Lover* and *The Homecoming*. Like *The Dwarfs* and *Old Times*, *The Basement* is about a threesome. The homeless Stott, with his lover Jane in tow, turns up at the basement flat of his old friend Law, and accepts Law's invitation to stay with him indefinitely. As the culmi- nation of a process which involves, as in *The Dwarfs* and *Old Times*, a fair amount of talking behind each other's backs, and which extends over several changes of season in the world outside and several refurbishments of the basement's own decor, each of the two men manages to snatch hold of something, but also loses something. Stott usurps Law's flat. Law commandeers Stott's girl.

In *The Lover*, too, a pair of characters both win and lose, but this time there is no third party. Richard and Sarah are a married couple, she a housewife, he something in the City, who have spent many afternoons pretending to be unfaithful to each other, but with Richard himself in the role of "Max", Sarah's lover. He now tells Sarah that he thinks of his partner in this mock-adultery as simply a whore: "Just a common or garden slut. Not worth talking about. Handy between trains, nothing more" (II, 155). When this rather disconcerts Sarah, he assures her that he thinks of his *wife* very differently: he respects and loves her. But then it turns out that he is actually tired of their charade in its present form, and Sarah realizes that the only way to hold the relationship together is openly to combine the role of whore and wife at one and the same time of day. She tells him:

> I have other visitors, other visitors, all the time, I receive all the time. Other afternoons, all the time. When neither of you [neither Richard nor "Max"] know, neither of you. I give them strawberries in season. With cream.   (II, 181)

This may remind the audience that, just before Richard turned up as "Max" this after-noon, John the milkman, realistically enough, but at first sight rather anomalously in such a tight-knit play, had knocked on the door to ask Sarah whether she would like some cream. "Mrs. Owen just had three jars. Clotted" (II, 163). But even if Sarah has not actually had sex with John the milkman and others, she is clearly capable of weav-ing her everyday life into the fantasized possibility, and perhaps this is all Richard really wants. "You lovely whore" are his, and the play's last words (II, 184). Sarah, that is to say, has forced him to stay with her, and he has forced her to allow him his rampant fantasy-life. But they will both be aware of the downside: that what is left of their relationship is not nearly as precious as a different kind of relationship would have been, a relationship which could have included, for instance, a glad acceptance of parenthood. When, in the role of "Max", Richard says he has had enough of afternoon infidelity, Pinter's notation – the scripted pauses – confirm that the dialogue now takes an especially significant turn:

> SARAH. Why?
>
> *Slight pause.*
>
> MAX. The children.
>
> *Pause.*
>
> SARAH. What?
> MAX. I've got to think of the children.
> SARAH. What children?
> MAX. My children. My wife's children. Any minute now they'll be out of board-ing school. I've got to think of them.   (II, 171)

Richard and Sarah may not have children of their own, or they may have children they have packed off to boarding school. But even though Richard is nominally in his fan-tasy role here, Sarah is clearly taken aback when he starts to talk about children, and about children as objects of concern, and in her next response she defensively moves the fantasy in a direction which both maternalizes her and infantilizes him:

> *She sits close to him.*
>
> SARAH. I want to whisper something to you. Listen. Let me whisper to you. Mmmm? Can I? Please? It's whispering time. Earlier it was teatime, wasn't it? Now it's whispering time.
>
> *Pause.*
>
> You like me to whisper to you. You like me to love you, whispering. Listen. You mustn't worry about … wives, husbands, things like that. It's silly. It's really silly.
>
> (II, 171)

As could also be said of Deeley and Kate in *Old Times*, Richard and Sarah are *psychologically* childless. Under their roof, their own little sexual "games" (their word (II, 171)) are the closest thing to the joys of children playing, and are not really very close at all.

Not that a larger household would guarantee greater happiness. In *The Homecoming*, Pinter's next play, coercion's Pyrrhic victories are fought within a fair-sized family. Teddy and his wife Ruth, both of London working class origins, return to his childhood home from America, where he is a university professor and they have two children. Since the death of Jessie, his sexually promiscuous mother, there has been no woman in the East End house, and his father Max, his Uncle Sam, and his brothers Lenny and Joey all perk up on the advent of Ruth. She for her part clearly feels more at home in lower class London than as a university wife in the States, and starts to exercise a sexual power over her male in-laws. In the end, Teddy returns to his job and his children without her, and she agrees to be the new woman of the London home, and to bring in an income as a prostitute working in one of the flats which Lenny runs for such purposes. According to Billington, Ruth is a feminist heroine, who rids herself of a domineering husband and achieves power over a whole houseful of men. According to Joan Bakewell, Ruth's final situation is utterly degrading. Both these views are correct, and the similarity to Sarah's self-demeaning containment of Richard in *The Lover* is close. Nor do the other characters do any better for themselves. In some senses Teddy is perhaps as well rid of Ruth as she of him, but he will smart from his loss of face and control. Lenny may make a few bob out of her, but his boasting of violent assaults on other women has already failed to cow her. Joey is drooling at the prospect of a live-in sex-object, but has already spent two hours in a bedroom with her without getting all the way. Uncle Sam is emboldened by the general upheaval to reveal what he knows about his dead sister-in-law's infidelity with MacGregor, Max's best friend and business partner, but then has a near-fatal heart attack *coram populo*. And Max himself, though accusing Sam of a diseased imagination here, and delighted to have what he thinks of as a new wife in the house, is tormented by a suspicion that she will be just as untrustworthy as he basically knows Jessie to have been.

10.4 Genuineness on stage

As this suggests, Max's attitude towards both his dead wife and his daughter-in-law is ambiguous. Jessie he remembers as follows:

> Mind you, she wasn't such a bad woman. Even though it made me sick just to look at her rotten stinking face, she wasn't such a bad bitch.   (III, 17)

And although on first being introduced to Ruth by Teddy he describes her "a smelly scrubber", "a stinking pox-ridden slut" (III, 49), at other times his talk of home and family, and of both women's place therein, is a flood of treacle:

> Well, it's a long time since the whole family was together, eh? If only your mother was alive. Eh, what do you say, Sam? What would Jessie say if she was alive? Sitting here with her three sons. Three fine grown-up lads. And a lovely daughter-in-law. The only shame is her grandchildren aren't here. She'd have petted them and cooed over them, wouldn't she, Sam? She'd have fussed over them and played with them, told them stories, tickled them...   (III, 53)

In one way the play presents the audience with a complete travesty of what commentators have variously called the Victorian or bourgeois or Jewish ideal of the family unit. Yet in words like these that ideal curiously lives on, and in the play's closing tableau can be sensed as superimposing itself on the entire array of relational dysfunction. Apart from the self-absenting Teddy and still recuperating Sam, as the curtain descends the males are all clustering around Ruth. Lenny is standing, as always keenly watchful. But Joey and Max are actually kneeling to her, Joey at peace as she gently strokes his hair, Max begging for a kiss and perhaps her blessing. Throughout the play we have been following the destiny of human beings whose relentless coerciveness brought none of them control in a form they would have wished. But these parodic echoes of an earlier age's dream intimate a capacity they might have had for habits of interaction that were less territorial, less possessive, less manipulative, less abusive. As Pinter himself put it, there is "a great deal of love" in this play but the characters "simply don't know what to do with it" (Pinter 2005 [1980]: 74). Selfish, coercive, manipulative they may be. But this is by no means the whole story.

According to Ruby Cohn, "it is by his bitter dramas of *de*humanization that he [Pinter] implies 'the importance of humanity'" (Cohn 1962: 58, her italics). This would be a good gloss on several of the dramas of both public and private coerciveness discussed so far. What makes the unspeakably sad *Old Times*, for instance, so completely unlike a tragedy by Shakespeare is that its three characters, for all their extraordinary flights of memory, fantasy and intellect, are fundamentally unselfconscious. Whereas Macbeth immediately knew, and could find the words to say, that by murdering Duncan he was also murdering sleep, Kate, Deeley and Anna simply do not see that their urge to mastery is stifling their own humanity. In a case like this, Cohn's word "implies" is exactly right, I think. It is Pinter himself who implies an explanation of why the three of them are so unhappy.

But in *The Lover*, the limitations of Richard and Sarah's infantile and degrading sexual fantasy is something they are on the brink of voicing for themselves, and in the case of *The Homecoming* "implies" would definitely be too weak a word, since characters themselves not only positively wish, in one corner of their heart, for a more genuine communication, but are actually beginning to express this longing, albeit self-mockingly or incoherently. Particularly important in channelling family feelings and the desire for decent behaviour is Uncle Sam, who, while fondly remembering Jessie's best qualities, has for all these years been trying to cover up the more dubious ones; who may himself have been in love with her; who tells Teddy how much she had loved him (Teddy); and who did not walk out of the family home even when Max sacked him from the family's butcher's shop in favour of MacGregor, the man who really won Jessie's heart.

Somewhat more articulate are the two literature-buffs Richard and Jerry in *Betrayal*, another play of the private sphere. Jerry and Richard's wife Charlotte, by having a long-drawn-out affair, have damaged *her* marriage with, and *his* close friendship with, Richard. The terrible pain which, underneath civilized exteriors, wracks all three of them is the measure of their self-awareness. All three of them know what has been lost, and by dramatizing the story in reversed chronological order Pinter is able to trace how their present misery grew over time, from the first small seed of a stolen kiss at a party, gradually developing several branches. On discovering his wife's adultery several years ago, Richard started to betray Charlotte through an affair of his own, and quite possibly started to abuse her physically as well. He certainly tells her that he has always liked Jerry more than he liked her. "Maybe I should have had an affair with him myself" (IV, 72). Equally harsh is his misogynistic refusal when she wants to join Jerry and himself for one of their *après*-squash lunches. But then again, Jerry, too, feels bitterly betrayed, and by Richard, since Richard did not reveal that he had already known for a long time that Charlotte and he were lovers. For several years already, Richard has been feeling that his relationship with Jerry, despite the squash, despite their shared literary interests, has gone sour. Now Jerry feels the same, but even more bitterly, perhaps because he knows that it was his own irresponsibility that started it all.

Most self-knowing of all Pinter's characters is Hirst, Spooner's potential benefactor in *No Man's Land*. Hirst is a true poet, even if part of this play's bizarre comedy stems from a running contrast between the free-wheeling volubility of the more mundane Spooner and Hirst's halting difficulty of utterance, a contrast which Spooner finds amusing:

> HIRST: Tonight … my friend … you find me in the last lap of a race … I had long forgotten to run.
>
> *Pause.*
>
> SPOONER: A metaphor. Things are looking up.   (III, 338)

Hirst achieves understanding only by a colossal mental effort, undertaken in the very teeth of death, and with lashings of alcohol to dissolve all shame or pride. Nowhere are Pinter's famous notational dots more profoundly effective than when this character staggers his way towards painful illumination. Where has he lived his life? "No man's land … does not move … or change … or grow old … remains … forever … icy … silent" (III, 340). Not that his life has seemed completely worthless to him. On the contrary, his past is now a hallowed memory, sustained by his most cherished possession, an old photograph album, from whose pages the faces of his friends, long since ghosts, now namelessly peer out at him. You must "[a]llow the love of the good ghost", he explains to Spooner. "They possess all that emotion … trapped." (III, 383). Yet he also senses that, in this important respect, he is already a ghost himself, and always has been. "There are places in my heart … where no living soul … has … or can ever … trespass." (III, 388). *Although* he is a poet, he has resisted an ultimately human communication, as have Len in *The Dwarfs* and Kate in *Old Times*. *Because* he is a poet, unlike Len and Kate he can put the human cost of his own coldness into words, part of that cost being that, unlike the more self-giving Aston in *The Caretaker*, whose brother Mick to some extent protects him against the liberties intended by Davies, he now has nobody who loves him enough to defend him against spongers. In his interchanges with Spooner's rivals, the thuggish parasites Briggs and Foster, he is well aware that his domestic circle during his declining years is not what it might have been, and his sardonic tone reflects this. "What would I do without the two of you? I'd sit here for ever, waiting for a stranger to fill up my glass" (III, 351) – a stranger such as Spooner, he doubtless hints, just to needle them.

The deep desire of some characters for genuine communication, and the ineradicable sense of other characters that genuine communication is something they have missed out on or have themselves destroyed or resisted, substantially qualifies many earlier accounts of Pinter's plays. Yes, he does show us people who are ruthlessly coercive in all the ways I have mentioned, and whose coerciveness, sometimes extremely violent, sometimes successful in its own way, sometimes less so, can be such an impoverishment in human terms. But there are also characters who have not lost contact with their own humanity. Even Douglas in the political play *Party Time*, whose clenched fist is going to make the whole country function properly, whose pulse races "rat-at-tat-tat" as the storms sweep across his island retreat, describes the peace which he and his fellows in the ruling class are aiming to impose in words whose appeal would not be restricted to that elite. You "know what God intended for the human race, you know what paradise is", he says, "when the storm is over and the night falls and the moon is out in all its glory and all you're left with is the rhythm of the sea, of the waves" (IV, 300). As it stands, this still has nothing at all to do with actively embracing the human other's otherness. But at least it is pleasant to think of Douglas's fist unclenching itself at times, and there are plays of the private sphere in which a hard-soft duality like his, sometimes polarized between two different characters, acquires more human depth. Seen in this light, the strand of orthodox commentary descending through Hall's remarks on characters operating "as if they were all stalking round a jungle, trying to kill each other, but trying to disguise from one another the fact that they are bent on murder" seems seriously unbalanced.

On Pinter's stage there is certainly huge scope for antagonism between one character and another, not least as a result of class distinctions. Susan Engel has commented that, until John Osborne's *Look Back in Anger* (1956), "working-class characters, or Irish characters – anyone who wasn't middle-class and English was written patronizingly, because they weren't written by working-class writers" (Engel 2005: 174). Pinter had a working-class background himself and was no more patronizing about working-class characters than Osborne. But when Engel goes on to remark that Pinter himself did not remain "imprisoned by his working-class origins", an important addition is in order. Working-class origins *do* imprison characters in his plays. He does not dramatize felicitous transgressions of class boundaries within a rainbow society. When characters of differing social origin rub shoulders, they retain their distinguishing marks of language and identity, there is absolutely no hybridization, and a person's class identity does not figure as an otherness that can be embraced in genuine communication. On the contrary, social difference is a sure-fire trigger to coercive agonistics. The literary Richard *versus* the match-selling vagrant in *A Slight Ache*; the poet Hirst *versus* the gangsterish Briggs and Foster in *No Man's Land*; the well-to-do Harry *versus* Bill, his toy-boy slum-slug, in *The Collection*: in cases like these, nobody on stage has even the slightest expectation that class distinctions are about to fade away, and in *The Homecoming* any such possibility is rejected quite explicitly. On revisiting his Cockney roots, the meritocratic Teddy feels no more comfortable than Ruth has felt as a university wife in America. "You wouldn't understand my [scholarly] works", he tells his father. "You wouldn't have the faintest idea what they were about" (III, 69).

But then there is Disson in *Tea Party*. Disson used to down ten or so pints a night, and still finds it difficult to tie a tie. His idea of a festive reception is still not a cocktail party but a tea party. He has certainly climbed the ladder. He now owns and runs a firm which markets the latest refinements in sanitary ware; he speaks the managerial jargon of success, efficiency, purpose; and Diana, his second wife, hails from the landed gentry. But the two sons of his first marriage adjust much better to upward social mobility than he does, and he feels deeply insecure in his new household, both culturally and sexually. At the wedding, his best man was Diana's brother Willy, who also gave her away, and who in proposing a toast for each of them clearly implied that Disson had had an extraordinary stroke of luck to make such a catch. Disson does everything he can for both Diana and Willy: he gives Willy a senior position in the firm and quickly makes him a partner; and on Willy's suggestion he makes Diana Willy's secretary. Partly, he is putting them in his debt so that they will forget his humble origins. But he also really wants them to be happy: happy members of his happy family. In bed, both on the wedding night and on their first anniversary, he is anxious to know whether he makes Diana happy, and keen to assure her that he has never been happier himself. But when he asks her point blank whether she married him for love, she says, honestly enough, that she admired his clarity of mind and surety of purpose. He cannot help feeling that she is more spontaneously fond of her brother than of him, and perhaps as a compensation for such marital anxieties he allows himself a coyly sexual relationship with Wendy, his own secretary. This is something he does not really want to acknowledge, even to himself, so that a routine develops whereby he touches Wendy only if he is wearing her chiffon scarf as a blindfold. And perhaps because there is much else that he does not really want to see in his situation, he begins to suffer attacks of psychosomatic blindness. At the office tea party he lays on for the first wedding anniversary, he again has himself blindfolded, and Pinter dramatizes the difference between the innocent things the groups of guests are really saying to each other and the products of Disson's paranoiac fantasy – not least, a vision of Willy making love to both Wendy and Diana on his own desk. Nothing could be more painful for an audience to watch, and what makes it all so pitiful is the urgency of Disson's desire for everything to turn out well for everyone. He is basically sociable and generous, and part of his idea for the tea party was that his smart new family and his own lower class parents should enjoy themselves by meeting and mingling with each other. Yet the only thing that brings Diana and his mother closer together is their attempt to shake him out of his hallucinatory fit, which hardly recommends itself as a model of genuine communication across lines of difference.

"Desire" is not a frequent word on Pinter's stage. But unbearable desire is exactly what characters often feel, most excruciatingly of all, as with Disson, a desire for the genuineness of reciprocated love. Nowhere is this more poignantly clear than in *Landscape*, the first of the plays usually described as memory plays, in which Duff and Beth are sitting on either side of the kitchen table in a large country house, each of them making both longer and shorter utterances throughout, but apparently without hearing each other's voice. Though married, they inhabit two different universes, which are minimally co-extensive.

Beth remembers a beach, sand dunes, the sea, her man lying in the dunes, herself suggesting that they have a baby. "Would you like that?" (Pinter 1997: 167). She used to feel beautiful, and she remembers the gentleness, the lightness, as men held her arm through a door, down steps, or touched the back of her neck. But *with one exception*, she registers. Then there was that day after the party, when she went out with the dog into the misty morning in her blue dress, and later watched children running through the grass, up the hill. She used to draw, too, but did not draw her man. She drew bodies in the sand, trying to keep in mind the basic principles of drawing, "[s]o that I never lost track. Or heart", even though sometimes "the cause of the shadow cannot be found" (Pinter 1997: 186). Finally, he turned to look at her, though his own face was in shadow. His touch was soft. "Oh my true love I said" (Pinter 1997: 188).

As for Duff on his side of the kitchen table, the first thing he would like to tell her is that the dog has gone. Then he describes his walk in the rain: how he wondered what the youngsters under the trees were laughing at, how he saw a man and a woman who then disappeared from view. Near the pond there was "[d]ogshit, duckshit … all kinds of shit … all over the paths" (Pinter 1997: 170), and a bit later on a man in the pub criticized the beer, so prompting the landlord to give him back half a crown. But the man said his pint had cost only two and three, which meant that he now owed the landlord threepence. The landlord told him to give threepence to his son instead. But

> I haven't got a son, the man said, I've never had any children. I bet you're not even married, the landlord said. This man said: I'm not married. No-one'll marry me.
>
> (Pinter 1997: 174)

Then the man bought drinks all round and Duff, as an experienced cellarman, told him something of beer's mystery. Beth, too, he feels, is a professional. She made Mr Sykes an excellent housekeeper, and the two of them together were a good team. That Mr Sykes bought her a blue dress was only natural; he was concerned about what his guests would think. But he was certainly a gloomy bugger, and once when he gave a dinner party Beth was very late getting to bed afterwards, and fell asleep immediately. On one occasion Duff was unfaithful to her, but it was nothing serious, he says, and he told her about it, after which they walked to the pond and she kissed his face. Now, they live in the house alone, and

> I booted the gong down the hall. The dog came in. I thought you would come to me, I thought you would come into my arms and kiss me, even … offer yourself to me. I would have had you in front of the dog, like a man, in the hall, on the stone, banging the gong, mind you don't get the scissors up your arse, or the thimble [. …] I'll hang it [the gong] back on its hook, bang you against it swinging, gonging, waking the place up, calling them all for dinner, lunch is up, bring out the bacon, bang your lovely head, mind the dog doesn't swallow the thimble.
>
> (Pinter 1997: 187)

Duff and Beth's parallel streams of memory will leave an audience with some open questions. One of these has to do with the curiously insistent motif of children, and the couple's own apparent childlessness: a greater sorrow to Beth, one might assume, though it could be that Duff is taciturnly masculine here; some fellow-feeling certainly seemed to develop between him and the childless man in the pub. Then again, does Duff quietly suspect, and does Beth silently remember, that she and Mr Sykes made love on the night of the party? If so, was Duff's own infidelity in retaliation? And if so, in retaliation to his retaliation did Beth then go completely cold on him, so that in his desperation he has finally raped her? – which would perhaps be the one exception to all the gentleness she remembers. And *did* the dog swallow the thimble during some such violent commotion? – which could indirectly explain Duff's opening mention of the dog's absence.

But what is absolutely clear is the sheer power of their respective desires, which thanks to the way Pinter has spaced their utterances culminate at exactly the same moment, desires so different in tone – she ravished by the thought of an utter gentleness, he in a white-hot fury – yet both of them utterly dependent for full consummation on the self-giving of the other. Bearing in mind the way things seem to have turned out, both of them are clearly wounded. Yet on both sides of the kitchen table, the desire for a more genuinely communicational union lives vigorously on, fuelled by memory. So much so, indeed, that we can well ask whether the play is dominantly elegiac or open-ended. To apply Hirst's insight from *No Man's Land*, there are places in this couple's hearts where they have not allowed each other to trespass. But given the undying strength of their longing, given that they are twenty to forty years younger than Hirst himself, and given that, unlike Kate, Anna and Deeley in *Old Times*, they are now under no illusion that the final self-surrender they are hoping for in another person can be induced by coercion, each of them might still come to realise that the responsibility for maintaining the reserve between them has not been all on the other side.

In *Silence*, another memory play, we have a threesome once more, but are closer to *Landscape* than might at first appear. Once again there are unconnecting streams of parallel utterance. Rumsey, who is possibly a gentleman farmer, seems thoughtful and calm as he walks with Ellen on high windy ground. Once she came to his house as a child, and she was all curiosity, he all gentleness. Now, at an age when she can cook, she is visiting him there again. He notices that she dresses in grey for him, he refers to her as "my" girl, and he is still gentle. But he is also a willing solitary. Bates, on the other hand, whose social origins are possibly lower, is restless and more bitter. After a bus ride into town, he took Ellen "down around the dumps. Black roads and girders", and to a place his cousin runs. When she meets him he presses the smile off her face. One of his main memories is that he once had a little girl, and told her about the birds resting in trees at night-time. But now his landlady has asked him why he never smiles. As for Ellen herself, she wants Rumsey, but Rumsey says she should take somebody younger. Her female drinking companion tries to force sexual secrets out of her, and in the end she says she has been married. She *remembers* being married, she insists, but she also claims to have no sense that other people are real, and cannot remember ever having had something that would normally be called a thought. All she knows about is the silence at night. "My heart beats in my ear. Such a silence. Is it me? Am I silent or speaking?" (III, 201). From all of which we can gather that the kind of tenderness which Beth remembered and still desired in *Landscape* is at present not available to Ellen either, and that in Bates she faces a dogged roughness not unreminiscent of Duff. The situation seems to be prolonging itself indefinitely,

and she is living in a kind of dream, though she refuses to call it that. Also, she is childless still, which, again as in *Landscape*, is perhaps an underlying dilemma. The play's
only imagery of adult-child relations was of Bates telling the little girl about birds and
of her own childhood visit to Rumsey. It is almost as if both the men have already
made their contributions to parenting the next generation. Now Rumsey seems to be
retiring from active engagement, desiring only the well being of others. He is a bit pat-
ronising towards her, certainly, but in the last analysis is quite possibly a *kind* man, in
this respect resembling Disson in *Tea Party*, and quite unpredictable from orthodox
accounts of Pinter's murderous jungle beasts. The younger Ellen *could* presumably
still have a child, and Bates's agitated interest in her shows no sign of lessening. The
stalemate between them does replicate the one between Beth and Duff, but they, too,
are still alive, and their hopefulness not quite extinct. Here again, then, it may not be
really possible to speak of elegiac closure.

At the end of *Monologue*, another memory play, a step has perhaps been taken,
and life may be moving on. Throughout the play, a seated man is addressing an
empty chair. He has been very close to another man, possibly his brother, whom
he addresses in his absence as "you" and is imagining as seated next to him. They
have competed with each other for the affection of a black girl, and he now muses
that his rival ought to have had a black face to match his motorbiking gear. The two
of them have been the best of mates, truest mates. But now it is "as if our sporting
and intellectual life never was" (IV, 123). The other man was dangerously detached,
and that was "the web my darling black darling hovered in" (IV, 125). But he himself is now mentally busy, he claims, and can even take an ironical view of things.
"What you are witnessing is freedom. I no longer participate in holy ceremony. The
crap is cut" (IV, 126). Finally, though, he says that if "you" had a black face, then
"you could have had two black kids" and he himself – his next remarks here are
interspersed with pregnant pauses – would have died for them, would have been
their uncle, *is* their uncle, will take them out, will tell them jokes. "I love your children", he concludes (IV, 127). In the course of his monologue, then, we have seen
him resigning himself to his amatory failure, and acknowledging that he still loves
both the girl and the other man as much as ever. Despite the loss of his own former
hopes, he recognises their family unit, and is himself joyful when he thinks of their
children. Before our eyes, after a huge inner struggle his whole orientation to living
has changed to the more positive, and nothing could be more different from the
way the triangle situation works out in *Betrayal*, for instance. A nobler love, a more
generous friendship, would be difficult to find in English literature outside the pages
of *Euphues* or Book IV of *The Faerie Queene*. Or at least the speaker's *intentions* are
excellent, we should perhaps say. Happy endings are as little a part of this group of
plays as elegiac closure. The speaker is still addressing that empty chair. How genuine his communication will be when he next confronts the loved-ones in the flesh
we can only guess.

In *Family Voices* and *Moonlight* a passionate desire for meaningful family relationships is to the fore even more explicitly. The son in *Family Voices* has left his own home for a new one, a very strange one, where he is not sure whether the other inmates are members of the aristocracy or sex workers. His mother longs for him to return, and his father, although technically dead and inhabiting an "[a]bsolute silence everywhere, absolute silence throughout all the years", still has strong feelings for him. In the end, the mother gives up hope. She just wonders whether he thinks the word "love" means anything. But by this time the son is "longing to have a word with" his father and is planning to return home. Perhaps one day he will, possibly to a happy reunion with his mother, but doubtless to be shocked by the news of his father's demise.

An open ending yet again, then, and the same applies to *Moonlight*. As Andy is waiting to die, he is looked after by his wife Bel, and much of their discussion revolves around their loves and betrayals in the past. They both seem to have had sexual relations with Mary, and it turns out that Bel also had a soft spot for Mary's husband Ralph. In discussing these matters, they are robustly free-spoken, both of them giving as good as they get, and the play contains some of the funniest of all Pinter's ribaldries. One of Andy's jokes is that, as a consummate civil servant, he had "kept my obscene language for the home, where it belongs" (IV, 334), and it is the home and traditional family values that attract his most uproariously comic wit. So when Bel fondly remembers how their sons Jake and Fred used to clear the table and do the washing-up, he counters:

> You mean in the twilight? The soft light falling through the kitchen window? The bell ringing for Evensong in the pub round the corner?   (IV, 348)

But Andy is capable of other registers as well. Bel comments here, revealing her own flair for the ludicrous, that his habitual verbal coarseness may merely be the disguise of

> a delicate even poetic sensibility, the sensibility of a young horse in the golden age, in the golden past of our forefathers.   (IV, 335)

In fact they both have deep feelings, and at one point all their hilarity quite falls away, the stage direction indicating that "BEL *sits frozen*" when Andy asks why their daughter Bridget has not brought his grandchildren to "catch their last look of me, to receive my blessing" (IV, 357). As I say, Bridget has apparently died childless, and although she is a dramatis persona, she merely haunts the stage (except for in a scene set during her childhood), a ghost who anxiously wishes she could ease her parents' lot, and who well knows that Jake and Fred are not visiting the deathbed either, even though Andy longs to see them and Bel has tried to persuade them. The brothers spend their days in aimlessly witty dialogue with each other, and even if Jake says that "one day I shall love him [Andy]" and Fred, with a parodic literariness worthy of Andy himself, that "I shall not look upon his like again" (IV, 367, 370), they cannot yet overcome their deep sense of alienation from him. Whether or not they will snap out of denial in time remains unclear, and there is also no knowing what they would think about some of the play's stranger episodes. One of these is the tableau in which Andy sees and hears the ghostly Bridget, and responds in all simplicity: "Ah darling. Ah my darling" (IV, 360). Then Bel comes on stage as well, and he and she look at each other, only to turn away from each other, listening. Bridget remains in the background, and there is utter silence. Finally, the lights fade on Andy and Bel, leaving Bridget standing alone in the moonlight, before the light fades on her as well. A kind of family communion has outlasted death here, it would seem, with the parents and daughter reaching out to each other across the divide. And in the play's closing speech, similarly, Bridget tells how she once went to a party to which she thinks her mother and father may also have been invited. The only problem was that she had been told to wait until the moon had gone down.

> The house, the glade, the lane, were all bathed in moonlight. But the inside of the house was dark and all the windows were dark. There was no sound.
>
> *Pause.*
>
> I stood there in the moonlight and waited for the moon to go down.   (IV, 387)

The hard-soft duality we have seen in Douglas in *Party-Time*, Disson in *Tea Party*, the speaker in *Monologue*, the son in *Family Voices*, Andy in *Moonlight*, and polarized between Beth and Duff and between Rumsey and Bates in *Landscape* and *Silence* respectively, is present in both Lambert and Russell in *Celebration*. Lambert is taking his wife Julie out for dinner to celebrate their wedding anniversary, together with his brother Matt with his wife Prue, who is Julie's sister. In the same restaurant Russell is treating his secretary Suki to a meal, and eventually on Lambert's invitation they join the others at their table. The language of all the diners is coarse in the extreme, and they have absolutely no cultural refinement. Their personal lives, too, are shallow, their memories meagre. Lambert's topic of conversation with his guests on his wedding anniversary is a girl with whom he once truly fell in love, and who truly loved him back. And no, he does not mean Julie. Julie retorts that he fell in love with *her* on the top of a bus somewhere between Broadway and Shepherd's Bush. Prue then supports her, thanking Lambert for the expensive meal by loudly telling the restaurant owner that Julie was not impressed by the food: "she said she could cook better than that with one hand stuffed between her legs – she said – no, honestly – she said she could make a better sauce than the one on that plate if she pissed into it" (IV, 457) The restaurant owner and his staff are more civilized than their customers, and one of the waiters makes long speeches in which he recalls the literary Modernists, Hollywood in the 1930s and the Austro-Hungarian empire. His grandfather, he remarks in the final speech when everyone else has left the stage,

> introduced me to the mystery of life and I'm still in the middle of it. I can't find the door to get out. My grandfather got out of it. He got right out of it. He left it behind him and he didn't look back.   (IV, 508)

Which is enough to suggest that the waiter is not terribly impressed by the customers he has to serve every day. Yet at two earlier moments in the play it became fairly clear that both Russell and Lambert partly realise how awful they are. When Suki says that Russell's description of eating his mother's bread-and-butter pudding – "like drowning in an ocean of richness" – is poetry, he agrees, albeit in his usual awful way: "I wanted to be a poet once. But I got no encouragement from my dad. He thought I was an arsehole" (IV, 465). And Lambert says, perhaps tongue in cheek, but perhaps not altogether so, that in his next life "I'm going to come back as a better person, a more civilised person, a gentler person, a nicer person" (IV, 492).

Nor does Pinter's treatment of human interaction confine itself to coercive characters and to characters who merely desire a more genuine communication. There are also plays in which, despite huge obstacles, genuineness actually breaks through into the way some characters behave towards each other. Again, this is not what much orthodox commentary would lead one to expect. Yet in a Pinter play, it was always one of the things that *could* happen.

It happened very strikingly in the first play ever staged: *The Room*.[4] Here Rose is living in a room with the ominously silent Bert. In her monologues she tries to convince herself of the room's cosiness. By comparison, the weather outside is very bleak, and she urges Bert not to venture out into it on a job. No less worrying, apparently, are the damp glooms of the basement down below, where somebody dangerous could be lurking. Her peace of mind is fragile at best, and when the landlord Mr Kidd visits, the reality she would like to hold on to begins to elude her. Was the rocking chair already in the room or did she bring it with her when she moved from somewhere else? Was the room once Kidd's own bedroom? How many floors does the house have? And what about Kidd's sister? – under some pressure, Kidd says she must have been like his mother, who was perhaps a Jewess, but did not have many babies. After Bert, still without having spoken, has left to do his job, Rose's anxieties intensify when she is visited by the strangers Mr and Mrs Hands, who have apparently been down in the basement, where a helpful man told them that *this* room will soon be vacant. When they have left, Kidd returns in considerable distress. For the whole weekend he has been waiting to tell her that there is a man in "the black dark" downstairs who urgently wants to see her as soon as Bert goes out, and who, if she refuses, is threatening to come up while Bert is actually there. "He'd never do that", says Rose (I, 105). But when Kidd insists that he would, she relents and allows the man up. He turns out to be what the stage directions describe as a blind Negro, who says his name is Riley. She cruelly taunts him for his blindness, and rages at him for upsetting the landlord and disturbing the peace. "We're settled down here, cosy, quiet, and our landlord thinks the world of us" (I, 107). In the end the Negro says he has a message from her father, who wants her to come home, and before long it begins to seem that he himself could

---

4. See fn. 1 above.

be her father. Despite her initial protests, he begins to call her by the name of Sal, and says he has been waiting a long time to see her. She begins to soften, and admits that "[t]he day is a hump. I never go out". "Come home now, Sal", he says, and she then *"touches his eyes, the back of his head and his temples with her hands"* (I, 109). At which point Bert comes back and for the first time opens his mouth, launching into a vigorous tale about how he got his way with the feminized van he has just been driving. "She went with me. She don't mix with me. I use my hand" (I, 110). After which he kicks the Negro to death on the floor, and Rose, *"clutching her eyes"*, speaks the last words before the blackout: "Can't see. I can't see. I can't see" (I, 110). Until she touched the Negro, then, she was in denial, a victim of Bert's violent brutality. She turned the walls of the room into a protective shell against a world of larger realities she had excluded. The blind Negro sees human truths that she cannot see, until the eyes with which she has hitherto been viewing Bert and the room are blinded too. As her insistent curiosity about Kidd's family life perhaps anticipated, her fiercely defensive anger against her father has finally melted. Despite the imminent threat of appallingly atavistic coercion hanging over them, their love for each other has now expressed itself unmistakably. Her wordless touching of his eyes and head is Pinter's first staging of genuine communication.

Also early is *The Caretaker*, where Aston's kindnesses to Davies the tramp are obvious enough. He invites him home, he says he can stay, he gives him tobacco and money, he goes to great lengths to find a good pair of shoes for him, he tries to find his bag. And at times Davies's response suggests that what is going on is commendably genuine behaviour on both sides. "That's kind of you, mister", he says (II, 6). On the other hand, Davies does start to try and sponge on him, and one can easily begin to suspect that the tramp's initial success here is due to a certain gullibility, or even some sort of mental deficiency, in Aston. In his longest speech Aston tells how, like Lamb in *The Hothouse*, he was placed on the receiving end of psychiatric shock therapy. This, one might well assume, has left him permanently traumatized, and he is certainly rather helpless as a practical handyman – the plug never gets mended, the garden shed never built. Yet the truth is both more complex and more cheering. Aston resembles Simon in *Lord of the Flies*, Golding's novel of six years earlier, the boy whose visionary truth-telling led to his terrible death at the hands of some of the other boys in their fear of the demonized and non-existent "Beast". Aston, too, is saint-like in a way. He used to visit the café down the road and talk about his strange visions, until one day somebody started to interrogate him, which led to the electrotherapy. But unlike Golding's Simon, he is a survivor. Like Stanley in *The Birthday Party*, he resisted and, as Jimmy in *Party-Time* may not have a chance to do, he returned to ordinary life after the treatment. Although he tells Davies that he steers clear of the café nowadays, alert members of the audience will remember that it was precisely at the local café that he first met Davies and bravely rescued him from a punch-up there, just as he resolutely stands up for him again when his own brother Mick threateningly fools around with Davies's bag (or rather, the substitute Aston has found for it). In defending his protégée Aston is not merely thinking about Davies's need of a roof over his head and a bag for his possessions. Pinter himself once said to Václav Havel that this play was about a man looking for a home but, when Havel replied that in his own country there were not the problems of homelessness, refrained from pointing out that a home is more than bricks and mortar (Fraser 2010: 166). Aston clearly wants Mick to feel that Davies should belong to their family unit, and throughout the play he himself only increases in moral stature. His generosity is not weak-witted but principled. When Davies does finally go too far, and even threatens to have him sent back to the men with the electrodes, Aston does not allow himself to be either intimidated or fooled, just as in the café he had firmly expressed his dislike of drinking Guinness from a thick mug, and his lack of interest when a woman asked whether he would like her to have a look at his body. Yet in showing Davies the door he is still courteously friendly, even offering him some cash to help him get down to Sidcup where he says his papers are. Davies's scheming coerciveness has put him under enormous strain, but he is far too big a human being to repay him in kind. Whereas in *Monologue* the speaker addressing his absent friend or brother finally talks himself towards some very noble resolutions, Aston's nobility is immediately knowable in his spontaneous deeds.

In *A Kind of Alaska*, a memory play of two decades later, the memory motif is extremely prominent, in that Deborah was afflicted by sleeping sickness as a teenage girl and is now temporarily woken up and begins to speak, a middle-aged woman whose entire world of knowledge, assumptions and feelings still belongs to a distant past. But in contradistinction from *Landscape*, *Silence* and *Monologue*, the play does not consist merely of characters who reminisce and analyse their current situation. It centrally stages the real-time interaction between Deborah and Hornby, her doctor, and Hornby's wife Pauline, who is Deborah's sister. Hornby and Pauline's long years of caring for the dormant Deborah have in effect killed their own marital relation. Pauline "has suffered for you. She has never forsaken you", Hornby tells Deborah. "Nor have I." Pauline "is a widow. I have lived with you" (IV, 183, 185). Yet despite this enormous penalty, so much graver than the liberties Davies tries to take with Aston in *The Caretaker*, the two of them continue to do the right thing by Deborah, showing exquisite delicacy in the way they try to tell her what has happened, not only to herself, but to the rest of the family, and indeed to the world as a whole. "I suppose the war's still over?" asks Deborah. "It's over, yes", says Hornby. "Oh good. They haven't started another one?" "No." "Oh good" (IV, 174). At first Pauline tells her that her father, mother and sister Estelle have not come to see her because they are on a world tour. Hornby offers a more truthful narrative: that her mother is dead, and that her father, now blind, is being nursed by Estelle. But they force nothing upon her. In her final words before returning to her silent otherworld she says, "I think I have the matter in proportion. [*Pause.*] Thank you" (IV, 190). She has chosen only those of the explanations that she can take on board: much of the truth about her own position,

but together with the attractive story about the family's world tour. In their utter genuineness of communication with her, Hornby and Pauline have struck a finely balanced
compromise between truth to the facts and respect for their addressee's well-being
and autonomy. In ethical quality, this is exactly comparable to what, in the previous
study here, I found to praise in Lynne Reid Banks's way of treating the young readers
of *Melusine: A Mystery*.

The *Room*, *The Caretaker*, and *A Kind of Alaska* are all plays of the private sphere,
even though Aston in *The Caretaker* has had his brush with officialdom's electrodes.
But most surprisingly of all, genuine communication arises even in two plays of the
public sphere, where the odds against it seem highest of all: in *Ashes to Ashes* and
Mountain Language.

In *Ashes to Ashes*, Rebecca herself has not been sent to a concentration camp, has
not had a baby snatched from her by a camp guard on the platform of a railway station, and none of her friends has suffered that fate either. Yet she has had a lover who
was himself such a guard, who took women's babies away from them, who showed her
round a factory where there were no lavatories for the workers, and who told her that
those same workers would have followed him over the cliff into the sea if he had asked
them. With her own eyes, she has seen a huge crowd of human beings walk into the
sea on the command of their guards. She has also taken no comfort from the sound
of a fading siren, because she knew "it was becoming louder and louder for somebody
else. […] [I]t's always being heard by somebody, somewhere" (IV, 408).

At the beginning of the play, she is telling her husband Devlin that there was
once a time when she would kiss the fist of her ominous lover. Murmuring through
his fingers, she would ask him to put his hand round her throat, and he would do so,
with a little pressure, so that her body went back, "slowly but truly", her legs opening
(IV, 397). Devlin seems extremely interested to hear this, and does not want to discuss
the appalling things she has witnessed in the world at large. Instead, he responds to
details in her totally non-antagonistic utterances as if their implications were luridly
combative, as in the pen sequence discussed by Katie Mitchell. Above all, he wants her
to remember that she is happily married to him, that she has a beautiful garden, and
that she has a sister and her sister's kids to visit, even if, like so many other women
in Pinter, she apparently has no children of her own. He probably does *not* want to
hear that her sister is refusing to take her husband back. But he is keen to remind
her that he himself does not wriggle out of things. He is "[a] man who doesn't give a
shit. / A man with a rigid sense of duty" (IV, 415). In which, he stresses, there is no
contradiction, but much for her to think about. First and foremost, she should now
kiss his fist, let him put his hand round her throat and force her backwards. Her legs
should open.

But she, at least as Devlin might express it, ignores him, telling him instead how
she saw more victims, and empathized with a woman whose baby was snatched away,
feeling that the baby was her own, and that she herself had suffered its loss. During

her narration, Devlin's *"grip loosens.* [...] *He takes his hand from her throat"* (IV, 429). Whether the sinister lover of whom she told him was, as Mitchell assumes, another man with whom she had committed adultery, or whether, as I believe, it was Devlin himself in an earlier phase of their relationship, the full horror of violence, and above all of its destruction of the most elementary and important human relationships, has got through to her. Unlike Miss Cutts in *The Hothouse*, she cannot finally be aroused by a fascistic male who closes his eyes to that. She no longer accepts a dehumanization of either the public or the private sphere. Public ethics and private ethics are ultimately indivisible for her because, to return to Alastair Macaulay's summary, no man is an island.

Throughout the play, Devlin's own, coercive discourse has been a matter of trying to make her answer the questions in which he himself is particularly interested, and of urging her to accept, in effect, a politically passivizing separation of the domestic from the public. His appeal has been to the good of the body politic itself, to the ideal of marriage, and to the will of God, whose existence and authority cannot be denied, he explains, because that would be "like England playing Brazil at Wembley and not a soul in the stadium. [...] Not a soul watching" (IV, 412).

But if Devlin's manner of address confirms the widespread view of Pinter's characters as constantly battling for position, Rebecca's rejection of his coercion is of an ethically different order, and is even more courteous than Aston's rejection of Davies's coercion in *The Caretaker*. She at no point responds with a direct counter-claim, challenge or refutation. And why not? Ultimately, I suggest, because she could never champion humane values through a coercive mode of discourse which in and of itself denied them. Instead, her replies will have seemed to Devlin inconsequential in his own terms. He will have thought that she is changing the subject all the time, dodging the issue, or simply failing to concentrate, weak-headedly and – which amounts to the same thing in his book – womanishly. What she does is simply to tell him the dreadful things she has seen or thought about, and to give him, too, a chance to react like a human being. Loving him here, not in an erotic sense but charitably, she shows the genuine communicator's hope that a community of understanding can indeed be achieved, and she allows, because as a genuine communicator she cannot do otherwise, full scope to the autonomy of his human otherness.

As for *Mountain Language*, here two of Pinter's fullest, albeit shortest dramatizations of genuine communication occur in the context of a maximum official hostility to them. The following passage is one of only two instances in Pinter's entire dramatic production of a pair of lovers addressing each other without the slightest trace of coerciveness:

MAN'S VOICE
I watch you sleep. And then your eyes open. You look up at me above you and smile.

YOUNG WOMAN'S VOICE
You smile. When my eyes open I see you above me and smile.

MAN'S VOICE
We are out on a lake.

YOUNG WOMAN'S VOICE
It is spring.

MAN'S VOICE
I hold you. I warm you.

YOUNG WOMAN'S VOICE
When my eyes open I see you above me and smile.   (IV, 263)

And in Pinter's plays the only familial discourse completely unaffected by family-in-ternal coerciveness is the following passage from this same play.

ELDERLY WOMAN'S VOICE
The baby is waiting for you.

PRISONER'S VOICE
Your hand has been bitten.

ELDERLY WOMAN'S VOICE
They are all waiting for you.

PRISONER'S VOICE
They have bitten my mother's hand.

ELDERLY WOMAN'S VOICE
When you come home there will be such a welcome for you. Everyone is waiting
for you. They're all waiting for you. They're all waiting to see you.   (IV, 261)

In both cases, the words are only a brief voice-over against the surrounding horrors of the prison-camp. Extremes of inhumane treatment have been the catalyst to an almost unreal extreme of true humanity, to a communication almost impossibly genuine. The chances for its continuation could hardly be more bleak.

Even this, though, cannot be my last word on the subject, since there were also two occasions on which Pinter dramatized genuine communication as taking place without any obstacles or qualifications at all. One is the 1959 sketch *Last to Go*, in which an old newspaper seller and a barman compare notes. David Lodge (1997) has already analysed this as a prime example of phatic communication. Neither of the men is really informing the other of anything very important, and neither of them has any kind of axe to grind. They are simply being sociable. "I sold my last one about then. Yes. About nine forty-five." "Sold your last then, did you?" "Yes, my last 'Evening News' it was. Went about twenty to ten" (II, 234). The other case is the short memory play *Night*, which is Pinter's only other dramatization of completely uncoercive, genuinely communicating lovers. This couple are in their forties, and are reminiscing about their shared past, but each from their own point of view. Even their first kiss has lodged as two very different memories or, by now, fantasies: he is sure that he touched her breasts from behind her, she that she was facing him. He tends to remember "women on bridges and towpaths and rubbish dumps" and she her "bottom against railings and men holding [… her] hands and men looking into [… her] eyes" (III, 219). They disagree, then. And he even asks, "Why do you argue?" But she replies, "I don't. I'm not" (III, 215). Neither is he. He said he would adore her always, and he always has, and does so still. And one point of crucial importance in Pinter is that they seem to have children – they think they hear a child crying at one point. Perhaps partly on the strength of this, they can agree to disagree, even about the most fundamental thing they share: their memories of loving each other.

Why only two such cases in the whole of Pinter? Perhaps because in Pinter's experience unrestrictedly genuine communication is not very common in real life. And perhaps partly because, as I have stressed all along, unrestrictedly genuine communication has low tellability. Which could also explain why *Last to Go* and *Night* are both very short. Over any greater length, the topic might have been dramatically unsustainable.

But be that as it may, Billington's gloss on the situation of Kate, Anna and Deeley at the end of *Old Times*, though finely responsive to the extraordinary bleakness of that particular play, and though applicable to several of the other plays as well, becomes misleading when he raises it to a generalization. The conclusion of *Old Times*, he rightly says, strips away cowardly facades "to reveal the naked ugliness of the battle for possession". He then adds that the play

> also moves effortlessly from the particular to the universal by suggesting, in contrast to John Donne, that each man *is* an island, and that while we make necessary gestures towards each other of love and friendship, we are all in the end trapped inside our own skins and live in a state of inviolable loneliness. That seems to me the meaning of the final image with the characters all occupying their own space: what Octavio Paz … once called "cages for infinity".
>
> (Billington 2007:219, his italics)

Well yes, Kate, Anna and Deeley are trapped inside their own skins and live in a state of utter loneliness. And yes, Kate, Anna and Deeley may continue in their "cages" for the whole of the rest of eternity. But no, this does not necessarily apply to us "all", and it most certainly does not apply to us all *as Pinter sees us*. Throughout his career Pinter showed characters, not only longing to communicate genuinely, whether within families or friendships, but sometimes succeeding at it in the face of huge reluctances and obstacles, some of them political. In the case of Rebecca in *Ashes to Ashes*, the success is that of a private individual who comes to accept political responsibility, and for whom, as Alastair Macaulay was hinting, Donne's words would have a profound meaning. In the cases of *Last One To Go* and *Night*, success comes across as totally easy and ordinary. With reciprocal goodwill, genuine communication is, on Pinter's showing here, the most natural thing in the world. The friendship and love in such cases is not a mere "necessary gesture", but real.

That human beings not only desire but can actually achieve genuine communication is one of his most fundamental and lasting perceptions about them. He would surely have unpicked both Billington's generalization and the agentless passive construction in which he couches it: "*we are … trapped* inside our own skins". This does not correspond to what Pinter shows on stage, because it is too deterministic, as if entrapment happened inevitably, as the result of inscrutable forces over which human beings have no control. When individuals such as Kate, Anna and Deeley do find themselves very much alone, Pinter's implication, I have suggested, is that they are trapped by an aspect of their own behaviour: by an ethical failure on their own part, to which they could perhaps have been alerted by Macbeth, a more self-knowing individual who had landed himself in the same predicament.

10.5   Pinter's own identity and coerciveness

That a dramatist so convinced that human beings desire, and are even capable of, genuine communication unhesitatingly decided to emulate the negative capability he found in Shakespeare, Beckett and Proust is not surprising. Pinter's view of humankind included an instinctive sense that audiences would be able to respond generously to his own generosity: that if he respected their human autonomy, they would not simply jump to their own conclusions, settling on the first interpretation or judgement that came into their heads, but would consider matters in their full complexity, with no irritable reaching after fact and reason, to use Keats's phrase again. As a result, he wrote many plays which give the impression, not only that there is no character on stage who is supposed to be driving home the playwright's views but that, as John Stokes (2009: 40) puts it, the playwright is himself sitting in the audience, watching and listening.

Yet Pinter's negative capability is not a total annihilation of personal identity such as Keats fantasized in describing himself as a true poet, and Stokes, too, is misleading when he argues that the plays are basically existentialist in character: that they take no doctrines, ideals or values for granted, but show characters confronted by reality through their own experience and drawing unpredetermined conclusions about it. Both Pinter and his most sympathetic characters are historically rooted in a particular ideology, the same ideology, as it happens, which had already nourished Keats. It was bourgeois. It was secular, but without being rationalistic. And it placed a high value on personal feeling and the emotional life, and on bonds of family and friendship. In an earlier study here I have already dealt at some length with its inception, when

I was discussing the Romantic nervousness of Pope. The character who, though not a spokesman for the author, most fully embodies it in the plays of Pinter is Andy in *Moonlight*, who would be unthinkable in a play by Beckett, for instance, a writer who does deserve the existentialist tag. As Peter Hall puts it:

> I think that Pinter is concerned with the family unity, the husband-wife relationship, the child – the hope of making the bourgeois unit: whereas Sam's work is entirely concerned with "me alone in the dark tunnel" – or you alone in the dark tunnel. (Hall 2005 [1974]: 156)

Himself sitting, as it were, in the audience, Pinter assumes that he will be surrounded by playgoers who share his bourgeois values, or who will at least not mind empathizing with them for the purpose and duration of his communion with them. All things considered, this assumption does not expect much of them, and is not really an infringement on their autonomy. It is impossible to write a play without assuming some ideological common denominators, and the ones assumed by Pinter's plays are pretty minimal, which is doubtless one reason why he could be enthusiastically taken up in many different countries. To think of cultures in which close family relations and friendship have *not* been important is actually difficult, even if many playgoers and readers would now argue that bourgeois values have had their day, and have over the centuries been grossly unjust to homosexuals, women, single parents, and children born out of wedlock.

Pinter has certainly not been immune to ideological critique. Steve Waters says that the shorter political plays imply "a curiously passive notion of political theatre, more concerned with enacting the impotence of the stage or the liberal imagination itself, than with spurring audiences to resist an increasingly barbarous world" (Waters 2009: 307). Drew Milne, too, would prefer a drama more politically articulate and politically correct. According to him, Pinter's plays generate politically indeterminate interpretations, do not offer clear criteria, and have a misogynist blind-spot. Not least, complains Milne, in *Ashes to Ashes* Pinter's "imaginative juxtaposition of holocaust [sic] 'memories' and female desire for misogynist authoritarianism ... leaves political responsibilities disturbingly ambiguous" (Milne 2009: 247).

In his specific comments on *Ashes to Ashes* Milne is in denial, it seems to me. The hard reality is that many people, including many women, enter into relationships with lovers, including many men, who have a very dark side to their character. To place "female desire for misogynist authoritarianism" beyond the pale for a playwright on the grounds that it might lead people to believe that all women want to be abused and bullied all the time would be the sort of move that gets political correctness a bad name. No less unfortunately, Milne is insensitive to the text Pinter has actually written, quite missing its crucial contrast between Rebecca's opening narrative of having previously acquiesced in the Nazistic lover's foreplay and her present rejection of Devlin's attempt to replicate it.

More generally, reservations such as those of Waters and Milne have been brushed aside by critics who place a lower value on coercive dogmatism than on negative capability. Pinter himself commented on "the great trap in writing political plays as such if you know the end before you've written the beginning" (Pinter 2005 [1996]: 91), and some of the commentators who praise him for not retailing politically correct predictabilities also say that his political antennae are in any case very sharp. Mireia Aragay (2009) values his work for having rejected the postmodern assumption that the individual subject is determined by social discourse and has no space outside the dominant order. In her view, which is very typical of the present phase of post-postmodernity, Pinter's political plays, by reinstating categories such as truth, value, and knowledge, and by drawing a distinction between discourse and reality, effectively undermine this potentially quietist conception of language and subjectivity. Katie Mitchell, similarly, points out that in both *Ashes to Ashes* and *Mountain Language* Pinter

> put the emotional heart, and therefore the idea of the play, into the female characters, not the male. … There are strong political ideas contained in these plays – and they are carried by women, not by men. It's like *Hamlet* from Ophelia's point of view – it's a fascinating choice.   (Mitchell 2005: 194–195)

Basically, Aragay and Mitchell are assimilating Pinter's work as the latest development of Romantic nervousness, which in Pope began by challenging what was then the Humanist account of rational order, opening up a new, emotional reality, and encouraging the growth of a new, and feminized communion of sensibility. The first shot at *Hamlet* from Ophelia's point of view was arguably "Elegy to the Memory of an Unfortunate Lady".

Pinter's ideological assumptions will never have shocked anybody by seeming to propose a new social order. On the contrary, they have undisturbingly extended a culture of feeling that is nearly three hundred years old. If and when they do shock, it is because in one particular respect they are positively antiquated. In point of fact, complaints such as those of Waters and Milne are not without all ground, and there may even be a risk that spirited defences such as those of Aragay and Mitchell will either whitewash Pinter or de-historicize him. Especially, but not only, in plays such as *A Slight Ache, A Night Out, Night School, The Lover, The Homecoming, Family Voices, One for the Road* and *The New World Order*, he is preoccupied with male characters who in moments of male bonding tend to see woman as the root of all evil, except that they also often tend to draw a distinction between dirty whores on the one hand and clean virgins, wives and mothers on the other, a dividing line which in a traditionally English way they sometimes equate with a distinction between lower-class and genteel. They are particularly disturbed when they perceive a woman as transgressing this boundary, but in their traditionally English fantasy-life are also strongly aroused by such a prospect. In *The Homecoming*, for instance, there is the group of males for whom Jessie has been the disorienting whore-cum-*materfamilias*, but who now urgently nourish a group fantasy about installing Ruth as her replacement. Their Victorian offshoot of bourgeois ideology here – the same set of assumptions as underpins the representation of women, sexual relations and class in *David Copperfield* – was still vigorously alive in Pinter's own psyche, and nothing is to be gained by pretending otherwise, or by denying that *per se* this mind-set has become increasingly distasteful to audiences even in England. On the other hand, a mediating critic would hasten to add that a writer whose formative years were during the 1940s could not necessarily be expected to spearhead the 1960s' revolution in attitudes to gender and sex. And as a communicational critic, I am already trying to suggest the honesty and power with which Pinter explored the consequences of his own mental formation on stage. This, indeed, was no small reflection of his negative capability, of his being in the midst of uncertainties, mysteries, doubts, without any irritable reaching after fact and reason, and audiences have all along been bound to warm to it.

His negative capability did not cancel out his sociocultural identity, then. And although the plays of the private sphere generously refrained from didacticism and allowed audiences to make up their own minds, not even here was he totally uncoercive. The complexity and tight suggestiveness of his writing in these plays represented a level of Modernist difficulty which was not universally welcomed, quite simply because its challenge to a spectator's grey matter was so demanding. Magnanimous though he was, he was in effect telling audiences to like it or lump it, and thereby *forcing* them to think. Coercion in this sense has been somewhat overlooked in commentary hitherto, but Harry Derbyshire does relevantly point out that, especially in England, Pinter has been seen "as a representative of a high, bourgeois and, sometimes, avant-garde culture" that remains inaccessible "to those who are excluded from it by class, education and intermediaries such as the *Sun*" (Derbyshire 2009: 277). Even though postmodern sociological discourse spoke of a culture without hierarchy, in Britain a strong distinction sometimes still applies in practice between elitist high culture and low culture, and Pinter's plays of the private sphere are seen as decidedly high. Their pregnant artistry has often been experienced as intimidating in and of itself.

Given Pinter's own working-class background, given that many of his plays have lower class settings and characters, and given that his "faithful reproduction of the repetitions, hesitations and lacunae of everyday speech, alongside the exuberance of street argot" has been seen by Billington, his greatest critic, as "his single most important contribution to British drama" (Billington 2007: 91), there is a paradox here. But it is a very English one, which was no less apparent in the English reception of the flagship Modernist poem, *The Waste Land*, whose pub scene, with the Cockney conversation about Albert coming home from the war to Lil, who may not be able to hang on to him unless she gets some false teeth, did not immediately endear it to a mass audience. Among Pinter's own characters, probably the only ones of lower class origin who would themselves go to see a Pinter play, as it were, are Lenny in

The Homecoming, the meritocratic émigré to an American campus, and Disson in *Tea Party*, who would spend the whole evening wriggling in his seat. As I said earlier, Pinter did not write about people like himself, who moved effortlessly between any English grouping and another. His plays did not suggest the possibility of a rainbow society in England, and his own celebrity image in that country was structured on a pre-postmodern opposition between high and low culture.

As with his preoccupations with sex and gender, so in his class instincts he can easily be accused of political incorrectness. But he would doubtless have welcomed a significant improvement in English educational standards, so that people across the board could have appreciated a complex Modernist play, and he doubtless assumed that such a development was just not on the cards. In view of the crass vulgarity and levelling-down he saw all round him, unforgettably captured in *Celebration*, the assumption was not unreasonable. The "splitting of bloody popcorn all over the place" made it impossible for him to watch a serious film at the cinema (Pinter 2005 [1980]: 77), and the efforts of the serious theatre to make itself more audience-friendly simply appalled him, even if this particular capitulation was still more total in the programmatically democratic United States.

> Last year, [he told Billington,] ... I went to the American Place Theatre to see Sam Shepard's play *La Turista*. Right in the middle of the performance one of the actors suddenly left the stage and charged up the aisle inviting members of the audience to feel his muscle. I was furious. I watched this actor moving about the theatre and suddenly my spine chilled because I knew eventually he was going to come over to me. Sure enough, he did. All I could do was give him a look of utter devastation; he ultimately cast down his eyes and moved on. This kind of theatre produces propagandists who spout love and freedom and openness. But that's empty phraseology. They love themselves so terribly. I don't ... love myself.
>
> (Billington 2007: 195–196)

He dislikes this actor's populist exhibitionism because, by seeking to cultivate a quite extraneous relationship with the audience, it detracts from what is actually happening on stage. A film-maker or a playwright can be unreservedly generous to an audience in letting them make up their own mind about a film or play. But in Pinter's view, the challenge of the work is to be taken with absolute seriousness. The audience must concentrate, must sit still, must keep quiet for the entire duration. They shall not be invited to participate, except in the utter silence of their own most active mental life.

Judging by the direction our culture now seems to be taking, with blogs and Facebook, phone-in radio and reality TV all eroding distinctions between public and private, and between authority and laypersonhood, and with children learning to surf the net or the channels, and to follow regular short instalments of many different soaps well before they experience a full-length novel or play, the demand which Pinter makes on playgoers and readers may come to seem more and more unreasonable as time goes by. But given that his texts are as they are, that demand will remain. For anyone approaching his plays of the private sphere, the kind of attention and effort he expects is a *sine qua non*. Like any major Modernist writer, he presumes hugely upon our patience and concentration, expecting us to cede him the floor, to grant him an extensive and uninterrupted turn of conversation, so to speak, on the grounds that our attentiveness will eventually be rewarded. Those grounds are not something he spells out in an explicit line of persuasion. What do come into operation are rather principles of trust and delayed gratification. His assumption is that we will give him the benefit of the doubt – that we will be prepared to suck it and see.

As a result, the coerciveness involved is curiously of our own making. It is not a matter of Pinter telling us to watch or read his plays and explaining why we should do so. We are self-commanded to take that leap in the dark, and if we are disappointed by them shall partly have ourselves to blame. If the plays had had even as little as an eighteenth-century-style Prologue explaining their aim and inviting us to enjoy them, the situation would have been different. As things are, his Modernist apophaticism precedes our hearing or reading of a single word. In the situation within which we confront one of his plays, it is simply taken for granted that what he gives us will be a verbal icon whose value is symbolistically self-evident and unamenable to prior paraphrase or justification. In the event, discussion may well turn out to be extensive and richly rewarding. But we are expected to believe that, for any particular playgoer or reader, discussion cannot really begin until after the play has been experienced, and that even then it will inevitably be reductive.

To repeat, then, even in the plays of the private sphere there is an element of coercion: a coercion that is bound up with the irrationalism of Modernist aestheticism. As for the plays of the public sphere, here there is precisely the political coerciveness which earlier Pinter commentary leads us to expect. This is the coercion of a no less irrationalistic emotionalism.

Pinter belongs to that bourgeois culture of feelings partly initiated by Pope. This is a tradition which, despite its valorization of individuality and originality, came to involve a strong compulsion to gregariousness. However illogically, the great Romantic geniuses were supposed to stand as examples to everybody else. In order to have the sensitivities of a truly original individual, one only had to copy what they did! Like Pope and Pope's Romantic successors, when Pinter directly appeals to our sensibilities, he does so in the role of critic, sage or prophet. Or perhaps I should say that his appeal is surrounded with vibrant cultural memories of such roles, even though prime documents of the Modernist movement in which he also has deep roots – Strachey's *Eminent Victorians*, most obviously – debunked them. Certainly the appeal is attended with a strong implication that, if our feelings do not chime with his, then our sensibilities are less than fully human.

"*When* Pinter directly appeals to our sensibilities". He does *not* make this appeal in the plays of the private sphere, whether plays of menace or plays of memory. It is only the plays of the public sphere which are emotionally coercive in this way, both the three plays usually classed as menace (*The Birthday Party*, *The Hothouse* and *The Dumb Waiter*) and those classed as political. Here there is an undertow in the writing which to many playgoers and readers has seemed close to paranoia. Orwellian and Kafkaesque dystopias are in the near background, and so, too, are the anti-Fascist plays of Sartre and John Whiting, plus the disturbing kind of confessional poetry, British and American, collected in Al Alvarez's anthology *The New Poetry* of 1962, some of it about madness and psychiatric institutions, some of it processing mid-century Europe's worst horrors – a poem such as Sylvia Plath's "Daddy", for instance, with its references to Dachau, Auschwitz and Belsen, and with lines such as "Every woman adores a Fascist / The boot in the face, the brute / Brute heart of a brute like you" (Plath 1962: 65), which might have interested Devlin in *Ashes to Ashes*.

In his political activities outside of his playwriting, Pinter's highly emotive imagery, sweeping generalizations and conspiracy theories sometimes carried him away. This is registered even in the deeply loving account of him by Antonia Fraser, as for instance when she writes that, in the speech he made in 2002 on being awarded an honorary doctorate in Turin, there was one word which struck her as not quite right:

> Harold all too presciently referred to the possibility of an attack on the London Underground, saying "the responsibility will rest *entirely* on the Prime Minister's shoulders". I queried "entirely". "No, it won't," I said, "it will be shared. It will also be the responsibility of those who order it and those who do it. Free will and self-determination can never be eliminated from calculations of responsibility".
>
> (Fraser 2010: 267)

When he spoke in a debate on the Iraq war at the Imperial War Museum in 2004, similarly,

> I thought he was wrong to describe the American empire as the most barbarous the world has ever seen: what about the Nazis, Pol Pot, etc?   (Fraser 2010: 277)

At least in the first of these cases, Pinter accepted her reservation, and she also mentions that, for a reading of his own poems at the British Library in 1999, "he rejected reading his strident poem 'American Football' (thank goodness)" (Fraser 2010: 236). That poem, on the subject of the Gulf War, concludes:

> Praise the Lord for all good things.
> We blew their balls into shards of dust,
> Into shards of fucking dust.
>
> We did it.
>
> Now I want you to come over here and kiss me on the mouth. (Pinter 2009: 280)

The audience in the British Library was the Library's American Friends. "What a charming, civilized group!" Fraser remarks. For Pinter to have read "American Football" to them, would have been, she says, "his definition of bad manners", because it would have suggested that this "cultured, philanthropic group" was somehow

> responsible for the crimes of the American government – as though all Americans were bad Americans, the sort of crude generalization which did not belong to serious debate. (Fraser 2010:236)

In the end, then, Fraser is biased in his favour. It was not as if cultured and philanthropic Americans were not going to read the poem in print. If it would have been crudely bad mannered and unserious to read it aloud to an American audience, was it not, as the editors of the *Independent*, the *Observer*, the *Guardian*, the *New York Review of Books* and the *London Review of Books* all judged when they turned it down, crudely bad mannered and unserious to want to publish it in the first place? Although, as a celebrity, Pinter adopted the role of the Aristotelian, responsible citizen, his own language was sometimes *not* responsible, one problem being that in a poem like "American Football" he could himself become the thing he hated: angry, threatening, not clearly discriminating. In mitigation one could point out that this was something of a period style, adopted by certain politicians of all colours. A blunderbuss politics of conviction was the hallmark of Thatcher and Blair alike. But the popular image of Pinter as permanently and unreasonably bad-tempered was not without ground.

As described by Mary Luckhurst, Pinter's plays of the public sphere sound just as emotionally coercive and unreasonable as some of his non-literary political activity, but Luckhurst herself seems blandly unaware of the problem demanding critical scrutiny here. In reference to *The Birthday Party* she writes, "Political freedom of expression requires a bravery and a certainty which Stanley has never possessed" (Luckhurst 2009:110). Her implication that Pinter means that only the brave and the certain deserve to enjoy basic human rights is extremely worrying. Linking *The Birthday Party* with *The Hothouse*, she continues, "Stanley and Lamb do not fulfil their obligations as citizens: they do not ask the fundamental question: 'What is true? What is false?'" (Luckhurst 2009:111). This, too, seems to be implying that Pinter goes in for an awesome poetic justice: that he subjects Stanley and Lamb to terrible torture because their intellectual inadequacies deserve it. Luckhurst takes the Pinter of the Nobel Lecture, which is bound to remain his most famous public speech, at his word. This is a Pinter who speaks of the "crucial obligation" of citizens to apply "unflinching, unswerving, fierce intellectual determination" in order to "define the *real* truth of our lives and our societies" (Pinter 2009:300; Luckhurst 2009:111). Applying this to the plays of the public sphere, Luckhurst concludes that here Pinter is telling us how to get out of the hell we find ourselves in, but is also "intent on painting that hell precisely because it is incessantly glossed over, and with the passive agreement of many of his audience members". Pinter "would make adults of us. And citizens. He would compel us to speak out" (Luckhurst 2009: 117). If all this is itself "the *real* truth" about these plays, then they represent an extreme form of emotive coercion that quite lacks the common touch. In Luckhurst's account, they come across as the work of a hysterical fanatic, who believes that the entire population should down tools in order to devote themselves to a supremely demanding intellectual labour, and that all those who fail to do so will richly deserve everything they have coming to them.

To some extent the plays of the public sphere do support the impression Luckhurst gives. Pinter said that the staple weapons of the British establishment are derision and mockery, complacent malice and self-congratulatory spite (Pinter 2005 [1988]: 89). Especially in *The Hothouse* he shows a world of officialdom in which these qualities are deeply ingrained, but at the same time subjects the characters who are guilty of them to liberal doses of his own derision and mockery. Bubbling away under the surface there may also be some malice and spite as well. *Saeva indignatio* at the very least, anyway. In what can seem a rage for emotional battery, far from pandering to the sensitivities of an English audience, in *One for the Road* he even has that Nazistic interrogator Nicolas discuss his role with his detainee Victor in terms of a cricket metaphor: "You probably think I'm part of a predictable, formal, long-established pattern; i.e. I chat away, friendly, insouciant, I open up the batting, as it were" (IV, 224–225). No less shockingly, in *Ashes to Ashes* there is not only Devlin's description of the departure of God as England playing Brazil in an empty Wembley Stadium, but the babies are snatched from the mothers, the detainees are shepherded into the trains, on the platforms of what can only be English railway stations; the snow was not white, "as if there were veins running through it" (IV, 418), on the streets of an English city; and Rebecca watched the crowd of prisoners follow the bidding of their "guides" into what was explicitly the English Channel off the coast of Dorset. Not that Shakespeare refrains from staging some profoundly terrible things in England. But the blinding of Gloucester, and the blind Gloucester's attempt to throw himself from the cliffs of Dover, are presented as having happened far back in the mists of time. Nor are English audiences the only ones whom Pinter's plays of the public sphere might disconcert. His set-pieces of dehumanizing humiliation – Stanley reduced to a grunting animal in *The Birthday Party*, the blindfolded man in *The New World Order* being told about what will happen to his wife, Victor in *One for the Road* being told about his wife's duties in the staff brothel, being forced to drink whisky after the torture inflicted on his tongue, and being told, as if quite casually, about his son's murder – are universally horrendous. And as if to add insult to injury, Pinter frequently compels audiences to feel a deep guilt by association. Goldberg and McCann's interrogation of Stanley in *The Birthday Party*, or Lush's account in *The Hothouse* of how he lauded the institution to the mother of the patient who had mysteriously died there, will seem savagely funny, until it dawns on the audience that they have been lured into laughing with the victimizers at the victims' expense, an experience suggestively discussed by Christopher Innes under the heading "Harold Pinter: Power Plays and the Trap of Comedy" (Innes 1992: 279–297). In Pinter, the victimizers, Nicolas in *One for the Road* especially, can be quite dazzling in their Machiavellian mastery of language and situation. An audience, utterly appalled by its own reaction, can find them brilliantly attractive.

In this light, it begins to look as if the plays of the public sphere were Pinter's own instruments of torture, his way of bullying and blackmailing the audience into submission. That many people have resisted them is unsurprising, and such resistance seems likely to continue. Yet on the other hand, these plays *have* been performed, have been accepted, and praised even. On what grounds, then, can such brutal emotional coercion, if that is what it really is, be licensed?

For one thing, satire of the establishment is not in itself offensive or upsetting, and can even be richly entertaining. In free countries this has long traditions, and in the England of Pinter's time there were, for instance, the popular satirical review *Beyond the Fringe* (1960–1966) and the no less popular satirical television programmes *That Was the Week that Was* (1962–1963) and *Yes, Minister* (1980–1982). In *The Hothouse* especially, Pinter is often working in this vein, as in Roote's homage to the institution's great founder:

> As my predecessor said, on one unforgettable occasion: "Order, gentlemen, for God's sake, order!" I remember the silence, row upon row of electrified faces, he with his golden forelock, his briar burning, upright and commanding, a soldier's stance, looking down from the platform. The gymnasium was packed to suffocation, standing room only. The lucky ones were perched on vaulting horses, hanging without movement from the wallbars. "Order, gentlemen," he said, "for the love of Mike!" As one man we looked out of the window at Mike, and gazed at the statue, covered in snow, it so happened, then as now. Mike! The predecessor of my predecessor, the predecessor of us all, the man who laid the foundation stone, the man who introduced the first patient, the man who, after the incredible hordes of patients, or would-be patients, had followed him through town and country, hills and valleys, waited under hedges, lined the bridges and sat six feet deep in the ditch, opened institution after institution up and down the country, rest homes, nursing homes, convalescent homes, sanatoria. He was sanctioned by the Ministry, revered by the populace, subsidised by the State. He had set in motion an activity for humanity, of humanity and by humanity. And the keyword was order.   (I, 214)

Then as regards the shockingly English settings, in the post-war years Pinter was by no means the only writer in the West to imply that Nazism was not a peculiarly German phenomenon and could in principle have happened elsewhere. In England, his work was anticipated by Golding's *Lord of the Flies* of 1952, in which the English schoolboys who kill the visionary Simon are under the influence of the Nazistic Jack. In Robert Muller's novel *After All, This Is England* of 1965, England's susceptibility to Nazistic indoctrination and forms of control was suggested even more explicitly.

As for offering the audience spectacles of humiliation and trapping them into self-recriminating laughter, cases of this can equally well be found in Pinter's plays of the private sphere, as when, in *Old Times*, Anna and Deeley poke cruel fun at Kate for always having been, as they say, such an unrealistic dreamer that her head simply seemed to float away. If an audience accepts such unnerving moves in a play like this, then their presence in plays of the public sphere will not in itself be automatically off-putting, and the same consideration applies in the matter of attractive victimizers. In *The Caretaker*, for instance, the long speech in which Mick grills Davies is at once quite as frightening to the victim and quite as mesmerizing for an audience as anything said by Nicolas to Victor in *One for the Road*.

Seen this way, then, the plays of the public sphere do subject an audience to a pretty brutal emotional pressure, but not quite as brutal as may at first appear. Nor are these plays nearly as unreasonable and unrealistic as Luckhurst's account of them unintentionally suggests. When she sees them as arguing that all citizens have a "crucial obligation" to apply "unflinching, unswerving, fierce intellectual determination" in order to "define the *real* truth of our lives and our societies", she is reading them through the lens of Pinter's own non-literary activity as a political activist. As a member of the intelligentsia he certainly felt that he had such an obligation himself, and he lived up to it. But in these plays, the characters who resist tyranny, including even the educated young woman in *Mountain Language* and the bookish Victor in *One for the Road*, do so, not by way of intellectual labour, but simply by having their hearts in the right place. I have already quoted the beautiful simplicities of the genuine communication between the young lovers and between the old woman and the prisoner in *Mountain Language*. In *Party Time*, nothing can prevent Charlotte from honouring her husband's memory, or Dusty from steadily trying to put the fate of her brother Jimmy on the agenda. And in *Ashes to Ashes*, Rebecca is a less self-centred version of Pope's Eloisa. She does not so much consciously arrive at a decision as simply begin to live her life according to the perceptions of her self-awakening sensibility. What breaks Devlin's grip on her is that, having had her eyes and ears open all the time, she is finally starting to respond as a human being. True to Pinter's sense of the delayed-action fuses by which our emotional lives develop, she did not react at once, and it would be inaccurate to describe her as traumatized by the terrible things she has noticed. Shocked, certainly. But the shock now triggers a way of being in the world that rounds out her own humanity. So much so, that the most remarkable thing about her victory over Devlin is its sheer gentleness. Here Pinter has created a wonderful character who seems totally different from his own belligerent public image, an achievement which in the long run could have far greater historical consequences than the icy fury of his Nobel acceptance speech, for instance.

In their different ways, the collective coerciveness which he stages in the plays of the public sphere and the coerciveness in personal relations which figures so largely in the plays of the private sphere are equally unpleasant. We have seen that in both kinds of play the longing for genuine communication is also strongly present, and that this can even break through into the interaction of stage, sometimes in the face of huge inhibitions or obstacles, on much rarer occasions quite without effort. This makes Pinter's own two kinds of coerciveness – his Modernist assumption that we shall take the writing's verbal icon on trust, and the emotional pressure under which he puts us to agree with his political analysis – much easier to bear. And so, throughout his work, does our sense of his sheer truthfulness. Here I do not mean that he tells what he and, following him, Luckhurst call "the *real* truth" about anything, or that he has what Billington calls a "point". I am speaking, as so often, about negative capability: about the honesty with which he explores a situation *without* purporting to say the last word on it. The human dynamism of a character like Rebecca; the eloquent body-language of the speechless Devlin when his grip loosens and he takes his hand from Rebecca's throat: in these kinds of case we are dealing with a dramatic communication which raises genuineness to an apophatic dimension. We are not being told to swallow a dogma. We are being given the chance to compare notes with another human being's most thoughtful response to ways of being in the world.

In some of the earlier plays, and in *The Room*, *A Night Out* and *The Dwarfs* especially, the truthfulness is intensely serious. These are disturbing plays, and the only concession to an audience's possible craving for entertainment is the strong element of suspense – we are not far away from Hitchcock. But to suggest that, to playgoers who yield to his forms of writerly coercion, who pay close attention, and who are prepared to bring their own ethical judgement into play, Pinter never offers a more congenial trade-off would totally underestimate him as a man of the theatre. There was nothing he did not know about performance, and his plays lend themselves to histrionics in the most primitive and powerful sense. They overflow with sheer exuberance and energy, whose expression is sometimes formidably comic.

As time goes on, some of his humour will seem just as dated as Shakespeare's. He had a remarkable facility in sexual jokes, some of which already read like playing to his own time's groundlings, as it were. In *Old Times*, for instance, there are the ravenously Lesbian usherettes in the cinema Deeley says he visited. The otherwise magnificent *Moonlight* is in my view flawed by a similar flippancy, a flippancy actually in the face of death, not so much on the part of the dying Andy, in whom the anxious questioning about what death is actually like and the simultaneous determination to brazen it out ring very true, but in the scenes between the absent sons, which do not progress, and which surely play like second-rate cabaret. As it happens, the same uncertainty of tone occurs in the thematically related *Family Voices*, perhaps reflecting Pinter's personal lack of ease in face of his own father's death, and of his own son's self-distancing from him.

Be that as it may, of far more lasting entertainment value, it seems to me, is a distinctive tone of sardonic glee in alliance with lively imagination. Pinter characters exhibit this in many different forms, but it is seldom gratuitous, and can vitally move the interaction forward. One example from *Moonlight* is Andy's memory of Bel as a young wife. Out of context his words may seem cruelly misogynistic. But Bel, as I say, always gives as good as she gets, and her latest bombshell has been the revelation that she not only was unfaithful to him with Maria but also loved Ralph, Maria's husband and Andy's friend. Presumably thinking that attack is the best form of defence, Andy replies:

> And how I loved you. I'll never forget the earliest and loveliest days of our mar-
> riage. You offered your body to me. Here you are, you said one day, here's my body.
> Oh thanks very much, I said, that's very decent of you, what do you want me to do
> with it? Do what you will, you said. This is going to need a bit of thought, I said. I
> tell you what, hold on to it for a couple of minutes, will you? Hold on while I call
> a copper.   (IV, 375–376)

No less integral to the ongoing interaction, and equally generous in the licence it gives an actor to entertain at full tilt, can be Pinter's pastiches and parodies of other writers and genres. I have already quoted Roote's commemoration of the illustrious founder in *The Hothouse*. Another rich example is the speech Willy makes on giving away his sister Diana to Disson in *Tea Party*, which conjures up the world of a nineteenth-century romance:

> I can remember those long summer evenings at Sunderley, my mother and I
> crossing the lawn towards the terrace and through the great windows hearing my
> sister play Brahms. The delicacy of her touch. My mother and I would, upon en-
> tering the music room, gaze in silence at Diana's long fingers moving in exquisite
> motion on the keys.   (III, 100)

More than enough to recharge Disson's inferiority complex!

But Pinter's comic performativeness is not just a matter of particular speeches. Perhaps rivalled by only Peter Shaffer among his own contemporaries, Pinter is a creator of great comic *characters*, and it is no coincidence that, as a director of his own plays, he saw to it that the language of speeches did not draw all the attention to itself. As the actor Roger Lloyd Pack testifies, "He's very good at making sure you find the humanity in a character, that you're not carried away by the language, and that you don't separate the language from the character" (Pack 2005: 182). Some of his comic characters have fairly minor prominence, rather like a walk-on caricature in Dickens, but they can do much to lighten the atmosphere of an entire play, as with Willy's dotty old aunts in *Night School* and their shady landlord Mr Solto, who claims to have talent-spotted Don Bradman. As for a more major figure, Pack is eloquent on Davies in *The Caretaker*, who despite his problems as a social outcast allows himself his little airs and graces, and has a low cunning which eventually leads to his comic comeuppance, a rather Jonsonian comeuppance, one has to say, both funny and cruel. Then there is Spooner in *No Man's Land*: full of soul and fantasy, but incurably derivative in his

Eliotian literary aspirations, and unstoppably verbose; for ever on the lookout for the main chance, yet always likely to fall flat on his face, and constantly in danger of exposing his own shabbiness; at one moment appealing to Hirst by echoing Kent's offer of his services to Lear, next moment asking him whether he will not at least come and do a reading for a poetry society he runs in a scruffy pub. Even Nicolas, the appalling interrogator in *One for the Road*, is, as I say, entertaining, admirable even, and – I think we must face it – comic. An audience will indeed licence an extraordinary performance, and the chance to provide an extraordinary performance is exactly what the part of Nicolas means for an actor. In senses explored by Richard Poirier (1992), all literature, and not just drama, has performative potential. But in Pinter, and especially with a character like Nicolas, this is very directly felt, in a way reminiscent of Browning's dramatic monologues, one of Nicolas's most obvious antecedents being the Duke in "My Last Duchess": a Machiavellian manipulator of words and people who will stop at nothing, a sheer monster whom we loathe and detest when judging him, as we certainly do, by "normal" standards, but whom it is difficult not to enjoy for his sheer brio, energy and genius (Langbaum 1957: 75–108). In at once shunning and admiring in Nicolas what Blake would have called the proverbs of experience, an audience is responding to the presence of a life-force of enormous power.

Discussing this quality in Pinter's great comic characters of both the more amusing and more sinister varieties, his friend and fellow-playwright Simon Gray remarked that such characters are defined by their ultimate freedom from circumstance, a freedom which expresses itself "in an aria of free-wheeling lunacy, sometimes comic, sometimes frightening, but never in need of justification" (Gray 1985: 41). This is well said, I think, and it is small wonder that, when put in touch with freedom of this order, playgoers and readers do not much chafe against the authorial coercion that has brought them to it. Its energy is far too infectious and restorative – too liberating!

Nor are Pinter's insights into genuineness, his truthfulness, his comedy, and the sheer vigour of his writing the only compensations. What makes his coercion even more forgivable is that in the last analysis it paradoxically *improves* the chances for genuine communication. In urging spectators or readers to interpret the plays of the private sphere as Modernist enigmas, he is not only extremely challenging, but extremely empowering. He could not have knocked the ball into their court with greater panache. But how they then play it is entirely up to them. When he urges them to consult their sensibilities as regards the behaviour of collective ideology's minions in the plays of the public sphere, similarly, he is invoking Kant's notion of the universal human right to respect and fair treatment (Kant 1998 [1785]), the notion so central to the high modern, postmodern and post-postmodern sense of justice, and underpinning the concept of genuine communication itself. In short, his coerciveness, though prodigiously forceful, is responsibly deployed in the best of causes.

10.6   The genuineness of Pinter's dramaturgy

So Pinter's coerciveness itself implies a profound respect for human beings in general. This extends to his own addressees. Far from cancelling out his own genuineness of communication, his urgent force makes for a world in which genuine communication can thrive more widely, and in which his own truthfulness can indeed go hand in hand with a negatively capable deference towards every possible reader or spectator. If I now return to tellability, the concept introduced in my study of *Great Expectations* as one of the keys to a communicational narratology, I think I can show that this ultimate deference of Pinter's had fundamental implications for his dramaturgy.

Primary tellability in Pinter, his way of getting the audience immediately hooked on a story, varied from play to play, but mainly in parallel with the conventional tripartition of his career into phases of menace, memory and politics. In plays from his menace period, including those which I have also classed as plays of the public sphere, primary tellability is very strong. The audience will be in no doubt that something is happening, even if they are sometimes not at all sure what it is, and these plays also lead to a powerful curtain. *The Dumb Waiter*, for instance, ends with the climax of Ben pointing that gun at Gus and under orders to shoot him. In one sense this may seem open-ended. Will he shoot, or will he not? Yet in a larger sense, a story-line really has come to a definite end here, in that whichever way Ben chooses there will be no more business as usual. If he does shoot Gus, their partnership will be over. If he does not shoot him, they will both be out of a job, and probably both be shot by one of the organization's other assassination squads. *The Basement*, on the other hand, is transitional between menace and memory. Primary tellability is still strong, and the final curtain apparently very tidy, in that the play, having opened with Stott turning up at Law's door with Jane in tow, now closes with Stott himself installed in the flat and Law turning up at his door with Jane. At the same time, though, there is already a hint here that a process has reached a point at which it could start all over again, in a kind of *perpetuum mobile*, with Stott recovering Jane and Law recovering the flat, and so on and so on. In *Landscape* and *Silence*, plays of memory *par excellence*, some such recycling is definitely likely, and primary tellability is far lower. Nothing seems to be happening; characters are not even talking to other characters; and at the end of these plays there is not even phantom closure. A *perpetuum mobile* does now seem to be operating, so that the words of the play could be repeated over and over in a kind of eternal present, as in point of fact is already starting to happen within the text of *Silence*, where Ellen, Rumsey and Bates each have their own recurrent leitmotivs. Then in many other memory and post-memory plays, including, despite their lack of direct dialogue, even *Monologue* and *Family Voices*, primary tellability becomes a good deal stronger again. In *A Kind of Alaska*, for instance, on the one hand there is a welling-up of Deborah's memories, which are partly repetitive or circular, but on the other hand Hornby and Pauline make their intervention into the timeless silence in which Deborah has been sleeping, hoping to draw her into what they themselves think of as the present. In *Old Times* and *No Man's Land*, too, characters do a lot of reminiscing, but there is also a strongish story about them negotiating the detail of the past and its significance for the present. Often they fantasize new versions of what happened long ago, or fantasize things that never happened at all, using their fantasies as weapons in their battle here and now.

Secondary tellability, on the other hand, the story's appeal to something deeper than the audience's eagerness to know "what next?", is very high in all of Pinter's plays, and in *Landscape* and *Silence*, quintessentially memory plays, is almost the only kind of tellability there is. There, and in other plays, such as *Moonlight*, where the element of memory is high and primary tellability fairly low, the audience is not drawn in by an exciting story, but is faced with the challenge of having to work out the bearing of one thing on another so as to make some kind of overall assessment. The experience is similar to that of reading Eliot's *Four Quartets*, which like *Landscape* and *Silence* seem to be about to repeat themselves and to exist in an eternal present. Put the other way round, when secondary tellability is high, readers or playgoers feel that the work will reward a later visit. One of the things we take away from a great poem is precisely a sense of being invited back to it, and as Antonia Fraser has remarked, "One should never forget that Harold wanted to be a poet and in many ways sees himself as a poet. He would agree with the order on Shakespeare's grave …: 'Poet and Playwright', i.e. poet first" (Fraser 2010: 89).

Primary tellability is by definition something that gets hold of audiences in a very primitive way. When it *is* a factor, it is what draws them into the play sufficiently deeply for them to start thinking about secondary tellability. One might at first think, then, that in their temporal process of assimilating the play its story is what comes first, well before questions of meaning and value. But human beings are perfectly capable of *parallel* processing, and in Pinter even primary tellability can be far from blatant. This is reflected in the critical orthodoxy's commentaries on the masks which have to be penetrated before there can be any real grasp of what is going on. Earlier I noted that directors such as Hall and Mendes have assumed that people disguise their intentions in real life, that Pinter created characters whose intentions are realistically disguised, that rehearsals designed to pin down a play's "melodrama" or the "secret play" strip off the disguise, that other rehearsals put it back on again, and that the audience then has to repeat the detective work of the first rehearsals. There is much truth in this, it seems to me, but the reason why people in real life do not wear their heart upon their sleeve may sometimes be that their heart is still undecided. This, too, is strongly registered in Pinter's plays, and this alone was enough to make his dramaturgy radically different from Shakespeare's.

The convention adopted by Shakespeare was that characters themselves know what they think, feel, and are trying to do, and that they instantly say so, either to each other or to the audience in soliloquy. Macbeth fully understands, and explains, his own actions and their spiritual consequences, whereas even for the poet Hirst in *No Man's Land* self-knowledge is more tight-lipped and difficult. Most of Shakespeare's successors followed in his footsteps here, including George Bernard Shaw, who sometimes pushed the convention a bit too hard, producing those characters whom Penelope Gilliatt finds so inhumanly logical and transparent. Pinter's approach to character psychology revealed itself to Douglas Hodge when he played the part of Jerry in *Betrayal*. What Hodge found so refreshing was that the text did not require the actors to make their characters express an immediate reaction to what was going on. The converse, we can add, is that when a character on Pinter's stage does have a strong outburst of feeling, this is not necessarily a reaction to something happening in the present. As noted earlier, in *Ashes to Ashes* Rebecca's reaction to all the horror she has witnessed has gradually defined itself over a period time. In *Betrayal*, Robert's response to his discovery of Charlotte and Jerry's affair works on a similar delayed-action fuse, and because Pinter tells the story backwards, in the beginning of the play Robert seems bitter and misogynistic towards Charlotte, whereas in later scenes, which are chronologically earlier, he seems more controlled, and even courteous and care-free. To recall another earlier observation, *Betrayal* is very much suggesting that a person's present emotional life is not merely a matter of what is happening here and now, but continuously feeds upon things which happened long ago, things which in and of themselves may almost be forgotten. The similarity with plots in late Dickens is striking. It was by burrowing back into the distant past that Pip came to understand why Miss Havisham is now so strange.

As an audience becomes accustomed to Pinter's dramaturgical originality, they will begin to speculate for themselves about what it was in the past that is making a character behave so forcefully in the here and now. In *The Homecoming*, for instance, why is Max always so viciously bad-tempered towards his brother Sam, whom he himself, it turns out, has treated so badly by kicking him out of the family business? Why does he say that Sam "would bend over for half a dollar on Blackfriars Bridge"? (III, 56) Is Sam really gay, and Max homophobic? Or could it have something to do with Jessie, whose memory Sam so honours? *Could* there have been rivalry between the two brothers for her affections, and could Max, though victorious in that case, have been left with a suspicion that Jessie regretted her choice, and that it was this which led her to find sex and solace with MacGregor? This line of questioning could be carried much further, drawing in the other family members as well, whose immediate reactions may also bear little relation to what actually seems to be going on in the present.

Although all this kind of thing is in one sense a matter of primary tellability, of working out exactly who did or thought or felt exactly what, the implications for secondary tellability are substantial. In both *Betrayal* and *The Homecoming*, the strength of male feeling, so inexplicable to an audience at first glance, raises the whole question of sexual mores and gender roles. Both Robert in *Betrayal* and Max in *The Homecoming* are clearly deeply wounded. But are they wounded because their original feelings towards their wives were misogynistically possessive? If they had been more prepared to regard their wives as free agents, would their own pain and anger have been less? Or is the strength of their present mysogynistic stance largely epiphenomenal to their

wives' infidelities and, if so, would Pinter then think of this as a mitigating circumstance, or would he absolutely not take such a view? What, too, about our own assessment here? It is no part of my purpose to state a definitive judgement on any of these
questions for either of these plays, since definitive judgement is not actually possible.
If it had been, the plays would have ceased to be discussed, and would thereby have
ceased to be literature. My point is rather that the realism of Pinter's character psychology tends to interweave primary and secondary tellability in such a way as to
leave his audiences even freer than those of Shakespeare to let discussion arise and
flourish. It is one of the most crucial aspects of his negatively capable genuineness.

Closely bound up with his realism of character presentation is his obvious reluctance to exploit the three devices which were Shakespeare's principal means to
kick-start the audience's communal comparing of notes about his stories and subject-matter: soliloquies, choric statements, and dramatic irony. The paradox is that,
in largely dispensing with these possibilities, Pinter has himself set playgoers and
play-readers eagerly talking, by again allowing audiences much more freedom. It is
the relative absence of these devices in Pinter which explains Billington's impression
that he lessens an audience's sense of the dramatist's own presence. The only thing
Billington forgot to say here was that Shakespeare's heavy use of the devices did not
prevent him from achieving negative capability all the same, and was actually central
to his particular way of doing so, as I tried to show in my Introduction.

As for soliloquies in Pinter, the speeches characters make in the memory plays
are often not addressed to, or at least not heard by, other characters, but neither are
they soliloquies in the usual sense of the term. They are never directly addressed to the
audience, but are self-communing, and not with a view to future action, but as a way
of processing memory. So if such passages do not have the realism of spoken dialogue,
and if they often carry that high degree of secondary tellability which can remind us of
Four Quartets, they are nevertheless at least as authentic as a stream-of-conscious novel,
and equally dramatic in their mode of presentation, with no omnisciently pointing sign-
posts. In *The Dwarfs*, too, secondary tellability is at a poetically high level, and, exceptionally for a Pinter character, Len does have three longish soliloquies, plus the play's
last words. This may certainly prompt us to empathize with him, and to see the world
through Len's own eyes. Yet because of his envious insecurities his view of the world is
very strange and destructive, so that the soliloquies will most probably act upon us like
a dramatic monologue by Browning, not by *helping* us to form an opinion but by *challenging* us to do so in resistance to the character's own opinion (Langbaum 1957). Then
Jimmy does soliloquise at the end of *Party-Time*, Bridget at the end of *Moonlight*, and
the Waiter at the end of *Celebration*: Jimmy is reduced to that sense of sucking the dark;
Bridget meditates on that ghostly reunion with her parents for which she is waiting; and
the Waiter contemplates his grandfather's distinction in having managed to find the
door out from life and all its mysteries. But these soliloquies are all shortish, and they tell
us little more about the characters who speak them than we know already.

In point of fact, these three closing speeches are the nearest Pinter ever comes to choric statements, and in poetically summing up something of the entire play's mood they recall Feste's closing song in *Twelfth Night*. Here, too, though, Pinter is working through particular characters' own intense experience. Or to put this another way, his negatively capable dramaturgy springs from the same instinct as did his own style as an actor. As Katie Mitchell commented,

> [t]here are two types of actors generally. There are those who play the audience as the main relationship and there are those who play the other characters as the main relationship. There are some actors who are fantastically skilled, who always play the main relationship with the audience. Harold isn't like that. You could say (but not to him, of course!) that he's a great Stanislavsky actor, a great *interactive* actor, although for him it's just instinctive.   (Mitchell 2005: 198)

This makes it easier to understand why, in his own plays, there is such a shortage of authoritative generalization, rationalization, moralizing. The apparent exceptions prove the rule. When, in the final moments of *No Man's Land*, Spooner says to Hirst, "You are in no man's land. Which never moves, which never changes, which never grows older, but which remains forever, icy and silent" (III, 399), this is not seriously choric comment but pure Spooner: volubly unhesitating (no notational dots on Pinter's part), no syntactical breakdowns, glib, derivative. It is Spooner's travesty of the utterance that earlier came to Hirst himself through such grimly painful experience (with notational dots a-plenty), and in the play's last line Hirst, who began the play by mocking Spooner's boast that he could stick a needle through any "essential flabbiness of […] stance", delivers an appropriate *coup de grâce* to Spooner's own flabbiness of bardic wisdom: "I'll drink to that" (III, 322, 399).

As for dramatic irony, the situation which arises when the audience knows more than one or more of the characters on stage, Pinter's most Shakespearian use of this is in *The Collection*, when Harry goes to visit Stella. She tells him that she and his Bill have *not* committed adultery, and that the whole thing was simply something dreamed up by her James. An alert audience will know that this is not true, because in an earlier scene James and she have discussed the adultery as something about which *she* had informed *him*. As a result, the audience will later be very interested to hear Harry telling James and Bill that it was Stella who dreamed the whole thing up. The audience will probably *not* take this to mean that Harry is the type of gay man who thinks women are merely a nuisance. They have already seen, during his visit to her, just how much they understand each other's position. Now face to face with Bill and James, Harry does not want to accuse James of fabrication anyway, since it would only reinforce the two younger men's sexual union against him. But in saying that the fabrication was Stella's, there is also a sense, an audience can feel, that he has read her correctly. The misery he is suffering at the hands of his own unloving lover has helped him to understand her similar misery, and to understand the stratagems to which it might compel her. Uncharacteristically for Pinter, the dramatic irony here can have guided the audience towards an assessment.

In the early *A Night Out* there is another traditional use, of a kind with which Pinter was familiar from his roles in repertory thrillers and whodunits. Arthur, having in the previous scene murdered – or so he and the audience both believe at this point – his mother with the kitchen clock, now finds himself in the bed-sit of the girl he met on the street and begins to stare at the large clock on the mantelpiece. The girl, quite unaware of how her words are irritating him, continues talking, but the audience will already be fearing he will seize the clock as a weapon, as he eventually does, even though a second murder attempt does not materialize. This then is a dramatic irony which creates a sharp difference between the knowledge shared by the audience with one character on stage and the complete ignorance of another character. It is somewhat more typically Pinterian, however, in that its main product is merely an element of suspense. In no way does it stimulate the audience's meditation on the difficult issues which the play is otherwise offering for consideration.

In many other Pinter plays dramatic irony is, if anything, at an even lower level of interpretative relevance. One character overhears what another character says, or spies on what they are doing, but with few consequences of any kind at all. Stanley in *The Birthday Party*, for instance, finds out about the arrival of Goldberg and McCann well before they know that he knows about it. But this knowledge merely increases his anxiety without equipping him to resist them, and neither can it substantially affect an audience's assessments. Cases in Shakespeare which do remind us of Pinter are less typically Shakespearian. Polonius behind the arras is one of only fairly few characters in Shakespeare whose own ends are *not* immediately furthered as a result of overhearing something. In Pinter, that kind of situation is more common, though never so fatal to the character concerned. One example is in *Night School*, when Walter's old Aunt Annie, having tiptoed down the landing to try and hear what Walter and Sally are saying to each other in what used to be his room, is unable to hear, or understand at least, a word. The result is a pure comedy which, unlike the comedy of Malvolio being overheard by the perpetrators of the letter conspiracy, in no way furthers the action or affects the audience's assessment of any of the characters' life-goals.

In *Betrayal* and *Moonlight*, this kind of positively insignificant dramatic irony is built into the very structure of the play. In *Betrayal*, because the story is told in reverse chronological order, as the performance continues the audience becomes increasingly more god-like in perspective as compared with the characters on stage. The younger the characters get as the play continues, the more the audience already knows about their future. Yet the audience derives no help or benefit from this. They still have to make up their own minds about things, and the continuing play presents them with a steep learning curve, as they gradually work their way back to the apparently trivial incident which set the whole painful process of betrayal under way. In *Moonlight*, while Andy and Bel spend several scenes agonizing over whether their sons Fred and

Jake will eventually visit their dying father, the audience witnesses several scenes in which the sons' bitter sense of alienation from him becomes all too clear, so that the chances of a Victorian deathbed scene of the kind Andy would like seem to get smaller and smaller. Yet there is no sense in which the audience's knowledge here makes them superior to Andy, or more entitled than he himself to form an opinion of his moral judgement. The situation is totally different from that in which Shakespeare's Gloucester comes to think that his son Edgar is plotting against him, while the audience knows that Edmund is deliberately tricking him into believing this. Andy is simply *not* deceived about the basic situation. All along, his knowledge of the spiritual distance between himself and his sons is at least as certain as that of the audience. He does not *need* to hear what the sons are saying to each other.

In other plays Pinter's dramaturgical anti-Shakespearianism, as we can call it, is even more pronounced, because, as Philip Hope-Wallace noted, he totally reversed the normal pleasure of theatre, in that the audience sits in total ignorance while some of the characters on the stage must have a far better idea of what is going on and of what it means (Billington 2007: 176). In *Old Times* Deeley apparently surprises Anna, when he says that years ago he spent a pleasant evening in a London pub just staring up her skirt. The audience will perhaps be inclined to take this as a present-time fantasy on his part. But later on Anna says that it is true, that she had been aware of it at the time, that she had actually been wearing Kate's underclothes, and that Kate herself had been apprised of the situation and displayed a keen interest. But on the other hand, Anna also says, "There are things I remember which may never have happened but as I recall them so they take place" (III, 270). Here, then, the audience is presented with an enormous interpretative challenge, as regards the line between fact and fiction and the significance of both past and present. And an exactly similar case occurs in *The Collection*, where, as noted, only Bill and Stella can really know if any adultery has taken place. The audience, like Harry and Stuart, are left guessing, and left trying to evaluate what significance both truth and fiction would have here.

If Pinter's characters are not self-explanatory, if there is a dearth of choric comment, if his dramatic ironies tend to be interpretively irrelevant, and if he sometimes puts dramatic irony into reverse, so that the audience is more *ignorant* than one or more characters on stage, then the endings of his plays also depart from Shakespearian convention, which was again far less obviously conducive than Pinterian convention to negative capability. Shakespeare's endings are resoundingly final, leaving nothing of the story in doubt. A Shakespearian tragedy ends with one or more dead bodies and a new regime coming to power. A Shakespearian comedy ends with weddings and dancing. And Shakespearian tragi-comedies and history plays are hardly less clear-cut. Pinter said that theatre critics like to put plays into little boxes – this one is a comedy, that one is a tragedy – when they are stumped for anything else to say about them (Pinter 2005 [1961]: 44). He also remarked that although many commentators talk about his own comedy, his plays do not actually offer much to laugh about during the last ten minutes (Pinter 2005 [1996]: 95). He was clearly aware that his own work was resisting classification according to traditional genre conventions, and his avoidance of unambiguous closure was doubtless one of the things he had in mind. To return to *The Dumb Waiter*, immediately before the curtain we know that the story is about to come to an end one way or the other, but we still have to ask ourselves whether or not Ben will shoot Gus. This is the final "What happens next?" of the play's primary tellability. Yet we cannot decide what we expect here without getting deeply involved in its secondary tellability. On the play's showing, how strong is an individual's loyalty to an organization's mission statement likely to be? How strong the bond of a friendship? Is it only the order to take a buddy's life that will make an individual rebel against a boss's commands? Or can even that be tolerated? We find our minds circling from the story's "What happens next?" to that famous remark of E. M. Forster's in a radio talk of 1938 – "[I]f I had to choose between betraying my country and betraying my friend, I hope I should have the guts to betray my country" (Forster 1965 [1938]: 76) – and back again. Circling inconclusively: for unless I am mistaken, in the end we shall be *unable* to decide whether Ben shoots Gus, because the issues involved allow no certainty. Our negatively capable response to Pinter's own negatively capable genuineness will have been our pondering of the likelihoods.

All these un-Shakespearian yet negatively capable narratological and dramaturgical practices confirm Pinter's deep roots in Symbolism and literary Modernism. While giving audiences an arguably unprecedented freedom to work things out for themselves, he simultaneously maximized the interpretative challenge. Like a symbol in Baudelaire, like a haiku in the Imagists, like an epiphany in *Dubliners*, like a story as told by James, like a neo-Metaphysical conceit in early Eliot, a Pinter play is an aesthetic construct with its own kind of beauty and suggestivity. It is *about* the real world, and it *communicates – makes community* – within the real world. But it does so, not by numbingly spelling things out, but by inviting pleasurable contemplation. Ultimately, there *is* nothing to be spelled out. There are only lives being lived, or lives which have been lived in the past. More precisely, there is Pinter's life and our life, with the Pinter play as his way of inviting dialogue – a comparing of notes – between the two, his own perceptions in as refined and suggestive a form as he could make them, our perceptions as alertly open as possible in response to his generosity.

Pinter's Modernist communicational mode is especially evident in that poetically high level of secondary tellability. I have already mentioned parallels with the eternal present of *Four Quartets*, and Hirst's mention in *No Man's Land* of blackened tennis balls under the leaves in countryside gullies, once thrown by girls for their dogs, or by children for each other, brings "Burnt Norton" particularly close. But it would be easy to compile an anthology of widely varied poetic extracts. In *A Slight Ache* and *The Dwarfs* there are the astonishing hallucinations of Edward and Len's unstable minds as they become ever more unstuck. In *Landscape* there is the sustained contrast between the infinitely tender daydreams of Beth and the unblinking realism of Duff. In *Old Times* there is the magical evocation of post-war London as seen through the eyes of two typists sharing a flat. Every reader or playgoer would make a different selection. The only difficulty in the operation would be the leaving out of everything else, not only because, with few exceptions, everything else is written with equal skill and suggestivity, but because in a Pinter play everything coheres. To see this is the greatest poetic challenge of all.

Another aspect of Pinter's challenging Modernism is his use of song. This is not very frequent, but is extremely suggestive when it does occur, not, however, in the Shakespearian manner by wooing characters and audience into a single mood, but by hinting, at one and the same time, an acute desire for a human communion, and its sheer difficulty. In fact the music and its associations apophatically intimate the tension between genuineness and coerciveness, as when Lambert and Matt unite in song at the end of *Celebration*:

> LAMBERT *joins in the song, slapping his thighs in time with* MATT.
>
> LAMBERT *and* MATT:
>
> Who's in front?
> Who's in front?
>
> LAMBERT
>
> Get out the bloody way
> You silly old cunt!
>
> LAMBERT *and* MATT *laugh.*   (IV, 505–506)

There can be little doubt of their present wish to be good brothers and buddies to each other, but their lyrics are hardly very distinguished, and their raucous communion will leave them with a dreadful hangover tomorrow morning, when their more customary antagonisms, not altogether in abeyance even during this evening's bash, will also kick in with a vengeance. Another example is in *Old Times*, where Deeley and Anna have a long sequence in which they sing catchy tunes from way back when, so ensuring a strong infusion of nostalgia for the good old days, except that they are also using the songs strategically in their battle over, and against, Kate. Even more disturbing is the following passage in *Ashes to Ashes*:

> REBECCA
>
> [...]
>
> *(singing softly)* "Ashes to ashes" –
>
> DEVLIN
>
> "And dust to dust" –

REBECCA

"If the women don't get you" –

DEVLIN

"The liquor must."

Pause.

I always knew you loved me.

REBECCA

Why?

DEVLIN

Because we like the same tunes.

Silence. (IV, 425–426)

By this stage in the play it is clear that there is absolutely no ethical or emotional harmony between the two of them, and Devlin is soon going to make his attempt at aggressive foreplay. The earliest examples of the device, however, are in *The Birthday Party*, where Meg and McCann drunkenly sing Irish tunes together, hers sentimentally amorous, his sentimentally brutal (a discordant duo which curiously anticipates Beth and Duff in *Landscape*), and where earlier on Stanley and McCann alternately whistle lines from the "Mountains of Mourn" while McCann is beginning, and Stanley is already resisting, the bullying interrogation. They share the tune, and the tune's sentimental aura, but their enmity is total. In all such cases, the play's spoken words are coopting the music as a stimulus at once more generous and more challenging towards the audience's hermeneutic independence.

Finally, there is a Modernist cultivation of the visual. As noted earlier, Pinter said that his plays sometimes began with an image which he had to explore. His explorations took the form of words for characters to speak, except that the words can almost fall away again in the presence of apophatic tableau. This is where Pinter's dramaturgy does finally come closer to Shakespeare's: the Shakespeare who in *The Winter's Tale* provided the image of Leontes touching the "statue" of Hermione and finding it warm. There is not just Devlin's grip loosening and his hand falling from Rebecca's throat in *Ashes to Ashes*. There is Rose, or rather Sal, in *The Room*, touching the eyes and head of the blind Negro; there is Ruth at curtain in *The Homecoming*, seated with Joey's head in her lap, Max kneeling to her, Lenny looking on, Sam supine; there are Beth and Duff throughout *Landscape*, Rumsey, Bates and Ellen throughout *The Silence*, and Anna, Kate and Seeley at the end of *Old Times*, each character's loneliness defined as a particular area of the stage; there is the speaker in *Monologue*, sitting in a chair throughout the play, addressing another, empty chair; there are the apparitions of the ghostly Jimmy and Bridget in *Party-Time* and *Moonlight*; and so the list could go on. As Richard Allen Cave (2009) and Roger Davidson (2005: 190) have shown, no placing, no movement, on the Pinter stage is gratuitous. Everything the eye sees relates to what the ear hears and the mind ponders.

One especially beautiful example, it seems to me, which speaks volumes without a single word being spoken, involves Stella's cat in *The Collection*. At one point Stuart reports to Stella that Bill has told him that it was she who had instigated the alleged adultery, but that he (Bill) had agreed with him (Stuart) that she must have been somewhat hypnotized by him (Bill). "He agreed it can happen sometimes. He told me he'd been hypnotized once by a cat. Wouldn't go into any more details, though." Which obviously lets the audience have a good laugh. But it is a laugh which can sensitize them to something which happens later. When Harry visits Stella, they both know that they are both in danger of losing their loved-ones through betrayal, and Stella is sitting with her cat in her lap. Finally, Harry says, "Oh, what a beautiful kitten, what a really beautiful kitten. Kitty, kitty, kitty, what do you call her, come here, kitty, kitty." And then the following happens:

> HARRY *sits next to* STELLA *and proceeds to pet and nuzzle the kitten.*
>
> *Fade to half light.* (II, 137)

There is surely a terrible loveliness and sadness to this. Both characters are in anguish at their likely loss, sad for each other's sake, yet unable to offer each other moral support, let alone emotional and sexual consolation, both now merely fondling the cat, so beautiful and, yes, so hypnotic, but only a surrogate – only a cat, poor thing!

My paraphrase of the ineffable merely stumbles and simplifies. Yet challenged by such an amazing moment, paraphrase, commentary, are after all a discourse which we need. Tableaus like this are at once the most extremely aestheticizing, but also the most genuinely communicational device in Pinter's entire dramaturgical repertoire. They are Pinter at his most Pinter, and the link in such cases between wordless visuality and the community-making of genuine communication has been tellingly hinted in a remark by Richard Allen Cave: "A refined use of body language ... ensures the plays an after-life for audiences, as subject for debate or what Yeats would term 'excited reverie'" (Cave 2009: 138).

10.7 Towards better communication

I have tried to show that, both in the plays of the private sphere and in the plays of the public sphere, Pinter's characters can be very coercive, whether in their own purely personal interest or on behalf of, or in the name of, a collectivity. Sometimes their coercion is successful, but the advantages it brings are questionable. Sometimes it is totally unsuccessful, and sometimes several characters are unsuccessful at once.

Coercion's victories can also be Pyrrhic, and these, too, can be distributed between several different characters. Yet despite the widespread view of Pinter's dramatis personae as "all stalking round in the jungle, trying to kill each other", his characters sometimes fervently desire a world in which there was less coercion, and long to be less coercive themselves, to become better human beings, as some of them phrase it, and to have more meaningful and rewarding relationships. Even in plays of the menace phase, this is quite apparent, but in the memory plays it is explored in great depth. And throughout all four decades of his writing career, Pinter wrote episodes in which genuine communication actually comes about as a mode of behaviour on stage, often in the face of what seem hopeless odds. In *Night* it even seems easy and natural, because the two characters involved are both so ready to recognize each other's autonomy. On the whole, his perception can at first seem to be that genuineness of this order is *not* all that likely in human intercourse. But two considerations sharply qualify such an appearance. For one thing, genuine communication does not have high tellability, so that most of the world's stories have been about its breakdown or total absence. For another thing, from Pinter's very first play onwards genuineness was always a possibility, unlikely or not.

As for Pinter himself, he is a forceful authorial agent, who does nothing to water down his powerful individuality or his own cultural formation. This involves a bourgeois emphasis on the values of family, love and friends, a now somewhat dated view of women, and a tradition of sensiblerie going back to Pope. More than fully recognized in commentary hitherto, his menace and memory plays place their addressees under strong pressure from an irrationalist Modernist aestheticism, which forces them into serious interpretative difficulties. In the political plays, his coercion is every bit as strong as many commentators have alleged, and is basically that of a politically oriented emotionalism. But both these kinds of coerciveness are considerably mitigated by his frank truthfulness, and by the comic genius and sheer vigour of his writing. And paradoxically, his coerciveness itself improves the chances of genuine communication, in that his Modernist style is a liberating challenge to the audience's own powers of thought, while his emotive politics offers an invitation to humane fellowship that is difficult to refuse. His fundamental respect for the human otherness of his addressees is reflected in narratological and dramaturgical strategies that are significantly different from those of Shakespeare and the English theatre tradition. Despite much commentary to the effect that his characters *hide* their feelings, his representation of them is far from assuming that they always know their own minds in the first place, and by not using choric characters, soliloquies and dramatic irony in the conventional way he gives members of the audience an even greater responsibility as parties to the process of understanding and interpretation. He trusts them to work out things for themselves, to form their own assessments, to respond to poetic suggestivity, to build significance out intermingled words and music and image, and indeed out of wordlessness. He gives them something to think about which he has thought about very seriously himself, and then leaves them to draw their own conclusions, as citizens no less capable than he himself.

So in his own relationship with his audience, Pinter is actually tending to *do better* than most of the human beings he represents on stage. He is more fully satisfying the human yearning for genuineness, for communion, for a truer dialogicality. He invites his audience into a dialogue in which, while contemplating the dialogue on stage, he and they together begin to form a more rewarding community. Their new dialogue *replaces*, as it were, the less satisfactory dialogue between the characters on stage.

CHAPTER 11

Afterword

Exploring literature's new dialogue

The "new dialogue" between Pinter and his audience "*replaces*, as it were, the less satisfactory dialogue between the characters on stage." In the closing pages of the present book, such a comment will come as no surprise. At many points in the studies collected here, I have expressed or implied the same kind of take on other writers as well.

To move to a fresh example, there is a sonnet by Coleridge which, for all its brevity, has major paradigmatic significance.

> *TO A FRIEND WHO ASKED, HOW I FELT WHEN*
> *THE NURSE FIRST PRESENTED MY INFANT TO ME*
>
> Charles! my slow heart was only sad, when first
>   I scanned that face of feeble infancy:
> For dimly on my thoughtful spirit burst
>   All I had been, and all my child might be!
> But when I saw it on its mother's arm,   5
>   And hanging at her bosom (she the while
>   Bent o'er its features with a tearful smile)
> Then I was thrilled and melted, and most warm
> Impressed a father's kiss: and all beguiled
>   Of dark remembrance and presageful fear,   10
>   I seemed to see an angel-form appear –
>   'Twas even thine, beloved woman mild!
> So for the mother's sake the child was dear,
> And dearer was the mother for the child.[1]

What makes this poem so exceptionally revealing of literature's workings is the explicitness of its dual address.

In the first word of the first line, Coleridge addresses by name the friend mentioned in the poem's title as its recipient. Charles is the sonnet's addressee persona, to which any other reader can also imaginatively latch on for the purposes and duration of reading the poem, even though the original Charles (probably either Charles Lamb or Charles Lloyd) was of course a unique individual with his own historical position

---

1. Quoted from Keach 2004.

(Sell 2000: 158–175). Exophoric address to a particular reader or group of readers in the real world outside the text sometimes is explicit like this, but is most often implicit. Either way, though, it is not something a text can do without, and it is bound to be historically specific. No utterance can be directed to the whole human race throughout the whole of human history. Exophoric address always assumes addressees of some particular formation or range of formations, even though our powers of imaginative empathy allow us to process language that is addressed to somebody different from ourselves, as when we read this poem now.

Then in line 12 there is equally explicit endophoric address when Coleridge directs some words to his wife, whom he has so far been describing, together with the baby and himself, within the world of the poem. But what the poem fairly strongly hints is that his relationship with his closest family is a bit more problematic than his relationship with Charles. There is something spontaneous about that exclamatory opening word, and about its being the man's Christian name. Coleridge's little son, by contrast, is merely an "infant", complete with "face of feeble infancy", merely a "child", merely a sexless "it". Even if, at the time of writing, the boy still had no name (even if, that is to say, Coleridge had not yet persuaded his wife to let him be called David Hartley after the philosopher), words such as "he / him", "son", "boy" and "baby" are notably absent. When he addresses his wife, similarly, he does not call her Sara but resorts to the anonymizing poeticality of the archaic second-person-singular pronoun, plus an even more artificial apostrophe: "beloved woman mild!" Then again, although the poem's last lines do describe a moment of shared happiness for the three of them, that happiness seems oddly precarious. On the one hand, there is a suggestion that, as far as Coleridge is concerned, the baby boy is not actually welcome in his own right. On the other hand, the claim that both mother and child are angelic reads like a sentimental over-correction of what has gone before: not only of the diabolization of Coleridge himself, but of the prospect of the child's turning out to be no less disastrously sinful than his father.

Within the poem Coleridge is portrayed as a pathologically and self-knowingly introverted individual, who at first instinctively projects his intense guilt feelings on to the new-born baby. His difficulty in casting off his total self-absorption here is even marked in the punctuation. When he puts Sara's more outgoing response to the child within parentheses, it is as if he cannot at first bring her feelings into main focus, as if he does not immediately recognize and identify with them, and also, perhaps, as if he thought of them as merely womanly, and not the kind of thing to which he himself would immediately confess in the company of Charles and other cronies.

As represented within the poem, then, Coleridge's solipsism is detrimental to his family life. With Charles, by contrast, and with other readers who are able, willingly or reluctantly, to imagine their way into Charles's shoes, Coleridge's communication is in its own terms frank and untroubled. Here, then, we see even more clearly what I was pointing out in the case of Pinter: that literary writers' most important role within society and culture at large is to instigate a communion with their audience which can replace, and be a better model than, communication of the kind so often represented within the worlds of their texts.

Another of my earlier examples was from Wordsworth's Two-Part *Prelude* of 1799. It is Coleridge, perhaps Wordsworth's most important associate, who is the primary addressee in *The Prelude*, and "the poem for Coleridge" was always Wordsworth's own way of referring to this work. His loving affection for his dazzling yet difficult friend carries over, I suggested, to other readers who, though differently positioned, are willing and able to project themselves into the poem's addressee persona. For long stretches of text Coleridge in any case falls into the background, so that other readers will have the very normal experience of belonging to a valued audience which, though by no means universal, is large and only vaguely specific.

Here, too, though, the relationship which the writing promotes with its addressee or addressees can be far more humanly rewarding than the communication represented within the world of the poem. In the passage I discussed, the poem describes a total lack of communication between one human being and another – two solipsistic monads whose isolation, outside a literary work, would usually be quite without mitigation.

>   … I saw
> A naked pool that lay beneath the hills,
> The beacon on the summit, and more near
> A girl who bore a pitcher on her head
> And seemed with difficult steps to force her way
> Against the blowing wind. It was in truth
> An ordinary sight, but I should need
> Colours and words that are unknown to man
> To paint the visionary dreariness
> Which, while I looked all round for my lost guide,
> Did at that time invest the naked pool,
> The beacon on the lonely eminence,
> The woman and her garments vexed and tossed
> By the strong wind.   (First Part, ll. 314–347)[2]

My point was that the writing actually takes us into the poet's friendly confidence, almost as if in compensation for the starkness of the incident described: the total separateness of the two human existences, Wordsworth's and the girl's, each in their own desolate universe. Within the poem's mimetic world, Wordsworth is isolated and the girl is isolated. In the poem's discoursal world, isolation is broken down. True, readers who register the visionary dreariness of the a-human moment in the poem, do so

---

2. Quoted from (Jonathan) Wordsworth, Abrams and Gill 1979.

in their most private being, perhaps even acknowledging a tendency of their own to self-sufficient coldness. Yet thanks to the poet's self-conscious and prosaic intervention, they can also find themselves attracted into a warmth of dialogue, as it were, on the topic of language itself as an interface between perceptions held in solitude and perceptions shared. "*In*" the poem, Wordsworth has lost his guide, and he merely sees at a distance another human being, whose own defining relationship seems to be only with the wind. "*Through*" the poem, Wordsworth's readers can be brought into communion, both with him and with each other: a communion arising from a shared contemplation of the bleak gaps that can exist between one human being and another.

Sometimes, though not very often, literary texts do include representations of what I have been calling genuine communication. They have episodes during which characters recognize each other's human autonomy, that is to say, behaving in a way that is kind, generous, friendly, considerate, as when the couple in Pinter's *Night* love each other so much that they agree to differ about the history of their love itself. There are examples where even people less intimately related are shown as positively delighting in each other's company and strongly bonding, as in that wonderful passage in *The Prelude* about the shared pleasures of a village party where the music and dancing went on all night.

But the truth is that genuine communication is not strongly tellable, and usually figures as a mere temporary contrast to the sadness or madness of everything else taking place. In most stories it typically comes in, if it comes in at all, at the beginning or the end, as a condition which gives way to greater eventfulness, or into which eventfulness finally subsides. In many cases, including *Great Expectations*, the story both begins and ends in the *medias res* of ongoing communicational dysfunction. Having already lost both parents and all his siblings except his older sister Mrs Joe, young Pip's enjoyment of Joe's selfless love is circumscribed by Mrs Joe's firmness of hand. And even in the revised ending recommended by Bulwer Lytton, the ultimate communion Pip has always desired with Estella still seems, if it is anything at all, a thing of the future.

The interpersonal conditions described within Coleridge's sonnet, within Wordsworth's passage about losing his guide and seeing the windswept girl, and throughout *Great Expectations* are saddening and incipiently tragic. But even tragedy, thanks to our communion with the tragedian, and with other spectators or readers, becomes a source of pleasure, and I hasten to add that communicational breakdown can be just as much a focus of comedy. Think only of Malvolio's difficulties of interpretation and self-expression in his relationship with Olivia, and of the Baron's counterproductive way of channelling his adoration of Belinda in *The Rape of the Lock*. Or think of George Orwell's gentle ironies at the expense of George Bowling, whose wife and children are so much more important to him than the quality of his daily communication with them leads him to suppose.

My nominalistic definition of literature as the works which a great many people have admired, or seem likely to admire, for a very long time embraces many texts whose authorial genuineness of address is *not* contrastable with communication taking place within a human world described. But it is worth pointing out that, on the one hand, the Victorian distinction between non-literary factuality and literary fiction was never watertight anyway and that, on the other hand, poems, novels and plays never held a monopoly on narrative. Both Coleridge's sonnet and *The Prelude*, even though they are poems, are autobiographical, and Churchill's autobiography, though it is not a poem, novel or play, tells, like anybody else's, a story, as also do most history and travel books, for instance. Communicational genuineness, I have suggested, is a necessary (though not sufficient) condition if a writer's work is to achieve high cultural status. And in a large number of cases, including very many which would not have been encompassed by nineteenth century accounts of literature, the writer's own manner of address certainly will establish itself in contradistinction from represented modes of human intercourse on which, as addressees, we are invited to compare notes. Churchill's relationship with his parents is no less open to discussion than Coleridge's with his son and wife.

All major writers bring about communion in their own ways. They all have their own style and their own kinds of material and emotional range, and by an experienced audience none of them could ever be mistaken for another. Yet they have all in practice worked to the same effect. Although, as I tried to show *à propos* Shakespeare, their language has had not only strength but weakness, they have managed to promote between themselves and their public a renewed dialogicality in which all parties respect each other's human autonomy. This has applied even when, as in much of Pope and Pinter, the writing has also been coercive, even when, as in Banks's *Melusine*, it has been addressed to children, and even when, as in *The Waste Land*, it has ostensibly been predicated on a literary impersonality.

So the communicational exemplariness of the writings classed as literature ultimately has less to do with the relationship between characters within a world created by the texts than with the relationship between writers and their public. And paradoxically, the writers of many significant works of literature tell us, or agree with us, or convince us, through their depiction of human interaction, that relationships can be far from ideal, while at the same time giving us, through their own exophoric addressivity, an on-the-pulses experience of an additional, and far more comfortable human truth. Such works have always been basically *about* communicational dysfunction. But literature itself has been communicationally ameliorative within society as a whole, a dimension of literary history which is at last coming in for some detailed scholarly examination (Sell and Johnson 2009).

The studies collected here are samples of such examination when it takes the form of a post-postmodern communicational criticism. As I explained at the outset, what a communicational critic seeks to develop is a new form of that pleasurable kind of assessment that used to be called literary appreciation. The newness lies partly in a post-postmodern ideological goal, partly in the heightened sensitivity to communicational ethics, but above all in a pleasurability now consciously stemming from the satisfactions of genuine communication between writers and readers.

Such criticism draws particular attention to modes of literary address which, despite their historicity, acknowledge the human autonomy of any and every reader or spectator, so bringing about communities of respondents that are indefinitely large but also indefinitely heterogeneous. This is the kind of community-making which, in the many different ways in which it happens through many different kinds of text, communicational critics seek to identify and hold up for admiring emulation. If, as I believe it could, communicational criticism were in the long run to lead to a somewhat wider spread of self-consciously genuine communication in the world at large, then the post-postmodern ideal of a community both global and non-hegemonic would be that much less of a dream.

References

Appiah, K. Anthony. 1994. "Identity, Authenticity, Survival: Multicultural Societies and Social Reproduction." In *Multiculturalism: Examining the Politics of Recognition*. Amy Gutman (ed.), 149–163. Princeton: Princeton University Press.

Aragay, Mireia. 2009. "Pinter, Politics and Postmodernism (2)." In *The Cambridge Companion to Harold Pinter*. Peter Raby (ed.), 283–296. Cambridge: Cambridge University Press.

Armstrong, Karen. 2009. *The Case for God: What Religion Really Means*. London: Bodley Head.

Arnold, Matthew. 1888 [1880]. "The Study of Poetry." In his *Essays in Criticism: Second Series*. 1–55. London: Macmillan.

Arnold, Matthew. 1888. "Wordsworth." In his *Essays in Criticism: Second Series*. 122–162. London: Macmillan.

Ashcroft, Bill, Griffiths, Gareth and Tiffin, Helen (eds). 2002. *The Empire Writes Back: Theory and Practice in Post-Colonial Literature*, 2nd ed. New York: Routledge.

Attridge, Derek. 2004. *The Singularity of Literature*. London: Routledge.

Auerbach, Erich. 1969 [1952]. "Philology and *Weltliteratur*." *The Centennial Review* 13: 1–17.

Austin, J. L. 1962. *How To Do Things With Words*. Oxford: Clarendon Press.

Aviezer, Miriam Steiner. 1996 [1964]. *The Soldier with the Golden Buttons*. Lynbrook: Gefen.

Bagehot, Walter. 1972 [1850]. "Hartley Coleridge." In *Wordsworth, The Prelude: A Casebook*. W. H. Harvey and Richard Gravil (eds.), 55–57. London: Macmillan.

Baker, Juliet. 2001. *Wordsworth: A Life*. London: Penguin.

Bakhtin, M. M. 1981. *The Dialogic Imagination: Four Essays*. Austin, Texas: University of Texas Press.

Banks, Lynne Reid. 1990 [1988]. *Melusine: A Mystery*. London: Penguin.

Baron, Michael. 1995. *Language and Relationship in Wordsworth's Writing*. London: Longman.

Barrell, John. 1988. *Poetry, Language and Politics*. Manchester: Manchester University Press.

Bate, Jonathan. 1997. *The Genuius of Shakespeare*. London: Picador.

Bayley, John. 1960. *The Characters of Love*. London: Constable.

Bayley, John. 1976. *The Uses of Division: Unity and Disharmony in Literature*. New York: Viking.

Bell, Ian A. 1994. *Henry Fielding: Authorship and Authority*. London: Longman.

Bennett, C. E. (trans.). 1964. *Horace: The Odes and Epodes, with an English Translation*. London: Heinemann.

Bergonzi, Bernard. 1990. *Exploding English: Criticism, Theory, Culture*. Oxford: Clarendon Press.

Best, Geoffrey. 2002 [2001]. *Churchill: A Study in Greatness*. London: Penguin.

Bhabha, Homi. 1994. *The Location of Culture*. London: Routledge.

Billington, Michael. 2007. *Harold Pinter*. London: Faber and Faber.

Blake, Norman. 1989. *The Language of Shakespeare*. Basingstoke: Macmillan.

Block, Francesca Lia. 1994. *The Hanged Man*. New York: Harper.

Bloom, Harold. 1995. *The Western Canon: The Books and the School of the Ages*. Basingstoke: Macmillan.

Bloom, Harold. 1998. *Shakespeare and the Invention of the Human.* New York: Riverhead Books.

Boswell, James. 1906 [1791]. *Life of Johnson.* London: Dent.

Bradley, A. C. 1909. "Wordsworth." In his *Oxford Lectures on Poetry.* 99–148. London: Macmillan.

Bridges, Robert (ed.). 1940. *The Spirit of Man: An Anthology in English & French From the Philosophers & Poets made in 1915 by Robert Bridges, O.M. Poet Laureate & dedicated by gracious permission to His Majesty King George V.* London: Readers' Union and Longmans Green.

Briere, John N. and Elliott, Diana M. 1994. "Immediate and Long-Term Impacts of Child Sexual Abuse." *The Future of Children* 4: 54–69.

Brooks, Cleanth. 1968 [1947]. *The Well Wrought Urn: Studies in the Structure of Poetry.* London: Methuen.

Brooks, Peter. 1994 [1980]. "Repetition, Repression, and Return: *Great Expectations* and the Study of Plot." Extracts in *Great Expectations: New Casebook.* Roger D. Sell (ed.), 98–109. Basingstoke: Macmillan.

Brown, Laura. 1985. *Alexander Pope.* Oxford: Blackwell.

Brown, Marshall. 1991. *Preromanticism.* Stanford: Stanford University Press.

Brown, Penelope and Levinson, Stephen C. 1987. *Politeness: Some Universals in Language Usage.* Cambridge: Cambridge University Press.

Bullough, Geoffrey. 1939. *Poems and Dramas of Fulke Greville, First Lord Brooke,* 2 vols. Edinburgh: Oliver and Boyd.

Butler, James A. 2003. "Poetry 1798–1807: *Lyrical Ballads* and *Poems in Two Volumes.*" In *The Cambridge Companion to Wordsworth.* Stephen Gill (ed.), 38–54. Cambridge: Cambridge University Press.

Butler, Marilyn. 1981. *Romantics, Rebels and Reactionaries: English Literature and its Background 1760–1830.* Oxford: Oxford University Press.

Butt, John (ed.). 1963. *The Poems of Alexander Pope: A One-Volume Edition of the Twickenham Text.* London: Methuen.

Byron, Lord (= George Gordon). 1933 [1820]. "Observations upon an Article in Blackwood's Magazine." In *Pope: Poetry & Prose: With Essays by Johnson, Coleridge, Hazlitt &c.* H. V. D. Dyson (ed.), 26–27. Oxford: Clarendon Press.

Byron, Lord (= George Gordon). 1933 [1821]. "Letter on the Rec. W. L. Bowles' Strictures on the Life and Writings of Pope." In *Pope: Poetry & Prose: With Essays by Johnson, Coleridge, Hazlitt &c.* H. V. D. Dyson (ed.), 27. Oxford: Clarendon Press.

Carey, John and Fowler, Alastair (eds.). 1968. *The Poems of John Milton.* London: Longmans.

Carroll, Joseph. 2004. *Literary Dawinism: Evolution, Human Nature, and Literature.* New York: Routledge.

Cart, Michael. 1996. *From Romance to Realism: 50 Years of Growth and Change in Young Adult Literature.* New York: Harper Collins.

Cave, Richard Allen. 2009. "Body Language in Pinter's Plays." In *The Cambridge Companion to Harold Pinter.* Peter Raby (ed.), 123–145. Cambridge: Cambridge University Press.

Chandra, Sarika. 2008. "Reproducing a Nationalist Literature in the Age of Globalization: Reading (Im)migration in Julia Alvarez's *How the García Girls Lost Their Accents.*" *American Quarterly* 60: 829–885.

Chesterton, G. K. 1970 [1906]. *Charles Dickens.* Extract in *Charles Dickens* [Penguin Critical Anthologies]. Stephen Wall (ed.), 244–249. Harmondsworth: Penguin.

Churchill, Winston S. 1942. *The Unrelenting Struggle*. London: Cassell.

Churchill, Winston S. 1959 [1930]. *My Early Life: A Roving Commission*. London: Collins.

Cohen, Judi R. 1998. *Communication Criticism: Developing Your Critical Powers*. Thousand Oaks: Sage.

Cohn, Ruby. 1962. "The World of Harold Pinter." *Tulane Drama Review* 6: 58–68.

Coleridge, Samuel Taylor. 1815. Letter to Wordsworth, 30th May. In Baker, Juliet. 2001. *Wordsworth: A Life*, 329–330. London: Penguin, 2001.

Coleridge, Samuel Taylor. 1885 [1818]. *Lectures and Noters on Shakspere* [sic] *and Other English Poets*. T. Ashe (ed.). London: Bell.

Coleridge, Samuel Taylor. 1956 [1817]. *Biographia Literaria*. George Watson (ed.). London: Dent.

Coleridge, Samuel Taylor. 1960 [1834]. *Table Talk Recorded by Henry Nelson Coleridge and John Taylor Coleridge, Vol. I*, Carl Woodring (ed.). London and Princeton: Routledge and Princeton University Press.

Combs, Steven C. 2002. "The *Dao* of Communication Criticism: Insects, Individuals, and Mass Society." *Social Semiotics* 12: 183–199.

Conaghan, John. 1978. *Dryden: A Selection*. London: Methuen.

Cook, James. 1879. *Bibliography of the Writings of Charles Dickens and Many Curious and Interesting Particulars Relating to His Works*. Paisley: J. & J. Cook.

Crane, R. S. 1952. "The Plot of *Tom Jones*." In *Critics and Criticism: Ancient and Modern*. R. S. Crane (ed.), 616–647. Chicago: University of Chicago Press.

Creaser, John. 2001. "'Through Mazes Running': Rhythmic Verve in Milton's 'L'Allegro' and 'Il Penseroso'." *Review of English Studies* 52: 376–410.

Creaser, John. 2002. "Prosody and Liberty in Milton and Marvell." In *Milton and the Terms of Liberty*. Graham Parry and Raymond Joad (eds), 37–55. Cambridge: Brewer.

Cross, Gillian. 1996. *Pictures in the Dark*. London: Puffin.

Cruttwell, Patrick. 1966. "Alexander Pope in the Augustan World." *Centennial Review* 10: 13–36.

Culler, Jonathan. 1975. *Structuralist Poetics: Structuralism, Linguistics and the Study of Literature*. London: Routledge and Kegan Paul.

Damrosch, David. 2004. "World Literature in a Postcanonical, Hypercanonical Age." In *Comparative Literature in an Age of Globalization*. Haun Saussy (ed.), 43–53. Baltimore: Johns Hopkins University Press.

Darbishire, Helen. 1972 [1926]. "Wordsworth's *Prelude*." In *Wordsworth, The Prelude: A Casebook*. W. H. Harvey and Richard Gravil (eds), 81–98. London: Macmillan.

Davie, Donald. 1955. "Syntax in the Blank Verse of Wordsworth's *Prelude*." In his *Articulate Energy: An Enquiry into the Syntax of English Poetry*. 106–116. London: Routledge and Kegan Paul.

Davidson, Roger. 2005. Interview. In *Pinter in the Theatre*. Ian Smith (ed.), 184–190. London: Nick Hern Books

Davison, Peter. 1996. *George Orwell: A Literary Life*. Basingstoke: Macmillan.

Dean, Paul. 2003. "Current Literature 2002: Literary Theory, History and Criticism." *English Studies* 84: 558–572.

De Quincey, Thomas. 1893. *The Posthumous Works of Thomas De Quincey*, vol. 2. Alexander H. Japp (ed.). London: Heinemann.

De Quincey, Thomas. 1933 [1848]. Extract from "Essay on Pope". In *Pope: Poetry & Prose: With Essays by Johnson, Coleridge, Hazlitt &c.* H. V. D. Dyson (ed.), 28–30. Oxford: Clarendon Press.

Derbyshire, Harry. 2009. "Pinter as a Celebrity." In *The Cambridge Companion to Harold Pinter*. Peter Raby (ed.), 266–282. Cambridge: Cambridge University Press.

Derrida, Jacques. 2002. *Acts of Religion*. New York: Routledge.

de Saussure, Ferdinand. 1978 [1916]. *Course in General Linguistics*. London: Fontana.

de Selincourt, Ernest and Darbishire, Helen (eds). 1952–1959. *The Poetical Works of William Wordsworth*, 5 vols., revised edn. Oxford: Clarendon Press.

d'Este, Carlo. 2010. *Warlord: The Fighting Life of Winston Churchill, from Soldier to Statesman*. London: Penguin.

Dirlik, Arif. 2007. "In Search of Contact Zones: Nations, Civilizations, and the Spaces of Culture." In *Cultures in Contact*. Balz Engler and Lucia Michalcak (eds.), 15–33. Tübingen: Gunter Narr.

Dowden, Edward. 1906 [1875]. *Shakspere* [sic]: *A Critical Study of his Mind and Art*. London: Kegan Paul, Trench, Trübner.

Duncan-Jones, Katherine (ed.). 1997. *Shakespeare's Sonnets*. London: Thomson.

Ďurišin, Dionýz. 1989. *Theory of Interliterary Process*. Bratislava: Veda.

Edwards, Robert L. 1992. *Of Singular Genius, of Singular Grace: A Biography of Horace Bushnell*. Cleveland, Ohio: Pilgrim Press.

Eliot, T. S. 1951 [1919]. "Tradition and the Individual Talent." In his *Selected Essays*. 13–22. London: Faber.

Eliot, T. S. 1951 [1921]. "The Metaphysical Poets." In his *Selected Essays*. 281–291. London: Faber.

Eliot, T. S. 1951 [1929]. "Dante." In his *Selected Essays*. 237–277. London: Faber.

Eliot, T. S. 1951 [1936]. "*In Memoriam*." In his *Selected Essays*. 328–338. London: Faber.

Eliot, T. S. 1969. *The Complete Poems and Plays of T. S. Eliot*. London: Faber.

Eliot, T. S. 1975 [1918]. "Henry James." In *T. S. Eliot: Selected Prose*. Frank Kermode (ed.), 151–152. London: Faber.

Empson, William. 1952. "Sense in *The Prelude*." In his *The Structure of Complex Words*. 289–305. New York: New Directions.

Empson, William. 1961. *Milton's God*. London: Chatto and Windus.

Empson, William. 1961 [1930]. *Seven Types of Ambiguity*. London: Chatto and Windus.

Empson, William. 1962. *Collected Poems*. London: Chatto and Windus.

Engel, Susan. 2005. Interview. In *Pinter in the Theatre*. Ian Smith (ed.), 169–176. London: Nick Hern Books.

Evans, G. Blakemoore *et al.* (eds). 1997. *The Riverside Shakespeare: Second Edition*. Boston: Houghton Mifflin.

Fairclough, H. Rushton (trans.). 1966. *Horace: Satires, Epistles and Ars Poetic, with an English Translation*. London: Heinemann.

Fairclough, Norman. 1988. "Register, Power and Socio-Semantic Change." In *Functions of Style*. David Birch and Michael O'Toole (eds), 111–125. London: Pinter.

Farrell, J. G. 1975 [1973]. *The Siege of Krishnapur*. Harmondsworth: Penguin.

Faure, Guy Olivier and Rubin, Jeffrey (eds). 1993. *Culture and Negotiation: The Resolution of Water Disputes*. Newbury Park: Sage.

Ferguson, Frances. 2003. "Wordsworth and the Meaning of Taste." In *The Cambridge Companion to Wordsworth*. Stephen Gill (ed.), 90–107. Cambridge: Cambridge University Press.

Fernie, Ewan. 2007. "Action! *Henry V*." In *Presentist Shakespeares*. Hugh Grady and Terence Hawkes (eds), 96–120. London: Routledge.

Fielding, Henry. 1903 [1743]. "An Essay on Conversation." In *The Writings of Henry Fielding: Vol. 14*. William Ernest Henley (ed.), 245–277. London: Heinemann.

Finkelhor, David and Browne, Angela. 1985. "The Traumatic Impact of Child Sexual Abuse: A Conceptualization." *American Journal of Orthopsychiatry* 55: 530–41.

Fishelov, David. 2010. *Dialogues with / and Great Books: The Dynamics of Canon Formation*. Brighton: Sussex Academic Press.

Forster, E. M. 1965 [1938]. "What I Believe." In his *Two Cheers for Democracy*. 75–84. Harmondsworth: Penguin.

Forster, E. M. 1974 [1927]. *Aspects of the Novel and Related Writings*. Oliver Stallybrass (ed.). London: Arnold.

Forster, John. 1928 [1872–1874]. *The Life of Charles Dickens*. London: Cecil Palmer.

Foss, Sonja K. 2009. *Rhetorical Criticism: Exploration and Practice: Fourth Edition*. Long Grove, Illinois: Waveland.

Fowler, Roger. 1995. *The Language of George Orwell*. Basingstoke: Macmillan.

Fraser, Antonia. 2010. *Must You Go? My Life with Harold Pinter*. London: Wiedenfield and Nicholson.

Frye, Northrop. 1956. "Towards Defining an Age of Sensibility." *ELH* 23: 144–152.

Gadamer, Hans-Georg, 1986. *The Relevance of the Beautiful and Other Essays,* Cambridge: Cambridge University Press.

Gadamer, Hans-Georg. 1989 [1969]. *Truth and Method: Second, Revised Edition*. London: Sheed and Ward.

Geduld, Harry M. 1973. *Filmguide to "Henry V."* Bloomington: University of Indiana Press.

Genette, Gérard. 1980. *Narrative Discourse*. Ithaca: Cornell University Press.

Gill, Stephen. 1989. *William Wordsworth: A Life*. Oxford: Oxford University Press.

Gill, Stephen. 2003. "The Philosophical Poet." In *The Cambridge Companion to Wordsworth*. Stephen Gill (ed.), 142–160. Cambridge: Cambridge University Press.

Gilmour, Robin. 1981. *The Idea of the Gentleman in the Victorian Novel*. London: Allen and Unwin.

Glover, Jon and Silkin, Jon (eds). 1990. *The Penguin Book of First World War Prose*. Harmondsworth: Penguin.

Goodson, A. C. 2009. "The Voices of Others: Wordsworth's Poetics of Recognition." In *Levinas and Nineteenth-Century Literature: Ethics and Otherness from Romanticism through Realism*. Donald R. Wehrs and David P. Haney (eds), 44–60. Newark: University of Delaware Press.

Gordon, Lyndall. 1977. *Eliot's Early Years*. Oxford: Oxford University Press.

Gould, Gerald. 1969 [1919]. "Irony and Satire in *Henry V*". In *Shakespeare: Henry V: A Casebook*. Michael Quinn (ed.), 82–94. London: Macmillan.

Grabovsky, Ernst. 2004. "The Impact of Globalization and the New Media on the Notion of World Literature." In *Comparative Literature and Comparative Cultural Studies*. Steve Tötösy Zepetnek (ed.), 45–57. West Lafayette: Purdue University Press.

Grady, Hugh and Hawkes, Terence (eds). 2007. *Presentist Shakespeares*. London: Routledge.

Grant, Cynthia D. 1994. *Uncle Vampire*. New York: Atheneum.

Gray, Simon. 1985. *An Unnatural Pursuit*. London: Faber and Faber.

Greenblatt, Stephen. 1985. "Invisible bullets: Renaissance authority and its subvervsion, *Henry IV* [sic] and *Henry V*". In *Political Shakespeare: New Essays in Cultural Materialism*. Jonathan Dollimore and Alan Sinfield (eds), 18–47. Manchester: Manchester University Press.

Greene, T. M. 1976. "Petrarch and the Humanist Hermeneutic." In *Italian Literature: Roots and Branches: Essays in Honor of Thomas Goddard Bergin*. G. Rimanelli and K. J. Atchity (eds), 201–225. New Haven: Yale University Press.

Greimas, Algirdas Julien. 1977. "Elements of a narrative grammar." *Diacritics* 7: 23–40.

Griffin, Robert J. 1995. *Wordsworth's Pope: A Study in Literary Historiography*. Cambridge: Cambridge University Press.

Gurr, Andrew (ed.). 1992. *Henry V* [New Cambridge Shakespeare Edition]. Cambridge: Cambridge University Press.

Habermas, Jürgen. 1970. "Systematically Distorted Communication." *Inquiry* 13: 205–18.

Habermas, Jürgen. 1972. *Knowledge and Human Interests*. London: Heinemann.

Habermas, Jürgen. 1984 & 1987. *The Theory of Communicative Action*, vols. 1 & 2. Boston: Beacon Press.

Habermas, Jürgen. 1994. "Struggles for Recognition in the Democratic Constitutional State." In *Multiculturalism: Examining the Politics of Recognition*. Amy Gutman (ed.), 107–148. Princeton: Princeton University Press.

Habermas, Jürgen. 1998 [1985]. "On the distinction between Poetic and Communicative Uses of Language." In his *On the Pragmatics of Communication*, 383–401. Cambridge, Massachusetts: MIT Press.

Habermas, Jürgen. 1998a. *Justification and Application: Remarks on Discourse Ethics*. Cambridge, Massachusetts: MIT Press.

Habermas, Jürgen. 1998b. *On the Pragmatics of Communication*. Cambridge, Massachusetts: MIT Press.

Hall, Peter. 2005 [1974]. Interview with Catherine Itzen and Simon Trussler. In *Pinter in the Theatre*. Ian Smith (ed.), 131–157.

Hall, Peter. 2009. "Directing the Plays of Harold Pinter." In *The Cambridge Companion to Pinter*, 2nd ed. Peter Raby (ed.), 160–169. Cambridge: Cambridge University Press.

Hampshire, Stuart. 1992. *Innocence and Experience*. Harmondsworth: Penguin.

Hara, Eiichi. 1994 [1981]. "Stories Present and Absent in *Great Expectations*." In *Great Expectations: New Casebook*. Roger D. Sell (ed.), 143–65. Basingstoke: Macmillan.

Harper, George McLean. 1928. "Coleridge's Conversation Poems." In his *Spirit of Delight*. New York: Henry Holt.

Hart, Roderick P. and Daughton, Suzanne. 2005. *Modern Rhetorical Criticism*. Boston: Pearson.

Hartman, Geoffrey. 1971 [1964]. *Wordsworth's Poetry 1787–1814*. New Haven: Yale University Press.

Hastings, Max. 2009. *Finest Years: Churchill as Warlord 1940–45*. London: Harper Press.

Hawkes, Terence. 1986. *That Shakespeherian Rag: Essays on a Critical Process*. London: Methuen.

Hawkes, Terence. 1992. *Meaning by Shakespeare*. London: Routledge.

Hawkes, Terence. 2002. *Shakespeare in the Present*. London: Routledge.

Hazlitt, William. 1814. "Character of Mr Wordsworth's New Poem, The Excursion." *Examiner*, 21st August.

Hazlitt, William. 1818. *The English Poets*. London: Taylor and Hessey.

Hazlitt, William. 1826. "Of persons one would wish to have seen." In *The New Monthly Magazine and Literary Journal* 1: 32–41. London: Henry Colburn.

Hazlitt, William. 2000 [1823]. "My First Acquaintance with Poets" In *The Norton Anthology of English Literature: Seventh Edition: Volume 2*. M. H. Abrams and Stephen Greenblatt (eds), 513–526. New York: Norton.

Hilton, M. R. and Mezey, G. C. 1996. "Victims and Perpetrators of Child Sexual Abuse." *British Journal of Psychiatry* 169: 408–415.

Hirsch, E. D. 1967. *Validity in Interpretation*. New Haven: Yale University Press.

Hodge, Douglas. 2005. Interview. In *Pinter in the Theatre*. Ian Smith (ed.), 199–206. London: Nick Hern Books.

Hoffmann, Heinrich. 1848 [1845]. *Struwwelpeter* [the English translation]. George Routledge & Sons, Ltd.: London.

Holmes, Richard. 2005. *In the Footsteps of Churchill*. London: BBC Books.

Holsti, Kalevi J. 1991. *Peace and War: Armed Conflicts and International Order*. Cambridge: Cambridge University Press.

House, Humphrey. 1948. "G. B. S. on *Great Expectations*." *The Dickensian* 44: 63–70 & 183–6.

Howe, P. P. (ed.). 1930–1934. *The Complete Works of William Hazlitt*, 21 vols. London: Dent.

Innes, Christopher. 1992. *Modern British Drama, 1890–1990*. Cambridge: Cambridge University Press.

Jack, Ian. 1954. *Pope*. London: British Council.

Jacobus, Mary. 1994. *Romanticism, Writing and Sexual Difference: Essays on* The Prelude. Oxford: Oxford University Press.

James, Henry. 1963 [1884]. "The Art of Fiction." In *Henry James: Selected Literary Criticism*. Morris Shapiro (ed.), 78–97. Harmondsworth: Penguin.

James, Henry. 1968 [1881]. *The Portrait of a Lady*. London: Oxford University Press.

Jameson, Fredric. 1981. *The Political Unconscious: Narrative as a Socially Symbolic Act*. London: Methuen.

Jenkins, Roy. 2002 [2001]. *Churchill*. London: Pan Books.

Jenks, Chris. 1996. *Childhood*. London: Routledge.

Johnson, Paul. 2009. *Churchill*. New York: Viking.

Johnson, Samuel. 1925 [1779–1781]. *Lives of the English Poets*, 2 vols. L. Archer Hind (ed.). London: Dent.

Johnston, Kenneth R. 1998. *The Hidden Wordsworth: Poet, Lover, Rebel, Spy*. New York: Norton.

Johnston, Kenneth R. 2003. "Wordsworth and *The Recluse*." In *Cambridge Companion to Wordsworth*. Stephen Gill (ed.), 70–89. Cambridge: Cambridge University Press.

Julius, Anthony. 1995. *T. S. Eliot, Anti-Semitism, and Literary Form*. Cambridge: Cambridge University Press.

Kant, Immanuel. 1998 [1785]. *Groundwork of the Metaphysics of Morals*. Cambridge: Cambridge University Press.

Karshan, Thomas. 2009. "Evolutionary Criticism." *Essays in Criticism* 59: 287–301.

Keach, William (ed.). 2004. *Samuel Taylor Coleridge, The Complete Poems*. London: Penguin.

Keats, John. 1954 [1817, 1818]. *Letters of John Keats*, Frederick Page (ed.). London: Oxford University Press.

Kendall-Tackett, K. A. *et al.* 1993. "Impact of Sexual Abuse of Children: A Review and Synthesis of Recent Empirical Findings." *Psychological Bulletin* 112: 164–80.

Kermode, Frank (ed.). 1997. *King Lear*. In *The Riverside Shakespeare: Second Edition*. G. Blakemore Evans (ed.), 1303–1354. Boston: Houghton Mifflin.

Klancher, Jon. 1987. *The Making of English Reading Audiences 1790–1832*. Madison: University of Wisconsin Press.

Knight, G. Wilson. 1954. *Laureate of Peace: On the Genius of Alexander Pope*. London: Routledge and Kegan Paul.

Kokkola, Lydia. 2003. *Representing the Holocaust in Children's Literature*. New York: Routledge.

Kokkola, Lydia. 2007. "Holocaust Narratives and the Ethics of Representation." *Bookbird: A Journal of International Children's Literature* 45: 5–12.

Krell, Jonathan F. 2000. "Between Demon and Divinity: Mélusine Revisited." *Mythosphere: A Journal for Image, Myth and Symbol* 2: 375–96.

Langbaum, Robert. 1957. *The Poetry of Experience: The Dramatic Monologue in Modern Literary Tradition*. New York: Norton.

Lassén-Seger, Maria. 2002. "Child-power? Adventures into the Animal Kingdom – the Animorphs Series." In *Children's Literature as Communication: The ChiLPA Project*. Roger D. Sell (ed.), 159–176. Amsterdam: John Benjamins.

Lassén-Seger, Maria. 2006. *Adventures into Otherness: Child Meamorphs in Late Twentieth-century Children's Literature*. Åbo: Åbo Akademi University Press.

Lawrence, D. H. 1960 [1921]. *Women in Love*. Harmondsworth: Penguin.

Lawrence, D. H. 1967 [1914]. Letter to Edward Garnett, 5th June. In *D. H. Lawrence: Selected Literary Criticism*. Anthony Beal (ed.), 17–18. London: Heinemann.

Leavis, F. R. 1930. *Mass Civilization and Minority Culture*. Cambridge: Minority Press.

Leavis, F. R. 1948 [1943]. *Education and the University: A Sketch for an "English School"*. London: Chatto and Windus.

Leavis, F. R. 1962 [1948]. *The Great Tradition: George Eliot, Henry James, Joseph Conrad*. Harmondsworth: Penguin.

Leavis, F. R. 1962 [1952]a. "*The Dunciad*." In his *The Common Pursuit*. 88–96. Harmondsworth: Penguin.

Leavis, F. R. 1962 [1952]b. "Literary Criticism and Philosophy." In his *The Common Pursuit*. 211–222. Harmondsworth: Penguin.

Leavis, F. R. 1963. "Henry James as a Critic." In *Henry James: Selected Literary Criticism*. Morris Shapiro (ed.), 13–24. Harmondsworth: Penguin.

Leavis, F. R. 1964 [1936]a. "Milton's Verse." In his *Revaluation: Tradition and Development in English Poetry*. 42–61. Harmondsworth: Penguin.

Leavis, F. R. 1964 [1936]b. "Pope." In his *Revaluation: Tradition and Development in English Poetry*. 62–86. Harmondsworth: Penguin.

Leavis, F. R. 1964 [1936]c. "Wordsworth" In his *Revaluation: Tradition and Development in English Poetry*. 130–169. Harmondsworth: Penguin.

Leavis, F. R. and Thomson, Denys. 1933. *Culture and Environment: The Training of Critical Awareness*. London: Chatto and Windus.

Leggatt, Alexander. 1988. *English Drama: Shakespeare to the Restoration 1590–1660*. London: Longman.

Lévi-Strauss, Claude. 1970 [1964]. "Overture to Le Cru et le Cuit." In *Structuralism*. Jacques Ehrmann (ed.), 31–55. Garden City: Anchor-Doubleday.

Lewis, C. Day (ed.). 1977. *The Collected Poems of Wilfred Owen*. London: Chatto and Windus.

Lindley, David (ed.). 2002. *The Tempest* [New Cambridge Shakespeare Edition]. Cambridge: Cambridge University Press.

Lodge, David. 1997. "Pinter's *Last to Go*: A Structuralist Reading." In his *The Practice of Writing*. 270–285. Harmondsworth: Penguin.

Loe, Thomas. 1994 [1989]. "Gothic Plot in *Great Expectations*." In *Great Expectations: New Casebook*. Roger D. Sell (ed.), 203–215. Basingstoke: Macmillan.

Lonsdale, Roger. 1984. *The New Oxford Book of Eighteenth Century Verse*. Oxford: Oxford University Press.

Lonsdale, Roger. 1989. *Eighteenth Century Women Poets: An Oxford Anthology*. Oxford: Oxford University Press.

Lopéz, Silvia. 2004. "National Culture, Globalization and the Case of Post-War El Salvador." *Comparative Literature Studies* 41: 80–100.

Luckhurst, Mary. 2009. "Speaking Out: Harold Pinter and Freedom of Expression." In *The Cambridge Companion to Harold Pinter*. Peter Raby (ed.), 105–120). Cambridge: Cambridge University Press.

Lyotard, Jean-Francois. 1984 [1979]. *The Postmodern Condition: A Report on Knowledge*. Manchester: Manchester University Press.

Mack, Maynard. 1969. *The Garden and the City: Retirement and Politics in the Later Poetry of Pope*. Toronto: University of Toronto Press.

Mack, Maynard. 1985. *Alexander Pope: A Life*. New Haven: Yale University Press.

Marshall, Peter. 1997. *Positive Diplomacy*. Basingstoke: Macmillan.

McFarland, Thomas. 1981. *Romanticism and the Forms of Ruin: Wordsworth, Coleridge, and the Modalities of Fragmentation*. Princeton: Princeton University Press.

McLaverty, James. 2001. *Pope, Print and Meaning*. Oxford: Oxford University Press.

McLaverty, James. 2007. "Pope and the Book Trade." In *The Cambridge Companion to Alexander Pope*. Pat Rogers (ed.), 186–197. Cambridge: Cambridge University Press.

Mendes, Sam. 2005. Interview. In *Pinter in the Theatre*. Ian Smith (ed.), 218–230. London: Nick Hern Books.

Milford, Humphrey Sumner (ed.). 1906. *The Poetical Works of William Cowper*. London: Oxford University Press.

Mill, John Stuart. 1970 [1854]. Letter to his wife, March 1854. In *Charles Dickens* [Penguin Critical Anthologies]. Stephen Wall (ed.), 95. Harmondsworth: Penguin.

Miller, J. Hillis. 1995. "The University of Dissensus." *Oxford Literary Review* 17: 121–43.

Miller, J. Hillis. 2007. "A defense of literature and literary study in a time of globalization and the new tele-technologies." *Neohelicon* 34: 13–22.

Milne, Drew. 2009. "Pinter's Sexual Politics." In *The Cambridge Companion to Harold Pinter*. Peter Raby (ed.), 233–248. Cambridge: Cambridge University Press.

Milton, John. 1644. *Areopagitica*. London.

Mitchell, Katie. 2005. Interview. In *Pinter in the Theatre*. Ian Smith (ed.), 199–206.

Montagu, Lady Mary Mortley. 1967 [1754]. *The Complete Letters of Lady Mary Mortley Montagu, Vol. III*. Robert Halsband (ed.). Oxford: Clarendon Press.

Morris, Mowbray. 1882. "Charles Dickens." *Fortnightly Review* 32: 762–799.

Neale, J. E. 1965. *Elizabeth I and her Parliaments, 1584–1601*, 2 vols. London: Cape.

Newlyn, Lucy. 2003. "'The Noble Living and the Noble Dead': Community in *The Prelude*." In *The Cambridge Companion to Wordsworth*. Stephen Gill (ed.), 55–69. Cambridge: Cambridge University Press.

Newlyn, Lucy. 2004. *Coleridge, Wordsworth, and the Language of Allusion*, 2nd ed. Oxford: Oxford University Press.

Nikolajeva, Maria. 2002. "Growing Up: The Dilemma of Children's Literature." In *Children's Literature as Communication: The ChiLPA Project*. Roger D. Sell (ed.), 111–136. Amsterdam: John Benjamins.

Nobelprize.org. 25 Aug 2010. "The Nobel Prize in Literature 1953." http://nobelprize.org/nobel_prizes/literature/laureates/1953/

Nodelman, Perry. 1992. "The Other: Orientalism, Colonialism, and Children's Literature". *Children's Literature Association Quarterly* 17: 29–35.

Nünning, Ansgar. 2000. "Towards a Cultural and Historical Narratology: A Survey of Diachronic Approaches, Concepts, and Research Projects." In *Anglistentag 1999: Mainz Proceedings*. Bernhard Reitz and Sigrid Rieuwerts (eds), 345–373. Trier: WVT.

Obama, Barack. 2008 [2006]. *The Audacity of Hope: Thoughts on Reclaiming the American Dream*. Edinburgh: Canongate.

Orgel, Stephen (ed.). 1994. *The Tempest* [Oxford Edition]. Oxford: Oxford University Press.

Orwell, George. 1962 [1939]. *Coming up for Air*. Harmondsworth: Penguin.

Orwell, George. 1964 [1939]. "Charles Dickens." In his *Decline of the English Murder and Other Essays*. 80–141. Harmondsworth: Penguin.

Orwell, George. 1965 [1938]. "Charles Dickens." In his *Decline of the English Murder*. 80–141. Harmondsworth: Penguin.

Orwell, George. 1965 [1941]. "The Art of Donald McGill." In his *Decline of the English Murder*. 142–154. Harmondsworth: Penguin.

Orwell, George. 1965 [1942]. "Rudyard Kipling." In his *Decline of the English Murder and Other Essays*. 45–62. Harmondsworth: Penguin.

Orwell, George. 1965 [1947]. "Why I Write." In his *Decline of the English Murder*. 180–189. Harmondsworth: Penguin.

Owen, W. J. B. and Smyser, Jane Worthington (eds.). 1974. *The Prose Works of William Wordsworth*, 3 vols. Oxford: Clarendon Press: Oxford.

Pack, Roger Lloyd. 2005. Interview. In *Pinter in the Theatre*. Ian Smith (ed.), 177–183. London: Nick Hern Books.

Parsons, I. A. (ed.). 1965. *Men Who March Away: Poems of the First World War*. London: Chatto and Windus.

Perry, Seamus (ed.). 2000. *S. T. Coleridge: Interviews and Recollections*. Basingstoke: Macmillan.

Perry, Seamus. 2003. "Wordsworth and Coleridge." In *The Cambridge Companion to Wordsworth*. Stephen Gill (ed.), 161–179. Cambridge: Cambridge University press.

Petrarch, Francesco. 1971 [1348]. *Petrarch, A Humanist Among Princes: An Anthology of Petrarch's Letters and Translations from his Works*. David Thompson (ed.). New York: Harper & Row.

Phelan, James. 1994 [1989]. "Reading for the Character and Reading for the Progression: John Wemmick and *Great Expectations*." In *Great Expectations: New Casebook*. Roger D. Sell (ed.), 177–186. Basingstoke: Macmillan.

Pieterse, Jan Lederveen. 1995. "Globalization as Hybridization." In *Global Modernities*. Mike Featherstone, Scott Lash and Roland Robertson (eds), 45–68. London: Sage.

Pinter, Harold. 1986. *Plays One*. London: Faber and Faber.

Pinter, Harold. 1991. *Plays Two*. London: Faber and Faber.

Pinter, Harold. 1997. *Plays Three*. London: Faber and Faber.

Pinter, Harold. 1998. *Plays Four*. London: Faber and Faber.

Pinter, Harold. 2005 [1961]. Interview with Harry Thompson. In *Pinter in the Theatre*. Ian Smith (ed.), 43–48. London: Nick Hern Books.

Pinter, Harold. 2005 [1966]. Interview with Lawrence M. Bensky. In *Pinter in the Theatre*. Ian Smith (ed.), 49–66. London: Nick Hern Books.

Pinter, Harold. 2005 [1980]. Interview with Miriam Gross. In *Pinter in the Theatre*. Ian Smith (ed.), 67–78. London: Nick Hern Books.

Pinter, Harold. 2005 [1988]. Interview with Anna Ford. In *Pinter in the Theatre*. Ian Smith (ed.), 79–89. London: Nick Hern Books.

Pinter, Harold. 2005 [1996]. Interview with Mireia Aragay and Ramon Simo. In *Pinter in the Theatre*. Ian Smith (ed.), 90–106. London: Nick Hern Books.

Pinter, Harold. 2009. *Various Voices: Sixty Years of Prose, Poetry, Politics, 1948–2008*. London: Faber and Faber.

Pizer, John. 2000. "Goethe's 'World Literature' Paradigm and Contemporary Globalization." *Comparative Literature* 52: 213–227.

Plath, Sylvia. 1962. "Daddy." In *The New Poetry*. A. Alvarez (ed.), 64–66. Harmondsworth: Penguin.

Poirier, Richard. 1992. *The Performing Self: Compositions and Decompositions in the Languages of Contemporary Life*. New Brunswick, New Jersey: Rutgers University Press.

Pope, Alexander. 1933 [1715]. Extract from the Preface to *The Iliad*. In *Pope: Poetry & Prose: With Essays by Johnson, Coleridge, Hazlitt &c*. H. V. D. Dyson (ed.), 145–149. Oxford: Clarendon Press.

Pope, Alexander. 1933 [1725]. Extract from Preface to *The Dramatic Works of Shakespear*. In *Pope: Poetry & Prose: With Essays by Johnson, Coleridge, Hazlitt &c*. H. V. D. Dyson (ed.), 150–153. Oxford: Clarendon Press.

Potts, L. J. (trans.). 1968. *Aristotle on the Art of Fiction: An English translation of Aristotle's Poetics*. Cambridge: Cambridge University Press.

Pound, Ezra. 1963. Interview with Grazia Levi. *Delta* 22: 3–4.

Pratt, Marie Louise. 1977. *Toward a Speech Act Theory of Literary Discourse*. Bloomington: Indiana University Press.

Prince, Gerald. 1983. "Narrative Pragmatics, Message, and Point." *Poetics* 12: 527–536.

Propp, Vladimir. 1968 [1928]. *Morphology of the Folk Tale*. Austin: University of Texas Press.

Quigley, Austin. 2009. "Pinter, Politics and Postmodernism (I)." In *The Cambridge Companion to Harold Pinter*. Peter Raby (ed.), 7–26. Cambridge: Cambridge University Press.

Raphael, Linda. 1994 [1989]. "A Re-Vision of Miss Havisham: Her Expectations and Our Responses." In *Great Expectations: New Casebook*. Roger D. Sell (ed.), 216–32. Basingstoke: Macmillan.

Rawson, Claude. 2000. *Satire and Sentiment 1660–1830*. New Haven: Yale University Press.

Ricks, Christopher. 1974. *Keats and Embarrassment*. Oxford: Clarendon Press.

Ricks, Christopher. 1987a. "A Pure Organic Pleasure from the Lines." In his *The Force of Poetry*. 89–116. Oxford: Clarendon Press.

Ricks, Christopher. 1987b. "A Sinking Inward to Ourselves from Thought to Thought." In his *The Force of Poetry*. 117–134. Oxford: Clarendon Press.

Ricks, Christopher. 1994. *T. S. Eliot and Prejudice*. London: Faber.

Ricks, Christopher. 2001. "Defects of Kipling (1909)." *Essays in Criticism* 51: 1–7.

Ridley, Matt. 1997. *The Origins of Virtue*. Harmondsworth: Penguin.

Robson, W. W. 1960. "The Dilemma of Tennyson." In *Critical Essays of the Poetry of Tennyson*. John Killham (ed.), 155–173. London: Routledge and Kegan Paul

Rogers, Pat. 2010. *A Political Biography of Alexander Pope*. London: Pickering and Chatto.

Rose, Jacqueline Rose. 1984. *The Case of Peter Pan: Or, The Impossibility of Children's Literature*. London: Macmillan.

Rosenberg, Edgar (ed.). 1999. *Charles Dickens: Great Expectations*. New York: Norton.

Rousseau, George. 2007. "Medicine and the body." In *The Cambridge Companion to Alexander Pope*. Pat Rogers (ed.), 210–221. Cambridge: Cambridge University Press.

Rumbold, Valerie. 1989. *Women's Place in Pope's World*. Cambridge: Cambridge University Press.

Rybacki, Karyn Charles and Rybacki, Donald Jay. 2002. *Communication Criticism: Approaches & Genres*. Boston: Pearson.

Sadrin, Anny. 1988. *Great Expectations* [Unwin Critical Library]. London: Unwin Hyman.

Said, Edward. 1994 [1993]. *Culture and Imperialism*. London: Vintage.

Searle, John. 1969. *Speech Acts: An Essay in the Philosophy of Language*. Cambridge: Cambridge University Press.

Sell, Roger D. 1985. "Tellability and Politeness in 'The Miller's Tale': First Steps in Literary Pragmatics". *English Studies* 66: 496–512.

Sell, Roger D. 1991. Review of Leo Hickey (ed.), *The Pragmatics of Style*, David Birch and Michael O'Toole (eds), *Functions of Style*, and Alan Swingewood, *Sociological Poetics and Aesthetic Theory*. *Journal of Pragmatics* 15: 588–599.

Sell, Roger D. 1994. "Introduction." In his (ed.) *Great Expectations: New Casebook*. 1–40. Basingstoke: Macmillan.

Sell, Roger D. 1999. "Modernist Readings Mediated: Dickens and the New Worlds of Later Generations." In *Dickens, Europe and the New Worlds*. Anny Sadrin (ed.), 294–299. Basingstoke: Macmillan.

Sell, Roger D. 2000. *Literature as Communication: The Foundations of Mediating Criticism*. Amsterdam: John Benjamins.

Sell, Roger D. 2001. *Mediating Criticism: Literary Education Humanized*. Amsterdam: John Benjamins.

Sell, Roger D. 2002. "Introduction." In *Children's Literature as Communication: The ChiLPA Project*. Roger D. Sell (ed.), 1–26. Amsterdam: John Benjamins.

Sell, Roger D. 2004a. "Decency at a Discount? English Studies, Communication, Mediation." *The European English Messenger* 13: 23–34.

Sell, Roger D. 2004b. "What's Literary Communication and What's a Literary Community?" In *Emergent Literatures and Globalisation: Theory, Society, Politics*. Sonia Faessel and Michel Pérez (eds), 39–45. Paris: In Press Editions.

Sell, Roger D. 2005. "Social Change and Scholarly Mediation." In *Re-imagining Language and Literature for the 21st Century*. Suthira Duangsamosorn (ed.), 133–50. Amsterdam: Rodopi.

Sell, Roger D. 2007. "Gadamer, Habermas and a Re-humanized Literary Scholarship." In *Literary Criticism as Metacommunity*. Smiljana Komar and Uros Mozetic (eds), 213–220. Ljubljana: Slovene Association for the Study of English.

Sell, Roger D. 2011. "Dialogicality and Ethics: Four Cases of Literary Address." *Language and Dialogue* 1: 79–104.

Sell, Roger D. and Johnson, Anthony W. (eds). 2009. *Writing and Religion in England, 1558–1689: Studies in Community-Making and Cultural Memory*. Farnham: Ashgate.

Shankman, Steven. 2007. "Pope's Home and His Poetic Career." In *The Cambridge Companion to Alexander Pope*. Pat Rogers (ed.), 63–75. Cambridge: Cambridge University Press.

Shapiro, James. 2005. *1599: A Year in the Life of William Shakespeare*. London: Faber and Faber.

Shelley, Percy Bysshe. 1954 [1840]. "A Defence of Poetry." In *Shelley's Prose: or The Trumpet of Prophecy*. David Lee Clark (ed.), 276–297. Albuquerque: University of New Mexico Press.

Sherburn, George (ed.). 1956. *The Correspondence of Alexander Pope*, 5 vols. London: Clarendon Press.

Shusterman, Richard. 1992. *Pragmatist Aesthetics: Living Beauty, Rethinking Art*. Oxford: Blackwell.

Sillars, Malcolm O. and Gronbeck, Bruce E. 2001. *Communication Criticism: Rhetoric, Social Codes, Cultural Studies*. Long Grove, Illinois: Waveland.

Sitter, John. 1982. *Literary Loneliness in Mid-Eighteenth-Century England*. Ithaca, New York: Cornell University Press.

Sitter, John. 2007. "Pope's Versification and Voice." In *The Cambridge Companion to Alexander Pope*. Pat Rogers (ed.), 37–48. Cambridge: Cambridge University Press.

Sitwell, Edith. 1930. *Alexander Pope*. London: Faber and Faber.

Smith, Huston. 1989. *Beyond the Post-Modern Mind*. Wheaton, Illinois: Quest Books.

Snead, Jennifer. 2010. "Epic for and Information Age: Pope's 1743 *Dunciad in Four Books* and the Theater Licensing Act." *ELH* 77: 195–216.

Sontag, Susan. 1966. *Against Interpretation and Other Essays*. Farrar, Strauss and Giroux: New York.

Spaccarelli, Steve. 1994. "Stress, Appraisal, and Coping in Child Sexual Abuse: A Theoretical and Empirical Review." *Psychological Bulletin* 116: 340–62.

Sperber, Dan and Wilson, Deirdre. 1986. *Relevance: Communication and Cognition*. Oxford: Blackwell.

Stanhope, Philip Dormer (= 4th earl of Chesterfield). 1755. Letter, 21st August, 1749. In *The World*, 30th October.

Stephen, James Kenneth. 1891. "Sonnet." In his *Lapsus Calami*. 83. Cambridge: Macmillan and Bowes.

Stephen, Leslie. 1876. "Wordsworth's Ethics." *Cornhill Magazine* 34: 206–226.

Stokes, John. 2009. "Pinter and the 1950s." In *The Cambridge Companion to Harold Pinter*. Peter Raby (ed.), 27–42. Cambridge: Cambridge University Press.

Stubbs, Michael. 1983. *Discourse Analysis: The Sociolinguistic Analysis of Natural Language*. Oxford: Blackwell.

Sutherland, John and Watts, Cedric. 2000. *Henry V, War Criminal? and Other Shakespeare Puzzles*. Oxford: Oxford University Press.

Tallis, Raymond. 1997. *Enemies of Hope: A Critique of Contemporary Pessimism, Irrationalism, Anti-Humanism and Counter-Enlightenment*. Basingstoke: Macmillan.

Tannen, Deborah. 1987. "Repetition in Conversation: Towards a Poetics of Talk." *Journal of the Linguistics Society of America* 63: 574–605.

Tannen, Deborah. 1990. "Ordinary Conversation and Literary Discourse: Coherence and the Poetics of Repetition." In *The Uses of Linguistics*. Edward H. Bendix (ed.), 15–22. New York: New York Academy of Sciences.

Taylor, Gary (ed.). 1982. *Henry V* [Oxford Shakespeare edition]. Oxford: Clarendon Press.

Thackeray, William Makepeace. N.d. *Henry Esmond; The English Humourists; The Four Georges*. George Saintsbury (ed.). London: Oxford University Press.

Thomas, Claudia N. 1994. *Alexander Pope and his Eighteenth-Century Women Readers*. Carbondale: Southern Illinois University Press.

Tillotson, Geoffrey (ed.). 1962. *The Twickenham Edition of the Poems of Alexander Pope: Vol. 2: The Rape of the Lock and Other Poems*. London: Methuen.

Tracy, James D. 1987. "*Ad Fontes* The Humanist Understanding of Scripture as Nourishment of the Soul." In *Christian Spirituality: High Middle Ages and Reformation*. Jill Raitt, Bernard McGinn and John Meyendorff (eds). London: Routledge and Kegan Paul.

Traversi, Derek. 1940. "Henry the Fifth." *Scrutiny* 9: 352–74.

Trilling, Lionel. 1950. "Manners, Morals, and the Novel." In his *The Liberal Imagination*. 205–222. New York: Viking.

Trilling, Lionel. 1967 [1963]. "The Fate of Pleasure." In his *Beyond Culture: Essays on Literature and Learning*. 62–86. Harmondsworth: Penguin.

Trollope, Anthony. 1970 [1870]. Obituary on Dickens. In *Charles Dickens* [Penguin Critical Anthologies]. Stephen Wall (ed.), 177–183. Harmondsworth: Penguin.

Turner, John. 1988. "Introduction." In *Shakespeare: The Play of History*. Graham Holderness *et al.* (eds), 1–9. Basingstoke: Macmillan.

Vattimo, Gianni. 2007. "Towards a Non-Religious Christianity." In *After the Death of God*. John D. Caputo and Gianni Vattimo (eds), 27–46. New York: Columbia University Press.

Voigt, Cynthia. 1994. *When She Hollers*. New York: Scholastic.

Waldock, A. J. A. 1947. Paradise Lost *and its Critics*. Cambridge: Cambridge University Press.

Walker, Cheryl. 1991. "Persona Criticism and the Death of the Author." In *Contesting the Subject: Essays in the Postmodern Theory and Practice of Biography and Biographical Criticism*. William Epstein (ed.), 109–121. West Lafayette: Purdue University Press.

Walter, J. H. (ed.). 1954. *King Henry V* [Arden Edition of Shakespeare]. London: Methuen.

Warton, Joseph. 1806 [1782]. *An Essay on the Genius and Writings of Pope*, 5th ed., Vol. II. London: Thomas Maiden.

Warton, Thomas. 1762. *Observations on* The Fairy Queen of Spenser*: The Second Edition: Corrected and Enlarged*, 2 vols. London and Oxford: Dodsley & Fletcher.

Waters, Steve. 2009. "The Pinter Paradigm: Pinter's Influence on Contemporary Playwriting." In *The Cambridge Companion to Harold Pinter*. Peter Raby (ed.), 297–309. Cambridge: Cambridge University Press.

Watts, Isaac. 1808 [1719]. *The Psalms of David Imitated in the Language of the New Testament and Applied to the Christian State and Worship*. Boston: Samuel Hall.

Weigand, Edda. 2009. *Language as Dialogue: From Rules to Principles of Probability*. Sebastian Feller (ed.). Amsterdam: John Benjamins.

White, Ruth. 1992. *Weeping Willow*. New York: Farrar.

Wikborg, Eleanor. 2002. *The Lover as Father Figure in Eighteenth-Century Women's Fiction*. Gainesville: University Press of Florida.

Willcock, Gladys D. 1934. *Shakespeare as a Critic of Language*. London: Oxford University Press.

Willcock, Gladys D. 1943. "Shakespeare and Rhetoric." *Essays and Studies* 29: 50–61.

Willcock, Gladys D. 1954a. "Language and Poetry in Shakespeare's Early Plays." *Proceedings of the British Academy* 40: 103–117.

Willcock, Gladys D. 1954b. "Shakespeare and Elizabethan Rhetoric." *Shakespeare Survey* 7: 12–24.

Williams, Raymond. 1961 [1958]. *Culture and Society 1780-1950*. Harmondsworth: Penguin.

Williams, Raymond. 1971. *Orwell*. Glasgow: Fontana/Collins.

Williams, Raymond. 1988. *Keywords: A Vocabulary of Culture and Society*. London: Fontana.

Willner, Evan Willner. 2002. "The Arbiter-Critic" [review of Sell 2000]. *Essays in Criticism* 52: 155–61.

Wilson, Edmund. 1941. "Dickens: The Two Scrooges." In his *The Wound and the Bow*. 1–104. Boston: Houghton Mifflin.

Wimsatt, W. K. 1941. *The Prose Style of Samuel Johnson*. New Haven: Yale University Press.

Wolfson, Susan J. 1997. *Formal Changes: The Shaping of Poetry in British Romanticism*. Stanford: Stanford University Press.

Wood, Ian S. 2000. *Churchill*. New York: St Martin's Press.

Woodman, Thomas (ed.). 1998. *Early Romantics: Perspectives in British Poetry from Pope to Wordsworth*. Basingstoke: Macmillan.

Woodman, Thomas. 2005. "Pope and the Paradoxical Centrality of the Satirist." *Studies in the Literary Imagination* 38: 1–13.

Woodman, Thomas. 2006. "Augustanism and Pre-Romanticism." In *A Companion to Eighteenth-Century Poetry*. Christine Gerrard (ed.), 473–485. Oxford: Blackwell.

Woodson, Jacqueline. 1994. *I Hadn't Meant to tell You*. New York: Delacorte.

Wordsworth, Jonathan. 1979 [1970]. "The Two-Part *Prelude* of 1799." In *The Prelude, 1799, 1805, 1850*. Jonathan Wordsworth, M. H. Abrams, and Stephen Gill (eds), 567–585. New York: Norton.

Wordsworth, Jonathan, Abrams, M. H., and Gill, Stephen (eds). 1979. *The Prelude, 1799, 1805, 1850*. New York: Norton.

Wordsworth, William. 1805. Letter to Sir George Beaumont, 1st May. In *The Prelude 1799, 1805, 1850: William Wordsworth*. Jonathan Wordsworth, M. H. Abrams, and Stephen Gill (eds), 34. New York: Norton.

Wordsworth, William. 1814. First essay on epitaphs [as reprinted from Coleridge's *The Friend* in notes to *The Excursion*]. In *The Poetical Works of William Wordsworth*, 5 vols., revised edn. Ernest de Selincourt and Helen Darbishire (eds.), 444–456. Oxford: Clarendon Press.

Young, Brian. 2003. "Pope and Ideology." In *The Cambridge Companion to Alexander Pope*. Pat Rogers (ed.), 118–133. Cambridge: Cambridge University Press.

Zarhy-Levo, Yael. 2009. "Pinter and the Critics." In *The Cambridge Companion to Harold Pinter*, 2nd ed. Peter Raby (ed.), 249–265. Cambridge: Cambridge University Press.

Index